ACCOUNTING

FINANCE AND MANAGEMENT

ACCOUNTING
FINANCE AND MANAGEMENT

R. J. CHAMBERS
Professor of Accounting, University of Sydney

ARTHUR ANDERSEN & CO.
1969

Australian National Library Registry Number AUS. 69-3659

Registered in Australia for transmission by post as a book.

WHOLLY SET UP AND PRINTED IN AUSTRALIA BY
HOGBIN, POOLE (PRINTERS) PTY. LTD., SYDNEY

FOREWORD

We are pleased that Professor Chambers has given us his permission to assemble and publish the various papers he has written over a period of time. We have been motivated to do this because we want the logic and clarity of his writings to be made readily accessible not only to our personnel for training purposes but also in libraries of schools of business for professors and students.

ARTHUR ANDERSEN & CO.

August 1969

PREFACE

This collection of papers comprises the greater part of writing, other than books and reviews, done over some 20 years. The papers were written for different purposes, as scripts for addresses or as journal articles, and under different stimuli. Because of the different audiences or readers to which they were addressed, and because I have sought to learn by revisiting particular themes, there is a certain amount of overlapping and repetition. This could only have been avoided by extensive rewriting of the settings of some arguments, and then their connection with observed and experienced circumstances would have been confused or destroyed.

There are in these papers changes in definitions, treatments and positions I have taken from time to time. This being the case, it may be wondered whether the views I no longer hold are worth setting cheek by jowl with more recent expressions of viewpoint and argument. There are several justifications.

First, it is never possible in one piece of the length of an article or an address to marshal all the evidence or to argue all the points on any matter. One cannot think of them all. And there are limits to the patience of audiences or readers. The evidence and argument in this collection is therefore more extensive than can be found in any one piece, and more extensive that that given in the books which have emerged from these exercises.

Second, when one's views change over time, it seems tedious and pedantic to correct explicitly in any one piece the errors and inadequacies of prior work. To do so would also interfere with the clearest possible exposition of one's latest views. I have found it necessary on occasions, and at several points in this volume there are additional explanations. But there is no complete account of these changes. Taken chronologically these pieces represent the growth of a particular set of ideas. Later positions are understandable largely in terms of accretions to, refinements of and rejections of earlier positions, and the evidence on which those changes were based. In particular, the positions taken in *Accounting, Evaluation and Economic Behavior* (1966) depend heavily on prior work reproduced here, to which no direct reference was made in that book. And some of the papers here, which were written since the manuscript of that book was completed (1964), amplify and modify positions I then took.

One thing that has remained constant over the period is the search for notions which conform with what is observable and experienced in active commerce, whether or not those notions tally with extant doctrine. It is my belief that we cannot, by mere umbilical contemplation, solo or in committee, have better foundations for belief and practice than we can by observing and reflecting on the ways in which the world goes about its business.

A constancy of a different kind has been belief in the need for and the possibility of reform. I doubt whether it can be asserted that there has been any major reform in accounting practice over the period, or indeed in theory and teaching, in spite of the recurrent evidence in one country or another of deficiences. Much of what was said critically years ago, and earlier and since by others, can still be said today. The repetition with variations in these pages serves the same function as repetition in educational and similar processes; to teach or to induce action seems to demand it.

The articles have been grouped under section titles which are roughly descriptive. But I have never regarded accounting, economics, finance and management as isolates, nor the forms of inquiry, exposition, teaching and practice as unrelated. The sections of the book are thus not unique in content; similar themes will be found in more sections than one. How the main ideas developed, and at what points new positions were taken, can only be seen by looking at what was done in its chronological order; a chronological bibliography (p. xi) is therefore given.

Many of these pieces were first published in Australia, many first in the United States, some elsewhere. The local allusions, technical terms and spellings have generally been retained. These are not likely to mislead or to give rise to difficulties. In the interest of a uniform style some minor changes have been made. And, in a few cases, material has been added, deleted or re-arranged.

I am grateful to the publishers of articles who have granted permission for reproduction in this volume.

I am specially grateful to Arthur Andersen & Co. for the suggestion that the collection be published in this way, for undertaking publication and for the freedom to choose what is here included.

R. J. Chambers

July 1969

CONTENTS

BIBLIOGRAPHY

The list is chronological. Some minor pieces of work are omitted. Items starred * are not reproduced here. Page numbers on the right are references to this volume.

Books

	Page
Financial Management, Sydney, The Law Book Co., 1947, 442 pp. Revised 1953, 432 pp. Revised 1966, 433 pp.	*
The Function and Design of Company Annual Reports, Sydney, The Law Book Co., 1955, 322 pp.	*
Accounting and Action, Sydney, The Law Book Co., 1957, 248 pp. Revised 1965, 287 pp.	*
Accounting, Evaluation and Economic Behaviour, Englewood Cliffs, Prentice-Hall Inc., 1966, 388 pp.	*
The Accounting Frontier, Melbourne, Cheshire, 1965. Co-editor with L. Goldberg and R. L. Mathews, and contributor	*

Other

"How to Achieve Lower Costs in Australian Industry," *Bulletin No.* 10, Australasian Institute of Cost Accountants, 1947	*
"Business Finance and the Analysis of Financial Statements," *The Australian Accountant,* XVIII (August 1948), 253-65	*
"The Training of Accountants," *The Australian Accountant,* XVIII (September 1948), 321-8	*
"Accounting and Management," *The Australian Accountant,* XVIII (December 1948), 417-20	3
"Incentives in Industry," *Current Affairs Bulletin,* Vol. 3, No. 13 (March 1949), 203-15	*
"Accounting and Shifting Price Levels," *The Australian Accountant,* XIX (September 1949), 313-20	295
"The Spice of Accounting," *The Australian Accountant,* XIX (November 1949), 398-401	161
'Widening Responsibilities of Accountants: A Comment," *Proceedings of the Australasian Congress on Accounting,* 1949, 229-31	*
"Budgetary Control," *Bulletin* of Sydney Division, The Institution of Engineers, Australia, December 1949, 12-15	*
"Depreciation on Replacement Cost," *The Australian Accountant,* XX (February 1950), 68-70	305
"The Relationship between Accounting and Financial Management," *The Australian Accountant,* XX (September 1950), 333-55	7
"Accounting and Inflation," *The Australian Accountant,* XXII (January 1952), 14-23	309
"Accounting and Business Finance," *The Australian Accountant,* XXII (July and August 1952), 213-30, 262-6	39
"Effects of Inflation on Financial Strategy," *The Australian Accountant,* XXII (September 1952), 304-11	321
"Financial Practice and Fiscal Policy," *The Australian Accountant,* XXII (November 1952), 391-8	333
"Capital for Private Enterprise under Existing Economic Conditions," *Proceedings of The Australian Society of Accountants Convention on Accounting, Adelaide* (June 1954), 5 pp.	*

Page

"Company Losses—Safeguarding the Investor," *Current Affairs Bulletin,* 34 (October 1964), 162-76 204

"Measurement and Objectivity in Accounting," *The Accounting Review,* XXXIX (April 1964), 264-74 .. .. *

"Looking at Economists Looking at Accounting," *Economic Review,* Sydney University Economics Society, 10 (1964), 36-37 653

"Fallacies in Company Accounting," *A.I.S. Technical Society Bulletin,* 9 (1964), 29-32 .. .. *

"Are the Stock Exchanges in Australia meeting their Challenges?," *Record* of "Investment in Australia" Symposium, Melbourne, February 1965, 6 pp. 220

"Published Financial Reports and National Productivity," *Selected Problems in Accountancy, Papers from a Seminar,* Adult Education Board, The University of Western Australia, February 1965, 19-32 229

"Professional Education and the Vatter Report," *Proceedings* of Conference of the Australasian Association of University Teachers of Accounting, Melbourne, May, 1965, 17 pp. 656

"Measurement in Accounting," *Journal of Accounting Research,* 3 (Spring 1965), 32-62 554

"The Complementarity of Accounting and Economics," *Calculator Annual,* Singapore Polytechnic Society of Commerce, 1964-65, 78-86 583

"Edwards and Bell on Business Income," *T ehAccounting Review,* XL (October 1965), 731-41 426

"The Development of Accounting Theory," *The Accounting Frontier,* Cheshire, Melbourne, 1965, 18-35 .. .. *

"The Price Level Problem and Some Intellectual Grooves," *Journal of Accounting Research,* 3 (Autumn 1965), 242-52 .. .. .. *

"Accounting and Analytical Methods: A Review Article," *Journal of Accounting Research,* 4 (Spring 1966), 101-18 .. .. *

"A Matter of Principle," *The Accounting Review,* XLI (July 1966), 443-57 242

"Why Worry about Accounting?," *Proceedings* of The Fifth Annual Accounting Form of Hayden, Stone Incorporated, in the New York University Graduate School, November 1966, 7-16 260

"A Study of a Price Level Study," *Abacus,* 2 (December 1966), 97-118 .. 439

"The Foundations of Financial Accounting," *Berkeley Symposium on the Foundations of Financial Accounting,* University of California, Berkeley, January 1967, 26-44 595

"Prospective Adventures in Accounting Ideas," *The Accounting Review,* XLII (April 1967), 241-53 685

"University Education in Accounting," *Accountancy,* LXXVIII (July 1967), 469-74 673

"Price Variation Accounting—An Improved Representation," *Journal of Accounting Research,* 5 (Autumn 1967), 215-20 .. .. .. *

"A Study of a Study of a Price Level Study," *Abacus,* 3 (August 1967), 62-73 .. .. *

"Continuously Contemporary Accounting—Additivity and Action," *The Accounting Review,* XLII (October 1967), 751-7 612

"Uniformity in Accounting," *The New York Certified Public Accountant,* XXXVII (Ictober 1967), 747-54 283

The Relationships between Accounting, Finance and Management, Faculty of Business Administration, The University of Alberta, 1967, booklet, 16 pp. 143

"The Mathematics of Accounting and Estimating," *Abacus,* 3 (December 1967), 163-80 715

"Reality and Illusion in Accounting, Finance and Economics," *Michigan Business Review,* XX (January 1968), 1-9 272

"Consolidated Statements are not really Necessary," *The Australian Accountant,* 38 (February 1968), 89-92 631

ACCOUNTING FINANCE AND MANAGEMENT

* Dates are dates of preparation; publication dates are in some cases later.

1

ACCOUNTING AND MANAGEMENT*

The formal study of management has evoked not a little interest on the part of accountants in the last decade. But I fear that the concern accountants have displayed bears no relationship to the effort they are prepared to devote to an analysis of the function of management and of the contribution of accounting to modern management. This short note is intended as a criticism of some of the recent writings of accountants on the subject of management; no apology is made for the purely critical approach, for the writer supports the view that analysis and criticism are vital to reconstruction even though the critic offers no alternative approach or point of view. Such alternatives as I suggest therefore are not to be regarded as my unalterable opinion; they are offered as stimuli for other readers.

In several places within recent years I have found the accountant in business referred to as a unit in the group styled "management". No matter how much we accountants may like to think we are part of management we must be prepared to face the facts. Now, the fact of the matter is that the chief accountants in some organizations do exercise managerial authority, and are responsible for some managerial functions in every organization of any size. But this does not make them members of "management" except in rather a special sense.

The Functions Briefly Described

Without discussing in detail the content of the concept of management, it should be possible to obtain fairly general agreement with the notion that management comprehends decision-making, direction and supervision—and very little else. Accounting is generally understood to mean something entirely different. As taught today, accounting is mainly a body of rules and precepts for record-keeping; taken in what I believe to be its widest connotation, accounting cannot be construed to mean more than reporting to responsible persons the summaries of monetary records of business transactions.

It is most important, in my view, that there be an independent reporting or recording authority. Adequate and reliable information is the only sound basis for business decisions or for corrective actions; accounting should therefore be understood as a service by which reliable information is supplied to business executives on problems which confront them. Accounting is not a decision-making function, and accountants are not decision-makers in respect of the whole of a

---

* First published in *The Australian Accountant,* Vol. XVIII, No. 12, December 1948, pp. 417-20.

business unit, though they may be in respect of the operation of their own departments.

Consequences of Confusion

To imagine the possible consequences of confusing the two functions of data-collection and decision-making is not difficult. The subject of both functions is very often the supervisor of some operation or department of the undertaking. Can't you envisage the distrust with which both management and accounting staff would be viewed by supervisors who had any grounds for supposing that the data-collecting function was being used to bring undue pressure to bear on them, rather than to report the facts? I have frequently asked production supervisors whether their managements recognized, by requiring formal reports, the extent of idle time or time lost through departmental or extra-departmental inefficiency. The fact that very few managers require such information could be due to recognition of the futility of the procedure, or the failure to appreciate the significance of such facts. If it is due to the "futility" of asking such a question, one would be pardoned for believing that at some time the data supplied had been used in a way which, to the supervisory group, seemed quite unfair. And this in fact is often the case. One can hardly expect supervisors to report fully in the knowledge that they are making rods for their own backs; the only sure way to encourage accurate original documents is by demonstrating to supervisors an attitude of helpful co-operation rather than something in the nature of witch hunting.

Now, such co-operation cannot often come from the accounting personnel of an organization; seldom are clerical or administrative staff capable of or interested in making suggestions for technical or works management improvement. For this reason the managerial reaction to reported business facts should never find expression through the accounting personnel to the works managers, sales managers or supervisors. If it does, it is to be expected that the supervisors and executives of production and selling functions will come to regard the accounting department with suspicion and its personnel as incompetent bureaucrats.

Limiting the Meaning of "Accounting"

The confinement of accounting to the reporting of business facts may be thought by many to place an unnecessary and distasteful limit on the work of accountants. I do not believe however that such a limitation lowers the status of accounting or accountants in any way; and I should not be concerned, in any case, provided the limitation is logically sound. The provision of impartial reports on business developments is a vital function of modern business, and accountants should be much more interested in developing ways and means of performing their special function more satisfactorily, than in reaching out in all directions to annexe territory (e.g., by giving opinions and making communications which are strictly managerial) which they are imperfectly equipped to administer, and which will inevitably lead to confusion of functions and its consequences. The doing of one job well, the refining of original records, the selection of ways and means for obtaining reliable original data—these are much more important to business, in my view, than mere versatility.

It is admitted, of course, that accountants are not always to blame for the variety of non-accounting functions they may be called upon to perform; nor is it intended to suggest that accountants should refuse to undertake new and wider responsibilities in commerce or industry. But in so far as they are responsible for accounting they should be careful that their efficiency in that direction is not impaired by other types of relationships which may make non-accounting personnel suspicious of their overtures. Where, because of the relative smallness of a business organization, many different types of activity are carried out or supervised by one person (e.g., an accountant may be secretary, budget officer, office manager and personnel officer at the same time), it may be difficult for that person to act always in a manner appropriate to the function which he is, for the moment, serving. Thus, he may act sometimes in an advisory capacity, sometimes in a service capacity, and sometimes as an executive in his own right; and the executive capacity, being of the three most influential, may be allowed to encroach where, formally at least, it is forbidden. As one writer has said: "The germ of autocracy invests every situation involving the exercise of superior authority." Few are immune from its infection. It is therefore wise, wherever possible, to keep the different types of function separate. There will be no occasion then for the accountant to undertake activities which may prejudice his chances of procuring perfectly reliable data on business operations for the enlightenment of the management. . . .

Some appear to believe that checks and balances are unnecessary in business organization; that the cost accountant is a paragon of business knowledge, quite free of the lust for power which so often is evident in those with special skills, and quite capable of guiding the management he serves to halcyon days of continued efficiency and prosperity without other aid. That view is obviously unrealistic. Any discussion purporting to deal with the place of accountants in the managerial structure of business should deal very fully with the inter-relationships between accounting and executive departments; a treatment which lightly dismisses these relationships seriously over-simplifies a vital aspect of practical business management.

Managerial Accounting

What may be considered the classical example of confusion of management and accounting is the general concept of "managerial accounting" and the "managerial accountant". Writers who have used the terms over the past five years appear to have been most reluctant to discuss the implications of the use of the adjective "managerial"; it is used as though it were any other adjective, as though it were entirely free of potentially misleading insinuations.

This reluctance to be critical of terms used evidences a superficiality which ill-becomes a group of people who have a reputation for demanding accuracy. "The claims that are sometimes made, both from without and within the profession, that the scope of accounting should be enlarged should be carefully investigated" said Mr. A. A. Fitzgerald in his 1940 lecture "The Field for Research in Accountancy". The crux of the statement seems to me to be the last two words. An irresponsible or superficial approach to the question of the scope of accounting can only result in adding confusion to an already obscure problem.

The problems of formulating financial policies and of controlling the financial aspects of a business must always be examined in the light of the accounts; a special officer may conveniently be detailed to carry out continuous research into factors affecting the financial position and financial results; and because of the nature of the background necessary and because of the managerial importance of the work he does, this officer may be described as the managerial accountant. I believe that the precision sought in using this term is not really obtained, for the words "accounting" and "accountant" imply processes which are mainly synthetical (i.e., built up from observation), whereas the type of work suggested above is primarily analytical. I cannot at present countenance the view held in some quarters that the cost accountant is, or should be considered as, the managerial accountant.

Conclusion

The relationships between the theory of accounting and the theory of management, and between accountants and managers in practice unquestionably need careful thought and thorough investigation. Are we going to be content to let others point out the faults in our theories and the paucity of our concepts of the real function of accounting in business? If not, it's time we did some real thinking about accounting and management.

2

THE RELATIONSHIP BETWEEN ACCOUNTING AND FINANCIAL MANAGEMENT*

1.—Introduction

The general theme to which I am directing attention for the purpose of these research lectures is "Accounting and Financial Policy". The Accounting Research Committee of the Commonwealth Institute of Accountants should not, however, be saddled with the entire blame for selecting this subject. When it was suggested to me, it seemed to offer an opportunity of examining a kind of no-man's-land in business theory and practice[1]. I accepted the theme readily, for one could hardly wish for better territory to work in than a territory that is poorly defined and quite inadequately explored.

The acute controversy of the past 10 years on the accounting treatment of stock values and reserves and provisions for depreciation has thrown into sharp relief the inadequacy of business theory in some of its most vital aspects. These inadequacies have become apparent principally because of the impact of drastic social and economic changes on the financial problems of business enterprises; and the present seems an opportune time to examine them, while their effects are still in our minds. An inadequate theory does not become adequate merely because the environment changes: but it does attract less attention, and is therefore likely to be tolerated longer, if the environment presents no critical tests of its adequacy. It will help to give direction to our present study if, at the outset, we describe some of these difficulties more precisely and if we suggest the need for a new method of approach by which some of them may be overcome.

Confusion as to Objectives

One of these difficulties is the determination of the financial objectives of business enterprises. It has long been customary to consider that the prime objectives of the managers of such undertakings are to maintain the invested capital and to earn a profit commensurate with the risks undertaken. This bald statement continues to serve, even in the technical discussions in accounting journals where greater precision may be expected. But it bristles with inexact terms which

---

* First published in *The Australian Accountant,* Vol. XX, No. 9, September 1950, pp. 333-55. Text prepared for Commonwealth Institute of Accountants Annual Research Lecture in the University of Melbourne, June 1950.

[1] The discussion is, throughout, in terms of private business enterprises; but it is not generally restricted to corporate business, although corporate business provides some of the illustrations.

should be defined more precisely before any attempt is made to build a body of theory, such as accounting theory, upon them. What is capital? What is the invested capital which is to be maintained? What is profit? What is income? and expense?—for these determine profit. What is the criterion for determining whether or not a profit is commensurate with the risks undertaken?

Whenever the opportunity has arisen for a more precise definition of financial objectives, other issues seem to have crowded out this fundamental question. The procedure usually adopted among accountants anxious to elucidate the meaning of profit and capital is to examine first the dicta of eminent jurists, rather than to proceed by logical steps to develop pertinent concepts *ab initio*. In so far as accounting practice depends on decided cases for its basic concepts, it is bound to find those bases insecure, unless the findings in those cases may all be deduced from a single unstated generalization. A body of consistent theory and sound practice requires a more substantial foundation than isolated legal decisions, however eminent their source; for legal decisions are given to suit a single event or chain of events—anomalous or unusual events, moreover—and they are thus a poor foundation for rules and principles of general application. We should have a consistent theory of business, of managerial aims and enterprise objectives as a basis for accounting techniques (and as a guide for those who make or those who interpret the law) if we offer those techniques in the service of business and business management.

This is the first important question which the subject of "Accounting and Financial Policy" enables us to approach. Income, profit, capital, and similar concepts are the everyday concern not only of business managers, but also of accountants, economists, lawyers, and governmental policy makers. Where so many specialists are concerned, the subject of their interest may appear to be undefined and confused, as each puts forward his own point of view. But truth is many sided; if we carefully examine these viewpoints we may find some contradictions, but we will also find consistencies and complementarities. What view we should accept as the best reflection of business practice or the best recipe for ideal business practice we may only determine by attempting to appraise the concepts of each group of specialists concerned with these issues. We shall not be able to examine the question of objectives, except incidentally, in this lecture.

Problems of Method

A second kind of difficulty which confronts accountants and managers is deciding upon the most effective ways of achieving the financial objectives, whatever they may be. The problem of objectives mentioned above involves the external relationships of business entities, the expectations of owners and creditors; but the problem of methods is an internal one. It involves determining the formal relationships which will exist between specializing executives within an organization, and it involves decisions on the techniques necessary to keep a watchful eye on the attainment of the financial objectives.

But, as in the first group of problems, we will not materially advance our knowledge or our capacity merely by considering the precedents. Precedents are useful, even though their origin may not be as professionally eminent as the originators of legal precedents; but we need to get behind the precedents represented by established business organization and practice, and to discover which of the basic financial objectives has inspired a given method or a given form of organization, and which concepts and methods are most useful by reason of the assistance given to managers in their efforts to attain the objectives of their enterprises.

The methods which business managers have become accustomed to using in their efforts to attain the financial objectives of their undertakings may be dichotomously classified. The subject of accounting embraces a large group of these methods; the remainder are not classifiable as accounting operations, nor are they widely known by any other unifying subject title, but they are known to be important in business operations nevertheless. Two such groups of concepts and methods are recognized in contemporary accounting theory: for example, A. A. and G. E. Fitzgerald make reference "to the effects of *financial policies* on financial statements, and to the fact that *accounting conventions* and opinions based on *financial prudence* influence financial statements of all kinds"[2]. Here, observe, reference is made to two distinct sets of concepts: accounting concepts and financial concepts.

That such a distinction should now be made is, I believe, symptomatic of the difficulties which are confronting thoughtful accountants. More are becoming aware of the need to relate accounting practice to an accounting theory based on business reality, instead of basing accounting practice on a neat series of propositions, whose independence of reality grossly vitiates the end product of the accounting process. The subject of "Accounting and Financial Policy", enables us to work on this second group of difficulties also, and this lecture is devoted almost entirely to the development of a realistic statement of the relationship between the two groups of concepts referred to in the previous paragraph.

The last purpose of this introduction is to indicate the nature of the conclusions reached in the sequel. It will appear that several of the doctrines and concepts now deemed to be accounting doctrines and concepts, ideally have no place in accounting or in accounting operations. It will be argued that accounting statements are not merely "affected" by financial policies and financial prudence; they are the whole expression of the effect of business policies, tacit and explicit. Following these notions, accounting is considered as an integral but subordinate part of the body of rules and methods developed to assist in the attainment of the financial ends of enterprises.

---

[2] *Form and Contents of Published Financial Statements,* Sydney, Butterworth & Co., 1948, p. 16—italics not in original.

It is believed that this is a most important relationship to establish at this stage in the development of accounting theory. For:

(1) Such a standpoint will resolve the conflict between the points of view of the accountant and the financial executive evidenced by the juxtaposition of accounting and financial policy or prudence in recent discussions.

(2) It will lead to a better understanding of several concepts which have, hitherto, been accepted as accounting doctrines, but which are, logically, beyond the boundaries of a corpus of accounting rules.

(3) It will contribute to the development of a system of accounting which is intimately concerned, not incidentally concerned, with economic realities.

(4) It will have the effect of giving accounting a realistic organizational setting, an effect which will contribute materially to the clarification of executive relationships in business.

(5) By delimiting the field of accounting it will permit more effective discussion of accounting and related subjects.

(6) By demonstrating the closeness of the relationship between accounting and financial management it will save accounting theory from the sterility which follows sharp subdivision of business activities into independent and unrelated compartments.

2.—Policy and Management

Before we proceed to the main task it will be desirable to indicate what we understand by policy and how accounting and management are both concerned with financial policies.

The Meaning of Policy

In the growing literature on business management there is relatively little on the subject of policies and the meaning of "policy". The word is often quite loosely used not only in respect of decisions of top management to meet isolated problems but also to cover plans of operations which have been sanctioned by top management. The word "policy", for our purposes, will be used to designate "a standard governing present and future actions and decisions within a defined area of operations"[3]. If this meaning be accepted it will be apparent that neither isolated decisions nor detailed plans qualify for classification as policies; neither is sufficiently broad in scope or in application.

Policies may be laid down in order to economize the effort of the policy maker, or to be of general guidance to his subordinates. The policy maker may be the highest authority in an organization or a relatively junior executive; the definition we have accepted does not confine policy making to top management. But at whatever level policies originate they are the product of managerial necessity, the necessity of relieving busy executives of the burden of considering in detail each important recurrent problem as it arises. Policies do not

[3] N. Chamberlain, *The Union Challenge to Management Control,* New York, Harper & Bros., 1948.

arise out of technical criteria usually; unless they involve a choice between technical and economic ends they do not engage the discretion of executives. For example, the method of performing accounting operations is a matter of technique: a proposal such as—it is the intention of the management that the accounting system shall be fully mechanized—is not a policy; it is purely a matter of selecting one device from available recording and analysing devices, with known advantages and disadvantages. The provision of funds for this purpose, however, would conform to some financial plan or policy.

Financial policies are of three general varieties. One variety is the particular concern of top management. Policies relating to the financing of business operations, the financial structure of enterprises, the determination of income and its distribution, have such important bearing on the solvency and economic effectiveness of enterprises that these matters are very seldom left to the discretion of any but top management. We might observe two features of these policies. Because they deal with matters solely at the discretion of top management, only seldom are they committed to writing. For the same reason they seldom become known to subordinate executives. Secondly, as these matters affect the external legal and financial relationships of enterprises, and as these relationships are in a measure influenced by the changing financial environment, some policies of this variety are more in the nature of isolated decisions. At least they are more flexible, more subject to variation than many other kinds of policy.

Not only are these policies little known among subordinate executives in business enterprises: little is written about them as policies. One of the most comprehensive treatments of the financial operations of corporate business, Dewing's *The Financial Policy of Corporations*[4], offers no list of the subjects of financial policies of companies which would enable us to distinguish between financial policies and financial operations generally; nor does it give specific examples of the form which statements of policy on financial matters may take. That study is a series of inferences drawn from the external financial operations and financial statements of American companies, and it effectively illustrates the claim that financial statements are the expression of the effects of policies. This lack of examples is general in the literature of business finance; such occasional references to policy as occur are almost uniformly uninformative. In the interest of clarifying our concept of this first category of policies there follow some of the matters which may be considered to be the subject of top-level financial policies:

(a) the method of financing fixed assets of an undertaking;
(b) the method of financing working capital;
(c) the general financial structure of an undertaking;
(d) the giving of credit in any form (i.e. the assumption of a banker's function);
(e) the payment of dividends and the establishment of reserves.

[4] New York, The Ronald Press Co., 1920.

The second category of financial policies is mainly internal in application and effect. These policies are laid down by top management with the object of focusing attention on the long-run purposes of the entity, so that its financial resources may be deployed in a way that will serve for an indefinite period the general objectives of the entity. Within this group also are policies laid down by top management to guide subordinate executives on the financial aspects of their special problems and responsibilities. This category includes the following matters:

(a) the selection, for implementation, of specific projects requiring finance;

(b) the extent to which executives, below the chief executive may incur or authorize the incurring of expenditure without seeking the approval of higher executives.

The third category we may term quasi-financial policies; they are policies which are partly financial in purpose and effect. But because they are only partly financial, they are not thereby inconsequential or irrelevant to our study; they indicate, in fact, how extensive are the ramifications of financial factors in the operations of business. As examples of subjects falling within this category, the following are offered:

(a) pricing policies;
(b) wage and salary policies;
(c) merchandising policies (such as variety of lines stocked);
(d) procurement and stock-level policies.

The list may be considerably extended.

By way of further illustration, and because it is unique, a recent statement of the objectives and elements of an aggressive (financial) policy is presented:

"*Objectives*

1. The procurement of the maximum amount of new capital for improvements and for development and expansion, up to the point of the optimum rate of growth and so far as consistent with the maintenance of a sound financial structure.
2. The utilization of available capital for the attainment of the management's long-term objectives.

"*Elements*

1. The definition of aggressive but realistic objectives for:
   (a) Earnings, and
   (b) Operating capital.
2. A programme for the attainment and maintenance of a balanced financial structure consistent with the operating capital objective.
3. The definition of a common dividend objective.
4. Continuing procedures for the selective allocation of available funds."[5]

---

[5] D. R. Anderson, *Practical Controllership*, Chicago, Irwin, 1947, p. 459.

If we accept Chamberlain's definition of policy and if we admit that financial policies include the matters mentioned in the last four paragraphs, we must admit that the relationship between accounting and financial policy is quite intimate. It is much more than a casual relationship; fixed assets, working capital, financial structure, credit, dividends, long-term obligations, are all matters that accountants discuss and keep records about. Accounting thus assumes some of the importance of financial policies: if financial policies are designed to promote important ends, then accounting must share in the importance of those policies. "Accounting has to do largely with the financial policies of business, and policies of sales, production, labour, and other management problems are important elements in the success or failure of a business enterprise."[6]

But, although the relationship between accounting and financial policy may be close, it is not direct. Financial policies do not arise, Phoenix-like, from the records of past events. Some personal agency is interposed. Somebody or some group of persons determines policy; to describe conveniently this person or group (and also, very often, to describe what this person or group does) we use the term financial management.[7] Now I find it impossible, in the present state of accounting theory, to proceed to examine the subject "Accounting and Financial Policy" without at first examining the two concepts, accounting and financial management, at greater length.

For, firstly, I am unable to accept as a basis without modification the present concept of accounting and its functions. And, secondly, although there is an obvious difference between accounting and financial policy, the difference between and the relationship between accounting and financial management have not been formally demonstrated. My procedure will be to examine some aspects of contemporary accounting and of modern accounting theory which appear to need revision or excision; then, to present a view of financial management as a subject; and, finally, to attempt to establish their logical relationship.

3.—Accounting as a Subject

A most important task of the philosophy of any subject is the laying down, and explanation, of the relationships between that subject and other subjects to which it is conceptually contiguous. Not only does it seem to be a most important task; it is, ideally, the first task, for a subject can hardly be discussed logically or rigorously unless its boundaries are known. But, typically, that is not the way in which a body of theory grows, however desirable it might be. Practical solutions to pressing problems are more important in the origins of any technical subject of study, and in the infancy of the subject much

---

[6] G. R. Byrne, "To What Extent can the Practice of Accounting be reduced to Rules and Standards?", *Journal of Accountancy*, November 1937, p. 371.

[7] The disadvantage of using one term to describe two such different phenomena is recognized, but it is not expected to give rise to any confusion in the following analysis.

more attention seems to be given to developing methods than to developing a theoretical justification for those methods. For an example we have not to go far from our present subject. Economics is an excellent case in point; there was a vast literature on economic subjects before serious attempts were made to appraise the content of the body of economic theory, and during the infancy of economics many of the real issues with which the subject purported to grapple were so readily and so widely considered to be exceptions that the slowness with which unrealistic assumptions were abandoned does not now cause us surprise.

The development of accounting theory is no doubt going through the same processes. We are passing out of the stage where practicalism reigned supreme. Neither accounting theory nor accountants have passed entirely beyond that stage; the rate of progression appears sometimes to be annoyingly slow; but we are passing to a stage where the reasons for our actions, for our practical devices and techniques, are assuming some importance. With the gradual appraisal of our reasons will come inevitably some disillusionment, but out of it will arise a stronger and a more versatile body of theory; a theory that is more realistic, more logical, and more resilient than our present notions. That "the rules of accounting, even more than those of law, are the product of experience rather than of logic"[8] is no cause for satisfaction or complacence. Only in so far as experiences are reduced to a logical pattern of widely applicable generalizations do they become useful bases for future action.

As we move in that direction then, it seems to be a first task of theorists to describe the subject of accounting, its relationships with other subjects, and its function in that aspect of the life of the community to which it is relevant. The reason should be obvious; it lies in the need for a basic rationale, a body of fundamental postulates against which the propositions and developments of the theory may be tested. Only in this way may accountants be sure that their subject is not based on pretentious nonsense and humbug.

Accounting theory is very closely related to a number of other fields of study and inquiry. It is related to jurisprudence; for the legal characteristics of different kinds of accounting entities oblige accountants (when acting as accountants) to assume quite different obligations. It is related to business management; because the conduct of business enterprises necessitates specialization in the practice of accounting, and because accounting is used much more widely in the process of business management than in the conduct of most other types of group activity. It is related to economics; for, though its methods may be different, for the most part it uses similar symbols and deals with transactions the same as or similar to those which are the concern of economics and economists. It is related to government and to statistics and to logic and to mathematics in certain ways and by certain ties.

---

[8] G. O. May, *Financial Accounting,* New York, Macmillan, 1943, p. vii.

Some of these relationships are seldom disputed. But there are enough disputed areas to cause the greatest confusion if we are lax in argument or careless in definition; and with respect, it is submitted that accountants have been both lax in argument and careless in definition. That this is so should be apparent from the sequel, but a simple example of laxity in argument may be interpolated here.

The proposition that an argument or proceeding may be tested only by reference to its fundamental propositions, and not by reference to other propositions, will be assumed. Now, if it is desired to test the proposition that depreciation provisions should be permitted to influence the figures in published balance sheets to the extent of the Taxation Commissioner's rates, reference must be made, not to the problems of the Taxation Commissioner or the Federal Treasurer, but to the purposes for which the balance sheets of enterprises are prepared and published. It seems, however, that the practice of using the rates in the official schedule in deriving published statements is widespread and growing. In other words, accounting practice is being influenced by considerations not only beyond the field of accounting but also beyond the managerial purposes which are served by financial statements. This might not be recognized as an important defection in practice: but however expedient it may be it is quite indefensible logically. It is the kind of irrationality upon which much accounting is based.

But let us return to the "disputed areas" referred to previously. Why, it may be asked, is the definition of these areas so important? Why not accept the fact that there are specialists in, for example, economics, management, and accounting, and leave it at that? What imposes the necessity for determining priority as between these closely-related fields?

The need arises, firstly, from the problems of business organization. The establishment of a complex organization for the carrying out of prescribed purposes necessitates clear definition of the activities of the persons or groups of persons who will make up the organization; it also necessitates a clear statement of the relationships which should exist between such persons and groups of persons. In designing an organization structure there will be specified a series of positions ranging from those which are concerned with minor matters, involving very little discretion on the part of their incumbents, to the top executive position which involves a very wide area of discretion; and in this series, no position or group of activities may be ranked higher than another group of activities which involves a wider area of discretion in the same general field of activities. The determination of the areas of discretion appropriate to accounting, financial management, and management generally is, then, an important practical purpose to be served by a study of the differences of viewpoint expressed by specialists in these and other related subjects.

The need arises, secondly, from the desire to have a system of postulates and propositions which will explain the widest range of phenomena in the field of business. Such a system may be expected to integrate, to give meaning to, and to give direction to, the many specialized operations related to business management. The process of establishing rules for management and for accounting would thus be related to the whole function of business, and would not be carried on with scarcely any cross-reference between related specialties. This, I believe, is the only way in which accounting may become more scientific and less pragmatic, for this approach is a scientific approach, based on accepted scientific method. In an endeavour to establish generalizations which embrace progressively greater numbers of observed phenomena there are several general canons which may be used as guides. We need not discuss them at length; three of the most important will be given, any one of which may serve to check the state of accounting theory, so that some indication of the distance we have yet to travel may be obtained. These three are:

(1) That generalization is preferred which is simplest, or which involves the fewest assumptions.

(2) That generalization is preferred which explains the greatest number of the facts it is intended to explain.

(3) A generalization should be internally consistent.

What is here said of generalizations may also be said of systems of generalizations and of codes of rules.

Now, what is the character of our best generalizations? It is, to say the least, quite unflattering of the efforts of our profession to establish a claim to scientific status for the study of accounting.

Among such framework of theory as exists we have a number of doctrines; if we accept Gilman's survey[9], which we may do for the purposes of illustration, they are the doctrines of conservatism, consistency, disclosure, and materiality. There are also a number of conventions, which, again following Gilman, include the entity convention, the valuation convention, the accounting period convention, and the going concern convention. If these generalizations are to be adopted as a systematic description of accounting operations, it may be expected of the system that it demonstrates internal consistency and that it demonstrates economy of generalizations. What have we, in fact?

"Conservatism often *conflicts* with the convention of the 'going concern'... Conservatism may also *conflict* with the doctrine of disclosure... Conservatism is *opposed* to consistency... Conservatism also *conflicts* with that desirable but often unattainable accounting ideal of matching costs with income."[10]

"The doctrine of disclosure tends to *overlap* the doctrine of conservatism."[11]

"The monetary unit is generally assumed to be substantially constant in value, but at times this assumption of stability has to be abandoned, with the result that accounting conventions have to be *modified*."[12]

---

[9] S. Gilman, *Accounting Concepts of Profit*, New York, Ronald Press Co., 1939.
[10] Gilman, op cit., p. 235. Italics in this and following quotations not in original.
[11] Yorston, Smyth & Brown, *Advanced Accounting*, Sydney, Law Book Co., p. 9.
[12] G. O. May, op. cit., p. 7.

It must amaze people of philosophical, or even critical, tendencies to find in a field of study, the practice of which pretends to be so precise, conflicts, oppositions, overlappings, and modifications of the kind instanced here. What is perhaps most noticeable in the first extract is that "conservatism" appears to be the nigger in the woodpile. That this doctrine should have been assailed and deposed as a doctrine of accounting may well have been expected, in view of the damage it does to the system represented by the above conventions and doctrines. But it still retains its place in accounting theory; it has even been accorded quite an exalted place.

"The most important accounting doctrine in effect on accounting statements is the doctrine of conservatism, viz. that statements should be prepared in such a way as not to overstate profits or financial strength, nor to understate losses. It is motivated by the business maxim of prudence, of being always 'on the safe side', and can be defended from the standpoint of the owner or the creditor."[13]

But we digress. To conservatism we shall return at a later point in our analysis.

It would be most helpful if we could develop a body of theory and a code for practice which would make a unity of the present divided field of business theory. We need a revolutionary theory, perhaps, something as distinct in its field as the theories of, say, Copernicus, or Einstein, or Freud, or Keynes were in their fields. And I think we may expect sometime to have such a theory, for both economics and accounting are concerned in a major sense with one common subject—the business enterprise. Meanwhile there are areas in which the economist and the accountant question the validity of each other's approach, in which the business manager and the accountant cannot always see eye to eye, and in which the economist and the manager are obviously arguing at cross purposes—the existence of these areas is clear evidence of contending theories about business behaviour, and because these theories are quite effective in their own limited areas it is unlikely that they will be supplanted by anything less compelling than a universal system which serves the several viewpoints of economist, accountant, and manager equally effectively. The present study does not attempt a complete rationalization of the subject: but one of its purposes is to attempt to clairfy some of the concepts used in these poorly-defined areas: this is its contribution to a general theory.

The "Independence" of Accounting

Now, it seems to me that many accountants are deliberately fostering the partition of accounting from other related subjects; their arguments frequently betray an intransigence which seems to imply that accounting is an independent discipline or set of operations, having principles (or, as some prefer, standards) which it may more or less impose on business managers. The infrequency with which

[13] A. A. Fitzgerald, *Analysis and Interpretation of Financial and Operating Statements,* Sydney, Butterworth, 1947, p. 25.

some writers on accounting make reference to business management or business policy and the blithe indifference they show towards the needs of managers can only be construed as supporting this idea of the independence of accounting.

It is chastening when one is confronted with this kind of notion to go back to the realm of mathematics, of which accounting is a descendant; it may be said, with some reflection on the practical significance of accounting statements, that the two are not many generations removed. May I quote Lord Russell on mathematics?

"Pure mathematics consists entirely of assertions to the effect that if such and such a proposition is true of anything, then such and such another proposition is true of that thing. It is essential not to discuss whether the first proposition is really true and not to mention what the 'anything' is of which it is supposed to be true . . . . Thus mathematics may be defined as the subject in which we never know what we are talking about, nor whether what we are saying is true."[14]

Doesn't this precisely describe the degree of abstraction of accounting records, under contemporary rules and conventions? Do we not constantly carry out accounting operations in which it is vital "not to discuss whether the first proposition is really true"? For example, do we not habitually add and subtract money sums in accounting processes which represent quite different things; these are operations which would be impossible were it not for the high degree of abstraction (unreality) which is permitted in accounting.

And here's the rub! When "pure" mathematics begins to be applied it becomes essential that the numerical symbols have identical significance—"If measures are to be merged, the unit of measure must have a sensibly common significance throughout the measuring."[15] But when accounting operations begin, that is precisely when the numerical symbols are required to pretend they have identical significance, though in fact they have not. One hesitates to say of accounting that it is "the subject in which we never know what we are talking about, nor whether what we are saying is true"; but many who have followed the price level controversy might feel like heartily endorsing the sentiment.

This abstractness was lampooned by Sweeney; but much earlier than that it was observed by A. S. Dewing:—

"Accountancy is, like all mathematical sciences which assume a correspondence between number and material things, essentially abstract. It chooses to neglect all aspects and qualities of the material things with which it deals, except the mere correspondence to money value. In the same way, the science of celestial mechanics neglects every quality of its objects except forces of attraction exerted at physical points."[16]

---

[14] Quoted from Bertrand Russell, *Mysticism and Logic,* by E. P. Northrop in *Riddles in Mathematics*, E.U.P., 1945, p. 4.

[15] J. B. Canning, *The Economics of Accountancy,* New York, Ronald Press, 1929, p. 199.

[16] *The Financial Policy of Corporations,* New York, Ronald Press, 1920, Vol. 3, p. 4.

Dewing was writing, of course, before the experience of drastic inflation impelled Sweeney and his contemporaries to consider ways of overcoming the ineffectual abstractness of conventional accounting. But today, after a 30 years' period in which accounting literature has grown as never before, accounting practice is still fundamentally the same. The comment of Canning still rings true:—

"Many economists are grieved to find that the balance sheet valuations of accountants are of mongrel origin (from the economist's point of view). They find that cash has been counted (a present valuation); that accounts, bills and notes receivable have been valued at the number of dollars expected to come in (a future valuation); that interim receivable interest accruals are valued separately from the principals to which they attach (an earning); that inventories are valued at cost or market (a purely arbitrary index); that items like organization expense, purchased goodwill, etc., having no attributes in common with the assets grouped with them, are included (valuation account balances); that fixed assets are valued at an approximation to the cost of the future services expected to become available provided that cost does not exceed cost of available substitute services (a division of costs into past and future charges). They find, moreover, that these diverse valuations of diverse things are added to find an asset total that, dollar for dollar, cannot possibly have a common significance."[17]

There will, of course, always be "diversity of things" about which records are made; but it may have been expected that something would be done about the diversity of valuations and the diversity of practices in areas where uniformity is obviously advantageous to those using accounting statements. It appears, however, that the old practices and old concepts will die hard. Here we are in the midst of a period of violently changing conditions, having emerged from a period in which economic conditions have been changing at an even more violent rate; it is clearly a testing time for accounting theories and concepts, a time of extremes, an ideal laboratory for examining the effect of different ideas, a laboratory the equal of which has never yet been available to accounting theorists. It has undeniably set them thinking, and thinking in rather different ways from those of traditional accounting, but in only few cases has the divergence been sufficient to signify a major re-appraisal of accounting.

There has been a marked reluctance to assume the obligations which such an opportunity imposes. Many of us have taken the stand that these conditions are only temporary departures from a normal state of affairs to which we shall soon return, and that therefore our techniques need no augmentation or alteration. This inertia even takes the form of assertions that stability in accounting method through such period of change contributes to the stabilizing of business

---

[17] Op. cit., p. 319.

operations and economic activity generally[18]. But to assume there is such a thing as normality is to err. Normality may be a convenient conceptual fiction; it can be little else. Conditions may have been less erratic in the nineteenth century, when modern accounting methods received general recognition and formulation: but those conditions are useless as norms in the middle of the twentieth century. With Littleton we must agree:—

"It is no fault of nineteenth century theories, that they do not fully meet twentieth century needs; a better criticism would be that twentieth century needs are so poorly comprehended that we still try to make nineteenth century notions suffice."[19]

And as for the notion that traditional accounting contributes to economic stability, it is not difficult to demonstrate that "conservative" accounting has quite the opposite effect, depressing profits in periods of recession and exaggerating them in periods of recovery.

The wish to stand off from the hurly-burly of economic change implies the abdication of responsibility: it leads to what one may call Accounting in Wonderland. It is my contention, however, that we may not, if we value professional integrity, lightly put off the objections which have been raised to traditional methods; accounting cannot be independent of business reality, no matter how convenient it may be to draw accounts which yield information irrelevant to business purposes. The relevance of the accounting function to business purposes we shall develop at length in the succeeding sections.

Accounting and Management

The last 20 years have seen the growth of a much livelier interest in the formal study of management and management processes than had been evident before that time. This new body of ideas, as in the origins of economic theory and accounting theory, was, and still is, poorly defined; and like many new subjects, it is attracting much attention, by reason of its novelty, from technologists of all kinds. Among these technologists there appear to be some accountants who have been infected by the virus[20]; both local and overseas writers appear to want to dignify one or another accounting specialty with the epithets "management" and "managerial". Unless the relationship between management and accounting is clearly understood, such a step will only result in further confusing the already confused and fuzzy theory of accounting. It savours of an attempt by accountants

[18] Cf. F. Sewell Bray, *Precision and Design in Accountancy*, London, Gee & Co., 1947, p. 23: "Accountants have been reproached for their conservatism but in so far as such conservatism has sought to safeguard the long term financial stability of business enterprise it has been itself a factor making for economic well-being." One wonders to what extent this is an *a posteriori* rationalization.

[19] A. C. Littleton, *Accounting Evolution to 1900*, New York, American Institute Publishing Co., 1933, p. 217.

[20] The word "virus" is used with intent, for the awakening of interest in management theory seems to have induced a kind of pathological condition which militates against the maintenance of scientific neutrality in our thinking.

to dominate non-accounting operations by making rules and setting accounting standards which convey the impression of technical imperialism. But it is the part of wisdom for the accountant to stick to his last—or should I say to his ledger—even if it were not at the same time of great practical value in the management of business. To demonstrate this it will be necessary to consider the scope of the responsibilities of management and of accountants.

Now, unfortunately, although much has been written round the subject or around some aspects of management, there is as yet far too little that is analytical in the literature; and until the analytical approach supersedes the descriptive, management literature is likely to remain a confusion of tongues. It is suggested, however, that management may be tentatively considered to comprise three groups of activity: firstly, deciding on courses of action to be pursued; secondly, providing the means by which they may be pursued or executed; and thirdly, reviewing their execution. This is the bare minimum. It presupposes, of course, that in practice managers are obliged to attain certain goals and that these groups of activity are conditioned by those goals or objectives; but for the moment these goals will be taken for granted. The liberty will be taken, too, for the moment, of using the words "manager" and "management" to refer principally to top management, and of using "accountant" to refer principally to the chief accountant.

If managerial duties are envisaged as deciding on, facilitating, and reviewing operations, it is clear that managers assume the responsibility for the end result of these operations. The responsibility for this may be located at no other point, or assumed by no other group than top management. This is so whether the top managers are efficient or not; whether their methods are adequate, up to date, and relevant to the purposes they purport to serve, or just the reverse. Assumption of responsibility for the end product implies assumption at the same time of responsibility for the methods, intermediate steps, and devices used in producing the end product. In particular it implies responsibility for the forms of communication, of recording and reporting, of accounting that are employed, even though, as an eminent executive has recently opined: "Most businessmen do not know the kinds of information they ought to have to manage effectively." The sense in which this responsibility is imputed to management is that in the managers resides the final power of decision on matters of technique; that only methods which they judge to serve their purposes will be tolerated. The enterprise is conducted at their direction and, subject only to law, to their externally-determined goals, and to the will of those they represent, their discretion is absolute and unchallengeable.

None of these things can be said about the accountant in enterprise, however. Let us consider the position of the accountant, as accountant, leaving aside the diversity of posts which may be filled and functions which may be served by particular accountants in specific circumstances. The accountant in business is the servant of the management. He is engaged by the management to aid in the processes of managing, by specializing in the provision of certain kinds of information. His salary is at the disposal of the management. His authority, his duties and responsibilities are determined by the management. He may be dismissed at the pleasure of the management. This means that, vocationally, he owes duties to no other party, neither to creditors nor to investors nor to prospective investors. No creditor or investor may take proceedings against him if the statements eventually issued by his management as financial statements are grossly misleading. He is charged with no legal obligation to protect the interests of any group related to the enterprise or any person or persons at large in the community. If an accountant chooses to try to persuade his management to do certain things (e.g. issue better financial statements) in the interests of outside parties, he may be giving expression to what he feels to be a professional obligation, but he is under no legal duty to do such things. Such influence as he has is persuasive, not authoritative.

Furthermore, what is said here of an accountant employed by a business firm applies with equal force where an accountant in public practice is engaged, as an accountant, by a firm which has no need for the full-time services of an accountant. Taking the whole case, then, it must be obvious that what accountants do as accountants is in the interests of and for the purposes of managers or "that vague body known as the management".

4.—Accounting and Financial Management

The responsibilities of top management and of accountants are thus quite distinct; they are owed to quite different groups of people. To proceed with our analysis we shall have to move to a lower level in the business hierarchy, where functions subsidiary to general management are performed; we shall abandon the restricted use of "management" which we adopted for the previous section and consider management as it may be applied to one functional sector of business operations. We want to discuss the relationship between accounting and financial management because this relationship lies at the root of some of the confusion in contemporary thought.

Financial management is a unifying concept which is relatively new in the theory of management. Production management and sales management we know; like the poor, they are always with us. But though much has been written about the external financial operations of business enterprises, little has been done to reduce internal financial operations to system or to establish the relationship between both internal and external types of operation. The notion is so new that very few Australian enterprises include in their organization structure a financial executive (other than the accountant); so new that an English writer, after quoting the following opinion (1947) of the American Institute of Accountants: "Any basic change in the accounting treatment of depreciation should await further study of the nature and concept of business income. The immediate problem can and should be met by financial management," was moved to comment: "The term 'financial management' is not very explicit, but, in round terms, it would seem that the Committee of the American Institute solved the problem to their own satisfaction (with the exception of four dissenting members including the Chairman) by placing the responsibility for dealing with it squarely on the shoulders of some other body. This is scarcely a courageous decision and leaves unsolved the question of the relationship between the accountant and financial management who, on the face of it, would in industry appear to be closely related."[21]

Several notions are necessary for a study of this relationship. Firstly, financial management involves the same kind of operations as management generally, but they are applied to a restricted field of business. There occur, for example, problems of deciding on, facilitating, and reviewing financial operations and financial aspects of general operations. There are specific financial objectives, just as general management is concerned with the orientation of the whole of operations to the general objectives of an enterprise. There are certain discretionary areas in which the financial executive may operate for the purpose of maintaining the solvency and economic effectiveness of the enterprise.

Secondly, to be more specific, financial management includes the establishment of financial policies, the long-run financial plans of an undertaking. It seems particularly important to observe this: if there are financial plans or decisions to be made or policies to be laid down, that is a function of financial management; if there are adjustments to be made in financial relationships, if there are steps to be taken to ensure a steady flow of funds to an undertaking, if there are measures to be taken to ensure the protection of the financial interests of those who supply funds—these things are the function of financial management; they form part of the group of activities which the term "financial management" is used to describe, no matter who, in a particular undertaking, carries them out.

Thirdly, we may include in this idea of financial management the maintenance of the financial integrity of an undertaking, of preventing its existence being imperilled by reason of financial inadequacy or folly. Note here, however, the whole burden of preserving an undertaking from liquidation is not imposed on financial management. There are other resources needed by firms the lack of which may force their liquidation, and there is the question of demand for the services they render, the lack of which may also force liquidation. Financial management is concerned with financial considerations, both internal and external, only.

If the terms used above in describing financial management be perused, many things will be found which are fairly commonly found also in the literature of accounting. Works in which references to these matters occur should be read with discrimination, for it is relatively easy for the impression to be gained from them that accounting is the very process by which these functions are carried

---

[21] E. H. Davison, "Accounting for Survival", *Industry,* February 1949.

out. A few examples may be given to illustrate the ease with which one may confuse matters of record with matters of judgement.

The first example is from depreciation accounting. There is no point in citing any particular writer here, for it is almost universal practice to approve some systematic procedure for making the provision for depreciation, such as the straight line method. The method may be a convenient way of ensuring that some record is made of the fact that depreciation is occurring; but it may readily lead one to believe, or to accept without argument, that the formal calculation expresses a reality—a reality the measurement of which, however, entails judgement of a high order rather than obedience (of a high order, maybe) to a formal accounting rule.

Financial statement analysis provides the second example. The subject is frequently treated so formally that one may easily fall a prey to the idea that manipulation of financial statement figures has supplanted judgement in the arrangement of the financial affairs of business entities. This view is implied in Foulke's phrase "the growing importance of Arabic figures in the business world",[22] and seems to underlie attempts to justify the use of typical industry ratios in the financial management of enterprises.

There are other examples; not a little of the work on cost control overemphasizes the accounting formality and neglects the fact that the controlling of costs is a matter of the judgement of many executives not closely related to accounting or financial matters; the assumption that prices are based on any cost-plus system overlooks the judgement implicit in intelligent price determination. These four examples are sufficient to demonstrate that the functions of recording and of judgement bear on precisely the same business issues, and that great care is necessary in deciding where the one ceases to operate and the other begins. Furthermore, as formal representations of business facts are so much easier to handle than the unabstracted realities, it is no wonder that the formal aspects of such matters as depreciation accounting and policy, credit-giving, cost control, and price determination frequently appear to have impressed accountants as the aspects of dominating importance. All this boils down to the proposition that financial management has been generally ignored by accountants.

Two Tentative Definitions

In order that comparisons may be made, however, it will be necessary to offer rather more definite descriptions of financial management and accounting than may be conveyed by the above general comments. These descriptions are not tendered, however, as the last word in defining either subject; they are offered for the clarity their understanding will impart to the subsequent discussion. One of the errors to be avoided is describing accounting in more grandiose terms than is necessary: the definition of the American Institute of

---

[22] R. A. Foulke, *Practical Financial Statement Analysis,* New York, McGraw Hill Book Co., 1945, Ch. 1.

Accountants Committee on Terminology is the least pretentious in this regard. Accounting is defined as: "the art of recording, classifying, and summarizing in a significant manner and in terms of money, transactions, and events which are, in part at least, of a financial character, and interpreting the results thereof"[23].

"Interpretation" is included in almost all modern definitions, but until the implications of interpretation are fully discussed (as they have not been hitherto) judgement on this issue may be reserved. The above definition, which makes reference to the doubtful function of interpretation, will be accepted, however, for the sake of argument.

Of financial management there are far fewer definitions than there are of accounting. In 1945, when a course in financial management was first offered at the Sydney Technical College, an extensive study of the literature failed to unearth any comprehensive definition and we were obliged to define it, for our purposes, in terms of the field covered in the literature and the group of activities dealing with financial operations in the practice of business management. That definition is in roughly the following terms:—

Financial management comprises the planning, organizing, directing, and controlling of all activities relating to the acquisition and application of the financial resources of a business entity; its purposes are the maintenance of such a financial position and of such relationships with external parties as will be conducive to the economical supply, when necessary, of finance from external sources for the general purposes of the entity.

Neither criticism of nor comment on this concept has come to our notice since it was published in 1947. It is adopted for the purposes of this demonstration, however, not on that ground, but because it describes reasonably fully a group of activities which are of vital interest to management and which are concerned almost solely with financial matters.

5.—Possible Relationships Between Accounting and Financial Management

We may now consider at length the relationships which could possibly exist between accounting and financial management and, by a process of elimination, attempt to resolve the confusion which appears to exist both in theory and practice. There are six possibilities:—

(i) that accounting and financial management are identical fields (i.e., A ≡ B; see diagram);

(ii) that accounting and financial management are cognate fields, both being of equal rank and of equal significance in the management of enterprises (i.e., A is neither superior nor inferior to B);

(iii) that accounting is the senior field, dictating, on the basis of its own rules, the aims and processes of financial management (i.e., A is superior to B);

---

[23] Report of the Committee, May 1941, *Accounting Research Bulletin No.* 9.

(iv) that accounting is the subordinate field, its operations being based on and determined by financial management (i.e., B is superior to A);

(v) that accounting is the wider field, and that part of accounting is financial management (i.e., A includes B); and

(vi) that financial management is the wider field, part of it being accounting (i.e., B includes A).

The cases may be represented diagrammatically as follows:—

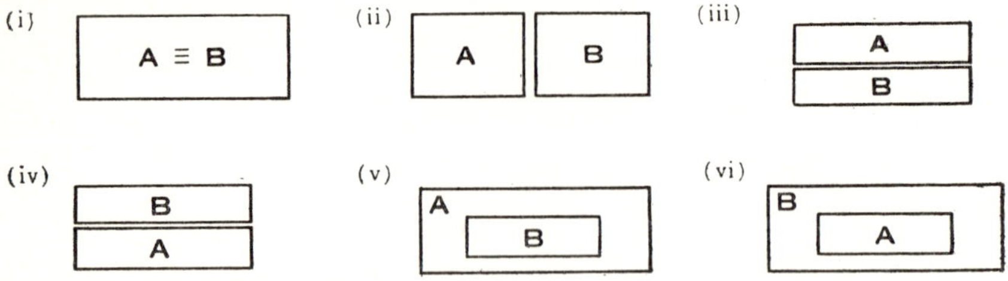

They will be dealt with *seriatim.*

(i) In spite of Davison's suggestion that in industry accounting and financial management are closely related, it is seldom seriously contended that the two are identical. Yet there are a number of business practices which are considered to derive their rationale from accounting reasoning, but which are in fact reasoning about financial management; and to that extent it may often appear as though writers assume tacitly that the two subjects cover identical ground. Consider, for example, the following:—

"Apportionments [of income and expenditure] are based on certain well-established rules, conventions, and doctrines of accounting, in the formulation of which conservatism... has been the over-riding consideration. In some cases, in the interests of financial prudence, the application to known facts of conservative accounting conventions may be carried to more extreme lengths than in others. For these reasons, profit and loss statements and balance sheets are conditioned both by accounting convention and by opinion and financial policy; the 'profit' disclosed by a profit and loss statement must be interpreted in the light of accounting concepts of profit, and must be regarded as an expression of opinions which have been formed with special care for financial prudence. . . ."[24]

Although the same source was quoted earlier for an example of the recognition of the two influences, accounting rules and financial policy, on the form of financial statements, this passage appears to mingle the two, as if they were identical in purpose and effect. Promiscuity is diagnosed here because the passage is not a statement "for the purpose of argument" but part of the general development of a case. Observe how the last sentence states two criteria for interpreting disclosed profit as if the two criteria could not be in conflict,

[24] A. A. and G. E. Fitzgerald, op. cit., p. 16.

i.e. as if the two criteria were derived from the one body of consistent propositions. Although there is no outright statement that the two fields are identical, identity may readily be inferred, particularly by inexperienced students learning the theory of accounting. Great care should be taken to avoid this kind of confusion arising in the elementary theory of the subject.

A second example is taken from the theory of management. T. G. Rose, whose work on techniques of managerial control is usually refreshingly informative, describes seven different "management functions"[25]: "Production, Distribution, Development, Accounts and Finance, Legal and Secretarial, Personnel and Industrial Relations, and General Management." This list may be expected either to convey the impression that "Accounts and Finance" is one field covered equally by both subjects, or to imply that "Accounts" is the dominant subject (something like the third possibility). Both views are logically untenable, and both are as dangerous in management as they are in accounting.

These may be regarded as tenuous examples however; it is not consciously argued, by those who are interested in accounting or financial management, that they are identical fields.

(ii) The second possibility, that accounting and financial management are of equal rank, is also to be denied.

For an instance of this view reference is made to the work of Henri Fayol. He commences his study of management with a division of all activities to which industrial undertakings give rise into six groups: numbers 3 and 5 of those groups represent financial activities and accounting activities respectively, giving them quite clearly an independent and, by inference, a collateral status. He describes them thus:—

"3. *Financial Activities*

"Nothing is done without this function entering into it. Capital is required for personnel, plant, tools, raw materials, dividends [*sic*], development, reserves, etc. Shrewd financial management is necessary to obtain capital, to make optimum use of available funds, to avoid foolhardy commitments. Many potentially profitable enterprises die suffering from lack of money. Nor is any reform or improvement possible without finances or credit. An essential condition of success is to keep constant watch over the financial position of the business.

"5. *Accounting Activities*

"This group is the visual organ of businesses. It must throw up at any given moment, present position and future trend, must afford

[25] *Higher Control*, London, Pitman, 1945, p. 25. The use of the phrase "management functions" is, in my view, misleading. The seven groups of activities mentioned are functions commonly found in business in respect of any one of which management may be necessary if that function is sufficiently important to a firm or if it is, of necessity, organized in a complex manner. These groups of activities may be more usefully designated "the common operating functions of business".

accurate, clear and precise information about the economic position of the concern. An efficient accounting system, clear and simple, giving an accurate idea of the firm's condition is a powerful managerial instrument. . . ."[26]

Fayol was not primarily concerned with the relationships between these two groups of activities, hence he does not directly contribute to the solution of our present problem. But the fact that these two appear as distinct in his analysis evidences a belief in the dissimilarity of their purposes. Furthermore, that they appear in a classification purporting to cover all business activities in industrial undertakings, suggests that Fayol regarded them as co-ordinate.

Now this view entails that the relationship between the two groups of activities should be a two-way relationship; each should in fact be the source of argument directed towards influencing the operations of the other, and at the same time each should be the subject of argument by the other; and lastly neither line of argument should be presumed to have less validity by reason of the status of its source than the other.

That this does not square with the facts of business is obvious. Accounting processes are frequently influenced by the exigencies of financial management[27], whereas financial policies and financial management as such are not to any appreciable extent influenced by accounting processes. If there is any jugglery, it is the accounts which are juggled to serve "financial" ends; financial structure and financial policies are not modified just to make the accounting easier or harder. The two fields are clearly not co-ordinate.

(iii) The third possibility stated above is that accounting is the senior field, dictating on the basis of its own rules the aims and processes of financial management.

Such a notion may be considered by the informed to be so patently erroneous that it may be dismissed out of hand. But examples may be drawn, even from authors most highly respected in the accounting fraternity, to establish the case that accounting is the superior subject. It may be said in defence of these writers that their statements are born of a concept of accounting which confuses accounting and managerial functions, but such a form of excuse does not validate the arguments put forward.

This confusion is so general that the examples given will be in terms of authors' approaches rather than by reference to the works of particular writers. Several examples are given.

Firstly, almost every argument adduced to support the traditional historical cost basis for depreciation computations is an argument which exalts accounting to a status senior to the discretionary field of financial management. The argument that the historic cost basis is

[26] *General and Industrial Management*, London, Pitman, pp. 4-5.
[27] Whether or not this should be so is not the concern of the present argument.

"generally recognized"[28] and is superior, for this reason, to any other basis, sets accounting custom above reproach from any angle, including the financial management angle. The argument that the historic cost basis provides a "systematic" way of dealing with depreciation also carries the implication of superiority; financial problems are presumably to be dealt with only by some neat, regular, systematic technique conceived by Procrustean accountants who are not averse to a little lopping or stretching of business facts provided they can be made to fit the system. The argument that "the uncertainty of any estimate of replacement cost makes it a less 'desirable' basis for computing depreciation than the original known cost"[29] implies that the historic cost method involves no such uncertainty (which is not true) and that in any case the criterion for "desirability" (however that is conceived) is accounting convenience and not service in financial management.

But more important than quoting specific arguments is the general attitude which underlies them and permeates all the apologia for historic cost. If one reads the official pronouncements of some of the institutes with an eye to this kind of rationalization, the conservatives appear almost to fall over backwards in their efforts to avoid this accursed thing, replacement cost. More significance appears to be attached to the record of a market fact written in a book 10, 20 years or more ago than to all the judgement and experience (which incidentally are part of the basis of market facts) which businessmen are accustomed to buy from their financial and other expert advisers. The written book entry seems to be a subject of veneration, of persistent but blind faith. The tone of this attitude is given by the impassioned peroration to an article on historic costs by G. Moller: "Let us therefore . . . cling to historic costs as a basis for depreciation charges, lest we come under suspicion of pretending to have superhuman powers of foresight."[30] One might be pardoned for feeling that to be condemned for having subhuman intelligence would be a worse fate; and, as the inadequacy of the traditional basis to reveal the pertinent facts of business under recent and present conditions is understood by a growing number of business people, that may well be the fate of the accountant unless he augments his technique.

The second group of indications of the prevalence of the view that accounting is the superior function is given by the attitude being adopted among accountants regarding the disclosure of business facts in financial statements. One of the major functions of published financial statements is the maintenance of harmonious relationships between the user and the supplier of finance; hence published

---

[28] E.g., editorial, *Business Week,* quoted in *Journal of Accountancy,* January, 1949. See also the present writer's comments in a note "Depreciation on Replacement Cost," in *The Australian Accountant,* February, 1950 (see p. 305, *post*).

[29] Sanders, Hatfield and Moore, *A Statement of Accounting Principles,* New York, American Institute of Accountants, 1938, p. 32.

[30] "Historic Costs—the Lesser Evil". *The Canadian Chartered Accountant,* July 1949, p. 28.

accounting statements are undeniably a tool serving financial management. Their form, content, and design should, it is submitted, serve the aims of financial management, and should be conducive to the creation of certain states of mind among the recipients. The formal accounting approach to report design is so general, and its treatment constitutes such a large part of the work so far done on design, that accountants appear to have appropriated, or are endeavouring to appropriate, this important part of the field of business communications to themselves.

Thirdly, the existence of any discretionary area higher than accounting but junior to top or general management is not contemplated in most of the literature. Just because accounting theory was already established before financial management began to be examined, there is a tendency to imagine it is senior in the business hierarchy even if only by reason of long service.

It may be objected that the case for believing that accounting is elevated to an unjustifiable status by some writers rests entirely on circumstantial evidence, on inference and imputation; but it is considered to be a strong one nevertheless; for, to judge from published contributions to accounting theory, there has been insufficient analysis to lay bare the distinction between accounting and financial management; until that is done, both subjects remain a confused and confusing tangle.

Strong disavowal of the third possibility, that accounting is the senior field, must be recorded. Further, and for the same reasons, we must abandon the fifth possibility; accounting is not the inclusive field of which financial management is an integral part.

(iv) The fourth possibility is the reverse of the third; it requires accounting to be viewed as a group of activities subordinate to financial management. This is, in my view, the most realistic approach of the first four. The criticism offered in respect of each of the former three possibilities establishes quite an effective body of argument in favour of this view.

But the relationship is not precisely determined: it is possible that although financial management may be senior in status in the hierarchy of business operations, accounting may be more extensive in purpose. It may serve many other business purposes than merely financial purposes. This possibility is examined below.

(vi) The sixth possibility is put forward as the most logical arrangement of the two functions. Its terms may be recalled: Financial management is the wider field, part of it being accounting.

Financial management is, by definition, a field of activities upon the adequacy of which the promotion of profitable enterprise, the preservation of entity assets, and the conservation of entity earning capacity depend. It is not only of major significance in aiding the execution of the objects of an undertaking; it is of such vital importance in the eyes of the highest authority in the hierarchy of most business undertakings that few of its aspects are delegated. This cannot be contested.

The only question now to be debated is whether accounting is to be regarded as part of the field of financial management or whether it represents quite an independent set of operations not subject to financial management principles (whatever they may be). What we have in fact to decide is whether accounting serves only the financial ends of management or whether it serves other ends as well.

This will require a short study of some of the other ends which management may be considered to accept. On the one hand management must accept the general objective of the undertaking served, that is to supply a socially acceptable good or service. What is an acceptable good or service, however, is not determinable by accounting processes, hence accounting is not relevant to this objective. It may be observed that no mention is made of price at this point, for to introduce price introduces financial ends.

On the other hand management may accept as a general aim the provision for workers of opportunities to earn a competence under conditions which are satisfying to the social and individual wants and drives of workers. The extent to which this is done is not measurable in any accounting terms: workers' psychic satisfactions are grouped among the intangibles about which accounting has absolutely nothing to say.

There are no other such general ends of management beside the financial ends, which accounting, by general agreement, ought to serve. It may be objected, however, that accounting can be and is used for other internal purposes than financial purposes. It may be pointed out, for example, that Hayes' *Accounting for Executive Control* is a book devoted to ways of applying accounting information or modifications of it in the management of supply activities (purchasing), of credit giving, of production and selling operations, of personnel administration, and so on. It is granted that accounting may be used in these directions; but still it serves only a financial end. Take the case of supply management, for example. The efficiency of the supply manager and his staff is measured largely by their ability to maintain an adequate supply of materials for production activities or an adequate supply of commodities for the selling unit of an undertaking. Whether a given supply is adequate or whether relationships with suppliers are happy is not determinable by any accounting procedure. What is determinable by an accounting procedure is the cost of goods procured and the costs involved in procuring them—but these are essentially financial matters, and in so far as financial aspects of supply operations should be observed and controlled, accounting techniques or modifications of them may be devised for the purpose. This is all Hayes' proposals amount to.

This is not to deny that non-financial incidents of supply management or any similar function are important, nor to deny that they are controllable: they are often quite as significant as financial aspects, and they are controllable; but the information reviewed for control purposes is a different class of statistics from that with which accounting is concerned. Only an adequate general statistical service will provide the data relevant to non-financial aspects of business management.

There is one last question we may ask: may not accounting be conceived as an independent source of general information which will serve top management by providing unbiased checks on the operations of the diverse functional executives of an undertaking? Accounting may be considered as independent of other functional processes (except financial management) but it neither provides general information nor unbiased checks. The mere fact that its concern is money figures restricts the generality of the information and introduces a monetary bias.

This discussion of the relationship between accounting and financial management has led us to conclude then, that the logical view to take, the view most consistent with observable business realities, is that accounting is part of the field of financial management and that it is subject in many respects to the financial policies of the undertakings it serves, even though at the same time it is subject through such policies to overriding considerations such as the law and the general interest of the community. To put it briefly, "accounting is the language of finance"[31]. It must be viewed in the same relationship to finance as language is to the human creature; it must serve the purposes of financial management just as language serves the purposes of man.

6.—Consequences of the Distinction

The distinction we have drawn has several immediate consequences. We are able to eliminate, by a matter of simple transplantation, quite a number of the obvious inconsistencies in accounting theory. That may seem to be of only academic consequence, but in such a field as accounting, with such obvious and important practical aspects, no theoretical issue can be far removed from practice. Theory is about practice. If we are informed about our subject, we can hardly be content with its frequent deficiencies, its incapacity to stand up to the canons of scientific method. If we are applying a method which lacks obvious inconsistencies, our practice will be the more confident, our conclusions more informed, our services to our managements or to our clients more valuable.

Conservatism has no Place in Accounting

The first object of our transplantation is the doctrine of conservatism; if our analysis has been satisfactory it will appear that this doctrine may be conveniently transplanted to the body of rules which guide the financial management of entities. This will immediately relieve the theory of all those unwelcome contradictions, conflicts, and oppositions which have hitherto been observed, and which have proved such a serious stumbling block to clear thinking about the function of accounting. But the practical accountant is perhaps entitled to greater compensation for such a change in his long-

[31] R. A. Foulke, op. cit., p. 29.

established *modus operandi* than a merely theoretical consequence; and the business manager, on whose behalf the financial statements are drawn, is perhaps entitled to expect some considerable advantage to accrue from such a change in the practice of accounting as this new notion implies.

To treat these practical consequences, it is necessary to consider conservatism in each of two distinct applications: there is the conservatism which is accepted as part of the accounting system and is thus a significant factor influencing the accounts to be used for the internal management of an undertaking; and there is the conservatism which is applied in the preparation of the published financial statements and which is a significant factor influencing the actions and attitudes of persons and institutions external to the undertaking. If this distinction is drawn, the first kind of conservatism will fall within the theory of accounting. The second will fall beyond such theory: it will form part of the theory of financial management.

One practical consequence of this division is to establish without equivocation who is responsible for submitting conservative figures to management and for submitting conservative figures (though the extent of conservatism may differ) to owners, investors, and creditors; the accountant is responsible for the former and the management for the latter. That any particular accountant may act for the one firm as accountant and as financial manager simultaneously is immaterial, provided this duality of function is recognized and provided a distinction is made between the concepts he uses in framing accounting statements relevant to the purposes of each function.

Now, I can imagine no valid reason why accountants, acting as accountants, should not draw their accounts so as to show as precisely as is possible the facts of business. If there are several aspects of the same set of facts, there can surely be no objection to the presentation of them all; in fact, one might say it is imperative that the accountant should present them all, for it is surely the most important justification of accounting in business that it is the means—the only means—by which business managers may judge the economic efficiency of their enterprises, and maintain the financial integrity and stability of those enterprises. But the facts should not be distorted by any accounting practice such as is justified by conservatism.

"... the accountant now functions at the right hand of the management of industrial enterprise. In such a connexion the accountant is required to provide information which shows the results of transactions which have taken place in the form of carefully designed periodical financial statements which reveal the points of equilibrium of an enterprise in both short- and long-term periods, so as to retain it on an 'even keel' and determine its general direction ... the preservation of both the short- and the long-term financial stability of business enterprise is more important than ever before, and consequently the work of the accountant in relation to management problems is likely to be more valuable and more essential than ever before."[32]

---

[32] F. Sewell Bray, op. cit., pp. 82-3.

When general economic and social conditions are as fluid as at present, the maintenance of stability can only be encompassed intelligently by intelligent use of the facts—all the facts. Concealment of even some of the facts on the grounds that they are difficult to extract or are not provided by the customary techniques of accounting is inexcusable. If business undertakings fail it is seldom the accountant who is deemed responsible; the brunt of failure is borne by the management. This being the case, to withhold information or to conceal information, even if under the guise of generally accepted practice, seems to be quite unethical; for the accountant takes for granted the responsibility of management for success or failure, but denies management the right to have the facts in their naked reality.

Particular examples where the accepted accounting procedures lead to misrepresentation of relevant business facts are the cost or market rule for stock valuation, the methods of providing for depreciation on any other basis than usage of physical facilities, and the charging of capital expenditures against current income. These things may all be done rather mechanically, and with a careless disregard for the managerial necessity of unbiased information. We are not unaware of the arguments that have been used to justify the accountant's conventional procedure in these matters, not the least of which, as we have observed before, is that the conventional procedure has contributed to the stability of business in the past. I have no quarrel with the effect, however; it is the method by which the effect is obtained that is invalid. Existing accounting methods involve a mingling of two distinct operations: the first is a fact-finding operation, the second an operation by which effect is given to judgement based on the accounting facts and all other facts relevant to the business situation. The first operation is within the competence of the accountant; the second is equally clearly beyond his scope. If the results of the fact-finding operation—the reported facts—include already some allowances for errors and contingencies, how may the second operation be performed in a rational and informed manner? For, the executive who must interpret the accounts into financially significant ideas will not know what margins are already provided, in the reported figures, due to conservative accounting rules; he will therefore perhaps allow for matters already given expression in the accounts, and the effect will be doubly conservative. This may be no disadvantage to a firm in the short run, but in the long run it may require extensive adjustments in capital structure or asset values.

In this connexion I recall a line of argument used by Mr. W. Scott in dealing with those who are unconvinced of the practical value of the break even chart; he quotes: "By every principle of aerodynamics and all known practical tests, including wind tunnel and other methods, the bumble bee cannot fly. But it does", and adds: "Perhaps the break even chart shouldn't work. But, with careful thought and preparation, it does."[33] This line of argument may easily be applied to modern accounting; one might well say "It may be illogical, but it

[33] "The Profitgraph," *The Australian Accountant,* March 1949, p. 81.

works," and consider that the end of the matter. But such an attitude is intellectually unsatisfying and scientifically unjustifiable. It suggests that managers make profits in spite of the lack of logic in their aids, not because of the service accounting renders. It implies that the secret of success in business is not so much a matter of rational, informed judgement as of sheer good fortune. If the flight of the bumble bee cannot be explained, it must only mean that "every principle of aerodynamics" is not yet known. The physicists are not content with a body of principles which leaves important phenomena unexplained; neither should accountants be satisfied with a confused system, even though it has unquestionably been useful in its time. Accounting must be freed of the incubus of conservatism; accountants must visualize their function as the presentation of unvarnished facts. Only in this way may the inherent inexactitude in contemporary accounting be eliminated.

Disclosure is not a Function of Accounting

The second application of conservatism covers the same ground as the doctrine of disclosure; and the doctrine of disclosure is the second object of the transplantation we referred to earlier in this section. If our analysis has been acceptable, it will be agreed that disclosure is correctly described as a technique of management, or, if we wish to moralize, a duty of management; it is a technique designed to influence in one way or another the recipients of financial statements, and is thus closely related to financial aspects of management. I am unable to agree with Professor Sanders' view:—

"In spite of all efforts to make accounting factual and objective, it cannot be wholly divested of estimate and conjecture, nor can it fail to take account of the impressions which different presentations will make on the minds of different groups of people."[34]

Accounting, in my view, must not take any account whatever of the "impressions" which might be conveyed by the accounts; the function of accounting is to convey facts. If any manager considers it necessary to detract from, to add to, to explain, or to belittle the importance of such facts, for financial or other purposes, that should be regarded as his affair. It is, I feel, largely because accountants have not kept their hands out of this field of managerial judgement and policy that the auditor was implicated in the Royal Mail Case.

Stephen Gilman describes the word "doctrine" in relation to accounting "as referring to a general statement of accounting or reporting policy"[35]. "Policy" gives the real clue to the nature of the concept of disclosure. Consider the policy: It is the intention of the Board that the published financial statements of the Company shall contain such information as will inform shareholders no less fully, for their purposes, than the directors are informed. This is not a policy about accounting, nor a policy arising out of accounting necessity: it is not an accounting policy, but it is a policy closely related to financial management.

---

[34] "Two Concepts of Accounting", *Harvard Business Review,* July 1949, p. 507.
[35] Op. cit., pp. 186-7.

Disclosure is to be considered as a matter of managerial policy, not a matter of accounting doctrine. According to this view, disclosure is the outcome of the action or agitation of interested groups (including the managerial group) in the community; it is the response of management to the demands of other groups. The merits and deficiencies of any published statement do not have to be judged by accounting standards of disclosure, but by what becomes necessary in view of the attitudes of and the relationships between different groups in a community. It is through the conflict of views of different groups in a community that socially acceptable codes evolve, in this field as in any other field of wide general interest.

Furthermore, to classify disclosure as a managerial policy or practice gives meaning to the otherwise meaningless epithet "adequate" often so lamely attached to disclosure. If we accept disclosure as a doctrine of accounting, there is no test within accounting theory, as it now stands, for adequacy of disclosure; but if we regard it as a business policy, the test of adequacy is the ability of a given amount of information to build and maintain mutually satisfactory relationships with the groups of people for whose benefit disclosure is made. "Adequate disclosure" is still a relative term, but at least we know to what it relates.

In removing disclosure from the doctrines of accounting I do not mean that accountants should thereupon cease to have any interest in the question; just as in distinguishing accounting from financial management I do not mean to suggest that accountants should ignore financial management. My purpose here is to tidy up the theory rather than to limit the sphere of interest of accountants. I consider accountants may contribute substantially to the improvement of published statements, even though at the same time I deny that disclosure is a question of accounting.

The Dependence of Accounting

The third point of impact of the distinction we have drawn between accounting and financial management is the notion of the independence of accounting theory and technique. But, whereas the first two points require the removal of two matters of policy from accounting theory, this third requires a new postulate to be added. Accounting justifies its place as a technique of business in the measure that it contributes to the management of the financial affairs of business. Its technique must be adapted if managerial problems necessitate a new approach or additional information. Its traditions must be abandoned if they are found to have no realistic rationale or if new techniques are conceived for serving business purposes more effectively. If it is accepted among business managers that "to insist on recovering historical costs is irrational, and people who obstinately insist on doing so must be phenomenally lucky to avoid the bankruptcy courts"[36], then, I believe, accountants must amend their procedures to conform with the requirements of management.

---

[36] G. J. Stigler, *The Theory of Price,* New York, Macmillan, 1946, p. 149.

To Auguste Comte is attributed the observation "that mathematical facts are the simplest, least complex, and most crude of phenomena, the most abstract, barren, and remote from reality, in contradistinction to social facts, which are the most complex and subtle"[37]. The facts of business and of the business environment are all social facts: so complex are they that many ways of presenting them must be used in the management of enterprises. The solvency of an enterprise, for example, may be indicated roughly by the appearance of its balance sheet; but the balance sheet hardly begins to tell the story. The nature of liabilities is scarcely explained; the attitudes of suppliers and bankers towards debtor entities are not translatable into accounting terms; there is not even a hint of the relationships of such a debtor with other sources of financial assistance than those being used at balancing date. When a businessman (say a banker) is confronted with the question whether he shall extend credit or not to a client or customer, he will seldom be satisfied to accept the balance sheet as conclusive one way or the other if he is in a position to get sufficient of the other information mentioned above.

There is no reason, therefore, to consider accounting practice to be beyond modification to suit the purposes of financial management. I would consequently like to have accepted as the first postulate of accounting: "Accounting is a fact-finding function, the aim of which is to assist in the financial management of enterprises by whatever means management considers adequate." This provides a foundation for accounting theory—what was described above as a realistic organizational setting—which leaves little doubt as to the relationship of accounting practice to management.

7.—Conclusion

As I look back over the ground covered in this study I feel that the results may appear to many to be quite meagre. We seem to have laboured wordily to bring forth quite a puny addition to accounting knowledge. In fact, after reviewing the progress that has been made over the last 20 years in codifying accounting concepts, some may feel that the discussion has upset the system of rules that was, till now, becoming accepted; with Pope, they might complain:—

> "Lo, thy dread Empire, Chaos! is restor'd;
> Light dies before thy uncreating word;
> Thy hand, great Anarch! lets the curtain fall,
> And universal Darkness buries All."

The outlook, however, is not as gloomy as that, I like to believe. Many accountants are restive because of the deficiencies in accounting theory and the irrelevancies in accounting practice which we have discussed. But the fact that the doctrines of conservatism and disclosure are still peddled as accounting doctrines suggests that many accountants can see no way out of the impasse. The concept of financial management appears to me to provide such a way, for it

[37] H. Fayol, op. cit., p. 86.

permits a splitting up of financial fact-finding and judgement on financial matters into two distinct functions and two separate subjects of study.

In conclusion, I should add (though in a research lecture this should not be necessary) that the view here put forward is to be regarded only in the nature of an hypothesis for further study. It seems to me to be a satisfactory hypothesis about the two subjects I have examined. It is, moreover, an hypothesis which I find necessary to any direct treatment of the problems posed by the general subject "Accounting and Financial Policy", even though no claim is made that its full implications have been examined.

The task of elucidating the operations of business is a worthy one, in view of the great social importance of business activity in the life of civilized communities today. It is a task requiring the effort of many minds, for the complexity of business operations offers a challenge to the inventive and exploratory genius of the accountant and the economist that few have the capacity to accept unaided. It was my wish, in demonstrating that there are new concepts to be developed and new techniques to be adopted, that more may be inspired to take up the challenge.

3

ACCOUNTING AND BUSINESS FINANCE*

1.—Point of View

In the first lecture of this series, delivered in the University of Melbourne last year[1], I endeavoured to clear away some of the contradictions and inconsistencies in accounting theory by proposing a reclassification of certain concepts relating to accounting and to business finance. In particular, I attempted to show that conservatism and disclosure are not rules or criteria of accounting, *per se*, but are rather devices used by businessmen to secure certain ends they deem to be important.

Attention will be directed, in this lecture, to one such end: the continued participation of parties external to the business organization. The title of this lecture and the first group of financial policies mentioned in the previous lecture may suggest that we refer here only to the participation of those who support business organizations financially. This shall be our main concern. But we shall not omit to observe that financial policies may influence for good or ill the willingness of those who contribute in kind as well as those who contribute in money; financial policies which secure the co-operation of workers and the goodwill of customers are just as much within the purview of financial management as policies designed to secure financial support, and, from the point of view of the organization, just as important.

It is customary when treating business finance to discuss the kinds of securities which are the instruments of private financing. Here, however, we propose to consider only the broad basis upon which all capitalization plans and adjustments are founded—the apparent relationship between capital invested and profits earned. "Apparent" is the significant word. We shall suggest that the actions of investors and of other parties entering into relationships with business organizations are influenced by what they can find out about those organizations, even though what they sometimes find out is incomplete and irrelevant. We shall be concerned throughout with the parties involved rather than with the instruments of business finance.

We do not propose a merely descriptive treatment of the connexion between conventional accounting statements and financial questions. The inquiry is oriented to the fundamental rationale of accounting.

---

* First published in *The Australian Accountant*, Vol. XXII, No. 7, July 1952, pp. 213-30; No. 8, August 1952, pp. 262-66. Text prepared for Commonwealth Institute of Accountants Annual Research Lecture in the University of Queensland, July 1951.

[1] See p. 7, *ante*.

Some of the forces and issues which influence the financial decisions of businessmen are discussed with the aim of bringing forward conclusions which bear directly and critically on the principles and practice of accounting. It is believed that an examination of this kind may provide an explanation of many business practices which are not explicable by means of, and are even inconsistent with, much currently-accepted accounting theory.

In the course of this examination we shall find cause to question the validity of the valuation convention, or the constant money value convention, for many purposes; we shall find opportunity to remark that the going-concern convention, although generally upheld in theory, is inadequate to explain much that is done in practice; and we shall find that many treatments of accounting statements omit to consider the ends which alone justify them.

Although much of the argument proceeds from the form and circumstances of corporate business, it is not believed that this in any way limits the generality of the conclusions. In all important respects, excepting only that of the personal influence, resources, and integrity of the owner or owners, the company is but a more elaborate entity than the unincorporated business. Our object is to consider accounting in general, not corporate accounting only.

2.—The Business Organization and the Accounting Entity

It is necessary at first to consider the nature of the business entity.

The social sciences are in a large measure concerned with the ways in which communities organize to attain their ends, the types of relationship which arise in this process of organizing, and the formal institutional devices and technical aids by which the attainment of social ends is promoted[2]. The social processes and types of relationship which are found to be used at any time will have arisen in various ways. Some will have been created deliberately; some will have arisen spontaneously, so that it is difficult, looking backwards, to discern the time or circumstances of their origin. Some of the organizations and relationships will be very flexible, capable of being influenced merely by changes in the opinions, customs, and wishes of the people concerned; there will be little certainty about the nature of these forms in the early stages of their development, but in time the general understanding or acceptance of customary relationships may become expressed in codes of rules, laws. Other features of social organization remain the subject of more or less free change; even though legislation recognizes their existence, it does not crystallize or ossify their form or their processes[3].

Entity Theory

In seeking to explain the characteristics of accepted relationships and processes, it has been found convenient to postulate the existence

[2] Cf. F. W. Eggleston, *The Search for a Social Philosophy*, Melbourne, Melbourne University Press 1941, p. 120: "The social pattern is the matrix from which all social sciences spring."

[3] Accounting is one such feature.

of an abstract being or entity which appears as the focus of the relationships under examination. The abstractness of the entity consists in the fact that it has none of the external appearances which we associate with any of the forms the entity may assume; yet it has certain features which constitute it representative of them all. One is thus enabled to speak of "the entity"—e.g., the legal person, the accounting entity—without having to consider the aspects of particular instances of the entity which are irrelevant.

But the value of the entity as an epistemological device does not inhere only in the fact that it enables generalizations of wide validity to be made in concise terms; that such an entity may be postulated is evidence of the recognition by the society of certain broad principles or ends which it considers, or at some previous time considered, important.

Most accountants will be familiar with the two types of entity theory to which reference has been made. They clearly illustrate the fact that the entity approach is a device for separating for consideration one aspect of the many complex attributes of persons and institutions. The notion "legal person" does not represent something additional to the natural persons and bodies corporate and unincorporated which the law recognizes; it represents a particular feature of those persons and organizations—the legal feature. The law is no different merely because jurists have found it convenient to conceive a legal entity as the object or focus of legal rules, relationships, and processes; but it is possible that, by resort to the entity concept, the extension of principles of law may be carried out more systematically and consistently than if all kinds of persons and bodies were treated as unique.

Similarly ordinary accounting processes are no different merely because we conceive an accounting entity, an artificial abstraction for the purpose of accounting. A businessman is no different biologically, psychologically, or legally merely because, for accounting purposes, we consider him as an accounting entity; but for accounting purposes his biological, psychological, and legal condition are ignored. The Commonwealth Institute of Accountants (N.S.W. Division) Accounting Research Committee on Accounting Terminology has adopted a definition of the accounting entity in terms similar to those appropriate to the entity in law: "The accounting entity is a conceptual point of reference at which a particular aggregation of acts and events require translation into financial language."[4] Appropriately this indicates that accounting is concerned with an abstraction, which may or may not coincide with any distinguishable legal, biological, or organizational entity. And there is nothing in this definition to suggest that accounting is any different because of it. Such a notion, however, may provide a better explanation of accounting practice than would be possible by an alternative hypothesis. For example, the entity notion explains why the accounting treatments of owners' and

---

[4] The definition arose from a submission to the Committee by Mr. S. R. Brown, early 1950.

creditors' interests do not differ: both owners and creditors are considered as distinct from the accounting entity. Furthermore, as in the case of law, the entity concept may permit accounting rules to be applied to unusual cases more systematically and consistently than if there were no such means of proceeding from the general to the particular.

Both the legal and the accounting aspects of business activities are of consequence to those who would understand the complexities of modern business; but there are other ways of regarding the business community. It may be considered as a complex of economic entities. "The firm" or "the entrepreneur" is the common term used by economists to signify an abstract economic entity, or a business undertaking in its economic aspects; the firm is the source of certain economic influences and the subject of other such forces. It is possible also to regard the congeries of organizations by which we achieve our ends or enrich our living as a body of social entities; business firms will only be one sub-class of such entities, and the term "social entity" will then imply that we are concerned with sociological aspects of organizations and are disregarding other aspects.

Those who become responsible for managing the affairs of business organizations, however, are not able to consider all of these aspects as separable problems. Any single managerial decision, though directed towards or arising out of one aspect of business, is likely to impinge on other aspects. A decision to distribute a bonus dividend does not only influence investors: it creates a legal obligation, it requires accounting adjustments, it may affect the attitudes of workers and creditors. Although it is convenient, therefore, for specialists to conceive abstract entities for the purposes of their specialism, the entities represent organizations which are anything but abstract. Consequently, to approach realistically even single special aspects of business requires an understanding of the organizational "wholes" which are the subjects of legal, accounting, economic, and other rules and restraints.

It seems to be necessary, then, to consider the nature of organized activity, or organizations in general, for one's notion of the forces which shape the fortunes of business firms will differ according to the view of organized activity which one adopts. What we want is perhaps a concept of the firm as an organization, or the "organizational entity".

The Organizational Entity

There are at least two ways of looking at a business[5] organization as a whole. On the one hand, an organization may be considered as the product of the inventiveness of a promoter, or of a group of promoters. The promoter or manager may be seen as the user of the opportunities and powers made available (or not forbidden) by law and commanding the support and assistance of others at market prices. With

[5] Much of what follows applies to organizations generally: the qualifying term only rivets our attention on organizations with which, for present purposes, we are more closely concerned.

this view goes the notion that what the organization is set up to do, how it operates, and what relationships exist between it and other organizations are matters determined uniquely by those responsible for its establishment and maintenance. It implies that only centrifugal forces are at work, proceeding from top-management both downwards in the business hierarchy and outwards. To be more specific, this theory of business organization postulates a very large degree of managerial autonomy, power, and influence, within the organization at least; power to determine the products or services provided by the organization, power to determine the methods of providing those products or services, power to engage and dismiss staff at will, to raise and disburse money, to make and discharge contracts.

Now merely to state these presumed powers is to draw attention to the inadequacy of this notion of the business organization and the power or authority which regulates its functioning. Authoritarian management is a thing of the past; the above concept of organization has to that extent been found wanting. Inasmuch as there are, numerically, more discernible forces acting upon business organizations today than ever before, it is easier to draw a more realistic picture. It is a common thing today to find the better-organized interest-groups expressing their views on a host of matters which were formerly considered to be within the prerogative of management alone. And not only expressing their views, but taking such determined action that their views are made to prevail.

It is becoming more and more obvious that as well as centrifugal, there are centripetal forces impinging on the organization from without and establishing a kind of equilibrium of forces. Business organizations are subject to pressures from competitors, from owners, from creditors, from suppliers, from workers, from customers, from professional groups, and from local and central government authorities. The interest in the activities of a business organization which any such group may demonstrate arises from an actual or supposed relationship between the ends of both. In so far as it appears that any one of the ends of both are inconsistent, that is, both parties may not obtain satisfaction simultaneously, their mutual attitude will be one of incipient conflict. Not necessarily open or violent conflict, however; it may amount to nothing more than "ca' canny", and on the other hand it may be so serious as to break down the relationship between the parties altogether.

Business organizations, as they require the continued support and active participation of other groups, are obliged to consider other group interests in the formulation and pursuit of their ends. This does not mean that they shall bring no independent aims or unusual methods or organizational point of view to bear on other groups, for the other groups are often as dependent on the organization as the organization is on them. It means only that the upshot of the relationship will be the resultant of the various forces brought to bear on the work of the organization. Describing formal organizations generally, Barnard brings out these notions with admirable verbal economy: a formal organization, he says, is "a system of consciously co-ordinated activities or forces of two or more persons"[6]. To amplify this he adds: "For convenience and purposes of simplification, I have usually restricted the derivation of organization forces to the persons who would ordinarily be called 'members', 'communicants', 'employees', etc. But I have been unable even here to completely restrict myself to this convenience. The actions which are evidence of organization forces include all actions of contribution and receipt of energies, so that a customer making a purchase, a supplier furnishing supplies, an investor furnishing capital are also contributors. What they contribute is not material but the transaction, the transfer, the control of things, or action upon physical things themselves. Thus, usually, the only organization action of an investor is often a simple one of the transfer of money or of credit which he owns or controls" (pp. 76-7). Observe that the actions here mentioned are "evidence of organization forces", not the forces themselves. The principal force is willingness to contribute or participate; it is psychic, not physical or material.

It becomes apparent now that entities external to an organization will be willing to contribute as long as they approve, or are induced to accept, the ends of the organization and the means by which it pursues those ends. This involves that there shall be an adequate system of communications between the organization and other persons or organizations, so that they may be informed of the aims, of changes in the aims, of the means, and of the rate of attainment of the aims, of the organization. It is part of the present thesis that accounting is one such system of communications.

May we summarize these comments on the business organization as a complete entity? Observation and experience convince us that a business organization should be considered the focus of certain attitudes and actions on the part of those who participate in it or contribute to it, in whatever capacity. None of these parties may be regarded as tied so closely to a given organization that it can afford to disregard their attitudes. As it is valuable to the organization to secure and maintain the esteem and goodwill of contributing parties, the merit of policies which express regard for their expectations cannot be gainsaid. In particular, the design of means of communication, their use to portray the relationships between the organization and its supporting groups, and the arrangement of affairs so that participants will not withdraw their support are of considerable importance from the point of view of the organization.

The Business Organization as an Accounting Entity

Using the term "organization" in the Barnardian sense, no organization is necessarily an accounting entity. The accounting entity arises from the articulation of accounting features from the multitude of features of an organization. If an organization has not in fact any accounting features it is not an entity for accounting purposes: it is a nonentity, if we may turn the phrase. Looking at this

[6] C. I. Barnard, *The Functions of the Executive*, Cambridge, Mass., Harvard University Press, 1938, p. 73.

proposition from another way, we may say that the accounting entity is not conceived for organizational purposes, but for accounting purposes only.

Business organizations, however, are almost invariably accounting entities; the fact that accountants are concerned with an accounting entity should not be allowed to delude us into thinking the entity is the reality. The reality is infinitely more complex than the accounting entity: it is the subject and source of psychic, impalpable, but nevertheless effective forces.

To what extent is accounting required to contemplate the interest of outside parties and the impact of external forces on the organization, then? Is accounting to be regarded as a method of handling such aspects of business as are measured in numerical terms, without any consideration of purpose, without any regard for the effect it may have on the willingness of outside parties to contribute? In the following section an attempt will be made to show that accounting is in fact considered to be the substance of a system of communication universally used in business, and it will be argued that the uses made of accounting information require that accounting should therefore be neutral with respect to the wishes and claims of contributing parties. Accounting should recognize the interest of outsiders; but only by strictly accounting for the entity will no violence be done by accounting technique to the interest of any outside contributing party.

3.—The Function of Accounting with Respect to External Parties

In a much-quoted section of *Financial Accounting*[7], G. O. May sets out 10 uses of financial accounts. I should like to examine his list, for it provides a useful nucleus for the argument which follows. It is not to be presumed, however, that May would either endorse the argument or approve the conclusions.

Firstly, the list is divided into "older" and "new" uses; at present all such uses are deemed to be made of accounting statements. The older uses are (1) as a report of stewardship, (2) as a basis of fiscal policy, (3) to determine the legality of dividends, (4) as a guide to wise dividend action, (5) as a basis for the granting of credit. The newer uses are (6) as information for prospective investors in an enterprise, (7) as a guide to the value of investments already made, (8) as an aid to government supervision, (9) as a basis for price or rate regulations, (10) as a basis for taxation.

Let us concede that (8), (9) and (10) are more recent uses. It seems hardly correct to classify (6) and (7) in the same way. Governmental intervention in the conduct of business affairs is a product mainly of the last 100 years, whereas investors have been concerned with the quality of their investments quite as long ago as items (1), (3) and (4) have been relevant. This should be obvious in the case of unincorporated businesses, and it can readily be shown to apply also to corporate undertakings. It lies behind the slogan of one of the early supporters of full legal recognition of the limited

---

[7] New York, Macmillan, 1946, pp. 19-20.

liability principle: "Limited liability, paid-up capital, perfect publicity."[8] And surely its use by investors is contemplated in the accounts provisions of the model articles of association appended to the English Companies Act of 1862 and, for example, to the New South Wales Companies Act of 1874. Uses (6) and (7) seem to be so old that the only reason why they are classified as newer uses must be because it is only in relatively recent decades that concern for the investor has been actively shown by the accounting profession.

Secondly, May's list seems to be incomplete. As it stands the uses are not uses made exclusively by managers; (5) and (8) and (10) are uses made of accounting statements by parties other than owners and managers. We may therefore add to the newer uses an item "(11) as a basis for action by workers and their organizations, or as a basis for bargaining between workers and employers". The use of accounts for this purpose has depended on the growth of the power of workers and their representatives and on their increasing awareness of the data on which business issues are resolved; both have reached the "threshold of effectuation" in only recent decades. There may be other parties whose uses we should add, but this is one addition which is clearly justifiable in view of the new forces which workers are bringing to bear on business organizations.

The Stewardship Notion

Furthermore, it seems that uses (1) and (7) are merely restatements of the same idea. A report of stewardship is a meaningless thing unless it is expected that some action may be taken by the principal; and the machinery of corporate business was designed to permit investors to retain, augment, or diminish their investments or, if they wish, to vote out of office some or all of the "stewards". At all events this idea of stewardship needs working over. I do not know by what subtle alchemy the change has been accomplished, but we find examples in various places of the view that "financial stewardship is the paramount objective . . . of accounting"[9], a view which is very far removed from May's simple statement of purpose, item (1), and which appears to give little weight to the other nine uses.

That accounting statements are considered to be and are accepted as reports on stewardship I will concede. But it does not follow that accountants therefore exercise a stewardship function; nor does it follow that accounting systems and accounting statements must be based on the historical money value convention. By a report on stewardship I understand a report on the use of certain resources and the exercise of certain powers. Stewardship is only another way of describing the "agent-cum-trustee" function which the courts have

---

[8] William Clay, c. 1836, quoted by B. C. Hunt, *The Development of the Business Corporation in England, 1800-1867,* Cambridge, Mass., Harvard University Press, 1936, p. 69.

[9] R. A. Irish, "Fundamental Concepts of Corporate Accounting", *The Australian Accountant,* June 1950, p. 216.

long imputed to company directors; it is not a responsibility of accountants, even though it be qualified by the word "financial". Financial stewardship is only one aspect of the general notion of stewardship; it is undoubtedly a function of directors, and would be even if the Companies Acts did not stipulate that "the directors of every company shall . . . lay before the company in general meeting a profit and loss account . . . and balance sheet . . .".

What represents responsible or effective financial stewardship no one seems prepared to say. If the accounting statements are to be regarded as a report of stewardship, exactly how are their recipients to judge whether the stewards are worthy of their confidence? Is it immaterial, for example, "that changes may occur in the value of money as property, so long as the resources entrusted by shareholders and creditors are accounted for"[10]? Does the idea of stewardship impose on directors only the obligation of presenting accounts that balance? Surely not!

The responsibility of stewardship does not require the directors to preserve the resources at their disposal regardless of the environment in which their undertaking operates. All that directors have ever been required to do is to operate within their powers and exercise a certain degree of prudence and competence. Under some circumstances, losses may not necessarily be the result of bad stewardship; but to abuse the powers, to fail to use the powers, or to exceed the powers available is always bad stewardship.

What may be said, then, of directors who allow their business undertakings to run down so much that they are unable to look the coming months in the eye? Is it not an important responsibility to see that the undertaking is always in a fit financial condition to carry on? That it shall be carried on is certainly expected by most parties in any way connected with it. Surely, then, this is a stewardship function, and one on which a report on stewardship should be expected to throw some light. Should not the investors and creditors be able to discern from the accounting statements whether the directors are capably discharging their duty in this matter or not?

But conventional accounting does not permit useful inferences on this matter. Indeed it is not difficult to see that a system of money-accounting (whatever its postulates) is scarcely adequate to provide a report on the kind of financial stewardship here considered; some reporting in other symbols than money is imperative if rationality of decision and action are valued. Nor should it be difficult to see at the same time that a system of money-accounting based on the historical money cost convention cannot of itself constitute a valid basis and criterion of rational action.

To clinch the matter it seems necessary to consider two questions: what is the aim of the statutory provisions for the publication of annual accounting statements? and what information is required by the parties whom the "stewards" represent to enable them to discharge their main duties rationally? The two are closely connected.

---

[10] R. A. Irish, loc. cit., p. 216.

The Aim of Statutory Publicity

During the prolonged argument which preceded the granting of the privilege of incorporation with limited liability in England, the safeguards which would be necessary seem often to have been discussed. "Publicity" seems to be the most important of these safeguards, or if not the most important at least the most generally urged. "Publicity" is hardly specific enough to enable us to deduce the intention of the architects of the corporation; but at least they were not satisfied with inconsequential disclosures by company managements. The "perfect publicity" of Clay's formula mentioned above echoes through the dicta of his successors. Witnesses before a Royal Commission in 1854 testified: "Full freedom of association, guarded by *well devised regulations to insure publicity* and to defeat fraud" should be the aim of legislation on the management of companies, and "to justify confidence in their stability and management, it should be an imperative condition annexed to limited liability, that all [joint stock companies] should be allowed only on the *most perfect system of publicity* as to their affairs". Robert Lowe, President of the Board of Trade in 1856, opined: "The only way that the legislature should interfere [with the right of freedom of contract and the right of unlimited association] is by giving the *greatest publicity* to the affairs of such companies, that everyone may know on what grounds he is dealing."[11]

But it seems doubtful whether the publicity contemplated by these people went much further than the requirements that the annual accounts should be published. The publication of accounts had been urged as early as 1833, and Hunt (pp. 68-9), paraphrasing Clay's proposals of 1836, observes: "the privilege [of limited liability for banking companies] was to be available only on condition that capital be fully paid up and 'entire publicity' be given to the affairs of the banks by obliging them periodically to publish their accounts". Although adequate knowledge for the investor was a most important consideration in the opinion of some people who were instrumental in bringing in the Joint Stock Companies Registration and Regulation Act of 1844, it is quite certain that annual accounts are inadequate to serve this end. An observation of the economist J. R. McCulloch is not without interest; discounting his firm opposition to the joint stock company, and remembering that this passage is in the spirit of the debate at the time, it still points out deficiencies in the service which published accounts may render even today: "It astonishes us," he says, "that anyone living in London and having intercourse with practical men, should have been found to lay the least stress on the publication of balance sheets, or accounts of assets and obligations. They are worse than worthless, being eminently calculated to deceive and mislead. To effect Clay's plan by leaving it to the *honour* of the parties; that is by allowing each bank to report as to its own credit and solvency! It is difficult to suppose that Mr. Clay can be

[11] Hunt, op. cit., pp. 134, 138-9.

serious. . . . [And] even though the parties were perfectly honest, the publication of a balance sheet would be good for nothing."[12]

Rationality of Investors' Decisions

The view that the publication of a balance sheet would accomplish nothing as far as investors are concerned, many may wish to oppose. And yet McCulloch's view is chastening. Investors' decisions will depend in part on what they are able to learn of the past operations of their enterprises and the policies of their management; in part on what they know of the present position; and in part on what they can ascertain about the prospective operations of their firms. Information under each of these categories may be further classified into accounting information and other information. Even supposing that accounting statements are objectively realistic, it will be apparent that only one class of information, of the six classes made possible by this dual classification, is provided by those statements. In other words, what was substituted for, or what was conceived to be, "the most perfect system of publicity" turns out to be much less than the situation demands.

But we may reduce the dimensions of the problem by confining attention to aspects of business operations which are measurable in terms of money. These aspects may, but need not necessarily, be handled by money-accounting techniques. The extent to which confining attention to these aspects of business operations ignores realities has been suggested for certain situations in the previous lecture. Here we shall have to consider how such a limited body of information as accounting statements provide, influences the quality of investors' decisions.

We shall assume that the decisions of investors are made rationally. If we disregard elements of the problem which are not measurable or expressible in quantitative terms, this is not to be taken as making an unrealistic case; whatever decision is made on these other aspects, the rationality of the whole decision will depend on the quality and quantity of numerical (including money) data used. Following Weber[13], we may describe as "formally rational" decisions based on a consideration of those features of a problem which are measurable and expressible in numerical terms.

Within the category "aspects of investment in securities which are capable of treatment in terms of money" are such matters as past earnings, past dividends (and dividend policies in so far as these may be deduced from past earnings and dividends), the present money position, and prospective future earnings. Of all these the most critical is the last, and of them all it is the most difficult to obtain relevant information about. If the system of accounting is designed with the needs of the investor in view, there will be available a statement showing the predisposition of the enterprise to trade in the future,

---

[12] Hunt, op. cit., p. 70.
[13] Max Weber, *The Theory of Social and Economic Organisation,* London, William Hodge & Co., 1947, p. 170.

but there is nothing in such a statement to suggest trading prospects. Such a statement tells the investor something about a firm's conditions of supply, nothing about the conditions of the demand for its product; for demand it is probably usual to assume that present trends will continue into the future.

Among the conditions of formal rationality in the field of investment are the following: firstly, for each possible investment there shall be a statement of the predisposition of the enterprise to trade, including a statement of the resources available at values appropriate to future trade and a statement of the relationship between the enterprise and its financial supporters; secondly, for each possible investment there shall be quantitative statements of the proposed courses of action and of their expected consequences; thirdly, for each possible investment there shall be statements of the proposed dividends or of the dividend policy in general.

Superficially, these conditions bear a strong resemblance to the balance sheet and profit and loss account with which we are familiar, but instead of being a report on the past the statements are drawn with an eye to the future. The first statement would resemble the conventional balance sheet closely in form, the essential difference being the method of valuing the expected services from fixed assets. The second condition may be satisfied by a form of income and expenditure estimate; but, as we shall observe presently a detailed estimate may carry too great an air of precision and authenticity for it to be accepted as an estimate only. The third condition may be satisfied by an estimate of the way net income shall be distributed or appropriated.

Assuming for the moment that this kind of information in sufficient quantity were available, would an "historical" balance sheet and income statement be of any use to the investor? Not as an aid to deciding about prospective yields; but if the estimates could be compared with the results, the investor could perhaps decide the margin of error to which those estimates are subject.

Now it is hardly likely that the legislative fathers of the limited liability company had any of the above estimates in mind when they referred to the necessity of the "most perfect system of publicity". And yet it is very clear that they had in mind the need for providing adequate information for investors, even though they may not have chosen the instrument very happily. If, as we are led to believe, change in technical and commercial affairs proceeded at a more leisurely pace 100 years ago than today, that very fact may have created a presumption in favour of historical, backward-looking accounts; but, from a logical point of view, this would make such accounts no more relevant, and no less irrelevant, to investors' purposes than they would be in a period of violent economic change. It is even possible that although they saw clearly and legislated wisely, the doctrinaire application of *laissez-faire* as a public policy may have stifled further development in publicity devices: as it happened, the obligation to publish accounts regularly, although it was regarded as a vital condition of granting limited liability, was allowed to lapse very soon and it was not till 1928 in England that it was re-imposed. Meanwhile an accounting has grown up which threatens almost to ignore the fact that investors are concerned with the future more than with the past.

In pointing out that it has long been believed that, in some way, accounts should be designed to assist investors to make their decisions, and in setting out some of the conditions of formal rationality we do not presume that investors' decisions are always rational, or that they desire to make their decisions rationally. Nor do we suggest the adoption of the system of estimates referred to immediately above. On the latter question we shall comment again presently: but on the former an opinion of Lord Keynes is worth observing: "Our knowledge of the factors which will govern the yield of an investment some years hence is usually very slight and often negligible. If we speak frankly, we have to admit that our basis of knowledge for estimating the yield 10 years hence of a railway, a copper mine, a textile factory, the goodwill of a patent medicine, an Atlantic liner, a building in the City of London amounts to little and sometimes to nothing."[14] Nevertheless "it is reasonable to be guided to a considerable degree by the facts about which we feel somewhat confident, even though they may be less decisively relevant to the issue than other facts about which our knowledge is vague and scanty. For this reason the facts of the existing situation enter, in a sense disproportionately, into the formation of our long-term expectations; our usual practice being to take the existing situation and to project it into the future, modified only to the extent that we have more or less definite reasons for expecting a change." The accounting statements provide the main body of "facts" on which investors' expectations, and consequently their decisions, are based, even though conventional accounting statements are "less decisively relevant" than other kinds of information we could suggest; unquestionably they enter "disproportionately" into the picture.

The Creditor's Point of View

The provision of information for investors was not the only end contemplated by the proponents of perfect publicity: in fact it does not even seem to be the foremost in point of time. The protection of creditors seems, in England, to have been the main concern of the opponents of freedom of incorporation with limited liability: and in the United States during the nineteenth century the greatest forces making for improvement in the published statements of companies came from the representatives of creditors or from creditors themselves.

In the case of unincorporated business undertakings and of unlimited companies, creditors have always been able to rely on the established rule that the private and business property of the owners constitutes their security, and that it may be realized in satisfaction of debts owing to them. In England the proposal to grant the privilege

[14] J. M. Keynes, *The General Theory of Employment, Interest and Money*, London, Macmillan, 1936, p. 148, 149-50.

of trading with limited liability was viewed by some as a measure by which the rights of creditors were sacrificed without any form of compensation. On the other hand, in so far as the supporters of the measure had in mind the public interest when they argued the necessity for publicity, it is clear that some compensation was to be vouchsafed; to know the amount of the capital invested, the objects, and the management of debtor companies is surely some compensation. Creditors would in future shift their attention from one aspect to another of the financial position and prospects of borrowers: they would lend only on closer investigation than before. To quote Robert Lowe again: "The sum of the reasoning [by which] the present law is sought to be justified is that *he who feels the benefit, should also feel the burden.* This is true enough as a principle of natural justice, and in the absence of contract; but there is a maxim equally true that anyone can renounce a right introduced for his benefit, and if people are willing to contract on terms of relieving the party embarking his capital from loss beyond a certain amount, there is nothing in natural justice to prevent it . . . . The received principle in commercial legislation is to leave people to act for themselves."[15]

It may be suggested that a firm seeking financial accommodation would be obliged by the creditor to supply adequate information or security even in the absence of legal stipulations about publication of accounts. This is no doubt true in respect of specific loan agreements, but a very great proportion of business credit consists not in formal lending but in lending by way of trade credit. Trade creditors probably have not found it possible to subject all accounts to close scrutiny, nor have they been in the same position to require information as other creditors. The publication of accounting statements provides trade creditors, of public companies at least, with a systematic way of testing capacity to pay.

The problem of estimating the means of debtors was taken up in the United States by the credit-reporting agencies, which were first set up in the second quarter of the nineteenth century. In the United States the question of publishing accounts as a safeguard for investors was scarcely raised until the end of that century, but balance sheets were sought by mercantile information services on behalf of their clients much earlier. R. A. Foulke[16] quotes the explanation accompanying a request for financial and other information used by The Mercantile Agency during the 1870's; it points out that "many dispensers of credit regard refusal to comply [with a request for definite information as to pecuniary resources and indebtedness] as an unfavourable indication, except in the cases of houses of undoubted wealth".

It will be clear that the accounting statements have long been viewed as aids to creditors. As before, we may ask to what extent these statements meet the conditions of formal rationality as for creditors.

---

[15] Quoted by Hunt, op. cit., p. 118. Italics in original.
[16] *Practical Financial Statement Analysis*, New York, McGraw Hill, 1945, p. 11.

These conditions are rather different from the conditions appropriate to investors. The need to make investigations with respect to the prospects of the debtor firm is not so great, for a debt represents an obligation to pay a certain sum, not a sum varying with profits. It is perhaps true to say that the capacity of an entity to pay its debts may be determined by its profit-earning capacity, but for most cases much less information will suffice than is necessary to appraise income-earning capacity.

The conditions of formal rationality include the following: firstly, there shall be a statement of the resources which are available or will become available by the date of maturity for the satisfaction of debts; and secondly, there shall be a statement of all other creditors equal or superior in rank and the extent of their claims. The first set of information must take into account the possibility that some fixed assets are financed out of borrowings, but otherwise there should be no great difficulty in appraising the resources usually considered to be directly chargeable with debts, namely cash, trade debtors, marketable securities, and stocks. But note, in any case, that the statement bears on a future settlement, so that the resources should appear at valuations appropriate to future settlement, not at merely formal or conventional values. In respect of the current assets no great problem need arise: cash needs no adjustment; the balance of trade debtors involves only slight adjustment to reflect the possibility that some accounts may not be collectible; and stocks valued at current prices may be a useful enough approximation for present purposes.

The second statement—of the nature and extent of other creditors' claims—needs no adjustment. It is a statement based on certain contracts and the liabilities appearing in it are dischargeable on maturity at the stated money sum.

It would appear, then, that creditors are no whit less interested in the future than are investors, and both classes are only incidentally interested—if we take the view that their actions are strictly rational—in the past. Statements of accounting position based on the historical record convention and the constant money value convention would thus appear to be almost, if not quite, irrelevant.

Workers' Interests

It may seem unusual to introduce workers and workers' organizations into a discussion of business finance. But, inasmuch as they represent some of the more powerful forces bearing on business organizations today, to neglect them would be superficial. It is not possible to discuss the kinds of information required by all contributing parties in great detail, but the worker's point of view is in such marked contrast with that of owners and creditors that it will provide a critical test of conclusions we may reach with respect to owners and creditors.

Today's industrial conditions are almost infinitely remote from those of Gopher Prairie in Sinclair Lewis' *Main Street*: no more is it possible for employers to be as aggressively independent as Jackson Elder when he thundered, "I stand for freedom and constitutional rights. If any man don't like my shop, he can get up and git. Same way, if I don't like him, he gits. ... They like what I pay 'em, or they get out. That's all there is to it! ... All this profit-sharing and welfare work and insurance and old-age pension is simply poppycock. Enfeebles a workman's independence—and wastes a lot of honest profit."

Within the last 50 years it has become accepted that workers' organizations should be represented on bodies set up to decide on wages and working conditions. But not because any such right has been voluntarily admitted by employers; rather because workers have been able to exert sufficient influence to obtain representation. Now it is widely considered that consultation on wages and working conditions is the limit to which the influence of labour organizations on management decisions will go. But it is quite possible that, in 50 years' time, such a view will seem as reactionary as the views of 50 years ago seem to us today.

There can be no question about the intention of labour organizations to intervene in such other or wider matters as they deem worth their attention. In Melbourne recently one representative urged that "the trade union movement should demand a voice on boards of management in various industries"[17]; commenting on the suggestion, another representative of workers observed: "The Food Preservers' Union... agree that an elected representative of the workers in the establishment should be on the board of management, with equal voice in making decisions and offering suggestions as directors."[18] Professor Chamberlain discusses the whole matter in general terms in a review of certain industrial disturbances in the United States in 1941: "The management and direction of others do not flow out of legal rights, but must be granted by those very people who are managed and directed. And the price of the grant may be... that management—and the owners—yield their independence in certain matters of business operation. What matters? Potentially none would seem to be excluded—whatever matters are deemed important to those whose co-operation is being sought."[19]

In what way is all this relevant to the subject we are here to examine? Although the law does not specifically provide that information about financial matters shall be made available to workers or their representatives, these parties may acquaint themselves with the contents of the published statements (of companies) in the same way as members of the public may do so; and where no information is available they may base their claims or decisions on conjecture and supposition. But for what purposes may workers even be concerned with the financial position and profit of an employer undertaking?

---

[17] W. P. Evans, Federal Secretary of the Federated Engine Drivers' and Firemen's Association, addressing the Trades Hall Council, reported in *The Australasian Manufacturer*, 5 May 1951.

[18] Editorial in *The Food Preserver*, May 1951.

[19] "What is Management's Right to Manage?" *Fortune*, July 1949.

They will obviously be concerned with the way in which profits are divided, for they will want to know whether their share is, in their view, reasonable. Arising out of this, they will be concerned with the way profits are calculated, for in general the relationships between workers and employers have engendered the suspicion that employer companies can and do arrange their accounts to conceal the true extent of profits. Thus they will look at balance sheets to see how far asset valuations conceal profits. Rational participation by workers does require that they consider the distribution of income—strictly, the proposed distribution of income; but to be quite rational would involve that they be concerned also with the probability that the conditions under which they participate will not deteriorate so much that the employer will be obliged to dispense with their services or reduce their share of entity income. In specific terms, workers are interested in the way income will be distributed and in the capacity of the employer to secure for them regularity of income. These are questions which will only be answerable in the future, and may only be considered profitably now in the light of what "now" can shed on "then". The statement of predisposition to trade mentioned above is quite as pertinent when considering the expectations of workers as when considering other parties.

But most discussions of the respective claims of workers and other parties get no further than income questions. For example, there have been issued in the United States several lengthy treatments by workers' organizations of the way disclosed profit is calculated: the title of one issued by the United Electrical, Radio and Machine Workers of America indicates the general tenor of these statements—it is *How Corporations Conceal Profits and How to Understand Your Corporation's Financial Report.*[20] It is clear from some of the adjustments to disclosed profit made by workers' organizations that the contribution of reserves and financial conservatism to continuity of employment is not appreciated. But whatever we may say about the criticisms of workers' organizations, they do constitute one of the forces or pressures that impinge on the business organization; one of the forces which business managers must take into account when deciding on how they shall represent the entity to outside parties through the accounting statements. And if workers base their decisions on their expectations of the future they shall certainly be interested in accounts which are oriented to the future, rather than based on the past of which they have had adequate experience.

In General

The layman may well wonder why such a great deal of space has been devoted to demonstrating what is surely obvious: that actions we take now are based on what we expect to obtain as a result in the future. The layman may also wonder why it is necessary to stress the proposition that the accounting statements are in fact used as a guide

---

[20] Professor Sanders discusses this and two other statements in *Company Annual Reports*, Cambridge, Mass., Harvard University Press, 1949, Chapter VIII.

to action, a form of communication expected to procure action. But neither of these rather obvious propositions is countenanced by accounting theory and practice. True, much is written about financial statement analysis: but the analysis of such heterogeneous statements as the usual profit and loss account and balance sheet is both mathematically questionable and logically insufficient to constitute fair warning of what lies ahead.

The present section has considered only a few of the interest groups which contribute to organization activities, and which may be concerned with the reports it issues. But the same argument may be demonstrated to be relevant to them all; people act on accounting statements as if they were strictly relevant to the future, whereas in fact those statements are relevant only to the past. There appears to be strong grounds, in this case, for seeking to make accounting statements relevant to the future.

It should not be assumed from this section, however, that a new set of statements altogether is proposed. The "statements" mentioned above as conditions of rational action are to be considered as specifications, or as a model, which we shall presently use to construct an informative, forward-looking accounting.

But before doing so we will examine some specific features of the relationship between accounting and financial position, in an attempt to show that often unnecessary pressures are brought to bear on business organizations because the accounting statements do not portray financial position.

4.—The Financial Structure of Business Undertakings

As we have already observed, much of the discussion of business affairs which takes place within and among the participant groups mentioned in the previous section centres around the rate of profit being earned. It is natural, I suppose, to be curious about what others are getting out of what we consider to be a joint enterprise. The rate of profit crops up in industrial arbitration proceedings, in parliamentary discussion, in tariff- and price-fixing hearings: it is the subject of discussion by taxation experts, economists, brokers and their clients, bankers, opinion pollers, accountants, men in the street—and even businessmen.

Sometimes it is the amount of profit which excites attention, but most people are familiar with a "rate of profit" even though they are hazy about the basis of the rate. For some purposes the rate of profit is a ratio of profit to sales, but by far the commonest use of the term is to describe the ratio of profit to capital, whatever that may mean. The relationship between profit and the capital of an undertaking assumes such importance that businessmen are continually obliged to consider whether the capitalization of their businesses is appropriate to the conditions under which they operate. For this reason, to deal with the problems of capitalization would appear to present opportunities for discussing most of the critical features of our subject.

Capitalization

The capitalization of business enterprises does not seem to have attracted much attention on the part of accountants, and among the writers on business finance there is no unanimity on the meaning attributed to the term "capitalization". A. S. Dewing defines it as "the sum total of the par value of all the shares"[21]. Others include in the notion the long-term borrowings of a company.[22] Yet others distinguish a process of capitalization carried out by promoters or managers as distinct from the capitalization of the business; "capitalization is the act or process of fixing the value of an enterprise for the purpose of determining the capital liabilities which the company may assume"[23]. This is similar to the calculation by which the capital sum necessary to yield a given money return at a known interest rate is found; as when we say that a yield of £10,000 capitalized at 12½ per cent represents a capital sum of £80,000.

There appears, from these views, to be some connexion between the capital liabilities assumed (or the sum of all long-term securities issued) and the yield expected from the enterprise supporting those liabilities. The connexion deserves some consideration, for from it arises the test of the appropriateness of the capital structure of an enterprise.

When the capital of an enterprise is under consideration, there appear to be several sets of data upon which it may be computed. Firstly, the outstanding securities may be valued actuarially or by reference to their market values. Taken at market values such a capital would represent something like the cost of acquiring the undertaking as a going concern under competitive conditions in the investment market. Inasmuch as market values represent the consensus of investors' expectations, there will clearly be some relating of market price with yield on the part of investors.

Secondly, we may have recourse to the accounting statements of the undertaking, and use for the capital invested the aggregate of shareholders' funds shown in the balance sheet. Although this sum may differ from the subscribed capital, the discrepancy will not bother us, for only in the least sophisticated circles is a security supposed to be worth its face value. The aggregate of shareholders' funds is not an unequivocal amount however; it is subject to all the rules and conventions adopted and opinions held by those responsible for the statements; and accountants are among those responsible. For this reason, the estimate of capital on the basis of book value is so conventionalized that it may often be suspected of being irrelevant; and this suspicion is sufficient often to induce businessmen to do something about it, as we shall presently see.

---

[21] *Corporation Finance,* New York, The Ronald Press Co., 1931, p. 4.

[22] For example F. F. Burchett, *Corporation Finance,* New York, Harper & Bros., 1934, p. 349; Husband & Dockeray, *Modern Corporation Finance,* Chicago, Richard D. Irwin Inc., 1948, p. 176.

[23] Bonneville and Dewey, *Organising and Financing Business,* Englewood Cliffs, Prentice-Hall Inc., 1936, p. 108.

Thirdly, we may, using the accounting statements again, take the earnings and capitalize them at the rate of profit, or the yield, common in the market at the time. Two different kinds of conjecture arise in this case: the figure for earnings, being the result of accounting processes, is subject to the same qualifications as is the aggregate of shareholders' funds; and the current yield for any given class of securities is not easily determinable even statistically.

Fourthly, we may have the assets and obligations valued and derive the equity of owners on the basis of current values. On the formation of a new enterprise there will be little difference between this estimate of capital invested and the book value of shareholders' funds, but as time passes discrepancies will arise if there is any change in property and equipment values.

There may be other ways of attempting to compute capital, but these are sufficient to permit us to draw out the important features of these alternatives.

In his attempts to grapple with the problem his portfolio raises, an investor is scarcely likely to be influenced by conventional values and estimates other than those he makes himself or has made to his orders. Current market values, past dividends, current expectations as to yield we may aver to be his main concern; he is unlikely to be very much concerned with asset values as they now appear in published accounts except perhaps to test a view that as an investment the undertaking is a borderline case. But can we say the investor is concerned about any precise relationship such as percentage of profit on shareholders' funds? There is no direct empirical evidence to help us resolve this question. But the practice of the commercial and financial press in reporting dividend rates as a percentage of paid-up capital and of many men in the street confirm us in the belief that it is not the return on aggregate shareholders' funds but the return on subscribed capital that is deemed to be important as a guide to investors' actions.

But the subscribed capital will differ according to the way adopted for computing capital needed. On the launching of a new venture the shares issued may represent much more than the cost of the tangible properties acquired or to be acquired. The excess will not be arbitrarily determined, but will bear some relationship to the expected yield from the investment. An anecdote of Boswell illustrates the point. Dr. Johnson, when acting as executor to an old friend, Thrale the brewer, was asked what he thought to be the real value of the brewery. He replied: "We are not here to sell a parcel of boilers and vats, but the potentiality of growing rich beyond the dreams of avarice."[24]

Now it matters not how carefully the promoters attempt to see the end from the beginning, their expectations will seldom be completely justified. In many cases the enterprise will be able to operate within reasonable distance of the level of returns expected. In some cases,

---

[24] Quoted by Hartley Withers in *Stocks and Shares,* London, John Murray, 1948 ed., p. 73.

however, achievements greatly exceed or grossly fall short of expectations. This may happen not only at the inception of a venture, but also, through allowing some matters to get out of hand, at later stages of its history. It gives rise to conditions of under- or over-capitalization.

These terms appear to be the subject of considerable misunderstanding, but we shall adopt the following as definitions. When the profit remaining after meeting interest on deferred liabilities and dividends on preference shares bears an unusually high ratio to the ordinary share capital for any considerable period, the undertaking will be described as under-capitalized. When the same residual profit is unusually low for any considerable period, the undertaking will be described as over-capitalized. The consequences of each may be discussed briefly.

Over-capitalization may injure the interests of owners, employees, consumers, and the undertaking itself. A low rate of profit does not inspire great confidence on the part of creditors; any attempt to rehabilitate an over-capitalized business may therefore need to be preceded by such an adjustment of the capital as will make it appear able to meet its periodic commitments for interest and dividends at least. A reorganization of capital may involve some immediate sacrifice on the part of owners, but this may be the only way in which the main part of their investment may be preserved and made remunerative. It may be argued on the same grounds that employment may only be secured by a correction of over-capitalization. Except in the case of over-capitalized public undertakings, reorganization may be the alternative to abandonment. The interest of consumers may be prejudiced in so far as the undertaking enjoys any monopolistic advantage: where competition is keen, price will be tied fairly closely to the prices of firms which are more efficient financially; but monopoly features may enable an over-capitalized firm to make the consumer pay. Finally, over-capitalization may predispose the managers to false economies, inadequate disclosure, and similar makeshifts to evade criticism and to avoid loss of confidence in the firm.

It would appear that the pressures arising from groups other than creditors are less compelling in this case than in the case of under-capitalization; for there are no evident excessive profits to arouse the active opposition of other parties than owners, and owners may, if they are dissatisfied, dispose of their interests.

There are, of course, some advantages in over-capitalization, but they are hardly advantages one associates with efficient business. For example, where funds are adequate or more than adequate for all purposes which management may wish to carry out, the firm may obviously have greater flexibility and versatility, but if this encourages unusual and easy optimism it may quickly aggravate the situation.

Under-capitalization also may adversely affect the participation of some groups, such as workers, consumers, suppliers; and it may induce action on the part of regulatory bodies to control such profits as appear to be excessive. If the rate of residual profits to ordinary capital is unusually high, worker groups may easily become restive, expressing their unwillingness to co-operate by making new claims for improvements in wages and conditions and even endeavouring to back up their claims by actual or threatened withdrawal. The reactions of consumer and supplier interests are not so easily observed: they are the subject of much less publicity than relationships between workers and employers. But adjustments in contract prices and conditions may be none the less real, provided the interested external parties show sufficient solidarity and determination. If the under-capitalized firm is recalcitrant in the face of demands for better prices, there is always the possibility that new competition may arise in the expectation of equally high profits.

And what of the investor? Under-capitalization would tend to raise the price of ordinary shares because of the high dividend rate of past periods and/or the expectation of high dividends or capital appreciation in the future. In some cases this may make the market price of such securities so high that few investors are able to trade in them. Negotiability is reduced, and the price at which bargains are struck is less a reflection of free market forces than if more investors were interested in the securities. Furthermore, the demands made on the under-capitalized firm by participating organizations may be such that the rate of profit is considerably reduced in future periods.

If these disabilities are to be avoided, who shall impugn the wisdom of taking steps to relate the capital structure of a business organization to its profits? Who shall say asset revaluation and bonus share issues[25] and similar methods of adjustment are unsound, from the point of view of the organization, when their purpose is to secure the co-operation and goodwill of parties having such diverse interests as owners, workers, and managers, and consumers may appear to have?

To judge by the current spate of capital adjustments in Australian companies, capitalization would seem to be important to company directors if not to their accountants. The adjustments referred to are those involving an increase in the potential obligation to disburse profits without a simultaneous increase in actual funds available: bonus share issues and the conversion of preference share issues and long-term debts into ordinary shares are the forms this adjustment takes.

An adjustment of this kind may not be lightly undertaken, but the conditions determining its appropriateness are few. The most important is that there must be evidence to justify the expectation that the enterprise will be able to support a larger dividend obligation (i.e., larger in terms of money, though the *rate* of dividend may be higher, the same, or lower) than before adjustment. Under what conditions, then, may it be feasible for a company's management to alter a capitalization which has been established as the result of various financial decisions in the past?

---

[25] Stock dividends arising mainly from share premium reserves and asset revaluation reserves. See also "Accounting and Inflation", p. 309, *post*, and "The Implications of Asset Revaluations and Bonus Share Issues," p. 95, *post*.

Pursuing a canon of financial prudence, funds may have been raised by issues at a premium in order to avoid the possibility of achievements falling far short of expectations or to provide against errors in estimates due to lack of complete knowledge: if neither of these contingencies eventuate and the premiums can be used effectively in the business, evidently it will be able to support a larger paid-up capital. The adjustment in this case is merely a matter of converting a dividend-free ownership interest into a dividend-paying interest without adjustment of assets values. The effect is to change the legal rights of members and the legal status of the company (things external to accounting), but in so far as the extent of disclosed profits is the mainspring of such adjustments, the method of accounting has obviously an important influence on decisions about the capitalization of an enterprise.

Alternatively, the profit-earning capacity of an enterprise may have been underestimated from the start. If retained profits can be put to equally profitable use, this will aggravate the relationship between profits and paid-up capital. It may then be deemed advisable to increase the paid-up capital by a conversion, as before, of a dividend-free ownership interest into a dividend-paying interest, to avoid the repercussions mentioned above. It will not matter whether profits have been fairly computed and fully disclosed or whether depreciation charges and similar value adjustments have been made in such a way as to understate profits; it will be the disclosed profits which will determine the need for adjusting the capitalization.

Finally, the profit-earning capacity of a business enterprise may at any time be higher than for its contemporaries because it was established when prices of capital goods were at a much lower level; the paid-up money capital determined with reference to the aggregate of the prices of the necessary capital goods and the market prices of the finished product will be more profitable than money capital subscribed to set up an identical enterprise at the higher level of prices. It may be considered advisable then to increase the dividend-paying ownership interest and the book values of the assets simultaneously. The two former circumstances justifying a change in the capital structure may arise at any time, even when there is no shift upwards or downwards in prices, for expectations of profits can at any time be found to be false. The third circumstance is not a question of expectations so much as changes in fortune, but its effect is very much the same, for the rates of profit being earned by old and new firms in the same industry will suggest that the old firm can support a much greater paid-up capital than it has in fact.

It seems important to note that an adjustment to the capitalization of a business may take place at any time, because some people appear to believe that such adjustments are unusual or even heretical. In accounting it is commonly considered that downward revaluations are virtuous, upward revaluations iniquitous; so that the directors of those companies which are today writing up their assets and making bonus share distributions are believed by some to be acting without prudence. As we have tried to show, this view neglects several important practical and legal considerations and makes accounting a mere formality rather than a vital system of business communications.

It is in the nature of conventional accounting that it subjects the relationship of profits to capital to continuous distortion when price levels are not stable. For profits are then computed in terms of units of purchasing power quite different from the units in which the paid-up capital is represented. When price levels are rising, the accounting statements, to the extent that stocks and fixed assets are significant, tend to represent as under-capitalized firms which would not appear to be under-capitalized if the investment were measured in the same terms as the profit. When price levels are falling, accounting statements tend, of themselves, to suggest over-capitalization; but the cost or market rule for stock is not the cause in this case; the treatment of fixed assets is to blame.

When the accounts represent a business undertaking in such a light, the forces and pressures mentioned in the paragraphs dealing with under- and over-capitalization are brought into play; unnecessarily, or from the entity viewpoint improperly, in most cases, for by fully delineating what has taken place it would become apparent that the entity is not functionally out of order, but that its communications system is. What is worse, once those forces are engaged, it is difficult to avoid making some compromise. It is not always possible to satisfy the claims of workers, investors, and taxing authorities, merely by a change in the figures, that things are not what they appear to be; they will demand some more substantial satisfaction usually, and this may be contrary to the interest of the participating parties as a whole, contrary to the interest of the organization.

It seems to be important that, to avoid improper pressures being exerted by specific groups, accounting should properly represent the financial position and structure of accounting entities, without bias conducive in any way to the destruction or inefficiency of the entity. A different view of the accounts than that commonly adopted is necessary to ensure this.

What of Management?

Throughout this lecture no lengthy reference has been made to the way in which businessmen may use the accounting statements for the purpose of formulating financial policies. The whole argument, however, clearly indicates that if the organization is to be managed effectively, managers will be obliged to consider the effects of such policies (and statements bearing on them) on the willingness of others to participate in organization activities. They will, as "stewards", be anxious to see that the entity is maintained in a fit condition to carry out its economic purpose, and to see that no unwarranted pressures are permitted to diminish its capacity to do so. This is a view of stewardship which appears to be realistic, but it requires a different kind of reporting than the historical record conventions yield.

5.—The Accounting Statements Reconsidered

In the previous sections we endeavoured to show that a series of statements similar to the conventional accounting statements but based on a different point of view—forward-looking, not backward-looking—was more in keeping with rationality of action by all participants than present accounting statements are. No attempt is made here to justify rationality; but it seems pertinent to observe that rationality is a basic assumption of economic theory, that it is the criterion of economic action, and that accounting would be almost if not quite dispensible if men did not at least try to act rationally.

We shall now consider the extent to which our conclusions suggest aspects of accounting which may be improved to enhance the probability of rational action on the part of users of accounts.

The Income Statement

The probability of making errors in estimating the extent of future business and income will not need emphasizing: it is repeated, as a charm, by those who protest that the accountant should not prognosticate. But this probability is not the same for all estimates. The probabilities of error in estimating the future yields of alternative security investments are similar, to the extent that the available accounting information about the respective firms is based on the same accounting rules. Any proposal that the information required to be given shall be the product of the hopes and expectations of the managers of firms suffers from the disability that it makes close comparison between investments impossible; rationality would be diminished by the fact that estimates in respect of the alternative securities are subject, to an unknown extent, to the errors of judgment of those responsible; and the estimating difficulties of those responsible will be more or less acute according to the way an industry is organized, according to its rate of change, according to the nature of the goods and services produced, and according to the remoteness of the matters being estimated.

These considerations are sufficient to make any detailed estimate of future income and expenditure a poor substitute for a fully informative statement relating to the immediate past; it would certainly help, just as such estimates may help in the flotation of new enterprises, but it would not be a satisfactory substitute. A detailed estimate would perhaps be less desirable than general statements of the main prospective developments, for it would carry too great an air of authenticity.

Instead of devising a new statement we may rather consider how the income statement may be made more informative, how it may conform to the requirements we have imputed to investors and creditors.

Firstly, the probability of rational action will be increased by any device which designates the real sources of income. The isolation of windfall losses and gains is one such device which is approved widely among practitioners and theorists; it is obviously and specifically directed towards increasing the information available to users of accounts. The isolation of losses and gains due to no action on the part of the firm but to the fact that its economic climate is deflationary or inflationary is one such device which is *not* approved by practitioners, although its rationale is identical, and the losses and gains are no less "windfall" than in the accepted case. The income statement should specify gain from operations, gain (or loss, where necessary) from incidental sources, and gain (or loss) from variations in the purchasing power of the currency.

Secondly, the probability of rational action will be increased by any device which permits users to draw reasonable inferences with respect to departures from the level of business depicted in the income statement for the period just past. Generic descriptions of items appearing in income statements (such as salaries, supplies, purchases, depreciation) are much less significant for the future than their characters as fixed and variable items. An income statement giving gross income and expenditure classified into their fixed and variable elements would enhance the investor's chances of determining whether a given expected change in supply conditions, or demand conditions, will affect his enterprise seriously, mildly, or not at all.

Thirdly, the probability of rational action will be increased by any other information it is possible to present, beyond the framework of the accounts, regarding the expected future level of trade.[26]

The second and third of these conditions may be provided without any fundamental change in accounting technique. The first, however, will involve a significant change in accounting theory and practice, a new point of view; but the above argument indicates that only consistent application of an established rule is involved. The first proposal would therefore remove yet another inconsistency from accounting.

The Balance Sheet

There are several ways of looking at the balance sheet of an accounting entity. It may be considered merely as a list of account balances, a piece of technical apparatus for ensuring the mechanical accuracy of accounting. The same idea also occurs in a different guise. It is represented as a form of statement of sources and applications of funds; and this is the view which is associated with the idea of financial stewardship to which reference has already been made.

The "funds statement" hypothesis, however, is inadequate to account for at least two aspects of accounting practice. Firstly, the usual balance sheet refers to a very small proportion of all the funds entrusted to the stewards over the life of the entity, and the ways in which those funds have been disbursed are treated very scantily on

[26] For an excellent illustration of such a projection for future plant capacity, see the 1950 Annual Report of Australian Paper Manufacturers Ltd. That the distribution of the company's securities is unusual does not detract from the example.

the assets side of the statement. The balance sheet may be analogous to the statement of sources and distribution of funds; the analogy may be useful for some didactic purposes; but, in fact, the balance sheet most inadequately represents the sources and applications of entity funds. Secondly, the balance sheets of a great many entities contain items which may not reasonably be described as sources or applications of funds, even by such circumlocution as the "funds statement" point of view permits. When assets are revalued and amounts are written into the accounts, there is no such thing as an application of funds, for there are no more funds than before. And if at the same time a reserve account is raised or paid-up capital account is credited, that does not represent a new source of funds; nothing that may be called "funds" has been received. In strict logic, the "funds statement" hypothesis would preclude entries of this kind being made in the books at all; and yet they are made.

The balance sheet may also be viewed as a statement of financial position. This is rather a better hypothesis at first sight than the former. The balance sheet is a statement of some kind of position rather than a summary of funds transactions. But it is scarcely a statement of financial position within the usual meaning of that term; for several reasons. "Financial position", it is reasonable to suppose, is generally understood to apply to the position of the finances of an entity; that is, such of its resources and obligations as are expressible in financial terms would be so expressed. At values appropriate to what date? Values as at the date of the statement. The conventional balance sheet does not pretend to do this; its exponents are at great pains to make it clear that it is a mere list of balances subject to certain modifying conventions. The terms "accounting statements" and "accounting position" have been used throughout this lecture precisely because the conventional statements do not disclose a financial position.

Now, because a balance sheet does not disclose the financial position of an entity, because its entries are only resultants of many past transactions, it appears to violate (or perhaps to adhere, only to an insignificant extent, to) one of the principal accounting conventions, the going-concern convention. The rule that assets should be valued as a going concern has been sanctioned a long time; but it is a rule,

"... a custom

More honour'd in the breach than the observance".

A long line of textbooks writers have pontificated: "Plant and machinery is not valued upon the basis of its realizable value, but upon the basis of its value to the particular business as a going concern; in other words, the value is based upon its earning capacity, and not upon its intrinsic worth.... The market values of similar machinery may be disregarded; for the plant of a manufacturer is held solely for the purpose of manufacturing for the whole of such asset's working life, and this period is unaffected by fluctuations in prices. The 'break up' or realizable values are also disregarded, for this asset is not held with a view to resale."[27] With respect, it is submitted that this practice regards the entity rather as a mummy in a tomb than as a going concern. I believe the going-concern idea is essentially realistic, but the above recommendation does not give effect to it. The usual argument assumes that money cost less depreciation. represents earning capacity: it does not. Earning capacity is represented by the discounted value of future net receipts, and this differs vastly from cost less depreciation; it is an altogether different kind of calculation. The above argument also requires us to accept the proposition that the period of an asset's working life is unaffected by market values of similar assets: that this is not so should not need demonstrating. Would any businessman hesitate to sell a piece of plant, new or old, for which the aggregate costs of operation, maintenance, and repairs exceed similar costs for alternative equipment, or where the profit on the sale exceeds his expected gain from using it?

The going-concern convention appears to be a notion which envisages an entity whose financial position at present and whose readiness to carry on trade must be the concern of managers and other parties. It seems to be entirely proper to expect statements which disclose a financial position rather than statements which express an accounting position; for, as even the orthodox are prepared to concede, if bankers, creditors, and other parties want financial information relevant to their interest in an accounting entity they will get it—but not from the accounting statements. This leads me to a third way of regarding the balance sheet which to my knowledge has not elsewhere been propounded, but which accounts for many devices and practices which challenge the validity of the conventional framework. To state the case fully I must include with the balance sheet the profit and loss and appropriation statements.

The Statements Taken Together

The accounting statements represent the financial conditions under which the contributions of participating persons and organizations are secured for an accounting entity. This proposition is stated in the positive form rather than the imperative; for even if, as we suggest, conventional accounting statements are "less decisively relevant" than financial statements should be, conventional accounting statements are the principal statements which are available, as a basis for making decisions, to actual or potential participants. The term "financial conditions" should not be confused with financial position or condition (singular), however; the statement of financial conditions will only be a statement of financial position when it contains values relevant to future operations. Until that time the financial position will be assumed by many people to be what the accounting statements disclose, and they will act accordingly, even though their actions are really not in their best interest or in the interest of the entity.

---

[27] The words are De Paula's (*The Principles and Practice of Auditing,* 7th ed., Australian, p. 148), but the same ideas are expressed in the same form by countless others.

This view of the accounting statements permits us to state some interesting consequences.

Firstly, this view—and only this view—enables us to justify the vast amount that has been written about, and the amount of work devoted in practice to, statement analysis. If it is believed that accounting statements should be regarded merely as an end-product of a series of book operations—and that this should be made known to all users of such statements—the responsibility of publicity, contemplated by the law, is being avoided. And if accounting statements are no more than the end-product of a series of book operations on events that have passed, and are not oriented to events about to come to pass, their analysis must result in findings which are irrelevant to the making of decisions about the future. On this hypothesis statement analysis would be, to take a strict view, illogical; no amount of subsequent manipulation of the figures in conventionalized statements can result in measures which are strictly relevant to actions and decisions in the real commercial world. Those who uphold the "list of balances" or "funds statement" view of the balance sheet and at the same time discuss financial statement analysis are really holding one view and acting according to another—acting according to the "conditions of participation" hypothesis put forward here.

Secondly, this view resolves the argument about which of the statements is more useful than the other. It has always been difficult to understand the grounds of those who assert that the profit and loss account is the more important statement, when so much is written about balance sheets and their analysis. The specific legal requirements of published balance sheets are more numerous than those for income statements; the amount of space devoted to the balance sheet in most works on statement analysis is no less than that devoted to the income statement; comments in company reports on balance sheet figures are commonly more elaborate than comments on income statement figures; and so on. Furthermore, if the balance sheet is not as useful as it might be because of the conventional treatment of items appearing in it, the profit and loss account is also affected by the treatment of those items; which of the two statements is affected most by the artificiality of the rules used in accounting depends on the relative magnitudes of balance sheet totals and sales income. And, further still, very little status is given to the appropriation account by those who dispute the superiority of the balance sheet or income statement; and yet it is important enough to command space in published accounts. The "conditions of participation" hypothesis attaches no more importance to one than to another; they are all part of the statement of conditions, and I think that all are used, without discrimination, in practice, by people who are considering whether to grant or refuse participation, as investors, creditors, bankers, workers, or what have you.

Thirdly, the view explains the practice, now being adopted by many companies, of indicating the distribution of sales income among the participating groups. Whether this is done by giving the dissection of total sales income, or by dissecting the "sales-pound", or by "share-of-the-cake" diagrams, no device has given greater colour to the hypothesis now put forward than this. These statements indicate precisely who the participants are, whether they are described as "wages, materials, taxes, dividends, etc." or "workers, suppliers, government, owners, etc.". And the form of expression used in some such statements even indicates that their designers have the idea of participation clearly in mind. The adoption of this practice which is so different from the customary ways of drawing up income statements is a reaction on the part of management to actual or expected pressures from participants; it is not to be explained merely as a bright idea conceived and executed voluntarily by officers of the entity.

Fourthly, this view explains how entries originating in ideas which are inconsistent with certain accounting dogmas nevertheless find their way into the accounting statements. In spite of fulminations against writing up tangible assets, assets are revalued; in spite of declarations that goodwill should not be written up, it is written up; in spite of the fact that some accountants say making bonus share issues is unwise, bonus share issues are made. Why? Because these actions are demanded by the situation in which managers find their entities from time to time. Because these measures are deemed by managers to be necessary to secure the continued participation of the parties upon which the entity depends.

6.—Conclusion

The conclusion to which this argument leads is perhaps obvious, and it is hoped that the argument will have made it palatable. To make their decisions rationally, the participants in business activity need a different kind of accounting: they want information which bears on the future. This may be had by superimposing on existing accounting technique machinery for taking into account by an index number correction the effects of changes in the purchasing power of money. Such a system would yield statements which, like Janus, would look both ways, backwards and forwards. I do not mean that we should merely have additional statements by which the customary statements are shown to be adjusted. I see no value at all in the customary statements. True, we should have records of historical money costs that help us in the future to decide unforeseen questions wisely. But such unadjusted costs, I submit, have little relevance to the financial position and results which are the focus of the attention of participants and competitors.

To adopt such a system will have two kinds of consequences.

Among the practical advantages that will arise, several deserve specific mention. As the accounts more clearly represent the effects of managerial policy and action by separately stating the consequences of unavoidable general changes in the economic environment, enterprises will be subjected to a more informed supervision and criticism. The participating groups will have fewer occasions to make special claims against the entity, for its financial position and results will for longer periods be consistent with its environment. Comparison of one firm with another will be facilitated, for their statements will be based on current purchasing power; financial statement analysis will be put on a logical and consistent footing. A great part of the mental "adjusting" now necessary will be removed, as more of the facts of the situation will be put into numerical form.

The proposal will substantially improve the quality and consistency of accounting theory; it will permit us to drop certain ideas which are unnecessarily restrictive and stultifying, ideas which conflict with what the community generally, and the business community in particular, expects of accounting and accountants. It will make of accounting a system of communication which is much more "factual and objective", which has fewer "blind spots" challenging its most useful generalizations. Accounting will account; and the financial statements will describe the financial position more realistically. And, what seems to me most valuable, we shall have a system of accounting attuned to one of the basic assumptions of economic theory and one of the commonest features of action in business, formal rationality. Every point of view from which we regard the matter seems to demand a change of the kind suggested. The recommendation is not new,[28] but it is hoped that the argument will have lain bare some of the important implications not commonly discussed among accountants as yet.

Though I have endeavoured to keep questions of professional sentiment out of the argument, I hope it will be difficult to escape the hortative element in this conclusion. It is surely not consistent with the accountant's sense of professional responsibility that his technique evades the obligations which the law and commercial practice enjoin on him! And it is surely not satisfying to the accountant's professional pride that his subject and technique contains so much that is contradictory, uninformative, and misleading! These are social and intellectual challenges which we will disregard at our peril.

---

[28] It is difficult to say to what extent I owe this idea to the general character of economic theory, to the writings of other accountants—in particular H. W. Sweeney—on the subject, and to my own dissatisfaction with the observable differences between accounting theory and practice, economic theory and the behaviour of businessmen. There is an extensive and growing literature bearing directly on the matter.

4

THE FORMAL BASIS OF BUSINESS DECISIONS*

This is the last of three lectures devoted to an examination of the relationship between accounting and the financial policies of business. In the first of the series[1], it was argued that accounting is a fact-finding function the aim of which is to assist in the making of decisions on the financial aspects of business and other organizations. A distinction was drawn between decisions which are strictly financial in character, and decisions which are not solely of a financial nature. The second lecture[2] dealt, in the main, with the impact of the financial statements on the actions of financial supporters; it was concerned with the decisions of parties outside the group responsible for the management and direction of business firms. The present lecture will concern itself with the relationship between accounting and the decisions of businessmen *vis-a-vis* the firms which they manage. A selection of financial and quasi-financial problems will be considered.

Limitation of the problem

A complete examination of the process of making business decisions would involve separate discussion of two main groups of decisions: those which are made by groups, such as boards of directors, financial committees and executive committees, and those which are made by single persons. The processes by which group decisions are made are the more complex. Any such group will have at its disposal certain general information, information known equally by each of its members. But the interpretation each places on this information may differ from the interpretations of others. Each member may, however, have some private information. Some he may divulge, putting other members on the same informational footing as himself. Some he may not disclose, because he wishes to keep it to himself, or because it cannot be disclosed, or because he believes that other members already know of it. Whatever the reason, private information will influence the course of action which a member of a group will support. Further, there are personal relationships between members of a group which will have some bearing on the outcome of the discussion of a problem situation, and differences in the esteem some

---

* First published in *The Australian Accountant,* Vol. 26, No. 4, April 1956, pp. 155-74. Text prepared for Australian Society of Accountants Lecture in the University of Tasmania, September, 1955.

[1] "The Relationship between Accounting and Financial Management," see p. 7, *ante.*

[2] "Accounting and Business Finance," see p. 39, *ante.*

members have for the competence and judgment of others. Analysis of the way in which group decisions are made is confounded by these possibilities. To simplify the problem, therefore, it will be assumed that either (a) the decisions to be discussed are made by one person, or (b) if decisions arise from the deliberations of many persons, the outcome is not influenced by the inter-personal relationships and feelings mentioned above.

The Utility of Information

Varieties of information

Although financial and quasi-financial problems are the focus of attention, no such problem is entirely free of some non-financial aspects. Certain ends are to be attained other than the immediate and obvious end. Suppose, for example, it is proposed to raise a company's dividend rate; the present availability of profits and cash is not a sufficient ground. It may be necessary to consider the effect such a decision may have on the future expectations of investors, on the attitude of workers, on the goodwill of customers. It is difficult for the mind to grasp all these features of the problem and to evaluate each simultaneously. The proposal is taken piecemeal; the financial aspects and the non-financial aspects are examined separately, and the decision reached is a compromise, based on the weight given to each aspect, between the consequences of the available courses of action.

If he tries to act reasonably, the businessman will seek to inform himself about each aspect of the problems demanding his attention. For information on the financial aspects of problems he will have recourse to accounting statements of some kind; for information on the other aspects of problems he will have recourse to information generally less comprehensive and obtained by less systematic means than information on the financial features of business. Some of the non-accounting information will have been compiled for the specific problem before the businessman; some will be fragmentary; some will be qualitative. It is thus distinguishable from information compiled regularly, over time, according to some more or less consistent method, such as is information derived by the accounting process.

The businessman can make reservations or allowances for the inadequacies of information obtained occasionally or by unsystematic means. He will know it is a fragment, taken from but not necessarily representative of its context. Even though it may be directly relevant, it may not be accepted as thoroughly reliable. This lack of reliability may have to be discounted because there is no more reliable information available which is equally relevant. But the decision to which it gives rise will be made with less confidence (and should, therefore, be reviewed frequently and rigorously) than a decision based on information known to be reliable.

Information derived from accounting

There may well be a tendency, however, for the businessman to accept without reservation information collected according to an established and widely accepted procedure. Accounting information is the example *par excellence.* It may be accepted because the businessman knows that his contemporaries also depend on accounting information, and because he knows that there is an established profession of accountants who follow the same procedures. Beneath the acceptance of accounting information would lie the belief that accountants are sufficiently knowledgeable and technically competent to provide information appropriate to the decisions he is called upon to make. The businessman may, in fact, assume that the accountant knows intimately the problems to be solved and can look at them from the businessman's point of view. And, if accountants claim or admit that their function is to serve management, the businessman's assumption is justifiable. It would follow that the accountant would collect and arrange just that information which is relevant to business problems.

The accounting viewpoint

There is abundant evidence that accountants generally believe that the practices which they follow yield information which is relevant. The evidence is to be found in the practical work and in the writings of accountants.

Observations about the validity of accounting practices are commonly introduced with the phrase "from the viewpoint of accounting" or some equivalent qualification. This is a great convenience; it comfortably limits the issues to be discussed. But it also evades the only test of validity that is worthwhile—the test of utility in business.

Again, one is frequently confronted with the rhetorical question: can there be anything wrong with a technique which has survived centuries of use through greatly varied conditions? It is unwise to assume that the persistence of an accounting technique is proof of the utility of the resulting information. It is feasible, but not necessarily true, that business firms have prospered in spite of accounting, rather than because of it. Or, to take a less extreme view, it is possible that conventional accounting gave closer approximations to realities in the past than it has done in recent years. To overlook this possibility is to ignore a reasonable premise. Logical errors of this kind are not uncommon in the arguments of those who see in the survival of a technique evidence of its utility. Two examples are worth noticing. One deals with financial accounting, the other with an aspect of cost accounting.

(*a*) Professor Dein writes[3] of the criticism that accounting reports in the post-war period of rising price levels have been and continue to be incorrect and misleading: "These should be serious charges when made in public (as they have been) and when fully documented and authenticated. The evidence submitted thus far fortunately [*sic*] seems not to have been fully convincing, for with no more visible progress than has been made to cure the alleged defects, the

[3] R. C. Dein, "Price-Level Adjustments: Fetish in Accounting", *The Accounting Review,* January 1955.

profession of accounting, as well as the financial statements which symbolize the profession, should certainly otherwise have gone into a state of eclipse." This conclusion rests on the undisclosed premise that imperfect performance of function is a sufficient condition for the "eclipse" of the functionary, and this premise is demonstrably false. For, in the first place, a functionary may develop ancillary functions, so that even though it performs its prime function poorly its existence is still on balance justified. In the second place, it is not universal imperfection but relative imperfection of performance which will lead to the displacement of any functionary. In the case of accounting and the accounting profession, relative imperfection of performance has not been permitted to be observed. The conventional method of determining income has long been taught and practised, to the point where it is almost accepted as dogma, and it has been adopted by governments for taxation purposes. Any proposal to change it is, therefore, met with the unwillingness to experiment and the conservatism of the profession, and the fiscal sanction of the established method.

These observations are supported by some comments in the 1947 and 1948 annual reports of United States Steel Corporation. In 1941 the company had adopted the last-in, first-out method of valuing inventories. "This method recognizes fluctuations in the purchasing power of the dollar by reflecting current costs of employment and purchases—whatever the price change—in the cost of products currently sold. It is the most acceptable method yet developed of recording in costs purchasing power equivalent to that originally expended . . . [By this method] rising wages and prices currently incurred by U.S. Steel to reproduce what is sold are recorded as cost and not as increased inventory valuation and seeming profit" (1947 report). The company stated its belief, in the same report, that the same principle should apply to long-term inventories. "If a business is to continue, it is necessary to recover the purchasing power of sums originally invested in tools so that they may be replaced as they wear out. Therefore, this added amount is carried as a reserve for replacement of properties. It is a simple truth that to buy similar tools of production takes more dollars today than formerly; to count as profits, rather than as cost, the added sums required merely to sustain production is to retreat from reality into self-deception." Effect was given to this idea by increasing the 1947 charge for wear and exhaustion of facilities by 30 per cent of the amount determined on an historical cost basis. In the 1948 report, however, the company announced that it had abandoned the practice adopted in 1947 in favour of accelerated depreciation. The reason? ". . . the disagreement existing among accountants, both public and private, and the stated position of the American Institute of Accountants, which is supported by the Securities and Exchange Commission, that the only accepted accounting principle for determining depreciation is that which is related to the actual number of dollars spent for facilities, regardless of when or of what buying power . . . ."

This case demonstrates the difficulty, almost the impossibility, of comparing one method with another in practice; as long as no alternative is permitted, relative imperfections cannot be observed, and it is impossible to tell how much better, or worse, the "accepted" method is than another.

(*b*) A similar *non sequitur* occurs in a note on the distribution of overhead costs by Professor Baxter[4]. "Despite the apparent strength of the . . . arguments against the practice of allocating overhead expenses, the fact remains that allocation is very common, not only where departmental accounts are concerned, but also in most kinds of cost accounts . . . . We should therefore expect to find that, if the logic of the practice were shaky, many businesses would have noticed bad results, and vigorous criticisms would have followed. But the reverse is the case. There has been no public outcry; on the contrary, many of the most successful and profitable enterprises rely on costing methods that involve allocation, and attribute their prosperity at least in part to such systems."

It is perhaps true that vigorous criticisms follow bad results. But, firstly, bad results may not be experienced, for the consequences of biasses or inadequacies in the costing system may be more than counteracted by efficiencies of the firm in other directions. Secondly, it is quite improper to suggest that vigorous criticism will be directed towards an accounting method when bad results are noticed. Bad results are usually attributed to inefficient operations; supervisory and executive personnel in the manufacturing and distributing divisions are more likely to attract criticism than the cost accountant and his method. Professor Baxter's argument is based on the erroneous assumption that the illogicality of a practice becomes apparent in use. As was shown in the former example, the detection of error in practice depends on the opportunity of comparing alternative methods. There are many reasons why the kind of inductive reasoning mentioned by Professor Baxter will yield nothing which may be used to test alternative costing procedures. The laboratory method would be to expose the same executive, in the same circumstances, to different arrangements or types of information; the consequences of his decisions could then be compared, the decision which turns out to be the most appropriate being indicative of the information which is most relevant or useful. This method is not, of course, available; for every experience, of examining information or of making a decision, makes an executive a slightly different executive as far as any subsequent decision is concerned.

Further, it is doubtful to say the least, whether any voluntary or solicited statement attributing the prosperity of a firm to a system of costing which involves allocation should be relied on. For, quite apart from the fact that it is impossible to disentangle the causes of many observable results, the executive making the statement may well feel

---

[4] W. T. Baxter, "A Note on the Allocation of Oncosts between Departments", *The Accountant*, 5 November, 1938.

obliged to support a method used by him or by officers under his direction; he would scarcely condemn his own judgement.

The argument quoted above is thus no proof of the validity of overhead allocation. One can agree with Professor Baxter's comment that "an accounting system may be illogical and yet prove to be useful in business". But it does not seem proper to ignore the logical defect, or to disregard the possibility of devising a more economical system or a system which gives information of a higher order of relevance.

Relevance of accounting information

What financial information, then, is relevant to the solution of business problems?

This question has attracted very little attention on the part of accountants. Relevance does not rank among the so-called conventions and doctrines of accounting. It seems, nevertheless, to be fundamental, deserving of every bit as much discussion as other concepts. Much of the opposition to innovations in accounting may stem from the fact that relevance is not deemed to be a critical concept.

The idea is perhaps more frequently used in reverse by opponents of the view that current costs and current values should appear in accounting statements. Thus, Professor Littleton enunciates a Principle of Irrelevant Effects: If fluctuations in price levels are ignored as a basis for changing directly the statistical effects of transactions previously entered in the account, this omission would tend to avoid the introduction of irrelevant and confusing modifications in the objective measurement of enterprise efforts and accomplishments[5]. This kind of question-begging is typical of much accounting theory, and in the price level controversy it appears in statements by supporters both of historical cost and of current cost. Irrevelant to whom? and, irrelevant for what? one may ask. Professor Littleton offers no discussion of these questions, no argument based on observation of the business world to justify his "principle". He describes it as an "inductively derived principle", implying that it arises from observation or experience. It appears, however, that he alludes to the observations and experiences of accountants rather than of businessmen, and this, it is submitted, leads right away from the very point at which relevance may be tested.

To return to the question: what financial information is relevant to the solution of business problems?

Every business problem requires the making of a decision which is expected to result in the attainment of a purpose in a given environment. Over time, both the firm and its environment change, but with few exceptions the general purposes of a firm remain the same. The general problems of the firm are therefore concerned with carrying out its purposes in spite of changes in its environment. Because each

[5] *Structure of Accounting Theory*, American Accounting Association Monograph No. 5, 1953, p. 222.

problem is unique in time (though many are similar in other dimensions) it must be resolved in terms of the values ruling at that time, as determined by the environment. If the environment changes slowly, the values at which transactions are entered in accounts may continue to be relevant for some time. But if the environment changes rapidly, the initial values at which transactions (e.g., purchases of goods) are entered in accounts may be quite irrelevant at the date of the consummation of those transactions (e.g., by sale of the subject goods). And, even when the environment changes slowly, the values at which purchases of fixed assets are entered in accounts may be quite irrelevant in subsequent periods in which the consummation (by exhaustion of the asset) of such a transaction occurs. These irrelevancies arise, it is emphasized, because the initial amounts of unconsummated transactions are inconsistent with the later environment, whereas the businessman's problems must be resolved in the later environment as it stands.

The information that is relevant to the businessman is, therefore, information about here and now, inasmuch as "here and now" is the closest time, to the period in which his decision will be carried out, of which he can have knowledge. Contemporary values, costs or prices are the relevant magnitudes. The costs incurred in acquiring assets are relevant to problem situations when those assets are acquired, but then only.

Representativeness

There is another aspect of the question which also leads to the same conclusion. That accounting is abstract and formal was pointed out in the first lecture. Any kind of accounting that can be imagined is necessarily so, for it involves converting unlike real things into like symbols.[6] In this respect accounting is confronted with a problem similar to that which faces communication engineers. In a recent article, on the relationship between information and business decisions, M. Shubik observes: "Communication scientists and engineers deal with information as a set of messages obtained by arranging a given set of symbols"[7]. He quotes an expert in the field: "Frequently the messages have meaning: that is, they refer to or are correlated according to some system with certain physical or conceptual entities. [However] these semantic aspects of communication are irrelevant to the engineering problem."[8] Shubik continues: "It is precisely the meaning attached to and action taken on receipt of a message that is of interest to the social scientist."

This rings bells. Accounting may be abstract and formal, but it does not follow that its symbols must be considered as symbols only.

---

[6] The writer would now (1968) say: it involves representing a common property of unlike real things in like symbols. See, for example "Measurement in Accounting", p. 554, *post.*

[7] "Information, Risk, Ignorance and Indeterminacy", *The Quarterly Journal of Economics,* November 1954, p. 629.

[8] C. E. Shannon, *A Mathematical Theory of Communication,* Bell Telephone System Monograph B-1598, 1948.

The engineering approach is inappropriate for the accountant; he must be concerned, as is the social scientist, with the content and significance of his symbols; for the businessman is engaged in the manipulation of real events, real things and real relationships, and symbols are only useful to him if they represent these realities.

Under the conventional accounting process, it is possible to find identical assets appearing at different values because of the different figures at which they were first entered in the accounts, and to find identical goods or services charged against gross income in different amounts for the same reason. Can it be said that at any time there are several values corresponding to a given type of goods or services, all equally relevant to the price, output and product decisions of the businessman? Surely not. The service rendered by an asset purchased in the past is relevant as long as technology remains unchanged, but the value of that service varies as the environment dictates, independently of the wishes of businessmen and independently of the original entries in the accounts. The value placed on that service in the accounts should vary likewise, if the accounts are fairly and consistently to represent the business firm, its properties and costs, in a manner useful to businessmen. The unliquidated balances of any transaction and charges against those balances should appear at values ruling on the dates at which such balances and charges are reported. Only thus will they represent real phenomena in a way that is meaningful to decision-makers.

Adjustments of conventional accounts

It should not be assumed that the proposal to report transactions in terms of current values completely solves the problem of providing relevant information. The proposal itself involves a formal, and to some extent abstract, correction of originally recorded figures. For inventories there are generally no insuperable difficulties to obtaining current market values. But for fixed assets the only feasible solution seems to be to correct money costs by means of an index number. And this introduces a formal component in the calculations which may result, over years, in the adjusted figures diverging from true current costs or values. The discrepancy, however, will not usually be anything like as great as the discrepancy between initially recorded money outlays and true current values determined in the market. The adjusted figures are not unassailable, but they will be more relevant than historical costs, and will involve less guess-work, judgement or intuition on the part of the decision-maker. Occasional revaluation of assets may still be necessary, but the amounts of such adjustments will not be as great as those which have in recent years arisen from revaluations for the purpose of capital re-organization.

It will be clear from the foregoing argument that there are two general observations which may be made about information needed for the solution of business problems. Firstly, all relevant information is necessary, relevance being specific to problem situations at definite points of time. Secondly, as all relevant information can seldom be obtained—either because some is not available, or because the available information is formally derived and thus, for technical reasons, is not the ideal information—every decision involves the exercise of judgement or intuition.

The second principle, however, is no licence for neglecting the first. Accountants are in a favoured position to know in great detail the problems of businessmen, the kinds of financial information businessmen need, and the mental processes by which, in a given situation, information is converted into a decision. And they ought to know how just those kinds of information can be obtained. The way in which information is put to use is greatly in need of empirical study; it would be particularly interesting to accountants, for it would provide a test of usefulness, and usefulness is a necessary criterion of accounting method. It is not sufficient for accountants to know how to provide some information; and it is not sufficient to hope that whatever information is provided will be useful.

The attitudes of businessmen towards information

The way in which information is accepted has probably as much effect on the outcome of deliberation as the quality of the information itself. Just as there has been little empirical study of the use made of information, there has been no study of the attitudes of businessmen towards accounting information.

In the previous section it was suggested that businessmen may accept without reservation information collected according to an established and widely accepted procedure. This *a priori* generalization may apply to accounting for several reasons. Accounting is not only a process which, because of its numerical content, the layman assumes to be exact; it yields statements which independent accountants are often required to check, and on which those independent accountants report that the statements truly or fairly or correctly represent the affairs of business firms. This kind of certification, though not designed to have the same effect as testimonials for medicinal panaceas, may well have such an effect. And the adoption of the accountant's method by the fiscal authorities, as was mentioned earlier, may lend further support to accounting in the eyes of the businessman.

But the class "businessman" does not seem to be homogeneous in respect of the attitude towards accounting information. It will be useful to consider some of the views which may be adopted.

Some possible attitudes

Some businessmen may believe that the information supplied by accountants is relevant and complete. It is to this group that the generalization mentioned above properly applies. This group may include the largest number of all businessmen—those who know little about the technique and limitations of accounting, whose business units are not large, and who therefore cannot afford to employ specialists capable of interpreting accounting statements in the light of changes in the environment. If the belief of such a businessman is justified, subsequent action will not be inappropriate through faults in the information, though it may be inappropriate through errors of judgement. If his belief is not justified, because the information supplied does not meet the requirements mentioned in the previous section of this lecture, subsequent action will always be inappropriate to the circumstances, except in the unlikely event that irrelevancies in the information are compensated by errors of judgement.

A second group of businessmen may believe that the information supplied is relevant but incomplete. If the belief of such a businessman in the relevance of the information is justified, he will feel the necessity to add to it such other information as he may have obtained personally, by hearsay or observation. He may feel free to speculate about the impact of factors about which his knowledge is imperfect, and he may go about this in an organized, methodical manner, or in a disorderly manner. The appropriateness of subsequent action will depend on the amount of additional relevant information to which he obtains access, on his ability to discern the potential impact on net income of the factors about which he obtains additional information, and on the rigour with which he examines the courses of action available to him. If, on the other hand, his belief is not justified—because his information is relevant and complete, or irrelevant and incomplete—he is just as likely to act inappropriately as if he believed the information to be relevant and complete when it was not.

The two foregoing groups include all businessmen who believe accounting information to be relevant to their problems. These are the persons on whose behalf accountants should study carefully the relevance of the information they supply.

There is a third group—those who believe the information to be irrelevant. If, in fact, the information is relevant, the decisions of this group will be inappropriate, for they will disregard their information. If, on the other hand, the belief is justified, the businessman is without guidance of a formal kind; having no dependable information he may be forced to rely on speculation and intuition. Whatever the outcome of his decision, it will be by chance, not by reason. It is likely, however, that many firms in this group will have the means of testing whether or not any information is relevant to their immediate problems. They will be able to employ experts to examine and report on changes in the environment and their effects on the firms' prospects. They will be in a position to rework or to ignore accounting information because of their superior means of obtaining relevant information from other sources or of other kinds.

Evidence of belief in the inadequacy of accounting information

These three kinds of attitude towards accounting information are all plausible, and each has features which should interest accountants. This brief consideration of them seems to be warranted by signs, probably originating from or relating to the third group, that the accounting statements are not universally accepted by businessmen as complete and relevant even in respect of the matters they cover. The evidence is scattered. It is neither representative nor conclusive. But it is indicative of the views of some able and ably assisted businessmen.

(*a*) There are a few statements made by or on behalf of business groups. For example, in 1947, Machinery and Allied Products Institute (U.S.A.) published a pamphlet, *Depreciation and the Postwar Price Level,* written by its research director. It may be presumed to represent the view of members of the Institute, who, besides being machinery manufacturers are also large machinery users. The pamphlet argues that the conventional method of computing depreciation on the basis of cost results in overstatement of profits. The concluding sections deal with two types of managerial decision—dividend distribution and capital investment: "Profits and dividends are of course essential if corporations are to raise outside capital, either by direct borrowing or by security flotations. The question here is not whether industry should make profits: it is whether it should *overstate* them. Specifically, it is whether investment in productive facilities benefits by the reporting of capital recoveries as income and by the distribution of these recoveries in dividends. We think not . . . it will be obvious when we consider managerial behaviour that a billion dollars of capital recovery, labelled as such and retained for investment, will generate more corporate capital expenditure than a billion dollars of such recovery, erroneously labelled profit and paid out to stockholders. Management will spend money it has in the till when it will not or cannot go out and raise it from the public . . . . Since capital investment must be recovered in real purchasing power, not simply in dollars, under-depreciation should be recognized for managerial purposes whether recognized for tax purposes or not."

It is clear that the Institute regards the accountant's concept of income, and statements based on that concept, as a poor foundation for decisions on dividends and corporate investment. A similar belief is evident from a study, *The Effects of Inflation on Industrial Capital Resources,* published by the Federation of British Industries in 1951. The problem is stated as follows: "The maintenance of capital intact, in the sense of preserving the productive capacity of the enterprise, is, in fact, one of the most important responsibilities of management. For the fulfilment of this responsibility only the balance remaining after provision has been made for the maintenance of capital can be regarded as 'profit' and as available either to meet taxation or for distribution as dividends. If the value of money remained constant, an increase or decrease in the capital resources of industry would be fairly easy to measure. But when the value of money is changing as progressively as it has done in recent years, then there is great difficulty in interpreting the published accounts of public companies so as to measure changes in capital. This difficulty arises from the use, in a long period of rising prices, of accounting methods which assume a stable value of money."

The F.B.I. study takes cognizance of the overstatement of income arising from the inclusion of inventory gains as well as from inadequate provision for replacement of fixed assets. It purports to show that for 80 companies, accumulated reserves and depreciation provisions in 1949 fell materially short of the amount needed to maintain the real capital of 1938: "The amount of undistributed profits put to reserve in the last few years has been inadequate to maintain industry's capital over the years. Yet the proportion of profits distributed has not risen but fallen. It is clear therefore that the levels of prices and profits have not been excessive, but too low to sustain the burden of taxation under existing methods of computation and to maintain the productive capacity of industry."

The points to be noticed are: (i) the finger is pointed at the assumption of stability, in real terms, of the unit of account; and (ii) the implication that disclosed profits computed in the conventional manner have misled business firms either into making excessive dividend distributions or into inappropriate pricing.

(*b*) The validity of the contemporary accounting concept of income has been criticized in the annual reports of a number of companies. The number is not large, relatively, but the companies individually are by no means negligible. Companies which have made such observations at some time during the last eight years include: in the United Kingdom, Courtaulds Ltd., Lever Brothers and Unilever Ltd., Patons & Baldwins Ltd., Peninsular and Oriental Steam Navigation Co., Shell Transport and Trading Co. Ltd., Tootal Ltd.; in the United States, Bristol Myers Co., National Steel Corporation, United States Steel Corporation, West Virginia Pulp and Paper Co.; and in Australia, Broken Hill Pty. Co. Ltd., Colonial Sugar Refining Co. Ltd., Jantzen (Australia) Ltd.

The comments of these companies are often tied to some criticism of the basis of determining taxable income; but they nevertheless indicate that the managements of these companies believe that income should be computed in such a way that the maintenance of capital is assured. The following example from the 1951 report of Peninsular and Oriental Steam Navigation Co. is a comprehensive statement of what may be involved: "... if old ships are to be replaced, a Company must set aside resources each year for three purposes:—

(i) To write off the *original* cost of each ship. This is usually done by charging a proportion of her cost (say one-twentieth) against the ship's earnings.

(ii) To increase the sum set aside under (i) in proportion to the increase in *current* shipbuilding costs.

(iii) To supplement sums set aside under (i) and (ii) *in past years* because, since they were set aside each year, shipbuilding prices have risen and have thus rendered *past* reserves inadequate for the purpose.

(iv) To set aside the amount by which those reserves made under (i), (ii) and (iii) above have fallen in value through depreciation in Government stocks since they were invested."

This is a complete formula for securing continuity of operations, as far as continuity depends on the adequacy of facilities. It makes no reference to decisions on the price of services given, though appropriate price decisions have a material bearing on a company's capacity to set aside the reserves or provisions to which reference is made. The nature of the market for the products of any firm may be such that it cannot recover, in its prices, sufficient sums under each of the four categories mentioned in the P. & O. Co.'s report, but there can be no doubt about the criterion underlying the above statement. Price decisions are discussed at greater length in the following section of this lecture.

(*c*) One other indication of the necessity for more information than conventional accounting gives will suffice. Several years ago *The Economist* Intelligence Unit in collaboration with the Association of Certified and Corporate Accountants offered a service designed to aid businessmen in the United Kingdom in making decisions in respect of which knowledge of trends in the price levels of fixed assets is necessary. Two specific matters mentioned in the original circular were the amounts to be set aside to cover the future replacement of fixed assets, and the values to be placed on fixed assets "for insurance and other purposes". Indices have been compiled of changes in the price levels of capital goods in a wide range of industries, and these are offered on a subscription basis.

For this project to have been undertaken and continued, there must have been some assurance of a steady demand for such information. It does not follow that this information need be incorporated in the financial statements on which businessmen make significant financial decisions; but if, as was suggested above, businessmen are concerned with an income figure which allows for the maintenance of real capital, the most convenient way of following through the effects of price level changes would be to incorporate adjustments in the accounting process. The important point for present purposes, however, is that businessmen find the information conveyed by conventional accounts inadequate for their purposes to the extent of supporting the service here mentioned.

Required information

Knowledge of what is an appropriate form of accounting for business purposes has generally been pursued in much the same way as knowledge is pursued in other fields, partly by reasoning from observed events and partly by deduction. But the view that conventional accounting adequately serves business purposes can only persist if observation and deduction are circumscribed by a "tendency to expect business to conform to an accounting pattern rather than the reverse".[9] If inquiry is limited in this way, the needs of businessmen can be overlooked or treated scantily. An attempt has been made in the foregoing sections to shake off this limitation and to consider the kind of information needed, regardless of what accountants supply.

---

[9] R. H. Montgomery in Foreword to Peragallo's *Origin and Evolution of Double Entry Bookkeeping*, American Institute Publishing Company, N.Y., 1938.

The conclusions are: (*a*) that businessmen are concerned with the maintenance of real capacity; and therefore (*b*) that they require a form of accounting which will show what remains of gross income after meeting expenses and maintaining real capital; (*c*) that for the purpose of forming expectations about the yield from future operations or additional investment, they need figures which show the profits earned and the capital employed in comparable dimensions; (*d*) that, for the purpose of making any decision involving the value of an asset, representative or contemporary values of assets are required. Conventional accounting provides for none of these things; it is thus an inadequate formal basis for business decisions. Its inadequacies may, however, be overcome by adopting "current cost" as the principle for computing income and financial position instead of historical costs.

It is worth emphasizing that these conclusions follow from both inductive and deductive lines of reasoning, observation supporting what seems, on *a priori* grounds, to be reasonable and appropriate.

Information for quasi-financial decisions

Up to this point the discussion has been focused on information required for the broader financial decisions in business. It is necessary now to pay some attention to the information needed for what, in the first lecture, were called quasi-financial decisions. These decisions include the determination of prices, of the composition of turnover, of the volume of turnover, of the efficiency of operations.

Cost accounting method

According to most writers on the subject, the rationale of cost accounting lies in its capacity to provide information in greater detail and of greater relevance for the above purposes than does financial accounting. The greater part, by volume and number, of the expositions of cost accounting, is devoted to the treatment of absorption costing. It is the purpose of the present section to consider whether the emphasis on this kind of cost accounting is justified, to ask whether absorption costing gives information which is as useful and as relevant as it is claimed to be.

The purpose of absorption costing is to derive the full cost of each product. A distinction is drawn between direct costs and indirect costs. Product costs are obtained by adding to the direct costs a share or shares of the indirect costs. The shares of indirect costs are computed by making several successive apportionments (e.g., as between factory costs and general administrative costs; and for factory costs, as between different departments).

The important thing to note, for the moment, is that costs are made to fall on products. "The main type of entity with which the cost accountant has to deal is the unit of activity which the business is concerned to produce."[10] The reasons given for this emphasis on the

[10] Yorston, Brown and Sainsbury, *Costing Procedures,* Sydney, Law Book Co., 1954, p. 5.

product are varied. Some writers aver that in order to make intelligent price decisions, management needs to know the average cost to make and sell each product. Some say that each job produced must bear an equitable proportion of the charges against income. Some argue that average product cost must be known in order that inventories may be correctly valued and that periodical net profit may be correctly computed.

Absorption costing challenged

None of these reasons, however, shows how the information on average cost influences a decision. There is a gap between the derivation of the information and the specific decision which is supposed to be based on it. It is quite possible, for example, that business may be taken which does not cover average total cost; and it is quite possible that business may be taken with no intention that it will bear an equitable proportion of the total charges of the firm. It is also possible that the complex calculations required to give the average total cost, when a change in volume is contemplated, would take so long that a decision to take additional orders must be made in ignorance of the average total cost.

There are reasons for believing that concentration on the average total cost of products does not give the kind of information needed for price and volume decisions.

(*a*) As long as business firms have only one product it would be proper to attempt to compute its average cost per unit. It would perhaps also be appropriate to do so in the case of firms which have several products for which no services are provided in common. In these circumstances a significant profit-per-product could be obtained, significant in the sense that both income and expense are directly obtained from transactions with external parties. The same cannot be said of a firm which produces a variety of goods or services with the same physical and organizational equipment. No unequivocal figure can be obtained for the average total cost of any product in spite of the pseudo-scientific formulae which have been developed for the apportionment of common costs. What may the businessman do, given the average total cost of his products? If he believes that the costs given by his cost accounting system are correct and unique figures, his decision may be inappropriate; for computed average costs may vary widely according to the method adopted in allocating indirect costs, and there is no certainty that the particular value he is given in the range of possible values will be the value of greatest significance to the firm at the time. If he does not believe that the information he is given is correct and relevant, that information cannot be considered to be the basis of his decision. Therefore, in the case of multi-product firms, and in these days that means most firms, average total costs are unlikely to be of notable assistance in decision-making.

(*b*) A further reason will become apparent from re-examination of the view that the product is "the main type of entity with which the cost accountant has to deal". It does not seem to be as important to consider what the cost accountant has to deal with, as it is to consider what the business manager has to deal with. And it is doubtful whether management is vitally concerned with the average costs of products. A business firm is a unit; from the point of view of many persons, an indivisible whole. This is the view held, for example, by all financial supporters. They look to the management of the firm for overall results, for their security and their income depend on the results of the firm as a whole. They do not normally think of the profitability of any product or department of the firm, but of the profitability of the firm. Management is necessarily aware of this, and it is natural that, whatever decisions are made about specific aspects of operations (prices, volumes or what have you), they will not be made without reference to the effect on the firm as a whole. In the case of a going concern, it is extremely likely that the total costs of the firm and its total income will be considered to be the significant factors rather than the calculated results of each of the parts of the firm. For, the firm has known markets, in which it obtains known prices, yielding a net profit the approximate size of which is known; any event or proposal involving variations in the known figures can be translated into a variation in the result far more directly and economically by reference to aggregate costs and income than by reference to the arbitrary costs and profits from each product. In effect this means that marginal cost and marginal revenue of the firm are more to the point than average total costs of products.

(*c*) Further still, it is doubtful whether average total cost has any bearing on price when a reduction of output occurs or is contemplated. In this case, the fixed cost per unit of product rises, suggesting the necessity to raise prices. This, of course, is quite the reverse of the appropriate action as businessmen see it; for, when demand falls the reaction is to seek ways of supporting it, and one of the most effective ways to do this is to reduce prices. This effect of absorption costing has long been recognized but it has not led to any marked aversion to the method.

Marginal cost v. full cost in Economics

Many economists have speculated about the manner in which prices and outputs are determined. In fact there is scarcely anything in the literature of cost accounting comparable with the argument and counter-argument among economists aimed at elucidating the facts and processes behind price and output decisions. It will be useful briefly to consider two alternative explanations of the way in which prices and outputs are determined, even at the risk of understating the cases for and against either.

One school assumes that the businessman seeks to maximize profits. He will, therefore, at any time adopt a different course of action than formerly if the gain arising from the change exceeds the cost involved in making it. In particular, for example, he will increase his output if the revenue obtained from the sale of additional output (his marginal revenue) exceeds the cost of that output (his marginal cost). The average total costs of products, such as cost accounting produces, are irrelevant if the assumption of profit-maximization reasonably represents the businessman's criterion of action.

The alternative assumption is that businessmen do not deliberately and persistently pursue a policy of profit-maximization, but fix their prices by applying conventional margins to calculated average costs. If profit is maximized, this is simply an accidental outcome of the method adopted.

It is of some importance to inquire whether this is, in fact, the method adopted by businessmen, and not simply a rationalization of their policies, for it appears to make the figures produced by absorption costing the critical information.

Some light may be thrown on the matter by reference to an empirical study of the pricing process, reported by Messrs. Hall and Hitch in a paper, "Price Theory and Business Behaviour"[11]. The authors summarize the results of inquiries, by interview and questionnaire, of 38 companies, mainly manufacturers. Thirty firms reported that they adhered (12 "rigidly", 15 "normally" and three "in principle") to the full cost basis of pricing. "An overwhelming majority of the entrepreneurs thought that a price based on full average cost (including a conventional allowance for profit) was the 'right' price, the one which 'ought' to be charged."[12]

This observation has three loopholes. Firstly, full cost may be the basis of a price decision in a direct or an indirect way. If it is the only formal information put before a businessman, it is easy to understand that he might say it was the basis of his decision when, in fact, he subsequently made calculations of his own in respect of the consequences of alternative prices; calculations, that is, involving comparisons of the additional costs and the additional gains from alternative decisions. Secondly, "a conventional allowance for profit" is anything but precise. One can easily rationalize the inclusion of the profit which did in fact arise from a transaction by describing it as a conventional allowance. And, is the conventional allowance applied rigidly? Only if each transaction is expected to yield the same (percentage) margin for a given class of commodities can it be argued that the full cost formula is being followed. Thirdly, many entrepreneurs may aver that such and such a price is the "right" price, the price which "ought" to be charged, without in fact charging that price. "Right" and "ought" have ethical overtones; a businessman might be expected to describe his practices in terms which it is not difficult to justify, and for this purpose "full cost" makes a much better story than "what the market will bear".

But the validity of the conclusion that price is determined by full cost is open to question on the basis of the information in the appendix to the Hall and Hitch paper. One column in the appendix gives the circumstances in which the policy of pricing on full cost would be

---

[11] *Oxford Economic Papers, No.* 2, reprinted in *Oxford Studies in the Price Mechanism,* O.U.P., 1951. Subsequent page number references are to pages in the latter.

[12] Loc. cit., p. 113.

departed from. In the case of only one company is this column empty; the others between them, but not individually, give a wide range of conditions under which, or purposes for which, departure from full cost may be justified. When reasons are given such as depressed trade, pressure of competitive prices, to capture new markets, to obtain large contracts, etc., it is quite feasible that these are the memorable, the critical price decisions, the cases in which marginal cost and marginal revenue were significant factors. It is also possible that, in respect of many of the prices not fixed under special circumstances, there was a sufficient monopolistic element in the market to enable a price to be fixed within a range of prices, the precise price being a matter of indifference to customers. If such were the case, it is no more likely that prices would be based on full cost than on any other principle. The information given in the tables and the appendix strongly suggests that businessmen are concerned both with the effect of a price on the demand and with certain cost figures; this comes very near to justification of the assumption that the businessman seeks to maximize profits. And, as has been suggested already, this implies that marginal cost, not full cost, is the essential information.

What "cost" is relevant?

The argument so far has not required a specific definition of what is meant by cost. It is necessary to be more precise, for an important element in the calculations of businessmen may otherwise be overlooked.

The appendix to the Hall and Hitch paper gives some information on the methods by which price is determined. For example, "Materials + labour + overheads + intended profit. Overheads split to departments, then spread 'evenly'" (p. 135); or, "Works cost + average selling cost + about 5%. Output assumed to be normal. Overheads distributed specifically" (p. 132). It is fair to assume from such notes that the firms under inquiry follow conventional absorption costing. What is obtained is the average historical cost per product.

The same idea suggests itself in the work of Mr. Andrews.[13] Andrews suggests that the businessman fixes his price "by adding a definite margin to his estimates of the average direct costs of producing a particular article" (p. 157). Direct costs are those which "are entered in the trading account" (p. 86). The trading account, as Andrews envisages it, includes only material costs, manufacturing wages and other oviously direct charges. But even though his revenue accounts do not follow the form to which accountants are accustomed, his case is clearly based on the kinds of information which accountants record—money outlays and money receipts. ". . . profit is what is left after maintaining intact the financial value of the assets. This is valid so long as it is understood that 'value' there implies merely the total of the sums of money laid out, i.e., it is a *cost*-value, and not value in the sense of market valuation" (p. 34). Andrews notices the "suggestion

[13] P. W. S. Andrews, *Manufacturing Business,* London, Macmillan, 1949.

that the depreciation charges should be increased, in order to take account of the rise in replacement cost, and that the Inland Revenue should recognize such charges for income-tax purposes"; he feels "some temerity about intervening in a dispute properly the business of another profession, but it seems to him that those accountants who resist the change on the ground that it would give a false statement of the profit that the businessman has in fact earned, are correct" (p. 35).

Price and real cost

One who wishes to challenge the view that price and output decisions are based on historical cost information is, therefore, confronted with several kinds of opposition. They include (1) the assertions of text-book writers that product costing (on historical costs) is useful for these purposes; (2) the kind of information supplied to Hall and Hitch; and (3) the opinion of one group of economists. This may appear to be a formidable array. But there is evidence that some businessmen, at least, do not regard conventional costs as the proximate basis of price decisions. Two short extracts will suggest that real cost or current cost is relevant:—

"The only way in which we can maintain that part of our capital which is invested in fixed assets is to recover in the price of our products an amount which truly represents the wastage in value of our fixed assets at present day prices. . . . Selling prices must be so fixed as to bear relation to real cost." (Chairman's address, 1948, Lever Bros. and Unilever Ltd.)

"In order to avoid impairment of its capital investment, a company should include in its basis for computing selling prices a sum sufficient to provide the funds necessary for the replacement of productive facilities at the expiration of their useful life." (Bristol Myers Co., 1950 Annual Report.)

Inventory gains in periods of rising prices have not attracted the same kind of attention; nor have they been linked specifically to the problem of pricing in the reports which have come under notice. But the reports of Patons & Baldwins Ltd. and A. G. Healing Ltd. make it clear that the managements of those companies take account in some way of the replacement costs of stocks.

It is submitted that public statements such as are given above are more likely to suggest the real method of making price decisions than direct inquiries into the relationship between costs and prices. In the latter case, common conservatism and canons of business prudence must be allowed for. But, in the case of a public statement, in a context in which costs and prices are subordinate to the preservation of the firm, reticence is not to be expected.

But support for the argument against the relevance of the traditional information is not limited to statements of the opinion of businessmen. It is possible to demonstrate in a reasonably satisfactory manner that current costs of all factors or services influence the prices of a wide range of manufactured goods.

The case of a monopolist in an industry into which entry by new firms is difficult presents no problem. It is reasonable to suppose that, as there are no competitors to force down the price, a price will be established which will ensure the maintenance of real capacity. It will be such that provision is made continuously for the replacement of stocks and equipment. Where entry into the industry is not so difficult, the firm will still be able to include replacement costs in its calculations for pricing purposes, for replacement costs to the established firm are the same as initial costs to new entrants into the industry.

In the case of monopolistic competition, whatever the conditions of entry into the industry, the same conclusion holds. It is only necessary to assume that competitors are of different ages, and that their plants are therefore of different ages, so that there is a more or less continuous demand for new items of equipment. In any year new equipment may have been purchased by some firms, and the charge for its services, by way of depreciation, will be based on its cost. But in the same year old equipment will be providing the same services for other firms in the industry. In general, if fixed assets and stocks are acquired at different price levels, firms which buy at higher prices will sell at higher prices. The firm which has the advantage of buying at lower prices is unlikely, in the assumed conditions, to sell at low prices simply because its historical costs are lower. Its selling prices will therefore approach those of new entrants, or those appropriate to the higher purchase prices of the fixed assets and stocks which it or its competitors have recently acquired.

The two conditions dealt with, monopoly and monopolistic competition, cover most of the circumstances in which calculations of cost are important for price and product decisions. The general conclusion is that, whether or not businessmen are given cost information which includes the current cost of goods or services used, prices will tend to be based on current costs. It is thus incorrect to assume that price level variations are irrelevant for the purposes being considered.

Objectivity considered.

It may, of course, be contended that, even if the above conclusion is correct, accountants should limit their attention to recorded cost or outlay because it is objectively determined. But to do so leads to information which is of, say, second-level importance, in the sense that it requires further processing or manipulation in accordance with the businessman's formally imperfect knowledge of changes in price levels. The result of this processing cannot be as objectively appropriate as would information derived from incorporation in the basic cost record of the effects of price fluctuations. The statements which could be obtained by incorporating these effects would, by contrast, give information of first-level importance, in the sense that it is in a form appropriate for direct use in making decisions.

Further, the reason given for adhering to historical cost, its objectivity, may be challenged. What is meant by the objective determination of figures entered in accounts is that they arise from transactions "at arm's length"[14] between two parties. It is true that the price agreed between two such parties may be objective and relevant at the time of the transaction. It establishes a claim of one against the other in an agreed amount, and it represents the expectations of the buyer at the time of purchase. But thereafter the price paid need no longer be relevant; the expectations of the buyer may be disappointed or exceeded. This may come about because the market price of the goods or services he has bought subsequently falls or rises, as an expression of the consensus of opinion of buyers and sellers at subsequent dates. Do the supporters of the historical cost principle claim that a price struck between two parties is more objective than a current valuation resulting from the consensus of opinion of many parties? Given that the element of time is important, it seems rather that a current valuation is more objective than historical cost, and more relevant; for objectivity surely increases as the number of interested parties having like opinions increases, and "relevant" surely can only mean relevant to particular problems and times, not relevant to all problems at all times!

It may also be contended that the view expressed in the first part of this section is not in accordance with the facts elicited by the F.B.I. inquiry quoted for another purpose earlier in this paper, and not in accordance with the complaints in some annual reports that real capital cannot be maintained under existing fiscal policies. But the F.B.I. study included the war years in which ordinary commercial practice was necessarily suspended. And, in the case of individual firms, it may occasionally happen that prices cannot be fixed at a level which provides for the maintenance of real capital because they are in competition with foreign firms which are subsidized or taxed less heavily. But even in these cases it is useful to know the extent of the loss of real capital, so that unintentional liberality may not contribute to further loss.

Some conclusions

The argument may be summarized. Conventional product costs, it is claimed, are not unequivocal, due to the variety of methods for apportioning common costs. Their derivation is clumsy, as it involves changes in the apportionments with each change in total volume or the volume of each commodity produced. They are irrelevant because, to the businessman, the firm as a whole is the entity of prime concern. They are irrelevant because marginal cost, not average cost, is the significant magnitude for decision-making purposes. They are irrelevant because they take no account of the current value of services and goods consumed in production. It is hard to escape the conclusion that Mark Spade wrote with some realism when he gave the following example of product costing:[15]

---

[14] A. C. Littleton, op. cit., p. 182.
[15] *How to Run a Bassoon Factory*, Hamish Hamilton.

		s.	d.
Wood for bassoon			4
Metal for bassoon			5½
Reed for bassoon			½
Making bassoon		7	6
Total		8	4
Actual cost of bassoon	£29	9	6
Therefore overhead costs (lighting, heating, office staff, rent, rates, directors' fees, experts' salaries, sales staff, insurance, assurance, loss on canteen money stolen by cashier, loss on investments, depreciation of plant, etc.)	£29	1	2

There is here a proper regard for the direct costs and a (proper?) disdain for all the other costs.

Of positive conclusions there are two.

The businessman needs to know the costs and gains which arise from any change in output, combination of products, prices or other features of the firm's operations. In effect this means that, to the extent that he is interested in cost of production, he is directly interested in marginal cost, not average total cost. Costs need therefore only to be allocated to products in so far as they can be identified with products. The time and ingenuity often spent in calculating apportionments of common costs could more profitably be spent in calculating the costs of alternative courses of future action, so that management would have more to go on than single-valued reports on past action.

Secondly, the businessman needs to know the current cost of the goods or services being consumed in production, for unless his decisions take cognizance of current costs there can be no assurance that real capital will be maintained. This does not mean that the selling prices of all the commodities produced by a firm are influenced by the current values of its fixed assets; the demand for some commodities may be more susceptible to change with changes in price than the demand for others, in which case the appropriate reaction to a rise in costs is to raise the price of the former less than the price of the latter. But whatever prices are established, and whatever products are produced in whatever combination, a businessman has a greater need to know the current costs of goods consumed and plant service used than to know the amounts originally laid out to procure them, if he expects to remain in business.

Costs and efficiency

Nothing has so far been said of one of the managerial problems for which the calculation of purely historical costs is relevant, the measurement of organizational efficiency and the control of costs.

The introductory pages of books on costing include the measurement of efficiency among the services which cost accounting provides. But one is left to assume that substantially the same processes of aggregation and apportionment which give product costs also provide the means for controlling costs and determining efficiency. The treatment of manufacturing expense budgets in many books on budgeting follow the same pattern. The costs of running the manufacturing and merchandising divisions of a firm are obtained by adding to the costs directly identifiable with departments allocations of costs incurred for the benefit of many departments in common. Does this procedure give useful measures of efficiency or promote the control of costs?

Those who believe it does argue in the following way. If costs can be traced to the points at which they are incurred, they can be treated as the responsibility of the supervisory personnel at those points. All costs should be borne ultimately by products, but the indirect costs may, at an intermediate stage in the calculation of product costs, be made to fall on the several departments of an organization. These costs are therefore the basis upon which departmental efficiency may be tested.

There are some rather loose connexions in this case. It is obviously not true that prorated costs are the responsibility of a departmental supervisor or manager. He has no say, either as to the amount spent or the proportion allocated to his department, in respect of the majority of items which commonly appear in a departmental expense account or budget. It is questionable, therefore, whether he can be expected to assume responsibility for them. Confidence in the information supplied and in the equity of the allocations has much to do with the effectiveness of cost statements for the purpose of controlling costs. An example of lack of confidence came under notice some years ago in a large firm which supplied its departmental executives with monthly statements of budgeted and actual costs. The indirect expenses were allocated to departments on the basis of a fixed amount per direct labour hour. The departments frequently worked overtime, so that month after month these departmental executives received reports showing overhead costs much in excess of budgeted overheads. This they could not understand, for when the annual summaries were subsequently supplied the results were much more favourable to each than the monthly statements had led them to believe. The works department executives were pleasantly derisory towards the costing department and its statements, and in such circumstances it was not to be expected that the statements would be used as a guide to directions in which costs could be reduced.

Secondly, to attempt to control costs by the use of statements involving apportionments is likely to distract attention from the fact that apportioned costs are incurred as lump-sum outlays. These outlays arise on the exercise of the authority of some person other than those in charge of departments to which they are subsequently allocated as costs, and it is therefore equitable that the authorizing person should bear the responsibility rather than departmental executives.

Thirdly, it is also possible that the diffusion of a specific cost by apportionment to departments may lead to disregard of significant changes in its amount. This may occur because when it is divided none of its parts is as significant in amount as the whole would be, or because each such part is relatively unimportant by comparison with the aggregate in which it is included.

These observations suggest the conclusion that, for the measurement of efficiency, apportionment is often inequitable, and for the control of costs apportionment is unnecessary. One can agree with the commonly stated maxim that the control of costs should be based on the structure of an organization, provided this means that the authority to incur expenditure, not the departments over which an expenditure can be spread, is the determinant of responsibility.

General Conclusions

This being the last of this series of lectures, it appears to be desirable to summarize the conclusions which have been reached.

In the first lecture an attempt was made to show that accounting is a service function, providing information for the management of the financial aspects of business. Its logic must therefore be based on the logic of business. Any accounting practice which interferes with the right of the users of accounting statements to exercise their judgement on the basis of the facts of business should therefore be abandoned. On this ground conservatism was challenged and disclosure was considered to be a matter of managerial policy, not an accounting doctrine.

The second lecture dealt with the kinds of information deemed to be necessary to financial and other supporters of business organizations. Intelligent participation can only be expected if investors, creditors and other parties are put in possession of adequate information. It was argued that accounts compiled on the conventional basis are inadequate, as they do not represent the firm at the time when they are prepared, except in a static economy. The financial statements were regarded as expressing the formal conditions of participation, and, since the historical cost basis leads to distortion of the capital and debt structure of firms, (*a*) investors may well make inappropriate decisions and (*b*) other parties may exert unwarranted pressures on business firms. Participants need therefore to be informed of the impact of changes in the general level of prices on the financial structure and results of the firms they support.

This lecture has been concerned with the internal use of accounting information. Consideration of the information provided by the financial accounts led to the conclusion that the same kind of information deemed to be needed by external parties is also needed by businessmen for their purposes. Accounting statements based on current costs were considered to be directly relevant, whereas accounting statements based on historical cost tend to become less and less relevant as time passes and conditions change. This view was supported by the practices and statements of businessmen themselves. Turning to cost accounts and the uses they are said to serve, the same conclusion was reached: current costs are the appropriate basis for, and marginal costing is the appropriate process for, deriving cost information which is to be used in making business decisions. For most purposes the apportionment of costs seems to be pointless and time could more profitably be spent in making studies of specific activities independently of the accounting framework.

The whole study suggests two thoughts which are worth setting down against the possibility that some may believe that the answers to all the questions raised have been given—either in these lectures or in the work of those who take opposite views.

The first is that parts of the fields of study of accounting and economics are concerned with the same things: the facts of business and the behaviour of business firms and businessmen. It seems strange that accounting and economics have for so long proceeded on quite different assumptions as to the information which is relevant to businessmen. For the sake of the development of both it seems desirable that there should be greater intercourse between accountants and economists; or, to stay closer to home and to be more specific, accountants should perhaps take a more lively interest in the economic theories of the behaviour of business firms.

The second thing that emerges is that very little empirical work has been done on the ways in which businessmen use the information they are given, and on the kinds of information they would like to have. Superficial study is not enough; assumption is not enough. Careful and patient field work will be required to establish the way in which formal information is used or modified by knowledge or impressions gained otherwise, and to discover what criteria businessmen in fact adopt when making their decisions. The justification of accounting practices must remain in doubt as long as there are gaps in knowledge of the part accounting information plays in decision-making.

5

THE IMPLICATIONS OF ASSET REVALUATIONS AND BONUS SHARE ISSUES*

1.—Introduction

In earlier research lectures[1] attention was directed to the relationship between accounting and financial policies. Evidence was drawn from a variety of sources indicative of the inadequacy of the information yielded by contemporary accounting for many important business purposes. In this lecture it is intended to examine closely some concepts of the nature and purpose of accounting; these concepts will then be confronted with the actual practices of Australian public companies over the past 10 years and with the explanations of those practices given by businessmen themselves.

In essence this is an exercise in testing, by reference to the facts of financial administration, the hypotheses represented by accounting doctrines. Of some of these facts most practitioners will be aware. But, as no work has been published which presents them collectively, it is possible that the cases known to individuals are considered to be aberrations, and, as such, they throw no doubt on the validity of accepted views. But the evidence points in a direction different from those views, and, far from being expressive of anomalies, it seems to be sufficient to support opposing views.

2.—The Nature and Purpose of Accounting

The general nature and purpose of accounting are seldom described in adequate terms. There seems to be considerable confusion as to what accounting is, does, can do and should do. Some examples will serve to show that this confusion is not simply a difference in the viewpoints of different persons, but that it is a feature of the writings of the same persons or groups at different points in their arguments. It arises not so much, perhaps, from lack of discernment as from the difficulties of reconciling an inherited technique with the exigencies of business.

---

* First published in *The Australian Accountant*, Vol. 27, No. 11, November 1957, pp. 507-31. Text prepared for Australian Society of Accountants Annual Research Lecture in the University of Melbourne, October 1957. Reproduced in part in *The Journal of Accountancy*, August 1958, pp. 55-68.

[1] "The Relationship between Accounting and Financial Management", see p. 7, *ante*; "Accounting and Business Finance", see p. 39, *ante*; "The Formal Basis of Business Decisions", see p. 70, *ante*.

Truth and Approximation

First, consider an observation of a general character. "Truth in accounting is partly economic truth and partly statistical truth... [This] does not preclude the use of approximate price-aggregates when the circumstances make it impossible to know directly the actual money price of the consideration exchanged... a good approximation often is more truthful than the omission of a fact."[2] This is a fair statement of the character of accounting information. It contemplates an ideal representation of transactions and affairs, but recognizes the inevitability of using approximations short of the ideal. Yet, when discussing the possibility of making adjustments in accounts to represent changes in the values of assets, an example of the use of approximations short of the ideal, the author says, as if it were final and utter condemnation: "Accounting, having lost [as the result of adjustment] its most essential characteristic [presumably, the representation of *cost* price-aggregates], would become purely statistical and completely utilitarian. ... The force of accounting logic would be lost; it would then come close to possible for accounting to be all things to all men, available to support whatever views it seemed expedient for men to hold."[3] Possibly Professor Littleton does not regard approximations to the current values of assets, made in good faith and with the aid of independent experts, as "good approximations"; but there is no *a priori* ground for believing that they would be less "good" than the approximations which in the former quotation are approved. There can be no reason for supposing that accountants who enter approximations to values in accounts would be less impartial or independent than accountants who, when they can, adhere strictly to invested cost, but when they cannot, must compromise.

It seems that what one permits as an approximation depends, not so much on the materiality of the resulting information as on the view one takes of the purpose of accounting. But, if, though convinced of the appropriateness of initial invested cost, one concedes that approximations and estimates are unavoidable, he can scarcely object to a procedure, designed to enable reasonable judgements to be made about asset values and earning power in a dynamic economy, on the ground that it involves approximations and estimates.

There is a further point. Condemnation of accounts adjusted to reflect current values, on the ground that it would be "possible for accounting to be all things to all men", is quite misdirected. Those who support the initial cost basis of accounting commonly state or imply that the meanings of profit and value which they adopt are useful to all men[4]. But the assumptions and procedures of such an accounting yield profits and values which have esoteric meanings, understood perhaps by accountants but inconsistent with the usage of

---

[2] A. C. Littleton, *Structure of Accounting Theory,* American Accounting Association, 1953, p. 10.
[3] Idem, p. 228.
[4] See, for example, the opinion which is the subject of footnote 44.

the market place. In other words, conventional accounting contemplates a privilged class of people who know what the accounts mean, and an under-privileged class of people who, by virtue of common usage and understanding, believe them to be something else; yet it is the latter class—investors and other financial supporters—which the published accounts are intended to inform. Where, then, is the truth in accounting?

In a dynamic environment what is true one day is not necessarily true the next; the values of one day are not those of the next or those of the day before. This is the fact with which the adjustment of accounts to reflect current values attempts to cope, and only by moving in this direction will accounting statements move towards the truth.

Proprietors and Stewardship

Consider, next, an official statement of the purpose of accounting. "The primary purpose of the annual accounts of a business is to present information to the proprietors, showing how their funds have been utilized and the profits derived from such use. It has long been accepted in accounting practice that a balance sheet prepared for this purpose is an historical record and not a statement of current worth. Stated briefly, its function is to show in monetary terms the capital, reserves and liabilities of a business at the date as at which it is prepared and the manner in which the total moneys representing them have been distributed over the several types of assets. . . . Historical cost should continue to be the basis on which annual accounts should be prepared and, in consequence, the basis on which profits shown by such accounts are computed."[5] But the architects of this recommendation had to provide for the fact that historical cost is not invariably used. Hence: "The writing up of fixed assets has the effect of treating the business as ceasing and starting afresh on a new basis as from the date of the writing up; and this is why it is in practice considered to be appropriate and desirable in certain special circumstances, such as where a subsidiary is acquired and the assets are written up to reflect the cost to the acquiring company, or where subscriptions for new capital are invited on the basis of the current valuation of assets."[6]

There are several difficulties here. It is granted that the primary purpose of annual accounts is to present information to proprietors; but it is denied that proprietors regard the balance sheet as merely showing how their funds have been utilized. This narrow stewardship notion, appropriate enough in the case of a trust, is inappropriate in respect of business investments. Most proprietors will have bought their securities not from companies directly but from prior holders, and at prices which bear no relationship to the contributions made to

---

[5] The Institute of Chartered Accountants in England and Wales, Recommendation XV, "Accounting in Relation to Changes in the Purchasing Power of Money", *The Accountant,* 31 May 1952.

[6] Idem.

those companies by original subscribers. The balance sheet will give them no clue as to what has happened to their personal outlays. The transferability of securities and the independent market in them breaks down the relevance of the stewardship concept in its original and simple form, and renders the relationship between proprietors' outlays and corporate assets of no use as a measure of real stewardship. That the simple stewardship concept has little relevance in practice is apparent also from observation of the reactions of shareholders to capital reductions. Failure to preserve the money capital of a company is not of itself culpable. Losses may, but do not necessarily, lead to changes in directorates, they do not give rise to legal action on the part of equity holders, for it is understood that capital contributions have been made at risk.

The second noteworthy feature of the views quoted is the description of what are very frequent occurrences as "certain special circumstances". The acquisition of subsidiaries and the flotation of new share issues are everyday occurrences, and for some companies they are relatively frequent events. If it is "appropriate and desirable" to write up assets in these circumstances, it is surely continuously appropriate and desirable.

Thirdly, there seems to be quite a shift from the purpose first stated to the circumstances referred to in the second quotation. Is the information provided by the accounts to be considered as serving the needs of future proprietors only, or those of current proprietors also? What happens to the proprietors of a company which is taken over, as a subsidiary, by another? The cost to the acquiring company may be much less than the assets are worth, and the vendors will have been in no position fairly to bargain. As for writing up assets as a prelude to inviting new capital subscriptions, this savours of making easy the task of inducing the support of new investors, rather than of enabling current shareholders to look after their interests.

Fourthly, the going concern or continuity concept seems to be invoked to support objections to the writing up of asset values. But it is not reasonable to assert that "the writing-up of fixed assets has the effect of treating the business as ceasing and starting afresh". The writing-down of fixed assets and shareholders' equity when earning power has fallen materially is a measure taken to preserve a business unit in the face of changed circumstances; the unit is not considered to cease business and start afresh. The writing-up of fixed assets and shareholders' equity when earning power has risen materially has exactly the same effect and purpose in opposite circumstances.

Two Kinds of Accounting

The Committee on Accounting Procedure of the American Institute of Accountants, in 1940, put forward the view that the needs of proprietors and management were distinctively different. In respect of published reports and statements "accounting for fixed assets should normally be based on cost, and any attempt to make property accounts in general reflect current values is both impracticable and inexpedient. Appreciation normally should not be reflected on the books of account of corporations". So much for the shareholder. But "there is no objection to showing estimated present values, nor to the computation of depreciation on that basis for internal administrative purposes. A distinction can be drawn between the internal accounting for an enterprise and the accounting for the corporation which carries on the enterprise. From the standpoint of the enterprise, cost to the corporation is not of controlling significance, but to the corporation itself, cost is the proper foundation of its accounting".[7]

One would like to know the grounds on which it is impracticable and inexpedient to do for shareholders what it is apparently practicable and expedient to do for management. One would also like to know the explicit reasons for the assertion that cost is the proper foundation for accounting to proprietors. It seems rather that cost can only be a proper foundation for accounting to those having financial interests where management is obliged, under penalty, to maintain a given fund. There is no such stricture in the case of business enterprises; the only restraint applies to the payment of dividends, not to the regular operations of business.

The same view and the same inconsistency occur in Paton and Littleton's *An Introduction to Corporate Accounting Standards*.[8] At p. 3 the writers observe: "Capital should flow into those industries which serve the public interest, and within an industry into those enterprises in which the management is capable of using capital effectively". This means that investors must choose between the enterprises which seek their support. But, if the choice is to be well-informed, it is necessary that the profits and affairs of companies formed at different times should be reduced to a common basis. It is not sufficient to know that the managements of different companies were, at different earlier dates, judged by investors to be capable of using capital effectively; it is necessary at the time of an investor's decision to know how effectively capital is then being used, so that the common basis to which their several results and affairs should be reduced is a contemporary basis. What is the answer of Paton and Littleton to this? "To the extent that these [current or replacement costs] are the costs which influence decisions it may be argued that neglect of management to observe the effect of rising or falling prices of plant components is likely to lead to unwise utilization of available resources and questionable policies of pricing product. But it does not follow that management can become aware of the significance of current prices only through changing the accounts" (p. 132). There is not a word here about the choice exercised by investors, by which management obtains command of the means of utilizing available resources. Management may become aware of the significance of current prices by means other than the accounts; but investors have no other source of information relating directly to

[7] *Accounting Research Bulletin No.* 5, *Depreciation on Appreciation*, American Institute of Accountants, paras. 2 and 8.

[8] American Accounting Association, 1940.

particular enterprises which is as useful as the accounts; the particular knowledge available to management they are therefore denied.

The view that owners are entitled to information less complete and less relevant than that available to management implies that management will and does always act in the best interests of company members, and that management is the best judge of what is in the best interest of members. The same implications lie beneath the view that as long as the accounts show a position no worse than the real current position they perform the function required of them and may be reported to give "a true and correct view" or to "fairly represent" the state of affairs and the results of a company.[9] But these implications are inconsistent (a) with the experience of the members of companies the management of which have been unskilled or inefficient, (b) with the statutory provisions giving company members the power of review, and (c) with the notion of reasonable choice by investors between the companies seeking their financial support. Review and judgement can only be effective if information of the same general quality, even if not in the same detail, is available to shareholders and investors as is available to management. A man's achievement cannot reasonably be appraised by another if he has acted on information inaccessible to the other.

Value and Valuation

One of the most vexed questions in accounting is whether or not balance sheet figures and operations on them represent values and evaluations. The reluctance to accept "value" as what accounting purports to show is widespread; but it is sufficient, to illustrate the point, to take again an example from Paton and Littleton. Granting that at the date of a transaction cost represents value, they add: "With the passing of time . . . it becomes clear that the actual cost of the unit still in service or still attaching to operating activity is not fully acceptable as a measure of immediate economic significance." But, "would accounting meet more adequately the needs of the various parties concerned if, in the process of separating the charges to revenue from the unexpired balances, the estimated replacement costs or other evidences of current values were regularly substituted for recorded costs incurred? There seem to be no convincing reasons for an affirmative answer"[10]. Now, current value is "a measure of immediate economic significance". It is hard to agree that this is not a convincing reason for an affirmative answer.

The impediment to accepting it as a reason is the emphasis on income measurement, by the systematic matching of costs and revenues, as the primary purpose of accounting, a point which is taken up presently. But this, it seems, suggests either that income measurement is unaffected by the values of assets carried forward in balance sheets, or that cost has a unique meaning, i.e., money outlay; and neither is true.

---

[9] This view was probably first formulated in the judgement in an English case, Newton v. Birmingham Small Arms Co. Ltd., [1906] 2 Ch. 378.

[10] Op. cit., pp. 122-123.

There is, in contemporary explanations and descriptions of accounting, a valuation concept, notwithstanding the desire to avoid referring to "values". "Non-homogeneous assets and claims to assets are translated into financial equivalents or money values . . . [Such a process is] a convenient method of symbolizing. . . . Essentially all that the convention of valuation really accomplishes is substitution . . . [A valuation is] a substitution symbol for record purposes."[11] ". . . events [strictly, evaluations of events] are recorded as they occur, and are retained in the records as facts; for example, machinery [strictly, an evaluation of machinery] is recorded and the record maintained at the actual original cost."[12]

But what is the justification of such a valuation concept as this? Gilman avers: "The concept that valuation is no more than a convenient method of symbolizing is helpful in simplifying accounting problems."[13] True enough; but is the simplification of accounting problems the justification of a basic proposition? Gilman continues: "Only when this question of valuation is approached from the ownership, credit or legal viewpoints does a non-cost basis become of serious import. It is only when the task of interpreting accounting figures is faced that the convention of dollar valuation causes trouble."[13] Only when? These viewpoints are pertinent all the time; interpretations and judgements are being made all the time. If the entity concept is called into play and it is asserted that in accounting for an entity the interpretations and judgements of its supporters may be disregarded, the very nature of the entity is therefore disregarded; for any entity exists by virtue of the co-operation of its supporters; it exists in a specific ownership, credit and legal environment, in which, as Gilman admits, conventional valuations based on cost are inadequate.

It is often said that a balance sheet is not a valuation statement and that balance sheet figures do not purport to be valuations. The Cohen Committee on Company Law Amendment stated the conventional view as follows: "A balance sheet is thus an historical document and does not as a general rule purport to show the net worth of an undertaking at any particular date or the present realizable value of such items as goodwill, land, buildings, plant and machinery, nor, except in cases where the realizable value is less than cost, does it normally show the realizable value of stock in trade. Moreover, if a balance sheet were to attempt to show the net worth of the undertaking, the fixed assets would require to be revalued at frequent intervals and the information thus given would be deceptive since the value of such assets while the company is a going concern will in most cases have no relation to their value if the undertaking fails."[14] It is

---

[11] S. Gilman, *Accounting Concepts of Profit,* New York, Ronald, 1939, pp. 26, 56, 247.
[12] *Carter's Advanced Accounts,* ed. C. A. Reid, Melbourne, Pitman, 1956, p. 4.
[13] Op. cit., p. 56.
[14] Report of the Committee, Cmd. 6659, H.M.S.O., 1945, para. 98. The first sentence is quoted directly from evidence given by the Institute of Chartered Accountants in England and Wales.

questionable whether the Cohen Committee considered its function to include an appraisal of the basic premises of accounting; it is more likely that this statement was based on expert testimony. But it will be shown presently that some published balance sheets at least do purport to show net worth at a particular date. Further, if the restatement of asset values is deceptive, then large numbers of company officers have, according to the evidence to be presented in Part 3, been guilty of deception, and the auditors who have reported without qualification subsequent to revaluations are implicated in the deception. Further still, it is unrealistic to make such a direct contrast between going concern values and liquidation values. There is an intermediate possibility, the sale of the whole interest (on a take-over), or part of the interest (e.g., on the formation of a holding company to acquire the interests of shareholders in an operating subsidiary) in a going concern. This is far more common than liquidation, and for this purpose current valuations are essential.

Despite assertions to the contrary, the balance sheet is a valuation statement. Each asset is stated at some value, even when the basis of valuation is not given, and for many items it is given. These values may not be current values, they may be values long irrelevant, but they are values. Whatever attempts are made to belittle the utility of estimates of value and to avoid speaking of valuation, valuation and revaluation are everyday phenomena which may not be dismissed without destroying the significance of accounting.

The Profit and Loss Viewpoint

The difficulty of coping with dynamic events by means of concepts which are appropriate in a static situation seems to have led to an oversimplification of the main purpose of accounting. This takes the form of assertions that the most important product of the accounting process is the income account.

In 1932, the Special Committee on Cooperation with the Stock Exchanges of the American Institute of Accountants opined: "earning capacity is the fact of crucial importance in the valuation of an industrial enterprise . . . therefore the income account is usually far more important than the balance sheet"[15]. The Committee on Accounting Procedure of the same Institute in 1939 noted the tendency "to regard the balance sheet as the connecting link between successive income statements"[16]. Gilman, at numerous points, refers to the shift from the "balance sheet viewpoint" to the "profit and loss viewpoint", alleging that much of the dispute regarding the adoption of specific rules is due to the differences in viewpoint of their supporters[17]. Paton and Littleton contend: "Earning power—not cost price, not replacement price, not sale or liquidation price—is the

---

[15] *Audits of Corporate Accounts,* New York, American Institute of Accountants, 1934, p. 10.

[16] *Accounting Research Bulletin No.* 1, American Institute of Accountants, 1939, p. 2.

[17] Op. cit., p. 430.

significant basis of enterprise value. The income statement therefore is the most significant accounting report. . . . Accounting exists primarily as a means of computing a residuum, a balance, the difference between costs and revenues for individual enterprises."[18] The same view is carried into the present and the words and phrases of these writers are repeated in more recent texts.

It is not intended to deny that the income statement is significant. It is contended, however, that the swing from the balance sheet viewpoint to the profit and loss viewpoint has gone too far. It has gone so far, it is believed, because of the desire to bolster conventional accounting methods. In changing conditions the conventional profit and loss account gives a closer approximation to current net profit than the conventional balance sheet gives to current financial position. If one claims that the profit and loss account is the more important statement, one can make light of the defects of the conventional balance sheet.

The balance sheet, however, has always been of considerable importance. Professor Littleton gives seventeenth century examples which show that the balance sheet, representing the "estate" of a merchant, was significant of itself, and that the income statement served the purpose of "proving the estate". He alludes to a fifteenth century Italian tax on property; and to a seventeenth century French ordinance requiring merchants to make a biennial statement of all assets and liabilities, presumably as a guide in bankruptcy proceedings[19]. Both imply that the balance sheet was then of superior significance to that of the income statement. Throughout the nineteenth century too the giving of credit was based on statements or estimates of a debtor's worth; balance sheets were desired as a source of this information.

There is evidence, of course, of the preparation of income statements (as distinct from venture accounts) as early as the sixteenth century. But in an era when owner and manager were identical, and when profits arose from separate successful ventures or from monopolies, it is unlikely that annual income statements were of use for the purpose of testing the profitability of operations as a whole as a guide to future action. It was probably not until the late eighteenth century at the earliest that income accounts would be used for this purpose; for factory units, with limited, specialized processes, it would be feasible to compare the income accounts of successive years; and, in attempting to cover the fixed charges consequent upon the use of durable equipment, through changes in tastes, technology and competition, to make such comparisons would be the part of wisdom.

But, it was probably not until the late nineteenth century and the early twentieth that the income account became as significant to external supporters of business firms as the balance sheet had long been. By then corporate business and private investment in corporate

---

[18] Op. cit., pp. 10, 16.

[19] *Accounting Evolution to* 1900, New York, American Institute Publishing Co., 1933, pp. 133-36.

business had become widespread. Transferability of interests in business corporations and the divorce of management from ownership are the real factors which have tended to make the income account more significant.

But, these factors do not make the balance sheet any less significant. The Committee on Accounting Procedure of the American Institute observed that the tendency to regard the balance sheet as the connecting link between successive income statements "should not obscure the fact that the balance sheet has significant uses of its own"[20]. One of these uses, and the most important for the purpose of this lecture, is the provision of the amount invested to earn the income shown in the profit and loss account.

And, here, it may be observed that some of the above quotations contain non-sequiturs. It does not follow from the statement "earning power is the significant basis of enterprise value" that "the income statement is the most significant accounting report". The income statement does not show earning power; it shows earnings. Earning power is only ascertainable from a comparison of earnings with the sum employed; net profit of itself is not significant. It follows that the income account and the balance sheet are of equal importance for this purpose, and that the further asset values move from invested cost without restatement of those values and of the shareholders' equity, the greater is the distortion of the current relationship between net profit and the sum employed.

* * * *

The terms and views which have been considered are indicative of a struggle to reconcile observed business practices with what accountants have long found it expedient to do. The supporters of conventional procedures in some cases have treated the practices which deviate from them as exceptions; in other cases, specific terms which have a widely understood general connotation are given esoteric meanings to avoid the obvious conflict between the avowed purposes and the accepted procedures of accounting. The facts now to be presented will enable some idea to be obtained of the seriousness of this conflict.

3.—An Analysis of Australian Bonus Issues

The Facts

The financial practices of Australian public companies over the last 10 years seem to provide some evidence of the inadequacy of conventional accounting. Every revaluation of assets expresses disagreement with the concept that initial invested cost is appropriate and relevant. It was not possible to examine the published accounts of all companies to ascertain the frequency with which revaluations occur. Instead,

---

[20] *Accounting Research Bulletin, No.* 1, p. 2.

[21] Bonus issues are stock dividends arising mainly from share premium reserves and asset revaluation reserves. Under Australian and English law companies may revalue assets upwards and downwards.

it was decided to discover as much as possible about the companies listed on the Australian stock exchanges which have made bonus issues since the beginning of 1948, as a first approximation to the number and extent of asset revaluations, and because bonus issues themselves have certain implications.

The information presented in this section has been accumulated from press announcements, stock exchange publications, financial journals, published annual reports and new issue announcements, and from direct inquiries of companies. The population examined consisted of all Australian companies listed on the Australian stock exchanges except metalliferous mining companies. It is certain that some companies which should have been included in the bonus issue figures have been missed, but the cross-checking of a variety of sources of information has given the impression that these are few.

The number of issues and their aggregate amounts for each of 10 years are given in Table 1. A rough check of the coverage may be obtained by reference to the new issue series currently published in the Quarterly Survey of the Australia and New Zealand Bank Ltd. the figures in the column "A.N.Z.Q.S." of Table 1 are described as stock exchange new listings of bonus shares issued by non-mining companies. A footnote to the A.N.Z. list indicates that prior to 1953 the figures refer to the Melbourne Stock Exchange, but thereafter to all stock exchanges. The discrepancies between the two sets of figures may be due in part to differences in what is regarded as a bonus issue, but they are probably due, to a greater extent, to omissions in the information supplied to the A.N.Z. Bank.

The figures of the present study do not include ordinary dividends or small bonus dividends satisfied by share issues and appropriated from operating profits; nor do they include shares issued in consideration of a re-arrangement of the rights, *inter se*, of two or more classes of shareholders. They do include the bonus element in issues of shares, on the formation of holding companies, to shareholders of operating companies which were at the time already listed.

TABLE 1

Bonus Share Issues by Australian Listed Public Companies

Year	Present Study: No. of issues	Present Study: £000's	A.N.Z.Q.S.* £000's
1948	7	308	—
1949	5	340	6
1950	84	10,500	3,269
1951	79	12,450	10,066
1952	9	1,019	1,671
1953	20	2,088	1,245
1954	44	13,157	2,424
1955	71	16,943	8,043
1956	56	15,852	7,828
1957	29	31,686†	6,528
	404	104,343	41,080

*A.N.Z. Quarterly Survey, July, 1957. 1957 figures to May.
†Announcements made prior to 1 September, 1957.

These bonus issues were spread over the whole of corporate business. Table 2 has been compiled to show their incidence in particular classes of business.

Table 2 is to be taken as a general indication only. Comparisons of the number of companies issuing bonus shares with the total listed in each class will be in error, as some companies included in the bonus issue list were no longer listed on the stock exchanges in 1956. Comparisons of the amounts of bonus issues and paid-up share capitals are subject to greater error because of the inclusion of 1957 bonus issues in the bonus issue column. However, the general impression that one-quarter of all companies listed in 1956 had made bonus issues over the 10-year period in an amount equal to about one-eighth of the 1956 paid-up ordinary share capital is not likely to be greatly in error. It is worth nothing again that these figures do not give a complete tally of all bonus issues which have augmented the share capital aggregate in the period. Bonus issues made prior to conversion to, or on conversion to, public company status, or prior to listing on the stock exchanges, are excluded.

TABLE 2

Industrial Analysis of Bonus Issues, 1948-1957

	Listed Companies		Bonus Issues		
Class	No. of Cos.	Paid up Ordinary Share Capital—1956 Accounts* £000's	No. of Cos.	Total Bonus Issues £000's	% of Cos. making Bonus Issues
Retail distribution	94	66,932	35	10,160	37
Distribution, n.e.i.	104	56,945	23	4,622	22
Food, drink, etc., mfg.	125	110,748	38	21,271	30
Textiles, clothing, mfg.	93	50,649	25	3,305	27
Paper, publishing, etc.	59	51,637	19	4,074	32
Timber millers, furniture, etc	47	17,718	12	1,694	26
Hardware merchants	36	8,643	5	459	14
Paints, chemicals, oils	30	45,013	10	4,184	33
Leather, rubber, plastics, glass	19	33,672	8	4,745	42
Cement, bricks, etc.	50	22,408	19	4,469	38
Engineering	222	161,231	58	30,186	26
Machinery and elec. distribution	32	13,144	9	1,258	28
Automotive distribution	57	20,002	18	3,629	32
Coal, gas, etc.	38	21,033	6	936	16
Tansport, hotels, theatres	75	23,462	18	2,796	24
Finance, insurance, etc.	140	88,391	12	4,916	9
Miscellaneous	83	22,166	7	1,639	8
	1,304	813,794	322	104,343	25

*From information contained in Jobson's Digest Year Book, 1957. The aggregate amount of paid up preference share capital was £94,074,000, and of other share capital £923,000.

The 404 issues of Table 1 were made by 322 companies; 256 companies made one issue in the period, 54 made two issues, 8 made three issues and 4 made four issues.

These bonus issues were made from a variety of sources; as the underlying reasons may be different according to the source of the sums appropriated, those sources, as far as they have been ascertainable, are given in Table 3.

Table 3 does not give an exact analysis of all cases due to inadequacies in the information given in published statements, annual reports and other communications examined. The descriptions follow closely those given by the companies themselves. It is reasonable to assume that some part of amounts described as tax free reserves or profits arose from asset revaluations, and that a considerable part of the amount drawn from "unknown" sources also arose from revaluations. The bonus element in issues by newly formed holding companies may also be taken to represent an increase in the valuation of some assets. The general sense of the Table, therefore, is that

TABLE 3

Source of Bonus Issues, 1948-1957

	No. of Issues	Sum Appropriated £000's
Revaluations of—		
Land, buildings, property	143	29,275
Land, buildings, plant and/or machinery	27	2,384
Plant	5	365
Plant and goodwill	1	127
Goodwill	3	135
Shares in subsidiary or associated companies	51	12,183
Shares and freehold	3	325
Assets	50	10,008
Assets and share premiums	5	418
Total	288	55,220
Formation of holding company	27	31,364
Other sources—		
Tax paid reserves, tax free profits	15	682
Capital profits	4	502
Trading profits	7	199
Share premiums	75	14,348
Unknown	24	2,028
Total	125	17,759
Grand Total	*	104,343

*The grand total number of issues exceeds the number of issues shown in Table 1 because some of the latter were made from two sources.

something of the order of 75 per cent of the issues were made from asset revaluations, in an amount approximating 82 per cent of the total sum appropriated.

The Explanations

It is possible to develop one's own reasons for asset revaluations and bonus issues; but it is useful to consider the avowed reasons of those who were responsible. These reasons are not always given in communications from companies to their shareholders; generally, circulars to shareholders and notices of meetings called to approve recommendations of the directors simply state the intention without argument. But there are sufficient cases in which some explanation is given to permit reasonable inferences to be drawn. These cases are augmented by others which, in response to inquiries regarding the reasons, have given, often in great detail, statements relating to their issues; for the information supplied the writer is grateful to the directors and secretaries who have responded.

The reasons which are examined below, though separately stated and separately considered, have overlapping elements; the general features of all cases will be taken up at a later point.

(a) Restoration of acknowledged rights. In a number of cases, bonus issues were made to restore the nominal value of securities to amounts at which they stood before an earlier capital reduction. The writing-down generally occurred during the 'thirties, when loss of earning power and consequent over-capitalization made capital reduction and corresponding reductions in the values of assets a condition of survival.

Bonus issues out of share premium reserves may also be regarded as a form of acknowledgment of equity holders' rights. It is true that a premium issue, at the time it is made, tends to maintain the respective rights of existing and new shareholders, and to keep up the capital value of earlier issues of the same class. The premium also provides the company with capital, free, to some extent, of dividend obligations. The capitalization of share premiums when the funds they represent have been put to profitable use does not give equity holders any greater rights than they had before; but from the point of view of the shareholder the premium is a capital outlay, as it is, in a sense, a capital receipt of the company, and the issue of new scrip acknowledges this.

(b) Preliminary to new issues of securities. In many cases, bonus issues have been followed, by, or have been contemporaneous with new ordinary share issues for cash. Whatever the source of the sum appropriated for the bonus issue, the intention seems to have been to avoid attaching too high a premium to the new cash issue (in view of the high ruling market price of pre-bonus shares) in order to ensure that the cash issue is readily placed. The larger base for the new cash issue would make the market value of each new share smaller, and would make it easier for small investors to acquire a marketable parcel.

The preservation of the equity of existing shareholders is also borne in mind. Said one company: "The Company contemplated the acquisition of further subsidiary Companies, the consideration being on an exchange of share basis, and it was felt that existing shareholders were entitled to the benefits of the Company's improved financial position before the new shareholders were admitted."[22] The same reasoning applies to the cash issues mentioned in the previous paragraph.

Issues of loan securities may also make capital adjustments and asset revaluations desirable. Although loan creditors may be interested in net profit rates as indicating capital security, their direct measure of capital security is the tangible asset backing of their loans. As a safeguard against the debasement of their security, trust deeds commonly include provisions, based on asset and capital values, restraining further borrowing. The following provisions relating to an unsecured note issue are illustrative:—

"(i) The company shall not at any time charge any of its tangible assets if the aggregate amount of the contemplated charge or charges together with every existing charge by the company exceeds or would exceed two-fifths of the amount of the tangible assets of the company as disclosed in the last published balance sheet of the company and adjusted to include the introduction of further paid-up capital (if any) since the date of such balance sheet in so far as such further capital is represented by further tangible assets . . .

"(ii) The company will not borrow any sum or sums if the borrowing thereof would have the effect that the aggregate amount owing by the company exceeds or would exceed the amount of shareholders' funds plus one-quarter thereof . . .

"(iii) The company will not borrow by means of other notes any sum or sums if the borrowing thereof would have the effect that the aggregate amount owing on notes of the present issue and other notes would exceed one-half of the paid-up capital for the time being of the company."

Restraints of this kind make occasional adjustments imperative if a company is to squeeze all the flexibility it can from the capital and asset structure under its control. It would be foolishness to suffer the further restraint which out-of-date statements of value would impose.

(c) The most common reason given where revaluations have been made is the desire to portray the company's affairs more realistically.

"The Board feels it is desirable that the Company's Balance Sheet should reflect the value of the Company's fixed assets more in relation to present day values than the values at which they were purchased many years ago."[23] "[Following revaluation of freehold property] the Balance Sheet should present a truer and fairer picture of our net

[22] Letter dated 22 November 1955. In this and subsequent quotations, "Letter dated . . ." refers to a letter in reply to an inquiry by the writer; the originating company's name is given only when extracts are taken from published circulars and reports.

[23] East African Coffee Plantations Ltd., circular, 17 November 1954.

worth, even though such assets as Plant and Machinery will remain unaltered in the books at a figure substantially below replacement cost."[24] "For some time your Directors have been of opinion that the value of the Company's assets is greatly in excess of the figures shown in the books of the Company. The effect of this is that the equity of the shareholders has been understated and a more correct value of the shares has not been disclosed."[25] "Your Directors considered it desirable to increase the valuation of such shares in the Company's books to an amount representing a closer approximation to their true value."[26] "Your Directors gave careful consideration to the value of the shares in the two marketing Companies, and, having regard to the actual assets of those Companies and their earning capacity, your Directors consider that the real value of those Companies is at least 27s. per share and consequently the writing up of the value of such shares was fully justified."[27] "... it was considered advisable to bring the Balance Sheet values into line with present day realities."[28]

The sources of the new valuations are varied. Some real estate revaluations were based on recent valuations by Valuers-General; some on the valuations of expert private valuers; plant and machinery were revalued on the basis of expert opinion; shares were revalued on the basis of ruling market values, where applicable, or on the basis of the net tangible assets of subsidiaries (which may have involved anterior revaluation of those assets). In many cases the amount of the new valuation is given, but often it is not. In many cases only part of the increment in value is brought into the accounts, and there is evidence that some businessmen still are proud of the non-disclosure which is euphemistically called conservatism. Nevertheless, the bases of revaluation are obviously independent of managerial estimates.

(d) In a number of cases the nature of the relationship between profits or dividends and stated capital is suggested as a ground for revaluation and/or bonus issues.

"The principal reasons for the revaluation and bonus issue were (a) to show assets and shareholders' funds at a figure related to reality and (b) to overcome the ludicrous position of declaring a 12½ per cent dividend [upon a capital which was only one-sixth of the shareholders funds' employed]."[29] "In view of the Company's increased level of income... and the high premium at which the Company's shares are quoted... ."[30] "The greater earning capacity of the company warranted the issue of bonus shares."[31]

A number of companies have struck directly at the inflationary conditions which tend to make nonsense of static accounting. "The

[24] Henry B. Smith Ltd., Chairman's Address, Annual General Meeting, 1951.
[25] Hotel Metropole Ltd., circular, 11 June 1954.
[26] Humes Ltd., circular, 25 October 1954.
[27] Smith Wylie (Australia) Ltd. (later Purr Pull Oil Industries Ltd.), circular, 8 October 1951.
[28] The Victoria Ltd., circular, 25 March 1954.
[29] Letter dated 6 March 1956.
[30] Garratts Ltd., circular, 6 March 1951.
[31] West Australian Newspapers Ltd., quoted in *The West Australian*, 11 December 1954.

reasons underlying the issues were to allow the shareholders to participate to a greater extent in the prosperity of the company and to give them some further return on their investment to offset the decreasing value of the £1 without increasing dividend rates."[32] "The dividend rate was commencing to appear high in relation to the funds employed. The bonus issue allowed a lift in the amount of dividend without magnifying the published rate."[33] Among the factors in favour of revaluation and bonus issue one company noted that "the rate of dividend declared can be smaller, while still resulting in the same distribution to shareholders. Your Directors think it important in these days that dividends should be expressed as a percentage of real capital employed when there is much uninformed talk about excess profits being made by companies."[34] "The progress of the Company justified an increase in the dividend rate and it was socially desirable that this be given by way of a bonus issue, and from the shareholders' point of view, a better proposition than a straight out increase in the dividend rate."[35] The phrase "socially desirable" is probably intended to indicate aversion to the "uninformed talk" alluded to in the previously quoted circular. Another company seems to have had a similar purpose in mind when in addition to stating its shareholders' funds in the customary manner (i.e., paid-up capital, reserves, unappropriated profits) it also stated the same funds "as if" its ordinary shares were of no par value.[36]

(e) Revaluations and/or bonus issues are made by some companies as counters to actual or possible take-over bids.

"It is dangerous to underestimate the value of fixed assets when take-overs are so prevalent. It is to shareholders' advantage to have assets shown at their correct value. I do not think for a moment that the company is likely to be taken over, but, should anyone try, shareholders would know what their assets were worth."[37] The company referred to in footnote 35 gave, as an additional object of a bonus issue made partly out of share premiums and partly out of asset revaluation, "reducing the risk of a take-over bid". In 1955, as a counter to an offer by Myer Emporium Ltd., the directors of Finney Isles and Co. Ltd. announced their intention to recommend to stockholders a one-for-one bonus issue out of revaluations of assets. A subsequent offer by David Jones Ltd. was successful, but by this time stockholders were in possession of the knowledge that the company's freehold properties were worth more than twice their latest balance sheet values. Prior to a one-for-one bonus issue out of asset revaluations, another company advised its shareholders: "Just recently

---

[32] Letter dated 9 December 1955.
[33] Letter dated 21 November 1955.
[34] Strachan & Co. Ltd., circular, 28 February 1951.
[35] Letter dated 23 December 1955.
[36] A. G. Webster & Sons Ltd., 1955 Annual Report.
[37] London Stores Ltd., Chairman's Address at 1956 Annual General Meeting, reported in *Sydney Morning Herald* 11 May 1956. The company had revalued its assets.

a verbal offer was received to purchase the whole of the issued shares of the Company at a figure considerably in excess of par value but well below the true value of the Company's assets and profit earning potential."[38]

Whether the directors' actions in such cases are spontaneous or arise from specific offers, the fact remains that contemporary circumstances have rendered necessary the recognition of contemporary values.

(f) All these explanations seem in themselves to be reasonable. But there is one factor without which no revaluation and no bonus issue can be justified. That factor is the adequacy of corporate net profits to serve the capitals stated to be employed in earning them. No company, for example, could make a bonus issue if the profits available for dividend represented six per cent or a smaller percentage of the paid-up capital. Without adequate actual or expected divisible profits (after making all necessary provisions and appropriations to reserves) no increase in paid-up capital, by way of bonus issues, can have meaning. It is most difficult to obtain any significant aggregation of ordinary share earnings to demonstrate that the rate of profit earned on pre-bonus capitals has been increasing. Not only are the figures complicated by cash issues and issues on the acquisition of other businesses or shares in them; the profit figures themselves seem, in many cases, to have peculiarities suggestive of inconsistent reporting (e.g., as when disclosed profits show little change year by year until the year of the bonus issue, when the disclosed profit rises sharply).[39] But an examination of individual cases shows exactly what was to be expected; disclosed profits have been sufficient to service the augmented capital (except in isolated cases); dividend rates may have fallen, but dividend amounts have commonly been maintained or increased.[39] Those 66 companies which made more than one bonus issue were evidently earning ample profits on the capital employed after the first issue.

---

[38] The Griffin Coal Mining Company Ltd., circular, 5 September 1955.

[39] The figures of one company which made no change in its share capital other than a bonus issue illustrate the point. The absolute amounts have been changed by a constant factor.

	Ordinary Share Capital £000's	Ordinary Share Earnings £000's	Dividend Rate Actual	Dividend Rate On pre-bonus Capital
1950	276	49	9%	9%
1951	276	56	11½	11½
1952	276	46	9	9
1953	276	49	9	9
One-for-one bonus issue				
1954	552	82	15	18
1955	552	106	12½	25
1956	552	109	15	30
1957	552	123	15	30

Rather than attempt to indicate the growth in earnings or earning power by reference to aggregates of disclosed net profits, this growth may be shown to have been quite substantial by reference to the bases on which bonus issues have been made. Table 4 gives the distribution of bonus issue ratios; ratios falling between those shown have been included in the nearer class.

Changes of such magnitude as the first four classes suggest that

TABLE 4

Bonus Issue Ratios, 1948-1957

Ratio	Frequency	Cumulative Percentage
Greater than 1 for 1	37	9
1 for 1	73	27
1 for 2	102	52
1 for 3	50	65
1 for 4	46	76
1 for 5	37	85
Less than 1 for 5	52	98
Unknown	7	100
Total separate issues	404	

current profits and sums available for distribution were well in excess of those needed to service pre-bonus capitals; in other words the adjustments were made to correct apparent under-capitalization, a condition in which the relationship between currently earned profits and currently reported capital gives a distorted impression of current earning power.

Some accountants may make light of the consequences of apparent under-capitalization. "Businessmen are oppressed by the fact that prices and profits look high in comparison with the capital investments made some years ago, when price levels were lower. They find themselves the targets of demand from workers for higher wages, demands from politicians for higher taxes, demands from consumers for lower prices, and demands from their organization for the renewal of depreciating plants and equipment.... Thereupon they find fault with accounting procedures which subject them to these pressures."[40] But these pressures are real, not imaginary. Businessmen may well be expected to find fault with a technique the results of which are not real, but imaginary (i.e., a technique which treats events and transactions "as if" time had no effect on values).

This then, is the evidence. To what conclusions does it point?

4.—Some Corollaries

The Propriety of Bonus Issues from Unrealized Profits

Doubts have long been expressed about the propriety and the desirability of allotting shares against appropriations of unrealized

[40] Howard C. Greer, "Depreciation and the Price Level", *The Accounting Review,* April 1948.

profits. These doubts still exist, as, occasionally, correspondence in professional journals shows.

They appear to stem from the cases in which the legality of different kinds of dividends has been considered. In most cases the profits in question were realized profits. In one case the profits were unrealized, but the dividend in question was a cash dividend. In no case has the legality of a share dividend made from appropriations of revaluation reserves been tried; but the restraint and care with which directors are obliged, in marginal cases, to consider the sources from which they propose to pay cash dividends seems to have induced a timidity among accountants who write on the matter which is not shared by large numbers of directors. There are two lines of reasoning which should abate this timidity.

Although bonus issues may be referred to as "share dividends" and unrealized accretions in asset values may be described as "profits", both are rather loose usages. A bonus issue as such does not give shareholders any greater rights in the assets or profits of the company than they had before. No question can therefore arise as to the legality of any dividend subsequently declared on the augmented capital; nor can there be any question as to the legality of the "share dividend" itself, for, strictly, nothing has been divided. Further, although the Income Tax Assessment Act refers to "profits arising from revaluation of assets not acquired for the purpose of resale"[41]—and the phrase may be much older—is it reasonable to call a restatement of value a profit-making operation? The real effect has been stated clearly in a recent bonus issue announcement: "It should be understood that a share issue of this kind is not something for nothing for shareholders. It results in part from a restatement, as share capital, of cash previously contributed by shareholders in the form of a premium on the last issue of shares, and in part from a restatement of the value of existing assets in up-to-date monetary terms following inflation. Already shareholders as a whole own the assets of the company and the revaluation and share issue will not affect the intrinsic value of those assets. Speaking generally, each shareholder will own the same proportion of the same company, the same assets and the same enterprise after the issue as before."[42]

It seems probable that objections to making share issues out of revaluations are sustained with greater vigour than objections to the revaluation of assets.[43] If this is so, one may ask whether, if shares of no par value were common, objections to share-splitting would be taken with the same force. As no noticeable objection has been taken to share-splitting, one may surmise that the objection to bonus issues out of asset revaluations is simply a consequence of a system which contemplates shares having a par value.

---

[41] Section 44 (2)(b)(iii).

[42] The Chairman, Colonial Sugar Refining Co. Ltd., in *Sydney Morning Herald*, 19 June 1957.

[43] Cf. A. E. Barton, "Can Divisible Profits be Created by Writing up Fixed Assets?", *Post War and Commercial Legislation*, Law Book Co., May 1947, pp. 260-62.

The second line of reasoning which may assure the irresolute is the well-known unwillingness of the courts to interfere in company affairs, and their practice of searching for precedents in the behaviour of other honestly and judiciously managed companies. As the companies in the present study range from some of the largest to some of the smallest, and occur in so many separate industrial and commercial categories, if an action could ever have been brought to challenge the legality of making share issues from revaluation reserves, it is unlikely now that the practice could be condemned. There may, of course, be unwise and frivolous examples; but these do not warrant rejection of what is, on so many other grounds, a reasonable and prudent course.

The Needs and Expectations of Investors

From the number and variety of companies which have redrawn their balance sheets, and from the explanations given, it appears that many directors believe, or have come to believe by force of circumstance, that investors need more information than accounting on an invested cost basis gives. The explanations are liberally spiced with "actual value", "present day value", "true value", "present day realities", "up-to-date valuation", "current valuation", "present day or market price". There is no double talk, no squeamishness about using the term "value", and an obvious rejection of the view that "cost is the proper foundation" of a company's published accounts. It is impossible to avoid the conclusion that those who evade reference to values and insist on the inherent correctness of conventional methods of accounting either have not troubled to look at the real facts of commerce and industry, or, having done so, have been forced to find rationalizations for ignoring what they see.

The mark of realism is stamped on the explanations from which examples have been drawn. The businessman is not concerned with arid argument about the relative merits of the two general accounting summaries. He knows that both are used, separately and together, in important transactions in which he engages; he speaks of the asset value of shares, and of the relationship between capital employed and net profit, as if they meant something quite significant.

Beside the evidence many of the assertions about the propriety of accounting on the basis of original money cost stand condemned. Accounts kept on this basis, it is said "tell the owner, the investor, the manager, and the public, something definite, tangible and significant"[44]. Why, then, have so many companies abandoned initial cost? "It is obvious from the size of many businesses that a revaluation of assets for inclusion in the annual financial statements is neither possible nor desirable."[45] How, then, have so many businesses, large and small, found it possible and desirable? "Any attempt to depart from [actual cost] and to reflect the changing general price levels

---

[44] Howard C. Greer, loc. cit.

[45] Yorston, Smyth and Brown, *Advanced Accounting*, Sydney, Law Book Co., 1953, Vol. 1, p. 7.

would be extremely dangerous and difficult."[46] If so dangerous and difficult, why and how have so many companies managed to do it?

It may well be argued that the directors of companies which have not made bonus issues during the period under consideration have been less responsive to the needs of investors, and less concerned with the efficient allocation of resources between firms, than the directors of those companies which have done so. Prudence and conservatism —worthy enough features of financial policy—may be reasons. But if current disclosed profits do not favourably compare with a current valuation of the assets employed and the equity they represent, either earning power has not kept up with the level of the past or secret reserves are being accumulated. Old valuations conceal the former, and deliberate action the latter; neither is in the interests of the contemporary investor.

Every person who buys a house or a car buys it in the first place to hold and use. He does not contemplate selling it at the time, but at any subsequent time, due to changes in his preferences, or in his fortune, or in the level of market prices, he may decide to sell even though he bought to hold. He does not know at what time he may be faced with such a decision, but consciously or unconsciously he keeps himself informed of current valuations of his property. The managers of a business are in the same position. Even though some assets may be bought "not for resale at a profit" but "to assist in earning income", market conditions may make resale more profitable than continued possession and use. And what applies to single assets applies also to going concerns and to share interests in them. When the choice exists of selling specific assets as such, or selling an undertaking as a going concern (or a share interest in it), it is a mere quibble to contend that current valuations of assets have no relationship to the value of the going concern. Now, how is an investor to judge, if confronted with an offer to take over his company, or even with the choice of switching his investment, when he has no personal knowledge of the contemporary values of the assets in which he holds interests? He depends on the objective representation of the current state of affairs; he takes the accounts supplied by the management to be objective and representative.

In another place[47] the objectivity of initial money cost has been criticized on the ground that representativeness and relevance are sacrificed. Attention is now directed to the effect on objectivity of the attitude on which support of conventional processes is based.

The array of opinions, arguments and doctrines examined in Part 2 are not only internally inconsistent; they are found to be inconsistent with the facts and explanations of Part 3. They rely on the sanctity of tradition, the fear of innovation or reverence for the figure once written. Every statement that an alternative method of accounting is impossible, impracticable, inexpedient, difficult, dangerous or deceptive is a protective measure, the product of a defence mechanism,

---

[46] *Carter's Advanced Accounts,* p. 4.
[47] "The Formal Basis of Business Decisions", see p. 70, *ante*, at p. 89, *ante*.

enabling one to turn one's back on relevance and the problems of devising an alternative accounting. The accounting viewpoint takes precedence over the viewpoint of the users of accounts. The results are coloured by the self-imposed limitations of those who practice the art, and for that reason, if for no other, they cannot be described as objective.

There is still another lapse in objectivity; it is common to many companies which have revalued some assets only and to those which have revalued none. It will have been noticed that the greater part of all revaluations, in number and amount, consisted of revaluations of assets charges in respect of which do not appear in income accounts—freehold land, buildings, shares, etc. Few companies have revalued plant and machinery, yet there must have been in the interval a substantial rise in the value of all plant in existence at the beginning of the period and since acquired. There may be various reasons for failing to restate plant values, financial prudence and the protection given by conservatism among them. But it is also probable that income taxation provisions have something to do with the reluctance to shift from the cost basis for such assets.

Now, income taxation provisions are designed for the purpose of computing taxable income, and for no other purpose. It is certainly easy to use the same figures—the same asset values and the same depreciation charges—for the purpose of reporting to shareholders; and because it is easy it is commonly done. But this is another practice which results in the withholding of information which is necessary for a reasoned and informed appraisal of corporate results and prospects. A true and fair view cannot be had when the statements are clouded by computations made for other purposes than efficient administration and investment.

Much of this section, so far, has dealt with the position of an investor *vis-à-vis* a single company; in such a case revaluation by the company adds to his knowledge. But the typical problem for large numbers of investors is choosing between alternative investments. Taking listed companies as representing the opportunities available to the investing public, what does the aggregate body of knowledge look like? Some companies show their fixed assets at cost; some at valuations established on the occasion of previous capital reductions; some companies show some assets at cost and other assets at or below recent upward revaluations; where revaluations have been made, some companies continue to give the date of revaluation, others do not; where assets have been acquired subsequently to a revaluation, commonly one figure is given for all assets in each class with the notation "at cost and valuation"; and, as revaluations will have been made at different dates under the conditions then prevailing, their significance as between firms will differ. Confronted with such a melange, investors cannot be expected to choose wisely in their own interest or in the interest of the efficient distribution of resources between enterprises and industries. In the *Press Caps Case*[48] one of

[48] *Re Press Caps Ltd.*, [1949] 1 All E.R. 1013.

the appeal judges suggested that "a perusal of back balance sheets would show when the property was bought and what it cost. The broad relation between that figure and its valuation today would have been readily apprehended". With respect, the experience of endeavouring to compile the figures of Part 2 is tendered. In some cases it was only with great difficulty possible, and in other cases it was quite impossible, to discover the specific changes which had taken place in company balance sheets over time. A re-appraisal of asset values when there are so many ways of representing asset values in balance sheets is beyond the competence of investors at large.

A widely applied procedure is necessary to reduce this chaos to order. Some have suggested revalorization as the answer. All companies would be required to restate the values of assets simultaneously; this step would be taken under direction of the legislature when, after a period of rising or falling prices, price levels have reached a new plateau. This has the merit of occasionally bringing all companies into line. But when can it be said that price levels have reached a new plateau? The difficulty is illustrated spectacularly by the history of the New York stock market in the late 'twenties. The *New York Times* industrial securities price index rose from 106 in May 1924, with some reversals, to 245 at the end of 1927. In March 1928, some felt that the bull market had been checked, but at the end of the year the index had risen to 332. Again in March 1929, a wave of selling suggested a settling down, but by the beginning of September the index had risen to 452. Just prior to this Professor Irving Fisher had given his opinion: "Stock prices have reached what looks like a permanently high plateau." Yet, by mid-November the index had fallen to 224, from which by July 1932, it had slumped to 58[49]! The new plateau is like the pot of gold at the end of the rainbow.

Even if there were such plateaus, in the interval between revalorizations the accounts would fall out of step with market realities and would be misleading. The only solution is the incorporation, in accounting, of a dynamic principle by which the current position and results would be fairly represented, not now and then, but continuously. The fact that some companies have made three and four adjustments in 10 years shows that such a principle would be more acceptable than the initial cost principle which so many simply ignore.

The Independent Auditor

While examining the role of financial statements as means of communication the independence of the auditor is worth considering. It will be of interest to note what was expected of auditors and what auditors were expected to say of accounts from the early years of corporate business in Australia. The changes in what was required

---

[49] Digested from J. K. Galbraith, *The Great Crash,* London, Hamish Hamilton, 1955.

may be assumed to parallel in principle the changes which were taking place concurrently in Britain.

The first half-yearly report of the Commercial Banking Company of Sydney Ltd.—the earliest company whose accounts have come under notice—was for the period ended 30 December 1848. It includes a profit and loss account and balance sheet; at the foot of the balance sheet is the simple notation "Examined and found correct", signed by two auditors who were shareholders of the company. The private Act by which the company was incorporated contained no audit clause, and auditors' reports had no consistent form for the first few years. The statement appended to the accounts in the fifth report reads "The Auditors have to report that the Coin, Securities and Balances are correct as expressed in the accompanying account of Liabilities and Assets for the [period], and that they consider that the affairs of the company are in a sound and prosperous state"; it is signed by two shareholder-auditors.

The first New South Wales Act containing specific auditing provisions is the Act incorporating the Bank of New South Wales[50]. It required that each year at one of the two half-yearly meetings two proprietors shall be elected to be auditors for the year next ensuing. "Within three weeks next before every such half-yearly meeting the auditors for the time being shall fully examine into the state of the accounts and affairs of the corporation and shall make a just true and faithful report thereon which shall be submitted by them to the directors of the corporation one week previously to such meeting and which shall be by such directors submitted to the proprietors at every such meeting and the said auditors shall and they are hereby required to make a declaration before a Justice of the Peace that such report is to the best of their several and respective knowledge a just true and faithful report and statement of the accounts and affairs of the company and that the same is made by them after diligent and careful examination into the state of such accounts and affairs . . . ." Notice that the auditor was required to be a shareholder.

The inclusion of audit provisions was not common in the early acts of incorporation. The next case in which they occur is the Sydney Exchange Company Act[51] which required three persons each possessed of five shares to be appointed; it was permissible for two of the three auditors "to examine and pass the accounts" of the company. The Australian Joint Stock Bank Act[52] contained a clause substantially the same as that in the Bank of New South Wales Act. New features were introduced in the Hunter River Railway Company Act[53]. Two auditors were to be appointed; each was to be a holder of at least 10 shares; auditors were not to hold "any other office in the company nor be in any other manner interested in its concerns except as a shareholder". After providing that the auditors shall examine "the

[50] Private Act, 14 Vic., assented to 23 September 1850. Section 18.
[51] Private Act, 15 Vic., assented to 19 December 1851.
[52] Private Act, 17 Vic., assented to 3 September 1853.
[53] Private Act, 17 Vic., assented to 10 October 1853.

accounts and affairs" of the company, the Act stipulated that the auditors "shall be at liberty to employ such accountants and other persons in such examination as they may think proper at the expense of the company. . . ."

Some features of these provisions are indicative of underlying ideas which have since been obscured. Auditors were required to be shareholders. This means that they did in fact have the same interest in the adequacy of the accounting statements as did the remaining shareholders. Those who did not have access to a company's books and records were assured, by having two or more persons in the same position as themselves report on the accounts and affairs, that those affairs were represented in a manner consistent with their needs. The auditors were independent of the management and were, as owners, in a strong position if the need arose to express that independence. They may not have been accountants, and to that extent their views were not conditioned by professional conventions; they had not to be consistent with any customary method of procedure; they were free to examine company affairs as real things, and the accounts of those affairs as representations of real things, not as conventional symbolization. To the extent that expert assistance was necessary, in some cases they were empowered to obtain it; but the report was their responsibility.

With the growth in the size and number of corporate businesses, the specialization of the auditing function was inevitable. The first general Companies Acts provided in Table A that auditors may be shareholders, but the link between audit and ownership must, by now, have been broken. This does not necessarily mean, however, that the basic idea of reviewing affairs as through the eyes of shareholders need have been abandoned. Yet, step by step it has been abandoned.

The greater the refinement made in the form of the auditor's report the greater is the difficulty of discovering what it means. The auditors of one New South Wales company for 50 years used the following form of report: "We have examined the books, accounts and vouchers of the company . . . and certify that the foregoing balance sheet and profit and loss account are correct statements of the company's affairs as shown by the books of the company." The company's affairs may not have been according to the books, and this perhaps is a departure from the view postulated above. But this report clearly goes no further than saying that the statements agree with the books.

Quite a different position is presented by the contemporary Australian audit report. The relevant portion reads: "In our opinion, the balance sheet is properly drawn up so as to exhibit a true and correct view of the state of the company's affairs and the profit and loss account is properly drawn up so as to exhibit a true and correct view of the results of the business of the company for the year, according to the best of our information and the explanations given us, and as shown by the books of the company." What is to be made of this kind of report, when, in one year the auditors can report that a true and correct view of the company's affairs is given by a balance sheet in which assets are shown at £x, and make the same assertion of the following year's balance sheet in which the same assets are shown at £2x? In the first year were they reporting that the balance sheet was according to the books of account, or that it gave a true and correct view of the company's affairs? It may have been the former, but it could not have been both simultaneously. How can "true and correct", in the context of the auditor's report have any meaning when, subsequently, chairmen of companies can state that, following revaluation, "the balance sheet should show a truer and fairer picture of our net worth", or that "assets are now shown at their correct value"? The situation is Gilbertian; indeed, it is Orwellian. One is reminded of the stage in the history of *Animal Farm* when, according to its chronicler, the elite adopted the principle, "All animals are equal, but some animals are more equal than others."

Some have endeavoured to justify the phrase "a true and correct view" by saying that the phrase is "*a* true and correct view", not "*the* true and correct view"; and that there may be many true and correct views of which the balance sheet they report on gives one. Truth may be many-sided; but no shareholder is to know what side he is seeing if this kind of justification is valid.

Further, whereas auditors were, in the century-old examples cited, required to examine and report on the accounts and affairs, the modern phrase "the state of affairs" is much more precise. But because of the conventions adopted and the widespread view that if the real state of affairs is at least no worse than that shown in the balance sheet it serves the interest of shareholders, the very precision of the phrase is misleading and dangerous. If, according to the apologists there are more than one true and correct view, presumably also there are more than one state of affairs at a given date. But this is difficult to concede. The phrase is "*the* state of affairs" not "*a* state of affairs", if one may turn the argument. That the balance sheet is intended to show the financial position or the state of affairs, and that some believe this to be its purpose is indicated by practices other than those discussed in Part 3 of this paper. A number of companies have described their published balance sheets as statements of "financial position"[54] and others have drawn their balance sheets to show assets as what "we own", liabilities as "what we owe" and shareholders' funds as what "we are worth".[55] "Financial position" and "we are worth" carry strong suggestions of value, present value, moreover.

5.—Conclusion

Summarily, contemporary accounting practice and thought have the following characteristics.

Instead of attempting to represent affairs dynamically in a dynamic environment, the processes generally accepted are static, giving static results.

---

[54] See, for example, Holeproof Ltd., Commonwealth Engineering Co. Ltd., Ballarat Brewing Co. Ltd., Tooheys Ltd., Rosella Preserving and Manufacturing Co. Ltd., Buckley and Nunn Ltd., Myer Emporium Ltd.

[55] See, for example, G. J. Coles & Co. Ltd., Ampol Petroleum Ltd.

Instead of correcting those processes, attention is diverted and directed towards the need for educating the public to understand the limitations which the processes impose.[56] But no auditor, in the interest of furthering public education and understanding, will depart from the stereotyped report which, except in stable conditions, asserts two incompatible things. If and when consideration is given to company law amendment, it seems highly desirable that this incompatibility between "a true and correct view of the state of affairs" and what is shown "by the books of the company" should be the subject of close examination. A report which unequivocally states one thing is to be preferred to the present doubly-qualified report.

Instead of pursuing discussion of the investor's interest to the point of precisely defining and examining the tests which he adopts, inquiry comes to a halt and argument centres about the relative merits of the balance sheet viewpoint and the profit and loss viewpoint.

Instead of grappling with the problem of representing current realities, shelter is taken behind convenient rationalizations and half-truths.

Excuses, apologetics and sophistry are of no use to investors, to creditors or to managers. They are no better than folk-lore; and if practice is to be governed by folk-lore instead of by observation and reason, accounting will not continue to enjoy the respect which it has so far been accorded.

* * * *

The impression one gains from the internal inconsistency of many of the arguments upon which the justification of conventional accounting is made to rest is strongly reminiscent of the underlying philosophy of the rulers of Oceania in George Orwell's *Nineteen Eighty-Four.* The distinctive feature of this philosophy is *doublethink.* "Doublethink means the power of holding two contradictory beliefs in one's mind simultaneously, and accepting both of them . . . . The process has to be conscious, or it would not be carried out with sufficient precision, but it also has to be unconscious, or it would bring with it a feeling of falsity and hence of guilt . . . . To forget any fact that has become inconvenient, and then, when it becomes necessary again, to draw it back from oblivion for just so long as it is needed, to deny the existence of objective reality and all the while to take account of the reality which one denies—all this is indispensably necessary." The vocabulary of *Newspeak,* the official language of Oceania, "was so constructed as to give exact and often very subtle expression to every meaning that a Party member could properly wish to express, while excluding all other meanings . . . . This was done partly by the invention of new words, but chiefly by eliminating undesirable words and by stripping such words as remained of unorthodox meanings . . . ."[57] These sentences describe succinctly and pungently many of the features of accounting apologetics. The interest of

---

[56] Cf., for example, Greer, loc. cit.
[57] Op. cit., Penguin, pp. 171, 241.

investors in accounting statements is recognized; but their interest is pushed aside when it appears to require unorthodox accounting. Valuations are incorporated in balance sheets—even in orthodox accounting—but the balance sheet is said not to be a valuation statement. "Value", "true and correct", "cost", "going concern", "consistency", are used to give exact and sometimes subtle expression to ideas which accountants wish to express, but they are used with very special connotations; they are stripped of their commonly accepted meanings while, at the same time, those commonly accepted meanings are depended on to lend an air of propriety to the established processes. New terms have even been invented to do away with the inconvenience of using words with commonly accepted meanings, e.g., "price-aggregate" for "cost".[58] The theory of the subject cannot be expected to progress in such an intellectual climate; expedience and custom must give way to knowledge of the determining conditions of financial actions and policies.

* * * *

It may be the consequence of the individual and isolated acts of boards of directors that the published accounts of companies are, in respect of statements of asset and equity values, out of step. But what the canons of conventional accounting will not sanction those boards have been obliged by circumstances to do. And, it should be remembered that many of the directors concerned are themselves professional accountants and auditors. Has the initiative in the disclosure of realities been taken, or is it to be taken, from accountants? An observation, again from Orwell, on the fate of oligarchies seems appropriate to the power and influence of accounting and accountants. "All past oligarchies have fallen from power, either because they ossified or because they grew soft. Either they . . . failed to adjust themselves to changing circumstances, and were overthrown; or they . . . made concessions when they should have used force, and once again were overthrown."[59]

Unless accounting is forever to be wedded to doublethink and doubletalk, its purpose and its principles must be continually re-examined and its place in the economic fabric of contemporary society must be frequently re-appraised. A dynamic accounting, in which consistency, relevance, objectivity and representativeness are dominant concepts, may be difficult to devise. But, if one holds that the service of providing relevant information to those interested in corporate business is a significant purpose of accounting, the difficulty must be faced. It should not be left to the piecemeal adjustment which this study has shown to be so common. Rather should the adjustment be regular, based on some official or generally adopted measure of the change in value of property and other assets through time.

---

[58] Paton and Littleton, op. cit., p. 11.
[59] Op. cit., p. 171.

Is this beyond the ingenuity of accountants? With George O. May, one would hope not: "Some objection [to accounting techniques incorporating current values or replacement costs] has been based on the supposed difficulty of applying them. I have seen too much of the ingenuity and resourcefulness of accountants in solving problems in administration or tax accounting to attach weight to this objection."[60]

[60] G. O. May, "Business Income", *The Accountant,* 30 September 1950.

6

MEASUREMENT AND MISREPRESENTATION*

The possibility of measuring does not necessarily lead to the presentation of relevant information for decision-making in business. This is demonstrated by reference to accounting methods and to profit computation in particular. Accounting processes have become formalized to the point where they misrepresent financial results and position; the probability that resources will be used efficiently and that equity between parties of interest will be served is materially reduced by lack of care in the definition of significant concepts and the concurrent acceptance of procedures which have directly opposite justifications and consequences. As the speed of information processing increases and computational refinements develop, a corresponding effort is necessary to redefine in operationally relevant terms, or to sharpen the definition of, such key concepts as profit, capital, cost. The history of the development of accounting and auxiliary calculations illustrates the consequences of permitting a measuring and communicating system to become institutionalized. Some suggestions for improving the relevance of accounting and similar information are made.

The conventional concept of economic man, of whom the businessman is the archetype, endows him with the capacity for and the habit of careful, informed and calculated action. It is a commonplace, on the other hand, that businessmen are informed within limits and calculate within limits. These limits may be data to the macro-economist, or they may impose restraints on the validity of his generalizations. The situation of the "business metrologist", concerned with the designs of systems for accumulating, processing and communicating information, is quite different. When he assumes the role of expert, he assumes the responsibility for ensuring that the information supplied is, within his field, complete, pertinent and, as far as possible, objective. That the information may be ignored or misused does not relieve him of this responsibility. Though it has been said that "without measurement there can be no science", it does not follow that the possibility of measuring creates a basis for optimal action. Many widely used business measurements and calculations are inadequate or invalid; their failure to meet the criteria mentioned above offers a challenge to administrative science.

---

* First published in *Management Science,* Vol. 6, No. 2, January 1960, pp. 141-8. Presented at the national meeting of The Institute of Management Sciences, Chicago, June 1959.

The challenge is only perceived if one finds it necessary to take a more sophisticated view of the criteria of business action than the common traditionalist view. The common view arises out of the limited, sporadic and often poorly evaluated experiences of participants in business—of investors, financiers and businessmen themselves. By constant usage and the unconsidered transmission of commercial and financial "lore", tests which had significance and an easily discernible meaning in a less complex environment continue to serve; radical changes in the form and milieu of business have had no impact on them, except perhaps to knit them more securely into the fabric of commercial practice.

The oldest form of information processing in business is accounting, based on a monetary scale of measurement; this paper will deal primarily with accounting methods and concepts. But, first, some observations on its scope. Accounting is concerned with the measurement and representation of transactions and events; the effects of the majority of these can be measured readily at the time of their occurrence. It does not follow, though it is generally taken as axiomatic, that simple arithmetical manipulation of the measurements of separate events will give a clear and unambiguous representation of the effects of an extensive series of such events. Growth in the variety and number of events to be described creates the need for rules, if only to ensure consistent recording. These rules may be justified on grounds related to the recording process or on grounds related to the real operations represented. In the sense that rules reduce the area for the exercise of opinions or judgement at the point of recording, the resulting summaries may be considered as objective statements of what has transpired. But to the extent that rules incorporate widely held beliefs, judgements or criteria of the information processors, the result is not independent of the processors; it loses in objectivity and may communicate signals which are irrelevant to real operations.

One's conception of the nature of a business unit will affect what is envisaged as the ideal product of information processing. At any time a business unit has some of the features of an organism. It has purposes or goals to which its parts are expected to contribute. Criteria and measures of the effectiveness of the whole are therefore required. If its parts or its sub-goals are considered piecemeal—for convenience or ease in considering potential actions and their consequences—measures of the effectiveness of the parts and of the whole should have a consistent basis. But a business unit also has some of the features of a system of separate co-operating instruments and organisms. Though the unit as such may continue in existence for a long period, its separate machines, plants, properties, financiers, investors and other contributors may change or be changed as the market values of their separate contributions to the goals of the unit change. Consequently, the contemporary market value of any feature of the unit is the relevant basis of any system the purpose of which is to inform the actions of participants. If, on the other hand, its components are considered to be irrevocably committed or tied to the unit, a different basis of measuring operations and results will be adopted. This assumption is among the foundations of contemporary accounting; with consequences which will be demonstrated.

It is commonly held that the most important piece of information yielded by the accounting process is net income or profit. But what is profit and what in fact does a calculated profit represent? The profit from a single venture promptly consummated is easy to conceive and to measure. The profit from a series of diverse transactions consummated in a relatively short period is similarly easy to conceive and measure. Out of such simple circumstances arose the general idea of profit and its acceptance as a simple measure of the effectiveness of a business operation. But the intermediaries and intermediate functions and operations which characterize modern business have increased the complexities of calculation and rendered the primitive concept of profit irrelevant. Profit as it is now computed, and (by corporations) publicly reported, is a conventional residue, determined periodically from a series of completed and uncompleted operations; and determined in such diverse ways that its amount may differ widely according to the views of those who compute it and the wishes of those responsible for its publication

Consider first the influence of those who compute profit. Profit may be conceived to be a monetary measure of the residue from a series of transactions (including service-flows) whose individual effects are expressed in terms of initial price. This is not far removed from the primitive concept of profit; it is simple to compute and is the concept underlying most contemporary accounting. But it is appropriate only in limited circumstances, for example, where the enterprise is of a short-term liquidating nature, or where prices do not change through time and money has a constant purchasing power through time, or where the function of the accounts is deemed to be the representation of a true trusteeship operation. Most businesses fall outside these categories. Alternatively, profit may be conceived as a monetary measure of the residue from a series of transactions whose individual effects are represented by market values, whatever these happen to be from time to time. As value at the time of action, rather than price at some other time, is relevant to action, this concept is relevant for continuing businesses in a changing economic climate. But it is not an easy concept to evaluate; the simpler notion continues to be used, though it misrepresents the enterprise, in that the effects of changes in the context of operations are ignored. Even when the rate of change in technology or in price is small, the misrepresentation over a period of years may be material.

Typically, business operations are continuous, and reporting is periodical; this creates problems in timing the recognition of transactions. One may adopt as the criterion for allocating transactions to specific periods the dates on which legal claims in fixed monetary amounts, by or on the subject enterprise, arise. This satisfies a legalistic view of the rights and obligations of the enterprise and because of historical emphasis on the legal position it has become generally accepted. But a business firm is not simply a congeries of legal rights and liabilities; it is also an economic instrument; and other ways of viewing its operations can be envisaged. Transactions could be accounted for according to the dates on which cash flows take place; or according to the dates on which value is deemed to be created. Each of these methods would express a reality no less significant than the legal position. For some purposes they are in fact used, but not for the purpose of providing a general measure of performance such as profit is expected to be. The consequence of adopting the legalistic viewpoint is to shift the recognition of profit from the period in which value is created to the period in which its creation is finally realized by sale. This shift may be quite inconsistent with the scale of aggregate operations in consecutive periods; it will misrepresent the operations of those periods.

Whatever basis is adopted for evaluating and timing transactions, certain figures entering profit determination must be computed, because there is no market transaction in the period from which an objective price or value can be obtained. The principal figures of this sort are depreciation allowances and inventory values. The ways of evaluating these are manifold, each with its justification. Some of them derive their popularity from their sanction for taxation purposes; and practices which at one time lack favor and support have often found supporters "on theoretical grounds" once they have received the *imprimatur* of the courts or the legislature. But the tax-paying obligation has no necessary relation to the basic economic function of business; profits computed on the basis of taxation rules cannot be expected to represent business operations as such.

There are other possibilities of distortion. The processing of information is (in any firm except the smallest) performed by many people. Their separate opinions about the treatment of different items may have contrasting justifications, and the profit figures of any firm for consecutive periods may have different meanings, because methods having quite contrary effects are concurrently accepted in the business community. Further, there are no rigid rules governing the broad lines of profit computation by different firms, and profits of different firms may differ in kind as well as in degree. The effects of computational differences cannot be dissociated by any interested party from the effects of efficiency, or from the impact of external factors on each firm. Comparison of the results of a given firm in consecutive years, or comparison of a single year's data for several firms (even within the same industry) cannot fail to mislead, except in the most improbable combination of circumstances.

These strictures arise from the nature of the processing operation, an area where there are some generally accepted rules. But profit figures may be deliberately distorted, quite obviously in some cases. Company A published its profit, a six-digit figure, for three consecutive years, with a range of only four units; this in spite of the fact that it is an operating company, a holding company and an investment company, a combination which suggests far greater potential variation. Company B published its profit, again a six-digit figure, for three consecutive years showing an identical sum, this in spite of the fact that five of the six separate items shown in the income statement were different from year to year.

The difficulties of making informed decisions are compounded by the fact that profit calculation is a prior operation to the determination of the rate of profit on capital or resources employed. In some circumstances marked differences between methods may arise. Accounting on an initial price basis will, in inflationary periods, give a higher profit and a lower capital employed than accounting on a current market value basis. Both tend to give a higher rate of return on an initial price basis than on a current market value basis. Now, one of the functions of a profit rate is to suggest profit expectations; and the function of profit expectations is to direct the flow of funds available for investment into the most profitable projects, firms and industries. This function is improperly performed unless profit rates represent economic efficiency. The price basis of accounting does not have this effect. By its nature it shows better profit rates for well-established firms than for newly-established firms through periods when price levels are steadily rising; or looking at the other side of the coin, it permits older firms to decline in efficiency as prices rise without indicating the decline. It puts the established firm and the established management beyond criticism (or at least gives them a distinct advantage, as far as external support is concerned, over new firms and their managements). In deflationary periods the opposite occurs; and in neither circumstance has the capital market a valid means of assessing real efficiency.

Much of the above argument assumes that profits and profit rates are in fact used by investors in business securities. As there is some evidence to the contrary, this assumption should perhaps be justified. Lay persons (all not thoroughly familiar with the process of profit computation, including many managers) tend to accept profit and profit rates as carefully calculated and unequivocal figures. They have in mind the primitive concept of profit; they expect what is described as profit now to have some relationship to that concept. This is perhaps natural. It is common to rely on precise-looking figures, when so many other things bearing on one's judgements are difficult or impossible to quantify. And it is convenient to have one or few figures which may be taken to represent a very complex unit and its operations. This tendency is strengthened by the fact that financial statements, used to present profits, carry the signed reports of experts; and the fact that comparative figures are given in such statements carries a strong implication that the figures are consistently calculated and strictly comparable. It may be thought that institutional investors (through which much of the money for industrial investment passes) would take a less naive view. A tendency to use cash flow analyses may suggest that they do not depend on too precise a measurement of profit. But this is evidence of the importance to them of the liquidity of firms in which they invest; it does not involve or imply abandonment of the profit test. One does hear of investment companies which do not make searching analyses of profit records, but invest on the general reputation of a security in the market. This is "guessing about other people's guesses"; it is not the outcome of reasoned and informed decision-making. Aggregate operations of such companies may be profitable, but only because of satisfactory hedging or averaging.

It is possible to show that conventional methods are misleading in other ways. Some of the commonly used indicators of liquidity are open to criticism on the ground that although they contemplate a going concern, the primary indicators of liquidity do not suggest the real rate at which liquid assets will become available. And the capital gearing or leverage have been so significantly misrepresented by accounting reports that, when new capital was to be sought, restatements of asset values have been made on a large scale, where regulatory provisions have not restrained the practice. Misrepresentation of profit is only illustrative of the wider scale on which the products of conventional methods may mislead.

To external supporters, published profit and financial position are bases for appraising success and prospective success. For this reason the published figures and the conditions they indicate occupy the attention of managers. Being in a position to know a firm's condition in more detail, managers would presumably be able to appraise performance by more efficacious methods than those available to outsiders; so that even if the allocation of resources between firms is less than the optimum, the allocation of resources within a firm may be efficient. By budgeting, costing, project planning and other techniques, efficiency is pursued; but are these methods, in themselves, efficient?

The value of budgets, standard costs and other anticipatory calculations is said to lie in the fact that they give measures of what is expected in the period for which they are prepared: they are thus more rigorous bases for appraising performance than recorded measures of performance during a prior period would be. They may still be misleading. They frequently conform to accounting patterns, following conventional classification, cost allocation, inventory and fixed asset valuation methods. Comparison of subsequently recorded achievements with budgeted operations is useful, and comparison is facilitated, if the forecast and the record have the same formal arrangement. But this can be taken too far. It is not uncommon to find elaborate budgetary methods in which, due to routine adoption of conventional overhead cost allocation methods, monthly figures create unfavorable impressions which are contradicted by the annual result. If adaptive behavior is based on recent short period statements, it may clearly be inappropriate to the real conditions. (There are numerous accepted methods of overhead cost allocation, yielding quite different measures of divisional performance. Divisional performance may be made to appear better or worse simply by changing the method, a further example of the slackness in information processing which results in misrepresentation.)

On the other hand, some argue that budgets and cost estimates may be prepared without regard for the restraints of conventional accounting and in accordance with operationally relevant concepts and values. (Note that this carries an implicit admission of a deficiency in accounting information.) The consequence of a difference in concepts used in accounting and budgeting is that there will be two scales in use for appraising performance, one by external parties and one by management. Which, then, represents the enterprise? Unless the methods of accounting and of the auxiliary devices are reconciled, management thinking may imperceptibly or unwittingly shift from one point of view to another. There is a loophole through which the chance of consistent pursuit of efficiency may escape. At the same time it is obviously improper for external parties to judge the efficiency of an enterprise and its management on the basis of information of one kind when the enterprise is being managed on the basis of information of another kind. As was observed above, what is operationally relevant is also relevant to external supporters.

To many accountants the charges against conventional methods may be well known; and these charges have been challenged. Rebuttal has been attempted by multiplying justifications. But the contemporary use of the horse and buggy can be justified only on decorative or sentimental grounds; no one would claim that they provide an efficient means of transportation in the modern urban configuration of living, working and shopping areas. This is not simply a picturesque analogy. There are real and critical differences between the nature and operations of business units today and two generations ago; every new form of combination of businesses, every new method of financing operations, every new intermediary in the processes between the conception of new products and their consumption, creates the possibility of new differences arising and a potential need for new kinds of information. Rebuttal of the emphasis given to profit rates in this paper may be attempted on the grounds that no single profit figure can serve the informational needs of all participants. This is only a way of avoiding the difficulties of definition. Belief that there is a single relevant concept and the emphasis here given are derived from the inherent nature of a market economy. Profit is the price paid for the use of capital; if the profit test is abandoned, what alternative is there? That a price must be paid for the use of capital is one thing that remains constant, within an entrepreneurial context, no matter how production and distribution are arranged. To deny the importance of knowing the price, simply because of the present confusion of concepts, is to throw out baby, bath-water and bath.

Because they have as yet had little impact on practices, the foregoing charges against conventional information processing methods are worth repeating. The following consequences of faulty measurement and misrepresentation are pervasive: (a) Averaging persists (in cost determination, in inventory valuation, in investment policies). Reliance on averages prevents the refinement of decision-making processes. (b) Economic ill-fare results; securities and money change hands through poorly informed bargains; and the privileged few benefit to the disadvantage of the technically ignorant majority. Such inequity is not conducive to maintenance of the system. (c) Industrial and commercial power is held by firms or managements beyond the point where it is warranted by real performance; errors of judgement, loss of skill and sheer inertia, are masked by the very processes which should reveal them. (d) General economic inefficiency may result through funds flowing in directions other than where they could be used most efficiently (profitably). (e) In so far as the defects of one system for providing guides to action are perceived, auxiliary systems arise, leading at least to duplication of effort and waste of resources, and possibly to confusion, indecision and error.

What may be prescribed to eliminate or reduce the effects of contemporary methods?

(a) The firm should be viewed as an organic unity, inasmuch as every sectional operation has effects on the whole, and any external factor which affects the whole affects sectional operations. These effects arise from the conscious actions of participants, employed and independent, whose co-operation is activated by a communication system. The factor unifying these viewpoints is the market; the communication system must therefore convey signals relevant in the market place—signals based on contemporary values. Conventional or private values are inappropriate bases, as the market alone provides the tests of continuity or dissolution.

(b) Some signals originate from within the firm; they are the product of information processing systems. No single measure is adequate to represent the various facets of the firm. A pattern of measures is required: the pattern will be suggested by the tests in current use in the market.

(c) The pattern of measures must be self-consistent. If there are several information processing systems (e.g., financial accounting, cost accounting, budgeting) their basic criteria and methods must be consistent.

(d) The pattern of measures may be considered to comprise at least three layers: primary measures, the aggregates, differences, etc., resulting directly from processing systems; secondary measures, relationships (ratios, percentages, etc.) between the primary measures; and tertiary measures, rates and directions of change in primary or secondary measures. The latter are at least as significant as the other measures.

(e) As, in respect of certain matters, only estimates of market values are available, it should be indicated that primary aggregates and differences are selected values within a band of possible or probable values; and an attempt might be made to indicate the limits of the band, at least for administrative purposes. (Given consistent calculation on a market value basis, the band would be much narrower than under the varied alternatives now permissible.)

(f) As increasing efforts are made to quantify, as computational aids increase and as methods of selecting optimal courses of action are developed, an equally serious effort should be made to clarify key concepts; if maximizing profit or minimizing cost are objectives, it is necessary to know what concepts of profit and cost are operationally relevant in particular problem settings.

Some final comments. The misrepresentation contemplated in this paper is not deliberate in the sense of planned deception. The use of conventional accounting methods, however, is deliberate, and is vigorously defended on traditional and legalistic grounds; but the consequences of conventional methods are not widely understood. Hence the conventional patterns persist. The case under consideration demonstrates what may happen in any field, if methods of measurement become institutionalized; they cease to yield the independent and objective information which is their *raison d'être*. The preceding observations are not to be understood as over-emphasizing financial aspects of business. But if more efficacious methods of accounting were developed, participants in business would be able to place greater reliance on formal measures of success and would have less need to fall back on unquantified or unquantifiable considerations.

7

THE ROLE OF INFORMATION SYSTEMS IN DECISION-MAKING*

The growing literature of decision-making focuses attention on the selection of an optimal course from a series of hypothetical courses. Discovery of the position from which future action is to be taken has received rather less attention. Information systems are considered as means of discovering the facts antecedent to decision and action.

Introduction

Information systems may be dealt with from a large number of viewpoints and in a variety of contexts. Here we give attention to information systems as parts of organizations consisting of two or more persons.

An information system is itself the consequence of choice, whether choice is exercised by analysis and deliberation or by simple inertia. As information systems are costly to devise and to maintain we shall suppose that by deliberation an information system may be devised which is the most effective and most economical in terms of the means sacrificed and the ends attained. We are concerned therefore with the choosing of systems for producing information which will facilitate the choosing of substantive courses of action.

In the literature of decision-making, much attention has been given to the derivation and manipulation of hypothetical statements and to the relative degrees of confidence with which alternative hypothetical statements may be accepted. This is proper enough, for decision-making is directed to a future about which only hypothetical statements may be made. However it is generally assumed that the facts of the present, the present being the datum for all expectations, are known. This assumption is not necessarily warranted; it is warranted only in so far as information systems are designed to avoid losses, omissions and distortions of information.

Objectives of Information Systems

The objective of all decision-making in organizations is one general effect: the promotion of the ends of participants to their satisfaction. There is no end of an organization which is not an end of some person or persons. All persons whose ends are served in any way by an organization are participants in it. In so far as participation is voluntary, persons will only participate as long as they perceive their ends to be served. And inasmuch as all participants have different personal values, an organization is constantly susceptible to conflict.

---

* First published in *Management Technology*, Vol. 4, No. 1, June 1964, pp. 15-25. Delivered at a Seminar on Administrative Studies, Canberra, Australia, 15 August 1963.

It is the object of the agents of an organization so to arrange rewards and inducements that all participants are satisfied. The pursuit of one general effect entails that there shall be a means or a process by which co-ordination of the decisions and acts of the agents of an organization is secured.

Co-ordination entails that (a) all agents shall know the affective properties of the environment of the organization; (b) all agents shall know the general ends of the organization at any time; (c) all agents shall take account of the substantive facts of the environment in so far as they affect the pursuit of ends; and (d) all agents shall interpret alike the signs of substantive facts. As organizations increase in size each of these requirements becomes more difficult to satisfy. The difficulty is resolved in part by the provision of specific information collecting and disseminating agencies. But this of itself is not a sufficient condition of co-ordination. For in the first place all generally denominated ends are represented by word-signs; profit, efficiency, social welfare are examples. These mean different things to (they evoke different responses in) different people, according to their past experiences and their values. Similarly there are differences in the ways in which different people take account of substantive facts, and there are differences in judgements as to the facts which may affect the pursuit of ends. In the second place, these differences arising from aptitudes and experiences may be overlaid with specific points of view which are different in effect. The difference in point of view between factory and sales people is a matter of common experience. In the present context, there may be differences in the points of view of those responsible for acting and those responsible for an information system.

Records as Information

An individual person acting on his own behalf depends on his memory and on his immediate observations as to the operating stimuli and the means at his disposal when considering future courses of action. His memory is a store of signs; his recollections are in effect communications between himself at one point of time and himself at the time of recollection. But memory and the capacity for recollection are limited. The greater the number and variety of experiences which he may wish to draw upon when considering actions in the future, the greater will be his need to supplement his memory with a formal record. The capacity for observation and the time available for observation are likewise limited. So that even for those experiences which are remembered not all aspects of them may be recollected; for not all aspects may have been observed with such attention that recollection is assured. Further, every past experience is an experience in a particular setting—each has a time dimension, reference to which is necessary for the subsequent interpretation of past experiences as guides to action. But the time of experiences is less readily remembered than the experiences themselves. A formal record is the surest safeguard against faulty recollection in this respect, and hence against the misinterpretation of past experiences.

Organizations have greater difficulties. An organization is more extensive in terms of its agents than an individual actor. It has no natural memory other than in the form of the memories of its agents. As agents may be assigned different functions from time to time and as agents may join or terminate their association with it, the organization will lose the advantage of its accumulated experiences unless it augments the memories of its agents for the time being with a formal records system. For an organization as such its records are its memory. Thus all written records and communications at any time serve not only their immediate function, but also the function of memory. It is a matter of some importance then that all original communications and records should be adequate to enable them subsequently to be placed in their original time and environmental context. This may seem to be obvious but it is a condition often given less weight than it deserves.

Languages and Communication

Every organization has its own technical vocabulary. For different aspects of its operations it may use different technical languages. There are technical languages for dealing with its organizational structure; its legal problems; its manufacturing, merchandising or service operations; its financial problems; its personnel problems. Each of these languages consists of a set of signs (e.g., words) and a set of rules by which they may be formed into other signs (e.g., sentences). For each simple sign there are rules which determine how the sign may be applied to other objects. Each sign is interpreted by a person, in whom past experiences of the objects of experience and of related signs have developed the habit of responding to signs in the same way as he would respond to objects if they were present.[1]

In any given organization these rules and habits may be developed in such a way that they serve the organization well internally. Any description of its structure, for example, is a description serving its agents (or employees) primarily, if not exclusively. The word-signs employed may have no counterparts in any other organization, but they may be quite specific and be appropriately interpreted by the agents of the organization which they describe. The same applies to a number of the other language systems within their limited contexts. A manufacturing process may require a language system which is predominantly metrical and mathematical in character. Within its context the rules and habits developed may serve well the execution of the process; but they may have no counterparts in other divisions of an organization. If however any division has relationships beyond its own boundaries, with other divisions of the same organization or with persons or organizations external to that organization, a purely local language is inadequate. If effective communication is to take place the language used must be such that the signs employed evoke in others the same response as if those others were to see the objects represented instead of the signs.

---

[1] See, for example, Charles W. Morris, *Foundations of the Theory of Signs*, International Encyclopedia of Unified Science, Vol. 1, No. 2, University of Chicago Press, 1955.

For this reason many technical languages are supra-organizational. They are the languages of the basic sciences which are common to many organizations; of mathematics, chemistry, physics, law and so on. A supra-organizational language does much to overcome the problems of the mobility of agents with which organizations must contend. In the same way any language which is intended to evoke responses in persons beyond any division of an organization will necessarily be supra-divisional.

It is necessary to make these points because of the tendency for specialist divisions to emphasize their specialism. We have to consider two sets of circumstances. In the first case, the technical language serves limited and highly localized purposes. In this case there is little necessity for the signs to be interpreted by non-experts. There is little likelihood that experts will be misled. In the second case, the technical language serves a wide variety of purposes and in particular the purpose of co-ordinating the actions of many different agents. An information system of this kind is commonly provided through a centralized staff or service agency. To expect to have the advantages of specialization from such an agency is reasonable. But the creation of such an agency may have consequences which are not expected.

Firstly, a centralized information agency is in many respects removed from the situations in which actions are taken; it may be removed spatially, but it may also be removed intellectually and experientially. It may be removed intellectually by reason of the different skills, aptitudes and attitudes needed in the small back room by comparison with those needed in the factory or the market. It may be removed experientially by virtue of the lack of direct contact with the environment and by failure of operative persons to report unequivocally on misunderstandings or on maladjustments arising out of actions taken on messages received.

Secondly, a centralized information agency is staffed by persons having a specific expertise, one which is different from others in that it has, so to speak, universal rather than localized importance. It is a short step, and easily taken, to the view that its point of view overrides that of agents in other parts of the organization, particularly as there is a collection of persons serving to strengthen each others' beliefs as against the diverse and scattered views of others. If this tendency is supported by a professional orientation which is believed to be above organizational ends, the conditions of co-ordination may be destroyed rather than established. One does not have to look far to find the librarian who prefers tidy shelves to littered desks; to the central filing clerk who has a proprietary interest in his files; to the accountant who prefers delayed accuracy to expeditious approximation. In each case the service element of the agency is subordinated to personal ends.

Processor, Process and Actor

We are concerned with the consequences of differences in perception and orientation on the information processing and communication system of an organization. They may be illustrated by the use of a diagram which is a development of others used by Ogden and Richards[2] and by Cherry[3]. (See figure 1.)

An observed thing (designatum) is associated (the dotted line) with a signal which, in the context of the environment and his memories, organizes thoughts or responses in a processor. These he

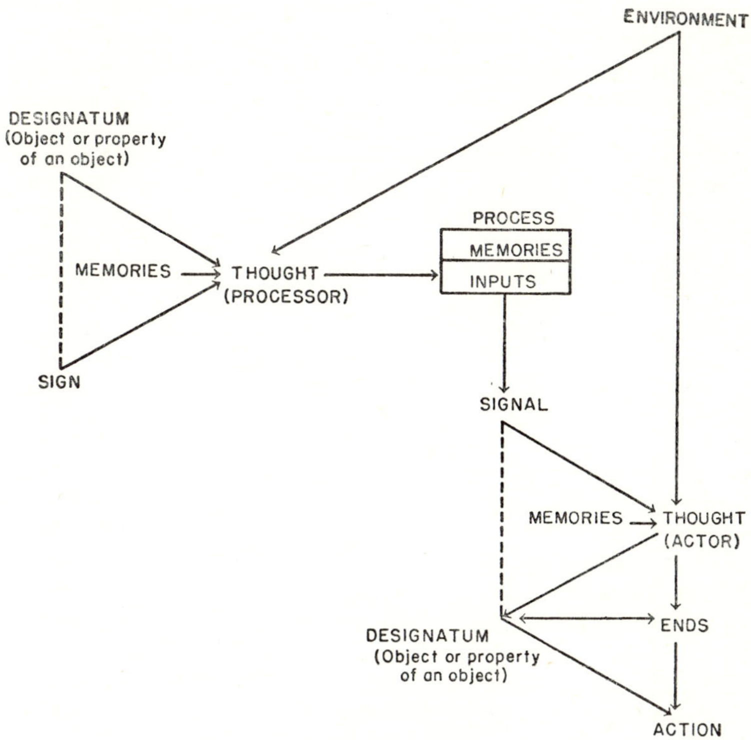

Figure 1

processes, the result being a signal to the actor. The actor associates the signal with an object, and interprets the signal in conjunction with his environment and his memories as denoting that object. Ideally his interpretation of the signal in the context of his environment will be the same as would be his interpretation of the object which was the experience of the processor if he were to experience it directly. The diagram represents only one stage in the handling of information. The designatum associated with the processor may in fact be a signal from another agent of an organization. But the diagram is sufficient to indicate the problems which may arise. We may suppose that the occasion of a communication between a processor and an actor is an event or an object which has just become of significance for action.

[2] C. K. Ogden and I. A. Richards, *The Meaning of Meaning,* London, Routledge & Kegan Paul Ltd., 1949.

[3] Colin Cherry, *On Human Communication,* New York, Science Editions Inc., 1961.

(a) Any technical language deals with specific properties of events or objects. It does not deal with all properties; to do so may require several technical languages. The processing of information involves the denotation of designata by signs in the technical language in accordance with the rules governing the use of those signs; the formation of simple propositions of the kind permitted by the rules of the language; and if necessary the transformation of those propositions into other propositions which in the circumstances are entailed by the original propositions. The constraints implied by this description may seem to be formidable. But they serve to emphasize the point that if the resulting propositions are to evoke in actors the responses (decisions) which the designata themselves would evoke, and if the class of actors includes actors of divergent skills, the formation and transformation rules will be such that they conform with the understanding and experience of persons of divergent skills. Otherwise the results will be esoteric, incapable of evoking unequivocal responses in actors; and if there are more actors than one, incapable of promoting co-ordination of actions.

(b) The processor must be regarded as an extension of the sensory and manipulative apparatus of the actor, but not of his selective apparatus. Among the memories of a processor there may be recollections of the actor's past responses to designata or signals. He may suppose that the ends or values of the actor are the same as they were in the past, and consciously or unconsciously "read" new objects (new in point of time) as if the actor's ends were unchanged. He may imagine this to be part of his service function. But strictly he cannot know the actor's ends, for they may change in the light of the very signals he is to communicate. Note that the consideration of ends comes late in the diagram and under the actor's own thought processes. We may state a principle; the denotation of events and objects by signs and the processing system shall be neutral with respect to the specific possible ends of actors. We speak here exclusively of information, not of advice. Advice is necessarily predicated upon certain hypothetical ends; but advice cannot be given without information which is free of such hypotheses.

(c) An information system will include records of past events. A processing system may require the formation of propositions relating events of the immediate past (an event or object which has just become of significance for action) and events of the more distant past. If the relationship to be expressed is a simple comparison, the time dimension will necessarily be specified for events of the remoter past; for the time dimension is a first indication to the receiver of differences in context. If the relationship to be expressed involves the merging of propositions, then any proposition of the distant past will necessarily be transformed into a proposition which is capable of being merged with propositions relating to the immediate past. This is on the one hand a matter of logical necessity. On the other hand, the actor is to infer something, from the signals he receives, in the context in which he receives those signals. The context in a sense conditions him to interpret whatever signals he receives. The merging of propositions without appropriate conversion to the context of the signals cannot be expected to evoke responses which are relevant in that context.

(d) Consider now the actor. Actors and processors are persons: all persons have different capacities for perception. It may seem unlikely then that any sign representing an event as it is perceived by a processor will evoke in an actor the response which the event itself would evoke in the actor. And indeed it would not, were it not for the fact that habits of making inferences from signs may be, and are always being, developed. But intermediary signs, such as those produced by a contrived processing system, have not the same reliability as events themselves or the signs which denote them to an observer-actor. If the signs are found by the actor to be unreliable in the context in which they are received, he may come to depend on other systems and his own observations rather than on the system found to be unreliable. In which case the latter system has simply failed in its function. This does not mean that it will be abandoned; it may have some useful elements and it may be preserved for these despite its defects. In this case the actor is faced with several information systems, yielding signals with differing modes of representing facts and events, a situation conducive to doubt, whereas the proper function of an information system is the removal of doubt.

An Illustration

We have framed these observations in the most general form, for they apply to all types of languages and information processing systems. It happens that one of the most widely used systems for co-ordination and for supplying information as a basis for decision-making is the system of recording and arranging the financial properties of events and things. No assertion need be made about the relative importance of financial and other properties in relation to any kind of decision. It is simply a fact that all organizations which have relationships with persons or other organizations are subject to monetary or financial constraints: in a market economy using a monetary medium, scarcely any decision has not a financial property. The budgetary systems and accounting systems of government and business, of cultural, political or ecclesiastical entities are evidence of the ubiquity of financial constraints. The processing of information relating to financial properties of events and things provides a useful illustration of the possibility of breakdowns in information processing systems.

Now money and market prices are things of which every person who is an agent of an organization has direct personal experiences. But these experiences are unique, for no two persons have the same ways of spending their own money. And their experiences as persons differ from the experience of an organization, for no person spends his money in the same ways as an organization. Here is one particular difficulty, differences in perception of the significance of money signs, which confronts an organization.

However, although there may be differences of this kind there is one thing common to the experience of all persons—the significance of any money sum (its purchasing power) is variable through time, under the influence of the supply of and the demand for goods and money. Notwithstanding this, there is widespread evidence that systems commonly used for processing financial information proceed on the assumption that the significance of any money sum is invariant, at least over long intervals. This is in flagrant violation of a number of the observations made above on the characteristics of the link between observed designata and inferred designata through processed information. It results in the merging of propositions containing signs having different time dimensions, and therefore different significances, as if they were signs having the same significance. It results in carrying forward, without appropriate transformation, signs of the past as if they were signs of the present. The only protection of decision-makers against irrelevant responses is not to respond at all to such signs but to respond to their own observations. Yet, in so far as some decisions are necessarily taken in the light of aggregative information, and as no actor can himself observe aggregative effects but must resort to processed information for this purpose, there is a high probability that decisions of wide and far-reaching importance are made on the basis of irrelevant information.

Systems and Sub-systems

In the preceding discussion we have spoken of actors and processors severally. This is a convenience. But it may not be allowed to overshadow the fact that information processors are also actors or agents of an organization within the field of their specialism. Co-ordination includes co-ordination of their operations and the operations of those who may affect the position of the organization with respect to its environment. This would result from the kinds of rules which have been suggested. But this result may be defeated if information systems are treated as independent sub-systems, deriving their rules from sources other than the obligation to promote co-ordination within, and adaptation to, the environment of an organization. An information system is not simply an information system: it is a system - for - supplying - information - to - actors - who - must - take - co-ordinated - adaptive - actions. The operative word is "information" not "system".

Information processors who regard their operations as a sub-system may imagine that economies on their part are justifiable in the same manner as are economies in affective operations. They may take the view that it is more economical to persist with an established system than to devise another which may seem to have some arguable but not experienced merits over the old. To do so will surely be less costly to the processors themselves, in terms of the strains of invention and of learning new habits: and consequently it will be less costly to the organization. But cost is only one side of the assessment of an economy; the other is the benefits which accrue by virtue of costs incurred. This is not a matter on which processors necessarily have a worthwhile opinion: it is not surprising that they commonly tend to disregard it, for they have not to use the information they produce in making decisions themselves. Here, as in other circumstances, sub-optimization may be incompatible with optimization for the whole organization.

There is a related point. We have noticed that a technical language can give expression to limited properties only of events and things. Yet events and things have an extensive, if not unlimited, range of possible properties. At a certain point in the development of an organization it may be of importance to know in considerable detail information relating to a phase of its operations. A program or system will be set up to provide this information. At a later stage information on the same phase of operations may be required, but simply by virtue of the differences in scale of the operations, the information may now be required in aggregative rather than particular form. The question arises whether a new system shall be substituted for the old or whether the old should be simply extended to cover the new requirements. Inertia tends often to result in the latter course being adopted. But, further, this course is justified on the ground that it is better to have all the information which could conceivably be used rather than just that information which can be used in the new circumstances.

Now the mere fact that detailed and aggregative information is produced, and by a group of expert processors, may predispose receivers of it to believe that the whole is relevant. But Millikan cites some work by Bavelas and Perlmutter "which suggests that an individual's capacity for making sound judgment about a complex situation may be seriously impaired by supplying him with a lot of information which he believes should be relevant but whose influence on the situation is not clear to him"[4]. There is then a point at which the marginal cost of differentiations of information and comprehensiveness of information exceeds the marginal utility of information to the receiver. A percipient processor will recognize this and design his system accordingly. But it is a matter of experience that information processing is done according to habitual modes far more commonly than according to deliberate assessment of the requirements of receivers. There is in any case a euphoria associated with the demonstration before others of one's mastery of a technique, particularly a technique that is beyond the competence of observers, which stands in the way of the reduction of complicated processes and complicated information to their essentials. Both factors cut across the objectives of information systems.

Information and Judgement

There is a view, held by practising decision-makers as well as by some observers, to the effect that, notwithstanding all the information

[4] Max F. Millikan, "Inquiry and Policy: The Relation of Knowledge to Action", in Daniel Lerner (ed.), *The Human Meaning of the Social Sciences,* New York, Meridian Books Inc., 1960.

available, the successful executive and the successful organization are successful because of personal judgement or flair. In the first place the implied casual connexion is difficult to sustain. To say that a successful decision-maker has a flair in his field or has good judgement is not necessarily to do anything more than to give another description to success. Another person, recognizing that unforeseeable events have much to do with the consequences denoted by "successful", may simply say the successful decision-maker was lucky. But, in the second place, we may admit that some people have superior judgement to that of others. Judgement subsists in the capacity to perceive actual or expected events as being related to other things and events. Superior judgement is the capacity to do this in a superior manner—to perceive more interrelationships or to perceive given relationships more clearly.

In so far as these perceptions stem from direct experiences of events and things, judgement depends on the breadth of experiences and the extent to which experiences have been organized in the experiencer. To improve one's game one prefers to compete against a better player. It is not just a question of how many experiences one has undergone. But in so far as one's perceptions stem from experiences through the receipt of processed information—and all experiences of aggregative or general effects are experiences of processed information—the quality of judgement depends on the reliability of the information as an index or a sign of relationships which actually exist and of events which actually occur. It is quite possible that superior judgement in matters of detail and of direct experience may be accompanied by sheer foolishness in matters of which one cannot have direct experience, simply because the processed information on which one has depended has been a quite imperfect reflection of the consequences of actions and of the state of affairs in the past.

Whether then we regard processed information as the basis for presently contemplated actions or as the basis upon which the judgements of persons will be improved by experience, the necessity stands that it shall evoke in receivers the responses they would make if they themselves were to have direct experience of the events and things of which they receive only signs.

The possible sources of interference in an information and communication system and its setting, are sufficient to give rise to the belief that no actual system will have or will maintain the ideal characteristics we have suggested. The mobility of agents, the time it takes to develop habits of mutual understanding between actors and processors, the self interest of processors and their lack of contact with substantive problem situations and so on, suggest that an information system must be regarded as a developing instrument, in the same way as an organization is constantly developing. In the organization as a total system, an information system serves not only to provide the premises of decisions but also to provide a feedback so that decisions may be reaffirmed or abandoned in favor of others. The development of an organization and the development of the judgement of its agents alike depend on this feedback. It is clearly no less necessary for the development of an information system. Some observations of Churchman on science as a control device are by analogy pertinent in the present setting: "... scientific procedures provide policies of such a nature that if a decision is selected wrongly the procedure will indicate the incorrectness of the wrong solution earlier or more economically than any other method. That is to say a method is scientific in so far as it presents control at the best possible moment for the individuals involved. The perfect scientific method would thus provide perfect controls at every instant, and approximations to such an ideal are more or less scientific according to the degree of approximation.[5]" As an information system is a device for continually bringing under notice new facts, new knowledge, its scientific orientation should be apparent. Direct observation, even on a modest scale, of information systems will reveal that they are much less amenable to correction than are the decisions they are intended to inform. This is a curious situation; a case of the tail wagging the dog. It is a situation in which faulty judgements may develop, incorrect decisions may be made, and the costs of maintaining the system are unwarranted by the nature of its contributions to the selection of environmentally appropriate actions.

Summary

1. An information system is a contrived or designed system employing a technical language relating to one property or class of properties of observable events and things. Information is distinguished from hypothetical propositions; it is here used of propositions denoting experiences.

2. The role of an information processing system with respect to decision-making is to produce and supply propositions or statements which, in conjunction with the context of their receipt, will evoke in persons responses (decisions) which will effect substantive changes in an organization or in its relations with its environment.

3. A decision emerges from assessment of information received, in the light of an actor's other observations, his expectations, and his ends or values at the time. An information system which anticipates an actor's valuations, which admits hypothetical values, or is affected by values of the information processors, interferes with the freedom of the actor to choose on the basis of the existent facts and his own contemporary values. If freedom so to choose is to be preserved, information will necessarily be neutral with respect to specific values or ends.

4. An information system is an abstracting system; its justification lies in the reduction of the information available to the information that is relevant to action. But abstraction may not be carried to the point where differences in significance are obscured (as, for example, by use of the same signs through an interval during which the relationship between given signs and their designata have changed).

---

[5] C. West Churchman, "A Pragmatic Theory of Induction", in Philipp G. Frank (ed.), *The Validation of Scientific Theories,* New York, Collier Books, 1961.

5. As information systems produce signals in technical languages, the denotation of signs, simple and complex, and the rules of the language, are required to be understood alike by processors and actors; processors shall respond, after their fashion, to objects and events in the knowledge of the relationship between their signals and the responses of actors.

6. An information system of an organization having many agents will necessarily produce signals capable of evoking similar or related responses in persons of different skills and competences, if it is to serve as a co-ordinating device.

7. Information will fail to evoke responses (decisions) relevant to the pursuit of ends if it is found by receivers to be inconsistent with other information, particularly if it is inconsistent with direct observations. The system which produces it will serve to increase doubt rather than to reduce doubt: it will cloud rather than clarify issues confronting decision-makers.

8

THE RELATIONSHIPS BETWEEN ACCOUNTING, FINANCE AND MANAGEMENT*

The Face of Accounting

Accounting may not seem to be much of a thing to entertain any sentiment about. That, at least, is the impression one has from the limited pre-occupations of accountants when they get down to talk about their art. The things that occupy, that even attract and hold, the attention are not infrequently the minutiae of book-keeping—how to save an operation by producing two or more similar records at the same time; how to use book-keeping machines, and now computers, to do routine tasks. Certainly if there is a more efficient way of doing routine operations someone should investigate it and apply it; but the impression is often difficult to avoid that these matters are the core of the accountant's concern. That this is the face accounting shows to the world may be judged by the allusions and comments of others when they make reference to accounting and accountants. But if Victorian vignettes of book-keepers and the slick phrases of Elbert Hubbard stick in people's minds, we may suspect that they have been nurtured by the experiences they continue to have in dealings with accounting and accountants.

Yet there is something vast and significant about what accountants do, or can do. It is not to be discovered, however, by looking inwards, at the technicalities of their operations. It is only to be discovered by looking outwards on the world in which accountants play a part. The complex arrangements of business and government could not have been built and could not be sustained without it. Billions of dollars pass through the treasuries of some governments and some private corporations each year; billions pass in domestic and international trade and commerce; billions are invested in business assets at any time. How much passes and to what effect is a matter of concern to millions of people; someone must keep account of it. This may seem like mere book-keeping—on a large scale, perhaps, but book-keeping just the same. If that is the best light in which it can be seen, then perhaps it's not worth a wisp of sentiment. But the information which emerges, or can emerge, from the process is much more than mere book-keeping. We will only understand the critical place of accounting in the complex system of economic interaction

---

* Text of an address given in The University of Alberta, Edmonton, in February 1967; published in booklet form by the Faculty of Business Administration and Commerce.

which surrounds us, if we realize that these summaries are the source of many of the "full speed", "slow down", "detour" and other road signs by which business managers and financiers are guided.

The Glamor of Finance

By contrast with accounting, no one doubts the importance of finance. There is glamor of a kind to it. Financial wizardry is something of which most people feel in awe, probably because, like nuclear physics, they do not understand it. The wheeling and dealing involving millions of dollars is the stuff of which fascinating biography and fiction are made. Great failures and great amalgamations alike tickle the popular imagination. The Daniel Drews, the Jay Goulds, the Carnegies, Vanderbilts, Rockefellers, Morgans are almost legendary figures. But no one seems to have seen fit to sing in praise of their accountants.

Indeed there may not have been many praises to sing. For on the one hand the art of accounting was little developed in the age of the powerful and wealthy manipulators. And, on the other hand these men were often much closer to the operations they controlled, and by direct experience much more knowledgeable of the contemporary facts than the managers of today's far flung enterprises. The self-attested impatience and distaste of Henry Ford, one of the last of the personal builders of an industrial colossus, towards accountants and their kind is perhaps indicative of a past age, as was the eventual necessity of "counting the costs" of the same enterprise indicative of a new age.

This new age is the age of the corporation, financed by the savings of many small investors. One of the opportunities created by this age was the possibility of promoters gaining control over large sums of money on the basis of promises and prospects. The classic case was the prospectus which offered magnificent returns from "a project hereafter to be disclosed". There was also the opportunity of capitalizing on future expectations based on past performances. This would seem to be less open to abuse than initial flotations of securities. But the naiveté of investors on the one hand, and the optimism, and in some cases the sheer bad faith, of issuers of securities on the other hand, were contributory to the sale of vast quantities of watered stock in what turned out to be the nemesis of many small investors, and in some cases the nemesis of the promoters. Since the popularization of investment in marketable commercial securities there seems to have developed a belief in the possibility of making money merely by shuffling paper[1]. The belief would not have arisen, nor have persisted, unless of course some people did make some money in this way. But unless there is some real substance to the

---

[1] Thurman W. Arnold (*The Folklore of Capitalism*, New Haven, Yale University Press, 1937) has some pointed observations on the uses of paper and the manipulation of financial symbols which are as pertinent today as when he wrote. See Chs. V and VIII. Ferdinand Pecora's *Wall Street Under Oath* (London, The Cresset Press, 1939) has numerous examples.

paper, some assets of discovered value as well as the prospect of putting them to work profitably, what some make others lose. And it so happens that those who make money are not uncommonly those who control the paper issuing business—the sale of stocks and bonds; and those who lose it, irretrievably because they have no resources to seek redress or spread their risks, are much smaller fry.

It is easy to see how ordinary people, accustomed to the immediate necessity of having money or other tangibles, would find the world of high finance, with its expectations, watered capitals and the like, beyond comprehension. Yet it ought not to be incomprehensible. It is as true for the largest companies as for the smallest households that only the application of human skills to actual non-human resources can produce an increase in the resources available for consumption or investment; and it is as true for one as for the other that the prospects of increasing resources depend on the actual amount of resources which can be committed to enterprises of one kind or another at a given time. As small householders may, under the corporate form of business, become stockholders in large companies, it is a matter of public interest that they should be informed about the companies in which they invest or may invest; a mere paper certificate, however finely engraved and notwithstanding that it may have an exchange value, is no basis upon which an investor may safely invest, as he judges safety and income prospects.

The Quasi-public Role of Accounting

The quasi-public role assigned to accounting and auditing, from the time of the first English companies legislation, seems to have been designed to provide the financial facts from time to time, so that investors would know what lay behind the paper they held as the fortunes of companies changed. Apart from occasional lapses, and what must be regarded as occasional mistaken judgements by the Courts, this function of accounting and auditing has never been altogether lost to sight. In the United States, the competition between States for the "incorporation" business was accompanied by very loose requirements generally in respect of financial publicity. They drew the fire of Professors Ripley, Berle and Means[2]. It was not until after the crash of 1929 that public sentiment focused on the necessity of legislating for improved financial publicity "in the public interest and for the protection of investors".

Ideally the publication from time to time of contemporary financial information makes visible the performance of managers and corporations. Ideally it would enable the informed financial community to set against the facts the optimism which managers and directors often express in the face of reverses, and to judge for itself whether censure or support were the appropriate response. Ideally it would

[2] William Z. Ripley, *Main Street and Wall Street,* Boston, Little, Brown and Company, 1927. Chs. II, VI and generally. Adolf A. Berle, Jr., and Gardiner C. Means, *The Modern Corporation and Private Property,* New York, The Macmillan Company, 1932, pp. 202-3, 310-11.

provide the factual basis on which the community would distribute, as between firms, and as between public enterprises and business firms, command of resources, so that the more efficient firms were encouraged and the less efficient were forced to improve efficiency or go to the wall.

As it has happened, these functions have never been performed in the manner signified by the above use of "ideally". The idea underlying the prescription of periodical publication of audited financial statements cannot have been other than the fact that changes in the prices of goods effect changes in the profitability of corporate ventures and changes in the safety of capital invested in them. This is a fact known to all having even the slightest understanding of business. It follows that no out of date information could possibly serve the investing public and the financial community in the manners suggested in the previous paragraph. Balance sheets and income statements containing items for which initial purchase prices constituted the basis of the amounts shown would not do. Now although this should have been apparent to everyone, the English and American legislation disregarded and still disregards it. The detailed statements about the contents of financial statements, both in companies acts on the English model and in Regulation S-X under the United States legislation, contemplate and even direct that initial purchase prices may, or shall, be the bases for determining the amounts at which certain items are subsequently shown.

Deviant Accounting

One can only speculate about the causes of this deviation, in the specific directions of the detailed rules, from the basic principle that only contemporary representations and measures are significant in making and subsequently following out financial arrangements. One possibility is that stockholders were regarded as long-run stockholders, so that, even if in the short-run the figures were not contemporary, in the long-run (strictly at the termination of the life of a company) any misrepresentations on paper in the interval would not matter. There are traces of such arguments in justifications of the use of historical purchase prices. But this view is at odds with the facts. Stockholders are not necessarily long-run investors; the stock exchanges would support very few operators if this were so. And in any case, no company can survive to a "long-run" unless its financial affairs in the short-run are managed satisfactorily. It is not impossible however that these facts were overlooked or disregarded in framing the rules.

But there is another possibility. Laws relating to legal contracts involving money sums deal generally with fixed money sums. The laws relating to agencies, estates, bankruptcies, transactions in goods and services, and all legal cases arising from disputes about such matters contemplate particular amounts in respect of which some person is accountable. When the laws relating to company accounts were being formulated, it is not unlikely that, in seeking for precedents, the legal draftsman would rely on the notion of fixed money sums which is so common in experience in the law. But the analogy between trusts or agencies and corporations of the commercial variety is by no means perfect. A business manager is not in the same position in relation to the funds invested by stockholders as a trustee is in relation to funds held in trust; and the operations of business are subject to risks, while the holder of funds in trust is expected to avoid risks. However, given that legal draftsmen accepted the precedents or the analogy, it is easy to understand that keeping accounts on the basis that there was a definite fund to be accounted for would lead to stipulations that assets should be accounted for on the basis of their initial purchase prices.

But we cannot blame the law-makers entirely. Businessmen found it necessary occasionally to revalue assets, upwards and downwards; the effects of such adjustments are of course in direct opposition to the rule that initial purchase prices are the proper basis for periodical reporting to stockholders. These revaluations have never been called in question in law; the only questions which have been raised relate to the legitimacy of divisions among stockholders of the surpluses which may thus have been created. Most of the upwards and downwards revaluations could not indeed have been upset. For the recognition of increases and decreases in market values is necessary in all calculations bearing upon the contemporary financial positions of firms; and such calculations are necessary in or preliminary to all significant rearrangements of the finances of firms.

Consider this latter point more fully. It is necessary to know the contemporary values of assets at any time so that one may estimate how much could be borrowed on the assets as collateral security. This information is obviously necessary to managers. It is also useful to stockholders as suggesting whether, in the light of existing assets and liabilities, the next source of funds a firm will tap is likely to be lenders or stockholders. It is necessary to know the contemporary values of assets at any time so that one may decide whether and to what extent some assets may be sold to finance more profitable alternative operations. This information is necessary for managers, and in some cases depending on the nature of the assets it may be indicative to stockholders. It is necessary to have the contemporary values of assets at any time to determine what the current rate of return is, for a rate of return calculated on an out of date denominator is useless. This information is necessary to managers who wish to compare the performance of their firms with the performances of other firms. It is equally necessary to investors for the same reason; but also it is necessary to enable stockholders to form some opinion, in extreme cases, about the relative merits of liquidating a firm or allowing it to to continue. All of these are financial questions. As they are all recurrent in nature, we must ask why, in the face of experiences of these things, accounting has not been geared either initially or by subsequent improvement to providing contemporary figures in financial statements.

The reason must lie, it seems, in the failure to link up financial statements with financial problems and their solution. That this failure is a distinct possibility may be evidenced in two ways. The conventional mode of teaching and studying accounting has never included any substantive material on business finance and financial problems. This may seem open to question but a glance at the textbook materials of accounting over three generations will prove its truth. Book-keeping, formal exercises in drawing up financial statements, tax problems—these are the kernel of the materials; there is scarcely any questioning, if there is any at all, of whether and in what way the resulting information is linked with financial decisions. The second type of evidence subsists in the concentration, in textbooks and the periodical literature, on the accounting for firms singly. Seldom if ever is the view taken that the accounts of one firm are part of the flow of the accounts of all firms to the securities market, and that the accounts of any selection of firms in which an investor may be interested must be contemporary to be comparable.

A Limited Perspective

In general, the three types of activity, accounting, financing and managing, have tended to be studied by novices in watertight compartments. And in so far as any study of economics has been required, that too has been another compartment. I, and in their turn many of my students, had their early exposure to these matters in just such environments, as no doubt many readers did. The ostensible evidence is extensive. The literatures of accounting, finance and management are separate literatures. Undoubtedly each makes passing reference to the others. But the world's work is not done, and the way in which it is done is not adequately described, by passing references. The subject-matters of each are taught by specialists in each. Perhaps this is necessary to some extent, but students must form some quaint impressions of how the world works when specialists deal with facets of the world's work in quite contradictory, not complementary, ways. Students of accounting and finance, for example, should surely think it unusual to find no mention of stockholders in a well-known book on the corporation. Students of business economics and accounting should surely find it odd that the marginal analysis which is such an important element in the analysis of economic behavior is almost disregarded, where it is not categorically set aside, in accounting. Perhaps students don't find it so odd. But if that is the case, it can only be because specialization has prevented the juxtaposition of such contradictions, or because learning is a formality unrelated to understanding.

These students in due course become practitioners, experts, specialists. But if they lack a coherent framework into which their various pieces of knowledge fit, and fit well, it would not be surprising if they failed to see accounting as a means by which important functions of great public interest are performed. Professional accountants find themselves in all kinds of positions—from boards of companies to the halls of the legislatures. Their breadth of view, one might suppose, would be extensive. Their familiarity with the intimate processes of choosing, manipulating, negotiating, dealing, should be a fine foundation from which to view, clearly and critically, the role of their especial expertise. But if one is to judge from the periodical and hard-cover literature, the interest focuses on such purely immediate matters as keeping records, attending to the preparation of financial statements (which seems often to be regarded merely as a necessary evil), and helping individuals to avoid estate duties and corporations to avoid taxes. It is an illuminating exercise to examine the popularity of taxation as a subject-matter for books and articles. I am not for a moment decrying the desirability or necessity of minimizing individual tax burdens, in so far as this may be done within the law. But such exercises are almost negative in effect. For clearly if Corporation A is saved some taxes, the burden will have to fall on some other corporations or individual taxpayers. A country is no richer for such operations. It may indeed be poorer; for if highly skilled people spend their time shifting burdens from one taxpayer to another, they will have little time to spend on seeing how the whole efficiency of a community can be improved by application of their skill. Further, in so far as the profession sees as one of its significant objectives the socially non-productive business of lifting burdens from some and placing them on others, it can scarcely conceive itself as filling a vital public role in the affairs of an economy. Nor is it ever likely, on such a footing, to be able to make much public play of its functions, for the purpose of recruiting to its ranks the idealistic and capable adolescents who are seeking to do something significant with their lives.

However, I am less concerned at this point with the image of the profession than with its functions. The functions of accounting are not to be discovered by looking inwards at its technical operations. They are to be discovered by examining the socio-economic framework which has given rise to the widespread use and necessity of financial information. Now it may seem that, in the relatively recent past and the present, accountants have begun to sense this, for there is a great deal of talk about the relationship of accounting to management and decision-making. Unfortunately much of it is at a very superficial level.

Two kinds of examples will suffice. First, there is the view that managers somehow make decisions in an absolute sense. It is supposed that managers know or can know in advance what a firm may be expected to do in a forthcoming period and that failure of performance to match expectations must be regarded as evidence of faulty planning and incorrect decisions. We have only to adopt a wider framework to see that this is a superficial notion. For suppose three firms A, B, and C in a given industry expect to make the same profit rate, 15 per cent, in a given period. And suppose that A makes 13 per cent while B makes 10 per cent and C makes 9 per cent. It would appear that the whole industry has been affected by some external factors, and it seems impossible to assert that the management of A has failed to make correct decisions, or to assert the same of B or C for that matter. We can say however that A did better than B and C in the circumstances common to all. Second, there is the view that managers can judge the performances of their firms from time to time on the basis of periodical figures which themselves contain managerial estimates affected by still future expectations. This view is entailed in all suggestions that, for the purpose of periodic financial reporting, the appropriate method of asset valuation is some method of obtaining discounted expected net proceeds. But again we need only to adopt a different framework, though of a similar kind, to see that this is a superficial view. If we set out on a journey expecting to cover 200 miles in 4 hours it is pointless to assert at the end of the first hour that we have travelled 50 miles. By checking the actual distance, say 44 miles, we will know that we must average 52 miles per hour in the next three hours to cover the distance in 4 hours. Only by reference to some facts external to us can we discover progress, on the road or in business.

Financial, Managerial and Socio-Economic Frameworks

Accounting should properly be seen as occupying a place within a set of wider frameworks. The innermost frame is the administration of the financial aspects of firms. But financial aspects are only one class of firms; the financial administration is itself set in the next outer frame, the management of all aspects of firms. But the management of all aspects of firms entails winning and maintaining the support of all classes of other firms and persons on which continued operation of firms depends; the management frame is thus set in the wider frame of the economic aspects of society[3]. These frames do not of course close off any functional field, nor set bounds to it. Functional decisions and the facts on which they are based reach out from the centre of this nest of frames through the intervening frames to the outermost. No such decisions or facts can properly be inconsistent with what occurs in the frames outside of it. We cannot suppose that financial facts can or should be at odds with financial administration; yet accountants sometimes do this, as when they asset that "in accounting" or "from the accounting viewpoint" such and such rules determine what will appear in statements which turn up in the outermost frame. Nor can we suppose that the financial facts, which describe the relationship between the firm and its environment, depend on or must first be conditioned by the viewpoint of specific managers, for the wider framework of economic interaction between firms and individual persons or classes of persons is the superior frame.

There is thus an hierarchy of frames. It is not so much what managers decide or do which secures that firms shall remain in business, as that what they decide or do shall be consistent with what is expected by financiers, stockholders, workers, customers, suppliers—all of whom have connections in the outermost frame, and who thus are able to set what a given firm offers against what other opportunities offer. Similarly financial objectives or criteria of action are not

---

[3] See the figure on page 153. Such frameworks are used also in *Accounting, Evaluation and Economic Behavior*, Englewood Cliffs, Prentice-Hall Inc., 1966, Chs. 11, 12; and *Financial Management,* Sydney, The Law Book Company, 1967, Ch. 2.

the sole criteria; general managers must bring to bear other criteria in the course of making their choices. Now, all these people, from financial executives to general managers to those beyond the firm and those who enter into contracts with it, have different wants and

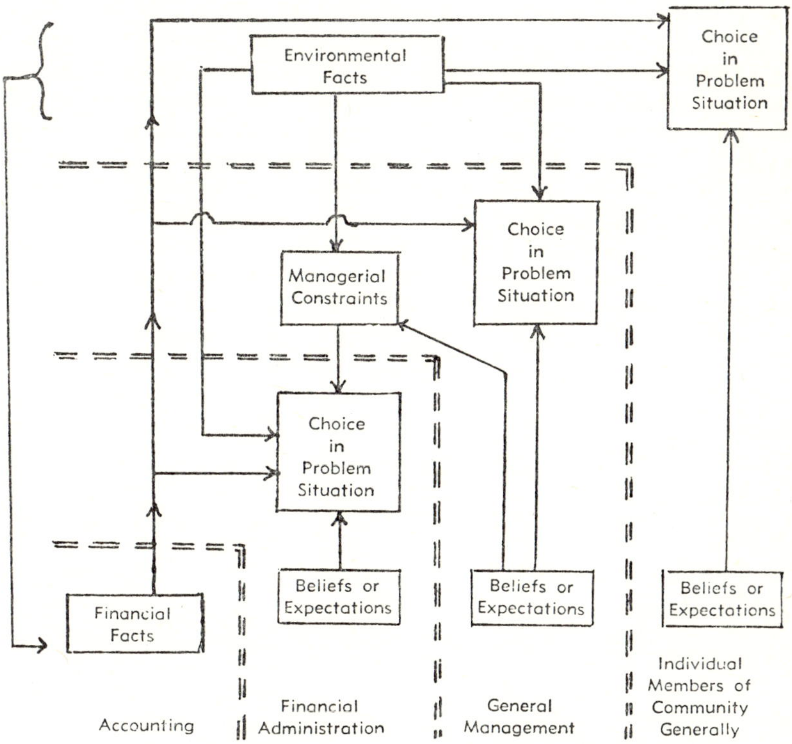

The Frameworks of Accounting and Decision-making.

different modes of evaluating a firm and its capacity to meet those wants. But none can evaluate or plan without knowledge of the state of the firm and of its demonstrated capacity as this is indicated by what it has done in the past. Facts of this kind are the things which are needed in common by all these parties; to produce financial facts of this kind is the function of accounting.

Accounting and Management

Accountants delude themselves if they suppose that financial statements may usefully be drawn which present anything less than the contemporary facts from time to time, on the ground that an immediate class of persons wishes for some reason that others shall have a modified version of the facts. Suppose, for example, that the immediate class of persons is the top management of the A company. Suppose that the accountant of the A company believes, or even is told, that the management wishes to present a conservative view of the company. And suppose that, in accordance with this, conservative valuations are placed on inventories and other assets by the use of, say, L.I.F.O. rules and long outdated durable asset values. The immediate effect of this is to give conservative numerators and denominators in rate of return calculations; the degree of distortion will depend on the effects of the conservative values of assets on the amount of income, but the degree is never explicitly indicated. We limit the example to this kind of calculation. Now suppose the same management wishes to know the rate of return of another company, B company. What is "good" for one company cannot be denied to another. Suppose B company's financial statements are also conservative. The A managers will surely want to know the facts about B company but all they will get is modified facts, modified by conservatism to an unknown degree! A similar situation will arise if accountants permit, or adopt at the direction of managers, optimistic statements of asset values and results. And the whole business becomes chaotic when rules prevail which permit firms at their option to adopt conservative or optimistic representations; for one would never know from the representations themselves whether one is considering a conservative or an optimistic statement.

The conclusion must be obvious. By an immediate distortion, supposedly in the interest of the firm or its managers or its stockholders, a situation is created in which the interest of the firm or its managers or its stockholders may be subverted by other firms which follow the same loose practices. The adoption of a wider frame of reference shows up the folly of adopting only a narrower or immediate framework.

The relationships between accounting, finance and management are intimate ones in principle. A firm and its management must satisfy its financial backers; satisfy, that is, by comparison with other opportunities. If its reported performance gives rise to superior or diminished expectations, its capacity for raising new money is correspondingly enhanced or reduced. But changes in expectations are not limited to financial backers. Customers, suppliers, workers, may also revise their expectations. If reported performance is factual the firm should not lack the means and the prospect of meeting all these changes in expectations. But if reported performance is a modified representation of factual performance, the disparity between the report and the facts may set up potentially destructive strains. Suppose that, for the purpose of maintaining the capacity to raise new money, an optimistic report is published, a report, for example, which is based on rules which mask a factual deterioration in results and position. The firm may indeed raise new money, but it will also have created other expectations—expectations of its executives for new plant, of its workers and suppliers for better wages or prices, of its customers for better goods or reduced prices. And all this at a time when its factual results and position are unable to support these expectations. There have been many examples, and recent ones, of failure subsequent to distortions of the factual results and positions of firms.

It is in one sense difficult and in another sense not so difficult to conceive that managers would countenance the production of reports which fall short of factual representations. It is difficult if we suppose managers to be as hard-headed about the facts which seem to be rather more remote from the market-place, as they are about the immediate facts of the markets in goods and services. We would suppose they would want the feedback of factual information. It is not so difficult if we suppose managers to take the same view of financial information, something to be used tactically, as they take of other kinds of information. But tactical uses cannot be hidden. They produce counter-tactics; they lead to takeover bids, and pressures of the kind mentioned in the previous paragraph; they lead to speculation on the quality of information, when the problems of speculating about the future of firms on the basis of facts is difficult enough.

There can be little doubt that there are managers of both kinds. Nor can there be much doubt about the possibility that even the hard-headed managers who prefer to face the facts may on some occasions wish to interpose statements of opinion of their own, tactically, to influence the opinions of others. If accounting rules are available which permit diverse representations to be made, from the conservative to the optimistic, it is only to be expected that managers will take the opportunity to interpolate their opinions, to insinuate the effects of their opinions, into statements which will be believed by others to be statements of fact; by doing so they avoid having to make any special statement of their opinions to influence the opinions of others. The opinions of others are influenced by a covert device. Reference to a covert device is not to be understood as necessarily indicating anything underhand on the part of managers, even though many cases have come to light in which managers have clearly wished to conceal the facts by recourse to extremely lax accounting rules. Rather it may be supposed that managers see the permissiveness of accounting as one of the rules of the game of managing. And as long as accountants hold to the view that the financial statements are the statements of managers, and tolerate rules which have extremely diverse effects, managers will be entitled to suppose that they may interpose their own valuations regardless of the facts.

Consider the implications of the reference to a covert device. Accountants may think that users regard financial statements as indicative of future prospects. But there is scarcely any doubt that users regard them as statements of fact. The figures are manipulated, recast into ratios and indicators of business trends, enshrined in serial tabulations over brackets of years—all as if they were facts. These operations would be unthinkable and meaningless if the financial statements were believed to represent facts modified by beliefs, expectations and tactics. Now if users believe the statements to be factual at a point of time when they are not, the widely upheld notion of disclosure is "more honoured in the breach than the observance"; the dependence of users on them as statements of fact is misplaced. The number of actions brought in recent years against accounting and auditing firms, whatever their outcome, must be regarded as evidence of the belief of many that their confidence was misplaced.

It would not be a difficult matter to cite particular companies whose reported results and positions have been gravely at odds with their actual results and positions on any realistic assessment. But it is unnecessary to do that. It is necessary only to draw attention to many well-known statements of accountants themselves. At various times professional bodies have drawn attention (a) to the inadequacy of accounts based on initial purchase prices when these are no longer close to prevailing prices, (b) to the necessity of reducing the diversity of rules having materially different effects on reported results and positions. A number of such bodies have indeed financed costly and lengthy inquiries into methods of overcoming the former difficulty and have published the results; this seems to indicate more than mere doubt about whether or not improvement is necessary. Many professional and academic accountants have illustrated the gross differences which may appear in the results of a given company using specific combinations of the available alternative rules. Many firms have chosen, or been forced by circumstances, to adopt valuations and modes of calculation not adopted by others, and indeed inconsistent with what are called generally accepted accounting principles. Many countries have, by special edict, more or less forced firms to adopt rules which are inconsistent with what in other countries are generally accepted accounting principles. This, and other evidence of the same kind, cannot but mean that there is no sound basis yet for having confidence in published financial statements even if they are audited; for no single user can know whether any statements he receives are close or distant representations of the facts of the firms which issue them.

Tendency towards Disorganization

We are forced to take notice of a principle which has been found to apply over a wide range of human interests in much the same way as it applies in its original field, physics. We may speak of the capacity of messages to induce responses consistent with the facts to which the messages relate as a form of energy. The principle we refer to is the principle of increasing entropy or disorganization; its purport is that any isolated system tends increasingly to disorganization or loss of energy[4]. To apply the principle to accounting we have to show that accounting has become an isolated system.

This is not difficult to show. In so far as accounting rules and procedures are conditioned by the demands of managers, the processes of accounting are isolated from the facts of the market, in which alone the relationship of firms to the rest of the community is discoverable. In so far as accounting rules merely follow out the expectations held at some previous time by managers or merely follow out the rules promulgated for calculating taxable income—as is the

---

[4] See also the references to entropy in *Accounting, Evaluation and Economic Behavior,* Prentice-Hall Inc., 1966.

case of accounting for depreciating assets—accounting is isolated from the market. In so far as there are no contemporary prices in any market which go by the descriptions "historical cost", "depreciated historical cost", "L.I.F.O." and, most common of all, "book value", accounting is isolated from contemporary affairs. In so far as there is no serious intercourse between accountants, managers, lawyers, and economists on modes of financial representation, which are of common interest to them all, accounting is isolated from the views of others. In so far as students of accounting obtain no integrated view of the role of accounting in the processes of economic choice, and consequently depend on indoctrination, accounting remains isolated. In so far as accountants insist on having "an accounting viewpoint" to justify what is unjustifiable on commercial grounds, accounting is isolated.

And what of the tendency to loss of energy of the product? One of the principles on which a system largely based on individual initiative and enterprise is justified, is that informed choice in such a system will tend to serve the needs and wants of the greater number, or to serve to the best possible extent the needs and wants of a whole community. Informed choice of investments is one facet of this. Choice in this direction can only be informed if all firms report in a substantially similar way and in terms consistent with facts which determine the contemporary states of firms as these are understood by users. But what have we? Every new rule, introduced as an accepted rule without the simultaneous rejection of an old rule, increases the difficulties of users, by increasing the degree of disorganization of the total flow of corporate financial information to the securities market. Given substantial acceptance of the historical cost doctrine, every new firm increases the difficulties of users, for it introduces to the total flow of information a different base date at which historical cost means something different from its meaning to all existent firms. Every rule justified by new tax laws, designed to tax differentially certain classes of taxpayers and which becomes incorporated in financial accounting, gives rise to increased disorganization of the flow of financial information. The compound effect of these several sources of disorganization must be formidable[5].

It would not be surprising if an economic system which depends on such information were far less efficient than it could be. For investors are unable to judge on the basis of reports of such mixed quality which are the more and which the less efficient firms. Managers likewise are unable to judge whether their firms are more or less efficient users of resources than other firms. Tax burdens and forms of governmental assistance are likely to fall on taxpayers other than those who ideally should bear or benefit from them. Pressures of workers, customers and others are likely to bear on firms inequitably. Managers, indeed, are likely to be praised or castigated for results

---

[5] For some observations on the extent of the proliferation of variety see "Financial Information and the Securities Market", p. 174, *post* and "A Matter of Principle", p. 242, *post*.

which turn to a considerable degree on the methods of accounting they accept rather than on the results which would be yielded by a neutral accounting.

Conclusion

The relationships between accounting, finance and management are not likely to be the intimate ones we postulated as long as these effects are possible. The solution is simple in principle. We indicated it at the beginning by the reference to the signs which guide managers and financiers. Accounting should, it seems, be regarded as an instrumentation system. In any deliberate competition, the parties work against one another and subject to the rules of the game. So it is with firms. As in any other competition, there is need for a scoring device which indicates how well the competitors are doing as the game proceeds. The competitors need such a device themselves so that in the light of the latest cumulative score they may devise their own tactics for the next step. And, if their capacity to compete depends on what others think of the score, they will want a scoring device which does equal justice to their respective performances up to any time. They will want a neutral, factual, scoring device.

These principles are recognized in all kinds of competitive activity. They are no less significant in business, though their significance is scarcely evidenced by the scoring rules presently adopted. Their significance in fact is much greater in business, for business managers play simultaneously a set of games against many different players, all of whom, though they have pay-offs of their own, may be influenced by a common scoring device—the financial outcome of the game to the firm. On the scoring may depend the rise and fall of individual incomes, the rise and fall of firms, the rise and fall of living standards. Its importance cannot be denied, unless one is prepared to take a narrow or short-sighted view of its effects—and then one will be mistaken. For the wider effects of the scoring system cannot be nullified merely by shutting one's eyes to them.

There are, doubtless, some who would regard the up-dating of knowledge, the keeping of the score, as a menial task; who fancy, rather, that they should be involved in the managerial process. But in doing so they fail to recognize that keeping the financial score in a volatile environment, in which the market indicators of the pay-offs are continually shifting and the score-keeping units themselves are gradually changing, is a highly specialized task—a task so demanding, indeed, that round the world it is still only imperfectly done. Let there be no pretension that managing and financing can be well done if accounting is not well done. Without a continuously contemporary system of accounting we cannot know how well managing and financing are done.

ACCOUNTING AND THE SECURITIES MARKET

9

THE SPICE OF ACCOUNTING*

Variety of mere nothings gives more pleasure than uniformity of something.
— RICHTER.

The extent to which the form and content of financial statements are discussed in recent and current periodicals and books may easily be taken as a measure of rapidly growing acceptance of the need for a clear and unequivocal public statement of business facts. The conclusion, however, seems to be contradicted, sharply contradicted, by the facts. There may be growing acceptance, but its growth is scarcely measurable in some respects, even if we examine the practices current during a period as long as 10 years. It is the writer's purpose here to illustrate this contention from the inventory notations in the published statements of a sample of 50 companies, large and small, whose securities are listed on one or more of the Australian stock exchanges.

Is Uniformity a Desirable Objective?

For the purpose of gaining some general idea of the changes in balance sheet presentation, a list was made of the various ways in which the different assets and their bases of valuation were described. It is granted that of all assets, the item "Stock in Trade" was likely to show the greatest variety of bases of valuation, and that the case made out here is stronger than if we were to take all the items in the assets side of the balance sheet together. But the writer was not at all prepared for the bewildering array of descriptions derived from the sample of 50. It seemed at first glance that the only generalization possible was that uniformity in accounting, or rather in the presentation of accounting statements, was not highly regarded amongst those responsible for published statements.

It seems that no case has been made out, by the institutes and individuals who proclaim the virtues of a standard terminology, with sufficient strength or cogency to influence the general body of accountants to adopt recommended forms and terms. And, it is submitted, no change of a general and noticeable character can be expected until accountants generally are persuaded of the real importance of uniformity. The fact that accountants are in reality subject to the directions of managers and boards of directors in these matters is not overlooked; but, unless accountants are convinced, they will have little in the way of argument or personal conviction to offer to their managers or boards as justification for a change to newer and better methods of presentation.

* First published in *The Australian Accountant,* Vol. XIX, No. 11, November 1949, pp. 398-401.

There are many reasons why uniformity in technical details (such as inventory valuation notations) as between companies should be widely adopted. Firstly, uniformity aids shareholders and investors, particularly those who have interests in a number of different undertakings; the present variety must be very confusing, so confusing, perhaps, that the whole purpose of giving a valuation notation is defeated. To know that stock is valued on a few widely accepted bases is better than having to decide on the effect of some of the vague and almost meaningless phrases now used. Secondly, it would aid all those who assist investors, for it would remove the need for much of the speculation which must take place about stock values and fixed asset values.

Thirdly, it would aid creditors and bankers, for these groups are concerned even to a greater degree than investors and shareholders in the liquidity of businesses, of vastly more business undertakings than individual investors; and in appraising the financial situation, stock may be a most important item.

Fourthly, it would give to all outside interested parties—the general public, the consumer, the worker, governmental authorities—more obvious evidence than they have yet had that there is a definite, recognized procedure among accountants, a form that is correct, a terminology that is widely accepted. The profession can well afford to take great pains to have this view established; otherwise it will lack cohesion, and hence social influence and strength as a profession.

The Table

A glance at the table will show how heterogeneous, in this one respect of inventory valuation notations is Australian practice. Thirty different notations are distinguished, and the variety is even greater, as may be gathered from the notations in parentheses (A4) and the use of "etc." (e.g., A5, B5). It may be objected, of course, that this list really contains relatively few different bases or methods of valuation; that, although the words vary, many items don't differ at all in meaning. That would have to be proved. But granting that is so; published statements are important not only for what lies behind them but also, and perhaps more so, for the impressions they create in the minds of people who have no access to the figures and facts behind the balance sheet. And their impressions must be gained from bald words and figures.

The different notations are listed in full so that the meaningless phrases and the unnecessary variety may be seen most readily. It is suggested that very little knowledge can be gained about the stock valuation methods of these companies in spite of these notations.

Meaningless Phrases

In the first place, the tag "as certified by . . ." conveys nothing at all to outsiders; they can know little of the competence (to value the stock) of the officer or officers mentioned in the notation. The phrase is quite superfluous unless an outside expert valuer has done the job.

Inventory Valuation Notations in Balance Sheets of 50 Australian Companies, 1938 and 1948

	Basis	1938		1948	
Cost—					
A1	Cost	6		5	
A2	Cost or depreciated cost	1		–	
A3	Cost less amounts written down	1		–	
A4	Cost or under (or lower, or less, at or below cost, at and under cost)	9		12	
A5	Cost or under as certified by, etc.	3		3	
A6	At or below cost, less depreciation	–		1	
		—	20	—	21
Cost and Market—					
B1	Cost or market	1		1	
B2	Lower of cost or market	5		6	
B3	Cost or current market value, which ever is lower	1		1	
B4	Cost or fair market value, which ever is the lesser	–		1	
B5	Cost price or market value as certified by, etc.	1		1	
B6	Not exceeding lower of cost or market	1		–	
B7	Lower of cost or market replacement price	1		–	
B8	Cost or replacement value, which ever is lower	3		2	
B9	Cost or replacement as certified by, etc.	1		1	
B10	Cost and/or replacement values	1		1	
B11	Cost, replacement value or under	1		–	
		—	16	—	14
Valuation—					
C1	Valuation	7		5	
C2	Valuation as per certified stock sheets	1		1	
C3	Valuation made by, etc.	1		1	
C4	Valuation after providing for possible obsolescence of stocks	1		–	
C5	Valuation after providing for diminution in value of stocks	–		1	
C6	Valuation not exceeding cost	–		1	
		—	10	—	9
Other Bases—					
D1	Fair market value	1		–	
D2	As certified	1		1	
D3	Cost and valuation	1		1	
D4	Lower of cost or valuation	1		–	
D5	Not exceeding cost, market or replacement value	–		1	
D6	Cost, market, or replacement value, which ever is least	–		1	
D7	No notation	–		2	
		—	4	—	6
	Total		50		50

The second type of phrase is much more serious, however. The "open end" notation (e.g., cost or under) sets an upper limit to the valuation basis, but who knows what the lower limit may be? In 1948 the cases described like this total 18 (groups A4, A5, A6, C6, D5), compared with 16 (groups A2, A3, A4, A5, B6, B11) in 1938—no improvement at all, in spite of all the work done by the institutes and individuals to promote better reporting in that interval.

The third quite useless term is "at valuation". However much it may be qualified by other phrases, it says nothing about objective tests of value at all, though admittedly the figures may have been quite objectively determined. The important thing, as far as outside parties are concerned, is to say so, if some objective basis, such as cost or market price, has been used.

On these counts and because two companies give no stock notation, we may say that in 1948, 30 of these 50 companies told outsiders nothing about their stock valuation methods except that they were conservative. How conservative no one outside could tell.

Unnecessary Variety

The previous paragraph has dismissed the whole of class C and most of classes A and D in the table. Let us examine class B.

These notations all carry slightly different shades of meaning, but I doubt very much whether such shades of meaning are intended. It is extremely likely that "Cost or Market" (B1) means "Lower of cost or market", but it need not necessarily do so. The adjectives "current" (B3) and "fair" (B4) complicate the descriptions. One might ask "What other market value than current market value would be used for this purpose?" and "What is fair, in any case?"

Class B really includes two types of notation, one referring mainly to market price or value and the other to replacement price or value. As there seems to be no precision in so many other respects, one may be excused for assuming that replacement means market price in at least some of these cases. But the recommendations of the Chartered Institute and the company represented by D6 in the table clearly envisage three possible bases of valuation: cost, market and replacement value, each with a definite meaning and each required to be stated to define with any precision the limits of the stock valuation.

Summary

We may say that of these 50 notations, in only those companies represented by A1 are stock values objectively determined, and in those cases the notation has a more precise meaning than in all the other cases.

If we ignore the defects imputed to conservative valuations, we may say that only groups A1, B2 and D6 (12 out of 50) comply with the requirement of clear and meaningful expression in financial statements. Or to put it another way, the only acceptable notations are:—

Cost Price,
Market Price,
Lower of Cost or Market, or
Lowest of Cost, Market and Replacement Values—

and only the former two can claim to be rigorously objective and consistent.

Changes in the Period

As appears from the table, there were relatively few changes in notation or basis during the period. There were 18 changes in all over the 10 years, four of them occurring in 1948. The greatest movement was into group A4, an open-end group.

More significant than the movements in the data as a whole, however, is the effect unplanned or capricious changes may have on the meaning of the accounts of individual companies.

Here are the changes one company made, taken not from the balance sheet but from the directors' report each year.

1938-42: "Stock valuations do not exceed cost or replacement price, which ever is the lower."

1943: "Stock in trade has been listed at or below cost."

1944: Similar to 1942.

1945: "Stock has been listed at values not in excess of cost price, market selling price or replacement value, whichever is the lowest."

1946-48: No mention of stock valuation basis.

Unless one is prepared to ignore these notations entirely, the task of interpreting the statements to which they refer is an unenviable one.

Multiple changes occurred in only this and two other cases of the 50 examined.

A change to the best method of presentation ought to be planned, so that the inconsistency made inevitable by change can be worked out of the accounts in the shortest possible period.

Time and Place

We may well agree with Dr. Johnson's statement that "the great source of pleasure is variety". But who reads balance sheets for pleasure?

Uniformity in technical details is as important in business as in science; accountants should recognize its importance even if only by analogy with the uniformity of accounting procedures commonly required in all branches of a single firm.

Variety may be the spice of life, but surely people expect to find their spice in other places than published financial statements! We may take our pleasure in "variety of mere nothings", but we could derive considerable professional satisfaction, perhaps even an improvement in status, from a greater measure of "uniformity of something".

10

THE FUNCTION OF THE BALANCE SHEET*

Accounting is a representative art. Its purpose is to represent acts, events and relationships by means of symbols. The symbols are not to be taken as complete representations of the acts, events and relationships with which accounting is concerned; a much more comprehensive set of descriptions would be necessary for complete representation. But, subject to its limitations, accounting may be expected to provide a reasonably useful representation of the financial aspects of the actions and affairs of business firms. The practical justification of business accounting lies in its capacity to do this; for, action taken in the absence of reasonable knowledge of the financial aspects of a firm's actions and affairs will only by chance be appropriate action.

The generally accepted (but not universally accepted) view of the function of the balance sheet permits and sanctions wide deviations from a reasonable representation of corporate financial affairs. Summarily stated, the essential feature of the process of accounting is taken to be the allocation of historical costs and revenues to successive accounting periods; costs unabsorbed in the earning of past revenues are carried forward as assets in the balance sheet, and, as far as those assets are concerned this is the sole function of the balance sheet. It follows that no increment in the values of assets, other than by new purchases, can be allowed to enter the accounting system, and thus to find its way into the balance sheet. Self-acknowledged supporters of this view assert that the income statement is the most important summary yielded by the accounting process, and relegate the balance sheet to a position of much inferior significance.

It is the purpose of this article to subject the generally accepted position to some logical and practical tests.

The Postulated Primacy of the Income Statement

It is undeniable that the expectation of income is a significant determinant of the actions of business managers and financial supporters. Figures representing past income are taken to be indicative of the level of future income, thus entering into the formation of income expectations. But how, specifically?

The income statement yields an absolute difference, net profit. The absolute figure by itself, however, is meaningless. It only derives meaning by comparison with some other magnitude. For example,

---

* First published in *The Chartered Accountant in Australia,* Vol. XXVII, No. 10, April 1957, pp. 565-70.

the amount of net profit stated to be earned in one year may be compared with the amount stated to be earned in other years. That the movement in the absolute amount is upwards or downwards is of some interest. But, much more interesting is the relationship between the amount of net profit earned and the capital employed in earning it. This relationship ties net profit to a financially critical figure, so that either for a single year or for a series of years it is a superior measure to the simple figure for net profit. It is suggested that a relationship of this kind, rather than the absolute amount of net profit, is contemplated when income expectations are being formed.

What then shall be taken as a measure of the capital employed in earning a given business income? It is notorious that paid-up capital is an insufficient and inappropriate basis on which to compute a net profit rate. Its insufficiency rests on the fact that share capital may be issued on a variety of premium or bonus terms and that undistributed profits may contribute in varying degrees to earning net profit.

A second possible measure of capital employed is the total of shareholders' funds. The resulting relationship—percentage of net profit to total shareholders' funds—is a measure of the effectiveness with which those funds are employed.

Now, total shareholders' funds cannot be obtained otherwise than as a result of accounting processes; the figure is in fact derived from representations made in the balance sheet. However, although the movement in the relationship of net profit to total shareholders' funds is not devoid of significance to the management of any given firm, it is not directly pertinent to the decisions of any specific group of shareholders or investors in any such firm. Preference shareholders (if any) may simply be concerned with dividend coverage, a different relationship altogether; and ordinary shareholders may seek a net profit relationship which more directly represents their own interests.

Theoretically, the appropriate relationship for ordinary shareholders to consider is that between net profit available to ordinary shareholders and the ordinary shareholders' equity; it may be called the ordinary equity earnings rate. To obtain this rate the interests of preference shareholders in net profit and in total shareholders' funds would be eliminated from the numerator and the denominator respectively of the relationship discussed in the previous paragraph. Although this involves a different measure of capital employed (and, incidentally, a different profit figure) from that contemplated in the foregoing paragraph, again the measure cannot be obtained otherwise than from an accounting statement such as the balance sheet.

In practice, however, the appropriateness of the ordinary equity earnings rate is partially obscured by the fact that shares have par values. Much of the agitation for no-par value shares derives point from the distortion which arises when profits are related to the par value of company shares. That there is agitation of this kind is evidence of the inappropriateness of the only other profit relationship to be discussed here—the relationship between profit available to ordinary shareholders and the par value of ordinary share capital, i.e., the ordinary share earnings rate. The importance attached to the ordinary share earnings rate is manifest from stock exchange publications and the financial columns of the Press. Because of the intervention of an artificial par value, this is the rate which is widely used in making comparisons between firms for management or investment purposes. The par value of ordinary share capital does not depend on accounting processes or balance sheet figures; but as the ordinary share earnings rate is only a stand-in for the theoretically appropriate ordinary equity earnings rate, and as many accountants support the no-par value share on the ground that it eliminates one kind of distortion, no essential violence is done to the point that a relevant measure of the capital employed can only be obtained from an accounting statement such as the balance sheet.

The postulated primacy of the income statement is thus a myth. Internal and external parties using net profit as a measure of general performance, as between periods, or as between firms (the typical case for investors), are obliged to link it with some more satisfactory measure than paid-up capital or the par value of ordinary share capital. A statement such as the balance sheet can provide this measure. The income statement and the balance sheet are thus equally necessary information for informed action. This equality is not impaired merely because, for internal purposes, the figures in the income statement may receive more constant and critical attention than many figures in the balance sheet.

Some have denied the relevance to investors of the balance sheet on the ground that asset backing is only a minor element in the choice of investments. But, as an offer to acquire any company, its assets and undertaking, may be made at any time, asset backing may not be as inconsequential as some believe. This will be more obvious at a later point in the article. In any case, the purpose of this section has been to show that a statement of financial position is relevant to action quite independently of its use for the calculation of asset backing per share.

Others have suggested that yield is the primary test made by investors, and that, as yield calculations do not depend on balance sheet figures, the balance sheet is unnecessary. But yield is not overlooked in the above discussion; it is simply placed in its proper position. A yield calculation depends on the values for a particular dividend rate and a particular share market price. As neither the dividend rate nor the share price may be typical, one must resort to the ordinary share earnings rate or the ordinary equity earnings rate to obtain some idea of the capacity of a company to maintain or improve its rate of dividend distribution. It is only on some such basis that one is able to judge whether (in his opinion) a particular share price undervalues or overvalues the long-run worth of a share.

The Relevance of Cost and Current Value

To make a valid comparison of the ordinary equity earnings rates of different firms at a given time (and this, it is suggested, is the task confronting all actual and potential financial supporters), it is necessary that ordinary shareholders' equities shall be computed on a similar basis. Balance sheets drawn up according to the generally accepted view do not satisfy this condition; companies similar in all respects except for the prices at which assets were acquired will have different values for the shareholders' equity. This is a perennial difficulty. New firms are continually being established to compete with existing firms, and the prices at which similar durable assets of new and old firms are acquired will generally differ by greater amounts the longer the interval between the dates of acquisition of those assets.

The crucial question is: are the prices paid by companies for durable assets acquired some years ago relevant to the present acts and decisions of persons having financial interests in those companies? If one is to judge from the view most commonly expressed in the writings of accountants, the answer is, yes. This answer, however, completely ignores the fact that a price paid is a function of expectations at the time of purchase; it may never again be relevant. A positive answer implies that the purchasing firm and its environment —technology, demand, prices, etc.—are static. This implicit assumption needs only to be stated for its absurdity to be apparent. At any date of reporting subsequent to the date of acquiring an asset, the relevant magnitude with which to represent the asset is its price at the date of reporting (subject, of course, to allowances for use, obsolescence, etc.); for that is the price which, at that time, is a measure of its earning capacity. Only in this way may investors be assured of a reasonable representation of the state of affairs of the ventures they support.

Those who give a positive answer to the question may take some comfort from the appeal judgement in *Re Press Caps Ltd.*, [1949] 1 All E.R. 1013. This case deserves closer attention, however, than it seems to have been given. It was an English take-over case in which one shareholder in Press Caps Ltd., the company taken over, objected to the basis for the exchange of shares on the ground that his company's balance sheet understated the then current value of the company's freehold property by some £60,000. Granting the dissenting shareholder's application, the judge said: "If you find admitted so large a discrepancy as an under-valuation of the most important asset in the balance sheet of this company, an admitted under-valuation of no less than £60,000, I should have thought that threw a great deal of doubt on the appropriateness of the balance sheet as an estimate of value, and through that, therefore, it also threw doubt on the market prices of the shares."

The conclusion seems to be reasonable, but this judgement of the lower court was reversed on appeal. The question at issue on appeal seems to have been what a balance sheet purports to show. The significant points brought out by the appeal judges were:—

(a) Balance sheet figures do not purport to be valuations.

(b) If a balance sheet shows the value of property at "cost less depreciation" there is nothing misleading about it.

(c) If the date of purchase or the date of a valuation of an asset or a group of assets is given in the balance sheet, interested parties may, by examining past balance sheets, readily discover the relationship between the figures given and the current valuation.

(d) The balance sheet does no more than represent the state of the asset accounts in a company's books.

Now, as to (a), whatever the balance sheet purports to be, assets are shown at valuations; the important feature of them is that they are (in the case of fixed assets, at least) out-of-date valuations. It is highly probable that lay users are unaware that they are as out-of-date as they often are.

As to (b), "cost less depreciation" means what it says; formally and perhaps legally, it is not misleading. But one wonders whether it was brought to the notice of the court that the calculations which investors make on the basis of such figures may be very misleading. In particular, the ordinary equity earnings rate would be vastly different according to whether the book values or the current values of assets were used in calculating it.

Point (c), by contrast with (b), is based on the assumption that knowledge of current values is relevant. (It is only proper to note that points (b) and (c) occur in the dicta of two different judges.) But to suggest that an interested party could discover the relationship between the balance sheet figure and the current valuation for a given asset or class of assets is, with respect, to assume that accounting is a much more effective instrument than it is. So complex may be the entries by which the residual figure "cost less depreciation" is obtained, that it would be almost, if not quite, impossible for an investor, or even an accountant asked to advise an investor, to discover the stipulated piece of information from past balance sheets. Scrambled eggs cannot be unscrambled.

Finally, if the view is taken that the balance sheet should only show the state of the asset accounts in a company's books, following point (d), what becomes of the phrase in the audit report which alludes to "a true and correct view of the state of the company's affairs"? If the report were to read "a true and correct view of what the books of the company show the state of the company's affairs to be", the stand represented by point (d) may be excusable, even if the results were meaningless for practical purposes. But the phrase relating to the books of the company is so far removed, in the customary audit report, from the phrase "a true and correct view" that it scarcely serves as a qualifying phrase at all; it would be strange indeed if many lay persons did not interpret the whole statement as a doubly supported assertion, rather than as a qualified assertion. If the balance sheet is only to show the state of the accounts in the company's books, it would be better to say so than to preserve the misleading formula now current.

In all, it seems that the most important practical feature of the statement of the judge in the lower court—that the understatement threw doubt on the market prices of the shares—was not given the attention which, for business purposes, it deserved. The balance sheet needs to be preserved from the futility and sterility to which some would condemn it.

Deviations from the Money Cost Doctrine

There is ample evidence to show that the business community believes that the figures appearing in accounts and entering a balance sheet need not be cost figures. In the early 'thirties many companies wrote down asset values to figures much less than "cost less depreciation". In the last decade many companies have written up asset values to figures far above "cost less depreciation". Over 20 per cent of companies now listed on the Australian stock exchanges have made bonus issues in this 10-year period, a significant proportion of them from revaluations of assets. Quite a number of other companies have written up assets without making bonus issues.

These processes have a definite rationale related to the function of the balance sheet.

Consider first the bonus issues from asset revaluations. At a casual glance it may appear that bonus issues are simply gratuitous distributions of "paper" rights; it has been suggested to the writer that they are a means of compensating shareholders for low incomes received during years of restricted dividends (e.g., war years). But, firstly, the impulse to make a bonus issue cannot arise simply from retrospection. If the rights they carry are to have meaning to shareholders, they must entail prospective increases in dividend distributions; otherwise, notwithstanding the tax-free element of certain bonus issues, the market value of the holdings of any shareholder would be no greater after than before a bonus issue. The issue would be quite meaningless, except in so far as a larger number of shares at lower prices per share established a wider market and allowed market prices to rise slightly above the market value of the original holding; and this effect can be obtained more simply by a straight share split.

Most bonus issues have been made in the expectation of a higher dividend appropriation than the pre-bonus capital would have required. Now, this expectation could scarcely have been countenanced without a rise in net profits. In most cases there has been in fact such a rise, to the point where the earnings rate on the pre-revaluation ordinary shareholders' equity appeared to be unusually high. So also did the ordinary share earnings rate appear, and the companies concerned began to show the symptoms of under-capitalization (just as, in the 'thirties, the ordinary share earnings rate of many companies fell to the point where they were obviously over-capitalized).

The appearance of under-capitalization in recent years has arisen from the failure of accounting practices to represent business realities. In reality values have risen; in books of account the rise is ignored—with two consequences. Firstly, the higher current values of the services of durable assets being consumed are not charged against the higher money incomes being earned, so that disclosed money profits are in excess of strict currently available surpluses (or economic incomes). Secondly, the present values of ordinary shareholders' equities are understated as long as they are computed on the basis of money outlays, which were relevant enough at the time of acquisition of durable assets but which are irrelevant to present action. As a result, ordinary share earnings rates are distorted upwards by overstatement of net profits, and ordinary equity earnings rates are distorted upwards both by overstatement of the net profit and understatement of the capital employed (under and over being relative to the current real state of the magnitudes referred to). These rates thus reach unusually high and misleading levels.

Now, the appearance of under-capitalization has its practical drawbacks.[2] To avoid these in the face of rigidities in the accounting processes, businessmen have been obliged to force on accountants adjustments of asset and equity values which accounting doctrine opposes. It appears that the original cost doctrine is not serviceable under conditions other than perfectly static conditions, and that those who assert its propriety under all conditions and who frown on revaluations and bonus issues are, in essence, denying that it is the prime function of accounting to provide information appropriate and relevant to informed and reasoned action.

Consider now the case of companies which have revalued assets without making bonus issues. This action cannot be attributed in any way to a patronizing desire to augment shareholders' incomes. In some cases revaluation seems to have been prompted by take-over bids or the fear of take-over bids. That take-over bids are made or feared is evidence of the existence of financial advantages which are not disclosed in the financial statements, but which, if those statements are to be realistic, can and could be shown. Explaining the decision of his board to revalue certain assets, one chairman of directors recently asserted that it was dangerous to underestimate the value of fixed assets when take-overs were so prevalent; he did not think his company was likely to be taken over, but, should anyone try, shareholders would know what their assets were worth. Another said that revaluation was made to enable the next published balance sheet to reflect more accurately the current financial position. Examples could be multiplied, but from such lines of thinking it is manifest that businessmen think of the balance sheet as something more significant than a mere "connecting link between successive income statements"[3].

Conclusion

The balance sheets of many companies may, in fact, be misleading. But that the balance sheet has a significant purpose is demonstrable. It may be used to assess the respective equities of creditors and shareholders, facilitating the choice between loan and share issues as new sources of funds; and it is the only source of some of the most useful criteria for judging the adequacy of net profits. To assert the importance of the income statement and to deny the balance sheet any function other than as a means of deriving subsequent income statements is simply to devise a conventional rationalization of

[2] As has also the appearance of over-capitalization; see the writer's *Financial Management,* 1967, Law Book Co., pp. 121-22 (revised note).

[3] Committee on Accounting Procedure, American Institute of Accountants, *Accounting Research Bulletin No.* 1.

conventional methods. The practical and constructive course of action would rather be to examine the reasons why contemporary balance sheets are misleading, why they lead to inappropriate decisions and how their deficiencies may be eliminated or modified. Balance sheet figures which do not represent the facts have much wider repercussions than many recognize. Obviously investors may be misinformed, to their disadvantage; less obviously, the distribution of resources among industries and firms may follow patterns which deviate materially from those which would arise from really representative information; even the forms of the organization of firms and industries may be influenced. If effects of these kinds may be induced, it is much more reasonable to seek to make the balance sheet a useful instrument than to write it off. At least this is the view of many company directors.

11

FINANCIAL INFORMATION AND THE SECURITIES MARKET*

Accounting as Language

Accounting has occasionally been described by its exponents as a language. The use of accounting summaries and of specific pieces of information contained in those summaries is so widespread that this communicative function of accounting has deserved much more critical attention than it has been given.

The general position taken in this paper is that accounting is a language system, whatever else it may be. Accounting, like other languages, is a social instrument. Like other systems of signs, such as morse code or the signs and symbols of mathematics, it is concerned with a specific facet of the interpersonal relations of the members of a society. But this facet—the economic facet—is so much a matter of common concern that the importance of having a system of signs which is widely understandable cannot be gainsaid.

One class of the common understandings which ensure the viability of a society subsists in the customs and laws which are accepted as defining the rights and interests of individuals and the relationships between them. As self-interested actions may adversely affect the rights and interests of others, the general laws provide the members of a society with remedies or with the means of discovering whether grievances are remediable. The balancing of interpersonal rights and interests depends on one person being able to discover whether his specific rights and interests have been promoted or prejudiced by the actions of another.

Discovery is in some circumstances relatively easy. If A builds a house for B, it is not difficult to discover whether the roof leaks: dripping water is an observable sign of a deficiency in fulfilling a contract. But if A puts his savings, as an investment, into the hands of officers of Company B it is not easy to discover whether those officers have used his savings in his interest. Small associations by their own rules, and larger associations by rules embodied in the general law, seek to provide the means by which individuals may discover whether their contributions have been used in their interests; generally, by requiring that the officers of such associations shall present periodically an audited financial statement or statements.

---

* First published in *Abacus,* Vol. 1, No. 1, September 1965, pp. 3-30. Prepared as the basis of the Australian Society of Accountants Endowed Lecture in the University of Sydney, September 1963. Mimeograph 1963.

In all voluntary associations (including companies) the right of each individual financial contributor to choose what is in his interest and to judge for himself whether continued participation is in his interest is generally assured. But there are two fundamental conditions which must be fulfilled if he is to judge in an informed manner on the basis of the financial statements he is given.

The first is general comprehensibility. In everyday language there are rules by which the signs (words) are interpreted. And there are rules by which signs are linked to form statements. We speak of the "meanings" of words and statements. There is nothing fixed or unalterable about these rules. They are accepted because they make communication possible. In everyday language there are many words which can convey a great variety of impressions, or which may be interpreted in a great variety of ways. If we wish to evoke in others responses of a specific kind, we resort to signs which have precise and unequivocal meanings. We specify by definition the interpretation to be given to the signs we use.

In face to face discussion the process of definition involves both parties. Unless the words used have agreed meanings, each party will explain, amplify or restrict the interpretation he intends to adopt, so that in the end a common interpretation is agreed upon. Communication at a distance, however, is only effective if the signs used have unequivocal or accepted interpretations or if the interpretations are specified. In the context of the affairs of corporate business the pre-eminent form of communication at a distance is the publication of financial statements. On such occasions there is no face to face discussion, no possibility of explanation. The community places great trust in the terms used and the statements made, and by implication it places great trust in the methods by which those statements are derived. But this trust is only justified if, in fact, the terms used have a uniform and accepted interpretation, so that no amplification, explanation or clarification is required.

We have noticed that accounting is a special purpose language, that it is concerned with the economic aspect of affairs. But it is not to be considered as a language privy to accountants. Balance sheets and income statements are not drawn up by accountants to inform other accountants. They are prepared so that persons and business firms may communicate with other persons and business firms. The terms employed in them will only communicate anything if those terms have the same interpretations as business usage generally.

The second condition of informed judgement is that the system of singular statements which constitute the financial statements shall have a structure which is identical with the structure of the objects or events about which those statements are made. We speak of this as the requirement of correspondence. Every event having financial significance changes the financial characteristics of an entity in a specific way. Persons having financial interests in the entity, but remote from the point at which such events may be observed directly, depend on the system of signs by which those objects are represented in making their responses to changes in the entity. Obviously any event not communicated will leave interested parties uninformed, and thus unable to judge the consequences of the event. Equally, any event communicated by the use of a sign which misrepresents its extent will also leave interested parties uninformed.

It is necessary to elucidate "the financial significance" of an event. The financial significance of an event is the money measure of its effects. If an event occurs at a certain point of time, say, a sale of goods for cash, the financial significance of the event is the amount of the price, which is also the amount of the cash received. If, on the occurrence of a subsequent event, say, banking the cash proceeds, it is discovered that the cash tokens are counterfeit, the financial significance of this event is the amount of the cash lost which is also the amount of the loss sustained. It would clearly be nonsensical to carry the counterfeit cash tokens in the safe as if they were cash and not to take cognizance of the loss. It would be equally nonsensical to say that the sale was not made. Every event must find its way into the system of statements which represents the system of events, and in the form of signs which represent its financial significance.

In the above example, the refusal of the banker to accept counterfeit tokens is an action beyond the control of the vendor of the goods. Yet it is an event which the latter cannot disregard. Similarly if the market price of goods held rises or falls, this also is an event which cannot be disregarded. For, if no statement of the financial effect is incorporated in the system, no recipient of statements issuing from the system will be informed, and no informed action can be taken. If the price has risen, the recipient of such a defective statement will not know that a greater flow of cash may be expected; nor, if the price has fallen, that a smaller flow of cash may be expected.

It is the thesis of this paper that the financial information made available to the securities market meets neither of these tests of general comprehensibility and correspondence. It follows that no investor is able to judge whether or not the officers of companies are conducting their business in his interest (subject to the interests of others); that many companies may therefore receive far less credit than they deserve and that many companies receive far more credit than they deserve; and that there is no firm foundation for any informed judgement as between deserving and undeserving companies.

Decline and Fall of Financial Reporting

The prevailing attitude towards the published financial statements should be interpreted against the background of over 100 years of developing opinion. We propose to examine some features of this history with the object of showing that habit and faulty arguments have led to a situation where reasoning from financial statements is almost pointless.

The English Companies Registration and Regulation Act of 1844 required that a "full and fair balance sheet" should be prepared annually and approved by the directors of companies before delivery to the auditors; the appointment of auditors was made a prerequisite to registration. The balance sheet and auditors' report were required to be filed with the Registrar of Companies. However, the Act gave the Registrar no disciplinary powers, and nine years later the failure of the Act to secure the provision of information was noticed in the course of an inquiry on assurance associations. The Acts of 1856 and 1862 relegated the financial publicity provisions to an appended, optional, model set of articles of association, leaving such publicity therefore at the discretion of incorporators.[1] There was thus far less occasion for critical examination of what was expected of balance sheets than may have been expected if publicity had been mandatory.

The model articles appended to the Acts of 1856 and 1862 provided that "the correctness of the balance sheet [shall be] ascertained by one or more auditor or auditors.... The auditors shall...state whether, in their opinion, the balance sheet is...properly drawn up so as to exhibit a true and correct view of the state of the company's affairs". The Act of 1900 made the audit of accounts compulsory and retained the phrase "a true and correct view". Apparently those who drafted these Acts believed that there was such a thing as a correct balance sheet and a true and correct view of the state of a company's affairs. It is evident that those who interpreted the law adopted substantially the same view. The following are extracts from judicial and legal opinions in some of the significant cases:—

1887—It was the duty of the auditor...to see that [the balance sheet] was a *true and accurate representation* of the company's affairs[2].

1894—...the *accounts must show the truth* and not be misleading or fraudulent[3].

1895—The auditor's business is to ascertain and state the *true financial position* of the company at the time of the audit. ...*a full and fair balance sheet* must be such a balance sheet as to convey *a truthful statement as to the company's position*[4].

1926—...an auditor [is]...responsible for ascertaining *the true position* of the business, whether disclosed properly by the books or not[5].

1931—...the fundamental object of the profession is to ensure that in the documents which are produced a *true and accurate account* of the affairs of the company is given...the law requires this, that the shareholders shall have put before them *true and accurate accounts*[6].

---

[1] For the history of these provisions see Bishop Carleton Hunt, *The Development of the Business Corporation in England* 1800-1867, Cambridge, Harvard University Press, 1936, pp. 96-8.

[2] Stirling, J., *Leeds Estate Building and Investment Society Ltd.* v. *Shepherd* (1887), 36 Ch. D. 787. Emphasis added in this and following extracts.

[3] Lindley, L.J., *Verner* v. *General and Commercial Investment Trust Ltd.*, [1894] 2 Ch. 239.

[4] Lindley, L.J., *Re London and General Bank Ltd., Ex parte Theobold* (*No.* 2), [1895-9] All E.R. 953. The last sentence is from the judgment of Rigby, L.J.

[5] Astbury, J., *Trustee of the Property of Apfel* (*a bankrupt*) v. *Annan, Dexter & Co.*

[6] The Attorney-General, Closing Speech for the Prosecution, *R.* v. *Lord Kylsant, and Another* (1931), reported in Collin Brooks (ed.), *The Royal Mail Case*, Edinburgh and London, William Hodge & Company Limited, 1933, pp. 210, 212.

There is persistent reference to the true position. All such statements are recognitions of the requirements of correspondence. But in fact practice did not and still does not conform with these precepts.

The early company laws appear to have assumed that the practice of accounting followed well defined rules which were directed towards the discovery of the "true" state of affairs. But in fact the profession had given little if any thought to the matter. Understandably so. Reporting for the protection of investors and creditors was in a sense a novel responsibility, thrust upon accountants whose methods were either habitual or *ad hoc.* They saw their duty as serving the demands of businessmen, a situation they were accustomed to and against which they had no grounds for complaint. The legal cases make it quite clear that there were no settled principles and that accountants were willing to make such entries as businessmen required, even if they required entries which were different in principle from time to time. The legislators and the accountants of the time were at the mercy of the prevailing spirit of liberalism and the doctrine of *laissez-faire* in economic matters. The rising strength of the mercantile classes in conjunction with the temper of the times was no doubt responsible for the relegation of publicity rules to the status of optional articles. They were subject to gradual attrition.

As an example we turn to a case of 1906, concerned primarily with internal or secret reserves. The court expressed the opinion: "The purpose of the balance sheet is primarily to show that the financial position of the company is at least as good as there stated, not to show that it is not or may not be better."[7]

Under the Act of 1900 auditors were required to state whether the balance sheet exhibits a true and correct view of the state of the company's affairs as shown by the books. Anything less than a true and correct view seems clearly to be inconsistent with the Act. A statement of financial position which is in any way inferior to the actual position surely does not comply with the Act, notwithstanding the above dictum.

In any event, if the purpose of the balance sheet is to show that the financial position is at least as good as there stated, how does it do this? The balance sheet contains a set of singular statements. No one can tell from the face of it whether it is at least as good as anything. In order to show that the stated position is at least as good as something else, it is necessary that the "something else" be shown also. If the balance sheet is to meet the implicit requirements of the Act and the dictum of the court, the "correct" position must be shown, as well as a "less good" position. But if the correct position is shown no one surely will pay any attention to the "less good" position.

Again, if it is contended that a less good position may be shown "by reason of prudence", how is any outsider to know whether a

---

[7] Buckley, J., *Newton* v. *Birmingham Small Arms Co. Ltd.,* [1906] 2 Ch. 378. The sense of this judgment taken as a whole is not given fully by the quoted extract. But this extract seems to have set the tone of a considerable amount of subsequent thinking.

company's management is prudent or not? Only by having also a statement showing the correct position as well. Without this, he is in effect obliged to take the prudence of management for granted. Not only does this make nonsense of the publicity provisions of the Act; it is a position which is quite imprudent from the point of view of investors and creditors, as the history of commercial failures and frauds amply demonstrates. Statement of a less good position may be, and has often turned out to be, as much a matter of sheer bad faith as of prudence.

This case strengthened the tendency to anarchy in financial reporting. "True and correct" became a mere formula. It came to be held that there are many "true and correct" statements of the state of affairs of a company, including the state of affairs represented by the books of account, no matter how diverse the rules employed in setting up the accounts. And this in spite of what is known to every businessman and to every intelligent person, that mere statements in books of account do not have superiority, as facts, over the facts of the market place. The consequence of this looseness of thinking is made clear in judicial dicta in a more recent case. What was referred to as "well established practice" in the course of an Australian judgment of 1939[8] turns out, on reflection, to be not one practice but a series of quite conflicting practices, apparently available to any and all companies. By direct statement or by implication from the judgment:—

(a) fixed assets may be shown at cost when *cost does not understate* their "true value" (e.g., at the time of purchase);

(b) fixed assets may be shown at cost when *cost does understate* their "true value" (e.g., after an "accretion in value");

(c) fixed assets may be shown at any selected figure higher than cost even though this *higher figure does understate* their "true value" (e.g., on revaluation);

(d) fixed assets may be shown at a given higher figure which *does not understate* their "true value";

(e) fixed assets may be shown at less than cost when *such figure does understate* the "true value";

(f) fixed assets may be shown at less than cost when *such figure does not understate* the "true value";

(g) fixed assets may be shown at cost even if cost *overstates* the "true value".

If all these possibilities can exist, what then is a balance sheet? A balance sheet is a statement which may understate or overstate or state the "true strength of a company's position". And if that is all a balance sheet is, it is nothing. It certainly cannot be expected that any balance sheet shall correspond with the substantive position of a company.

Complacency with this state of affairs has become general. The Institute of Chartered Accountants in England and Wales apparently

---

[8] Evatt, J., *Dickson* v. *The Federal Commissioner of Taxation* (1939), 1 A.I.T.R. 515, at p. 535.

had no difficulty in convincing the Cohen Committee on Company Law Amendment (1945) that "A balance sheet... does not as a general rule purport to show the net worth of an undertaking at any particular date or the present realizable value of such items as goodwill, land, buildings, plant and machinery, nor except in cases where the realizable value is less than cost, does it normally show the realizable value of stock in trade"[9]. This extract from the Institute's evidence is incorporated, uncritically, in the report. There is no discussion of whether a "true and correct view" results. What is more, of course, it is little help to know what a balance sheet is not. One would like to know what it is. For if there is no definition of what it is, there is no possibility of it being generally comprehensible. And if there is no definition of what it is, it is extremely unlikely that by sheer good fortune it will turn out to correspond with the state of affairs at the date it bears.

Laws and Regulations Relating to Financial Publicity

We propose to show in this section that, although the contemporary laws dealing with financial publicity express the best of intentions, they fail to achieve their purpose. There has been a growing tendency for laws and regulations to be more specific as to details, with the object, one may presume, of closing loopholes and securing greater clarity in published statements. The object is entirely worthy. But the more specific the laws become, the more likely are they to meet the firmly entrenched habits of practice, and the more difficult does it become to avoid inconsistencies. We wish to show that looseness of expression is widespread. We will consider some of the broad features of existing English and United States laws and regulations.

(a) United Kingdom

The Companies Act of 1948, in common with earlier acts, gives no statement of the general intention of its provisions in relation to the protection of the interests of investors and creditors. It is thus to be interpreted strictly in terms of its explicit provisions. On the face of it these seem to be quite clear:—

"Every balance sheet of a company shall give a true and fair view of the state of affairs of the company as at the end of its financial year, and every profit and loss account of a company shall give a true and fair view of the profit or loss of the company for the financial year." (s. 149.)

The Act provides for the appointment of auditors who shall report to the members on the accounts examined by the auditors and on the financial statements laid before the company in general meeting. The auditors are required to state, *inter alia*:—

"Whether the company's balance sheet and profit and loss account dealt with by the report are in agreement with the books of account and returns; and

[9] *Report of the Committee on Company Law Amendment*, London, H.M.S.O., 1945, para. 98.

"Whether, in their opinion and to the best of their information, and according to the explanations given them, the said accounts give the information required by this Act in the manner so required and give a true and fair view—

"(a) in the case of the balance sheet, of the state of the company's affairs as at the end of its financial year; and

"(b) in the case of the profit and loss account of the profit or loss for its financial year." (Ninth Schedule, 3 (1)(2).)

Some have taken comfort in the substitution of "true and fair" for the wording "true and correct" of the Companies Act of 1929. But verbal quibbling cannot overcome the continued use of "true". The Eighth Schedule to the Act sets out in detail matters which shall be disclosed in the financial statements; but s. 149 (3) of the Act makes it clear that mere compliance with the provisions of the Eighth Schedule is not to be considered sufficient if compliance fails to give a true and fair view.

Now some parts of the Eighth Schedule are curiously at odds with the "true and fair view" which the Act makes mandatory. Section 11 (7) of the schedule clearly contemplates that the current assets, or some of them, may be stated at amounts other than their value "on realization in the ordinary course of the company's business". It runs: "If in the opinion of the directors any of the current assets have not a value, on realization in the ordinary course of the company's business, at least equal to the amount at which they are stated, the fact that the directors are of that opinion [shall be disclosed]."

There seems to be little doubt that a true and fair view would be given, of the company's position in respect of any asset, if the amount at which it is shown is its value "on realization in the ordinary course of business". This basis seems to be a going concern basis without question. Any other amount would not give a true and fair view. If the statements were prepared on this principle s. 11 (7) would be pointless; and if they were not prepared on this principle they would not give a true and fair view. In fact, therefore, the Act contemplates its own defiance, and implicitly encourages defiance. It will be noted that the above Section entails that if the stated amount is equal to realizable value no comment is required; if the stated amount is less than realizable value no comment is required; and if the stated amount exceeds realizable value comment is required. These are three mutually exclusive and possible rules; but they cannot all give a true and fair view. What is more, disclosure is required in only one of the two permissible variants from realizable value, and even then the extent of the variation is not required to be stated. This is a further departure from the true and fair view, which the Act appears to condone.

Dealing with fixed assets, s. 5 (1) of the schedule provides that the method of arriving at the amount of any fixed asset shall be to take the difference between cost, or a valuation, and the aggregate amount provided or written off, since acquisition or valuation, for depreciation or diminution in value. We observe firstly that no restraints are placed on the valuations which may appear in the statements; valuations must therefore conform with the general test—the true and fair view criterion. But the schedule permits the balances in the accounts at the date of the commencement of the Act to be accepted as valuations, regardless of the true and fair view test. Secondly, the alternative basis, cost, is given special mention as if there were a certain magic about cost which constituted it a reasonable basis from which to derive a true and fair view. In fact, as time passes, cost becomes less and less significant as a basis, due to shifts in specific prices arising from changes in demand and technology, and shifts in the general level of prices. Thirdly, no rules are given as to what interpretation is to be placed on the "amounts provided or written off for depreciation or diminution in value".

The only precise thing about these three specifications is the reference to cost and, as we have suggested, costs may be plainly misleading. It would not be surprising therefore if the Act were taken as giving approval to cost as a basis, but otherwise as permitting all existing practices to remain as before. True, there is the overriding provision of s. 149 (3) of the Act, mentioned above. But where the legislation appears to give precise rules in amplification of a general rule, it would be reasonable to suppose they were amplifications and not contrary to the spirit of the Act. As Gower has observed: "These words [of s. 149 of the Act] ought to make it impossible to support the view, formerly held, that a balance sheet is an historical account only and that it need only give an accurate picture of the past. Nevertheless they do not appear to have had any effect on accounting practice regarding valuations, which, so far at any rate as fixed capital is concerned, remain on the purely historical basis of cost minus depreciation, which may bear little relation to value as at the end of the current financial year."[10]

We believe the absence of the expected effect is due to the inconsistencies between the body of the Act and the provisions of the schedules. In brief it is the existence of contradictions in the legislation which is responsible in some measure for lack of precision, lack of correspondence and lack of general comprehensibility in the financial statements which result.

(b) United States of America

Although the incorporation of business firms is regulated by laws of the several states, the major financial publicity provisions affecting incorporated businesses occur in Federal statutes. The interests of investors are sought to be protected by the Securities Act of 1933 as subsequently amended, and by certain other acts which created the Securities and Exchange Commission and provided for the administration by it of laws relating to certain securities and of dealers in securities. The 1933 Act has been described as a disclosure statute.[11]

---

[10] L. C. B. Gower, *The Principles of Modern Company Law*, London, Stevens & Sons Ltd., 1954, p. 115, Note.

[11] Louis H. Rappaport, *S.E.C. Accounting Practice and Procedure*, New York, The Ronald Press Co., 1959, p. 4.

In the course of a recent report on the regulation of securities it was observed: "Disclosure is the cornerstone of Federal securities regulation. It is the *sine qua non* of investment analysis and decision. It is the great safeguard that governs conduct of corporate managements in many of their activities. It is the best bulwark against reckless corporate publicity and irresponsible recommendation and sale of securities."[12]

Whereas the English statutes make no mention of the purpose of the financial publicity they prescribe, the Securities Act is in this respect quite explicit. Its long title is: "An Act to provide full and fair disclosure of the character of securities sold in interstate and foreign commerce and through the mails, and to prevent frauds in the sale thereof, etc." The body of the act makes repeated reference to disclosure of things "necessary or appropriate in the public interest or for the protection of investors".

The Acts deal with the provision of information by means of prospectuses, by the registration of particulars relating to securities issues and issuers, and for the filing of supplemental or periodic reports, including financial statements, by all issuers of securities registered on a national securities exchange. Detailed rules relating to the form and content of financial statements required to be filed with the S.E.C. are given in Regulation S-X and Accounting Series Releases issued from time to time by the Commission. Disclosure is required of a large number of specified items, subject to the frequent proviso that amounts which are not material need not be disclosed. "Material" is defined as limiting the information required to those matters as to which an average prudent investor ought reasonably to be informed before purchasing the security registered (Regulation S-X, Rule 1-02).

The Securities Act gives a right of action to any person acquiring a security in respect of which the registration statement contained "an untrue statement of a material fact or omitted to state a material fact". Such an action may lie against auditors, but any such expert may prove in defence that "he had, after reasonable investigation, reasonable ground to believe and did believe . . . that the statements therein were true and that there was no omission to state a material fact required to be stated therein or necessary to make the statement therein not misleading". The standard of reasonableness "shall be that required of a prudent man in the management of his own property".

The character of securities: It is reasonable to suppose that the character of securities at the time of issue is represented by the whole contents of the registration statement; and that the character of securities at any time subsequent to issue is represented by the registration statement together with the latest supplemental or periodical statements filed with the Commission. The public may thus discover how the character of securities has been modified since the date of issue. But modification does not arise by mere entries in the books of account; it arises by the impact on a company of its own actions and

[12] Report of the Special Study of Securities Markets: abstracted in the *Securities and Exchange Commission News Digest,* 3 April 1963, at p. 20.

its environment (including rises and falls in market prices). Only if the books of account correspond with the impact of actions and environment will statements based on them represent the character of securities as modified up to the date of the latest statement. Such statements will then be true statements.

True statements: The right of action for untrue statements implies that true statements are expected. Now if we find in a balance sheet long after their date of purchase the statement "Land and buildings (at cost) . . . $200,000", we may say this is a true statement; but only if we consider the date of purchase not to be a material aspect of the truth of the statement. Unless the date is specified, no two persons are likely to interpret the statement in a similar manner; the statement does not in fact meet the test of general comprehensibility. Now suppose further that the market price has, since the date of purchase, risen by 50 per cent. Has this rise any impact on the character of the company's securities? Certainly; its occurrence may make it possible to issue new securities having the same asset-support as issues made before the rise. If the filed financial statements fail to incorporate this change they cannot be said to disclose the character of the securities, or to be a true statement of the character of the securities at the time; and they do not meet the test of correspondence.

It may be argued that to show the assets at cost may be a true statement of what the books of account show. But the books of account are not to be taken as evidence on their own of the truth or falsity of any statement. The S.E.C. report on the McKesson and Robbins case (1940) and statements of the American Institute recognize the practice of examining inventories and receivables independently of the books of account[13]. It is of little use to verify the existence of these assets without giving equal care to their monetary representation at that date. And indeed the 1933 and 1934 Acts refer to material facts, not to facts as they are represented in books of account. If the books of account fail to represent material facts, financial statements based on them fail to meet the requirements of the Acts.

Reasonable ground for belief: A prudent man in the management of his own property would be concerned with any rise or fall in its price by comparison with cost. Any such rise or fall will influence his insurance cover, for example. It will affect the amount he can borrow on the security of it. It will affect his expectations of cash receipts if he has to dispose of it for any reason. There seems to be ample reason here for reflecting rises and falls in the market prices of property held; and there seems to be no defence for auditors who accept, as true, statements which fail to do so.

The above comments on the "character of securities", "true statements" and "reasonable ground for belief" are not made for the

---

[13] S.E.C. *Accounting Series Release No.* 19 Summary and Conclusions, para. 8. A.I.C.P.A. *Statement on Auditing Procedure, No.* 1, October 1939. It will be noticed that these practices conform with the judicial dicta quoted above.

purpose of comparison with prevailing practice, but to point out the inconsistency of the Acts and Regulations themselves. It almost seems as if, when formulating Regulation S-X, care was taken to give the balance sheet the most amorphous character possible. Rule 5-02 reads, in respect of marketable securities, inventories, securities of affiliates, property, plant and equipment, patents, etc., all severally, "State the basis of determining the amounts". The word "amount" can mean anything. It could mean physical quantities. But in the context of a balance sheet it could mean cost, or market price, or any other money amount. In fact, in the detailed schedules required there is a strong suggestion that the preferred amount is cost, and, to judge from American literature and practice, the cost basis is indeed preferred. But cost does not meet any of the three tests we have just discussed—tests which are embodied in the very regulations and laws which are expected to serve as "the best bulwark against reckless corporate publicity". The lack of precision in the rules defeats the very good intentions of the Acts themselves. As we shall presently show, the vagueness of the rules has permitted extensive proliferation of sub-rules; to the point where George O. May was moved, in 1955, to observe: "today it is difficult to decide just what significance may be attached to the annual accounts of a corporation"[14].

Professional Recommendations

The laws and regulations of the United Kingdom and the United States leave many matters to the discretion—of someone. Or they presuppose that the terms and expressions they use have a limited and not markedly divergent interpretation among those whose behaviour they prescribe. But in this they are mistaken, as an examination of professional recommendations and practices will show. We will deal with limited features only of these recommendations and practices for the two countries—but in reverse order.

(a) United States of America

An extensive treatment of inventory pricing is given in the Research Bulletins of the American Institute of Certified Public Accountants[15]. The opening paragraph states that "inventories are required both for the statement of financial position and for the periodic measurement of income". At a later point it is stated that "the major objective in selecting a method of [inventory pricing] should be to choose the one which, under the circumstances, most clearly reflects periodic income". This latter statement represents at least some recognition of the principle of correspondence. But no reason is given for the emphasis on periodic income; some reason might be expected in view of the

---

[14] Talk with G. O. May on his 80th Birthday, *The Journal of Accountancy*, June 1955.

[15] References are to *Accounting Research and Terminology Bulletins*, Final Edition, 1961, Ch. 4.

inclusion in the first quoted statement of reference to financial position[16].

The statement goes on to permit cost as the primary basis, cost being interpreted as "the price paid or consideration given to acquire an asset". But this interpretation is not simple. The *Accountants' Handbook*[17] presents 10 acceptable "cost" methods. For partly processed and processed inventories, determination of cost commonly entails allocation of at least some overheads. Vance[18] gives seven methods of distributing overheads (including depreciation) to products. Further, the allocation of depreciation to particular periods (an operation antecedent to the allocation of overheads to products) may be made on 13 different bases, according to Grant and Norton[19].

It will be clear that there are $10 \times 7 \times 13 = 910$ different ways of arriving at the cost of items of inventory which are semi-processed or processed goods. Further as some specific items of the inventory of any one company may be valued on bases different from other items, clearly the number of methods available for arriving at the cost of a mixed inventory is much greater than the number given above.

The A.I.C.P.A. statement goes on to say that inventory may be stated at less than cost, when the market price is lower than cost. And, "in exceptional cases", inventories may properly be stated above cost. As no definition is given of exceptional cases, it is permissible for any company to claim it is an exceptional case and thus to state all or some part of its inventory above cost. These are open-ended possibilities; there is no effective limit to the variety of numbers of money units which may be assigned; and there is potentially a large number of permissible rules.

The statement further permits the lower of cost or market as a basis. It gives three interpretations of "market". It permits the application of this cost or market rule, to each item, or to the total inventory or to categories of inventory. Now if there are 910 ways of obtaining cost, three ways of obtaining market, and three ways of applying the rule, there are $910 \times 3 \times 3 = 8190$ ways of obtaining a figure for "cost or market whichever is the lower".

Given 910 ways of finding cost and 8190 ways of finding cost or market whichever is the lower, there are 9100 ways of valuing an inventory, disregarding the two open-ended methods, above cost and below cost. But even this is a very conservative estimate. For example, in applying the cost or market rule to categories of

---

[16] Throughout this paper we deal primarily with balance sheets, notwithstanding the popular emphasis on income accounts in the literature. Strictly, the income account is only an amplification of one item in the balance sheet—the change in the capital account, or the residual equity account. The popular emphasis has been challenged in "The Function of the Balance Sheet", see p. 166, *ante*.

[17] Fourth Edition, Wixon and Kell, eds, New York, The Ronald Press Co., 1956, s. 12.

[18] Lawrence L. Vance, *Theory and Technique of Cost Accounting*, New York, Henry Holt and Co., 1959, p. 189.

[19] *Depreciation*, New York, The Ronald Press Co., 1955, p. 185.

inventory, any two firms in a given industry may have different numbers of categories. And, again, in finding depreciation charges, any two firms in a given industry may use different expected service lives. The number of ways of ascertaining the price of an inventory is thus indeterminate, but very large indeed. So therefore is the number of ways of computing a net profit and the number of ways of obtaining the financial position.

(b) United Kingdom

The Institute of Chartered Accountants in England and Wales has an even more comprehensive statement on the valuation of commodity stocks[20]. We will vary the analysis from that given to the American statement. We will notice only variations in methods which are explicitly given in the recommendations.

The broad bases permitted are cost, net realizable value and replacement price. There are five "principal" cost methods: unit cost, first-in first-out, average cost, standard cost and adjusted selling price. The first four of these may be computed differently for partly processed and processed stocks; cost may include only direct charges, or direct charges plus portion of all overheads. There are thus three explicitly stated possibilities. In choosing between cost, net realizable value and replacement price, the total stock may be considered as single items, as categories or as an aggregate. There is also a possibility of using a price greater than cost in special cases, but as in the treatment of the American pronouncements this will be disregarded.

Given three bases, four cost methods, three methods of finding cost (i.e., of treating overheads) and three methods of choosing the final figure, there are $3 \times 4 \times 3 \times 3 = 108$ explicitly permitted methods. If we were to include the various alternative ways of finding depreciation charges and allocating overheads, the total number of possibilities would run into thousands, as in the case of the American pronouncements. But for variety we will extend the example.

The recommendations in respect of fixed assets stipulate that historical cost shall be the basis for stating their amounts. But under some circumstances revaluation of assets is permissible (Recommendation N15-30). There are thus two bases. Four methods of writing off depreciation are mentioned (Recommendation N9). It is recognized that for different types of assets different depreciation methods may be appropriate (Recommendation N9-9). If we suppose that there are three clases of fixed assets in most balance sheets, then any combination of three methods is possible. The number of permissible sets of rules for a three-item statement of fixed assets is thus $2 \times 4 \times 3 = 24$.

The recommendation on the treatment of investments (N20) permits four methods of stating the amount of trade investments,

[20] The Institute of Chartered Accountants in England and Wales, *Treatment of Stock in Trade and Work in Progress in Financial Accounts,* Recommendation N22, 16 November 1960.

four methods for quoted investments, and three methods for shares in subsidiaries. For any company having all three types of investments the number of possible sets of rules for arriving at their aggregate amount is $4 \times 4 \times 3 = 48$.

We will desist. From the above it will be apparent that the number of possible methods, or sets of rules, for obtaining the aggregate amount of the assets of a company which has commodity stocks, three classes of fixed assets and the above-mentioned three classes of security investments is $108 \times 24 \times 48 = 124{,}416$! And this is only a conservative estimate, which, by considering alternatives implicit in some of the rules such as those for depreciation, could be increased at least tenfold.

A million sets of mutually exclusive rules, each giving a true and fair view of a company's state of affairs and its profits! This is absurd. Where there are so many possible rules there are in effect no rules, and where there are no rules there can be no correspondence, no general comprehensibility, no language—a set of signs, maybe, but no language. It is as if there were a million people with different foot-rules, or a million motorists with different road rules. Reason and order are deposed and chaos is enthroned in their place.

Suppose we put ourselves in the position of any investor or creditor who has the choice of buying the securities of one of a number of companies. We will be told on the face of the best balance sheets the specific rules adopted by each company for each asset or class of assets. But it is highly improbable that the sets of rules for those companies will be the same; and even if they appear to be the same (e.g., by the use of multivalent words like "cost", "valuation", etc.) it is highly improbable that the compilers of the accounts of the several firms will have used the descriptive terms for similar things. Now the conditions under which an investor or creditor may make valid comparisons between the substantive features of two or more companies—e.g., their profitability, liquidity, solvency—include the condition that the rules for deriving the figures to be compared shall be identical for all companies. The superabundance of alternatives makes this highly improbable; any attempt to make comparisons is thus defeated at the outset by those who choose the specific rules.

Some Empirical Evidence of Inadequacies

Those who believe that an historical examination of the origins of confusion has little bearing on contemporary affairs will be unaffected by observations on the decline in the quality of financial reporting. Those who accept legislation as authority will be unmoved by demonstrations of inconsistencies in the law. And those who regard professional group pronouncements as the distillation of practical wisdom will brush aside the observations of the previous section as curious but unconvincing arithmetical exercises. In this section we present three pieces of empirical evidence for the view that contemporary financial reporting is misleading, and seriously misleading, in the securities market.

(a) THE BASES OF INVENTORY PRICING

The adjoining table gives the results of three studies of methods of reporting the bases used for valuing commodity stocks in company balance sheets in the U.S.A., Canada and Australia. We select the treatment of commodity stocks for its obvious importance both in deriving net profit and in deriving the statement of financial position.

Bases of Stock Valuation

	U.S.A.	*Canada*	*Australia*
Year	1959	1958	1959
Number of Companies	600	300	300
A. *Disclosed bases*			
Cost	165	40	49
Market; contract price	10	9	2
B. *Mixed bases*			
Lower of cost or market value; cost not in excess of market*	524	257	67
Cost or less than cost	20	12	126
Cost or market	–	–	10
Lower of cost or replacement ..	–	4	9
Market or less than market ..	3	–	3
Lower of cost or valuation ..	–	–	7
Lowest of cost, market or replacement value	–	–	10
Lowest of cost, market or adjusted selling price	1	–	–
C. *Undisclosed bases*			
Valuation	1	2	26
Cost or (and, and/or) valuation	–	–	7
No basis specified	–	5	16
Various bases not separately stated in Sources	3	13	–
Number of bases used	727	342	332

Sources: U.S.A.: American Institute of Certified Public Accountants, *Accounting Trends and Techniques, 1960.*

Canada: Canadian Institute of Chartered Accountants, *Financial Reporting in Canada, 1959.*

Australia: Author's survey of Australian Company Reports.

* "Cost not in excess of market" is treated as a "lower of cost or market" basis in the American study; "not in excess of market" is thus treated as implying an alternative basis rather than as a descriptive phrase. The Canadian data have, in this table, been treated in the same manner.

The groupings in the table have been chosen to indicate the degrees of preciseness in the descriptions given, on the ground, mentioned at the beginning of the paper, that there is some possibility of general comprehensibility if the terms used are unequivocal. The groupings of the American and Canadian data thus do not agree with the classifications in the original publications.

"Disclosed bases" state categorically the method used. (For present purposes we disregard the observations made earlier about the varieties of interpretation of "cost" and "market".) Whether or not these bases result in information which is useful to investors and others, there can be no doubt about the description of the method used. It will be noted that of all "bases used", disclosed bases represent, for the American data, 24 per cent; for the Canadian, 14 per cent; and for the Australian, 15 per cent.

In the three countries "mixed bases" occur most commonly. The characteristic feature of all mixed bases is that they do not disclose which of the alternatives has in fact been used; note that every basis here listed contains an "or". They all introduce an element of uncertainty which destroys any expectation of common interpretation or understanding. What is a user to make of such a statement? He has neither a cost price, which represents an actual past outlay, nor a market price, which represents the present significance of an outlay. Mixed bases thus describe neither an element of past experience nor a basis for future expectations. They describe nothing relevant to past or future experience. They describe nothing. Mixed bases are nothing more than instruments of non-disclosure.

"Undisclosed bases" may represent a greater or smaller degree of uncertainty. But again the user has no means of knowing how the assigned money amounts are to be interpreted; who knows what "valuation" means, when it appears beside a money sum?

It is a striking commentary on the disrespect or disregard shown for the ordinary intelligent user of financial statements that over 75 per cent of all the companies covered by these three studies employ methods which are mixed or not disclosed and which therefore interfere with the making of useful comparisons between companies.

The possibilities of confusion are by no means exhausted. The American survey disclosed that there are at least 14 methods of stating how cost was determined; the Canadian survey disclosed the same number. (By contrast, the Australian practice is not to disclose the method or methods by which cost is determined.) It is commonly supposed that if companies disclose the bases of valuation and the methods used, any user of financial statements will be able to make due allowance for the differential effects when comparing statements having different bases. He may notice that they are different, but he has no means whatever of knowing the effects of the differences. In such circumstances, all statements on methods of determining cost are simply multiplications of the amount of useless information given. Whereas the purpose of information is to reduce areas of doubt, such disclosures only tend to increase doubt in the mind of the user.

(b) Some Australian Takeover Bids

One of the few opportunities available to investors as a check on the adequacy of the information relating to the results of operations is the making of takeover bids. A selection of Australian bids made in the last decade, not all of them successful, is given in the adjoining table.

The fifth column gives an indication of the extent of the offer for each ordinary share of companies for which bids were made. Generally it is the final bid, and where the terms of the offer involved an exchange of shares, the figure shown in this column is the market equivalent of the bidder's securities offered, at some point during the currency of the offer. These market equivalents would, of course, vary with the market prices of the bidder's own securities. The absolute amounts shown in this column are not critical in themselves; but they indicate the order of magnitude of the difference between the market's appraisal of the company which is the subject of the bid and the appraisal made by an external company which has some knowledge of the subject company's trade.

The sixth column indicates the quoted prices of the ordinary shares of the subject company towards the close of negotiations. These are not necessarily the highest prices quoted in the negotiation interval. The final column gives the percentage increase of the average of the column (6) prices over the column (4) prices. The following features of the table deserve notice.

All companies, bidders and subjects were public companies, listed at the time on Australian stock exchanges, and they are all companies of no mean size. There would be a substantial number of shareholders involved in every bid. As examples they are not open to the objection that only a few persons are involved, as may be the case where a bid is made for an undertaking conducted by a few proprietors.

In almost all cases the bid was made by a bidder having familiarity with, because of experience in, the same line of business as the company which was the subject of the bid. This suggests, in the first place, that some person or persons are particularly well placed to have knowledge about another company of a kind which is not available to the members themselves of that other company. The members of subject companies are at a clear disadvantage because they are denied information which is procurable by others who are not members. This is, to say the least, a curious position for shareholders to be in. In the second place, the fact that bidders have experience in the same line of business as subject companies suggests that their bids are not mere kite-flying. They have some substratum of sound business sense. It may be supposed that acquisitions of similar businesses may be expected to yield certain operating economies; but this is certainly not sufficient to justify bids which are so far in advance of pre-bid market prices of the securities of subject companies. It is more reasonable to suppose that bidders regard their bids as a cheap method of acquiring the assets and operations of subject companies. But what is a bargain

Selected Australian Takeover Bids

(1) Bidder	(2) Subject	(3) Date bid announced		(4) Price of Ordinaries of subject Co.—first week of previous month		(5) Final Offer for Ords. (Cash or market equivalent of shares and cash)	(6) Market Price of Ordinaries			(7) Percentage rise in market prices
							Buyer	Seller	Date	
David Jones	Charles Birks	Sept.	1954	35/–	(A)*	100/–	68/–	80/–	Sept. 8	112
Cox Brothers	Foy & Gibson	April	1955	45/6	(M)	53/–	55/9	56/3	May 25	23
G. J. Coles	Manton & Sons	May	1955	15/9	(M)	58/9	56/–	56/3	July 27	256
Elder Smith	C/wealth Wool	June	1955	27/3	(S)	54/10	54/6	57/–	Aug. 31	102
David Jones	Finney Isles	June	1955	47/–	(B)	126/6	119/–	–	July 27	153
Myer	McWhirters	Oct.	1955	46/9	(B)	92/6	79/9	80/–	Nov. 2	71
Hicks Atkinson	Georges	July	1956	34/6	(M)	80/–	60/–	62/–	Aug. 15	77
Buckinghams	The Hub	Aug.	1957	12/–	(S)	17/–	–	16/3	Sept. 4	35
G. J. Coles	John Connell	Mar.	1958	12/6	(M)	29/3	27/7	27/9	July 2	121
C.S.R.	Masonite	July	1959	14/10	(S)	30/3	32/6	33/–	Aug. 19	120
Myer	Allan & Stark	Aug.	1959	37/9	(B)	90/–	66/–	66/6	Aug. 26	75
H. C. Sleigh	Adelaide Steampship	Aug.	1959	28/3	(A)	105/–	69/6	70/6	Aug. 26	148
Ralph Symonds	Beale	Mar.	1960	16/3	(S)	45/6	55/–	45/6	May 5	168
G. J. Coles	Matthews Thompson	July	1960	11/4	(S)	22/6	19/–	19/6	Sept. 28	72
W. R. Carpenter	Claude Neon	July	1961	32/6	(S)	58/–	–	56/–	Sept. 20	72
Howard Smith	Melbourne Steamship	Oct.	1961	29/–	(M)	79/6	80/–	80/6	Nov. 29	177
George Weston	N. B. Love	Mar.	1962	8/3	(S)	13/2	12/10	13/6	May 14	59

Source of basic data—Various press reports. Market prices from *The Australian Financial Review*. Prices are in shillings and pence.
* Initial of Stock Exchange on which prices were quoted: generally the "home" exchange.

to a buyer in the securities market is commonly a sacrifice on the seller's part.

The pre-bid prices of subject companies will have been based on their reported results and positions in the past. They represent the market's assessment of income and capital prospects in the light of what the market has been told of the performance of directors and management in the past. Any bid substantially above the market price appears to be a clear indication either of the inadequacy of the management in the past, or of the niggardliness of management in the past in giving information to shareholders. On neither count can it be suggested that shareholders have been well served. On the other hand, it may well be suggested that niggardly reporting is a device which serves to veil the inadequacy of management and directors, whereas one might expect that a form of communication required by law would serve to unmask inadequacies and inefficiencies without the necessity of a takeover bid as a catalyst.

The comparison of pre-bid and post-bid prices has been made because these are actual reported prices; they are above conjecture. This comparison, given in the last column, may be taken as some indication of the extent to which, prior to the date of the offer, shareholders of subject companies were being misinformed. The percentage rise in market prices is in many cases staggering. In only eight of the 17 cases was the rise less than 100 per cent. In four cases the rise exceeded 150 per cent, that is, the post-bid price exceeded two and a half times the pre-bid price[21]. In rebuttal of the suggestion that shareholders were being misinformed, it may be contended that the bids made were unrealistic. Some of these acquisitions may not have turned out to be such good investments as their bid prices may have suggested. But who can tell, when the operations of subject companies have become merged with those of bidders, whether the buying price was over-optimistic, or whether the management of bidding companies was inadequate for the increased size, or has since deteriorated?

Consider now the shareholders in subject companies as individuals. If all shareholders were long-term shareholders they would perhaps, in the long run, suffer no losses by reason of poor information in the short run. This is a comforting, but quite unrealistic, thought. Individual shareholders have personal difficulties which from time to time, and at unpredictable times, oblige them to liquidate their

---

[21] Over some months of 1963, I quizzed a variety of business people (executives, professional accountants, bankers, security analysts) on their opinions as to the probable rise in market prices of the shares of companies for which bids were made in the last decade. The inquiry was informal and the question was stated in general terms.

Many of the respondents thought the rise would have been less than 25 per cent. The great majority thought the rise would have been no greater than 50 per cent. In fact, as the Table shows, in only two cases was the rise less than 50 per cent. No respondent suggested a rise as high as 100 per cent; whereas in half the cases given in the table this figure was exceeded. I am grateful for the co-operation of the participants in these slight experiments.

investments—death and taxes, to name an obvious couple. It must surely be a matter of considerable chagrin to investors who sold shares, under circumstantial pressure, on one date, to find two or three months later that the same shares in the same company are changing hands at twice the price they received and more. There can be nothing more destructive of confidence in a system which, through no fault on the investor's part, submits him to such sharp disappointments, and drops such unrequited windfalls into the lap of his successor. Investors thus have not only the risks of business to contend with; they have also to contend with the unpredictability of takeover bids to put them in a knowledgeable position, which they have a right to be in as a matter of course under the law.

The one feature common to all the cases is the appearance of additional information. The shareholders of subject companies came to know that some other party or company placed a higher value on their securities than they themselves placed. Further, although we may be accustomed to shifts in security prices as technology changes or as the structure of a market changes, there is no change which can produce over a few months such marked shifts in share prices as we have shown to arise from additional financial information. Confirmation of this in the reverse direction is given by the publication of losses which can longer be concealed or rationalized.

(c) Asset Revaluations

What seems to be convincing evidence for the emptiness of the phrase "true and fair view" under present practices is given from a different direction, the extent of asset revaluations by Australian companies. Some indication of this was given in an earlier paper[22]. Some later unpublished work of D. J. McKee and D. S. Clarke[23] attempted to assess the extent of asset revaluations by Australian and New Zealand companies over the 10-year period ended June 1960. They found that of 1354 public companies they noticed, 591 had made at least one revaluation of some assets in the period; and that of 658 companies for which information was available for the 10-year period (because they were for the whole time public companies), 388 or 60 per cent made at least one revaluation. This seems to be incontestable evidence of the fact that there are some circumstances which make adherence to past values (including costs) quite irrelevant in the opinion of directors, and that in those circumstances they are obliged to pay at least some respect to the principle of correspondence. But only from time to time.

It is evidently quite possible for a company to make a statement at one date to the effect that the amount (?) of a certain asset is 100 money units, and one year later to state the amount of the same asset at 375 money units, when the change in the financial significance of

---

[22] "The Implications of Asset Revaluations and Bonus Share Issues", see p. 95, *ante*.

[23] Corporate Asset Revaluations, a paper prepared in part fulfilment of the requirements for the award of the degree of B.Ec., University of Sydney, 1962.

the asset was nothing like the order of the change in the statements[24]. What is more, it is quite possible for directors and auditors to assert that the statements made at both dates gave a true and correct view. The emptiness of the latter phrase is only too obvious.

The occasional revaluation technique, useful though it is in the long run, leaves investors very much in the dark in the short run—and the short run may run for years. Investors may go on buying and selling securities, not knowing what those securities represent, until directors choose, or are forced, to disclose. They may go on believing that the profits reported are a reasonable basis for the dividends declared, not knowing the date at which a revaluation and a bonus issue will be announced, followed, for no obvious reason, by higher reported profits. Occasional revaluation is no substitute for a systematic procedure for reporting in a manner which corresponds with the facts.

The purpose of these three kinds of empirical studies has been to show that the defects detected in the law and in practice have consequences which cannot be lightly brushed aside. The stock valuation survey showed the extent of non-disclosure, in spite of the common belief that statements of the methods used are an advance in disclosure. The demonstration could be extended by reference to the varied methods of reporting valuation bases for fixed assets. The takeover survey showed the extent of the discrepancy between informed evaluations and the uninformed and misinformed evaluations of investors. The asset revaluation studies showed the extent to which businessmen themselves recognize the inadequacies of conventional procedures—even though for individual firms revaluation is only sporadic, the very number of instances shows that the recognition of inadequacies is widespread.

We hold no views about the acuity of investors or on the other hand about their ignorance and indifference. Whether they use the information or not does not affect the professional accountant's and auditor's position or his responsibility. Investors have a legal, and, indeed, a moral right to information which can be interpreted against the context of contemporary commercial affairs. Contemporary law and practice on the other hand take away the substance of these rights and proffer in their stead an insubstantial shadow, a chimera which vanishes under the light of criticism.

Comprehensibility and Correspondence Through Time

We return now to our original specifications of the properties of accounting if it is to serve as a language—general comprehensibility and correspondence.

---

[24] The figures are based on the change in the reported values of the security investments of The Adelaide Steamship Company Limited. The Sydney Stock Exchange share price index for ordinary shares of non-financial companies rose from 263 in June 1959 to 361 in June 1960. The company's investments included debentures, so that the rise in the value of its holdings would have been relatively less than the rise in the index. The asset was revalued from £630,000 to £2,373,000.

As to comprehensibility, as long ago as 1845 a newspaper editorial stated the principle that the system of accounting employed by companies should be "distinctly avowed and understood by the shareholders"[25]. Fifty years later Pixley opined that a finally approved balance sheet "should be so clearly stated that every shareholder of ordinary intelligence can understand it"[26]. The principle is, today, as valid as ever. But today the conflict of rules and the diversity of rules, not to mention their complexity, give rise to a situation in which no professional accountant, however qualified and experienced, can interpret or understand the meaning of the statements relating to the most significant non-monetary items in any balance sheet. The purpose of a language system is to communicate ideas or meanings, not just symbols. But if financial statements cannot be interpreted by professional people (except with access to the original computations) clearly no ordinary intelligent shareholder stands a chance.

Comprehensibility has, however, two facets. The first has to do with the words and other signs used; we have demonstrated the impossibility of interpreting some of the words deemed by the laws and professional bodies to be necessary in the interest of disclosure. The second facet of comprehensibility is closely connected with the second stipulated property of communications—correspondence or isomorphism.

Interpretations of signs are made in specific contexts, or at specific times. If a statement is made to the effect that the population of Australia is 11 million people, its interpretation is that there are at the time of the statement that many people in the territory designated as "Australia" at the time. The verb "is" does not mean "was" or "will be"; it will not be interpreted as "was" or "will be". Balance sheets bear on the face of them an indication of the date as at which the statements they contain are to be interpreted. They do not say "this balance sheet is dated 31 December 1962, but this item is to be interpreted as for 1952, and that item is to be interpreted as for 1957". If any such statement were made it would be a clear indication of the uselessness of the balance sheet. For firstly no user can cast his mind back to the setting of 1952 or 1957 for the purpose of interpreting specific statements, however well he may recollect the broad settings of those years. And secondly, it would be pointless to do so; for the purpose of reading the balance sheet is to be informed about the actions he may take now, not about the actions he could have taken years ago.

As this is the user's purpose, he will be entitled to suppose that the information he is given is relevant to action at the stated date. Even if the balance sheet indicates that certain items are stated at cost, and even if the date of purchase is given, the user will suppose that the amount stated is the presently relevant amount and that the

---

[25] Leading article in the *Morning Chronicle,* 17 May 1845. Cited in Hunt, op. cit., p. 112.

[26] F. W. Pixley, *Auditors, Their Duties and Responsibilities under the Joint Stock Companies Acts,* London, Henry Good & Son, 1889, p. 165.

supplementary indications are mere descriptions. He is given no other information as to what is presently relevant; he can only interpret what he sees and the date it bears as being relevant at that date. It may be argued that these suppositions as to the interpretations of users are unfounded. But there is no other supposition which one may make.

What, then, is relevant at any specified date? Only specific statements which correspond with contemporary market conditions at that date; statements which at that date are indicative of the capacity at that date to borrow on the assets; statements which at that date are indicative of the cash which could be made available, directly or by disposing of other assets, to pursue any course of action which might be chosen; statements which are a reflection of the effects of actions and the impact of the environment up to that date. Correspondence of facts with statements descriptive of contemporary facts is a condition of intelligent interpretation.

We anticipate an objection to the requirement of general comprehensibility. It may be argued that the company laws relating to financial publicity concern themselves principally with protection of the interests of actual shareholders, whereas we have frequently referred to investors making comparisons between two or more companies. This objection could perhaps be well taken while the publicity provisions were part of the optional model articles. But it is a position which can no longer be sustained. For in Britain the publicity provisions are now incorporated in the Act, and by the Act "every balance sheet shall give a true and fair view", not to its shareholders, nor to anyone in particular, but to everyone in general. The American Securities Act is likewise generally pervasive in intention.

But we do not even have to fall back on this defence. Shareholders no less than potential shareholders require to have a true and fair view. For among their powers as shareholders are the right to elect directors and to remove them, the right to appoint inspectors, and the right to resolve that a company shall be wound up. Only if they have a true and fair view which corresponds with the actual state of a company's affairs can any of these rights be exercised intelligently. Then, if every company is to serve its shareholders in the same way, with information of the same objective kind, all companies will necessarily be comparable in respect of their financial disclosures. In any case, the argument that the law only seeks to protect shareholders is invalidated by the requirement that annual returns including financial statements shall be filed in public offices where they may be inspected by the public; this requirement has no point if the protection of shareholders' interests only were contemplated.

The Quality of Financial Information

The Australian securities markets operate under substantially the same laws, practices and institutional arrangements as in Britain. In both countries the stock exchanges have no statutory status or function. They are recognized contractually by companies which seek a ready market in their securities, and those companies agree to abide by the financial publicity requirements of the exchanges. In many respects the requirements of the exchanges have been in advance of the requirements of the company law; their rules are able to be varied to meet the interests of investors more readily than is possible by the protracted processes of introducing new legislation. But in England and Australia, and indeed also in the United States, the publicity requirements have always been directed towards increasing the quantity of financial information made available, in terms of specific items to be disclosed or frequency of disclosure. In no case has attention been given to the quality of information required. The members of the exchanges have recognized the problem of quality to lie within the competence of another group, the accounting profession. This deference seems to express reasonable professional respect.

In a similar way the accounting profession has shown great respect for the wisdom of the legislators, and for the rights of brokers and investors to interpret the published statements in the light of their own expertise and circumstances. But it, too, has concentrated on quantity of information rather than on quality. And over all are the legislatures which have provided statutes, which for the purposes they envisage depend more on quality than quantity, but which give such detailed treatment to quantity that the disregard of quality by others is reinforced.

There are thus at least three main groups of people, all concerned in some measure with securing an informed market in securities—the legislators, the members of the exchanges and the members of the accounting profession. Each group recognizes and respects the area of competence of the others—but each relies on the strength of the rules of the others to make its own rules effective. Only by chance is it likely that such a system, of inter-group respect coupled with group independence, would produce information of that contemporarily relevant character which would enable investors intelligently to guard their interests. And chance has not been on the side of investors.

The primary problem of the whole question of financial reporting lies in the character of the accounting process adopted in the books of account which companies are required by the law to keep. The linkage of the requirements, "true and fair view" and "as shown in the accounting records" or books of account, is, to say the least, unfortunate. It is a matter of common knowledge that for all kinds of reasons, through errors made in good faith as well as fraud, the books of account may diverge from a representation of a true and fair view. The only form of words which may avoid the implication that what is shown in the books of account may be considered as a true and fair view is, "Every balance sheet shall give a true and fair view, *notwithstanding* anything contained in the books of account." This is plainly what the law should contemplate.

The only alternative is to abandon all accounting rules which fail to yield statements giving a true and fair view. The accounting system required is one giving always contemporary representations in balance sheets and profit and loss accounts. Out of date information simply will not do. There is no accountant who does not, in his own private affairs, make his calculations in contemporary terms; yet in the practice of accounting it is common to suppose that contemporary terms are not just as relevant to investors and creditors.

There is only one rule which will give a true and fair view. It may be expressed thus: the amounts representing assets in balance sheets shall be such as give the closest possible approximation to contemporary monetary equivalents. In a general way "contemporary monetary equivalent" is to be interpreted as current market prices, for they are the critical determinants of future actions. The above rule will of course need to be supplemented by subsidiary rules for the cases in which current market prices are difficult to obtain. But a profession which has been able to discover a million ways of representing the financial positions of firms has obviously sufficient ingenuity to devise the relatively small number of supplementary rules which would be required. Certainly it will require some ingenuity. But the general rule stated above gives a clear indication of the direction in which ingenuity should be exercised, an indication which contemporary practice so obviously lacks that it acquiesces in a million true and correct views.

It is not possible to argue at length here in support of appropriate subsidiary rules for particular assets. But some of the effects of the basic rule may be indicated:—

(a) there would be no "this *or* that" rules for stating the method of assigning money amounts to assets, rules which we have shown to be devices which disclose nothing interpretable;

(b) there would be a common basic rule for assigning money amounts to all items; this would eliminate the doubts which exist where there are diverse possible rules, and it provides the only basis, for logical and mathematical reasons, on which the different money amounts assigned may be added or related;

(c) the periodical resort to market prices would avoid the compounding of errors or deviations from contemporary relevance; compounding of deviations is an unavoidable feature of the consistent application of formal rules to basic data which, as time passes, become less and less relevant;

(d) consistency with reality would be substituted for consistency of application of formal rules;

(e) there would be no ground, save fraud, for supposing that the true and fair view was other than that represented in the books of account.

There are several objections to any changes of rules in the direction we suggest. It is important to be clear about what these are, and if possible to answer them.

There is firstly the objection that the difficulties of discovering the rules and carrying them out are so great that no acceptable solution will emerge. This is counsel of despair and an abnegation of professional responsibility. Accountants who proclaim the difficulties of changing their rules are obviously refusing to recognize the great difficulties which confront them if they are to follow existing rules seriously. For, if there are a million possible ways of drawing up a balance sheet, and if there is a specific way appropriate to every company, then every accountant must of necessity have to discover which of the million ways is appropriate to his company. One cannot believe that such an exhaustive examination is ever carried out: it would be too difficult, and it would take a lifetime.

The real question, of course, is who shall be confronted with difficulties—those experts who compile the financial statements, or those less expert persons who have to interpret them? The resolution of the difficulties seems clearly to lie in the hands of the experts; that is what is expected of experts. Any attempt to approximate contemporary financial significance is better than no attempt at all. We venture the opinion that if the professional competence of any accountant were at stake, some method would be found, whatever the difficulty.

The second objection we notice is the assertion that our proposals would be much more costly than existing methods. Many years ago Sweeney anticipated this objection and demonstrated that for the three companies which he used as examples the additional cost was modest[27]. But what is costly can only be judged by the utility of the product. A defective product is costly however small its cost. It is impossible to make assertions about the costliness of information which is not interpretable to the detriment of information which is interpretable. Those who emphasize the greater out-of-pocket costs of relevant information clearly overlook the potential improvement in business effciency which may flow from closer scrutiny of business. They overlook the enormous costs to investors of the spectacular failures which from time to time shake the confidence of the investing public—failures which we contend are only permitted to become so spectacular by the inadequacy of the accounting information published. They also overlook the incidence of losses and windfall gains which affect individual shareholders in companies for which takeover bids are made.

A third objection which is raised is that current valuations will subject periodical profits to marked fluctuations and this, it is contended, cannot be in the interests of buyers, holders or sellers of securities. Now, if contemporary changes in the market place raise or lower the financial capacity of a company, this is surely of consequence to all investors; to report the change is to conform with the principle of correspondence. But there are some, on the other hand, who strongly support the principle of "smoothing" profits and averaging out or disregarding these fluctuations. Of all principles this is one of the most vicious; for its effect is non-disclosure[28]. If profits in fact fluctuate, this is a piece of information which an intelligent investor will wish to know; for fluctuating profits are indicative of the risks he will want to take into account in bidding for or holding

---

[27] Henry W. Sweeney, *Stabilized Accounting*, New York, Harper & Brothers, 1936.

[28] See "Measurement and Misrepresentation", p. 125, *ante*.

securities. Profit smoothing makes a risky business appear to be much less risky. It makes it possible for a risky business to become more risky still to its ordinary shareholders, for it deludes them into supposing that a higher gearing or leverage is warranted than the underlying variability of income warrants. Profit smoothing enables companies and their managements to go on declaring profits for some time after profits have ceased to be earned. How often this has happened and how often it has deferred the day of reckoning, at great cost to old and new investors, can only be a matter of conjecture. But it is a conjecture with a high degree of probability.

A fourth objection is that new methods should only be adopted when they have been tried out in practice and found to be as effective as they are claimed to be. But the objection must fail. Valuations in contemporary terms have been made in respect of some items at least, by many companies. The dangers and difficulties which have been said to follow departure from cost have not in these cases been experienced. In any case the complete procedure has been tried out in practice over many years by at least one international company, without any ill effects[29]. And, in any case the defects of the conventional system are so demonstrable that a change which removes many of them is overdue.

Who is Responsible?

No specific class of persons may be held to be responsible or culpable for the present state of affairs. Legislators, accountants and brokers alike became involved initially with corporate financial publicity at a point where there was no evidence of the consequences of the procedures adopted. In the absence of restraining principles, managers and directors were obliged to argue their own cases, and because they are a group holding the reins of economic power they were able to make their proposals heard and accepted. Investors were and are, by contrast, a diffuse and scattered group, depending on the verbal formulas of the law for protection but, except in very unusual cases, unable to voice their protest against default in giving substantially what the law requires. Through a century and a quarter, old habits have hardened, particularly habits of belief in the virtue of old habits. New shibboleths have been heaped on old; and every group has depended on the intelligence and integrity of other groups to patch up defects in the structure which it felt itself incompetent to remedy.

More recently there has been a tendency to suggest that the financial press is responsible for failure to throw light on the defects of specific companies. The suggestion is entirely unjustified as long as published financial statements fail to represent the positions of the companies which publish them. There being no dependable basis for

---

[29] N.V. Philips Gloeilampenfabrieken (Netherlands). The company is in some respects unusual; its practices must be interpreted against the background of theoretical developments in the Netherlands. Its practices have not prevented the listing of its securities in the United States.

intelligent analysis, the financial press is forced to set up some assumptions as a foundation for interpretation; for example, as to the relationship between disclosed tax provisions and actual profits, when the tax provisions bear no obvious relationship to disclosed profits. The questionable character of the financial statements makes such guessing inevitable—on the part of all who wish to understand, not solely on the part of the financial press.

There is also a tendency to believe that the protection of the interests of secured creditors may be assured by appointing as trustees for debenture-holders only companies of considerable standing. But whoever the trustees are, they can do no better than the financial information supplied to them. As we have shown, the legal requirements are defeated by established accounting practices. No satisfactory supervision of debenture-holders' interests can be expected while this is the case.

Although, therefore, we believe that none of the parties involved—legislators, businessmen, brokers, accountants, the press, trustees and investors themselves—is to blame for the present situation, the better informed of these groups have some duty, a professional and a social duty, to remedy its defects. Re-examination of their own position by specialist groups is unquestionably valuable; but an examination of the general field in which all have some common interests promises to be much more fruitful.

Searching inquiry should be made into the whole question of financial publicity. As the quality of financial information is very much a matter of the accounting principles employed, inquiry should be directed towards the discovery of principles which will give a true and fair view; that is to say, principles which conform with the requirements of general comprehensibility and correspondence. Notice that we do not suggest an inquiry which by democratic process will yield an agreed set of principles. There have been inquiries of this kind, but their outcome has usually been that old habits are simply given a new look. We contemplate an inquiry of the nature of a rigorous scientific examination. The discovery of new technical devices has never been the product of democratic deliberation.

We do not pretend that the best results of any such inquiry will do away with company losses through lack of technical adaptation or mistakes of judgement. But we do believe that an adequate system of financial publicity, reflecting the realities of changing market conditions, would reveal the consequences of such mistakes much earlier than the present system, and would thus materially reduce the severity of losses. But we are more concerned with efficiency than with avoiding losses. As companies and their operations affect, in one way or another, the lives of us all, as they have such an extensive impact on incomes, employment, the development of industry and the distribution of economic power, there can be no doubt about the social value of efficient corporate business. And as every member of the community is a potential investor who may base his income expectations and capital protection decisions on published financial statements, there can be no denying that an efficient means of financial communication, enabling investors to judge in an informed way the the efficiency of corporate business, is a critical necessity.

Improvement in the quality of published financial information is commended as one suggestion for removing the ignorance and many of the uncertainties which now bedevil the securities markets, for changing the character of the securities markets from that of a casino with loaded dice to that of an instrument of rational and informed economic development.

12

COMPANY LOSSES—SAFEGUARDING THE INVESTOR*

On Friday, 13 December 1963, the financial Press reported that on the previous day—since described as "Black Thursday"—six companies had declared losses totalling £3.6 million for the year ended during 1963. Within a week two other companies had reported losses totalling £2.9 million. A year earlier, to the day, the Press had reported losses of four companies totalling £3.8 million for the year ended during 1962. Within a week of this another firm had reported the largest loss for a year announced by an Australian company up to that time, £3.5 million. On one day a month earlier, 21 November 1962, two companies reported losses aggregating £3.3 million and eight other companies were "declared" with the object of official investigation—a day described at the time as "the blackest day in Australian company history". These figures have since been overshadowed by the scale of the losses of the Reid Murray group.

One would suppose that these events, all within the space of a little over a year, could not help but shake the confidence of Australian investors. But investors as a class are not vocal. There have been some stormy company meetings; receivers, committees of inquiry and official investigators have been appointed; but once this kind of action has been taken the opportunity for complaint by investors seems to pass, and there is little evidence of the extent to which confidence has been shaken, if at all.

The spectacular losses which have attracted the greatest attention should be seen in perspective. In the three financial years since the restraining measures introduced by the Commonwealth in November 1960, some 150 companies listed on the Australian stock exchanges have reported losses in one or more years. Some 60 reported losses in at least two years and nearly half of these reported losses in all three years. These losses may be estimated at six to eight per cent of the total reported results of listed companies over this period.

This may not seem a large proportion, nothing large enough to shake the general state of confidence, and if the companies concerned are examined more closely many of the losses are, in a way, understandable. Credit restrictions are bound to affect firms in the building, building-materials, engineering and land-development industries, and about one-third of the loss companies were in these groups. Motels, hotels and TV stations, which had been developing over this period,

---

* First published in *Current Affairs Bulletin,* Vol. 34, No. 11, October 1964. (Department of Tutorial Classes in the University of Sydney.)

seem to account for 10 per cent. Textile and clothing manufacturers (about 12 per cent) and merchandising companies (about 20 per cent) are the other principal groups involved.

But of all loss companies, just three groups—Korman, Latec, and Reid Murray—accounted for over half of the £50 million losses reported in these three years. On the face of it, each of the three appeared to have rather diverse activities and might therefore have been expected to suffer less disastrously than companies operating in, say, the building or engineering trades solely. It seems not unlikely that some such belief lay behind the capacity of Latec and Reid Murray to go on raising money long after difficulties should have been apparent to investors.

Consequential Losses

The losses mentioned above are computed losses, arrived at by the methods used to calculate the net financial result of yearly operations. But they do not represent consequential losses borne by individual investors indirectly, through the effect the computed losses have on dividends and share prices. High share prices help companies to raise new money from the public by further share and debenture issues; and they make it easier to acquire other companies by issuing shares at a premium in consideration for the shares of the companies taken over. Companies seeking to take advantage of high share prices will tend to keep up dividend rates, even if this means distributing almost the whole of calculated profits. They may, as will be seen, keep up profit rates by adopting unusual methods of profit calculation. They may stimulate the confidence of investors by expressions of great expectations.

All these measures tend to boost share prices, but, if circumstances show the beliefs of investors to have been poorly founded, share prices will collapse. And the severity of computed losses must therefore be multiplied, because of the peak from which share prices fall.

To take one example, Latec Investments 5s. shares commanded a premium during 1958, 1959 and 1960. They reached a peak price of 17s. in 1960, on which basis the business was reckoned by investors (or some of them) to have a capital value of about £6 million. During the financial year ended in 1961, the company issued a further £1 million in shares. By the end of 1961, the year in which the company reported its first big loss of £1.5 million, the shares had fallen in price to about 3s. On this basis the business was reckoned by investors to be worth about £1.6 million—a drop of £5.4 million in the market's evaluation, for a disclosed loss of only £1.5 million. Since then the shares have dropped to 4d., making the market's evaluation of the equity less than £200,000. Even if one considers only the drop from the par value of 5s. paid in to 4d., or 93 per cent, this is scarcely a loss which investors individually can lightly brush off. But this is not the whole picture.

In 1962, Latec Investments owed to secured lenders and debenture-holders £5 million and to unsecured creditors £5.5 million. The receiver appointed on behalf of debenture-holders in that year has since paid off part of this debt, but as at June 1963, it appeared that assets worth only £6.5 million were available to pay off debts of £9.7 million. Thus, besides the complete loss of their equity by shareholders, creditors of the company stand to lose some £3.2 million.

This company's creditors are not alone in this predicament. The Reid Murray group has outstanding debentures to the tune of £23.5 million. These debentures were traded at about 25 per cent of their face value in May 1963, indicating a possible loss of £18 million. The situation has improved somewhat following the examination of the company by the receivers, but the currently quoted price suggests that debenture-holders stand to lose some £13 million. In the Korman group, Chevron Sydney debentures and Rockmans debentures stand at heavy discounts, but none so great as the 92 per cent discount on £2 million registered unsecured notes of Stanhill Development Finance.

The direct consequences of such losses are not trifling. The sums invested by shareholders and debenture-holders represent their accumulated savings. They are invested either in the expectation of increasing income or in the expectation of resale if and when personal needs make resale necessary. The latter precautionary element is often thought to be important when it comes to investment in debentures. The losses being considered have had the effect of converting the capital of one part of the community into the consumption of another part of the community.

It should be remembered that credit retailing, financing, hotel operation and real-estate development are not wild-cat operations like oil prospecting, to which investors would ordinarily attribute considerable risk of loss. They are activities in which many other companies have long engaged successfully—notwithstanding the restraints following the "little budget" of 1960. There was no reason why investors should suppose their investments to be at inordinate risk, though it might have been naive to suppose that the risks had not been increased by the Government's measures. There was some reason, on the other hand, for supposing that integrated and diversified activities under a single management would enhance the earning capacity of a group of companies. Why then were these expectations disappointed?

Contributory Incidents

Credit Restriction

Of all the factors which might have given rise to the spectacular losses (and to the even modest losses) of companies in the engineering and construction trades, the most commonly blamed is the Commonwealth's measures of November 1960. Sales tax on motor vehicles was raised; bank overdraft rates were raised, tending to reduce the resort to overdraft accommodation; and bank deposit rates were raised, tending to narrow the margin between the returns from bank deposits and alternative uses of idle funds. Limits were announced on the allowance of interest paid on company borrowings as a deduction for taxation purposes; and life offices and superannuation funds were required to hold 30 per cent of their investments in government securities. These all tended to reduce the funds or opportunities available to corporate business.

That these restraints need have had serious effects on some companies is debatable. Companies whose operations and policies are fundamentally sound provide themselves with room to manoeuvre under critical conditions. Although all new money raised by listed companies fell from the 1960 peak of £248 million to £219 million in 1961, and to £176 million in 1962, new money from share issues rose substantially, while new loan money fell by greater amounts. On the whole companies were thus able to turn from loan finance to share capital issues, indicating capacity of earnings to justify these new issues. Profits of companies receded from their 1960 level in the following years (see table below), but as was seen earlier the number of companies reduced to losses was not relatively large. The companies which were crippled simply lacked the disciplined management necessary to maintain adaptability. And this lack now seems to have been inherent and therefore independent of the credit restriction policy, which, in a sense, did no more than bring it to light.

Profits of Australian Companies listed on Stock Exchanges

Year	1958-59	1959-60	1960-61	1961-62
Number of Companies	941	909	876	841
Net Profit before charging depreciation	£m.	£m.	£m.	£m.
and taxation	309.4	355.9	339.9	354.1
Net Profit after charging depreciation				
and taxation	142.1	162.6	136.8	138.0

Source: Reserve Bank of Australia, *Statistical Bulletin Company Supplement,* November 1963.

New Money raised by Australian Companies listed on Stock Exchanges

Year ended June	1959	1960	1961	1962
	£m.	£m.	£m.	£m.
Share Capital	48.7	47.9	98.5	76.3
Debentures, Registered Notes and Deposits	142.2	200.4	120.4	99.9
Total	190.9	248.3	218.9	176.2

Source: Commonwealth Bureau of Census and Statistics, *New Capital Raisings by Companies in Australia,* July 1963.

To be more specific, the Commonwealth's policy seemed to be directly pointed at credit retailing, financing and real-estate development. And one might be tempted to regard this as all the more reason for the losses of companies operating in just those fields. But it is not. The appropriate policy of a company in such a case would appear to be a tightening of its credit control; trimming its operations in all directions to meet the likely if delayed effects of the measures on the disposable incomes of consumers and ability to pay debt instalments. In particular this would mean closer examination of applicants for credit and prompt action to recognize bad debts. In some cases it has become clear that the drive for growth was in no way modified by such considerations; and the number of companies which have written off bad debts on a large scale suggests that care in granting and managing credit was scant.

Debt Financing

A likely additional factor contributing to the collapse of some companies was the growth in popularity of financing by debentures and note issues. It was not until the early 'fifties that financing by these means became a common practice among Australian companies. The dangers—to companies, shareholders, debenture-holders and note-holders alike—of depending heavily on debt finance were not known from critical experience. Nor had the weakness of some of the protective rules become obvious.

Debentures are one of the instruments by which companies may raise loan moneys. They are usually regarded as a safe form of investment, in which the debenture-holder forgoes, for a fixed annual interest payment, the prospect of high dividends which might flow to shareholders. They confer priority over shareholdings in the payment of interest and the repayment of capital. Some debentures are styled mortgage debentures, the understanding being that something in the nature of a mortgage over real property stands as security for the loan given by debenture-holders. They are issued under terms which provide both expert supervision, through the appointment of trustees in the interest of debenture-holders, and a limit to moneys the issuing company may raise by further issues of debentures.

These are the provisions which give debentures the element of "safety" by comparison with shares. Generally speaking they work quite satisfactorily. But the investigations of recent months have shown that they are not as effective as they seem.

The terms of issue of debentures may provide, among other things, that a company's borrowings shall not exceed, say, four times the amount of shareholders' funds, or net tangible assets of the company. The strength of this constraint lies in the interpretation given to "shareholders' funds" or "net tangible assets". The word "tangible", like the word "mortgage", suggests that borrowings are backed by some assets of real substance. Yet in the case of Reid Murray Acceptance, which raised from the public £43 million on "mortgage" debentures over four years, almost the whole of the so-called "tangible" assets consisted of unsecured debts owing to it by other companies within the group. Being unsecured they could scarcely be considered to be assets of real substance. The investigators reported that the company "as its principal asset had an unsecured debt owing by a partnership of companies whose history was a history of losses and whose existence as a firm was without substance". Small wonder that in 1963 the company reported a loss of £20 million, most of which was due to bad and doubtful debts.

There seems to be no doubt that if there is to be any element of safety in debentures the use of the words "mortgage" in relation to debentures and "tangible" in relation to assets must be so restricted as to make their implications more than an illusion. Fortunately, the present lax situation is in process of legislative correction. Also it seems that when trustees need to assure themselves that the financial limits imposed on a borrowing company are not exceeded, their status as trustees should require them to engage auditors who are independent of the borrowing company. The Reid Murray debenture-holders did not have the benefit of this elementary precaution.

Further, shareholders' funds or net tangible assets consist of the sum of the amounts paid in by shareholders and the amounts retained by the company out of past profits. Thus the methods of calculating profits in the past become an important consideration. If profits are calculated without regard for their consequential effects on the representation of assets, a protective provision which links borrowings to net tangible assets can give little warrant of safety. If past profits have been calculated without adequate provision for bad debts (and even secured debts may be bad), or without proper charges being made for interest paid, or without proper charges for depreciation, the amount of the net tangible assets will be fictitiously high. And the security of debenture-holders is then, in part, based on pure fiction.

The methods of calculating profits thus have much to do with the security of debentures, and any examination by the trustees for debenture-holders of the effectiveness of constraints on borrowing companies can mean little unless it includes an examination of these methods. From the evidence available it seems that much greater care in this respect should be required of trustees.

In addition to defects in description and the bases of calculation, there may be delays in the supply of information. Only recently did some States introduce legislation requiring more frequent financial reporting by borrowing companies. Until then it was possible (and still is in other States) to raise money on debentures, citing financial information (included in a prospectus) which might be anything up to 15 months out of date by the time the issue closes. The legal provisions permitting this are quite inadequate to enable prospective debenture-holders to protect themselves. The new provision for half-yearly reporting is a great improvement. But there seems to be no good reason why there should not be a provision that prospectuses include fully audited financial statements up to a date no earlier than three months before prospectuses are issued. This would be particularly valuable when material changes in the financial structure of a company could have occurred, or when changes in the climate of business could have altered the prospects of a company. The costs of this additional scrutiny is a small price to pay for the advantage of borrowing and for the better information of lenders—except of course to companies which fear scrutiny.

The Freedoms of Promoters and Managers

Promoters and managers have considerable freedom under the law in their conduct of corporate business. In one sense this is necessary. If enterprise were unduly shackled by tight and specific restrictions, innovation, in respect of goods and services and in commercial and industrial methods, would be severely hampered. Without the freedom to exercise initiative, ingenuity and inventiveness, corporate business would have been less attractive to the skilled and knowledgeable men who fill its senior managerial ranks. But there are limits.

It is not long since companies were required to specify the avenues of commerce and industry which they intended to exploit. This gave investors some idea of the possible risks involved. But diversification promised to spread, and hence to minimize, risk. The desires of promoters and managers to keep open a wide range of possible activities led to such extensive statements of company objects that the specification of limits became pointless.

For other reasons it is proper that promoters and managers should have considerable freedom. Under modern conditions, technical and economic aspects of even one class of business have become so complex that they are beyond the comprehension of all but those closely connected with them. It would hopelessly clog the administration of companies if their day-to-day operations were open to question by investors or creditors.

But these two characteristics—diversification and complexity—make it a matter of great importance that investors and creditors should have some means of knowing how efficiently companies are being managed. The Companies Acts provide several means. They provide for the appointment and the removal and rotation of directors by shareholders; they provide that the directors shall present annually to shareholders financial statements and reports on the operations of companies. They also require that the statements of a company give a true and fair view of the state of its affairs and its results; and that auditors be appointed to report on whether the statements presented give a true and fair view of the state of affairs and of the results.

There are several objects of these provisions. Given adequate information it is possible to get some idea of the skill with which the investors' and creditors' funds are being employed. The rate of return, obtained by comparing the year's net profit with the funds invested, may be compared with rates earned in previous years, or with rates earned by other comparable companies in the same year. On this basis some judgement can be made about both the skill of the management and the relative profitability of the company.

Given adequate information, it is also possible to form some idea whether it would be better to wind up a going concern or to persist with it. If, for example, the rate of return on the funds currently invested were below the rate on alternative investments (and in the limiting case below the rate on government bonds), investors might well choose to liquidate or to sell the company, either piecemeal or as a going concern.

These choices cannot be made without adequate financial information; that is the crux of the problem. A company may have an extremely efficient sales organization; its technical equipment may be the latest; its industrial relations may be exemplary; but unless the combination of all its divisional operations is such that it meets the tests of investors and creditors, divisional efficiency is pointless.

Does the market have adequate information? The evidence made available from some of the investigations of loss companies clearly suggests it does not. It may be objected that the number of companies subject to investigations on which full reports have been published is too small to provide sufficient evidence; but they do furnish evidence, which is strongly supported by other evidence to be mentioned later.

Regulating the Flow of Information

The information made available to the market can be described most clearly as a regulated flow—regulated by those whose performance and efficiency are to be judged.

Latec Investments operated as a finance company. Almost all its assets were for some years represented under the heading "Cash and Debtors". The distinction between cash and debtors is material in any company; it is critical in respect of a finance company. Only in 1962, by which time the company had already declared £5 million losses, was the figure split. This is a clear example of regulating the flow of material information to shareholders. Again, no provision for doubtful debts was disclosed by the company up to 1960; but in September 1961, the company announced that £1.9 million of bad debts had been written off in that year—an amount almost double the reported net profits of the group over its previous seven years of existence. The conclusion seems to be inescapable that recognition of doubtful debts had been deferred notwithstanding the fact that much of the company's business involved financing of vehicles of old makes and models. Indeed it was admitted in 1961 that adequate provisions had not been made in previous years.

Between June 1958 and August 1961, the company issued £1.15 million in shares to shareholders for cash, and £1.2 million in shares and £600,000 in debentures in eight takeovers. One wonders how many of these invitations would have been acceptable to shareholders and vendors if profits of previous years had been reduced by adequate provisions for doubtful debts. There seems to be little doubt that delaying the flow of information enabled the company to maintain its attractiveness, and in the sequel to cause investors much greater losses than if realistic financial statements had been published.

The Reid Murray Group also was heavily engaged in financing consumers' goods. Of the group's assets of £67 million in 1961, £36 million consisted of debtors. Against this the group had provided £780,000 for doubtful debts or about two per cent. It is now known that the group was experiencing difficulties as early as mid-1960, and it seems probable that two per cent was a very slight recognition of the possibility of bad debts. In August 1963, the receivers and managers estimated that of £38 million owed by debtors of the group only £18.4 million would be realizable. It seems improbable, though it is not impossible, that this £20 million loss on book debts was attributable to business written in the previous two years. When, in 1961, at the instigation of the auditors, the group's provision for bad debts was raised by £350,000 to the figure of £780,000 mentioned above, the amount was not charged against the year's profits, but against past accumulated profits. The consequence was that this amount was never charged against profits of any specific year, so that the profit record continued to look impressive.

But this was only one device which regulated the flow of information. Many companies in the group followed the practice of accounting for the whole of the profit on terms-sales at the time sales were made. Now the greater the length of time of collection of a debt on consumers' goods the greater the profit risk, for changes in a buyer's preferences or circumstances may give rise to a default. The above practice therefore involves bringing forward the time of recognizing profits—i.e., taking account of profits before they are in fact made. Similarly, in respect of lands being developed by the group, interest on the cost of land was added to land values instead of being charged off against profits—another device having the effect of giving a better showing than the facts warranted. And again, in 1961 the methods used in previous years for calculating net profit were changed. The investigators have calculated that whereas the net profit before tax in 1961 was reported to be approximately £1.25 million, £1 million of this was due simply to changes in the method of computing net profit by comparison with the methods used previously.

It is only possible to speculate upon the effects which adequate provision for doubtful debts, taking profits into account only when they had been realized and charging interest against profits as interest was paid, would have had on the disclosed profits of years before 1961. But it seems highly unlikely that if these matters had been properly brought into account the group's prospects would have been promising enough to secure the subscription, at least, of the £17 million raised on debentures after May 1960.

These two cases only illustrate the many devices available for regulating the flow of information. Even companies which are not in the "loss" class may determine the rate at which information of interest to investors is made available to them. For example, the announcement of a takeover bid has frequently forced company directorates to disclose that company properties were worth far more than their financial statements had shown; this presumably is regarded as a defence against bidders. But it implies that the rate of profit on funds was not nearly as satisfactory as it appeared to be before the higher contemporary values were revealed. And up to the time of the revelation investors and creditors were deprived of a true and fair view of the state of affairs and of the results of operations.

Business Morality and Efficiency

Following upon the reported losses, the ultimate failures, and the investigations of the Ducon affair, the Moulton group, the Sydney Guarantee Corporation and others, it is natural that questions should be raised about the ethics, or the morals, or the sense of duty of business and professional men. Do these cases indicate a decline in the standard of competence and integrity of managers, advisers and expert consultants to industry, of accountants, auditors, solicitors and underwriters? To any such general question the general answer must be, no. Specific instances of incompetence, dishonesty and even fraud there may be; but no profession or vocation is entirely free of black sheep. Consider some particular circumstances.

Was it wrong of the Reid Murray management to seek to grow as rapidly as possible to being the largest company of its kind? In some senses, no. Growth has generally meant to investors the prospect of capital gains, new share issues on favourable terms, and increased cash returns by way of distributed profits. Growth can mean benefits from economics of large-scale operations. Growth by way of geographical and operational diversification can mean stability of earnings. All of these things may be said to be in the interests of shareholders. But a company depending heavily on the support of debentures cannot disregard the interests of the debenture-holders without threatening the interests of shareholders. A heavy debt, built on overstated assets and profits, and requiring a constant or increasing flow of new money to pay interest charges and to repay maturing debentures, is the surest way to defeat the interests of shareholders and debenture-holders.

On the other hand, is it wrong of a company's management to show its assets in an amount of say, £2.25 million (an actual case) when the present commercial value of those assets is known to be double the amount? Some would say, no; and advance plausible reasons for the practice, which is no less misleading than overstating the amount of assets. They may contend that the practice is prudent, conservative, tending to the preservation of a company, and therefore of the interests of shareholders in it. But this view is just as one-sided as that just mentioned. It is based on the idea that all shareholders in a company are long-term shareholders and that all shareholders prefer the continued existence of the company to its sale or liquidation. This is far from the truth. Many shareholders are relatively short-term holders. It would be in the interest of a shareholder contemplating selling his shares to have a realistic rather than a conservative showing of profits and asset values, for "conservative" profits and asset values could only tend to lower selling prices. There may be many shareholders who, if they had access to realistic instead of "conservative" information, would perfer to wind up a company rather than keep it going.

Indeed this paternalistic care for the interests of shareholders, expressed in conservative financial statements, leaves the way open to abuse. If it is generally believed that financial statements are conservative, any directorate—from the unscrupulous to the merely unfortunate—may reverse the process, at least for some time, and still have its statements believed to be conservative. There is no way, then, of knowing whether the figures of any particular company are conservative or not. Even if directors assert that their statements are conservative, this can be no assurance: conservatism amounts to tampering with the evidence on which the performance of the directorate and management is to be judged. No court, no jury, takes the simple assertions of a man on trial as proof of his innocence; but that is exactly what commercial practice in relation to company administration has accepted and condoned.

Again, is it wrong of auditors to report that the balance sheet of a company gives a true and fair view of its state of affairs and that its profit and loss account gives a true and fair view of a year's results, when assets are known to be conservatively valued and profits are known to be conservatively stated? Some would say, no; for surely prudence on the part of the directorate and management is to be encouraged in the interest of shareholders. This, again, is a one-sided view.

The law provides for the appointment of independent auditors for the very purpose of ensuring that shareholders shall not be misled. If auditors do not mind shareholders being misled by "conservative" reporting, who is to know whether they mind shareholders being misled in any circumstances? It is not implied that auditors generally act wilfully in disregard of shareholders' interests or dishonestly or carelessly; generally they may be supposed to act with good intentions and in good faith. But good intentions and good faith are no substitute for the true and fair view which the law requires, or for the independence which would ensure that directors give more than just a conservative view.

If directors are to be allowed to act prudently, the same right should surely be allowed to shareholders, by whom and for whose benefit the auditors are appointed. But shareholders cannot act prudently as long as they are denied the very information which will tell them whether directors have been prudent or not.

The three classes of circumstances considered demonstrate that quite respectable justifications may be advanced for actions which turn out to be to the direct disadvantage of investors and creditors and to the indirect disadvantage of many others such as the suppliers and employees of companies which overreach themselves. The defect of these justifications is that they all arise from a one-sided view. Promoters, directors, managers, auditors, brokers—all see themselves as acting from the best of motives, but overlook the consequences which may fall on others. Thinking highly of their own judgements is a fault to which all men are at some time or another prone.

Company securities are bought and sold in a market in the same way as other goods. They represent claims against the assets of companies or against the product of the use of those assets. But there is one important difference. No investor can inspect the assets of a company of which he holds shares or debentures or notes. They are constantly changing; they are commonly spread over a wide geographical area; and even if an investor were to see them he would be in no position to say what they were worth individually. An investor may form some general notions as to the stability and growth of a trade or industry, and even of particular companies in a trade or industry. But, to be realistic, his beliefs, expectations or hopes need to be conditioned by some firm knowledge of the financial capacity of any company to share in the growth or stability of a trade, or to adapt itself to unfavourable conditions. Inspection being impossible, he has no other resource than the company's financial statements.

Business firms, and in particular business corporations, are co-operative devices, but the various groups which constitute them are, by the provisions of industrial and commercial law, able to withdraw their co-operation if it seems to them that one group interest is being disregarded in favour of the interest of another. Creditors may seek to enforce their claims if management acts to their detriment. Investors may cause a run on their shares if management appears to offer them reduced prospects. Workers may strike if it seems that customers or investors are offered better inducements than workers believe themselves to be offered. Brokers may refuse to support new issues. It will be clear that most of these "disciplinary" or "remedial" actions depend on the availability of reliable financial information. And company law has long provided that reliable information on the finances and results of public companies shall be made available to holders of their shares and debentures.

Statutory Protection

The law is in effect the express will of the people. If the law grants the right of incorporation with limited liability—both incorporation and limited liability not being rights available to ordinary members of the community—it is only reasonable that there be some *quid pro quo* for this. The law guarantees the privacy of individuals with respect to their own affairs. But a corporation or company is not a private instrument. It is a publicly permitted instrument of private co-operative action. In so far as the community grants, by law, the privileges of incorporation and limited liability, it is only reasonable that the public have the means of knowing clearly with what effect these privileges are exercised. And the only means of knowing this yet devised is the publication of financial information.

The problem of drawing up a companies statute to regulate the complex relationships between the parties who become shareholders and creditors is by no means simple. Since the first modern Companies Act in England, enacted just over a hundred years ago, there have been many changes in it. This is as it should have been, for the whole apparatus of corporate business and widespread public investment in companies has much developed in that time. The earlier acts did not give any clear direction as to the expected character of the books of account and other records which companies were required to keep. As a consequence an extensive set of practical rules developed, many of them quite arbitrary, many of them contradictory, and many of them serving quite other purposes than the communication of up-to-date information as a guide to investors and others. From time to time the defects of these rules have become apparent.

It was once a widely held view that it was proper to represent assets in balance sheets in smaller amounts than they were really worth. This practice—the creation of secret reserves—came under severe criticism in *R.* v. *Kylsant* (see *The Accountant*, Vol. LXXXV, n.s.) in the 'thirties and opinion turned against it. It enabled annual profits to be distorted by undisclosed book entries at the discretion of company directors. But as recently as 1961, before the Jenkins Committee on Company Law in England, it was argued that this practice should be admitted as appropriate for banking, insurance and similar companies. Curiously, its supporters contended that while the community should have the utmost confidence in its financial institutions, it should not have the information on which to decide whether or not that confidence was well placed. This argument a leading London financial journalist described as "sheer sophristry".

There was once a widely held view also that an auditor's function did not extend to the independent observation and verification of the correctness of amounts shown in balance sheets as commodity stocks and amounts owing by debtors. But an American case (*McKesson & Robbins*), also in the 'thirties, demonstrated that, without proper checks of this kind, extensive frauds could be perpetrated over many years without discovery. Again opinion hardened against the previously held view.

These cases are examples of the fact that entries in books and other records of a company may, for fraudulent or accidental reasons, fail to correspond with the real state of affairs. Recent legislation has attempted to enforce the closing of this gap. The English Companies Act of 1948 states an overriding rule that "every balance sheet of a company shall give a true and fair view of the state of affairs of the company as at the end of its financial year". By implication, the books of account may diverge from a representation of the state of affairs in the course of a year, but the divergence must be corrected, by reference to the real state of affairs, for balance sheet purposes. The recent Australian legislation is quite specific. It requires that every company shall keep "such accounting and other records as will sufficiently explain the transactions and financial position of the company and enable true and fair profit and loss accounts and balance sheets . . . to be prepared from time to time". Again, by implication, if errors or divergences from the real state of affairs occur in the records, these are continually to be corrected.

Some Loopholes

Such mandatory provisions are good law from the point of view of securing an informed market in company securities. But they are clouded by a series of permissive provisions which in practice tend to be given more weight because they are more specific.

Thus, it is permissible for any company to choose its own methods of arriving at and showing the values of its assets. Consider two companies each owning freehold property. One may show its property at "cost"—perhaps what it cost many years ago. Another may show its property at "valuation"—and the valuation may be recent or long past. Which of these gives a true and fair view of the state of affairs at present? Everyone who buys durable goods knows that the initial price has little, if anything, to do with market or other values at a later date. Yet the act implicitly gives approval to the initial price or cost as a basis for showing a true and fair view. In any case, if two methods with widely differing effects on the values shown may be used by different companies at the same time, we can bid farewell to comparability as between companies.

Companies are required to state the methods they use to arrive at the amounts shown in balance sheets, but they may use any form of words they choose. Suppose two companies are set up and purchase their assets—one in 1950 and the other in 1960—and both companies state in their 1964 balance sheets that the basis used in stating their assets is "cost", without specifying the date to which cost applies. Readers of the two balance sheets will readily suppose that the information about the two companies is comparable. But a moment's reflection will show that it is not. No one believes that £100 spent in 1950 would buy the same as £100 spent in 1960. Yet that is exactly what the use of "cost" without specification of the date requires to be believed. If the dates of purchase had to be shown, it would become apparent that the two companies were not giving comparable views of the states of their affairs in 1964.

Companies are permitted to change the methods they use to arrive at the amounts shown in their financial statements, provided they state that they have done so. But they are not required to state the magnitude of the effect of the change in methods. If methods may be changed there can be no clear notion of what a true and fair view is, or by what particular methods the showing of a true and fair view will result. Again, if on a change of methods the magnitude of the effect is not shown, the state of affairs and the results of a company in two successive years may not be compared. Yet one would suppose comparison of this kind to be necessary if investors are to exercise a knowledgeable choice.

All these permissive provisions are clearly at odds with the mandatory provisions requiring a true and fair view at a stated date. English experience after the 1948 Act, which had similar mandatory general provisions and permissive specific provisions, has been that the mandatory provisions have been disregarded. The recent Australian legislation cannot be expected to have any better effect on the quality of published information.

It may be wondered what all this has to do with company losses. In a large measure it is the crux of the matter. The ideals of comparability and a true and fair view are written into the statutes. But the machinery provisions are so loose that the processes of regulating the flow of information are given ample opportunity for exploitation.

While it is possible to defer showing profits and losses to the full extent to which they occur and when they occur, it is possible for companies and their managements to avoid scrutiny.

It is impossible for shareholders to tell whether a company is a potential "loss company".

It is impossible for creditors to discover the extent of their security.

It is impossible for trustees for debenture-holders fairly to appraise either the financial position or the trend of results of a borrowing company.

It is impossible for the financial press to criticize, praise or blame, in an informed manner.

On the other hand it is possible for potential loss companies to go to the public for new share and loan capital, to make advantageous takeover bids, to continue to pay out commissions to their officers—forcing prices to ridiculous heights, increasing the risk of loss and ultimately the scale of losses to all parties.

But these defects, so vividly brought to light by the spectacular losses of the past few years, are of much greater consequence than as a mere explanation of how those losses arose. They strike at the very root of the system which permits them. The respect of the community for the private property of individuals is represented in laws against theft and fraud, by laws relating to the sale of goods and the making of contracts. In the same way the law seeks to ensure that investors shall know what they are buying and selling—but substantial protection vanishes through the loopholes previously mentioned.

Again, an important role of investors is to make sure that companies which can make better use of the community's resources than other companies shall be given preferential access to those resources. But if the information available makes it impossible to judge which companies can make better use, there can be no assurance that any company is efficient, or that companies generally are efficient. The level of efficiency may sink to the level of the least efficient company still in business, taking with it the contribution of the corporate business sector to the national product.

Investors invest at risk. But the risks of business are sufficient without supercharging them with unreliable or irrelevant information. It took the crash of 1929 to stimulate the regulation of securities markets by the creation of the American Securities and Exchange Commission. Even the comparatively few "crashes" experienced recently in Australia should serve to indicate that the community may be grievously misled in spite of the law. Legislation restricting borrowing powers has been suggested as a remedy for some abuses. But such restrictions may indiscriminately hamper the efficient as well as the inefficient. More frequent reporting by borrowing companies is being tried. But if the reported information is unreliable, more frequent reporting means simply a greater quantity of unreliable information.

It has been suggested that debenture-holders should be represented on boards of companies. But this would saddle them with conflicting allegiances, for a director's duty lies towards a company, not towards any particular group transiently interested in it. It has been suggested also that company officers should be made personally liable for debts incurred during winding up if there is no reasonable expectation that the company can meet them. But this does not strike at the cases where debts are incurred without reasonable expectations by going concerns.

The situation calls for no other instruments than are readily at hand. But it does require that those instruments be sharpened and actually used.

The legislation requires that a true and fair view of financial position and results shall be given. To make this effective all permissive rules tending to its avoidance should be eliminated from the statutes.

The legislation requires that auditors shall independently assure themselves that the financial information gives a true and fair view. Independence means nothing if the financial information is allowed to be coloured by the hopes, fears and ambitions of directors and managers. The auditing profession should therefore take all steps to ensure that their opinions are independently established, accepting no certificates or valuations by managers or directors as sole evidence of truth or fairness. If the profession itself cannot establish the principles which will give a true and fair view, legislatures should take steps to do so.

The legislation requires the appointment of auditors for the protection of shareholders. But no protection is vouchsafed unless auditors are free of doubts as to their legal position in respect of actions for defamation which may arise from their reports. So long as such a threat exists auditors cannot be expected to disregard it. But as knowledge of public corporations has become a matter of public interest, this threat should be decisively and unequivocally removed. The obligations of auditors to the public investor—and not to the company as such nor to its officers—should be firmly established.

13

ARE THE STOCK EXCHANGES IN AUSTRALIA MEETING THEIR CHALLENGES?*

No observer of the development of the Australian securities market over the last 20 years could fail to notice the changes which have been brought about by the stock exchanges and their members. Mr. Mellor has drawn attention to the ways in which the exchanges have regulated their affairs in the interest of expeditious service to the investing public; to the information and educational services they provide; to the fact that their requirements, directed towards an informed market, have been in advance of the legal requirements imposed on companies. The record is impressive, and is evidence enough of the keenness with which the exchanges and their members have faced the problems of an increasingly interested investing public in a community undergoing rapid and diverse development.

We take our cue from a number of observations made in Mr. Mellor's paper. They are all comments on "the paramount importance" of the disclosure of all relevant information on the nature of securities traded, and the avoidance of a false market in companies' securities. In concentrating attention in this way we are concerned with a universal feature of all stock exchange trading. There is considerable merit in the view that an annual financial report is insufficient information on which investors should be expected to act for a full year, and in the drive of the exchanges to secure to the investing public more information on "company results, accounts and activities". But it seems to be widely believed that more frequent information of the same kind is all that is necessary. We question the grounds for this belief.

Comparable Information

The essence of informed behaviour, in the securities market as elsewhere, is comparison. Hence on the one hand, the comparative figures over successive years of each company listed in the bulletins and information services of the exchanges and of individual broking firms; and on the other hand, the comparative figures of companies in particular industries and between industries for any one year. But comparative figures of a given company over years or for any group of companies in a given year may be quite misleading, tending to a false market, if the component figures are not of their nature uniform in

---

* First published in *Proceedings of Investment in Australia Symposium,* Melbourne, February 1965; comment on a paper by Mr. A. B. Mellor, Chairman, The Stock Exchange of Melbourne.

derivation. Mr. Mellor observed that one of the early objectives of the exchanges was to "to ensure that the intrinsic characteristics of a security offered for sale by one member meant exactly the same to all other members". Only by such kinds of uniformity is it possible to deal fairly. By a simple extension, only by uniformity in representing the intrinsic characteristics of a security many buyers and sellers deal sensibly. Now the intrinsic characteristics of a security do not simply subsist in the words and provisions of the forms which constitute a security. Thousands of security holders at present could wish it were so; but wishing does not make it so. The intrinsic characteristics of a security are in part in the legal forms, but in a far greater part in the economic substance of the issuer. The only way in which buyers or sellers can learn of the economic substance of companies and make comparisons of their financial features is through their financial statements.

Now it is undeniable that the financial statements of companies are not prepared on a uniform basis. Both the statutes and the stock exchanges have laid down rules which no doubt are expected to produce the uniformity of understanding which characterizes a fair market. But neither have reckoned with the factors which make for diversity notwithstanding superficial uniformity.

The Companies Acts require companies to publish annually balance sheets which shall give a true and fair view of their states of affairs as at the dates they bear. But the rules by which these balance sheets are derived have no such effect. What is commonly done in compiling balance sheets is to take the sum of money spent years ago on land and buildings, the sum of money spent more recently (less some allowance for depreciation) on plant and machinery, the sum of money spent some months ago on commodity stocks and the sum of money on hand at balancing date, to add these sums and to give the total as part of the state of affairs at balancing date. No individual would dream of adding such sums to find his present financial position; he would find it by getting some idea of the present purchasing power he commands from the present market prices of what he holds. We mentioned "some allowance for depreciation"; there are many different ways of calculating the amount of this allowance; all of them are equally acceptable, but all yield different amounts and therefore show different balances of the plant, etc., accounts and different net profits. There are also scores of ways of finding the money sum by which commodity stocks are represented; again all are equally acceptable, all result in different asset totals and in different net profits.

Consider what this means in terms of comparison of the intrinsic features of the securities of any small sample of companies. As their assets may be purchased at different times the total sums of money representing total assets will not be comparable even if the assets are the same. As the nominal amounts of their liabilities to creditors are contractually fixed, the difference between total assets and total liabilities, which is the shareholders' equity, will not be comparable. And as different methods of depreciation and stock valuation may be used their net profits will not be comparable; and the rates of net profit to shareholders' equity will not be comparable.

It is demonstrable that there are so many sets of rules by which balance sheets and profit statements may be derived that every single company on the Australian stock exchanges could use a different method every year for at least 10 years without exhausting their variety—and every method would be acceptable to the business community at present, and within the provisions of the law. And although the Companies Acts require a statement of the method used to obtain the values shown against certain kinds of assets, so many different methods go by the same name that it is impossible to tell which method is in fact used. To attempt to compare the characteristics of different companies under these conditions is to attempt the impossible. The intrinsic qualities of different securities cannot be ascertained, let alone compared; neither the terms used nor the numbers appearing in published financial statements mean the same thing in themselves; they cannot possibly have the same meaning to all investors and all brokers, and if they did, it would be a misleading meaning.

The situation was perhaps even worse in the United States some 30 years ago. The Securities and Exchange Commission was then empowered to require general uniformity of the financial statements of corporations traded on the national exchanges. In some respects it has not succeeded, due to the diversity of stock valuation rules and depreciation methods already mentioned—and there are more alternatives in both respects in the United States than in Australia. But in another respect it has succeeded too well. Adherence to the use of cost as the basis for showing durable assets and for calculating depreciation is more general there than here, if its use is not absolutely uniform. But this uniformity is uniformly misleading. What a company paid for a durable asset 10, 20, 30 years ago has no necessary relationship to its present financial position. The asset may now be worthless or worth 20 times as much as was paid for it. And if the cost basis is used, an investor can make little use of financial statements of different companies, one of which was formed 10, another 20, another 30 years ago. Only if the statements are all brought to the common basis of the present can companies be compared in the present. We understand that the S.E.C. is by no means satisfied with the results of its dependence on professional groups to develop of themselves methods which are uniform enough to provide comparable information as between companies; and there have in recent years been suggestions that it may yet exercise the powers it has "in the public interest and for the protection of investors". But the time is not yet. And the British investor is no better off.

In another sense, too, the common procedures for deriving financial statements are illogical and misleading. We all know that the pounds earned in business today have not the same significance as the pounds invested in business 10 or 20 years ago. If in comparative statements of single firms there are shown the capital contributed by shareholders originally, the initial purchase prices of durable assets and depreciation based on those prices, the initial price of commodity stocks, the cash on hand at successive balance dates, and the net profits of each year, every one of these figures will be in pounds of a different purchasing power—units of a different dimension. The folly of comparing the figures of any singular year will be obvious. It should be equally obvious that through a period of rising prices the rate of profit on the capital invested will tend to rise through no superior capacity of the company or its management, tending thus to mislead users of the figures. And it will also be obvious that a table covering a number of years in which all the figures are in units of different purchasing power cannot sensibly be used as a guide to the trend of a single business. And no trend derived in this way will be comparable with trends derived in the same way for other companies.

These practices of adding the unaddable and comparing the non-comparable are ritualistic; bits of folk-lore which scarcely conform with the scientific spirit of the twentieth century. We all conform with road rules for the better regulation of traffic, and with the rules of language for the better understanding of one another. There is no reason why companies may not be made to conform with uniform rules for the derivation of comparable financial information for the better conduct of the securities markets.

Relevant Information

Mr. Mellor has told us that "the Australian Associated Stock Exchanges consider that disclosure of all relevant information is of paramount importance". We wish to ask what relevance means; relevant to whom and for what?

In terms of the operations of the securities market, relevant can only mean equally relevant to all operators, buyers and sellers alike, and relevant to every course of action they may take in the market. If information is not relevant both to buyer and seller, the market cannot be fair. If it is relevant to neither it is useless, if it is relevant to the judgements of one but not of the other it creates inequities. The actions open to shareholders (to a less extent to lenders) are several. They may buy additional shares, sell off shares, maintain their holdings, change company boards, and in the last resort they may resolve to sell off the assets of a company piecemeal or in total. Only if the financial information enables them to choose between these possibilities is it relevant to them all. If financial information is not relevant to them all, it prevents shareholders from exercising their best judgement; it is unfair to them all. To be relevant, and fair, the information must be up to date, brought up to date from time to time, always contemporary.

We have already said that balance sheets generally contain statements about assets which may well be long out of date. A classic example is that of J. Sears and Company, an English company for which Mr. Charles Clore made a bid in 1952. The company's board on hearing of the offer advised shareholders that, although the book value of the company's properties was £2.59 million, at least £6 million could be raised on them if necessary, even disregarding the 350 or more branch shops which were occupied by tenants. It appears that the properties therefore had a contemporary realizable price of over £10 million, though they were being shown at only one-fourth of that sum. There have been similar cases of gross understatement among Australian companies in the not-distant past, though not perhaps on the same scale. Could it be said that this information, released under pressure by the Sears Board, was previously irrelevant to the market? Certainly not, if buyers and sellers are to judge between shares on the basis of the rates of return earned by companies. For in the above case the rate of return was clearly four times as high as would have been shown by a contemporary calculation.

It is unnecessary to multiply examples. The very rules by which financial statements are prepared at present yield information which is more or less out of date. And depending on prevailing economic conditions, shareholders and investors generally may as likely be given balance sheets which overstate the "state of affairs" as they are to be given balance sheets which understate the "state of affairs". Some of the companies which have been the subject of official inquiries provide memorable examples of continued overstatement. But whichever way the statements vary from the contemporary facts, out-of-date information cannot be relevant information; if balance sheets are out of date profit statements will also be irrelevant, for they are statements of contemporary revenues against which are set out-of-date costs; and profit rates based on such irrelevant information cannot be relevant. More frequent publication of information of the same irrelevant kind will do little to help the judgement of the investor.

No doubt the stock exchanges have believed that they are entitled to rely on the relevance of the financial information which companies publish. Any reasonable person would suppose that, if the law provides that published financial information shall give a true and fair view of the state of affairs and the profits of companies from time to time, the intention of the law could not readily be evaded; and that the result would be relevant, particularly when the financial statements bear an auditor's report to the effect that they give a true and fair view at a specified date. But our "reasonable person" would be quite wrong in his supposition. For though the law—the provisions of the Companies Acts in Australia and in Britain—is a good one, so much latitude has been taken with it that the results are anything but true and fair.

What has happened, it seems, is that the notion of a true and fair view has become completely inverted. The intention of the law seems to have been that users of the financial statements shall have a true and fair view of the state of affairs and of the profits from time to time; and that consequently the processes of deriving the statements would be designed to give this effect. What has happened on the other hand is that "true and fair" has been considered as a quality of the judgement of the producers of the information, company managements and auditors. One writer, a non-accountant, has said of accounting statements: "they may be untruths, but they are not lies".

What the certificates and reports appended to financial statements seem to assert is that "this statement seems to us (directors or auditors) to be true and fair". Only on some such interpretation as this is it possible to understand how the great number of different devices we have already mentioned have come to be adopted. If what is true and fair is a matter for the judgement of managers and directors, and as the financial statements are the basis of judgements by investors on the performance of companies and their managers and directors, it is easy to see how diverse views may be considered to be true and fair, or may be represented to be true and fair; and it is easy to see how relevance to shareholders and potential investors may be disregarded altogether.

Rules

The law in fact reckoned without the persistence of old rules for producing balance sheets and income statements. These rules date back to the time when there was no public market in company securities, and when businessmen could inform themselves by direct observation of the state of their business affairs. The revolution in the organization of business which gave us the public limited liability company has virtually left untouched the rules of a far less sophisticated and complicated age. And whereas the auditor was introduced to authenticate the statements given by the managers and directors of companies, if the auditor's report uses the words "true and fair" as an assertion about his own views, as we have suggested, the authenticating function, the task for which he is appointed by and for the shareholders, is in a critical sense unperformed.

Notice that we are not referring to the cases in which departures from the existing body of rules have drawn the censure of auditors. We are referring to the general body of rules itself. The reasons for the persistence of illogicality in the operation of, and irrelevance of the results of, constructing financial statements are several. The first is that the practical necessity, to investors and their advisers, of contemporarily relevant information was not a matter of concern when most of the rules now used were developed; and no serious consideration has been given to it since, except by a relatively small number of people on the periphery of business. The second is that the users of the information have taken for granted its contemporary relevance without examining the rules to discover whether that is what they produce. Perhaps this has been due to a feeling that the technicalities of the process are beyond the grasp of the ordinary man. But in so far as the ordinary man, as investor or manager, or broker, must use the information produced, there should be no mystery about the process of deriving it. The third reason for the practices referred to is that the law provides primarily for the supply of information periodically to existing investors in companies; and notwithstanding that published accounts have also to be filed in a public place, so that they are available to the public at large, those who prepare them have long held to the view that the existing investor is the only class to which a duty runs.

It is this last-mentioned view which may be used to justify all kinds of rules, and the abandonment of them, too. It is easy to justify giving shareholders a "conservative" view—one which understates their present position—on the ground that it is in their "long-run" interest. But such a view is unfair to many investors, for "long-run" may mean very long-run and they may not hold their shares long enough to get the benefit of what is not disclosed; they may sell them in the belief that the intrinsic characteristics of the security include assets worth, say, £2.5 million when in fact they are worth £10 million (the Sears case mentioned above). On the other hand it is easy to justify giving shareholders an "optimistic" view—one which overstates their present position—on the ground that a conservative view might cause them to sell, and that, too, is is not in their "long-run" interest. Common knowledge of the Reid Murray affair will suggest what may happen to the "long-run" interest if this is done. The freedom of companies to choose their own rules may thus defeat all desires to get at the facts if one wants to buy or sell: for particular views chosen to suit the circumstances of a company can never be known with confidence to be conservative or optimistic in effect. In any case, if all investors were long-run investors there would be no stock exchanges. The notions of long-run interest and reporting only to existing shareholders are clearly fanciful and unrealistic and should be abandoned.

Obligation

This more or less legalistic view of the obligation of companies and auditors to existing shareholders has no place in the affairs of the stock exchanges. As Mr. Mellor observed, it is just as necessary that relevant information shall be available to intending investors in securities as to existing holders. A market is only fair if it is fair both to buyers and sellers, if the information circulated in it is biased towards neither. A fair market, not a market fair to one side only, is the ideal which apparently has motivated the policies of the exchanges.

In this respect the concern of the stock exchanges with the quality of published financial information transcends other interests. The law does not make a market in securities; it lays down minimal rules. If there is such a thing as the spirit of the law on published financial information then that spirit tends in the direction of contemporarily relevant and uniformly derived information. But a narrow interpretation of the law tends in the other direction. Similarly the financial officers and managers of companies do not make a market in securities. They have specific interests to preserve and promote; and if they believe that limiting the supply of information tends to preserve those interests, they will limit the supply. The securities market is made by the buyers and sellers of securities, and their agents, and the machinery by which the characteristics of securities are put on display. That is where the rules of the law are put into effect; that is where the rules for deriving financial information have their impact; that is where the comparability and the contemporary relevance of information should be recognized as the prime qualities which distinguish a biased market from a fair one.

A Challenge

Now the stock exchanges may not for a moment be thought to be responsible for the rather chaotic state of the information supply we have suggested. In an interdependent world one class of experts necessarily depends on another. And we imagine there is an ethic which to some extent restrains professional people from trespassing on the domain of others. What we suggest, however, is that corporate financial information is not the domain solely of lawyers, or accountants, or company managers and directors. It is in a real sense part of the domain of the stock exchanges. The function of a market is not simply to enable exchanges to be effected; it is also to enable the things to be exchanged to be examined by buyers, and to enable the offerings of one seller to be examined by other sellers; and, as we said at the outset, the offerings subsist much more in the substance behind documents of title than in those documents themselves.

We do not suppose that brokers like being connected with companies which, on inquiry, have been found to be regulating the flow of information until its falsity can no longer be concealed; yet many companies have been found to fall into this class. We do not suppose that the stock exchanges are complacent about the long delays between the setting up of official inquiries and the release of the findings—delays during which the securities held by individual investors are either tied up in hope or are turned into the flimsiest of flotsam. We do not suppose that brokers are unaware of the fact that companies which give out-of-date information to the market subject their shareholders to marked and unforeseeable swings in prices when takeover offers are made by outsiders who have knowledge relevant to shareholders, and which should be available to them, but which is denied them by their own managements. And the exchanges have made it clear that they have no love for "inside" deals which can only be as lucrative as they occasionally are because knowledge of the present state of affairs, to which the general run of investors is entitled, is in fact withheld from them. These and other like anomalies may all be laid at the doorstep of faulty information. If comparable up-to-date, relevant information were available, it seems reasonable to suppose that incipient failures would more readily be discovered, faulty management would be more readily eliminated, the efficiency of companies would be promoted and the securities market would be a much better device for distributing control over investible funds than it is at present. Operations in the market would be much more a matter of informed judgement than is possible when investors are misinformed or poorly informed.

We suppose that no group of people is more competent to judge the quality of the information presently made available or potentially available to the securities market than those who, as experts, operate in it—if they would give critical attention to it. There are many features of regular operations which demand attention as the market develops. But this one feature, the quality of the information supply, is so general and fundamental that it seems to warrant the most serious examination.

Irrelevance and diversity present a challenge which is nowhere being met at present. Work in this direction could give a lead to those in other countries who are confronted with the same problems. It would certainly command the sympathy of many who have come to disrespect the information now available and who hope for something more reliable. One could hope it may give a lead to the amendment of the law in respect of published financial information in much the same way as stock exchange requirements have advanced practice in this respect in the past. The challenge appears to be worthy of the skills which have made the stock exchanges as significant and their operations as efficient as they are now.

14

PUBLISHED FINANCIAL REPORTS AND NATIONAL PRODUCTIVITY*

It is a commonplace, at least among accountants, that financial statements relate to the affairs of particular entities—partnerships, companies and so on. Consequently it is commonly supposed that so long as the best judgement of those who publish accounts is exercised in their preparation the published financial statements will serve their functions as well as can be expected. It is our purpose to challenge this presumption. We will contend that the present attitude towards the design of published financial statements is far too liberal to provide effective checks on the capacities of enterprises and the skills of their managers; and that those statements therefore serve poorly a function which they alone can serve, and which they are generally depended upon to serve.

Information and Motivation

An exercise of this kind is timely. We live in an age which is concerned with efficiencies of many kinds. It is an age in which men seek to measure things large and small, aggregative and singular, so that they may compare their measurements with the findings of others in pursuit of efficiency. Means have been devised by which the expected general consequences of singular actions or classes of action may be deduced, for such singular actions or classes of action are seen as integral parts of the complex system of actions which is a functioning society. Public institutions and authorities have become concerned with national productivity and with the discovery of ways of measuring and of increasing productivity. Among the ways of increasing productivity one of the most widely noticed is increasing the skill and knowledge of the populace, for productivity in the aggregate depends on the performance of the individuals who do the producing whatever form production may take. By knowledge, in this context, we do not refer only to knowledge of general principles. We refer also to the continuous supply of information which taken together with knowledge of general principles enables men the more efficiently to perform their chosen or allotted tasks. If then we speak of increasing the knowledge of the populace, we include also increasing knowledge of principles for the discovery of the facts so that the knowledge of facts as they occur is also increased.

---

* First published in *Selected Problems in Accountancy, Papers from a Seminar* (February 1965), The University of Western Australia Adult Education Board, 1965, pp. 19-32.

This is our cue. When we speak of skill we usually refer to some specific skill. And as we live in an interdependent society, the skill of some of us can be defeated if those on whom we depend overlook our dependence on them. When we speak of knowledge we usually refer to some specific kind of knowledge. And as we live in an interdependent society, only knowledge which is of a public and generally interpretable kind can serve to make fruitful our intercourse with others. Now although accounting has been, historically, a way of informing individuals about their individual affairs it has long since ceased to be merely that. The growth of public interest and investment in private corporations has made accounting a social instrument, a form of social communication, a way of disseminating in society at large knowledge of the operations of socially significant institutions.

This is no mere "puff", put forward to give ground for exaggerating the role of accounting and accountants. It is simply facing the facts. Facing these facts is not likely to give comfort to accountants or to others implicated in the affairs of public companies. The view has long been held that the obligations of companies and their auditors in respect of published information are limited to persons and institutions having present financial interests. This view is a relic of the days when business firms were small, even if they were incorporated, and when changes in shareholdings were presumably infrequent. If shareholders could be considered as having committed themselves for long terms to investment in any given company it may matter little whether accounting methods yield statements which are peculiar to particular companies. Long-term commitment implies disregard of interim signals relating to performance and financial position. Long-term commitment gives some colour to the notion of a form of accounting in which the stewardship idea might find a place, as it does in the affairs of trusts. But the assumption of long-term commitment entails also the absence of a market, or at least the absence of an active market, in securities.

Information and the Securities Market

This assumption is quite inconsistent with the conditions which now prevail; and indeed it is inconsistent with conditions which have prevailed for at least half a century and probably longer. The mere existence of the stock exchanges is evidence of an active market in company securities generally, and the special forms of financial journalism testify to the liveliness of the interest of the public generally in operations, results and financial positions of companies. The shareholders of a company today may be entirely different from its shareholders a month hence or a month ago. The market in fact arose out of the company legislation of over 100 years ago. With the right to invite public subscription to security issues went the obligation to make available financial information. By this one stroke accounting was transformed from its purely private character to a quasi-public character, a character which it appears to have been slow in assuming, if not quite reluctant to assume.

The existence of a market in securities made it possible to rely on the operations of the market to do what other markets do. The markets in goods enable exchanges to be effected. They enable prices to be made by some and discovered by others. The discovery of prices and movements in prices is the spur to actions which affect future markets. If the price of a good tends to fall suppliers are warned against continued production at the same cost. If the price of a good tends to rise, suppliers are warned of the possibility of future gains from augmenting the supply. On the demand side, buyers are able to compare qualities and prices of all offerings by suppliers, and again the discovery of prices and movements in prices influence the timing of actions on the part of buyers. The informative function of the market is implied in all responses of buyers and sellers to their observations of prices and qualities. The upshot of these interactions is the tendency of the market to indicate the directions in which economic resources should be deployed; and if because of specialization certain resources may not be switched to other employments, to indicate the necessity of a higher degree of efficiency in their employment. In brief, the goods markets ration the available supply at any time and provide stimuli to buyers and sellers influencing the choices they exercise as between present and future actions on their part.

An analogous function is performed by the securities market. Behind much of the production of tangible goods and services lie the aggregations of the savings of individuals which are turned to work under the control of the officers of business and public corporations. Personal resources which may otherwise be idle are deployed by persons in ways of their own choosing among the security investment opportunities which the ingenuity of promoters and directors and the exigencies of governmental and other authorities provide. The supply of and the demand for investible funds determine at any time the price at which the control over such funds is exchanged. Like the buyers of goods, the buyers of securities entertain different expectations of the satisfaction to be gained from securities of different qualities—not only as between different types of security but also as between securities of the same type but of different suppliers (companies and other issuers). The prices of particular securities will rise or fall under the influence of these expectations. Again, like the expectations entertained of goods, the expectation of satisfaction from investment in particular securities depends on the knowledge available to the market of the qualities of the securities offering.

This knowledge does not subsist solely in the formal or legal stipulations of the rights and obligations attaching to the securities as such. The qualities of a security depend on the legal and economic features of the issuer. But, unlike the qualities of marketable goods, these qualities of a security are not open to direct inspection. Envisaging the necessity of some indication of quality the architects of company law provided that the legal and economic features of companies shall be made accessible to the investing public from time to time, and that the authenticity of the information shall be vouchsafed by auditors properly appointed by and, or, on behalf of investors.

This is the function of periodically published financial statements. They represent the different kinds of resources under the control of companies, their assets; the legal and equitable rights of others in those assets; and the income earned periodically by the use of resources under the control of companies. Given that the magnitudes of all these items are discovered and represented in a way readily interpretable by investors, it is possible to discover the relative efficiency with which different companies employ the resources under their control; this is given by the relationship between the measure of periodical income and the measure of the risk capital employed in earning it, commonly called the rate of return.

The Rate of Return as an Indicator of Efficiency

Now the rate of return thus obtained for any given company is not a rate which may be judged to be satisfactory or unsatisfactory in isolation. There is no such thing as the rate of return appropriate to any class of enterprise or risk. Rates of return may only be judged to be better or worse than rates of return earned by other companies during the same interval or by the same company over different intervals. Intertemporal comparisons are valuable if one wishes to obtain some guide to the possibility of growth or decline. But at any particular time the rate of return revealed by the latest summarization of a company's results and position is the only measure which may be compared with that of other companies. The function of the rate of return is thus to enable actual and potential investors in, and suppliers of money to, companies to discover which companies are superior to others in the one respect which is common to all—the derivation of income. If the rate of return of a company rises, and if its trading environment promises the prospect at least of maintaining the new higher level, money will tend to flow into its securities, advancing the company's prospects of increasing its scale of operations and its command over non-monetary goods and services. The rate of return is the price yielded, by the market in its products, for the enterprise and temporal command over resources which in effect constitute a firm.

This price like all other prices serves both to ration the available investible funds among companies and to indicate the firms which are for the moment the relatively more efficient. If the securities market does not know this price the allocative function will be performed in a less satisfactory manner than if it were informed. If businessmen themselves do not know this price for their own firms and other firms, they will not know whether they are more or less efficient than others and whether therefore renewed efforts to increase efficiency are necessary.

If the rate of return is regarded as a price, it is to be regarded as an all-inclusive price. The efficiency or productivity of a firm has many facets. Of any selection of firms at any time, one may have a superior marketing policy, another a better balanced product line, another a technically superior manufacturing establishment, another a superior wages and labour relations policy, and so on. And over any lengthy period of time a given firm may occupy the top rank successively in respect of different features of its operations—if any such ranking could be made. It is improbable however that any firm will at any time be superior in all respects, or that it will maintain its superiority in any respect indefinitely. The continual processes of product and technical innovation, the shifting of market preferences, and the thrust of ambitious young executives within and of new entrepreneurs without all tend to unsettle the habits of older firms. Not for nothing did Schumpeter describe the processes of capitalism as "creative destruction". It is the resultant of all these facets of the operations of a firm, all these factors within it and all the forces of the markets beyond it, which the rate of return represents. The rate of return therefore does not necessarily indicate relative superiority in any one phase of the firm's operations; by comparison with the rates of return of other firms it indicates the relative efficiency of the whole co-ordinated set of policies and activities which are the firm.

It is emphasized that there is no absolute measure of efficiency or productivity available, or indeed conceivable. There is no device which a firm in isolation can use as a test of its efficiency as an economic instrument. There are exchanges of technical information of diverse kinds between firms all tending towards the improvement of technical performance in one field or another. But these exchanges relate only to partial performance, whereas the skill of managing an enterprise subsists in the capacity to organize all its parts and to adapt the whole to its opportunities and constraints. There is no other test than the performance of others operating through the same time within the same complex of markets. Not only that, the productivity of capital which is indicated by the rate of return is directly connected with the securities market. Investors do not invest in industries, they invest in firms. They do not want more steel or more beer; they want more money whether they invest in steelmakers or brewers. There is no indicator other than the rate of return which can reduce the diversity of firms to comparability, to a point where performance as a whole in the markets for supplies and for products may be judged in a single scale.

Necessary Qualities of Financial Information

The implications of this are clear. If published financial statements do not represent the capital invested and the periodical income from the investment in like terms, the rate of return will be meaningless, for it is a maxim of elementary arithmetic that the numerator and the denominator of a ratio must be in like terms if the ratio is to be interpretable. If published financial statements do not represent capital invested and periodical income in contemporary terms at the dates up to which they are drawn, the rate of return will be neither relevant at that time (the time from which action is to be taken), nor interpretable at that time (for all interpretations of money quantities at a point of time depend on what is understood at that time by the meaning of the unit). If published financial statements do not represent capital invested and periodical income in contemporary terms uniformly for all companies, no company will be able to assess its own performance by reference to the performance of others in the same settings. There being no absolute scale of efficiency, contemporary comparison of this kind is the only guide to the general rise or fall in efficiency and the only spur to the pursuit of greater efficiency. Similarly investors will be unable to choose the more efficient from the less in the absence of uniformity.

Present Deficiencies of Financial Information

It should be common knowledge to accountants that none of these conditions we have outlined—measurement in like terms at a given time for any company, in contemporary terms, in uniform terms for all companies—is satisfied by the financial information presently produced and published. But we outline the evidence.

The effects of present accounting rules are to represent so-called current assets by the use of quite different rules than those by which so-called fixed assets are represented. Broadly the distinction is that current assets are represented by monetary amounts which approximate their present prices; while the methods of representing fixed assets are generally based on initial purchase prices. Further the derivation of income is done in a way which treats numbers of monetary units of revenue as of like quality with numbers of monetary units representing depreciation, when the latter units, being based on initial purchase prices of plant, may be and commonly are of very different quality. The sum representing total assets is thus a mixed measure; the sum representing total liabilities is a sum of like measures; the difference should be a measure of capital invested, but it is also a mixed measure; the difference representing income is a mixed measure; and what the ratio of a mixed measure of income to a mixed measure of capital invested can mean can only be left to the imagination. It should give the rate of return, but what it does give is incomprehensible. So much for like terms.

The last paragraph suggests that the present rules do not give information in contemporary terms by virtue of the use of initial purchase prices for durable goods and depreciation charges in respect of them. For variety we look at a different facet of the matter. Suppose that a company shows the same rate of return on its invested capital over a series of years in which the level of prices rises, both income and invested capital being computed by rules of the present kind. The inference that would usually be drawn is that the company had maintained its efficiency as an income producer. But the result shown is due in part to the rise in prices of its products, that is to the rise in its revenues, while the statement of its invested capital is in terms very different from contemporary terms. In reality the rate of return which would result from showing income and assets in contemporary terms would be declining, and knowledge of the decline would either spur its management to make good the decline or induce its shareholders to think of preferable alternatives. Both possibilities would not come to attention under presently used rules.

As for uniformity as between companies the diversity of practices is notorious. We have elsewhere indicated that by considering only a selection of the methods available for valuing different kinds of assets there are at least a million different sets of rules by which balance sheets may be prepared. And even the notations, required by the Companies Acts to be given, of the general bases upon which various classes of assets are valued in balance sheets do not help the reader to decide which set of rules has been used by any company; for every one of the commonly used notations itself stands for a great variety of quite different rules. But not only is there diversity of practices; it is commonly held that diversity is to be expected. This view however disregards the whole function of financial information in the modern securities markets. That function is to enable investors, at least, to make comparisons between the financial features of companies so that they may judge in an informed way those companies which appear to have superior capacities for earning income, those which are the more efficient. A function related to this, because the tenure of managers and the preservation and promotion of their own interests depend on it, is to enable managers to make similar comparisons so that they in turn may maintain or improve the efficiency of company operations.

Two Kinds of Entropy

There is a tendency in many physical and social systems towards increasing disorganization, or inefficiency, if they are, or become, isolated from sources of energy which counteract the tendency. The tendency is expressed in the second law of thermodynamics, and it has been applied by analogy in many other fields. It is styled the principle of increasing entropy.

In the first place, business organizations are subject to entropy if in any respect they isolate themselves from the world at large. That is to say, if their norms are internal, their standards of performance are of their own choosing, their methods of operation are of their own devising, and their personnel become habituated to their own modes of thinking, their efficiency will tend to fall. The counter to this tendency is the inflow of new information—about the state of markets, performance of others operating in the same or similar markets, the changes in technology occurring elsewhere and so on. This information flows in, if at all, in the form of messages in the vernacular or a special technical language. But languages are also subject to entropy. Unless efforts are made continually to preserve the common meanings of at least a considerable part of a language, the meanings of words become so diffuse that messages in the language cease to inform. For this reason, when in any field of discourse precision is of paramount importance, artificial languages are invented in which the terms have unique meanings and messages in those languages are interpretable equally well by all who use the language.

Now financial statements are messages in a technical language. Much of what we have described in the preceding section is evidence of a language which has degenerated through its isolation from the modes of thinking necessary in the practical conduct of business organizations. If then one of the technical languages in which messages may flow into business organizations breaks down, the potential of those messages for reversing the tendency to disorganization is reduced. Furthermore, the whole system of business is itself subject to increasing entropy, if, by failure of the technical languages which serve to acquaint different sections of the systems of business with the state of other sections, each section is obliged to act independently rather than interdependently.

The looseness of the whole system thwarts any desire on the part of managers to profit by the comparison of meaningful figures of other companies with their own. Indeed it encourages further looseness. It must be clear to businessmen that if there are many alternative accounting rules, and if the choice is at their option because every such rule is itself acceptable and respectable, there are no effective constraints at all on the representations they make in balance sheets and income statements. If every man can choose his own rules there are obviously no rules. And if there are no rules, it is quite useless to seek a guide to one's own efficiency by comparing one's own meaningless figures with the meaningless figures of other companies.

It should not be supposed that we are engaging in hyperbole for effect. There is ample evidence of the inadequacy of financial communication in the history of takeovers and mergers. The new information which has come to light under the threat of absorption has often shown what a travesty of the idea of disclosure much previous accounting has been. There is also ample evidence of inadequacy in the reports published as a result of official inquiries, and in the statements of directors of loss companies over the past few years. We may well speculate that this is only the surface appearance of a phenomenon of which nine-tenths is still submerged but which may come to the surface at any time.

The whole system of business does not collapse under these inadequacies because other sources of information (and there are many) besides accounting information compensate at least to some extent for the deficiencies of the latter. The constant inflow of information on market prices, technical developments, economic changes, tends to reverse the entropy of firms and of the whole system. But every such kind of information bears on one facet of business at a time. It has always been a peculiar claim of those who calculate in terms of money, and particularly of accountants, that their methods cut across sectional facets and their results represent business as a whole and all its operations in terms of a common denominator. If in fact it did so it would supplement in a valuable way all other specific information by which managers are provoked to improve efficiency. But it does not do so. The mere use of numbers of units bearing a common name does not constitute the named unit a common denominator. The question is what any such unit denominates at any time. If the unit denominates different purchasing powers at different times it is not a common denominator;

the results of supposing that it is are the "mixed" aggregates we have referred to; and the likelihood of them being provocative of increased efficiency is almost infinitesimal.

Productivity and the Allocation of Resources

What can happen to national productivity under these circumstances? Business firms may be efficient in one or more respects, but relatively inefficient as wholes, for there is no observable information which enables their relative efficiencies as wholes to be ascertained. Their managers may persist in following courses of action which they believe to be individually advantageous, without the benefit of the corrective of a co-ordinated grasp of their affairs as a whole, such as well-designed financial statements would give. It is thus quite possible that routine, day-to-day decisions may be well taken, but that these decisions taken as a whole may be lop-sided, undisciplined and injurious. As no legitimate comparison between firms is possible, none is spurred to greater efficiency by the comparison which contemporary and relevant information would give; and the possibility that industry as a whole will settle down to a common level of mediocrity, a level far below its potential productivity, is ever present. Indeed it is not merely a possibility, it is inevitable.

Consider the question also from the point of view of the allocation of control over economic resources. Whatever the quality of published information the securities market must depend to some extent on what is published. But published information being what it is, the market is misled, often grievously. Some of the stock exchanges publish monthly bulletins, giving for all listed companies such figures as last year's disclosed profit, the amount of published reserves and the net tangible assets per share. One would presume that the details relating to particular companies in these lists would be comparable, but this is just not so. There is quite a deal of evidence to the effect that the information published by companies is tailor-made to their circumstances from time to time. When confronted with takeover bids many have been able to find overnight many more tangible assets, and indeed bigger profits, than previously published information would have given the share market cause to suspect. And on the other hand, many companies when confronted with liquidity crises such as the necessity to pay dividends or interest or to repay debts, have been unable to find the tangible assets they have led the share market to believe existed.

There can be no doubt about the possibility that in these circumstances the control of resources often passes to the optimistically inefficient much to the chagrin of investors. Millions of pounds worth of the savings of individuals have in the last five years passed, through such companies, out of productive employment as part of the capital of industry, into the hands of consumers (either as defaulters on terms purchases, or as buyers at bargain prices on the liquidation of firms in the business of consumers' durables). Whether the legend of Robin Hood, with his ideal of mulcting the rich for the sake of the righteous, has been the model of some of the leaders of business, we do not know; but it sometimes looks that way.

We do not believe in the monistic view, quite prevalent among the apologists for management but we believe less prevalent among managers themselves, that managers are the repository of economic wisdom. We adhere rather to the pluralistic view that the ends of the community are best served when the views of members of the community, on the widest possible scale, enter into the decisions of the business instrumentalities of the community. Thus we believe that the facts of the performance of business, whether good or bad, should be available to investors, potential investors and the public at large. Businessmen may wish to explain them, to extricate themselves from censure now and then, and also to enjoy the satisfaction of commendation now and then. But unless the facts are made available in contemporary terms, there can be no surety that explanation is demanded, that inefficiency is exposed or that informed decisions on the allocation of resources will be made.

Some Side-effects

Now some may suggest that our fears, or our assertions, about the potential mediocrity of business performance are ill-founded. They will point to the fact that businessmen do not depend simply on published financial information, but also on the breakdown of the details by "management" accounting analysis. The fact of the matter is that the raw material of cost accounts and calculations of departmental and product cost is the information contained in the financial accounts of business. If then the financial accounts of business are deficient in the respects we have mentioned, the cost calculations will be equally deficient, equally lacking in contemporary relevance. It may further be suggested that cost analyses are not directly related to the financial statements ordinarily published. If this is is so then there is no possibility that the consequences of the individual operations of firms will be or can be judged by reference to their impact, as a co-ordinated whole, on the operations of the firm as a whole. Under present conditions, from whatever direction our views are approached, the fact remains that present practices in accounting do not produce the kinds of messages or signals which, because they are presently relevant, will promote the further pursuit of efficiency.

There is a further feature still, of the problem we are considering. For individual firms, taxed as they are at what they consider to be high rates of taxation, there is much to be gained, or saved, by attending to the incidence of taxation rules. Now, nationally, this exercise is unproductive. It adds nothing to the *quantum* of goods and services which, collectively or individually, we consume. It may shift the burden of providing collectively consumed services from one taxpayer to another, but it makes the community no better off. The rules on which taxation levies are based are admittedly at the discretion of government. But they had their source primarily in the accounting practices used by business firms. It is our opinion that the complexities of the tax laws are due in no small part to the looseness of the accounting framework on which they are based; and that, on the other hand, these complexities give rise to extraordinarily complicated exercises aimed at removing gains of one kind or another from the taxable class. On this we make three observations. Firstly we do not challenge the right of any taxpayer legitimately to minimize the incidence of taxation on his gains. But secondly, if the diversity of practices in computing income were reduced to a rational, consistent system, there is every hope that the taxation code could be simplified. There is consequentially some expectation that the expensive hours devoted to the minimization of individual tax burdens might be directed towards the improvement of the efficiency of communication within and beyond particular companies, and through this to the improvement of the productivity of industry. And thirdly, in some respects the taxation rules have been accepted as the criteria of accounting practices, and in other respects they have been rejected; hence the disparity between published net profits and taxation provisions often alluded to in the financial press. In this respect, as in others, the users of the financial statements do not know which rules are being used in any given case and with what effect. The important thing at this point, however, is that in so far as taxation rules are allowed at all to influence reported results and financial positions they interfere with the proper function of financial statements as indicators of operating efficiency and therefore as auxiliaries to the allocative function of the securities markets.

Productivity in Information Production

To focus the preceding discussion directly on productivity we return to some of our opening remarks. The production of information relevant to action on the part of managers of all kinds, investors, and a variety of other users is the distinctive role of accounting. The productivity of any firm, and of any class of persons, is measurable in terms of the ratio of outputs to inputs. But defective or unusable products do not rank for inclusion with outputs, unless by further inputs a usable product emerges. Consider then the inputs to the process of financial information production in Australia. Of necessity we make some rather wild guesses.

There are probably no less than 30,000 persons qualified as accountants or occupying the position of accountant even though not professionally qualified. Let us suppose that 25,000 of them are employed in business or are engaged in professional practice. Let us suppose their average incomes from accounting, in auditing and similar work to be £2000 per annum. This will allow for the fact that many accountants who earn much larger incomes also engage in work which does not fall within the classification of accounting and similar work. Let us suppose that for every accountant there are four other persons who are assistants, clerks, machine operators and similar persons engaged on clerical and information processing tasks; and that the average incomes of these persons are £1000 per annum. Disregarding all other costs of the production of financial information, this guessing gives an annual bill of £150 million.

But our conclusions from an examination of the rules in use are that the intermediate product, the information produced, is defective in many respects and is not therefore usable in the form in which it is produced. The end product of the process is, of course, a reaction or a response on the part of some user. In so far as the information is irrelevant, even if it is used it cannot be said to have an end product. In so far as users are prompted by other observations or circumstances, to question its relevance additional inputs on their part are necessary to produce the end product. It is a matter of quite common experience to find financial information disputed within firms; and as for the class of information which is published much time and effort, on the part of the financial press and the compilers of investment bulletins and security statistics, is devoted to discovering what the implications of the information are, for only then can the end product, response on the part of investors, be a product of the information. There is thus a very considerable additional input not already counted in the treatment of the direct costs of information processing work. Nor have we counted the costs of printing, publishing and circulating financial statements.

It can be no exaggeration that the costs of merely producing the financial information now made available is in excess of £200 million annually. Nor can it be doubted that the potential of this information for selecting economically appropriate responses in those to whom it is supplied is small indeed. We are not asserting that an expenditure of the above order is unnecessary, though we do believe that a rationalization of the methods now in use would cut the costs of processing by a considerable sum. Who now knows how many hours in total are spent on the task of selecting (e.g., by internal discussion, consultation with auditors and legal advisers) from all the available rules those which will be used by each single firm in any given year? We leave it for others to judge in the light of our earlier remarks how much of the expenditure we mention is productive. But the sheer magnitude of the sum unquestionably warrants serious consideration of the utility of the intermediate product, information, with reference to the end product, action on the part of managers and investors which is appropriate to the real conditions and environments of the firms.

The greatest difficulties in grappling with the productivity of information production processes lie in the intangibility of the product, and in the fact that most actions are the consequences of many kinds of information and valuation brought to bear on a time-bound situation. It is pointless therefore to argue in support of, and to persist in using a method of deriving, information on the ground that its products have been found to be useful in the past; for past actions may just as much have been provoked by one of the incidents of the situation as another. The only guide we can have to the design of a system yielding information which is useful and usable is our sense of the fitness of things, of the logical relationships between ends and means.

No ordinary person would add the price he paid for his house 10 years ago to the balance he has in the bank today and suppose that the result is significant for any purpose; yet this is an illustration of a universal practice in the preparation of published financial statements. No ordinary person would compare the income he earns today with the cost of living 10 years ago, and hope to be informed by the comparison; yet this illustrates an effect of the rules generally employed in deriving published financial statements. No ordinary person would suppose that comparative performance in sport is judged without regard for the conditions of performance and the equivalence or uniformity of the measuring devices; yet the methods of deriving financial information include no corrective for establishing the uniformity of the measuring devices. Rules have been devised for overcoming all these defects and in the interest of increased productivity the wisdom of their adoption seems unquestionable. But, as long as the illogical is preferred to the logical, as long as things are added which cannot legitimately be added, and as long as things are compared which cannot legitimately be compared, the efficiency of individual firms, the efficiency of the business sector of the community and the level of national productivity will fall short of what they could be.

Published financial statements are one of the means by which large numbers of people of varying skills and knowledge are able to focus their attention on the productivity of firms. The wisdom of their decisions depends to a considerable extent on what they are able to discover from those statements. But when some of the important terms used in financial statements are simply jargon and others have a multiplicity of meanings, when no figures except perhaps cash and long-term debt have unequivocal and therefore understandable meanings and no totals therefore have a sensible meaning, the community's wisdom in spending £200 million annually on the production of such information is open to serious question. The very instrument which should serve to provoke criticism, self-criticism and the release of energy, to promote greater efficiency and a higher standard of living, serves rather to prevent these things occurring by making every enterprise informationally isolated. The tendency to disorganization, to loss of efficiency, will not be defeated in this way. One might, with some justification, claim that whatever steps may be taken to increase national productivity, the most urgent is improvement of the means by which comparative performance may be judged.

15

A MATTER OF PRINCIPLE*

It seems to be time to try to find our way out of the wood. We have been worried for a long time. We have tried to assuage our worries and uncertainties by pointed attacks on critical contemporary problems, as in the *Accounting Research Bulletins* of the American Institute and similar exercises by other professional groups. We have tried to tidy up the untidiness made apparent by frauds, indictments for negligence, and similar commercial disorders. Also, we have on occasion mounted massive offensives against what seemed to be serious threats to our self-respect; as examples there are the Institute-Stock Exchange co-operation in the early 'thirties and the Study Group on business income in the early 'fifties. But almost continually the smaller sources of worry have been so many, so varied and so insistent that we have become almost insensitive to the larger. In trying to avoid the trees we have become so preoccupied that the wood has been forgotten. It seems necessary to retrace our steps, perhaps a few, perhaps many, before we are again able to proceed with a sense of direction and confidence.

Observations such as these may very well represent the feeling which inspired the Accounting Principles Board to approve the preparation of the "Inventory of Generally Accepted Accounting Principles for Business Enterprises", *A.R.S. No.* 7. No indication of the sentiment of the Board is given in the prefaces. Indeed the author suggests in another place that the study had its origin in a context apart from reflection on confusion[1]. Be that as it may, its appearance as *A.R.S. No.* 7 suggests that the necessity of retracing steps may have arisen from the inconclusive and cacophonous reception of earlier studies.

The remarks which follow require some basic justification. They would be pointless if the propositions of the Inventory were stated categorically only. Many must have long wished for an inventory of generally accepted accounting principles; for whether one wishes to adopt, to rebut, or even simply to think about these principles, it would be useful to know what they are. But the Inventory is not a simple listing. A great deal of *A.R.S. No.* 7 is devoted to justification of the listed propositions and to the rebuttal of objections to them. The study is argumentative. As such it invites cross-argument in a way which would not be open if it had been simply a descriptive list. It invites cross-argument because both the justifications and the

* First published in *The Accounting Review*, Vol. XLI, No. 3, July 1966, pp. 443-57.

[1] Paul Grady, "Inventory of Generally Accepted Accounting Principles in the United States of America", *The Accounting Review*, January 1965, p. 21.

rebuttals seem to be incomplete and inconclusive. In what follows, therefore, we do not consider whether the list is complete, though we do consider the characteristics of principles in general. Rather we are primarily concerned with the arguments on which it is sought to establish the propriety of the principles listed.

Professional Responsibility

The first of the arguments deserving attention occurs at the very outset, where the limitations in scope of the inquiry are given. It is not easy for another to identify specifically the limits set, or to know unequivocally the weight attached to parts of a line of argument. This is merely the consequence of the shades of interpretation which may be put upon any written statement.

Dealing with the responsibility of the C.P.A. for the accounting principles followed by a client corporation, the author writes: "... we are not referring to legal responsibility, which would rest upon determination by the courts, but rather to his professional responsibility as reflected in the Code of Ethics and other technical literature ..." (pp. 15-16).

Whether or not the Study deals with legal responsibilities, there is a presumption that at least the legal responsibilities of C.P.A.s are to be recognized by them. But the phrase "which would rest upon determination by the courts" seems to imply that until the courts have ruled, and only in so far as the courts have ruled, is the law effective. Nor does the quotation or its context make clear whether the legal responsibilities referred to are those arising from statutes or those arising out of litigated cases of alleged negligence or fraud or other misdemeanors. In the framing of principles it seems quite proper to exclude from discussion the case law on negligence and such matters, for this is clearly at the lower fringe of behavior. It does not seem proper, however, to exclude from the discussion any statute law which is pertinent.

If on any matter there is a stated law, or regulation in pursuance of a statute, such a statement is, prima facie, the law. Legal responsibility rests upon determination by the courts only where the statute or regulation is in dispute; it does not so rest of necessity. The law is written for the general regulation of the relationships of all members of a society, whether or not they are also members of other groups which have views on matters treated in statutes. If the law imposes obligations on any class of persons, it does so regardless of the obligations which members of that class may impose upon themselves. But the law does not in principle countenance the self-imposition of obligations on the members of a class among themselves which is inconsistent with the general law; oppressive or minatory combinations of members of a class, for example, may be broken up. Nor does the law countenance the imposition, on persons beyond a given class by members of that class, of burdens additional to the general burdens of the law.

It seems, therefore, that in so far as the law is superior in effect, as representing the will of a whole society, no discussion of the responsibilities of C.P.A.s which neglects or passes over statutorily imposed duties can be complete. Now the law does indeed lay specific responsibilities on C.P.A.s. The Securities Act and the Securities Exchange Act regulate the affairs and the reporting on the affairs of certain corporations "in the public interest and for the protection of investors". There can strictly be no rule of practice that fails to conform with this statutory principle. It may happen that, on the occasion of a dispute, the courts are required to interpret the principle; but the principle is in any case stated as a rule of general behavior.

If a given class of persons wishes to enjoin on its members a higher "morality" or ethic than that of the general law, that is to some extent the concern of its members. But no such class may enjoin on its members a lower "morality" than that of the general law, for to do so would "outlaw" its members. No code of ethics is complete which does not fully satisfy the law. If a professional body enjoins on its members a specific behavior, it cannot but be a behavior which is equal to or superior to the behavior which reasonable lay persons would interpret the statute as enjoining. In the present case, a code of ethics for C.P.A.s could enjoin a behavior no less, and ideally even more, "in the public interest and for the protection of investors" than the lay person would suppose. It is curious, however, that the Study makes no reference to this phrase which is, if anything, the keynote of the basic securities legislation.

Generally Accepted Principles

The phrase quoted from the statute seems in fact to have been largely ignored since it was written into the law. Instead of drawing out the implications or meaning of the statutory principle, professional attention is commonly drawn to "generally accepted accounting principles". We will attempt to show later that these principles are contrary to the purport of the statutory principle. But for the moment we concern ourselves solely with the status of generally accepted principles in an ethical context. Under what circumstances are generally accepted practices invoked or relied upon as a test? There is a range of problems in other kinds of professional practice—medicine, law, engineering—in which the same phrase is invoked. This range is on the fringe where competence is questioned or incompetence is alleged; where, in medicine for example, a practitioner appears to have failed to take precautions or appears to have failed to exercise an adequate level of professional skill to the detriment of a patient; or where, in engineering, a practitioner has specified or used materials of inadequate quality or other specification. In such marginal cases the law steps in. At this point it is open to the accused to plead, in defence, adherence to generally accepted practices.

At the opposite end of the scale there are also marginal practices. But it is certain that no person acting on the basis of the general practices of his profession plus his own special or extraordinary knowledge or skill would be accused of violating generally accepted practice if he were, say, to perform a unique operation, the first of its kind. In so doing, he puts himself beyond what is generally accepted; but he does not endanger his reputation, even if he fails, provided that in all other respects he acts with the greatest care. Only by exceeding the general standard is a profession promoted: at the upper fringe of practice, adherence to generally accepted practice would impede the progress of the science and art. That a given behavior exceeds the level of generally accepted practice does not invoke social wrath and censure.

Only at the lower margin of practice then does the violation of a general standard become of importance, professionally and socially. But not with the object of lowering the standard to a new level. The test at this margin is not even what is good average practice. It is almost certain that indictment would be secured only if the behavior in question were clearly below the minimum standard of practice. The minimum is not, of course, a point on a scale, easily determinable either by individual practitioners or by jurists on the evidence of practitioners. But there are minima; practitioners are occasionally indicted; and the test of minima is the evidence of what is generally accepted practice in the context of the knowledge of the time. Anything at all above the minimum will pass the test; but that does not make the minimum the ideal of professional performance. If professional pronouncements are made they would tend, in keeping with an advancing ethic, always to be well up the scale of skill and competence, and to change as knowledge in the field of expertise changes, not only as other external changes occur.

The status of generally accepted practices in accounting seems to be in marked contrast. Whereas the phrase is invoked in other fields only at the point where professionally or socially unacceptable behavior is alleged, in accounting it is almost the touchstone of respectable practice. The phrase tends in other fields to be used as the defence of the incompetent, never as the ideal of the competent. It would almost seem that, by using the phrase, professional pronouncements would be advertising a mediocrity their originators would not wish to imply. In any case it seems that any statement purporting to have an ethical or idealistic foundation should claim much more than mere general acceptance.

Quite apart from these observations there should be some discomfort from the fact that the origin of the phrase "generally accepted accounting principles" can be traced to a point of time when in fact general acceptance was not required to be the criterion of use. The proposals resulting from the discussions of the early 'thirties included a provision that each company should register with the stock exchange its own practices[2]. The possibility of uniformity was denied; and by implication the generality of acceptance was not considered as a test of the propriety of a practice. The possibility of uniformity is still

[2] See Bishop Carleton Hunt (ed.), *Twenty-Five Years of Accounting Responsibility,* 1911-1936, American Institute Publishing Co. Inc., Vol. 1, pp. 112ff. The proposal was not adopted.

being denied, notwithstanding that the use of the phrase "generally accepted" strongly suggests uniformity. Something quite similar in a different field suggests what has happened: "... all the great mechanical brains, translating machines, learning machines, chess-playing machines, perceiving machines, etc., accounts of which fill our press, owe their 'reality' to a failure to use the subjunctive mood. The game is played as follows: First, it is asserted that except for trivial engineering details, a program for a machine is equivalent to a machine. The flow chart for a program is equated to a program. And finally, the statement that a flow chart could be written for a non-existent program for a non-existent machine establishes the existence of the machine. In just this way Uttley's 'Conditioned Reflex Machine', Rosenblatt's 'Perceptron', Simon, Shaw and Newell's 'General Problem Solver', and many other nonexistent devices have been named in the literature and are referred to as though they existed."[3]

In brief, the appropriate formulation of statements about generally accepted accounting principles would be something like: If there were a body of generally accepted accounting principles, then ... (for example, readers of accounting statements would be able to rely on their contents, their comparability, and so on). Stated in this way, the proposition may have induced a search for these principles. The omission of the subjunctive enabled the phrase to be adopted without the search.

It is in fact curious that in *A.R.S. No.* 7 no attempt is made to provide any kind of empirical evidence to support what are said to be generally accepted principles. It seems not unreasonable to suppose that investors, whose protection is the object of the legislation, would interpret generally accepted as accepted generally, that is, accepted by the great majority of companies or the great majority of accountants. Authoritarian statements are quite different; they may, but need not be generally accepted; many outmoded statutes fall into this category. It seems quite pointless to say that a principle can be "generally accepted even if not generally followed" (p. 51). The difficulty of determining whether a generally accepted principle is being followed lies in the fact that many of the principles assert two contradictory things at once. Thus: "fixed assets should be carried at cost ... in the historical amounts, unless such cost is no longer meaningful" (Principle C-2). In other words, fixed assets should be carried at cost or not at cost; which, because it includes all possibilities, cannot be infringed, provides no guidance, and cannot therefore be regarded as a principle. The corresponding objective is similarly contradictory: "Account for the assets ... in a meaningful manner .... It should be understood that financial position or balance sheet statements do not purport to show either present values of assets to the enterprise or values which might be realized on liquidation" (Objective C). For the protection of investors, the very things that are meaningful are the things

[3] Mortimer Taube, *Computers and Common Sense,* Columbia University Press, 1961, pp. 59-60.

excluded by the last sentence. The objective thus seems to be "to account meaningfully unmeaningfully".

The Character of Principles

One of the more serious omissions of all statements on accounting principles is adequate preliminary discussion of the manner in which "principles" is to be interpreted. There is a tendency to suppose that we can get along quite well without exercises in definition. In no other field having any pretension to rigor of thought or development is this presumption entertained. A nail or a screw is a definitely shaped piece of metal; a carpenter does not use any old piece of metal for the purposes for which nails or screws are used. Likewise in the process of thought we can make little progress without shaping the materials, the ideas, we use. There is also a tendency to suppose that, if we must shape our ideas, references to dictionaries will yield adequate definitions. This too is mistaken. Dictionaries seldom go further than giving commonly accepted and acceptable alternative words and phrases for a given word, substitute symbols; and generally the alternative or substitute symbols are those in lay use—they are not adequate for specialist use. A novice in the study of physics might be helped by what he finds under "atom" or "neutron" in a dictionary; a physicist would have no use for such a source. To choose from a series of possible lay usages one which will serve for the development of a technical field is to bind technical development to lack of precision, or to a precision that is good enough for lay use only. To suppose that lexicographers know all the uses to which a term may be put in all technical fields is to suppose they are omniscient.

Likewise, the interpretation given in dictionaries to "principle" is inadequate of itself. For better guidance it seems useful to resort to interpretations found to be serviceable in technical, generally in scientific, discourse. Even in such fields the nature of postulates, principles, laws, and rules is not entirely beyond dispute. But it is possible to make a distinction between postulates, principles, and laws on the one hand, and rules and descriptions of practices on the other.

In empirical science all have to do with some observable phenomena. Principles are statements of a general nature about classes of events or occurrences in the abstract. But they are no less useful because they are abstract. In the field of optics there is a principle of the rectilinear propagation of light in a medium of uniform density. But in fact a medium of uniform density is an abstraction, and so is a straight line. "A straight line has no width, no depth, no wiggles and no ends. There are no straight lines. We have ideas about these non-existent impossibilities; we even draw pictures of them. But they do not exist."[4] All principles are of this general abstractive kind. They are conceptual. They represent a grasp of the general form of certain regularities, without specification

[4] Billy E. Goetz, "The Usefulness of the Impossible", in William L. Schaaf (ed.), *Our Mathematical Heritage,* New York, Collier Books, 1963, p. 187.

of what will or might happen in the case of any particular phenomenon of the class with which they deal. They emerge from observation and contemplation of some aspect of the universe of experience. Their usefulness subsists in their capacity, as premises, to inform actions of great variety in contexts of which the phenomena they describe are a part.

In this sense principles are not usefully described as generally acceptable or generally accepted. The test for their use by any person or class of persons is whether or not they are consistent with "the nature of things". Each can make the test anew for himself; that others agree with him may be satisfying, psychologically; but the usefulness of such principles is not a function of general agreement or acceptance.

Statements of the second class referred to above are characteristically different from principles. Rules and statements of practice are normative or positive statements descriptive of desired or actual responses to particular problems. If we wish to formulate rules of behavior which are consistent with the nature of things, as that nature is conceived and expressed in principles arising from observation and contemplation, we will do so with those principles in mind. What we do is take a principle as a major premise, a particular circumstance or objective as a minor premise and deduce a consequence, which even though expressed in the indicative mood, is a rule of behavior[5]. In choosing minor premises, of course, we necessarily have to decide the circumstances in which principles are applicable and the extent to which they are applicable; but this is nothing more than the application of more or less common sense discrimination.

We do not have to do this, however, if we simply wish to formulate rules of behavior—only if we wish to formulate rules of behavior that are consistent with the nature of things. Rules that are not consistent with the nature of things can be formulated, and they can be imposed on others and enforced among the group which sponsors them if the sponsoring group is able to surround its operations with an effective mystique. But however consistently such rules are applied, they are not the better for this kind of consistency. Experience constantly informs us that to act on beliefs that are inconsistent with the nature of things is to court disgrace and disaster. King Canute tried it, but we seem constantly to have to relearn it.

If we have no principles that are representative of our understanding of the nature of things, it is common wisdom (based upon nothing more substantial than the gregarious instinct) to seek support in numbers, to base our rules of behavior on general acceptance. It is no less common wisdom to base our rules of behavior on general acceptance even when we have identified and endorsed principles representing our understanding of the nature of things. But in this latter case there is more than mere agreement or general acceptance

[5] See Bertrand Russell, *An Inquiry into Meaning and Truth,* Penguin Books, pp. 24-25.

to support the rules we adopt. Thus, although general acceptance of rules of behavior (or practices) may be a necessary condition of lay respect for a given expertise, it is by no means a sufficient condition. Much of the confusion about the criterion of general acceptance may, it seems, be traced to failure to distinguish between conditions which are necessary and conditions which are both necessary and sufficient.

Something like the distinction we have drawn is built into the report of the Special Committee on Research Program, reproduced at p. x of *A.R.S. No.* 7. But the distinction is blurred at the point where "principles" is introduced. It seems reasonable to say that "the principles . . . should serve as a framework of reference for the solution of detailed problems". But this does not entirely clarify the question of the nature of principles. It could be interpreted as saying that general rules should serve, just as easily as saying that principles (in the more fundamental sense) should serve, for the solution of detailed problems. And it is apparent that the former interpretation is the one most commonly adopted. The Study points out that in some of the Institute-Stock Exchange correspondence of the 1930s "practices" and "principles" were used interchangeably (p. 49). But the glossing over of the difference in that correspondence provides no valid ground for persisting in the manner of a generation ago. Yet this is done in the Study. The substantive part of the Inventory is presented in the form of directives or rules: "the objectives" and the "principles" are all cast in the form of imperatives. We are left with no statements which are the product of contemplating the nature of things, no principles at all in this sense.

It seems therefore that the so-called generally accepted principles of accounting are strictly nothing more than generally accepted rules of behavior, at best. This conclusion is supported by a number of features of the Study.

Authoritative Support

The rules are ostensibly founded to a material extent on the authority of persons rather than on the authority of reason. The author accepts an earlier description of accepted accounting principles as "those principles having substantial authoritative support back of them" (p. 16). The sources from which substantial authoritative support may be inferred are business practices, views of the stock exchange, regulatory prescriptions including those of the Securities and Exchange Commission, opinions of practising and academic C.P.A.s, and published opinions of the A.A.A. and the A.I.C.P.A. (pp. 52-53).

No evidence is adduced to show that any one of these sources has formed its opinions on the basis of analysis of the nature of things. We are not suggesting at this point that the views of the sources were not formed on the basis of analysis; we merely point out that "authority" appears to be taken as sufficient warrant for the designation of a practice as a generally accepted practice.

But even here there are difficulties. "Whether a given principle or practice has authoritative support is both a question of fact and a matter of judgement" (p. 16). The judgement referred to is the individual practitioner's judgement. In fact then, what comes to be done or accepted in any particular case is a matter of an individual judgement; and no person using the resulting statements may have any assurance that the practices used are endorsed or followed by other business firms whose statements he may consult in forming his opinions, or followed by the profession. The lay user of such statements, of course, may not be expected to know that the choice of practices is left to individual judgement, the more so since the auditor's opinion includes references to generally accepted principles and to consistency, both of which tend to give assurance of a useful degree of uniformity. Such terms therefore give an impression of the adoption of practices the justification of which is beyond individual judgement, whereas the initiated know that there is no such justification.

In effect, the dependence on authority, the authority of persons or groups of persons, is completely eroded in practice by the permissive exercise of judgement. It would be quite different if the views of all the persons or classes of persons converged on a specific given set of practices. But the Study makes abundantly clear, as we shall presently see, that there is little in the way of convergence, and the authorities are therefore authorities for little in the nature of guidance.

Authoritative support is not the only foundation on which the propositions of the Inventory purport to be based. There are some conceptual foundations which approach the kind of thing we would designate as principles. But even these are not entirely consistent with the nature of things.

Accountability

We are told that accounting information has a function in relation to the "fiduciary accountabilities" of management. There is no discussion of accountabilities of any other kind.

In the first place there is some confusion about the accountability referred to. It is said that "the separation of ownership from management of the business entity is a primary factor in imposing *on the entity* the fiduciary accountabilities to its stockholders" (p. 26, emphasis added). At a later point reference is made to the fiduciary accountabilities *of management* (p. 57). As fiduciary accountabilities are the basis on which the generally accepted accounting principles are "set forth" (p. 26), it seems that no distinction as between accountabilities of the entity and of management has any bearing on the sequel. Yet it is a matter of importance to know who is being held accountable. It seems undeniable that the business entity ("an organization of persons and properties," p. 26) cannot be held accountable, and that in fact it is the management of such an entity which is accountable.

Now the relationships of managers "to stockholders, creditors, government, and others having bona fide interests" (p. 57) can scarcely all be described as fiduciary relationships, without warping the meaning of fiduciary. None of these relationships is a fiduciary relationship in the customary sense. It is no doubt reasonable to say that directors and managers occupy positions of trust, in the sense that others trust them. But not in the sense that they are trustees. They are appointed or engaged contractually, under the charter or rules of a business firm and under specific contract within such rules, to assume business risks on behalf of equityholders; and to negotiate with creditors, other groups and governments, when necessary, on a contractual basis. They often have contractual rights of indemnity. They are not committed to the preservation of a capital sum held in trust (notwithstanding the use of "corpus" in Principle B-2), and no action can lie against them, in the absence of fraud and such offences against the general law, for the recovery of any part of the sum contributed by equityholders which is lost in the course of business. Their relationship with equityholders we see as one of agency, not as one of trusteeship; and their relationship with all other parties is one of contract, as contracting agent of the corporation proximately (in the case of a corporation) or as contracting agent for the equityholders (both in the cases of corporate and non-corporate business enterprises). We venture to speculate that the notion of a fiduciary relationship is in fact a vestigial remnant of the form of trust, which in the days before the recognition of corporate rights in real property was the only device available legally for the holding of titles in real property for the use and benefit of a large group of persons.

The object of these observations is not to clarify a simple verbal point. It is to strike at the root of what seems to be an error in conception. If the accountability of management is seen as a fiduciary accountability in the usual sense, it will lend support to the idea that management is accountable in respect of the sums of money "entrusted" by equityholders, and a balance sheet showing aggregate outlays from such sums may be held to be justified; the initial costs of assets will be acceptable as balance sheet figures (as in Principle C-2). But, in the first place, not even the proponents of the cost basis hold that balance sheets shall show initial costs without deductions (Principle C-2). Nor in the second place do they hold to the cost basis for all assets (p. 258). In both respects the fiduciary notion is not in fact respected, though it is held as a rule for durable assets: the inconsistency should be regarded as fatal. In the third place, if management is held accountable, not simply in the fiduciary sense but for the exercise of all powers and the use of all assets under its control at any time, it follows that it cannot be held accountable at any time if the money sums which designate assets are not money sums which correspond in the best possible way with the money equivalents of those assets at that time. We hold that this is the only realistic way in which accountability may be viewed, and that it clearly points in a different direction from the initial price or cost basis. To hold management accountable in sums of money spent under conditions no longer prevailing, and in all likelihood spent by persons who are no longer managers, and sums which have no logical or discoverable relationship to a present monetary equivalent, is to fly in the face of the nature of things and to make accountability a ludicrous notion.

Consistency

Another conceptual foundation is consistency of practices from year to year. There is a strong presumption that financial statements drawn in conformity with generally accepted principles applied on a basis consistent with that of a previous year can, and will, present fairly the financial position and results of operations of an entity (p. 31).

Now, at first glance, consistency commends itself as a principle which might enable us to devise rules which will result in comparable information for successive periods for a given firm. If rules were devised to secure comparability of such information, their consistent application would be a valuable rule of behavior. But in fact the practices of accounting as they are represented in the Study were not devised with this object in mind; they are themselves virtually inconsistent, and the consistent application of mutually inconsistent rules cannot yield comparable results. We demonstrate the point.

The Study devotes no attention to the elucidation of "financial position" and "results". There is no definition of financial position or of income, though there is some discursive but inconclusive discussion of the latter in the section on the Terminology Bulletins of the A.I.C.P.A. Perhaps it was supposed that these terms are so generally used and understood that no definition is required. But the acreage devoted in the literature to argument about income and the absolute neglect of financial position should suggest that this supposition is unwarranted. If these terms had a specified meaning we could consider what steps should be taken to quantify them, and we could grasp what we are expected to be able to compare and what therefore is the precise object of consistency of application of rules. We are left without such help, and consistency seems therefore to be unconnected with practical necessity. (One may lie, or talk nonsense, consistently; is consistency then a virtue?)

It is demonstrable that the result of applying generally accepted accounting principles does not give financial position as it is understood by merchants or financiers in the market-place, or even as it is understood by laymen. Let any man ask himself or another what is his financial position. He will not for a moment think of giving what he paid for his house and land, his securities and other assets. Ordinary knowledge of personal transactions in markets informs him that if he wants things other than what he holds (and that is one of the reasons for wanting to know financial position), he must think of what he could get on the market for some of the things he holds. This is "in the nature of things". Financial position is a position of an entity in relation financially to the rest of the community at a point of time. Past transactions may have left the entity in possession of certain physical things at a point of time; but it is the resale prices of those things, not the things themselves, which determines the relationship, financially, of the entity to the rest of the community.

Consider also now the idea of income. The idea has no meaning other than that, by virtue of some event or events during an interval, an entity has improved its relationship financially with the rest of the community during that interval. Now if, for the sake of consistency, income is calculated by setting off against contemporary revenues the measure of contemporary costs given by the L.I.F.O. method, there remains in the balance sheet a series of residues which are increasingly less contemporary as time passes. The balance sheet represents financial position less and less fairly at each successive balancing date. In fact therefore, generally accepted practices, of which L.I.F.O., is one, are found to lead to internal inconsistencies in any period, the income account being more or less contemporary in our example, the balance sheet becoming increasingly out-dated; and the comparison of inconsistent statements over successive periods cannot but be deceptive.

In so far then as consistency is held to be a basic principle it is found, like the notion of fiduciary accountability, to be applied as long as it is wanted; as long, that is, as it serves to lend support to practices which otherwise have no standing by reference to the nature of things.

Diversity

The next presumption we consider appears to have some foundation in contemplation of the nature of things. It is that "diversity in accounting [is inevitable, or tolerable, or permissible] among independent entities" (p. 32). But here again the critical objective of analysis of observable things is bypassed, the objective of finding the essential uniformity among diversity. The "overwhelming" arguments against "a minority view which urges uniformity in accounting" (pp. 32-33) appear to be entirely without foundation.

We are told that "judgment and estimates play a substantial role in accounting on an accrual basis . . . and . . . when there is diffusion in decision-making, a necessity in the free enterprise system, there is bound to be diversity in the accounting results" (p. 33). But we are not told precisely how far judgement and estimates play a role. Does judgement extend to the concepts which shall be quantified or only to the quantification of stipulated concepts? The difference is significant. Every different method of accounting entails a different concept of income and financial position. If every pharmacist were to have his own concept of poison, and every lawyer his own concept of crime, there would be not only diversity but chaos; yet these and other groups of persons could claim the necessity of judgement no less than accountants. As for the application of judgement and estimates to the quantification of specified concepts, accounting is in this respect no different from the exact sciences. It is freely admitted in the sciences that there is an element of judgement in every measurement process. Measurements are only approximations, their accuracy depending on the variables of the object, the context, the instruments, and the observer. The judgement and estimate argument is no argument for diversity; for if there is any skill in the practice of accounting the divergences arising from different measurements of the same property will be nominal only.

As for "diffusion in decision-making", this is the very circumstance which makes uniformity of rules obligatory. Within firms, manuals of rules and procedures are written with the object of ensuring that different persons doing similar things do them in a similar way, so that, wherever in an organization action must be taken on the result, the result is always interpretable in the same way. People acting at different points in a firm could not act in a co-ordinated manner if their informational premises were at variance. For even greater reasons, if the decision-making is really diffuse, if the users of the information are both internal and external to the firm, uniformity of information is imperative; negotiations between one firm and another or choices of external parties as between contracts with alternative firms, cannot be seriously considered unless the information produced by all firms is equally interpretable.

We are told, further (p. 34), that uniformity would require detailed manuals covering every conceivable rule for all firms. It is questionable whether any advocate of uniformity has ever contemplated any such suggestion. Uniformity in principle and in effect is what has been advocated. Advocates of uniformity have in mind uniformity of "principles" in the "framework of reference" sense in which "principle" is used in the report of the Special Committee; not in the sense of rules or directives in which sense "principles" is commonly used in the Study. We are told, too (p. 35), that "recognition of the concept of diversity in accounting among independent entities . . . in no way imperils the objective" of narrowing the areas of difference and improving the comparability of financial statements. On the contrary, the stated concept and the stated objective are flat contradictories as conceptual foundations.

Much of the discussion of the matter over a long period has been confused by the idea that business firms are independent (p. 35). It is a matter of direct observation that they are not; they are all interdependent. They are interdependent in the money market; for when money or credit is scarce, what some firms get others do not. They are interdependent in the commodities, the labor and the finished goods markets for the same reason. They are creditors of one another, investors in one another, suppliers to one another. They are all interlinked by market processes, and none can intelligibly communicate or negotiate with another unless the symbols they all use are equally interpretable, as symbols, at a given point of time. This is why uniformity is in principle imperative. Not only that. Investors, whose benefit has been at the heart of legislation and regulation in respect of financial information, cannot and do not think of firms or corporations independently. They consider them comparatively. Indeed, all forms of choice are fundamentally based on comparison; but comparison is pointless if the methods used themselves are capable of producing greatly divergent results and aggregates from the same data.

What the diversity argument entirely overlooks is that, although different firms have different operations, all persons interested in the financial characteristics of firms are interested in the same things, such as solvency, rate of return, and so on. At the same time, all interested persons are so interested because they have alternative opportunities of lending or investing. They cannot choose sensibly unless the financial statements, which yield such information for different opportunities, are comparable; and they will only be comparable if they are based on uniform rules. It is the common concern with money outcomes that makes common rules necessary. This is in the nature of things. A free enterprise society which condones anarchy in its communications system will not long remain rational or free.

The Consequences of Diversity

Consider now the alternatives explicitly indicated in Chapter 10.

It should be clear that if there are two methods of assigning a monetary quantity to one asset, and three methods of assigning a monetary quantity to another asset, and that if each method yields a different monetary quantity, there are in total six methods of finding the income of a firm and its financial position at the close of an income period, and six different results of applying those methods. In the following we limit the variants to major classes. We presume that each of the methods listed in Chapter 10 is a true variant, yielding a different result from each other method listed in its class; otherwise there would have been no point in its separate inclusion. Further we regard every such method as a legitimate method; being described as generally accepted, we are entitled to suppose that each is acceptable to all accountants regardless of the selection of particular methods to suit the circumstances of particular accounting entities. The results of our exploration will therefore indicate the methods of accounting which are embraced by "generally accepted accounting principles". They do not give the number of methods available to any singular firm or corporation. They do give the number of methods to which any reader of two or more sets of financial statements may be subjected.

(a) Revenue (p. 373). There are at least four methods: recognition at time of sale, and subsequent recognition of cash discount; recognition at time of sale and immediate recognition of cash discount; recognition at time of collection; recognition on completion of product.

(b) Pension payment charges (p. 374). There are apparently at least four different methods each of which will yield different magnitudes in any period.

(c) Taxes (pp. 374-5). Disregarding allocation alternatives, there are apparently eight methods each of which will yield a different magnitude in a given period.

(d) Depreciation. There are at least two basic sums on which a depreciation charge may be calculated, cost (three permissible methods) or an appraised value (p. 377). Whichever is adopted, there are at least six methods of calculation, each giving different magnitudes for the charge. Whichever of the methods is applied to the basic sum chosen, there are three ways at least of obtaining the aggregate for a class of depreciable assets—composite, group or individual calculations. There are thus $4 \times 6 \times 3$ ways of finding the amount to be shown for any aggregate set of depreciable assets.

(e) Inventory. There are five named cost methods: F.I.F.O., L.I.F.O., average cost, base stock, standard cost. We omit the many possible combinations of these for any given inventory. In respect of each, cost may or may not include "overheads". There are thus at least 5×2 methods. The suggestion of "combinations" entails that each of these methods may be applied to the whole inventory, to groups or to individual items. There are thus at least $5 \times 2 \times 3$ cost methods. There are two named market methods, replacement cost and net realizable value. Further, there is the method of the lowest of cost, replacement cost, and net realizable value; this will in any year provide a magnitude potentially different from any of the straight cost or straight market methods. The number of potentially different magnitudes is thus the number of cost methods multiplied by the number (3) of the alternatives, for under this formula no reader of the statement will know which of the three in any given period is the lowest. There are then $5 \times 2 \times 3 \times 3$ methods of this kind. The total number of methods is therefore 30 cost methods, 2 market methods, and 90 cost or market methods; total, 122 methods.

(f) Miscellaneous. There are five classes of items in respect of each of which there are two possibilities (pp. 376-7). There are thus $2 \times 2 \times 2 \times 2 \times 2$ ways of representing these items in any set of accounting statements, 32 ways in all.

There are also many ways of treating other individual items found in financial statements (pp. 378-9). But we disregard these. It should be clear that "generally accepted accounting principles", in respect of the items specifically considered above, countenance (a) 4, (b) 4, (c) 8, (d) 72, (e) 122, (f) 32, methods; or for any financial statements in which these may all occur—over 30 million possibilities!

Now the Study warns against making such "astronomical" calculations[6]. To do so "would be useless because it would merely confirm that accounting is not an exact science" (p. 379). We disagree. The purport of the exercise is not to indicate that an astronomical range of possibilities is open to any specific business or to say that an astronomical array of results could be obtained for any specific business. Its object is to show that, as the range is so vast and the results may be so divergent, any user of the resulting statements cannot know what precise set of methods has been used and cannot therefore know with what provisos he must accept any of the financial statements of different companies he may wish to consult at a given time to inform his choices.

Defences of Diversity

Attention is drawn to the observations which are adduced in support of the diversity which is disclosed. It is said that "the basic

---

[6] We do not know whether this warning was induced by some earlier exercises of ours: "Financial Information and the Securities Market", see p. 174, *ante*.

concept of 'diversity in accounting among independent entities' is fully supported by the variety of methods" (p. 380). The circularity of this should be obvious. We start with a basic concept, which one may suppose to be one of the premises on which accounting is based; it permits diversity; we then find diversity and believe it supports the concept!

The Institute-Stock Exchange correspondence is cited as authority for the view that "if the significant practices were adequately disclosed and consistently followed, the effect of differing methods on periodic income would soon be unimportant, although there might be considerable difference in balance sheet items carried forward to future periods" (p. 380). The correspondence appears to give no reason at all for this hope. It is in fact impossible to justify; for if the significance of differences in income calculations becomes unimportant the significance of differences in balance sheets would at the same time become unimportant. There could only be a divergence in the degree of significance of the differences if the rules for calculating the one were substantially at odds with the propriety of the other. The divergence which has in fact arisen has been due to just that—disregard for financial position and, in consequence, a notion of income which is of even more bewildering complexion than it was 30 years ago.

We are told that adherence to "consistency and disclosure standards" permits comparability from year to year for the same entity. In fact it does no such thing. If it did there would be no point in the suggestion that financial statements in dollars of current purchasing power would improve comparability (p. 382). The figures which appear in contemporary financial statements are mixtures of measures taken in scales of monetary units having different purchasing powers at different times. People may in practice compare them, but this does not mean they are comparable. In no other discipline is this disregard of a basic mathematical rule tolerated.

As for "comparability between entities", we are told that investors have the protection of a "qualitative standard of comparison" (p. 381). What this is is not at all clear; it can mean very little if there are literally millions of sets of rules for deriving financial statements. It is almost certain that if the difference in the ultimate effect on income or financial position of the adoption of either of two rules were immaterial, there would be or there would have been no cause for adding an alternative rule to the first one used. It is therefore almost certain that every rule which has survived has survived because its use made a material difference to the result at some time or for some firm. It seems odd therefore that rules which were adopted because of the material effects they procured are now held to be justifiable, yielding results which satisfy a qualitative standard of comparability. It would be useful to know what this means and how this standard is set, particularly as methods of accounting are at the discretion of "the management and directors of each enterprise". It would also be useful to know how "the leading financial and business executives and financial analysts" can "fully understand the value of the qualitative standard of comparability" (p. 381). It is far more likely that, where there are millions of sets of possible rules, they are simply unable to differentiate between them, much less understand them.

Finally some words on the view of Mr. Justice Holmes, which has been widely quoted in support of variety and the *status quo* in accounting. The words of the learned jurist are, with respect, far too laconic to do justice to the problem that confronts us. In practical affairs, as in the law, logic and good sense are only in apparent conflict if one regards them as two distinct and contradictory manifestations of mind. Good sense surely is seeing things as they really are; if we see things as they are, we are able to apply to them the disciplined thought (logic) which enables us to reach conclusions consistent with them. Good sense and logic seem to be complementary, not contradictory, manifestations of mind. The mind that longs for certainty and repose can achieve it at little cost—by inventing a simplified world in which the problems of the real world have no counterpart; a world, for example, in which numbers can be added regardless of their individual significances; a world in which changes in prices or price levels are non-existent or wholly without significance; a world in which all business firms are independent of one another; and so on. To imagine that the world is like this is to elevate fiction above good sense; this gives the illusory certainty which is the butt of the remarks of Justice Holmes. This is the illusory certainty which has given rise to, and comfort from, the whole idea of "generally accepted accounting principles". If there were in fact a set of such principles there would be uniformity. It is only because no accounting principles are generally accepted that there is diversity and hence the need, psychologically not logically, to defend diversity and to challenge uniformity.

We have not attempted to lay out the system of ideas we would substitute for the arguments put forward in the Study. This has been done elsewhere[7]. Our object has merely been to join issue with the argumentative sections of the Study. Some final words on the propositions which are represented as generally accepted principles, and which we accept as fair representations. Accounting has for too long suffered from overdoses of weasel-words. Attention has been explicitly drawn to a long list of them by Kohler[8]. A variety nevertheless occurs in the stated principles: proper (A-1), proper (A-2), appropriate (A-3), proper (A-4), misused, arbitrarily (A-5), misleading (A-7), properly (C-1), meaningful (C-2), appropriate (C-3), ordinarily (C-4), applicable (E-1), meaningful (E-2), appropriate (E-3). Similar words occur in many places in the argument as well. The reader may well ask himself what each of these means in its context; he will not find it easy to give a generally accepted answer. And he will not therefore quite know to what he is supposed to assent.

---

[7] *Accounting, Evaluation and Economic Behavior,* Prentice-Hall, Inc., 1966.
[8] Eric L. Kohler, *A Dictionary for Accountants,* Prentice-Hall, Inc., 1963, p. vii.

The Study is unquestionably valuable. It makes very clear the massive difficulties with which the users of financial statements have to contend—which brings us full circle to an observation made earlier in this paper. We suggested that the law does not countenance the laying of burdens, additionally to legally stipulated burdens, by one class on another. And we suggested that an important element of the law in the present context is that it provides for the publication of information "in the public interest and for the protection of investors". As all choices involve comparisons it seems beyond argument that the multiplicity of available methods will defeat every serious attempt to choose as between companies or to choose between the continuation and the liquidation of specific companies on the basis of published information. The burden of discovery imposed on the public and the investor seems unconscionable; it is far from the ideal, of disclosure of the facts upon which the general public and the investor can act to protect themselves. The Inventory, at least by implication, makes it abundantly clear that great changes are necessary to put contemporary practices on the footing of the requirements of the statutory principle, and even greater changes to establish practice on the ethical footing which we have suggested is ideally more solid and dependable than a statutory specification.

16

WHY WORRY ABOUT ACCOUNTING?*

I am not sure whether I should be addressing myself to the question "Why should you worry about accounting?", or to the question "Why should I worry about accounting?" We may all have personal reasons for worrying or not worrying; with these I shall not be concerned. Accounting occupies a place of some importance in the machinery by which the relatively small savings of millions of people are put to work in massive parcels by the corporations we confidently expect to improve living standards; and there are clearly some who think its function is not well performed. This is a kind of worry without barriers; accountants, investors, brokers and men in the street may well be equally concerned. That broad problem is the basis of what I have to say.

There is a sense in which accounting is concerned with small things. That is the sense which most novelists and laymen seize upon when they wish to make a denigratory assertion—"just like an accountant" or "just like book-keeping", they say. "What to one man is sheer poetry to another is mere book-keeping", one has said, as if the highest and lowest extremes in some scale were thus amply indicated. However, were it not for the safeguards which the designers of the legal rules for incorporating business firms believed accounting and financial statements would give, the whole history of business and present standards of living may have been vastly different. That belief stems from a fact known to all from childhood, if you haven't money or money's worth you cannot buy things you want; and perhaps a second fact, if at some time you have a different amount of money or money's worth than at an earlier time the difference is explicable. That belief in the usefulness of financial statements is not a naive belief; it applies as much today as it did before the corporate revolution, and as much to corporations as to men in the street. We may temporarily "get around" our insufficiences by resorting to credit, but usually we must have something to back our credit. A trader in securities on margin has to find more collateral if the stocks he is dealing in fall in price or worth; and similarly for all other kinds of credit.

It was expected that financial statements would give the financial positions of companies at yearly or other intervals and income statements showing their results during those intervals. Because corporate business depends on the initial contribution of money or money's

---

* First published in *Proceedings* of The Fifth Annual Accounting Forum of Hayden, Stone Incorporated in the New York University Graduate School, November 1966, pp. 7-16.

worth by investors, and because investors are interested in the money outcome of their investments, and because all buying and selling boils down to transfers of money, statements in money terms could reasonably be expected to show how successful a company and its management had been. The statements would give the resultant of good and bad trading, good and bad decisions, good and bad management (and every company has some of each) in two summaries which would be easily understandable because everyone knows what money and goods and trading transactions are. These expectations have been realized only imperfectly.

Accounting the Language of Finance; Financial Instrumentation

Accounting has often been described as the language of finance. One of the necessary qualities of a language is that its terms and statements shall be intelligible to the people who require messages expressed in it. We will return to intelligibility presently. Of equal importance is the fact that, if there is a dated time series of such messages about a given firm or corporation, everyone expects the later statement to bring up to date any information given or representation made in the last previous statement. The stock exchanges and the S.E.C., for example, would not require annual or half-yearly or quarterly summaries (as the case may be) if it were not expected that those summaries would provide an up-dating of the last previous statements. The demand for more frequent releases of financial information over the past 20 years is indicative of the drive for up-to-date information. That demand is also the plainest recognition of the fact that the prices of goods, of properties owned by companies, and so on, are volatile, and that movements in those prices may from time to time modify the status of corporations and modify the opinions which investors, financiers and other creditors hold about them. Now, whether or not corporate financial statements do bring the picture up to date each year, the commercial and financial world is obliged to believe they do; it acts as if they do. It must; there is no other information supplied. To this also we return presently.

The usage of financial information to which we are referring is usage for financial purposes, usage having to do with the issuing of stock, the raising of loans, the repayment of debts, the payment of dividends. In so far as financial information affects the opinions of investors, financiers and other creditors, it affects the capacity of management to command goods and services for business purposes. On the other hand, in so far as financial information describes clearly and unequivocally what has been done by a company in the recent past and the present relationship of the company with the rest of the community (the resources it controls and the obligations it owes), it enables investors, financiers and other creditors to look after their own financial interests. This usage of financial information is the primary justification of accounting. The financial statements of a country's corporations are, in effect, the measuring instruments which guide the country's investors in fostering or damping down activity in different types of commerce and industry and the activities of particular corporations.

The presumption underlying what is described as private (or free, or competitive) enterprise, is that if all seek their own interests within the law, the interests of all will be served most effectively. In the same way as there are laws requiring sellers of goods to enable buyers to ascertain what they are buying, so that buyers can judge knowledgeably whether to buy is in their interests, there are also laws relating to disclosure of the character of securities, laws requiring the publication of prospectuses and periodical financial statements. But buyers of initial issues of securities, and buyers and sellers of securities already issued, will only know what they are buying or selling if the financial statements, the measuring instruments, faithfully represent what has gone on and how companies stand from time to time.

Financial Analysis

There will be some who will say that the general run of investors do not take any notice of balance sheets or income statements of the companies they invest in, that they are concerned with share prices and movements in share prices only. There may be many people of this kind—speculators. But the greater part of the country's millions of stockholders are not just speculators, price-watchers; and even though we may suppose that a great part of those investors cannot make sense of the financial statements of corporations, they act upon the advice of those they believe to be able to make sense of the statements. We cannot, in all conscience, suppose that when one seeks advice from or is tendered advice by one's stockbroker, or attorney or any other source of advice, that advice is simply based on an attempt to outguess other guessers. This would make a farce of all the legal and other requirements for the publication of financial information.

Whether an investor makes his own analyses or has the task done for him by a security analyst, broker or other adviser, the only sensible basis on which to found expectations is the composite set of facts at the time of choice. One may consider the general state of the nation's business, the state of the money market, the state of international balances, the political climate—to name a few very general factors. One may consider the states of particular industries, whether they are growing or declining, whether their markets are wide open or nearing saturation, and so on. But then one must consider particular firms. Investors do not invest in "the United States" or in "the chemical industry". They invest in firms, and they need to know whether the record of previous performance and the present position of a company suggest that it—and its stockholders—will be able to benefit from whatever conditions they expect will arise in its industry and the whole economy. Not only that; they need to know the past records and positions of other firms, in the same or other industries, if they are to choose knowledgeably what they believe to be in their own individual best interests.

The conditions to be satisfied, then, are that any investor shall be able to have similar and up-to-date knowledge of all firms in which he may invest, and that the financial statements on which investors depend shall be intelligible to anyone who knows what economic resources and legal rights are.

Accounting satisfies neither of these conditions. This seems good enough reason to worry.

Among the things we may want to compare are the rates of return we may expect from alternative security investments, and the resources presently available to the companies which issued them. The rate of return we expect is a function of what we know about past performance, past rates of return, and the beliefs we have about the impact of future conditions on the continuation of past performance. If we are to calculate a rate of return at all we require to know the resources employed (the denominator) and the income of a period (the numerator, which is the difference between the resources employed at two successive dates). This requirement embraces all the singular pieces of information in a set of financial statements. We will therefore consider some of the difficulties in discovering from a balance sheet the present extent of the resources employed by any one company.

Financial Measures and Representations

The amount of cash on hand at a year's end would have been obtained, we may suppose, by adding up all the amounts of cash and things equivalent to cash (such as bank deposits). It would be an equally simple matter, we would suppose, to obtain the balances of receivables and payables. We know what cash, receivables and payables are, and we know the process of counting involved.

We may also suppose that the figure representing marketable securities would have a similar homogeneous character, particularly if beside the notation there appeared the words "at cost". But for all other items than cash, receivables and payables there is no such homogeneity. The amount shown for marketable securities may represent, say, three parcels of stock. For every such parcel there is a number of units of stock, a purchase price per unit, and a date of purchase at which the purchasing power of money was at a certain level. Suppose the stocks were purchased at different dates. The only thing that is likely to have remained constant since the dates of purchase is the number of units of stock. Yet the aggregate amount shown will imply that the price of the stock has not changed (for even though the figure is said to be "at cost", the balance sheet bears the latest balancing date), that the purchasing power of money has not changed, and that all three parcels were purchased when the purchasing power of money was the same. In fact nothing has been brought up to date except the date on the balance sheet. If the security holdings were listed in the balance sheet or footnotes, of course, we could find out for ourselves what the market prices at the balancing date (up-to-date prices) were. Or, the aggregate of the market prices may be given in parenthesis on the face of the balance sheet. But to obtain an up-to-date picture of the company we would then have to change the total for assets and the total for stockholders' equity from the figures at which these appeared on the face of the balance sheet. And if the prices of the securities had risen or fallen during the period, but the rise or fall had not been brought into the accounts (they are shown there "at cost"), we would have to change the amount shown as profit of the period if we wanted to find out all that had happened to the firm in the period. It is, of course, quite unlikely that any user of the statements will make all these adjustments to bring the out-of-date figures up-to-date, even if the footnotes and parenthetical statements gave him the means of doing so.

We will meet even greater trouble in trying to understand what is meant by the inventories figure. The most common description of the method used for finding the number of dollars at which an inventory is stated is "lower of cost or market". Although we may have a general idea of how this figure would be obtained, it is impossible to know in any particular case what it means or what its relevance is to the company's profits or position. In the first place, we do not know whether cost has been used or whether market has been used. To know this could be important. Suppose that in one year market prices had been rising; a company using the above formula would use the cost basis at that year's end; if, in the following year, the market turned down, at that year's end the company would use the market price, not the cost price. The rule will have been used consistently, but we will not know how much the reported profit has been affected merely by the shift from using cost to using market prices. It is even possible that the management of the company itself does not know the effect of the shift, through simple belief that the rule is a proper rule. But the problem is much more complicated than that. The word "cost" has an almost unlimited variety of meanings. Cost may be calculated on a L.I.F.O. basis, a F.I.F.O. basis, an average basis and about a dozen other bases. And almost every one of these bases is really a whole family of bases. Even if we were to know what L.I.F.O., F.I.F.O., average, and so on, mean in general, we would not know the exact consequence on profits of the way the company has applied these bases. Here is one full descriptive note from a recent balance sheet on the method of valuing inventories, modified only to exclude reference to the company's products:—

"Finished goods have been stated at amounts (*less than cost*) based on selling prices *less allowances for* selling expenses, profits and possible losses from style changes. *Substantially* all of the raw raw materials and the raw material content of the work in process have been priced at *cost* (*last-in, first-out method*) *not in excess of market*. All other inventories and supplies were priced at the *lower of cost* (*first-in, first-out method*) *or market*."

The inventory was stated as one figure. It is impossible from any such statement to understand what the figure means. Every one of the italicized words or phrases (the italics have been added) can have a host of meanings. And in any case there is a strong presumption that such a motley lot of figures derived by different means cannot possibly have a sensible meaning. The report showed a rise of 15 per cent in sales, a rise of less than 5 per cent in net profit before taxes and a fall of 15 per cent in inventory. Is there any possibility that the fall in the amount of the inventory and the relatively slight rise in profits for the rise in sales are due merely to the application of the above complex of rules (for the impact of each of the italicized phrases could have quite different, but unknowable, effects on reported profits in different periods)? This is a legitimate question for any analyst or investor to ask. But we have no means of knowing the answer.

Take another: "Inventories, stated at the lower of cost (currently adjusted standard, average, or first-in first-out) or market, were as follows:", and there follow separate figures for raw materials and purchased parts, work in process, and finished goods. Which method was applied to which class of inventory could be a material piece of information, but this notation can only leave the reader quite confused unless he refuses to be bothered with such trifles. Examples could be multiplied.

But inventory valuation is no trifle. The measure of the inventory affects both the amount of the profit for a year and the total of the current assets which is used in measures of solvency, as well as affecting both the numerator and denominator of rate of return calculations. Just as in the case of marketable securities, the valuation of an inventory can be years out of date if the L.I.F.O. method is used, and it is widely used. No reader of the financial statements can tell how out-of-date L.I.F.O. valuation is, either. Some companies try to help by giving, in footnotes, valuations on both L.I.F.O. and F.I.F.O. bases. In the latest report of one company the two figures are given; their difference is $6 million, and the reported earnings for the year were $18 million using the lower L.I.F.O. basis. If we wanted to bring the figures up to date we could add $6 million to the assets and the stockholders' equity; but we could not just add $6 million to the profits of the year if the company also used the L.I.F.O. basis for the opening inventory. Which means that if we wanted to find out the results, position and rate of return on an up-to-date basis we could not do it; and we would be quite unable to compare the profits or the solvency or the rate of return of the company with those of another company which used the F.I.F.O. basis. And, in general, using the lower value, as in the lower-of-cost-or-market rule or the L.I.F.O. rule when prices are rising, always tends to understate income and understate solvency; if these are important as foundations for investors' judgements, such understatements clearly leave investors uninformed.

Passing on to the investments of companies in durable goods (plant, buildings, land), the figures usually shown are even more out of date than those for inventories, simply because these assets last longer. They are generally shown at original purchase prices, less depreciation charges based on those prices; and these do not give up-to-date representations of what the assets are worth or what the costs of wear and tear have been. If prices have risen since purchase, the stockholders' equity, and hence the company's borrowing power, will be understated; and if depreciation charges are out of date, because they are based on out-of-date purchase prices, the amount of income will tend to be overstated. For both reasons the rate of return will be overstated by comparison with the rate which would be given if the asset values and costs had been represented by up-to-date figures.

Financial Trends

The first general observation about these out-of-date figures and the technical terms used to describe their derivation is that no one, with the sole exception of the persons who drew up the statements which contain them, can know how they were derived, and therefore what they mean. No investor can know how out-of-date they are, nor how relevant they are to anything at the last date of publication. Take a modest example. Suppose there were two similar companies with reported earnings of $75,000 and reported stockholders' equities of $500,000 and $600,000 respectively. The stock of the first may be expected to sell at a higher price than the stock of the second. But if the first was established when the prices of industrial goods of the kind required were much lower than at the later time when the second was established, the difference in the stock prices could be quite unwarranted. If, on an up-to-date basis, the assets of the first were $560,000 and the earnings for the year $70,000, and all other things were equal, there should be no difference in the price at all, taking account only of the earnings rate. The main point, however, is that no investor could make any such adjustment to bring the figures of the older company up to date. Furthermore, although an analyst could, by diligent inquiry, find answers to some of the questions he might ask about methods of calculation, the task of up-dating out-of-date statements is so involved that I doubt whether anyone attempts it. In effect then, the whole business of choosing investments is based on information which is out-of-date to a degree which no one knows.

The second point is that, as we do not know what the figures mean, we cannot even rely on trends in them. There is a widespread, and justifiable, belief to the effect that the foundations of judgements about future prospects are not the absolute amounts of profits or assets for the latest year or the rate of return for that year, but trends in these figures. It is consequently believed that, even though the absolute amounts may be somewhat out of date (or conservative, as some say), the observation of trends will avoid the effect of this. Of course it will do no such thing. Trends depend on the propriety of the measures on which the trend line is to be based. Suppose we have three companies whose operations over a number of years were absolutely identical. Different but equally acceptable rules for inventory valuation and depreciation charges will result in the net incomes and rates of return of the three companies being quite different. Suppose we represent the range of "possible profits" under all these different rules by a band, the vertical line shown for each year in the adjacent diagram. And suppose that each company uses a different one of these many sets of accounting rules. It is conceivable that the trends of reported profits will be materially different, as the diagram shows. In effect, A has chosen rules which were ultraconservative in the early years, reporting profits near the bottom of the band. Because of this it was able to show rising profits through the whole period, and still be using acceptable principles, even though the band has shifted downward. B has adopted a set of accounting rules which gives a steady net income notwithstanding that the band has shifted up and down. C has adopted rules which give a net

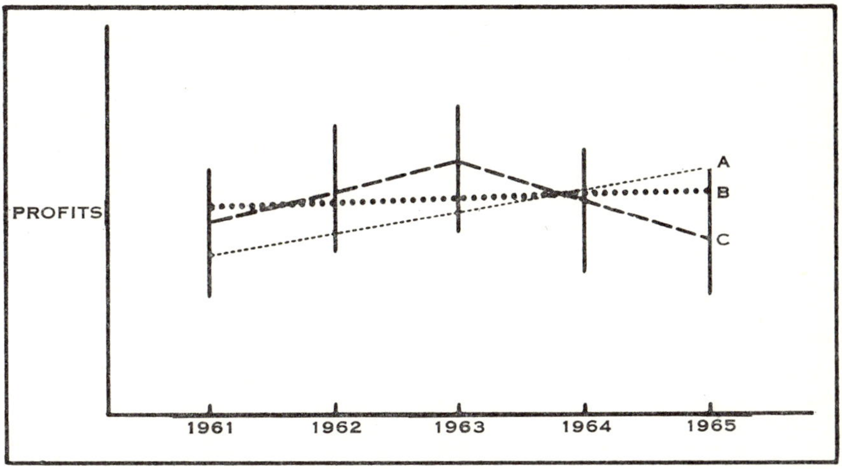

income more consistent with the shifts in the band. The extrapolation of the trend lines beyond 1965 is deliberately not given, for as of 1965 investors must form expectations. But on the evidence of reported past profits A would surely be preferred, on the "income growth" test, to B and C; B would be preferred, on the "income stability" test, to C; whereas the trends of both A and B are both inconsistent with the behavior of the band, and only the trend of C represents approximately what has occurred. If the prices of A stocks after 1965 are based on expectations of a continuation of the trend shown by the past figures, investors may well find they have burned their fingers. As we have said, no outsider can tell where any company's net income lies within the band provided by acceptable rules. But clearly if the band shifts down again in 1966, A will have to report a fall in net income.

This introduces a further important point. What A has been doing is "lagging" the effects of what has been going on in the markets of the firms. To keep up a firm's "earnings image" when the band is falling, it can feed on the effects of the "lagging" during the periods when the band was rising; it is obviously possible also to feed on previously undisclosed gains (undisclosed because they were not previously realized, for example) to show profits when there were none. But, if and when the turnback comes it is all the more severe. And, when it comes, because share prices are a multiple of earnings, it falls with multiplied severity on share prices. There are strong grounds for believing that many major re-organizations are simply the consequences of trying too long to sustain an "earnings image" (because it helps new financing) and of disregarding the right of stockholders to know what is occurring, so that they can let themselves down gently or move to replace or re-energize the management. The collapse is often said to be due to "inventory losses" or some such obscure-sounding thing, but the goods markets are seldom so perverse that they dump enormous losses in the laps of companies in one year. It is more likely that the looseness of the accounting rules results in it appearing that way.

What Do We Know?

I would like it to be clear just what these observations mean. I am not saying that all financial statements are uninformative, partially informative, or wrong, or misleading. All I am saying is that the words used are so hazy and the methods used are so complex and yield such varying values for the same things, that we have no means of knowing whether what they say is up to date or out of date, right or wrong, relevant or irrelevant. If we are investors, wishing to choose between a number of companies, we do not know which of the statements of those companies are more right than wrong, or more right than others. The unexpected failure of many large and apparently well-managed companies surely attests to this; and the stocks in our own portfolios may include the next one to fail in the same unannounced way. We do not know. This seems to be good reason to worry about accounting.

There can be no question, however, that accounting can provide the kind of up-to-date representations which the needs of investors demand and which the designers of the safeguards for investors—those, for example, who drafted the Securities Exchange Act of 1934—had in mind. There has not yet been invented any other device which can so knit together the consequences of all the varied acts of firms and the events which affect them, with such economy, that men of ordinary understanding can grasp them. To make accounting do what it is expected to do requires only a resolute will to find out the facts of the relationships of companies to the rest of the community from time to time. How then, it will be asked, has it happened that accounting does not now do this? What is the cause? Who is to blame? It may seem to be a digression to attempt to answer these questions. But an attempt to answer them will throw additional light on our main question.

Origins of Confusion

The present state of accounting is not entirely, or even largely, the fault of accountants. If by hindsight we may think accountants have been short-sighted, so by hindsight may we think that everyone else implicated in the development or use of accounting information has been short-sighted. In most of the critical situations, indeed, accountants have been in positions of subordinate influence only. The real trouble has been the very convenience of accounting and its products, a convenience which has led to its use for purposes quite unrelated to the financial purposes which were described above as the primary purposes of accounting.

We go no further back than 50 years. At that time accounting was relatively unsophisticated, its rules few and simple. So were business firms; but they were growing in complexity and there were some signs that accounting might parallel that growth. But 50 years ago income taxation was re-introduced. A ready to hand aid in the implementation of income taxation was the existence of the accounting framework, the methods of calculation and the terms, classifications and usages then current. Notice that this usage, for the calculation of a taxable income or a tax liability, serves quite a different purpose and one quite unrelated to the primary financial purpose. There is at least a potential conflict of interest between individual taxpayers and the Treasury; it is understandable, therefore, that the rules for calculating taxable income would be stated with some definiteness, even if they were simply codifications of what was then done in ordinary accounting. In particular, allowances for depreciation became limited in total amount to the original money outlays on durable goods. Before the 'twenties it was already being said that such a rule could lead to the attrition of business capital; but this in no way impeded the rule from becoming embedded in the tax laws. In the second place, reliance came to be placed on the times of receipt and payment of cash as indicators of the emergence of taxable income. Both these ideas can be justified in relation to the determination of tax liability—as a separate exercise from financial reporting to investors. But both tend to inhibit the up-dating of financial statements.

The acceptance of these rules had become quite firm by the 1930's, when the S.E.C. rules for registration statements were written; they became even more so by virtue of those rules. Thus the S.E.C. rules for financial statements, intended to serve the primary purpose we have mentioned, came to embody rules which were more appropriate to tax administration than to an informed securities market. The whole objective of accounting had become quite confused, and the confusion was not helped by the fact that business managers were faced with the problem: how to show a hopeful aspect of the firm to stockholders and a woebegone aspect to the Internal Revenue, simultaneously. As tax rates rose this was bound to lead to more regard for tax aspects than for stockholders' informational needs.

But about the same time, it was found that some of the established rules were imposing or were likely to impose heavy tax burdens on traders, as the prices of goods rose and necessitated the employment of greater quantities of money to do the same physical volume of business. In 1938 a tax measure for the relief of this was introduced, permitting the use of L.I.F.O. to some taxpayers; in 1939 it was permitted to all taxpayers (later its use was permitted even in cases where there were no continuous holdings of the same inventories). And one of the conditions for its use for tax purposes was that the same method be used for reporting to stockholders and for credit purposes. Notice what had happened. (1) A rule adopted to remedy a defect (the harsh tax effects) of an existing rule was permitted; it was not made obligatory; some taxpayers could and did adhere to the older rule. (2) The rule was for the purpose of giving tax relief;

it had nothing to do with the kind of information necessary for the efficient management of business, or for the proper judgement of business by investors. (3) The rule forced those using it for tax purposes to use it also for financial reporting purposes. The effects were threefold. Companies which used L.I.F.O. were reporting assets on a more out-of-date basis than before; the financial results and positions of companies as they were reported were less comparable than before because of the permissive use of the new alternative; and the dominant orientation of financial statements had virtually become a tax orientation rather than an investor orientation. Whatever divergences already existed between the accounting practices of firms, and whatever divergences between the tax and investor viewpoints, were multiplied by these events, and they have gone on multiplying since. The stockholder, though there were now millions of him, was forgotten.

In retrospect it is understandable that many of the steps which have vitiated the usefulness of accounting statements were regarded as the easiest steps to take at the time. But it is also clear that the consequences were not envisaged. The cost of making financial statements for investors conform with rules found to be convenient for tax purposes has, I am sure, been enormous; but even if it were small the coercion would be unjustifiable; for it conflicts with another law of Congress which seeks to guarantee to investors the opportunity of knowledgeably choosing their investments. The same may be said of any set of regulations, whether for rate-fixing or administration of the anti-trust laws or any other purpose, which tends to prevent the published financial statements from giving up-to-date information, or which requires to be incorporated in and as part of published financial statements information (such as divisional net incomes) which cannot be better than crude guessing.

Accountants are at present ground between the upper and nether millstones of serving the investing public and of obeying a tax law in the interest of their client companies. If they follow the tax law in the interest of stockholders as dividend-receivers, they fail to satisfy stockholders as information-receivers. Their defence against stockholders as information-receivers is certainly the conflict of laws. Unfortunately this is cold comfort for stockholders. But it is good reason to worry about accounting.

Accounting in a Rational Securities Market

The provisions of the Securities Act and the Securities Exchange Act were obviously intended to secure to investors knowledge of the characteristics of securities when first offered, and up-to-date knowledge of subsequent changes in the affairs of their issuers. Given such knowledge investors could protect themselves. Whatever excesses of optimism investors may allow themselves, whatever overreaching expectations they may entertain, whatever glowing hopes promoters and managers might hold before them, there would always be the hard facts of trade in the goods and services markets, as represented in corporate financial statements, to bring those expectations back to earth. Given that the financial statements represented the positions and results of firms in the context of the current market from time to time, they would be equally fair to all—actual and potential buyers and sellers of securities alike. The statements would be intelligible because they would be in contemporary terms; there would be no need for esoteric methods of valuation of unknown degrees of senility.

Until accounting is refined to the point of giving figures which are continuously up-to-date, and therefore continuously relevant to investors; and until those figures are derived by uniform principles, so that they are comparable as between firms, accounting will not serve as an efficient form of financial instrumentation in the securities market. I do not speak of "up-to-date" or "uniform" in any absolute sense; but accounting now falls seriously short of meeting those criteria. And that, I think, answers the question.

17

REALITY AND ILLUSION IN ACCOUNTING, FINANCE AND ECONOMICS*

We all have some sense of reality. We all have had experience of illusion. We have found what we thought to be real to be only an illusion. Sometimes we prefer illusions; we are comforted, entertained, amused by them. And we are fond of pointing out what we think are the illusions of others. But doubtless we are convinced that what we do in all seriousness—in business affairs—is realistic, and not illusory. This comfortable conviction should be questioned now and then.

There is at least a possibility that our convictions are merely habitual, that we have been so conditioned by what we learn from others that we cease to learn by our own experiences. We may prefer the shared illusion to the face of reality. In particular, this seems to be done on a substantial scale in the fields of accounting and finance as we shall try to show.

We shall take as the context of discussion an economy in which goods, services, and money change hands in an organized way through a system of linked markets. Even though operations in these markets may be influenced by governmental constraints—differential taxes, differential credit rules, regulation of markets, for example—there is a large degree of freedom of choice by buyers, sellers, producers, lenders, borrowers, and investors.

Markets as Information Sources

It is characteristic of markets as they are generally conceived by economists, and as they generally operate in common experience, that they provide both means of exchanging goods and services and information about the prices and qualities of goods and services. In fact they provide information to more people than they provide occasions and means of exchange. For, as the market is a rationing device, there must be more people who observe the price and quality signs given in markets than those who consummate exchanges. Markets are thus more than anything else providers of information.

There have long been rules about the information given or required to be given by sellers to possible buyers. Many are codified in laws relating to the sale of goods. *Caveat emptor* has not been the only rule. As products have become complex so that individual users cannot readily discriminate, and as vendors have resorted to practices ranging from fair to sharp, there have developed laws relating to the

---

* First published in *Michigan Business Review,* Vol. XX, No. 1, January 1968, pp. 1-9. Presented in the University of Michigan, January 1967.

testing and specification of food and drug products. Consumers' associations have done, in respect of many products, what legislatures have hesitated to do. These rules, laws, and appraisals have as their object and justification the maintenance of a fair market.

As with goods, so with securities. It has long been apprehended that, if a fair market in securities is to be established and maintained, potential buyers (and sellers) must have the right to some information about the underlying characteristics of securities and their issuers. Hence the laws relating to prospectuses and the periodical publication of financial statements of companies whose securities are publicly traded. Companies are required to put on record at the outset the nature of the securities they issue and the underlying facts of their businesses; and subsequently to publish financial statements which bring up to date the earlier reported facts.

Putting this information on record and distributing it is a costly business. Take any selection from today's company reports. A vast amount of expensive time must go into the preparation of financial statements, the accompanying text, and illustrations, and a deal of money into the printing and distribution of reports. Much expensive time goes into the preparation of statements to be registered with the S.E.C. Much expensive time is then spent by analysts in analyzing, and by executives explaining to analysts, what companies are doing, and how, and how well. Much time is spent by the information services in digesting financial reports and by hosts of other firms and persons in interpreting these reports. Why all these costs, and why is the publication of information mandatory? Because it is believed to be in the public interest that investors should be able to choose in an informed manner the firms in which they shall invest; and because it is believed that if informed investors act in their own interests they will distinguish the more efficient firms from the less efficient, support the former, and thereby promote the more efficient use of the community's resources.

The efficiency of a firm is some function of its efficiency, relatively to other firms, in acquiring factors of production, in combining them, and in selling them. These separate efficiencies are undoubtedly important; but they are not readily comprehensible to investors, and in any case investors need some comprehensible indication of their combined affect. The only overall measures of efficiency are financial measures, such as rates of return and measures of solvency. We hold these to be readily comprehensible notions, for every adult has some acquaintance with the rate of return on an investment and of the unpleasant consequences of insolvency or limited solvency.

The Quality of Securities

It is reasonable to suppose that the common factual bases of choice among buyers of food, drugs, automobiles and so on are price and quality. Individual buyers, of course, may have preferences which determine their choices for any given range of products having varying prices and qualities. Sellers may take account of these idiosyncrasies; but having done so the buyers are confronted by common facts—price and quality. To a limited extent buyers may force up prices by favoring a given product; but even among speculators there comes a point at which the price is regarded as ridiculously high for the quality. Quality does count. But, turning from the commodities markets, what is the quality of a security?

The quality of a security depends to some extent on the industry of its issuer at a given time. From time to time different industries go through stages of growth, improvement in efficiency, and so on; at other times the same industries stabilize or decline. But even in growing industries some firms grow faster than others, and some even decline and disappear. The mere trend in an industry cannot be the only determinant or even the main determinant of the quality of a particular security. To choose intelligently investors must know about the characteristics of particular firms. And to know whether an industry is growing in the only sense relevant to investors, financially, investors must be able to compare the financial characteristics of particular firms. Hence the uniform prescription that all firms which make public issues of securities shall report periodically in a manner which fairly presents their financial results and positions. If all firms were to report uniformly on these matters differences in the quality of securities in this one respect would be apparent—both differences in the quality of different securities at a given time and differences in the quality of any given security over time. And in so far as all other respects in which firms differ work themselves out in financial consequences, periodical financial reports give the resultants of all particular qualities of firms; in a real sense they represent the qualities of securities.

The Securities Market

But do operators in the securities market take any notice of these indicators of quality? Keynes, himself no mean investor, was sceptical, if not cynical: ". . . professional investment may be likened to those newspaper competitions in which the competitors have to pick out the six prettiest faces from a hundred photographs, the prize being awarded to the competitors whose choice most nearly corresponds to the average preferences of the competitors as a whole . . . . It is not a case of choosing those which, to the best of one's judgement, are really the prettiest, nor even those which average opinion genuinely thinks the prettiest. We have reached the third degree where we devote our intelligences to anticipating what average opinion expects average opinion to be. And there are some, I believe, who practice the fourth, fifth and higher degrees."[1] There can be little doubt that this graphically portrays the behavior of investors on many occasions. The great preoccupation with prices and prices alone, which forces some securities to ridiculously high prices, entails some such process. Underlying quality is regarded scantily; if any consideration is given

---

[1] J. M. Keynes, *The General Theory of Employment, Interest and Money.* London, Macmillan, 1936, p. 156.

to it, it is limited to the gross consideration of the state of a given industry.

In the guessing game that Keynes used as illustration nothing very serious hangs on the result. But in the securities market a very great deal may hang on the result—whether resources are rationed in favor of the efficient, whether there is any incentive to efficiency or any curb on inefficiency, depends on securities market operations being something more than a guessing game. Guessing there must be to some degree; but as Keynes observed also: "Speculators may do no harm as bubbles on a steady stream of enterprise. But the position is serious when enterprise becomes the bubble on a whirlpool of speculation. When the capital development of a country becomes a by-product of the activities of a casino, the job is likely to be ill-done." (ibid., p. 159).

What is necessary to prevent the market from pursuing illusions, to break the circle of expectations of expectations of expectations, is some facts independent of the expectors, some facts other than mere prices (which represent expectations), some facts to which investors may legitimately hitch their expectations. Now the theory of business finance does assume rational and informed behavior on the part of investors. The substantive basis for choices of investments must then be presumed to be some facts about the quality of securities, beside the prices at which they are currently traded.

We may appear to approach this requirement if we accept a view such as the following: "To serve as an effective resource allocator it would appear that the market should value a stock in some manner on the basis of the capitalized value of the company's expected future earnings as determined by the investment opportunities available to it."[2] But we still have no reference to facts. Can the market or any investor form any opinion about a company's expected future earnings without some financial facts specific to the company? It seems to be impossible. The work cited does not leave us altogether without facts. "The most direct measure of its efficiency of operation is the company's stream of earnings" (p. 67). But there is no reference to earnings statements and balance sheets. We find also the following remark: "Response to apparent irrelevancies such as presidential illness, instead of appearing a manifestation of panic or caprice, is seen as a rational response to a conspicuous signal which is seized upon by people seeking desperately for information" (p. 53). It is hard to understand in what sense people are "seeking desperately for information" when companies are obliged to publish directly information about their results and positions at least annually and, generally, more frequently; and when, as all company reports are not published simultaneously, there is an almost constant flow of such reports to the securities market. Unless, of course, financial statements are deemed to be illusory.

---

[2] William J. Baumol, *The Stock Market and Economic Efficiency.* New York, Fordham University Press, 1965, p. 6.

Financial Information

But at least if financial statements were deemed to be illusory we would expect some attempt by writers on business finance to examine their defects and to make some proposals for reform. However, it seems that in many cases the emphasis given to earnings quite overrides any usefulness that indications of financial position may have as a guide to a company's prospects. The solvency of companies surely has, or should have, some bearing on stock prices and resource allocation; the liquidity of the assets of a company surely serves, or should serve, as a guide to its capacity to advance with advances (or to adapt to reverses) in its industry. And the contemporary amount of its net assets or capital is surely necessary for the calculation of a company's rate of return, which one would suppose to be an indicator of prospects superior to the absolute amount of earnings. Typically it is the firm with available liquid assets or low leverage that is best able to take advantage of the inevitable changes in demand and technology; and there is evidence to the effect that firms with relatively small liquid resources, high leverage, and big ideas are the firms which cause enormous losses to stockholders and bondholders. In so far as these characteristics of a firm's financial position are passed over, one cannot help feeling that a significant part of the realities of the business community and the stock market is being overlooked.

The emphasis on earnings and the neglect of financial position may stem from, but at least it parallels, the concern of economists with income and their unconcern with financial position. And it has affected much accounting. The principal area of economic analysis which is of concern is that which deals with the determination of optimal price and volume policies of firms, and the principal device is marginal analysis. The greater part of the exercises in this field are concerned with the incremental effect of one prospective policy by comparison with another. Incremental effects clearly presuppose some base earnings, and some base investment, but with the magnitudes of these marginal analysis is unconcerned; at least they are covered by *ceteris paribus* assumptions. Further, incremental effects are computed on the basis of expected input and output prices, not on past input and output prices.

But we cannot suppose that the management of any particular firm can be unconcerned about the magnitudes of immediate past earnings and the current amount of the investment at any policy-making moment. These magnitudes give the rate of return which was earned and hence some idea of the rate of return which could be earned, *ceteris paribus*, in the succeeding period. If this rate appears to compare unfavorably with the rates obtainable by other firms or by adopting different policies, the contrast of rates will indicate the extent to which past policies must be supplanted. And if any new proposal involves the liquidation of some assets for the purchase of others, the statement of the current amount of the investment and its composition will provide an indication of the cash which could be made available by various combinations of disposable assets; and hence a starting point for working out the marginal consequences of feasible alternatives. It should be clear that the attention given to income calculation by accountants and their dismissal of the balance sheet as a mere repository of account balances is the product of an illusion; an illusion induced, as it seems, by adopting the forward-looking viewpoint which is quite proper in economic analysis.

Diversity of Accounting Rules

The concentration of attention on the calculation of income or earnings in the accounting process might be supposed to have led to refinement of the concept of income and refinement of the methods of computing it. But this too is an illusion. There is no generally accepted notion of income among accountants. Income is the residue obtained from performing certain operations on the numbers of monetary units representing purchases, sales and adjustments of some asset values. The residue can have no meaning unless the operations referred to are designed to produce the quantification of an income concept. In the absence of such a concept the operations cannot have been so designed. In fact, in the absence of such a concept there has been no way of constraining or disciplining the development of *ad hoc* rules for dealing with particular items of revenue, expenditure and assets. The number of rules available for dealing with such things as inventory values, the values of plant items and depreciation charges, and of other classes of assets is extensive[3]. And many of the rules are extraordinarily divergent in effect. It has been demonstrated repeatedly that any two particular selections of rules applied to the same basic data can yield enormously different periodical income figures[4]. And there are on record cases in which reported profits far exceeded the profits subsequently computed by applying different combinations of the acceptable rules. As every company can make its own selection from the permitted rules, and may indeed vary its selection from time to time, there is no possibility that the earnings or rates of return of any two companies are intrinsically comparable, except by a chance against which the odds are millions to one.

Writers on business finance and financial analysis are aware of some of these divergences. But they treat them in much the same piecemeal manner as accountants do. It is all very well to say that if one is comparing two companies, one of which uses L.I.F.O. for its inventories while the other uses F.I.F.O., some adjustment must be made to eliminate the effects of the different methods. No attempt is made however to say how the amount of the adjustment should be obtained; for the obvious reason that no one can tell from published figures what the effect of using a L.I.F.O. basis instead of F.I.F.O. has

---

[3] "Financial Information and the Securities Market", see p. 174, *ante,* and "A Matter of Principle", see p. 242, *ante.*

[4] See, for example, Leonard M. Savoie, "Accounting Improvement: How Fast, How Far?", *Harvard Business Review,* July-August 1963; and R. J. Chambers, *Accounting and Action,* Sydney, The Law Book Company, 1965, p. 182.

been. The advice is therefore banal. If the time and space devoted by writers on financial analysis to the peculiarities of accounting were turned to a demonstration of the necessity of up to date information of uniform quality, the chances of getting comparable information on the quality of securities could be greatly improved.

The acceptance of the (illusory) reliability of income figures can have some quaint consequences in the field of empirical analysis for theoretical purposes. Common sense suggests that the growth of the assets of a firm (as by retaining part of the assets which represent past earnings) would be accompanied by growth in the firm's earnings. Some work done in England, first published in 1962 and published in augmented form in 1966[5], purports to test this supposition for a selected year in the mid-'fifties. It was found that there was no discernible relationship between profits ploughed back and earnings growth. The plough-back variable chosen was "reported earnings less dividends as a ratio of earnings". Now, if reported earnings is a function of both actual earnings and the method of calculating earnings, and if the method of calculation may vary from firm to firm, and for any firm from year to year (these are both possible and demonstrable), the *a priori* probability of finding a relationship between plough-back and earnings growth is zero! In general, any attempt to use data in the mass to test suppositions of the above kind is likely to be defeated by the varying ways in which firms may calculate earnings, or at least reported earnings.

In the same study there are examples of year to year comparisons of the percentage growth of pre-tax earnings for individual firms with industry averages. Many of the instances yield zig-zag effects year by year. The question arises: does earnings growth really exhibit such swings, or are the reported figures affected by the modes of calculation adopted by the firms? As accounting methods are not uniform in effect, and as methods may be changed from year to year, it is quite possible that the swings are due either to "unconscious bias" inherent in the methods of accounting used, or to deliberate bias due to the choice of a method which will yield the kind of earnings figure the managements of particular firms may want to report in a given year.

There are no *a priori* grounds for rejecting the common sense view that growth in assets should be accompanied by growth in earnings. The empirical evidence of this study may be interpreted as demonstrating the folly of relying on non-uniform data, just as readily as it was interpreted as demonstrating the random character of earnings growth. That annually reported earnings mean much the same thing for all companies is an illusion. Notwithstanding the widely stated objection to secret reserves, varied and variable modes of calculation still make it possible for companies to smooth out earnings, or to report less than is actually earned in some years and to be less conservative in others.

---

[5] I. M. D. Little and A. C. Rayner, *Higgledy Piggledy Growth Again*. Oxford, Basil Blackwell.

Stale Information

The securities market is faced with a supply of information which is subject to two serious impediments to interpretation. The first is the sheer diversity of methods of accounting available to and used by firms. The second is a built in bias by virtue of which published information is systematically out of date. This latter effect is due to the suggestions made in the companies legislation on the English pattern, and the almost mandatory requirement of the S.E.C. regulations in the United States, that assets shall be reported on the basis of their initial purchase prices, or historical costs. These are curious provisions for laws which purport to secure the disclosure of relevant information. Investors at any time are investing or considering investing today's money, up to date money. The alternative opportunities open to them—real estate, mutual funds, savings accounts or other money loans—are all expressed in today's money. If they know or seek out any information on the prices of the products bought or sold by the firm in which they might invest, these too are in today's money, in units of today's purchasing power. Yet the information on which they might base judgements about the solvency, leverage, and rate of return of companies in which they might invest is all out of date. And if there are, in the final select group of companies from which they are to choose, companies of different ages, the information about some will be more out of date than the information about others. If investors do attempt to act in an informed and rational manner it is inevitable, or at least understandable, that stock prices will have a random character—not for any intrinsic reason, but because the information is irrelevant or confusing.

Security Analysis

But perhaps we have not yet the whole picture. Investors may not depend on their own unaided judgement, but on the skill and advice of investment advisers and security analysts. Security analysts do or may do a number of things.

They may study the differences between industries, and they may study particular industries intensively. But such studies are only background material for recommendations about specific companies or their securities. They may study particular firms. What is there to study? There are statements made by managers and other senior officers of firms; some such statements are publicly made, others are made orally in response to direct inquiry. Without in any way impugning the honesty or good faith of managers or other executives, these statements must be regarded as potentially biased. But because their subject-matter is privy to the firm, there is no way in which an analyst can corroborate them.

Secondly, there are the firm's financial statements which purport to be independently tested for corroboration; they are required to be audited by independent experts. It might be supposed therefore that the independently audited financial statements would be accepted as of greater value than the assertions of managers and executives;

or that they might serve as a basis for checking the validity of assertions or claims made by executives. But it is said that the practice is common among auditors of obtaining a statement from management to the effect that things are as they are represented to be in the financial statements. And we have shown that the financial statements embody figures which may be years out of date, particularly balance sheet figures for inventories and durable assets and items in income accounts which are based on balance sheet figures. Clearly they could not be used as a check on the recent general performance of the company, or as evidence of the effectiveness of any of its policies. But, we are told, analysts and advisers are able to get much more information than is available to the public in published financial statements. Let us admit they do. Several points may be made.

In respect of the relationship between a broker-dealer and a customer, the S.E.C. has gone on record as follows: "... the making of recommendations for the purchase of a security implies that the dealer has a reasonable basis for such recommendations, which, in turn, requires that, as a prerequisite, he shall have made a reasonable investigation. In addition, if such a dealer lacks essential information about the issuer, such as knowledge of its financial condition, he must disclose this lack of knowledge and caution customers as to the risk of purchasing the securities without it."[6] The reference to financial condition would be pointless if it did not refer to the condition at a date not far removed from the date of recommending, say, the latest balancing date. But, as we have already contended, the representations in balance sheets may be years out of date. Does the above statement imply, then, that the analyst or dealer must somehow discover the up to date position? If it does, all investors who act without this special "investigation" are not served by the balance sheets and income accounts which companies are required to publish! But this surely was not intended. The securities laws were devised for the disclosure of things "necessary or appropriate in the public interest or for the protection of investors"—not, be it noticed, as a starting point for investigations by analysts of financial positions and results.

Next, what in fact do security analysts do with the financial statements? We may read about financial statement analysis in many books; see analysts going through the steps in many back rooms; see the results in reports in all kinds of format—newspapers, periodicals, published investment services, private subscription services. But we will not find a book which tells us how to bring out of date information up to date, how to correct published financial statements so that they give reasonably up to date indications of financial positions and results. In fact most of the textbooks, and all the published ratios, percentages and whatnot are based on the presumption that the figures are up to date. The whole exercise is based on an illusion—or a delusion.

There have been some attempts to discover what analysts want to know from financial statements and what kinds of financial statement

---

[6] S.E.C. Securities Act Release No. 4445.

they would like to receive. One of the questions asked has been something like this: If accounting methods were devised which would take account of the effects of price changes or price-level changes on the positions and results of companies, would you prefer them to accounting on an historical cost or initial purchase price basis (that is, the present basis)? The answer which has been obtained in general is "No"[7].

What inference may be drawn from such an answer? Either analysts have some sixth sense, by virtue of which they can tell the up to date position even when the audited statements do not give it; this is hard to believe. Or, they do not want those who may consult analysts to believe that up to date information can be obtained without the intervention of analysts; this can scarcely be believed, for it would impugn the professional integrity of analysts. Or, they do in fact get up to date information from companies; this cannot be believed, for if it were so there would necessarily be some widely used form of accounting which somehow has never been mentioned in the literature. Or, they honestly believe that the statements they get are the best and the most up to date statements it is possible to get. Or, they, like many of us, are creatures of habit, and find it difficult to shake off old habits. These last two inferences are, at least, the most charitable.

But consider the consequences in the securities market. The informational bases of security investment decisions are not likely to be the facts as they are, but the facts as analysts see accountants' representations of them. Given that accountants' representations are diverse in quality, and that their measures of capital invested are generally out-of-date, and given that analysts have a preference for statements of the presently published kind, it is difficult to see how the advice of analysts serves the function of efficient distribution of the command of resources through the securities markets.

Reality or Illusion?

We have indicated only some of the points at which, in accounting and finance, illusion seems to have the better of reality. The view is no doubt still held, and the laws and constraints are so framed, that informed choices made in market places should ration the available goods, services and money in favor of the more efficient firms. But if the choices are badly informed, if the quality of securities is judged on inadequate financial information, the technically and commercially more efficient will not necessarily be preferred to the less efficient. The upshot is a less efficient economy, a lower standard of living, a lower national product, than existing technical expertise warrants. A greater concern for the value of contemporary financial information, and a more satisfactory integration of the theories of accounting,

[7] See, for example, Charles T. Horngren, "Security Analysts and the Price Level", *The Accounting Review,* October 1955.

finance, and management seem to be demanded if we we are to avert these consequences[8].

The burden of this falls to a considerable extent on the academic community. The academic is not merely a teacher of inherited techniques and folk-lore. His independent position permits him to stand off and look critically at the mode of operation of the whole economic apparatus, to distinguish what is real from what is accepted as real but is in fact illusory. Academics themselves, however, are not free of the tendency to cherish illusions, a tendency which is strengthened as narrow specialization increases.

We hear much of the virtue of free enterprise. But the enterprisers are not simply the managers of firms; investors, creditors, financiers are also enterprisers. If we prefer effective devices for securing economic efficiency above comfortable illusions, we will prefer that all who take part in the allocation of resources shall be free to choose with knowledge the risks they will run and the investments they will make. We will be impatient alike with those who would restrain our knowledge of what is going on and with those who adopt such limited frameworks that they foster such restraint. If we would escape the thraldom of outworn or outmoded dogma, we will examine more critically the relationships between business specialisms—the theory and practice of economics, law, management, finance and accounting. Partial views will bind us forever to respect for the illusory above the real.

---

[8] The writer has attempted such a synthesis in *Accounting, Evaluation and Economic Behavior*, Englewood Cliffs, Prentice-Hall Inc., 1966.

18

UNIFORMITY IN ACCOUNTING*

The debate may have become tedious. Although there have been some strong statements in favour of greater uniformity[1], and some less strong indications of the need to reduce diversity[2], there is still strongly entrenched opposition to the possibility and even the desirability of uniformity in accounting. All kinds of arguments and criteria—social, quasi-political, professional—have been adduced, on both sides. But there has been relatively little argument or illustration of the kind one might loosely describe as scientific.

We do not wish to be pretentious. By scientific we mean only having a proper respect for the observable world about us, attempting to discern the similarities which underlie observable diversities, and proceeding from these by careful argument to a reasonable conclusion. One cannot help noticing the frequency of occurrence of abstract nouns and turgid verbalizations which have characterized the debate; nor the infrequency of specific references to or illustrations of the particular kinds of mental operation by which choices in financial matters are made. But unless we look closely at the processes of choice, no amount of abstract discussion is likely to yield conclusions geared to the choices which users of financial information must make.

One of the most noticeable features of the world about us and our own actions in it is the respect for facts. Our claim to distinction from civilizations which respect or respected mysticism lies in the willingness with which we have recourse to facts. In this paper we concentrate on this aspect of the problem. It leads, as it has led others in other fields, to a disciplined set of procedures which will produce financial information which is uniform in effect[3].

The Diversity of Firms

That firms are diverse needs no argument. But it does need amplification. Firms are factually diverse; they do different things and their particular factual relationships to their environments at any time are different. From time to time a given firm does different things or

---

* First published in *The New York Certified Public Accountant,* Vol. XXXVII, No. 10, October 1967, pp. 747-54.

[1] See, for example, Herbert E. Miller, "Audited Statements—Are They Really Management's?", *Journal of Accountancy,* October 1964.

[2] *Report of Special Committee on Opinions of the Accounting Principles Board,* A.I.C.P.A., 1965, p. 7.

[3] The argument which follows amplifies positions taken by the writer in *Accounting, Evaluation and Economic Behavior,* Englewood Cliffs, 1966; see Chs. 4 and 7 especially; "Financial Information and the Securities Market", see p. 174, *ante*; and "A Matter of Principle", see p. 242, *ante*.

similar things in different ways, and from time to time its factual relationships with its environment changes.

But in some other senses firms are not so diverse. Their general objectives or functions are substantially similar. They aim to produce wanted goods and services at prices which will suffice to meet the outlays necessary to call for the supply of factor inputs—labor, materials and money. In the factor markets they are in competition, as they are in the product markets. The competition may be direct or indirect; for although markets may seem to be isolated they are all interrelated through the processes by which, as wants change and prices respond, the production and sale of some things increase and of other things decrease.

Firms are similar in other respects. If their operations are to be modified in such a way that, despite changes in their environments, they will continue to command the support of an adequate number of the classes of workers, suppliers, investors, financiers and customers, their managers will necessarily have recourse to the facts which, for the time being, are indicative of the extent of this support and the conditions under which it is given.

So that firms may match these conditions, or any subsequent conditions which their managers may expect to arise from these conditions, the managers will necessarily have recourse to facts relating to the operations and the states of their firms. Knowledge of the facts performs two functions. The discovered facts are the feedback which indicates what has occurred as a consequence of previously chosen courses of action, and which provides the basis of judgements about previous choices, and hence also of judgements about future kinds of action. Second, the facts are the basis on which any choice of actions from that time forward will proceed.

Factual Knowledge

The demand for factual knowledge is general and extensive. But there are many kinds of facts. There are output figures, sales figures, inventory level figures, quality control figures, labor force figures, labor turnover figures, and so on—each class or kind being required for its particular bearing on a particular class of problem. Now, even though these figures may be obtained for the solution of a particular class of problem, they may not be compiled with any bias, if the firm is to know what has happened and from what present position to proceed. Objection would be taken, for example, to any figures which showed a larger output, or a smaller, than the factual output, whether by mistake or deliberate intention; for such figures constitute an interference with the basis of judgements by those whose judgements are expected to be informed by the facts.

Further, as the firm itself is a system of differentiated, interacting parts, it would be reasonable to suppose that things which occurred in one part of the system will have caused things to occur in some other part. For example, we may suppose that labor turnover figures may be compiled as an indication of changes in "morale", or, to put it more objectively, in the comparative holding power of one firm as against all other employers. Having obtained the figures, the management may inquire whether a change in labor turnover has had an impact on output or sales turnover. Strictly, this use of labor turnover figures should be possible without any consideration of the original or primary use; facts are facts, however they may be used. What is more, the compilers of the figures cannot know whether or when they will be used in contexts quite different from the originating or primary context; the only safe rule for the compilers, therefore, is to get at the facts with all the skill and other resources at their disposal.

Now, of course, some facts are fuzzy things; and statements purporting to be statements of fact are often even fuzzier. There is a tendency to push this known limitation of human capacity for observation and description too far however. If we do this we are apt to conclude that there is nothing we know or can know.

But, men have not been daunted by their acknowledged deficiencies. They have sought to improve observation by the concentration of attention on one thing at a time, and to improve the consistency of observation and statements about observations by defining the things to be observed, by stipulating the steps to be taken in observing, and by stating the forms in which descriptions of observations should be cast. The reader may contemplate the steps to be taken, of these kinds, for the discovery of labor turnover. The same steps are taken in all strictly scientific work. Their effects are to reduce the fuzziness and increase the accuracy of observations and statements about observations. The resulting statements we describe as factual, provided no goal of the observer other than the goal of discovery has been interposed in the process.

The illustrations we have used have related to the "internal" facts of a single firm. We have held definition, description and stipulation to be necessary because many different persons may be involved in the discovery and use of the facts and because the facts may be put to varied uses of which the compilers are not necessarily aware. For greater reason these steps are necessary if any serious attempt is made to compile data on a given matter, which firms experience in common, for their better information.

Financial Facts

We return to financial information. Let it be noted that accountants are presumed to be expert in compiling financial information. The subject-matter of their studies, their qualifying examinations and their practices is financial information. It is not market information, nor technical information about physical facilities and their capacities, nor information about labor forces. Firms may be extraordinarily diverse in many respects, but financially they have many things in common. They all use money; they all need money from others to finance their holdings; they all are judged by others to be worthy or unworthy of financial support, in part at least, by the manner in which they deploy the money contributed by others, and by the monetary outcome of so deploying it.

If the managers of a firm wish to know whether one mode of operating is better than another, at least one of the criteria will be the monetary outcome, for the reason last stated. If the managers wish to know whether the outcome of one period's operations is better or worse than that of another, at least one of the criteria will be the monetary outcome. And if two such outcomes are to be compared for the purpose stated it is just as necessary that the key concepts shall be defined, that the method of obtaining measures of them shall be described, and that the components shall be stipulated clearly, as these steps are necessary for the determination of labor turnover or any other factual matter.

As in the illustration relating to labor turnover, the case for definition, description and stipulation is even greater if, for any purpose, the financial results and positions of different firms are to be brought into juxtaposition for comparison. We can have only general ideas about the manner in which the facts may be used; but we can have general ideas. We do know that some firms get into financial difficulties—meaning that their immediate command of resources is inadequate to meet immediate claims; and when they get into financial difficulties, financial supporters need a great deal of convincing, if they are convinced at all, that such companies can extricate themselves. We do know that some firms fail, some temporarily and some hopelessly, to earn net incomes of the size adequate to maintain the confidence of supporters. Clearly on financial position and results we need factual information so that we can make the comparisons which help us to distinguish the good from the poorer and the bad, financially.

The User's Standpoint

It is shocking to find it asserted that experts in the compilation of financial information do not know what kind of information is used by or is useful to those (managers, investors, financiers) having interests in the financial characteristics of firms. Those who make such assertions thereby set themselves below the level of sophistication, and even ordinary awareness, of quite unsophisticated persons—the untrained who clearly perceive that savings deposits, commercial bonds and stocks and direct investments in business operations yield different net incomes and different rates of return and are subject to different risks. If any manager, investor or financier wishes to know what are the relative incomes or rates of return of two or more firms, and what those rates are relative to the rate of return on riskless investments, the amount of the income and the amount of the investment in every case must be based on the same concepts of income and investment.

It seems so obvious, from the user's standpoint, that the concepts must be the same, that one can only suppose the user's standpoint is disregarded by those who support the notion that there can be many such concepts. The common retort to this suggestion is that users require a peep into the future, and that merely to tell them what has occurred in the past does not satisfy that need.

But first, income statements and balance sheets purport to represent fairly what has happened and the resulting position at a certain date. If they were to do this their contents would be entirely factual, subject only to the limitations of observation which affect all observers even in the most scientific fields. Second, no peep into the future can be useful of itself, without some indication of what has been done in the past and some indication of the position from which a firm faces the future.

Third, no peep into the future can be factual; so that if future expectations are embodied in financial statements, those statements must lack in some respects the factual qualities we have held to be necessary. And as the non-factual elements embody the expectations of someone, there is no possibility that they may be independently confirmed, as by a process of audit.

Fourth, the peep into the future can be only the peep of managers; yet accountants have long justified conservative accounting on the ground that managers are notoriously optimistic; the two positions can scarcely be reconciled.

On no ground, therefore, does it seem that a peep into the future can, or should be satisfied within the accounting framework. And, in so far as managers, and most of us, are so often wrong in prognosticating the future, it even seems very doubtful whether anything but the broadest descriptive indications of the future should be given.

Uniformity of Key Concepts:

Contemporaneity

We return to our contention that from the user's standpoint the concepts of income and investment must be the same. To be of contemporary or approximately contemporary use they must embody a strong element of contemporaneity. Unless they have reference to contemporary markets and prices they will have no relevance to contemporary or approximately contemporary judgements.

It is of no consequence that different firms operate in different fractional markets. All markets are linked directly or indirectly, competitively or complementarily. It is within the framework of those markets at any time that a firm's financial position is to be found, that the financial positions of all firms, indeed, are to be found. Given that financial positions are so found at successive dates, changes in financial position and the amounts of net income may be obtained by direct inference. Contemporaneity is conducive to uniformity.

Rate of Return on Investment

But contemporaneity is not the only element in the definitions of income, investment and financial position; nor is it the only element which has been neglected in whatever definitions have been offered. It is almost beyond question that the most common reference point which all users of financial statements have in judging the performances of firms is the rate of return currently obtainable on some such limited-risk investment as government bonds. In this case the investor obtains a money sum per period which is surplus to the amount of his investment.

It is beyond question that some such reference point is a useful reference point for investments at greater risk. That being so, users of financial statements will expect those statements to yield analogous information to that obtainable for, say, government bonds. They will expect to have an indication of the surplus generated in a period, on the footing that the opening investment is maintained—and as the financial statements bear the terminal date of a period they will expect the figures to be in terms of money measures taken at that date. They will expect this even though the component assets and equities are diverse in kind for a given firm, and diverse in kind and composition as between firms; for they know that the existence of markets provides a means of establishing equivalences and the existence of a monetary medium provides a common denominator for the prices of all goods in possession of firms at a given time.

Lay Persons' Expectations

We will admit that lay persons may have an oversimplified idea of the difficulties of finding the facts and reducing them to intelligible order. But that is in the nature of all lay persons. As a layman, looking at the tasks of engineers or astronomers, I can have only a limited and oversimplified idea of their difficulties, though I may have a very clear idea of what I and others expect them to produce, a clear idea of their functions. Laymen expect scientists, reporters, statisticians and accountants to get at the facts—for these people all have one product in common, ideally; reliable information of the most up-to-date kind. Given the facts laymen may make their own uses of them in their own interests as they see them. Without the facts, or given distorted facts, the layman's capacity to choose in his own interest is prejudiced from the outset. And in the present context, the getting of information, let it be noted that managers themselves are laymen.

Uniformity of Effects

It may seem odd that in a paper bearing the title of this one the words "uniformity" and "comparability" have appeared so seldom. But the reason is not hard to find, if it is recalled that we have been speaking of facts. A service dedicated to the discovery of facts of a stipulated class will develop rules which are uniform in effect. But it does require prior stipulation of the nature of the facts to be discovered.

Give two cubes of metal to two boys in a school laboratory, and ask them to find their volumes. One will measure the sides and compute the volume; another will drop the cube into a calibrated flask of water and read off the amount of water displaced. The results are uniform in effect. Give one of the boys a cube of wood with the same task. He will measure the sides, knowing that he cannot easily measure its complete displacement in water. But in all cases the property, volume, is the same property, defined to the point of understanding at the outset.

The Influence of Book-keeping Rules

Much of the argument about uniformity has turned on uniformity of details of operation, not on uniformity of effects. Attention has been riveted on book-keeping rules rather than on the character of the product they are expected by others to yield. Thus, it has been said, almost in derisory fashion, that uniformity would entail a complete prescription for all types of transaction for all types of firm. This, of course, is mere quibbling; for I doubt whether any proponent of uniformity would contemplate such an exercise. Concentration on book-keeping rules has almost certainly hindered the possibility of producing uniform information, for the allegiances of business firms and professionals to long-established rules is much greater than allegiance to the ideal of up to date information.

Allegiance to book-keeping rules has almost certainly obscured the fact that many such alternative rules are extremely diverse in effect, and has led to the elevation of mere consistency of application to a level it does not deserve. Consider again the boy with the block of wood. If he had been told that the way to find volume is to drop an object into a calibrated flask of water, and that he must always be consistent, his answer for the volume of the wood block would be wrong if he acted consistently. The result is what counts; not the process or the consistency of its application.

If, of course, a process has been designed so that in any circumstances it will yield a result of the specified kind, consistent application of the process is unobjectionable. But in accounting the process has not yet been designed to that end. A simple example will suffice. Suppose a company adopts the lower of cost or market rule. When prices are rising this reduces to the cost rule; when prices are falling it reduces to the market rule. If a period of rising costs is followed by a period of falling costs, the latter period will benefit from the fact that opening inventories are represented at less than market; and although falling prices are generally suggestive of poorer profits, the profits will be sustained merely by the benefit conferred on the second period by the rule adopted.

The rule itself is inconsistent; the results it produces will be inconsistent with the events which occurred. Consistency of application of this rule can only produce inconsistencies. Similarly for many other rules. If in the above case the rule were cost (in the traditional sense), it could be applied consistently, but it would never be up to date. If the rule were market, it could be applied consistently and it would always be up to date.

Mixing Facts and Judgements

We can develop rules for discovering facts which are uniform in effect, even though there may be alternatives for difficult cases provided they are similar in effect. But it is impossible to develop rules which are similar in effect for discovering mixtures of fact and judgement. This is one of the difficulties which confronts the traditional, permissive accounting.

Judgements are unique to their makers in the situations they are in at the time of judgement; judgements in short are relative and subjective. The kinds of judgement which are germane to the present arguments are judgements, opinions or valuations of assets. Suppose we ask the managers of a firm to put a value on an inventory for the purpose of including that value in a balance sheet which contains also cash and current obligations. In effect we ask managers to do this before they know what the financial position of the firm is.

Now suppose, following a line of argument which has become quite common, that the value is the discounted net proceeds of the item. Suppose that the usual production and distribution process takes six months—a fact which must be known to obtain the discounted net proceeds. And suppose that the resulting balance sheet contains: cash $1000, inventory $5000, owner's equity $2000, short term liabilities (due within three months) $4000. It is highly probable that immediately this position comes to the notice of the managers they will place an entirely different valuation on the inventory.

To avoid financial difficulties they may be forced to decide to liquidate some of the inventory in a much shorter interval than is usual, putting up with a cash "sacrifice" in order to maintain solvency. Such a decision involves weighing up the gains expected from sale in the usual interval against the gains expected from avoiding insolvency; and the valuation the managers effectively place on the inventory in the light of the revealed position may well be inconsistent in any given case with the valuation included in the statement of position. In brief the recourse to judgements of the above kind entails that managers must know the position in order to find the position—a circularity which is surely an affront to reason.

Now a statement of fact can lead to no such position. A statement of fact is certainly time-bound; but it does not depend on the specific expectations or evaluations of any person, and is therefore open to use by all or any persons. Consider again the above balance sheet.

The amount of cash is a fact. (I know of no assertion to the effect that a firm goes on using cash in the same way as it is using it (idly) at a given balance date, nor of any assertion to the effect that the discounted net proceeds of cash used in such a way over some future period should be shown as the amount of cash on hand.)

The amount of inventories is not a fact, but the result of some manipulations based on hypothetical outcomes of hypothetical courses of action. In the first place there is no process by which such different amounts may be added to give an aggregate having a sensible meaning. But in the second place, the managers of a given firm may place quite different valuations on an inventory at different times, due to changes in their "visceral apprehension" of future possibilities; and the managers of different firms will place quite different valuations on their own inventories at a given time due to individual variances in "visceral apprehension". The same effect is produced by the admission of conservatism in accounting.

Clearly, the results of an accounting process which depends on such judgements can never be uniform in effect—uniform in representing results and positions—nor comparable. This, of course, is exactly what the opponents of uniformity in accounting have been saying. What is noteworthy, however, is that the conclusion has been reached without any reference to the diversity of accounting rules. We may regard the existent diversity of permissible rules in two ways. Either it serves to compound the diversity of judgements yielding figures for financial statements. Or it gives the appearance of orderliness to what is nothing more than "rationalizations by rule" of judgements based on quite other and undisclosed considerations.

There is a second form of mixing facts and judgements which is equally insidious. It is commonly said, in a pejorative way, that the limitation of accounting to monetary aspects of affairs is a serious limitation; that the quality of management and the morale of workers and so on are most important elements in any judgement by outsiders. But, first, if the length and the weight of any object are of some consequence, we do not condemn foot-rules because they do not also measure weights. And, second, the quality of the management and the morale of the workers and so on can themselves only be judged, independently of mere assertion, by what they do in conjunction—and the only measure of what they do in conjunction is the inference from discovered facts which we call the ratio of net income to capital employed. By their fruits they are known. To judge is the function of users of information. To judge on an informed basis—informed by the facts—is the right which laws relating to financial disclosure seek to secure for external parties, and which the establishment of specialisms in fact-finding is expected to secure for managers.

Conclusion

The basic issues are quite simple. Do businessmen and investors need financial facts indicative of what has been achieved from time to time? Do they need facts indicative of the financial position from which companies face the future from time to time? Do they need facts which can be reduced to ratios indicative of the relative positions and results of a given firm at different times? Do they need facts which can be reduced to ratios indicative of the significant financial differences between firms at any time and from time to time?

If the answers to these questions are "no", managers and investors will be cast loose in a jungle of facts and opinions or expectations, mixed in a manner which it is impossible to discipline or to disentangle. If the answers are "yes", the discipline of fact-finding will ensure uniformity of effects; firms will be managed, scrutinized and judged on facts, not on a mash of facts and expectations; and the rules of accounting will be purged of the paraphernalia which now introduce so many non-facts into financial statements. Accounting, and management, may tend towards the scientific character of other modern exercises in human ingenuity and away from the present mysticism and confusion which are so reminiscent of the medieval scholastics.

ACCOUNTING AND PRICE VARIATION

19

ACCOUNTING AND SHIFTING PRICE LEVELS*

The valuation of stock and provision for depreciation have long been recognized as the two most complex problems in accounting. Their complexities have been increased by actual changes, and by expectations of changes, in price levels, during the past decade particularly. Though business managers are really closely concerned, the technical aspects of providing for these changes have largely been left to accountants—depreciation and valuation theories have been regarded as part of accounting practice rather than of management theory.

This paper deals with some of the implications of changes in price levels as they affect depreciation accounting and the basis of accounting practice generally. This is not to deny or to minimize the importance of inventory valuation theory and practice; the limitation enables us to concentrate on a particular group of problems more effectively than if we had to deal at the same time with two such groups. The principal intention is to present some other views than those so widely supported by accountants.

On the bases and methods of providing for depreciation of fixed assets, different views prevail in the camps of accountants, managers, economists, taxation experts and advisers of governmental treasurers. It is impossible that these points of view can all be conducive to the most satisfactory conduct of business operations, meaning, by "most satisfactory", those operations which yield the greatest long-run social benefits. It is also impossible that all these points of view are compatible with the aims of the managers of many individual business undertakings. Though we are constrained in practice to follow one of the accepted methods by reason of external influences, we should not therefore abstain from examining the advantages and deficiencies of other methods.

The Problem of Depreciation Accounting

The common bases of provisions for depreciation are (a) actual money costs and (b) estimated replacement costs. In stating the alternatives thus baldly it is sought to emphasize what is important for present purposes and to avoid introducing the complications which arise from the variety of methods applied to both bases.

---

* First published in *The Australian Accountant,* Vol. XIX, No. 9, September 1949, pp. 313-20.

The former basis is commonly favoured, for some theoretical but mainly practical reasons, by accountants, and for sound practical reasons by taxing authorities. The replacement cost basis is championed by businessmen mainly, by men with an eye to the important business problems of fixing prices and of maintaining the solvency of their business units; it is also in a measure supported by certain economic considerations which some economists, in America particularly, have rather graphically pointed out in recent utterances on business profits. The decision one reaches is not a mere bagatelle; it must have far-reaching effects, not only on business practice but also on accounting theory, as will be shown. The basis adopted by business managers or accountants or by taxing authorities can be readily shown to affect directly company profits available for distribution as dividends, the prices of goods and hence the general price level, and the capital structures of business undertakings in the future.

The Purpose of Depreciation Accounting

When the repercussions are so wide the importance of the issue must be granted. Little progress can be made, however, without some concept of the real purpose of depreciation provisions and of the objective of depreciation accounting. At this point we meet confusion. The purposes of making depreciation provisions have been variously described as:—

(a) to recover money costs;

(b) to replace assets;

(c) to maintain invested capital;

(d) to maintain earning capacity;

and a moment's reflection will suggest that these stated purposes may, in almost all real circumstances, mean different things.

The first is the purpose ascribed to depreciation provisions by the traditional accounting approach; it is supported by the great bulk of accountants and associations of accountants on the ground that money cost is an "objective" basis, a matter of record, whereas other cost bases must inevitably be a matter of unverifiable opinion. This argument has an appeal about it which is very satisfying to those who are conservative in their views. But in so far as, by accepted accounting practices, there is applied to this objective basis a yearly correction which is anything but objective, the merit of the above argument is diminished. One may further criticize the "objectivity" argument by denying the relevance of values which were objectively determined some years ago (in quite a different economic environment) to the problems of business today.

By Whose Authority?

Recognition of the fact that there is a variety of purposes which could be adopted for depreciation accounting forces us a stage further back than accounting technique to the question, "By whose authority are financial statements prepared and by whose authority are depreciation provisions determined?"

The ideal answer to this is not hard to find; financial accounts are drawn up as a report of the stewardship of the management, and therefore we may say that their contents are and in particular, the depreciation provision is, a reflection of managerial decisions. But the ideal answer is not always the correct description of practice. In fact, not all managers, a minority of managers perhaps, give any considerable thought to the extent of the depreciation provision or to its purpose; the matter is left in the hands of the accountant very often.

Now, I imagine it is largely due to the more critical approach, in recent decades, both to accounting theory and to business management that the accountant finds himself in difficulties. The accountant has developed a theory of his subject in which he accepts the fact that his balance sheet is a hotch-pot of money items with no common purchasing-power base: in other words, he is wedded to preparing statements on the basis of money cost. Traditionally the accountant's basis for depreciation accounting is cost; and traditionally, by a convenient rule, accountants provide for depreciation on some formula which is applied consistently year after year to original cost or residual cost.

But the war, and more forcibly the post-war years have upset this rather pleasant, because formalized, scheme of things. Price levels have moved considerably more than they had done almost for a generation, and the anomalies the movement has forced upon us have become the stamping ground of the financial press, businessmen, economists and some adventurous accountants.

Financial Statements Must Inform

As stated above, accounting statements are commonly regarded as reports of stewardship, reports not of purely detached interest to accountants but intended to inform, to advise, to provoke action when necessary. And they are not regarded in this way solely by the ignorant. The authority of the law, and of many distinguished accountants backs up this view. "Financial statements are usually intended to be acted upon, and once issued they may be put to any one of many uses by those into whose hands they come. They are significant even more on account of the inferences that are likely to be drawn from them on account of their character as statements of fact or opinion" (G. O. May, *Financial Accounting*, p. 19).

It is largely because of this notion of external usefulness that we have, put forward by leading theorists, a concept or doctrine of disclosure; and today disclosure is considered very widely to be a duty of fundamental importance. The examples commonly given of the idea of disclosure turn on the proper grouping and description of items in financial statements. But, no matter how explicit the descriptions are, it may be contended that in so far as historical cost is used in computing depreciation, shareholders and investors are being led up the garden path; they are being fooled by the talk of disclosure to rely on statements which may give an egregiously incorrect view of the states of their companies.

Nor is this all; the historical cost procedure puts in the hands of less scrupulous business people a first-class tool for deliberately evading the issue of rising prices and for window dressing in the guise of correct or accepted practice.

But let us return to the main argument.

Real and Conventional Costs

Economists and business managers have been slow to approach the problems of the accounting treatment of depreciation, but now there is a widespread conviction among them that the traditional methods of the accountant are inadequate and unsatisfactory. They generally believe that in times of rising price levels the depreciation provision should be greater than the provision which would result from using the money cost basis.

Economists justify their view on the ground that provisions which give effect, in some measure, to changes in the price level, enable a better approximation to be made to real income or real profit, as distinct from the book profits which traditional accounting methods would yield. Or to put it another way, when price levels change, the profits computed by traditional methods include profits or losses on trading and profits or losses on movements in the value of the currency, and these two should be segregated in the interest of all parties affected by those profits or losses.

Conventional methods give rise to grave inconsistencies when price levels change. In periods of sharply rising prices, money incomes tend to increase just as other prices increase, but real incomes don't necessarily change at all; the real incomes of fixed money-income groups decline. Now, out of the money incomes of businesses, depreciation provisions are made, dividends are paid and reserves are augmented. The depreciation provision in particular is thus an amount in, say, 1949 £'s set off against an amount which appears in the balance sheet as an asset expressed in £'s, but which really should be expressed in, say, 1939 £'s. If 1949 £'s are worth, in purchasing power, anything less than 1939 £'s were worth, then firstly, the provision is inadequate to maintain the real capital (e.g., productive capacity), and secondly, the effect is like subtracting a precise number of little red radishes from a given number of large green cabbages, to use the terms of F. Leger, quoted by Sweeney. In short the illusion of preciseness is the only significant reality to those who disregard changes in the value of money.

The businessman thinks in rather different terms, but his conclusions are not very different from those of the economist. Some recent statements on the general problem will be given.

The first example is that of Lever Bros. and Unilever Ltd. The Chairman's address at the Annual General Meeting in August, 1948, includes the following statement: "The cost value of our fixed assets at the end of 1947 was £88 million, and depreciation is being charged in the normal way, which will lead to the accumulation in due course of this sum for replacements, as and when they are required. Today, however, we estimate that to replace our existing fixed assets would cost £148 million, so that at present price levels our depreciation fund would be about £66 million short of our requirements . . . . The only way in which we can maintain that part of our capital which is invested in fixed assets is to recover in the price of our products an amount which truly represents the wastage in value of our fixed assets at present-day prices. If we cannot do this, then we shall be fixing our selling prices on a basis below real cost, and if the business community as a whole does the same thing, then the country will be consuming a part of its capital instead of paying its way . . . . Selling prices must be so fixed as to bear relation to real cost."

Some Criticisms

Some comment on this way of fixing prices seems necessary at this point. The method suggested has been lampooned by accountants. *Fortune* (January, 1949) quotes one as saying, "what is really proposed is a N.I.F.O. system (a new addition to the I.F.O. family, meaning next-in-first-out) since plant not yet acquired would be written off against current income". But this view doesn't scratch the surface of economic reality. If it is the purpose of depreciation accounting to maintain the earning capacity of an undertaking—and no accountant yet seems to have challenged this assumption—pricing on the basis of known changes in purchasing power is a logical way of giving effect to that purpose. As Sir Geoffrey Heyworth said, "Selling prices must be so fixed as to bear relation to real cost," i.e., economic cost not some probable future cost.

This seems to be a critical point in the controversy. We noticed how one supporter of the historical cost basis claims that basing the provision on something like replacement cost is writing off an asset not yet acquired. Another view is that using the replacement cost basis is tantamount to making a capital levy on the community to enable a business to replace its fixed assets. Before a joint committee of the United States Senate and House of Representatives at the end of last year, the major labour organizations made this claim in respect of American industry generally. These views seem to place far too much weight on the idea of actual replacement and lose sight of a significant feature of the economics of rising prices, due, it is suggested, to misunderstanding or confusion about the nature of costs.

These arguments miss the point which is of immediate concern to economists, who dislike the unqualified term "cost" and seek to be much more precise in their terms, and to businessmen who find they have to pay at current rates for everything else they use—labour and all materials and services used in production. Fixed assets like buildings and plant may quite realistically be considered as bundles of services (e.g., factory space, machine hire, etc.) purchased in advance, services which if purchased from month to month would be charged at prices adjusted almost automatically to changing price levels. The object of providing for depreciation at a rate estimated on probable replacement costs is to do just this: to give to current usage of assets bought in previous years a value, at today's prices, of equivalent services. It is submitted that replacement of identical assets doesn't enter into the question; and the idea that replacement cost in effect makes a capital levy on the community seems to me to violate the meaning of a capital levy. It is true to say that failure to provide at a figure approaching replacement cost results in counting as profits what are really unrecorded, but nonetheless definite, costs. Harvard Professor of Economics, Summer H. Slichter, has estimated that over the past three years American corporations have thus overstated profits by some 15,400 million dollars, and the National City Bank of New York has estimated that for the 100 largest manufacturing corporations in U.S.A., 1947 profits, after allowing depreciation on money cost, was 14.3 per cent, whereas corrected to meet replacement costs at 1940 values, only 8.8 per cent would have been shown.

Practice in Australia

Here are the views of some Australian directors on the same theme. Sir Norman Brookes, addressing the annual general meeting of Australian Paper Manufacturers Limited, in September last, said: "The net figure of £2,881,407 appears in the Balance Sheet before you against the item 'Fixed Assets' and it will be seen, this is after a total provision for Depreciation, Amortization and Obsolescence of £3,498,528 has been made over the years. To replace these 'Fixed Assets' would cost today well over 10 million pounds. On the one hand we have the very conservative position that our Fixed Assets in terms of today's values for equivalent capacity are nearly four times greater than appears on the Balance Sheet. On the other hand, your directors must ask themselves whether the provision of £3,498,000 for depreciation, etc., based largely on the pre-war basis adopted by your company, is adequate in the light of today's changed and changing values."

Mr. Maurice Shmith, at the twenty-fourth annual general meeting of Yellow Cabs of Australia Ltd. dealt with his company's problem in the following terms: "I am afraid it is not generally recognized that the preservation of effective working capital is a matter of fundamental importance, not only to private enterprise, but to the nation as a whole, and that the effectiveness of capital is greatly reduced by the incidence of rising prices, particularly in a business such as ours, where so much working capital is represented by fast-depreciating assets which must be replaced continuously at relatively short periods of time. For example, if before the war taxicab units cost, say, £400 each, as compared with the present price of £800, it follows that the effectiveness of part of the fixed capital of the company has been reduced. There are two ways of making good this loss of effective capital:—

"1. By the creation of reserves within the business, either as a charge against or an appropriation of profit; or

"2. By making a new fixed capital or share issue.

"It is the opinion of your Board that losses of effective working capital by the incidence of rising prices should be anticipated as far as possible, and provided for by the first method, namely, as a charge against or an appropriation of profits."

A number of other companies have recognized the effect of rising prices on the maintenance of effective capital. Hume Pipe appropriated from profits in 1948 £20,000 to augment a Plant Depreciation Reserve. Dunlop Rubber set aside £50,000 from the 1948 profit to make up for the material increases in costs of plant and equipment. Yarra Falls added £25,000 to its Machinery and Plant Replacement Reserve which was set up to meet the greatly increased cost of new machinery.

Now one can imagine the supporters of the money cost basis feeling quite satisfied with this treatment of the rise in plant costs. To appropriate extra sums from profits for replacement purposes seems quite excusable, whereas to charge extra sums in arriving at profits seems to be anathema. This inconsistency arises, we believe, from the formalities of accounting rather than from any underlying reality. We cannot believe that shareholders alone carry the burden of earmarking such extra provisions from profits. Consideration of the problem of pricing goods must convince one that prices will, subject to external controls, be so fixed that current costs, taxation, dividends and reserves are all provided for. Dividends cannot be made to suffer indefinitely from a failure of management to raise prices to meet real costs, or as managers may state it, to meet replacement costs. (Note: Replacement cost is, I believe, to be construed liberally rather than literally. It seems to be only a convenient way of saying "considerably more than money cost when prices are rising" or "considerably less when prices are falling". The difficulty of accurately determining replacement cost is not belittled, but accurate determination is not critical to the theory which claims that greater provision must be made than historical cost allows.)

Product Pricing

Some have said that the adoption of a real cost, or replacement, basis for depreciation provisions will have the effect of intensifying booms and depressions, by increasing the incomes of shareholders when prices are rising and creating a new pressure on the price level and the supply of goods, and by the reverse process when prices are falling. But, the effect of the depreciation basis adopted on the prices of goods is dependent on several things.

It depends, for example, on the relationship between price and cost. For, in an industry in which demand is far in excess of supply, or in which for other reasons there is no great price competition, it may not matter what the provision for depreciation is; in the absence of external price controls, price will be more closely related to what the consumer is prepared to pay than to cost, however cost is determined. In industries in which there is keen competition, price, however determined, will be much closer to cost, and the meaning of cost becomes much more important for individual firms. The general level of prices in a given industry then will be related to the system of cost computation used. If real costs (i.e., money cost adjusted for the rise in the price level) are used, prices in general may be higher when prices are rising than if money costs were used, but that is not inequitable, particularly where incomes are readily adjusted when changes in the general price level occur.

But look for a moment at the manufacturer's point of view. As the price level rises, the greater will be the loading which real costs impose, and production will appear to be less profitable than if historical money cost were used. Expansion is not so sharply indicated, and hence the postulated pressure on supplies and services need not occur. In addition, of course, high prices may induce new competitors to enter industry, depressing the prices of finished goods. (Note: This is only a brief statement covering the situation where competition is keen, manufacturers have reasonably full knowledge of their costs and act mainly from economic considerations. A similar argument would cover falling prices.)

Other critics of the replacement cost basis have pointed out that it cannot be consistently applied: for, when prices begin to fall, businessmen will want to recover depreciation at a higher rate than the replacement cost basis would allow or to make greater reserves to meet losses in the value of fixed assets; i.e., they want extra provisions both ways. Three arguments rebut this view.

Firstly, when prices fall, business undertakings are unable to provide out of current prices reserves or provisions for these purposes. Prices are cut generally in order to sustain demand, and extra allowances are not readily included in estimates of cost.

Secondly, if the replacement basis had been used in the upswing of the cycle there would obviously be less to write off as depreciation in the period of falling prices, and that is what would happen if replacement cost continued to be used.

Thirdly, as the depreciation charge is lower compared with the charge made during the period of high prices, production would not appear to managers to be as unprofitable as if the money cost basis were adopted and there would be greater opportunities for reducing prices to bolster demand and possibly less willingness to relinquish the entrepreneurial rôle.

Business Capitalization and Profits

It is notoriously difficult to "foresee all of the value-destroying factors which constitute entrepreneurial risk". But it is not impossible to try, or to forestall at least in a limited measure some of the effects of such value-destroying influences as currency depreciation. W. Hosmer in *The Accounting Review* of March 1938, gives some classic examples of the effects of failure adequately to provide for depreciation, without specific reference to the effect of currency depreciation: he gives American cases in which, over a 10-year period, profits were overstated by 41 per cent, 108 per cent and 830 per cent of the profits as corrected by subsequent adjustments in capital values.

Reconstructions or surplus adjustments such as these companies had to undergo can be made less severe (not to say avoided) if prices are such that adequate reserves can be built up and if managers are cognizant of the effects of shifting price levels on profit calculations.

Failure to provide depreciation provisions or reserves on a real cost basis will result, if a long period of rising prices occurs, in the general over-capitalization of business undertakings. To say that recourse to the capital market is the only reasonable method of meeting increased costs of capital goods is to force on business and industry a situation in which profit rates must fall lower and lower as prices rise, not because business is less profitable but because capital, paid-up capital, is steadily increasing. If all undertakings accepted the same accounting and price-fixing technique, this may not place any one company at a disadvantage. But when these processes differ, some companies less conservative and less sound, would be more attractive to investors, and more conservative undertakings would be much less attractive. This increases the speculative aspect of investment in securities, particularly in post-depression years.

Acceptance of the real cost basis of providing for depreciation would contribute thus to the stabilization of investment values to the general advantage of investors. The effect generally will be to foster conservatism in the financial management of companies and to ensure a better description of the real character of business capitalization.

Summary

To summarize the argument for replacement cost to this point:—

(a) Money cost does not represent the value of facilities used at current rates, due to changes in the level of prices.

(b) Some extra provision is widely recognized to be necessary, and its extent may be gauged roughly by the difference between money cost and current costs of replacement (the latter is approximately real cost in the economist's usage).

(c) This does not mean that physical replacement is contemplated, it only suggests agreement with the need to maintain company earning power or working capacity.

(d) No matter how the extra provision is made, it must be provided for in prices; and that is as it should be, for incomes have risen with the rise in all prices.

Some Methods

With this outline in mind we might indicate some ways in which the extra provision may be effected:—

(a) Compute depreciation provisions on historical money cost, and appropriate from profits depreciation reserves (as distinct from normal depreciation provisions).

(b) Compute depreciation provisions on probable replacement cost without revaluation of the fixed assets.

(c) Revalue fixed assets occasionally and compute depreciation provisions on the new value.

(d) Revalue fixed assets regularly by using a construction or plant price index and compute depreciation provisions on the new value.

The mention of revaluation stirs up another hornets' nest. Whatever one's feelings in the matter, however, it is a useful and accepted device among some business managers for correcting, or giving a better description of, the financial position of companies. Admittedly the Institute of Chartered Accountants in England and Wales frowns on the writing-up of fixed assets, but when the practice is found in the financial histories of many of the best companies one must ask quite seriously whether the accountants are being realistic in their recommendations.

Conclusion

The main point it was desired to bring out in this paper is that there are important reasons for seriously considering the replacement cost or real cost basis in depreciation accounting. It is not put forward as an interesting variant of accepted procedures; it suggests some very important and necessary changes in attitude on the part of many participants in business management.

It creates problems for management, such as whether the effects of changes in price levels should be determined and reported separately in internally used or externally published financial statements. It aims some serious blows at accepted accounting techniques; for example, it demands consistency in a vital sense, not mere lip service to the idea, and it demands that some efforts should be made to develop a practical technique for meeting the need by management of definitive reports of cost. It poses some questions for business theorists and economists, particularly in the direction of the assumptions underlying much business theory.

Many recent articles on this question have been so markedly partisan in their approach that, while making useful points often, they have tended to belittle or ignore opposing arguments. Furthermore, there is no known attempt to work over the whole problem systematically, and this paper is certainly no attempt to do so. It is hoped that it has lain bare some of the problems seen and viewpoints held by economists, business managers and a minority of accountants in respect of depreciation accounting, and that it has shown that their arguments strike at some of the basic concepts of traditional accounting.

20

DEPRECIATION ON REPLACEMENT COST*

The August 1949 issue of *The Australian Accountant*, p. 309, reproduces an extract quoted in the January 1949 number of the *Journal of Accountancy* from a quotation, by George D. Bailey, in evidence before the Sub-Committee of the Joint Committee on the Economic Report from an editorial in *Business Week*.

These few paragraphs have been quoted in so many places that one would expect them to be pregnant with significance, to answer at least some of the arguments of those who support the replacement cost basis in providing for depreciation. But, it is submitted, the extract is so lacking in logic that it is hard to understand why it has been quoted in so many journals, except perhaps to display its deficiencies. The writer would like to expose some of those deficiencies, for he fears that the extract may mislead many into believing, or confirm many in their beliefs, in the system it is supposed to uphold, despite its lamentable lack of logic.

Sympathy?

"Fundamentally, we are inclined to sympathize with the attitude of ... companies that want to allow for extra depreciation before they give a figure for net income. A businessman thinks of himself as a going concern. And profit isn't profit to him if he has to plough it back just to keep his plant intact.

"But . . ."

Now, why are we inclined to sympathize with any person or any point of view? We are not inclined to sympathize with things which we feel to be unfair, unjust or inequitable, whatever we understand by fairness, justice or equity. No: we sympathize with people and with their views because we feel that there is some underlying justification for them, even though, at the same time, we are unable to lay our hands on effective arguments which satisfy us that their views are the most reasonable. It is suggested that this applies in the present case. The writer of the editorial we are dealing with is not alone in his bewilderment. The pseudo-arguments, the counter-claims and the occasional real argument around this question are so numerous that few people, if any, will have considered the problem in its entirety. It is no wonder that the common reaction to the confused state of mind resulting from the current cross talk is to stick to something we are used to, something that we know—and to smother that disturbing

---

* First published in *The Australian Accountant*, Vol. XX, No. 2, February 1950, pp. 68-70.

"sympathy" with the Dutch courage of a time-serving adage—"better the devil you know than the devil you don't". Our conservatism triumphs.

Indifference or Personal Conservatism?

There is also another reason why we may sometimes feel an ineffective sort of sympathy: and that is when we recognize the virtue in another's point of view; but, because of the bonds of professional or social custom and tradition, we feel indisposed to meddle. Again this might very well apply in the present case. The business manager's point of view is not represented by anything like the same volume of material as is the traditional accounting viewpoint. Management as such is very largely inarticulate. There are no strong bodies representing the opinion of managers; but let anyone consider the practitioners and the practices of accounting, and he will soon learn how closely they adhere, by a mutual consent which almost amounts to a faith, to the practices of their professional ancestors. So, in the present case, the writer says we may sympathize, but . . . ; but we must not be led astray, for the accounting profession is widespread, and the consequences of assailing its established practices are too terrible to contemplate. This, at least to me, is the implication of the quoted editorial note.

The conclusion drawn from this first part of the extract is that ineffective sympathy, such as is implied, is the product of indifference to the demands business problems make on the reasoning capacity of accountants, or the product of a slavish adherence to traditional forms. In either case we are convicted of a form of conservatism which compares unfavourably with the questing spirit of scientific inquiry.

If, of course, we admit no sympathy, the matter would be quite different. But very few supporters of the historical-cost basis deny categorically the validity of the current value point of view; so that the above argument seems to be of fairly general application.

System?

"First, there is no systematic or generally recognized way of doing it. Nobody knows what replacement costs will be in the future . . . . Hence any allowance now has to be arbitrary."

These are really quite pointless arguments for refusing the replacement-cost basis. The writer says, firstly there is no systematic way . . . . As if there is at present a systematic way of providing for depreciation. Now it is true that present accounting practice may be said to be systematic in that it abets the computation of depreciation provisions on a mathematical formula year after year. But this is no virtue. Depreciation is not only a book-keeping phenomenon! It is a real feature of business which must be met occasionally by severe cuts in the venture capital of business undertakings. And it must be so met because the accounting treatment of depreciation is quite unsatisfactory and inadequate.

To treat depreciation as a time cost—and that is the effect of all methods in which the provision is not based on physical output or usage of productive facilities—may be systematic, if by systematic we mean regular, thoughtless or automatic. We must decide whether accounting is to be systematic in this sense, and therefore highly unrealistic and even irrational; or whether we would have accounting to be realistic even if it fails to conform with this type of regularity. I would much prefer to abandon systematic ways, if "system" is their only claim to recognition.

Tradition?

As an alternative to systematic ways, of course, we have "generally recognized" ways. This too is no argument. If we study the origins of almost every particular aspect of modern technology we will find a time when what is now "generally recognized" practice was one rank heresy. We should not be fooled by what is generally recognized; in fact, what is generally recognized might well be an object of our suspicion, for general recognition suggests something which appeals to an emotional or non-rational element in our character, rather than something appealing to our reason.

Abiding by what is generally recognized is only another way of pandering to our conservatism or, to put it more bluntly, our inertia. A profession worth its salt cannot indefinitely accept what has been generally recognized in the past. It must contain within itself the germs of change, if its virility, its capacity to serve in a changing environment, is to go undisputed.

Uncertainty?

Between the two sentences quoted in the last extract above occurs the remark, "Nobody knows what replacement costs will be in the future", followed by "Hence any allowance now has to be arbitrary".

I have yet to learn how the straight-line method or the reducing-balance method or any other method not based on physical usage is anything else but arbitrary. The fact that a formula exists for determining the provision does not make it any less arbitrary. Admitting there is no arbitrariness about the initial cost, both the effective life and the scrap value of a piece of equipment are quite unknown; unknown in exactly the same sense as replacement costs are unknown. Clearly there is no difference in arbitrariness between the accepted method and its alternative.

Incompleteness!

The quoted editorial proceeds: "And when you start making arbitrary adjustments you open the door to all sorts of trouble. The financial statement becomes less and less an unbiased report of what happened during the year and more and more a picture of what the company officers want the stockholders to think happened."

This may be criticized along three main lines. Firstly, it implies that conventional statements are unbiased. They are not. They are compiled almost universally on the notion of conservatism, a bias against short-term investors and for the benefit of long-term investors, and favouring creditors as compared with investors.

Secondly, it is implied that conventional statements report categorically what has happened during the year. They do not. They do not report, for example, how much of the profit of an undertaking is trading profit and how much is illusory gain or loss due to changes in purchasing power of the accounting unit. Conventional statements conceal these important economic realities; the replacement-cost idea does attempt to keep up with them.

Thirdly, it is implied that there is no check on what companies report to their members that would prevent members being hoodwinked. The sentiment may suit *Business Week*, but it should hardly be tolerated by the accounting profession, whose members claim to prevent, and on whose members there has been imposed a legal obligation to prevent, misleading statements being published.

Monkeying with the Books?

This is the last point I wish to take. "As soon as you abandon the strict rules of accounting you lay yourself open to a charge of monkeying with the books—no matter how good your intentions are."

Suspicion may be aroused if disclosure is incomplete or if only isolated undertakings adopt the procedure of adjusting accounts to reflect changing values. That however, should be only a minor consideration if the correct thing to do is to show the effects of changing values. One way of avoiding the charge of monkeying with the books, of course, would be for the whole profession to adopt, and for businessmen to adopt, a new style of reporting showing the effects of changes in purchasing power of the accounting unit. The task of convincing those two vast bodies of people is Herculean.

Individual firms could make the change, however, without attracting unnecessary suspicion, I believe, provided they showed, while accustoming members to the new form, a reconciliation of the new figures with what would have been obtained under the old system.

Conclusion

Resistance to change is always strong and is frequently bolstered by quite irrational "argument". While ever nebulous argument and thinly veiled error befog the discussion of business realities, accounting will make little progress. The statement of the case for historical cost in the editorial of *Business Week* is so full of illogical or untrue statements and implications that it seemed important to drag them out, give them full publicity, reveal their lack of substance. That was my aim.

21

ACCOUNTING AND INFLATION*

The "Logic" of Accounting

Accountants are often pictured as cold-blooded individuals who consider not only business issues but also many private matters strictly in the light of ineluctable and remorseless logic. Some of us do not like the implication, but to be strictly logical is no cause for shame. My first proposition is that we do not merit the description, and that may well be regarded to our discredit.

Studies in pure logic involve the use of symbols to the content of which we may be quite indifferent. We often use symbols for the very reason that it enables us to concentrate on the form of the propositions we use without being bothered by their meaning in any but a formal sense. Likewise, in mathematics, we contend that $2 \times 2 = 4$ without regard for the content of the symbols 2 and 4.

But when we turn to practical problems involving logical or mathematical symbols we cannot continue to disregard their conceptual content. We cannot multiply 2 eggs by 2 eggs and get 4 "squared eggs"; but we can multiply 2 eggs by 2. We must be careful what operations we require our symbols to perform.

Accounting involves both logical and mathematical elements; if we wished, we could develop a set of accounts the symbols of which would be quite unrelated to any kind of business or economic problem. But accounting was never developed as an exercise in mathematics or logic; it is, and has always been, related to practical business issues, and for that reason accountants must inevitably be concerned with the content of the symbols they use. In accounting the commonest symbols are money symbols—pounds, pence, dollars, cents are terms in which accounting operations are carried out, and in accounting practice we assume that these symbols have precisely the same meaning whenever they are used. In all reasonable discourse, it is important that the symbols used shall have the same meaning; or at least that there shall be ways of transforming the symbols into some common unit if we propose to manipulate the symbols by aggregating, averaging, or relating them in other ways.

If accounting is to be regarded as a system for expressing meaningful ideas, its symbols, too, should have identity of content. But have they? The money unit of account is not the same in different countries: if we wish to incorporate in the accounts of a

---

* First published in *The Australian Accountant*, Vol. XXII, No. 1, January 1952, pp. 14-23. This and the following two papers were read to members of the Commonwealth Institute of Accountants as part of a refresher course in April-May 1951.

domestic organization some figures relating to foreign transactions we must convert the items expressed in foreign currency into terms of the domestic currency. That is a recognized practice. But the money unit of account has not the same purchasing power in the same country at different times. This fact, however, we choose to disregard: we do not attempt, in accounting, to convert our terms into units having identical meaning: we are content to manipulate the superficial features of entity transactions. So that, although we work with figures, creating an impression of precision, that does not mean that our technique is logical or scientific.

In the whole process of conventional accounting there is a basic illogicality in that we add, subtract, and compute relationships between things that are not the same in economic reality although they are denominated in the same term, "pounds". H. W. Sweeney, in *Stabilized Accounting*, described this illogical practice as one of the main deficiencies of accounting. He says: "The success of the whole system of business depends upon the truthfulness of reports. The truthfulness of reports depends mainly upon the truthfulness of accounting. The truthfulness of accounting depends largely upon the truthfulness of the dollar—and the dollar is a liar! For it says one thing and means another" (p. xi).

The champions of conventional accounting will object that, in any case, accounting does serve many purposes regardless of these technical, fine points at which it may be faulty. We must consider some of these purposes. It is not possible here to consider at length all the uses and functions of accounting as they have been delineated by G. O. May (*Financial Accounting*, p. 19), for example. We may, for convenience, break them into two groups. One function of accounting is to supply managers with information to assist them in making decisions and in discerning the consequences of past decisions. Another function is to supply other parties with information—for precisely the same purposes. It does not matter whether the "other parties" have access to accounting information by right (as shareholders have access to published accounting statements) or by any other process; accounting information is obtained and used by many "other parties".

Two criteria of an accounting system emerge from these functions. Firstly, accounting must be oriented to the problems of the groups or parties it serves. Secondly, the form of communications between accountants and these groups should in no way do violence to the information communicated; that is to say, the communication should not be marred by illogical propositions, false assumptions, or technical jargon. To these criteria we shall return in a later lecture. We should note now that the crux of the function of accounting is "information for decision-making". It is reasonable to conduct the argument on the assumption that businessmen wish to act rationally, with knowledge of the facts, the available courses of action, and their probable results; that is why they have accountants, statisticians, research officers, and similar experts. But it is difficult to be strictly rational. We may inadvertently overlook certain items which are really relevant; we may not be able to get all the relevant information; we may be able to get it all, but because certain matters do not seem to be vital we decide to be content with what we consider the "most relevant" information; or we may find it so complex that we choose to ignore some of the relevant information. Each of these possibilities may arise in connexion with the information accountants supply for the use of others—particularly the information which would enable others to gauge the effects of inflation on the profits and finances of business enterprises.

Why does Accounting Ignore Monetary Instability?

Perhaps the accountant may inadvertently overlook the fact that it is illogical to treat items which mean different things as if they were the same in essential character; but he can hardly excuse failure to make reference to the effects of price-level changes by claiming inadvertence. The matter is right under his nose, every day.

Is it impossible then "to get all the relevant information" on the matter? Maybe, because of the universal, "all". But it is possible to get much more information than is used and disclosed. Price-level changes are a matter of the past; there may be some difficulty in estimating the change which has taken place, but the problem is not insoluble. Perhaps we do choose to ignore the effects of inflation merely because they involve a more complex set of calculations than we are used to making! This is a poor criterion for a service activity.

Are shifts in price levels ignored, then, because accountants do not consider them to be significant to the business organization or to its management? Do accountants think that the matter can be adequately considered by management when no figures even remotely suggesting the consequences of inflation are supplied? Or do accountants shun the idea of making an approximation, even though there is ample precedent for approximation on other accounting matters and even though the doctrine of materiality would appear to demand some action on their part to treat price-level changes?

Whatever the reason, accountants choose to do nothing about inflationary effects in the accounting records and reports they compile. What is more, they seek to justify this by a convenient rationalization. Thus, it is said, the prices paid for goods and services purchased are objectively determined, i.e., by a transaction which actually took place. As accounting should only be concerned with such objective, independently ascertainable information, these prices are the only values with which accountants are concerned. Therefore accounts based on original historical costs are unassailable. But this is rationalization only. Adjustments made to the original costs by way of depreciation provisions are not objective in the sense that they are determined by a market or other external process. If we apply our judgement (subjective manipulation) to objective data, we cannot obtain an objective result. If the depreciation provision is based on a formula, that may reduce the extent to which short-run disturbances may influence the accounts, but it does not make the accounts objectively descriptive. On the other hand, current prices for the same services as old equipment yields are objectively determinable even if there is no sale. But to this point we shall return later.

Why should we be bothered by criticism of this kind? Is it not possible that, although accountants do not prepare any information or reports on the consequences of price movements, businessmen are fully aware of such movements; fully aware of the fact that if they have to replace equipment this year it will cost much more than its original cost a few years ago? Are we not overlooking the fact that businessmen are the persons who make these decisions, and they know all about the existing circumstances in any case?

Businessmen are certainly aware of the impact of inflationary forces. They know by observation, by contact with others, by the size of the allowances their wives demand of them, that prices are rising to an extent that involves some revision of earlier decisions. But unless some quantitative expression of the extent of the changes in price levels is available, I think it is extremely unlikely that all decisions will be made or revised with a clear understanding of the real impact of rising prices. Note an observation of Thorstein Veblen, an eminent American economist of a generation ago: "... among the securely known facts of psychology, as [it] touches the conduct of business, is the ingrained persuasion that the money unit is stable .... This persuasion or presumption prevails wherever the price system has gone fully into effect. It affects not only the businessmen, properly speaking, but the underlying population as well. It is known not to accord with fact, but it still remains a principle of conduct. It is something like an instinctive force, or perhaps rather, it is something like a tropismatic reaction, in that the presumption is acted upon even when it is known to be misleading" (*Absentee Ownership and Business Enterprise in Recent Times*, New York, 1923).

This clearly implies irrationality in conduct; but whether we doubt Veblen's diagnosis or whether we agree with it, the possibility of irrational decision-making can be substantially reduced by a resolute attempt to orient accounting to the purposes of businessmen by augmenting its technique. Economists have usually been content to speak in terms of general tendencies: they say prices tend to rise or tend to fall, employment tends to increase or decrease, sales tend to increase, and so on. This is a convenient way of expressing an aggregate or average movement which is in reality made up of a whole series of quite different (molecular) movements. But this is hardly sufficient for the businessman. He wants to know not that demand tends, but how much demand tends to change under the impact of certain forces. A quantitative expression of the effect of inflationary or deflationary forces on his enterprise is of far more value to a businessman than general knowledge of the change such as he may deduce from what he reads in the newspaper or from the price he pays for newspapers. The hunches and general ideas he gets are quite inadequate when he must make his own decisions in quantitative terms.

But although we often consider the problems of businessmen, we should not overlook the fact that they are not the only ones involved in making decisions connected with business enterprises. Much of the writing in local and overseas journals seems to concentrate on the viewpoint of the businessman or manager, when it is not concerned abstractly with accounting. By concentrating on the problems of business managers, we may easily overlook the fact that a great deal of business owes its support to the investing public. Businessmen and accountants may be indifferent to the interest of the investor, up to a point—but to be indifferent is both unwise organizationally, and irresponsible socially. Investors as a class are (among other groups) closely interested in the products of the accountant.

It seems reasonable to postulate, therefore, that besides aiding managers to make rational decisions, accounting (or accounting statements) should also help investors to decide the direction of their investments rationally. Much of the work of the institutes of accountants, the rules of stock exchange committees, and the legislative provisions on company accounts are directed to providing that their decisions are not unduly influenced by the hopes and fears of businessmen. The problem of the effects of inflation on accounting may not be overcome merely by saying "let us give the managers auxiliary statements and statistics" or "let us pass off the whole problem to the statistician and the economist, and let them work it out"! Accounting is, essentially, providing information, no matter for whom; and accounting ought, in my opinion, to cater for the demands for information of all other parties connected with business enterprises, besides the needs of managers. Particularly is this so because relatively few people, of all those who must read and use accounting statements, are able to take account of the limits which the accounting conventions impose on the value of those statements.

Two Opposite Attitudes Towards the Problem

There are two general ways of tackling this problem of providing all the information required by interested parties in periods when prices are unstable. The first is by admitting the inadequacy of accounting statements so that readers are put on guard, and no one is thereafter confused or misled. The second is by improving reporting techniques.

The first proposition is something very like the trade practice, *caveat emptor*—a practice which is quite inconsistent with professionalism. Further, to admit inadequacy would perhaps be professional suicide, so we make no such bald admission. We do, however, use a convenient circumlocution. We contend that accounting is not quite all it should be; but it is useful for all practical purposes. We even sometimes say something ought to be done to improve the understanding, by all who use accounting statements, of the limitations which traditional methods impose on them, and of the only uses to which they should be put.

But nothing is done, just the same. No institute of accountants, no independent person, no business firm, is going out of its way to teach the recipients of accounts how they should adjust the items appearing in the accounts so that they are presently meaningful. It appears that we like to go on assuring ourselves that something should be done, but ardently hoping in the interval that, before we get around to it, the present inflationary emergency will have passed and it will be unnecessary to do anything.

In any case, re-educating the users of accounting statements would be a stupendous task. It is much more promising to consider the second kind of remedy: improving reporting techniques.

In emphasizing the need for, and possibility of, improving accounting and reporting techniques, we have no wish to disregard the improvements which have been made. In matters of detail improvements are numerous. But one of the most vital potential improvements has been evaded. It is not nearly as important to omit the shillings and pence, to group items correctly, to give items descriptive treatment, and to add footnotes, as it is to describe fully the consequences of having been in business one year. And by describing fully I mean setting out unequivocally trading profits and the consequences for the enterprise of the supervening change in price levels. Experience of two post-war inflationary sprees and one catastrophic period of deflation should have taught us the value of exact accounting; but accounting is unaltered despite many years of campaigning by people who have thought that accounting can be made a more logical and more valuable technique. Accounting will still yield three different profits for the identical business position, depending upon whether prices are rising, are stable, or are falling.

Objections to Changes in Technique

Why have these deficiencies been ignored? We shall consider only five principal reasons advanced for not making anything greater than superficial changes in accounting.

Firstly, there is the objectivity argument, to which we have already alluded. Here is an Australian writer's comment on the objectivity of accounting: "Pure accounting is always objective; that is to say its conclusions are founded upon external evidence which is capable of verification. . . . This remains true in those many respects in which there is room for legitimate difference of opinion, for even then, accounting opinions are formed in the light of evidence as to the underlying facts and in accordance with generally accepted accounting standards and consistent interpretation of the facts which are available." This line of argument is used by many apologists for the existing system and technique of accounting.

But, I submit, opinion is opinion, no matter how well informed it is, no matter how extensive the range of considerations on which the opinion is based. It should hardly be necessary to show at length that methods extensively used for computing depreciation provisions depend not only on matters of opinion, but on more or less arbitrary opinion. The fact that over short intervals (say, three, five years) the rate of depreciation provision does not vary seems to be sufficiently clear indication that it is a matter of arbitrary opinion or of periodical indifference. The depreciation provision is not determined by any objective, market fact: it is based on a subjective estimate of residual value, and a subjective estimate of working life, applied to a market price which for most practical purposes is no longer relevant to the enterprise.

If accounting figures are influenced by and based on opinions, as they are in respect of depreciation and other provisions made in the accounts, one can hardly refuse to adopt a new technique merely because it also involves some element of judgement. What other judgements may be required, then? Some have suggested that depreciation provisions should be based on replacement cost, instead of on historical cost; some have said we should revalue the assets every year; and some have said we should adjust the depreciation provision so that it represents usage of the asset-services at current prices. (These proposals are not mutually exclusive, but they represent different kinds of emphasis.) Each of these involves the use of certain evidence: current market prices of the assets, current market prices of the services the assets yield, current knowledge of technical and commercial changes. But this is no different, surely, from the class of evidence referred to in the quotation at the head of this section. If one wishes objectivity, then a current market price is even more objective than a conventionally computed depreciation provision, for one can go out into the market and find current prices even though there is no intention to purchase.

An objection has been raised to this on practical grounds. The objectors would say: "Well, if you are going into the market to find prices, you can be as canny as you like. You can look for and use the dearest or the cheapest price to suit your own purposes". But this is not an objection to the technique; it is a slur on the honesty and good faith of the people who do it—and that is only ourselves. One may be pardoned from dissociating himself from an objection which shows little regard for the professional integrity of accountants.

The second objection we shall discuss is the difficulty of forecasting replacement cost, for, as we have observed, replacement cost has been suggested as one of the bases for adjusting balance sheet values and depreciation provisions. Recommendation 12 of the Institute of Chartered Accountants in England and Wales contains the following comment: "Owing to the inherent difficulty of determining in advance the prices which may have to be paid in the future for the replacement of assets, it is impracticable to forecast with any precision the additional reserves which will be required. This fact alone is likely to necessitate modification of any plan whereby the actual sums required to effect replacements are provided by instalments over a period of years either by way of supplementing depreciation charges or by setting up in lieu of depreciation a provision for renewals based on estimated replacement costs. Moreover, the gap between historical and replacement costs might be too big to be bridged in these ways".

The term "replacement cost" has been rather loosely used in some places; it is not always easy to discern what is meant precisely in some proposals. It could mean that future replacement cost should be used, or that replacement cost at present should be used—in both cases subject to depreciation that has occurred up to the date of the accounts; the former is admittedly more difficult to compute than the latter. However, I do not think the notion of replacement cost has ever been used with any other purpose than to express conveniently the need to recover, and a process of recovering, a gradual wastage of real capital. That, in any case, is my view of the proposal. It is not at all concerned with the replacement of specific fixed assets, but with the maintenance of earning capacity appropriate to the change in price levels—the maintenance of real capital. Once this difficulty of considering the replacement of specific assets is removed, it becomes possible to view the problem as one of keeping up the capacity of an enterprise to carry on at its originally intended level of business; and a much simpler method of doing this may be considered than replacement-cost proponents contemplate. The method is to adjust the accounts, by an index number, to take account of the decline in purchasing power of the currency. Here only the income-statement adjustments are discussed.

The adjacent table indicates how the adjustments to income may be made; it will be clear that there is nothing more difficult or intricate in the mechanics of the adjustment than in converting foreign balances into domestic currency values. The table postulates a firm with an annual income of £7000 in each of six years, by which time the plant acquired in the first year is worn out; we assume also initial depreciation of 50 per cent. On the conventional method of calculation, the distributable income is given in line A. The second part of the

COMPARISON OF DISTRIBUTABLE INCOME UNDER RISING PRICES

(A)—*Under conventional methods*

(B)—*After providing for changes in price levels (i.e., after providing for maintenance of real capital)*

Year:	*1*	*2*	*3*	*4*	*5*	*6*	*Total*
Income before depreciation	7000	7000	7000	7000	7000	7000	42,000
Depreciation on conventional basis	5000	1000	1000	1000	1000	1000	10,000
(A) Distributable income ..	2000	6000	6000	6000	6000	6000	32,000
Index of prices	100	110	120	130	140	150	
Depreciation at adjusted rates—							
For year of calculation ..	5000	1100	1200	1300	1400	1500	11,500
Adjustment for year 1 ..		500	500	500	500	500	2500
„ „ „ 2 ..			100	100	100	100	400
„ „ „ 3 ..				100	100	100	300
„ „ „ 4 ..					100	100	200
„ „ „ 5 ..						100	100
Depreciation adjusted for shift in price level ..	5000	1600	1800	2000	2200	2400	15,000
(B) Adjusted distributable income	2000	5400	5200	5000	4800	4600	27,000

table shows how an adjusted depreciation provision may be computed for each year on the straight-line method, assuming that the price index moves 10 points each year. The kind of index to be used is not considered here; the purpose is merely to show how the calculation is carried out.

In the first year, £5000 is written off as under the conventional method. In the second year, because the price index has risen by 10 points, the year's provision will be $^{110}/_{100}$ths of £1000: £1100. In addition, for the same reason, the provision for the first year must be augmented by $^{10}/_{100}$ths of its initial amount, so that the total provision for the second year is £1600. In the third year, the year's provision is $^{120}/_{100}$ths of £1000, and to it is added a further $^{10}/_{100}$ths of the basic amount for the first year and $^{10}/_{100}$ths of the basic amount for the second year, because of the further rise of 10 points in the index. The effect of these provisions will be to charge income with sums necessary to replace the wastage of real capital, and, if necessary, to replace the equipment at the new higher price when it is retired. The distributable income under this method is shown in the last line, and the depreciation provisions in the penultimate lines are clearly sufficient to meet the change in costs: £15,000 will presumably be needed to buy equipment originally costing £10,000 if the price index rises 50 per cent.

Many people may be inclined to say to this: "How, in any substantial way, is this different from appropriating an additional amount from profits each year to a special reserve account—a capital-assets replacement reserve or some such thing? Why all this palaver over a problem that can be met by additional appropriations?" The important difference is that this proposal would designate clearly more of the real facts of the business situation. There is no clear relationship between an additional appropriation and the assets or real capital contemplated when making the appropriation; there is such a connexion under the method here suggested. Furthermore, there is an element of price determination involved; this we shall consider at greater length in the following lecture.

Others may say that such computations, admitting that they are interesting, do not add a penny piece to the funds available for business purposes; including replacement. But, though they add not a penny, they may prevent sums being distributed which, under the conventional method, would be distributed because of the healthier profits and free reserves—to the tune of £5000 on the data of the table.

The third objection we shall notice is the contention that, if we start monkeying with the accounts now we will do great damage to prestige we may have built up in the past or are building up now. It seems that accountants must choose between alternative values or ends. We have to decide (a) whether it is more important to serve our own ends first, that is to hope that the sort of work we do now is sufficient to secure our prestige or the prestige of the profession at the expense of business management; or (b) whether we ought not rather to seek long-run prestige by making our accounting statements more reliable and more serviceable, by showing we can adapt ourselves and our methods to the changing needs of business. Accounting can and should be adapted as changes in the social and economic environment demand. There can hardly be any real argument about the proposition that a body of persons having as one of their principles "service to the community" should be concerned more with efficient service than with prestige. If we refuse to alter our technique merely because to do so would damage what prestige we now have, we sacrifice whatever we have of social conscience.

A fourth objection looms largely in the minds of some groups of people. It is said that the temporary nature of inflationary movements does not warrant us paying much attention to devising techniques which will truly record and represent economic facts. Unquestionably there is a cyclical tendency in price levels, for they reflect long-term movements in the economic condition of communities. By taking specific indexes one may infer that the prices to which they relate return to the level at which they stood at some earlier date. The interval between the two dates will vary with the commodities for which the index is prepared, but it is a relatively long period, of the order of 10 to 20 years at least.

We may make two observations on this matter. On the one hand, merely because we can find dates at which prices appear to be the same does not necessarily mean that prices will ever return to those levels in the future; the behaviour of prices 10 or 20 years from now is quite unpredictable, so we should not depend on the return of prices to present levels to validate our accounts. The capacity of a long-term index to represent changes in price levels when the composition of trade and commerce is changing may also be questioned.

On the other hand, we must take into account the frequency with which users of accounts vary their previous decisions. It does not matter very much to a shareholder who intends to hold shares in a company for 20 years whether the market price of the shares goes up or down—provided he stands fast to his original decision. Similarly, a manager who has to make one decision which must stand for a long period need not worry about intervening incidents—provided his decision is irrevocable. But there are really few decisions which people make for 20 years, or 10 years, or even five years together—decisions which are irrevocable for those periods. Decision-making in business matters is a constant process; past decisions are under constant review in the light of current circumstances. No manager, or investor, or other interested party can find useful accounts which reflect the prevailing economic circumstances only once every 20 years. And, as major business transactions do not occur at one time (e.g., every 20 years), but are staggered, the accounts can never be in step even if some items appear at their current economic values at odd times.

There are so many times when decisions are changed, both on major and subsidiary matters, that to say we can ignore the short-run effects of inflation because in the long run price movements cancel out, is quite unrealistic.

The last objection we shall notice is the difficulty of selecting a satisfactory measure of the extent of inflation. This is a favourite hobby-horse of the ultra-conservatives—those who can see no reason for wanting to improve present techniques. It is easy to say that no single index would be equally appropriate to all classes of business. In spite of some drawbacks, it is difficult to imagine a better solution than Sweeney's: an index of general purchasing power, a price index of consumption goods.

We shall admit that any index may be less accurate than we could hope for as an ideal; but we may also claim that any index will make the accounts a better approximation to current economic realities than conventional accounts. As we have observed, we have a certain amount of licence in accounting if we relinquish the pursuit of utter and unequivocal precision. But there is no reason why we should not make the best possible and the most useful approximations, if approximate we must.

To stand in the way of development over the choice of an index is almost the last resort. In Australia we are accustomed to having the level of wages varied by a price index which is, admittedly, not an exact reflection of changes in the cost of living; but although people complain about it now and then it is still generally accepted by the Australian community as a useful, if rough, measure of the changes. In other words, it enables wages to be related to living costs more realistically than occasional *ad hoc* changes in wages would permit. And, if we look further than Australia, we find that under the fiscal arrangements of France and Italy index number corrections are actually being applied to income calculations: surely the resources of the French and Italians for meeting inflationary problems do not differ materially from our own!

Impelling Reasons for Change in Technique

We have attempted to show that objections to augmenting accounting technique so that the effects of inflation are segregated are either unrealistic or inconsistent with present practices. In addition, there are many positive reasons why a new technique should be adopted. Some of these will be considered in the following papers. But, before concluding, I would like to show as clearly as I can the importance of the development of a system of accounting free of the deficiencies of the accounting we now practise.

If the whole of currently-earned business income—as computed by conventional methods—is distributed, when prices are rising the recipients are likely to be consuming part of their real capital. Several American calculations in recent years have shown that the "accounting" incomes of corporations have greatly exceeded their real incomes. Now the consumption of real capital is not perhaps a personal tragedy, but it may seriously affect the living standard of a community in the long run. If we consume our real capital in the mistaken belief that it is income we are consuming, our standard of living must become impoverished, for we will have fewer capital resources with which to sustain it. We must endeavour to increase, or at least to maintain, the relationship between the capital resources of the community and the population if we want to maintain our standard of living. This is a broad socio-economic problem, and the methods used in business accounting are strictly relevant to it.

A fully-descriptive accounting method is no less important for the rational solution of business problems. If the businessman knew precisely what changes were taking place in the structure of his business due to inflation, he could perhaps do rather more about it than when his knowledge is merely general and unspecific. De Paula observed in England a few years ago that businessmen do not know what they really want in the way of information. That may be true: but if accountants know it, they should do something about it, so that businessmen are not obliged to continue making business decisions on totally inadequate information.

Finally—and this touches us rather closely, we can hardly be proud of an accounting practice which evades or does violence to some of the important realities of business. We are essentially a service profession, and our actions and the information we provide must always be conditioned by the needs of the people whom we serve. If it is important that businessmen have more information, we should seek to provide it. Inflationary conditions have challenged accountants to stand by this ideal of service.

The accounting problem, the business problem, and the social problem outlined here appear to warrant the long and deliberate consideration of accountants today.

22

EFFECTS OF INFLATION ON FINANCIAL STRATEGY*

In this paper we shall consider the effects of inflation on the accuracy with which the profit and loss account and the balance sheet report changes occurring in the financial position of a firm. This question attracts our attention because changes in the financial position of a firm call forth changes in financial policy and strategy, and if changes in the financial position are inadequately reported it is unlikely that appropriate changes in policy and strategy will be made.

Some may object that the accuracy of the accounting statements can have no significant bearing on the decisions of their readers; for, if the accounts of all firms are kept according to the same conventions, relative inaccuracies arising from the conventions will be much less than the real inaccuracies discoverable in any single set of accounts: relative inaccuracies will be equally inconsequential for internal purposes if the accounts are kept on the same conventions from year to year.

This may be true, but the extent to which changes in the purchasing power of a currency affect accounts will vary considerably according to the content of those accounts. Changes in the financial position of a firm with relatively little current and relatively great fixed assets will be much less faithfully reported than changes for a firm with relatively great current and relatively little fixed assets in its balance sheet, when prices of fixed assets are rising more rapidly than material prices. Both the profit and loss statement and the balance sheet are drawn in such a way that items in each are recorded on inconsistent bases.

To demonstrate this is very easy. The "wages" figure in an annual income statement is certainly not a homogeneous aggregate; the wages paid in the first quarter do not represent labour service equivalent to that represented by the same money wages in the last quarter, under today's conditions. Neither do material purchases represent a homogeneous aggregate: the figure represents purchases at various levels of prices. Neither does the depreciation figure represent services consumed, valued at a single price level. In fact there are very few items in the whole of the two statements that are strictly homogeneous; and, to take a fine point, we could assert that they should not be added at all. We shall examine the items appearing in these statements more closely.

---

* First published in *The Australian Accountant,* Vol. XXII, No. 9, September 1952, pp. 304-311.

The Profit and Loss Account

The profit and loss account represents a section of a stream of business transactions by which money capital flows through a business enterprise. There are two distinct phases in this circulation of money capital. Firstly, money capital is invested in various other assets which for the time suit the purposes of the business organization. Secondly, those assets are re-converted—some in the short run, some over a long period—into money, so that the cycle may be repeated. A critical question arises here: after allowing something by way of profit to owners, should the re-conversion of the second phase yield an amount of money equivalent to that originally available, or should it yield such an amount as will permit the business to carry on the same volume of transactions as it was able to support in the beginning? Clearly, as prices rise, the ability of the business to carry on at the same level at each successive commencement of the cycle depends on whether or not the saleable utilities (in goods or equipment) are being replaced.

In the case of those things which enter directly into the composition of saleable goods—material stocks, labour, and other productive services—the conversion into cash is usually sufficiently rapid for it to become obvious that rising prices will impose on the firm an immediate demand for greater liquid funds if the level of stock, of employment, and of sales is to be maintained. In the case of plant, machinery, and other durable goods, long intervals may separate the money outlay from the entering of the appropriate cost in the profit and loss account, and the threat to the liquidity of the business or to its physical volume of trade is not so apparent. But, if no other accretion to money capital occurs, the effect will be as serious in the one case as in the other: either the profits will have to be reduced to maintain liquidity or the level of business will have to be adjusted to the actually available working funds.

If we seek in financial accounts for a measure or demonstration of the effects of increased price levels, it is difficult to disentangle the changes in financial position which are due to the variation in the physical volume of business from those which are due to the increase in the cost of the goods and services required by the business. In very few annual reports or addresses by chairmen of directors is any specific attention directed to the problem of replacing stocks and equipment at higher costs. The Burroughs Adding Machine Company's 1948 report makes the following comment on the problem of increasing investment in inventories: "When a company improves its volume of production, it is necessary to have on hand larger quantities of materials and supplies, and also to increase the number of products in various stages of manufacture. The money paid for the materials and wages going into this increase in inventories could not be charged to 1948 operations, since the products and materials affected had not yet been delivered and paid for by our customers. It was allocated instead to inventory investment, which totalled $24,043,449 on December 31, 1948, $14,377,189 more than was required on December 31st two years before. Approximately half of this increase occurred during 1948. In other words, to sustain present production levels, we are carrying an inventory investment of more than $1600 for every employee in materials and products in process of manufacture, almost two and one-half times that required at the beginning of 1947."

Note that this comment makes no reference to the part of the huge increase in inventory investment which is due to price increases: it is unlikely to have been negligible. A few local examples of the increase in stock levels since 1945 will give further indication of the increase in funds necessary to support the stock levels now prevailing. In 1945, David Jones Ltd. carried stock equivalent to 46 per cent of the net tangible assets: by 1950 the proportion had increased to 77 per cent. The increase was approximately £1,300,000, or nearly one and a quarter times the 1945 stock figure.

To take a manufacturer, Australian Paper Manufacturers had a proportion of stock to net tangible assets in 1945 equal to 31 per cent. By 1950 it had risen to 46 per cent, an increase over the period of something like £1,300,000, making the closing stock more than double the figure of five years before. Mauri Bros. & Thompson's accounts show a change in stock levels from 16 per cent in 1945 to 30 per cent in 1950—again an increase in money value of about one and a quarter times in five years.

But, as we have observed, it is most difficult to distinguish the increased investment due to change in the physical volume of business from that due to changes in the value of money. We may be quite sure that the latter is significant, however, and that the increase in investment due to increased prices of capital goods is no less significant.

The Problem of Pricing

The income side of the profit and loss account is as important as the expenditure side. The fixing of selling prices was mentioned in a previous lecture in this series, but it will be considered at some length now because it impinges directly on the proposals which have been put forward for taking into account changes in the value of the currency.

There are two limits to the price which may be charged for a commodity—an upper limit determined by users and consumers, and a lower limit determined by the costs incurred in producing it according to the system of accounting or costing used.

The upper limit is influenced by a variety of factors, of which three may be mentioned. The first is the prices of competing goods. For any single firm the prices ruling in the market are an important consideration: the prices of competing products or near-substitutes may be determined by independent decisions of traders, or by some form of trade agreement, or by some regulatory agency; but, whatever they are and however they are determined, prevailing prices of close substitutes are the concern of every trader. What other traders are charging is very often a major factor in the pricing process. The second influence to be observed is that of the prices of goods in competition only indirectly: the number of newspapers an individual buys may be influenced by the price of glasses of ale or of theatre seats, and sellers must take into account the possibility that a variation in the price of one of these things will affect the demand for another. Thirdly, the upper limit to price may vary with changes in the general level of incomes; and, where there is a wage-adjustment mechanism by which wages and living costs are related, the upper limit may be quite flexible—upwards at least.

For the lower limit of prices there is also a series of such considerations. The prices actually paid for the services which go into manufactured goods obviously influence the lower limit. But these prices are subject to certain accounting manipulation. Services are not always charged to goods produced during the period in which the outlay occurs: they are charged at some conventional or convenient time. The ways in which these costs are allocated to products comprise the second determinant of the lower limit: as the dissection of costs and their attribution to products are matters either of opinion or of habit, the prices which any two businessmen consider to be the lowest they can afford may differ significantly. Thirdly, the sophistication of the accounting and statistical aids used by businessmen will influence their estimates: different conclusions may be reached, for example, by studying any one of total costs, average costs, marginal costs, or differential costs, for each involves different assumptions and each emphasizes different aspects of the costs incurred. Lastly, all the uncertainties which businessmen consider they have to cope with must be allowed for in fixing prices. It is unrealistic to assume that in making price decisions businessmen take account of all the ordinary and easily discernible expenses and expect the net proceeds to cover these expenses and all other risks without specification. Some of the other risks are evaluated separately, it is certain. The general reserves which it is planned to set aside out of profits are based on some calculations of this kind. Prices are fixed to cover taxation, whatever its level. And it is fair to assume that businessmen do endeavour to cope with changes in the purchasing power of currency through price rather than through diminution of profits. And this is done, even though the accountant provides no figures directly bearing on the question.

The limits which an individual trader places on the prices of his products are quite wide: the point between these limits at which actual bargains will take place is influenced by two other distinct factors at least. If competitors use historical costs when computing prices, those prices may be lower in a period of rising prices than if competitors based their prices on current or replacement costs. In this way the accounting and costing practices of traders bear on the prices of the commodities they sell. In the second place, the cost to competitors of acquiring fixed assets and stocks will influence the price which any one of them can charge for his goods. If competing firms acquire fixed assets and stocks at different price levels, those who buy at higher prices will, in general, sell at higher prices. And as no businessman, as businessman, is a philanthropist, he who has the advantage in buying will tend to adopt the selling prices necessary for competitors: where operators combine to regulate the output and prices of an industry the tendency to fix prices on the basis of the highest costs is even more marked.

The fixing of prices roundabout the price which a recent entrant to a trade must demand is a mechanism by which all operators are more or less taking into account current costs of the services used. If a new entrant has to compute in his costs depreciation based on last year's equipment costs, and if older operators allow the new competitor to remain in business, they will tend to take the higher margin between their (historical) costs and prices rather than sell at lower prices. Thus current costs are taken into account in the calculation of prices, and affect the income side of the profit and loss account, no matter how we choose to manipulate the resulting income figures.

It may be of interest to test whether this is in fact a reasonable statement of the effects of rising prices on costs. An alternative method is to base prices on historical costs. In practice, other things being equal, this would mean a gradual reduction in profit margins and ultimate reductions in dividend distributions. There have been no complaints by investors on either of these grounds, so that it would appear that prices have not been such as to limit unduly the residue of profit: in other words, prices have not usually been fixed simply on the basis of historical costs. The different effects of historical- and current-cost pricing on the working capital are also of interest. The reducing profit margins implied by historical-cost pricing leave smaller sums to finance current operations, so that additional capital may be required to support the same physical volume of business. This can be met in several ways. Businessmen may change their general strategy and resort more frequently to borrowed funds at low rates of interest: many seem to be doing that. Secondly, greater use may be made of what were formerly idle liquid funds to support increased stock levels and debtors. In both these cases, the rate of profit earned need not be affected. The third way of meeting the problem is by raising new capital: by itself, this would lead to lower proportionate profits, and in the absence of complaints on this score we conclude that in few cases has new capital been raised merely to satisfy growing demands on working capital.

Balance Sheet Items

As in the profit and loss account, balance sheet items are affected quite differently by variations in price levels. They are bought and sold in quite different markets: the markets for different kinds of materials, capital goods, securities are not susceptible to the same extent to changes in price levels generally.

Some of the items are a reasonable reflection of current conditions and are therefore useful enough for the purpose of making general observations about changes in the financial condition of business enterprises. In this category fall cash, and book debts recently incurred. Even long-term debtors and obligations may stand at their face values, for such obligations involve undertakings to pay or to repay a money sum. For all these items no material adjustment is necessary to enable the balance sheet to reflect current costs and outlays.

On the other hand, quite a few matters fall out of step when inflationary movements supervene. In conventional accounts, all plant and stock items are affected. They fail to reflect the current prices of similar services, and the possibility of making useful comparisons between companies or between successive figures of the same company become more remote.

Furthermore, changes in these items will involve corresponding changes in the residuary account on the liabilities side—the undistributed profits account. The way in which these changes are represented in the balance sheet will affect the decisions of people who regard the published accounts as a statement of a company's financial position. If the amount of the reserves is large, there is a presumption on the part of shareholders and their advisers that, at some time, the company will make a bonus issue, or declare a special dividend, or take some other such action. If undistributed profits appear in the balance sheet without alterations or adjustments for changes in the price level, they may be presumed to be free or available for distribution. Such a presumption may give rise to agitation for distribution of those profits in spite of the fact that they may only be distributed at serious inconvenience to the company. This would be a direct consequence of making no mention of the fact that part of the apparent undistributed profits really represents the maintenance of the real capital of the enterprise. The possibility of pressure of this kind cannot be overlooked: ordinary dividends are not fixed, but may vary with the size of the profit for the year and the attitude or expected attitude of other parties towards the way the profit is divided.

The Financial Position Generally

The above argument implies that what is desirable practice—the maintenance of real productive capacity—is carried out in a rough way in the pricing policies of businessmen. But that is not the end of the matter. The form and contents of the accounting statements affect other ends, besides pricing. It is insufficient that these statements be considered a formal and obligatory presentation of prescribed data: they may be used as a valuable and very effective means of conveying organizationally important facts to interested parties. The consequences of taxing incomes determined by conventional accounting methods we shall consider in the next lecture; but we may consider here the effect of conventional accounts on financing operations and on the co-operation of workers, creditors, and others.

The problems of financing business operations are exacerbated by financial policies and accounting practices which ignore the necessity, during periods of rising prices, of providing an increased *quantum* of financial resources or an increased velocity of circulation of existing resources. The form of the accounts may readily influence the extent to which deliberate consideration is given to the maintenance of the money capital necessary to support a given physical volume of business. Not that the question is ignored: it has been observed that some attempt is made to meet it. But it is almost impossible to work through the consequences of a change in price levels unless that change is expressed in terms appearing in the accounting statements: it is most difficult to plan to meet changes in the financial position and prospects except through a set of accounts incorporating the price-level changes which have occurred or are occurring. Inasmuch as conventional accounts misrepresent as trading profits sums which are mixtures of trading profits and windfalls arising from price-level changes, they are rather less than is necessary to ensure the maintenance of real capital when price levels are rising or falling.

If, as the result of distributing the profits calculated by conventional methods, working funds become inadequate, a serious position may arise. The Chartered Institute of Accountants in England and Wales, in its recommendations, drew specific attention to this position. The shortage of funds is a most important thing to know about, and the accounts should show it up directly. It limits the extent to which businessmen can exercise judgement and foresight to improve business efficiency; it prevents them from varying methods of production, or from varying the composition of business; it limits the ability to buy on economical terms or in anticipation of price movements.

Further, under-capitalization, in the sense of an apparently excessive return on the risk capital employed, may arise if the invested capital falls out of step with current costs and current revenues. This may create false impressions in the minds of other parties: some may clamour for higher wages, some for better prices, some for socialization of the industry! An accounting system or financial policy which leads to these impressions is scarcely in the best interest of the firm concerned.

Approaches to the Solution of these Problems

Quite a number of proposals have been put forward for obviating the difficulties mentioned above. It is possible only to discuss in general terms four of them just now. It will appear that some are merely *ad hoc* expedients, designed to provide a temporary palliative rather than a permanent, continuing remedy for the discrepancy between accounting statements and financial realities.

1. *L.I.F.O. and Replacement Cost Plans*

The L.I.F.O. method for stock valuation and the replacement cost method for calculating depreciation are substantially similar in their effects on the measurement of income and on the statement of residues. The L.I.F.O. method has been used in America to offset the inflationary drift. It involves charging against revenues stocks at the most recent prices. This makes "cost of goods sold" a reflection of current costs in respect of this item at least: profits computed on this basis of stock valuation are closer to the profits appropriate to current operating conditions than if another method were used.

But what of the balance sheet item "Inventories"? Because the charges to revenue account are nearer to current costs, the valuation of stock in the balance sheet must be further from current costs and closer to costs incurred in the distant past. When prices are rising, this practice will have the effect of creating a secret reserve to the extent of the difference between the actual cost in the distant period and the current costs as at the date of the statement. But as secret reserves are on our list of taboos, this method as it stands is scarcely satisfactory, and one is tempted to wonder what is behind the American enthusiasm for it, except of course that it is a hedge against inflation. Although it makes the revenue statement a better statement, it makes the balance sheet a poorer statement in that it does not reflect anything like the values of items standing in the balance sheet at balance date.

The replacement-cost method of providing for depreciation operates in the same way. The depreciation provision more realistically portrays current costs, but the residue of the historical cost will be so much less than on the conventional accounting basis that, again, a considerable understatement of assets occurs in the balance sheet. The residue of the historical cost will tend to get smaller, faster, and again a secret reserve will have been created.

One may flee from the dilemma of having either a currently useful income statement or a currently useful balance sheet by arguing that the balance sheet, in any event, is not intended to reflect anything like current conditions, that it is merely a statement of balances. To contend this way is comforting but hardly realistic. This view implies that the balance sheet is of no practical or immediate use to business people: a list of account residues, as such, has no particular value. And yet, balance sheets are used extensively as the basis of business judgements, whether we choose to close our eyes to the fact or not; and, as they are used, a duty seems to fall on accountants to make them useful in other ways than merely as checks on clerical accuracy. This cannot be done by halves. If the L.I.F.O. and replacement-cost methods are used for calculating income, consistent action must be taken in respect of the balance sheet: it is untidy to allow the balance sheet to remain in a form which hides "secret reserves". To be consistent with charging against income expenses at current rather than past rates, some alteration must be made in the balance sheet to bring the items in it closer to current values. And so that the assets may appear at values closer to current costs for the same services during periods of rising or falling prices, there must be some adjustment account among the proprietorship accounts to take up the amounts by which the asset values are varied.

It is, of course, possible to argue that the adjustment should be made in the income statement rather than in the balance sheet. F.I.F.O. is a way of doing this in respect of stock. If stock is charged on the F.I.F.O. method, the balance-sheet figure for stock will be closer to current values, but the profit will have to be adjusted to take into account the change in the cost of stocks. Whichever method is adopted the discrepancy between money income and real income must be covered by a calculated adjustment.

Given that the L.I.F.O. and replacement-cost methods are generally received in America for the assets to which they are relevant, it is fairly easy to understand why preference has been expressed for the income statement rather than for the balance sheet as a useful statement of relatively recent affairs: the income statement, as we have said, reflects more or less current events; the balance sheet reflects only a series of residues. The L.I.F.O. and replacement-cost plans with an adjustment account for correcting balance-sheet items comes fairly close to what we should expect of accounting in the future in place of the conventional accounts of today—balance sheets and income statements that are consistent and at the same time relevant to the decisions business people have to make.

2. *Increased Reserves or Provisions*

A second method of coping with rising prices is to make increased reserves and provisions, so that distributable profits are diminished and working capital is maintained at the level necessitated by higher price levels. This method involves no change in accounting technique: it is easy to carry out, as it requires only decisions to be made regarding the calculation or the appropriation of profits. For this reason it is quite commonly found among those firms where specific attention has been given to the problems of inflation. Increased provisions are made against stock and fixed assets. There is no ostensible calculation of probable replacement costs; but, as we have already observed, making provision for contingencies of all kinds is inherent in the price-fixing process, and rising replacement costs is one such contingency.

Although this method presents no unusual technical problems, there is some argument as to whether income should be charged with the increased provision or whether increased reserves should be appropriated from profits. From one point of view this is scarcely important, for whichever is adopted the consumer will be found to pay. From another point of view, however, the difference is significant. The residue of income is available for appropriation, generally, to any specific purpose. It is difficult to say which of the possible purposes—dividend payment, general reserves, asset-replacement reserves, dividend-equalization reserves, etc.—is accorded priority. Often it seems that contingencies receive prior attention, and reserves of some kind are set aside before consideration of the dividend appropriation. But, if changes in price levels are overlooked, and if dividends receive prior attention, the available working capital may easily be reduced below the level necessary to maintain the physical volume of business. It seems therefore to be preferable to cover increases in the level of costs by charges against income, so that there is no possibility of the problem being overlooked when the appropriations are made. As we shall observe in the next lecture, the value of this practice is even more noticeable in contemplation of the effects of taxation on business finance in inflationary periods.

3. *Revaluation of Assets or Quasi-reorganization*

The third method we shall discuss involves the revaluation of assets at infrequent intervals. Often it is said that these adjustments should take place only when prices have reached a new plateau or level somewhat removed from the old. I find it difficult to believe in the possibility of prices reaching anything like a plateau, but in any case the objection seems to be quite irrelevant. People make business decisions on the basis of the information they can get about the immediate past and present rather than on the distant past. Short-run considerations, the reporting of recently past events and circumstances, appear to loom largely in the function of accounting, if not in its practice. We should not be deluded, by the desire to make comparisons over long periods, into disregarding the importance of reporting recent events in terms which are now relevant. Comparisons over five years are often of less value than comparisons over two years because of changes in the environment. We shall argue in the next section that short-run comparisons may be made more effectively under a modification of this method.

Periodical revaluation is not difficult, in a technical accounting sense: this is one reason why it is resorted to by so many undertakings. What are the effects? Assets are written up, and depreciation may then be based on the book values at the higher valuation. Costs will, to that extent, reflect more closely current operating conditions, and the balance sheet will contain values closer to current outlays for the same services than would be possible on the book values before revaluation. The two statements will be consistent, between themselves and with market conditions, temporarily.

But this is only a partial solution to the problem, at best, for it does not cope with changes in price levels between the dates of valuation. It is a reasonable palliative inasmuch as it brings book figures and business realities more into line than if they were permitted continually to diverge in the way conventional accounting allows. The method has been used both where book values have been found to be above, and where they have been found to be below, market values of the same services, that is during periods of falling as well as of rising prices. We are not particularly concerned here with consequential changes in the proprietorship accounts: it is sufficient to note that these changes may affect the shareholdings of owners or only their equity in the residue.

4. *Stabilized Accounting*

The last type of approach we shall consider is what Sweeney described as stabilized accounting: it involves the correction of all costs and asset values by an index number of prices, so that the resulting statements contain items which are homogeneous in essentials.

This method differs materially from other methods in that it is applied to all items in the accounts which affect the conclusions to be drawn from them, and it is applied continuously. That it is neither piecemeal nor intermittent gives it considerable advantages over the others. The double-entry technique is so applied that full account is taken, through the income account, of adjustments in asset values brought about by changes in the general level of prices.

Given the solution of the index-number problem, it is possible to compute adjusted values for the important items, stock, securities, and plant, and to arrive at a profit for the period which is divided into trading profit and profit on the change in price levels. Some of these items may vary in quantity during any year, so that the calculation of profit is complicated both by changes in quantities and changes in current values of assets remaining at the end of each accounting period. The adjustments which stabilized accounting requires have the effect of separating realized and unrealized profits, making quite clear the profit that is available for distribution as dividends. Total income is, of course, unaltered, but unrealized profits are earmarked, and they constitute a buffer for income when prices begin to fall.

If the items affected by price-level changes are adjusted continuously, the balance sheet and income statement will be consistent as between themselves, internally homogeneous, logical in form and process, and more relevant to the problems of business than conventional accounts are.

There are a few problems, but they seem to be machinery problems rather than problems of principle. What index should be used? How often should adjustments be made? What initial adjustments are necessary on the introduction of this method? These are the kind of questions which come first to mind. Only on the first are we able to comment here. It seems difficult to conceive a better solution than an index of general purchasing power. Specific indexes for particular trades would create difficulties and overlook the purposes of those for whose benefit profits are earned: inasmuch as the dividends of many represent consumption expenditures, an index of general purchasing power would yield information quite relevant to the needs of the increasing number of investors.

Conclusion

On the (not unpardonable) assumption that accounting statements should be used, some change in technique seems to be imperative, if misunderstanding and uninformed guessing about the financial structure of business enterprises are to be avoided. In our time the whole community is organized into special-interest or pressure groups, each promoting its own ends with the greatest of zeal. Investors, businessmen, workers, bankers are some of the groups with close interest in business enterprises. If these and other similar parties are not to receive erroneous impressions about the financial position and profits of business, the financial position and profits should be shown realistically rather than conventionally. It is technically possible to augment accounting practices to do this. Some will say we should wait until conditions settle down, or until the accounting profession as a whole accepts the change. That would put the idea into perpetual cold storage. No change of any moment has been accepted with alacrity, in any field of knowledge or practice: evolution is a much commoner social process than the *coup d'état*. One could wish, with G. O. May, that "some bold pioneer would present the results of his corporation's operations on both a monetary and economic basis, with as much accuracy as circumstances permit". It is possible that the advantages of another method of presentation would then become more obvious than they are as yet. If present opportunities for experimentation are grasped, the business world may yet have to thank inflation for drawing attention to some inadequacies of present methods of accounting, and for making of accounting an art of greatly enhanced social value and influence.

23

FINANCIAL PRACTICE AND FISCAL POLICY*

This paper is divided into two parts. In the first, consideration will be given to some local and overseas practices by which some problems of business in an inflationary economy are met. The second part is devoted to an examination of some aspects of public finance and fiscal policy which are closely related to the problem of accounting realistically under inflationary conditions. The taxation of business profits during active inflation may introduce acute difficulties, for businessmen, for it is quite possible, if conventional accounting is used as its basis, for an income taxation policy not only to tax profits but to impose a levy on capital in the guise of an income tax. Truth in taxing may follow from the adoption of realism in accounting.

Among the methods being used to cope with rising costs and growing capital outlays three groups may be mentioned: (a) increased provisions and reserves, and accelerated depreciation; (b) new issues of share capital; and (c) issues of other securities.

Increased Provisions and Reserves: Accelerated Depreciation

Ideally the rate at which the investment in a fixed asset is recovered by way of depreciation provisions should depend on the rate at which the discounted net returns from its use diminish. This involves an appraisal of assets on the basis of the going concern convention, a practice which is not followed in business generally. The methods which are used are convenient makeshifts which must lead at some time to adjustments in book values or changes in the basis of the depreciation provision.

Accelerated depreciation has been advocated as a means of recovering current money costs of asset-service out of past money outlays, and its effect can only be to increase the discrepancy between book values and going concern values: physical depreciation is unrelated to the formula used in computing depreciation provisions. Several methods may be used.

Large sums may be written off in the year of acquisition on the ground that immediately after installation a piece of equipment becomes second-hand and loses much of its original value. This reason is inconsistent with the going concern convention, and even though present taxation rules encourage the practice, the excess depreciation is not regarded by the prices authorities as a valid charge

---

* First published in *The Australian Accountant,* Vol. XXII, No. 11, November 1952, pp. 391-8.

against income. The initial heavy depreciation provision may have helped many businessmen to overcome post-war difficulties but it cannot be regarded as a permanent solution to the problem of rising replacement costs. High initial provisions may also arise from using the "diminishing balance" method provided the rate is of the order of 25 per cent. Under the straight-line method using conventional rates, comparisons of replacement costs with large unexpired balances in the old asset accounts may well give rise to objections from financial personnel to new proposals put forward by technical experts. On the other hand, the unrecovered balances will not be nearly so great if the diminishing balance method is used; it therefore may have the effect of encouraging the pursuit of technical efficiency.

A third method is to use the straight-line principle over a shorter period.

But as far as one can judge, there is a tendency to take for granted the rates approved for taxation purposes; and not only to use them for computing taxable income, but to carry them over and adopt them as appropriate figures, for managerial and ownership purposes. No objection can be taken to the Commissioner of Taxation having canons of his own for the computation of taxable income. But for the purpose of maintaining the stability or guiding the progress of a single business, to follow the Commissioner's practice is not necessarily wise or efficient. Much of the information which must be treated in a formal way for taxation purposes may, and should, be considered in detail by the executives responsible for the financial position of a firm; their considered opinion on depreciation is extremely unlikely to be the same as would arise from the approved taxation rates.

However, to say that new systematic methods are not being adopted does not mean that business managers and boards of directors are not considering the implications of rising replacement costs. They are; but the methods used suggest that rising prices and replacement costs are not being considered as recurring problems. They are met, rather, in piecemeal fashion, occasional adjustments being made to ease what businessmen judge to be the immediate problem. Some examples may be given.

Humes (formerly Hume Pipes) in 1948 set aside £20,000 to a Plant Replacement Reserve. This is not a very large sum compared with their total fixed assets, and since 1948 it has neither been augmented nor transferred to any other account. In 1947 Dunlop Rubber had a Development and Deferred Expenditure Reserve of £250,000; it was augmented by £50,000 in 1948, since when it has stood at £300,000. Hoadleys Chocolates, in 1949, created a £20,000 Stock Equalization Reserve. The last balance sheet of Electrolytic Zinc shows a reserve for new plant and development of £550,000 and the 1950 accounts of Foy and Gibson show a Fixed Asset Financing Reserve of £300,000 and a Stock Financing Reserve of £125,000.

Some of these account titles may be confusing and the origin of the sums remaining in them is sometimes mixed. It is also probable that the account titles are not exact descriptions of the way in which the sums so appropriated have been or will eventually be used. But in any case, they are occasional appropriations and not part of a systematic and consistent attack on the problem of rising prices over the past few years. Their general effect, however, is to retain some part of the profits to meet higher costs of replacement without creating new interest or dividend obligations.

The problem is kept in mind by many other company boards even though they do not give effect to their deliberations by making specific provisions of the above variety. In 1948 the Chairman of Australian Paper Manufacturers drew the attention of members to the fact that the balance-sheet figure for fixed assets was considerably below the cost of installing similar fixed assets at that time. He said: "The net figure of £2.8 million appears in the balance sheet before you against the item 'Fixed Assets' and it will be seen that this is after the total provision for depreciation, amortization and obsolescence of £3.5 million had been made over the years. To replace these fixed assets would cost today well over £10 million against an aggregate figure of about £6.3 million. On the one hand we have the very conservative position that our fixed assets in terms of today's values for equivalent capacity are nearly four times greater than appears on the balance sheet; on the other hand, your directors must ask themselves whether the provision of £3.5 million for depreciation based largely on the pre-war basis adopted by your company is adequate in the light of today's changed and changing values."

Accelerated depreciation may have the effect of creating secret reserves; this is a question which cannot be shelved if the attitude towards secret reserves which has grown up over the last 30 years is to be maintained. It may seem to be feasible to charge the provision approved by the Taxation Commissioner in computing taxable income, but to make smaller provisions for the purpose of reporting to shareholders. There is, however, a provision in the tax regulations that obliges taxpayers to adopt rates of depreciation no lower than the Commissioner allows; if a taxpayer is found to be consistently writing off depreciation at a rate lower than the standard rate, and there are no special circumstances to warrant the practice, the lower rate adopted by the taxpayer will be applied by the Commissioner. The only way to overcome the difficulty is to charge depreciation at rates at least as high as the standard rates and to designate the excess, allowed by the Commissioner (such as the special initial depreciation allowance) over the provision deemed necessary by management, as a reserve.

New Share Issues

The second device used to overcome inflationary problems is the issue of new share capital. It has been claimed that providing for increases in replacement costs is a matter of refinancing rather than accounting. But it has been submitted in these lectures that the two are inseparable, that the price set on goods or services does in fact take into account the contingencies businessmen expect to face, and that businessmen tend to provide out of business income sufficient funds to finance the continuation of operations. And in any case, accounting statements may influence the extent of current charges against income, and through their effect on investors and creditors they may influence the time at which and the form in which it is possible for businessmen to augment business funds.

It will be useful to distinguish issues of bonus shares from new issues for cash.

It has been quite common for bonus issues of shares to be made out of revaluations of assets. This process has the effect of giving a more realistic indication of the current income earning capacity of the assets in use. It represents an old established firm in much the same light as a new entrant to its industry, both in respect of the assets employed and the shareholders' funds which support them. Not all companies which have revalued assets have made bonus issues out of the surplus thus arising; but even if no such issue is made the return on shareholders' funds is stated more realistically than without revaluation.

Bonus issues, of course, help to make revaluation effective in the income claims of shareholders, and in some cases the justification for a bonus issue may lie in the wish to give shareholders something on account of the low returns earned in previous years, rather than in the desire to represent the financial position and earning power of a company with greater realism.

A fashion in bonus issues seems to have originated in Australia in 1949. The following figures suggest their growth in popularity among Australian listed companies:—

1949	2nd half	2	issues
1950	1st quarter	11	„
	2nd „	19	„
	3rd „	22	„
	4th „	28	„
1951	1st „	28	„
	2nd „	20	„
	3rd „	5	„

(Figures for the 2nd and 3rd quarters of 1951 have become available since the lecture was given.)

Not all of these issues arose out of revaluations of assets, but they have been confined to revaluations and share premiums. Bonus issues may be made out of any kind of surplus, but concentration on the above-mentioned varieties is induced by taxation regulations. Bonus issues are, in general, subject to tax in the hands of shareholders, but a specific provision exempts from such tax all "dividends paid exclusively out of profits arising from the revaluation of assets not acquired for the purpose of resale at a profit, or from the issue of shares at a premium, if the dividends paid from such profits are satisfied by the issue of shares of the company declaring the dividend".

Revaluations should be made only for bona fide increases in value; they need not be equal to but should not exceed the independent valuations of experts. Both assets purchased and advantages not purchased may be revalued. It was common in the past to object generally to attempts to write up the book values of assets, particularly the value of such things as goodwill, on the ground that the practice was not conservative. We do not know whether the spate of new issues is evidence of a change of opinion among those who used to object, but it becomes increasingly evident that businessmen will not heed the cautionary pronouncements of conservative accountants if they lead to glaring, unsound discrepancies between book values and realities. One of the main points here emphasized is that accounting should conform with, or give expression to, realities rather more closely than it does now.

Consider, secondly, new issues for cash. In the case of revaluation no additional cash is made available for increasing the money investment in plant, for replacing plant or for increasing the investment in stock. New issues for cash, however, make possible the maintenance of plant capacity and volume of business in spite of higher replacement costs. But unless the additional funds can be obtained at a low rate of interest or there is an increase in efficiency, the mere maintenance of business volume will result in a decline in the rate of profit on funds employed.

One way in which the available funds may be increased without increasing proportionately the interest or dividend commitment is by making new issues at premiums. This has an effect quite the opposite of making bonus issues. A bonus issue creates additional demands for interest or dividends without providing additional resources. A new issue for cash at a premium provides additional resources without creating additional dividend or interest commitments in the same proportion.

There appear to have been several changes in the popularity of the premium issue since the war, but over recent years the following issues have been made:—

1949	2nd quarter	27 issues
	3rd ,,	13 ,,
	4th ,,	9 ,,
1950	1st ,,	11 ,,
	2nd ,,	20 ,,
	3rd ,,	17 ,,
	4th ,,	21 ,,
1951	1st ,,	35 ,,
	2nd ,,	21 ,,
	3rd ,,	13 ,,

By themselves these figures do not indicate the proportion of new funds which are dividend free: this would be difficult to obtain, but some examples from the above issues will show that share premiums have augmented handsomely the working funds of some companies. Bradford Cotton raised £367,000 in this way; Felt and Textiles on two separate occasions raised £475,000, nearly a million pounds all told;

B.H.P. in two issues raised £5,578,000; C.S.R. £819,000; Australasian Paper and Pulp £569,000; Swan Brewery £312,000; Tooheys £216,000; Dunlops £470,000; Drug Houses of Australia £416,000.

Issues of Other Securities

A third way of meeting rising costs is to make new issues of securities involving reduced interest or dividend obligations. Trading on the equity is becoming much more common. Many issues of redeemable preference shares have been made, for small enterprises and large; and some of the investment funds of insurance companies are being diverted in this direction. Increasing numbers of mortgage debentures are being issued at various interest rates down to 3⅞ per cent.

Some companies are resorting to financial instruments which are new in the Australian capital market, although they are not uncommon in other places. Toward the end of 1950, Henry Berry raised £200,000 at 5 per cent on an issue of unsecured notes; the issue was received with some timidity by the market, only 70 per cent being taken up by the investing public. Early in 1951, Myer Emporium and Sargood Gardiner made issues at 4½ per cent.

Unsecured notes give rather more flexibility to the issuing company than a debenture issue; but whereas debentures may be accepted partly on the strength of the assets charged as security, the acceptance of unsecured notes turns rather on the prestige, reputation and prospects of the issuing company. The rationale of financing in this way was the subject of a press comment on the occasion of Sargood Gardiner's issue. "Caught between the pincers of rising costs and the need for larger investment in stocks, companies like Sargood Gardiner must strive to increase turnover to maintain profit margins. But this takes cash, and evidently the company's bank overdraft liability (£783,840 last June) needed to be reduced. Fortunately, the company appears to have sufficient stature plus net tangible assets of £1,347,434 to support an unsecured note issue of £400,000. Small companies might find difficulty in gaining public subscriptions at 4½ per cent, even for long-term debentures. In seeking this loan, the directors considered that, in common with other businesses in the wholesale softgoods trade, the trend of higher replacement costs might continue for some years. They therefore fixed the currency of the loan at eight years, with an option to redeem whole or part after six years . . . . The overall return had not been commensurate with the funds employed and the risks of trading on a highly inflated market. Following this line of thought, the directors considered it unwise to introduce permanent capital and, instead, sought flexibility through a note issue." (*Sydney Morning Herald*, 5 March 1951.)

Conclusion of Section

Each of the above devices has its uses. Some aim at conserving funds, some at augmenting funds, and all aim at maintaining the return on paid-up capital. Each may be financially necessary and appropriate, but none strikes at the root problem of inconsistency and illogicality in accounting. As long as accounting aggregates different value units as if they were identical, so long will it fail to reflect continuously business realities.

Fiscal Policies and the Maintenance of Capital

In this final section an attempt is made to show that present methods of income taxation, based as they are on conventional accounting, result in the consumption of real capital, an effect which is deleterious both to business organizations and to the community in which they operate.

Many people are reluctant to consider the possibility of different practices in accounting for depreciation and stock values than those permitted by the taxation authority. This attitude is based, apparently, on the view that the taxation authority—the government—is incapable of social error, or on the view that taxation rules are sacrosanct.

Now it is unquestionable that taxation rules are alterable. A government may waive or alter the rules in any way it thinks fit in order to achieve socially important ends. It is equally unquestionable that present taxation rules contemplate the use only of conventional accounting methods. The taxation rules happen to have been developed when accounting conventions were not explicit and their effects were not generally understood and when the tax on business profits was comparatively small. The same rules can scarcely be considered appropriate when the effects of the conventions under different economic conditions are understood and when taxation has reached its present high level. The task of government, it may be postulated, is to ensure that the institutions of the community are enabled to continue to discharge their functions effectively; not to tax them out of existence. If that is so, taxation practices should not be allowed to interfere with sound principles in business finance. Reference has already been made to the fact that a taxpayer who elects, for his own purposes, to write off depreciation at a lower rate than the Taxation Commissioner permits will presently be obliged to continue doing so. That seems to be quite a false principle. If a taxpayer elects to write off depreciation at four per cent on technical advice that four per cent is a reasonable figure, why should the Taxation Commissioner oblige him to use four per cent continuously? It would seem to be desirable that as conditions change, fiscal policy, rates of tax and methods of taxing should also change.

There is very little flexibility in taxation practice, and no way of meeting inflationary conditions systematically. There are provisions for additional depreciation allowances when operating conditions are unusually rigorous and where much overtime is worked, and there is the special initial depreciation allowance. This may be considered by some as a means of meeting higher replacement costs by conserving business income, but its real purpose has nothing to do with inflationary problems. It is permissible, also, to claim as a deduction from income the difference between selling price and book value if it is decided to dispose of plant before the end of its previously estimated life.

But none of these concessions aids the maintenance of real capital or productive capacity. It seems necessary to argue strongly that a taxation policy should be devised which pays regard to the effects on the business community in the long run rather than with an eye solely on the short-run revenue-producing aspect of income taxation.

Undistributed profits are a traditional way of maintaining capital and of promoting expansion and development. But in recent years it has become evident that the pool of funds available for these purposes is diminishing because of the high rates of taxation on personal and business incomes. High taxation hinders the accumulation of funds for developmental and other purposes, and can in the long run be economically dangerous. It has been argued by many businessmen and economists that unless there is an adequate supply of savings—particularly business savings which relieve firms of the necessity of recourse to the money market—it is likely that economic progress and improvements in the standard of living may be impeded. Notable technical advances have been made in the chemical, automotive, steel, rubber and petroleum industries which would scarcely have been attempted in the absence of undistributed profits; much of this research work has been of direct market value, but much of it has also been fundamental research of far-reaching social value.

Clearly, businessmen cannot go to the money market and ask investors to put up money for research work, work which as far as the investor is concerned must be a pig in a poke. No assurance can be given as to the results likely to accrue from protracted research work, so that it must be financed out of what business firms may accumulate themselves. As present taxation methods diminish business savings and may even eat into the real capital of business firms, it is difficult to see how technical improvements can continue to be made.

It may seem to be a strong claim to assert that present taxation may lead to the consumption of real capital. An attempt is made in the table to demonstrate this. Hypothetical figures are given for two non-private companies, A and B, for two periods; these accounting periods are not related in any way (e.g., consecutive years), but it is assumed that in Period 1 the general price level for the industry's capital equipment rose by 50 per cent, and in Period 2 it rose by 100 per cent. It may be observed, too, that the proportion of depreciation to "Profits before providing for depreciation" differs for the two companies.

The top half of the table gives an approximate calculation of tax at 1950-51 rates under present taxation methods. The maintenance of real capital is not contemplated under conventional accounting, and the retention of some profits to achieve this purpose is ignored to simplify the demonstration. The consequences are aggravated if profits are retained.

The second half of the table gives an approximate calculation of tax at the same rates after allowing depreciation at a rate which permits real capital to be maintained in spite of rising prices. The resulting real profits are given in line (g) and the tax is calculated on these figures.

TAXATION ON CONVENTIONAL AND REAL PROFITS

	A Company		*B Company*	
	Period 1	Period 2	Period 1	Period 2
Rise in the price level of capital goods	50%	100%	50%	100%
CONVENTIONAL CALCULATION—				
(a) Profits before Depreciation . .	10,000	10,000	100,000	100,000
(b) Depreciation at allowable rates	3,000	3,000	40,000	40,000
(c) Taxable Profit	7,000	7,000	60,000	60,000
(d) Taxation—1950-51 rates (minimum 30%; maximum 35%) . .	2,200	2,200	20,750	20,750
(e) Balance (assume distributed) . .	4,800	4,800	39,250	39,250
CALCULATION ON REAL PROFITS—				
(f) Deduct from above taxable income provisions to maintain real resources	1,500	3,000	20,000	40,000
(g) Real Profit	5,500	4,000	40,000	20,000
(h) Tax on same—1950-51 rates . .	1,675	1,200	13,750	6,750
(i) Balance (assume distributed) . .	3,825	2,800	26,250	13,250
(j) Capital Levy (Difference in Taxes)	525	1,000	7,000	14,000
(k) Conventional Tax, % of Real Profit	40%	55%	52%	104%

The last two lines of the table are the most significant. On the data used, A Company in Period 1 would be taxed at the rate of 40 per cent of real income if current practices are followed, but at only 30 per cent if the taxable income were to coincide with real income. B Company in Period 2 would be taxed at the rate of 104 per cent of real income on conventional calculations, but only at 34 per cent of real income if it were the taxable income. The difference in taxes under the two systems may be regarded as a capital levy, i.e. a levy on real capital, and the amounts of such levy are given in line (j).

It must be obvious that no business can carry on long under these conditions unless it can increase efficiency or raise new money cheaply. The greatest danger in the established method of determining taxable income, however, lies in the way the extent of the tax is concealed, because the methods of accounting ignore some most important business realities. It would be far better to have a system of taxation the effects of which are explicit than one in which capital is levied in the guise of income taxation.

Some may urge against all this that, in any case, the government regards company tax as a revenue-producing tax, and if the government needs money it must raise it in this way or in some other. The above argument, however, has nothing to do with theories of public finance. All that is suggested is, that if traders must be taxed to the extent of the money sums indicated in line (d) because the government needs that amount, it should be made clear that the rate of tax is much in excess of the nominal rates of six or seven shillings in the pound. In the case of B Company in Period 2, the rate is greater than 20 shillings in the pound of real income; in other words, real capital will be reduced by the amount of dividends paid to shareholders.

Furthermore, in so far as the tax income of government is used in providing consumable services—and most of it is so used—the capital resources of the community are being eaten away and the standard of living is exposed to assault. In addition to this, in a private enterprise economy, profits are considered to be the mainspring of economic progress; if the profit incentive is reduced by penal taxation, the spur to the development of new techniques, of new forms of satisfaction and to the improvement of variety, the reduction of work and the increase of leisure is removed.

Conclusion

Accountants may well consider it in their interest and in the interest of the community generally to draw attention, insistently and often, to the consequences of company financial policy and governmental financial policy in periods of shifting price levels. Very few companies are doing much to make clear to shareholders, to the public or to government, the effects of using the methods they have long been accustomed to in conditions like those of today.

It has been submitted throughout these lectures that the customary accounting techniques may be criticized from many angles; they have been described as illogical, as inconsistent, as irrelevant to the purposes they are supposed to serve. These criticisms cannot easily be challenged, but they can be met with alterations in accounting technique. Financial strategy has been changed to meet today's conditions: why should not accounting technique be changed to meet the circumstances, too? Financial makeshifts will not overcome the inflationary problem satisfactorily; they permit changes to be made in book values now and then to introduce a greater measure of realism into accounting statements. But surely the only way of ensuring continuous realism is to modify accounting technique so that it takes account of shifts in price levels in some way. The decisions of businessmen are essentially based on realities. If accounting statements are to help them positively, no effort should be spared to make accounting logical, consistent, realistic and relevant, rather than merely conventional.

24

CROSSROADS

The preceding papers in this section were written, as will have been seen, at a time when post-war inflationary and fiscal conditions were causing some uneasiness among businessmen. The positions taken by many accountants who wrote on the matter seemed to be "sympathetic" to the problems of businessmen. Frequently the taxation authorities and taxation policies were the butt of their complaints. There certainly is something in the view that the taxation of a "nominal" profit, defined without reference to changes in the purchasing power of money, may result in levies on capital. But whether it actually happens depends on whether or not there are compensating gains which are not taxed—and of course there are.

In 1953-54 an attempt was made by a group of accountants in Sydney to reconstruct the financial statements of an Australian company along lines which might overcome some of the crudities of traditional methods. I felt that this was pushing ahead too fast, for I felt confident that the full implications of what was proposed were not understood, either by me or by those who took part in the exercise. At the same time, although my own line of thought seemed to place me "on the side of" businessmen, a vague feeling of academic rectitude cautioned me against "siding" with business against traditional accounting. In effect, it seemed that if a proposal for a modified accounting could be justified only on the ground that it was a palliative for a transient circumstance (rising prices, high taxation), it scarcely deserved notice. On the other hand, if there were inherent defects, which those circumstances only served to highlight, they were the things worth study.

I resolved, therefore, to take no further part in what had become known as the price level accounting debate. For some 10 years I published no article the title of which alluded to the matter. I tried rather to tackle the problem of constructing a set of ideas which would provide an accounting appropriate in all circumstances of business. The "Blueprint" paper, with which the next section of this volume begins, was the first indication of the direction I would take. Variations in prices and price levels were never far from my mind; allusions to them occur repeatedly in subsequent work. But the solution of the general problem required the introduction of a series of other considerations, common to all business accounting. Only after exploring these did the variation of prices and price levels seem to fall into its proper place—as an instance of a number of observables which traditional accounting has disregarded or has respected only partially.

ACCOUNTING THEORY

25

BLUEPRINT FOR A THEORY OF ACCOUNTING*

It is 25 years since Professor J. B. Canning wrote "the accountants have no complete philosophical system of thought about income nor is there any evidence that they have ever felt the need for one". Even today the statement is true. In fact, accountants do not appear to have any complete system of thought about accounting—and this might well be considered a more fundamental lack.

There are unquestionably several systems of thought about the practice of accounting: systems which attempt to categorize the kinds of things accountants do in practice. These systems are almost all the subject can boast of in the way of theory, and for this reason accounting lacks the sharpness, the progressiveness and the vitality of other technologies. Other technologies are based on systems of ideas which serve as references or criteria of performance. Their systems of ideas are not simply descriptions of practice; they transcend application as, indeed, any theory should. Only if a theory deals with the ideal can it serve as a guide to developments and improvements in the practice of the related technology. The conditions under which the practitioner works will inevitably cause his work or his results to fall short of the ideal, for the conditions are never ideal. But if the points at which the conditions fall short are discerned, or if the deficiencies in the technique are known (by reference to the theory), there is hope that the practice will be gradually improved.

Theory and Practice

It is necessary to distinguish between systems of rules relating to the practice of accounting and a theory of accounting. A system of rules is necessary for the consistent practice of any art, and it is useful to attempt to sort out the rules which appear to be followed. Only if the rules are adequately described is it possible to discover inconsistencies in the system. But adequate description does not assist in determining which of two inconsistent rules should be adopted and which should be abandoned. The question must be referred to a more fundamental proposition or set of propositions, to the theory of the subject.

The early analytical writers on accounting appear to have been content to limit themselves to descriptions of practice. *Accounting Concepts of Profit*, by Gilman, *A Statement of Accounting Principles*, by Sanders, Hatfield and Moore, *Introduction to Corporate Accounting*

---

* First published in *Accounting Research* (U.K.), Vol. 6, No. 1, January 1955, pp. 17-25.

Standards, by Paton and Littleton, are examples of attempts to formulate and describe. Whether these writers deliberately or accidentally avoided the use of the phrase "a theory of accounting" or whether they could not envisage a theory of accounting as distinct from a description of practice is not known. But their works cannot be impeached on the grounds that they do not present a theory of accounting, for there is no expressed intention in them to do so.

It remained to post-war writers to attach the word "theory" to accounting.[1] But these writers seem to have been less discriminating, or more anxious to employ a respectable word, than the writers of the 'thirties. They have given to substantially similar sets of rules as were formulated in the 'thirties the description "accounting theory". Thus we have Norris's *Accounting Theory,* Bray's *Four Essays in Accounting Theory,* Littleton's *Structure of Accounting Theory,* not to mention chapters in recent texts and articles in accounting journals which incorporate "accounting theory" in their titles. This practice is misleading and for several reasons tends to hinder developments in accounting.

The practice is misleading because it implies that there is nothing more fundamental in the study of accounting than formulations of practices. It is misleading because it tends to create the impression that accounting now has a basis similar to the basis of other technologies, whereas no scientist or technologist would be content with such a contradictory set of propositions as those described, for example, by Gilman. It tends to hinder developments because students of accounting are not encouraged to consider the possibility of alternative systems of accounting; because there is so much in the formulations of practice that is doctrinaire; because the real nature of the propositions put forward is not carefully considered; and because the assumptions underlying practice are not critically examined.

But the so-called "theories" of accounting are not even complete descriptions of practice. Accounting on a cash basis was probably useful enough for centuries before the idea of matching costs and revenues was recognized; and wide sectors of the business community today find this form of accounting adequate for their purposes. How, then, is its omission from the "theory" of the subject to be justified? It is dealt with in textbooks describing accounting technique, but the "theorists" seem quietly to ignore it. This can only be because accounting on a cash basis does not conveniently fit into a neat (but in part unrealistic) system.

In some of the more elaborate descriptive studies, attempts are made to justify rules or propositions on historical grounds and this is a common habit among accountants. The protagonists of conventional accounting frequently appeal to the antiquity of widely used practices. But antiquity is no criterion: in fact the history of other arts suggests that antiquity makes a practice suspect from the start.

The environment and the conduct of organized activity has changed vastly since the days when double-entry book keeping was cradled. It

---

[1] An exception is Paton's *Accounting Theory* (1922).

would be fatuous to expect the same propositions to be valid now as were valid then, or to expect that no new propositions now require to be added. The resort to history is, in any case, unnecessary and restrictive. It implies that only tried and accepted rules can take an honoured place in the theory of the subject and it leaves little ground for speculating about more useful forms of accounting.

Let it be admitted that formulations of practice are useful, and that historical studies of practice and developments of practice are interesting and informative. This still leaves accounting short of what may properly be described as theory.

The Form of a Theory

If a theory of accounting is to go beyond practice and if the historical development of the practice is to be disregarded, upon what basis, then, may it proceed? Upon the same basis substantially as any other theory; that is, by building up a series of relevant propositions from a few fundamental assumptions or axioms. The system of Gilman and his followers can in no way be related to this idea of a theory: its structure of conventions and doctrines is artificial, having no counterpart in the theory underlying any other technology. Are there no assumptions, for example? There are; but they are not identified as assumptions. Are there no axioms? Yes, but they sail under different colours.

It is possible to build up a theory of accounting without reference to the practice of accounting. This does not mean that the theory will have no connexion with reality. To design a theory which has no relevance to reality is quite feasible: but the theorist in any field which has a practical counterpart can scarcely be as delightfully irresponsible as Lewis Carroll. Theory is not synonymous with remoteness from reality. It is, in fact, one of the greatest pleasures of the theorist to put his hypotheses to the test of reality. If one is confronted with what purports to be a theory of accounting, and finds that it deals with corporate accounting only, the existence in reality of unincorporated ventures will cast doubts on the validity of the propositions put forward. This process of checking back is of the nature of scientific method. It is followed to secure that no unreal or unjustifiable assumptions lie beneath the argument.

Premises

The fundamental premises for a theory of accounting lie outside of the field of accounting proper. There is no such thing as accounting in the abstract: accounts are kept for entities which are recognized in other fields of discourse, chiefly in economics and government. The following propositions therefore seem to be necessary:—

(a) certain organized activities are carried out by entities which exist by the will or with the co-operation of contributing parties;

(b) these entities are managed rationally, that is, with a view to meeting the demands of the contributing parties efficiently;

(c) statements in monetary terms of the transactions and relationships of the entity are one means of facilitating rational management;

(d) the derivation of such statements is a service function.

The first of these propositions is an observation from the real world. It is general enough to cover every circumstance for which accounts may be required. It embraces incorporated and unincorporated trading ventures; private non-profitmaking organizations; government and other public bodies; and a community as a whole. It is thus the foundation of private, public and social accounting.

The second proposition is also an observation from reality. It can be interpreted in the sense of maximizing economic returns or in the sense of maximizing all returns to the contributors. It is substantially the same proposition as one which underlies a great part of economic theory. The precise demands of the contributing parties are not set down because, for the variety of entities contemplated, ends or purposes will differ materially.

The third proposition simply recognizes that, in a money economy, money is a convenient common denominator. If it were desired to make a theory fit any other kind of economy, the proposition could be stated in more general terms. That there may be other means of facilitating rational management is recognized at the outset.

The fourth proposition is a corollary of the former two. But it has itself some significant consequences. It implies that there can be no proposition admitted in accounting theory which interferes with the rights of those whom accounting serves: for example, the right of management to have full information and relevant information on the efficiency with which ends are pursued.

Entities

Some further comments on the first of these propositions may emphasize the difference between the view here suggested and that put forward in other systems. The idea of an accounting entity is now generally accepted in discursive treatments of accounting. Gilman and his followers describe it as a convention: Bray thinks of it as a principle. But the "entity" is an anterior idea to the "accounting entity": an entity becomes an accounting entity because and when accounts are kept about it. In the writer's view the entity is a datum, the particular features of which must be taken into consideration in framing an appropriate information-providing system. Many writers note that the entity may have different forms; but in no case is an attempt made to work out propositions which are appropriate to those different forms.

Now this seems to be the crux of the matter. If entities differ it is highly probable that the kinds of information required by their managers and other participants will differ. It becomes necessary to inquire, for each type of entity, what information is required for its rational management. For purposes of illustration it is useful to set down some of the ways in which entities may differ.

Firstly, entities differ in expectation of existence. The possible alternative assumptions are continuity and liquidation. The kinds of information which enter into a system of accounts will differ according to the assumption adopted. Entities also differ in the nature and variety of their contributors; two of the possible assumptions are tight control over performance of the entity and its management, and a loose form of control: the required end-products of an accounting system may be different according to the assumption made. Thirdly, entities may differ in respect of the criteria of performance by which they are judged. Some are conducted on a "sustenance" basis, some on a break-even basis, some on a profit or dividend basis; and in each case there may or may not be assumed a desire to maintain real, or money, capital. The various combinations of assumptions about the "ends" of contributors will yield different models of accounting processes.

It is not sufficient to pass over these differences in the nature of entities or to assume that the environment, scope and criteria of performance are always the same. Such an assumption can never provide a theoretical basis for the many forms of accounting used in the administration of organized activity; it is unreal; it condemns all entities to lie in the same Procrustean bed. Each of the possible assumptions mentioned in the previous paragraph is entirely feasible, and to every one there is a corresponding set of real circumstances and an appropriate technique. Yet in what now passes for accounting theory, the half of these possibilities is disregarded. And the half that is disregarded has just as much right to consideration as the other half, because it represents certain practical situations. Only if a theory, or even a descriptive system, envisages all these possibilities can it pretend to embrace accounting for sole traders, corporations, clubs, fiduciaries, governments and communities.

The Assumption of Rationality

The second basic proposition is rational management. It would be useful to consider at length the conditions of rational action but it is not intended to do so here. There are many uncertainties which cannot be adequately canvassed before making decisions, but the system of accounts should in no way increase these uncertainties. Rational management entails the consideration of alternative courses of action, the making of decisions, the facilitation of their execution and the examination or review of their consequences.

It is therefore a corollary of the assumption of rational management that there shall be an information-providing system; such a system is required both as a basis for decisions and as a basis for reviewing the consequences of decisions. Part of such a system, in money economies, is the accounting system. Because of its formal nature—formal in the sense that all kinds of transactions are expressed in more or less abstract money equivalents—the fact that real things and real relationships lie behind the figures in accounts may easily be overlooked. To avoid this oversight a formal information-providing system should conform with two general propositions.

The first is a condition of all logical discourse. The system should be logically consistent; no rule or process can be permitted which is contrary to any other rule or process. In particular the symbols used should have a sensibly uniform meaning throughout the system. In accounting this involves that equal things should be represented by equal symbols. In the present practice of accounting this proposition has no place. Equal things are often represented by different symbols and the same symbol may represent quite different quantities of the same thing. This is illogical. It can scarcely lead to the same conclusions (decisions) as a logical system, and it is hard to see how it can lead to rational conclusions. One suspects that on many matters appropriate decisions are made in spite of, rather than because of, the system of accounts.

The second proposition arises from the use of accounting statements as a basis for making decisions of practical consequence. The information yielded by any such system should be relevant to the kinds of decision the making of which it is expected to facilitate. There seems to be nothing indefensible about this proposition. If decisions are to be made now to be carried out in the future it is only reasonable that the present state of affairs, expressed in terms now relevant, should be used as their basis. And if the consequences of past decisions are being reviewed, it is only reasonable that achievements and the costs of those achievements should be expressed in terms which recognize the fundamental criteria of performance for the specific entity in question. This proposition, like the former, is in marked contrast with contemporary accounting practice, as will be shown presently.

Symbols of the System

The symbols used or to be used in a system of accounts are units of currency. This is a corollary of the proposition just stated: no other unit is as relevant as the unit of domestic currency to the general body of contributors or to the entity itself. But here again alternative assumptions may be made about the nature of the monetary unit: it may be assumed that the monetary unit or unit of account has a stable real value or an unstable real value. Either assumption may be realistic in certain circumstances, and each will result in a different system of accounts. Thus, (a) if an entity is assumed to have a continued existence and (b) if the real value of the unit of account has changed over time and (c) if the test of relevance be admitted, the system to be devised is one which will set off against the current gross income the current costs of services consumed, and will show in current terms the financial position which is the result of past transactions. Such a system differs materially from contemporary accounting practice: but it stems directly from the notions of rationality and relevance. Contemporary practice proceeds on the obviously unrealistic assumption of monetary stability, and it is scarcely to be wondered at that businessmen, themselves the users of accounts, so roundly criticize the relevance of accounting statements. The assumption of monetary stability may have been realistic at one time, but to preserve a time-honoured system only on the ground that it is time-honoured is not consistent with the notion of a service function.

Form

An accounting entity is a thing about which accounts are kept; and monetary symbols are the symbols by which the transactions of an entity are described. The form of a system of accounts may now be considered. For convenience of exposition monetary stability will be assumed; but this assumption in no way jeopardizes the generality of what follows. It is convenient, too, to start with the simplest kind of entity: the liquidated venture. In this, the simplest case, inputs equal outputs. In the simplest case of a continuing entity inputs equal outputs plus residues. The model can be extended by introducing inputs of an enduring kind and outputs or outlays for enduring benefits; but always inputs equal outputs plus residues. This is a convenient basis for a system, in that it shows what relationship exists between inputs and outputs and what the residues amount to. The equality may be called the basic identity or axiom of accounting. If it is granted that the relationship between inputs and outputs and the size of residues are matters of importance, double-entry follows. If some aspects of these matters are practically less important single-entry accounting may suffice.

For the purpose of recording inputs and outputs a convention is adopted. Inputs will be shown as credits; outputs and residues as debits. Credits and debits will be shown in adjacent columns, credits on the right-hand side and debits on the left. The usual book-keeping paraphernalia could be introduced here but will not be discussed. The reason for discussing form is to indicate that only one kind of convention may be permitted in the system of propositions here put forward: conventions as to formal arrangement. Everything else is too significant to be treated as convention only.

Accounting Statements

A second corollary of the assumption of rationality may now be stated. It is an assumption that relates only to continuing entities. The necessity for making new decisions and reviewing past decisions requires that there shall be periodical statements of changes in the affairs of a continuing entity. It may be shown that in complex entities three kinds of statement are useful for this purpose: a statement of the affairs of an entity at the opening and the close of such periods (for example, balance sheets expressed in values relevant to their dates); a statement of the operating incomes and outlays during the period (for example, an operating or revenue account); and a statement incorporating total net additions to the funds of the entity and total net dispositions of those funds in the period (for example, a funds statement, incorporating both the effects of operations and the effects of long-term financial and other arrangements). In simpler entities, a simpler system of statements may suffice. It is not intended to discuss these statements here; although their general nature is suggested it may be possible to work out other statements which promote rational decision-making.

But one point deserves mention. The statements should adequately describe what has happened in the period. They should relate to the period and to that period alone. Where account must be taken of the unexpired values of durable assets or unliquidated assets, certain problems arise. The simplest model is based on the assumption of certain knowledge, and for the purpose of sorting out the issues involved and of devising ways of meeting them this model is useful. But in reality uncertainties exist and the simplest model must be modified to meet the case of uncertainty. This requires some flexibility in the rules formulated for the system. The point is made here because in the teaching of accountancy some of the rules (for example, with respect to depreciation) tend to be stated in a way which virtually assumes certain knowledge.

A third corollary of rationality is that all material particulars are required to be shown. Material particulars are details which may influence judgement. They will vary according to the real nature of the entity involved and according to the assumptions made regarding criteria of performance. This corollary also justifies the omission of non-material particulars, inasmuch as non-material details interfere with the process of comparison and contrast which is characteristic of ratiocination.

Having established a system based on the assumption of monetary stability it is then appropriate to modify the model on the assumption of monetary instability. This will require the introduction of additional rules, but in every case the test is required to be: "What is necessary for rational decision-making?" The problem of accounting under conditions of monetary instability has been neglected or deliberately put aside by most writers on the so-called theory of accounting. This was perhaps inevitable if, as is here suggested, the discursive treatment of accounting has been confined to descriptions of practice. There has been no recognition of the possibility that all that is involved is a regrouping of assumptions, or the substitution of a realistic assumption for an unrealistic one. It is not a question of working out entirely new "principles".

Conclusion

In conclusion it is useful to point out some of the features of the system of ideas indicated here. The system is only briefly sketched; many details have not been filled in, because the purpose of this outline is to suggest a procedure for developing a theory of accounting rather than to expound such a theory in detail.

Firstly, the system of propositions suggested hangs together. It proceeds from a few data and a few assumptions to which propositions are added as convenience of exposition or recognition of realities requires. It is thus in marked contrast with other descriptive systems the main propositions of which are not tied to a few unifying ideas but are isolated, sometimes artificial, and often contradictory.

Secondly, the method recognizes that there are many different entities which require different models. This prevents the gross over-simplification which is characteristic of some descriptive systems. Every type of accounting can be represented by a theoretical model built along similar lines. No descriptive system yet put forward has contemplated the application of similar (but not identical) basic propositions to the problems of private, public and social accounting.

Thirdly, the theory consists of propositions which are a framework for the development of ideal systems of accounts. It may then become easier to discover the deficiencies of existing accounting methods, to devise means of meeting new requirements—and this not in an *ad hoc* fashion, but as the logical consequence of the basic function of accounting, that is, the provision of information to be used in making rational decisions.

Fourthly, the same framework may be extended to provide a theory of cost accounting. For this purpose the broad functions of entities are considered to be the basis for all minor decisions affecting their operations, and the information required is such as will make it possible to make these minor or contributory decisions rationally.

Fifthly, the system incorporates features which economists have found it useful to adopt in studies of business behaviour and social problems. It seems to be likely that many differences of emphasis in accounting and economics may be resolved if it is recognized that both deal with substantially the same entities, and that both should therefore proceed on the same assumptions. In many respects the assumptions of economics are more realistic than the assumptions of contemporary accounting; but each subject is likely to be more helpful to the other if the assumptions are laid bare for comparison. The unfruitfulness of exchanges between accountants and economists in the past seems to have been due to the neglect to discuss assumptions. A theory of accounting in which the assumptions are disclosed may help in this direction.

Sixthly and finally, the training now offered to accountants consists largely of the routine learning of procedures, often of procedures for which no alternative is countenanced. The habit of rigorous, logical thought is not inculcated and it cannot be expected that the products of this training will, by criticism or construction, contribute to the development of a more relevant and realistic accounting. The outline offered in this paper suggests a form of training in which the real nature of the "conventions", "doctrines", "standards", "principles", which appear in descriptive treatments of accounting, is brought to the notice of students. It may be hoped, then, that an assumption, an axiom, a hypothesis will be recognized for what it is, and will not be accepted as inviolable dogma. Descriptive and analytical studies of practice are necessary: only if there are such studies is it possible to test what is done against what is required. But even more necessary is the development of a theory which provides an ideal system against which expedient and convenient and unsystematic practices may be tested.

26

A SCIENTIFIC PATTERN FOR ACCOUNTING THEORY*

Like all arts, accounting has become the subject of theorizing late in its life; by comparison with some arts, very late in life. The slowness with which concepts and generalizations about the relationships between concepts have been developed is probably due to the fact that accountants have always regarded their work as practical, an art which can be learned to the point of practical utility by applying the seat of the pants to the seat of the high stool. Most of the practical men have seen no need to reconsider, or to attempt to clarify, the methods they have used. Few indeed of the partners in the oldest and largest practices have left any contribution to knowledge about accounting by which they may have been remembered. They have gone about their work, as most practical men do, simply confident of the propriety of their methods and of the value of their services to the community.

Simple confidence is, of course, a comfortable state of mind. It allows one to go about his business without any gnawing fear that his technique may not be as efficacious as he has been led to believe. It relieves him of the painful problem of devising and experimenting with alternative techniques; it even saves him from thinking about the purposes for which his technique exists at all. It is natural, therefore, that those who have slipped into technical somnolence should be suspicious of theory, for it is the annoying habit of theorists to question established beliefs and customary procedures.

However, simple confidence is a poor foundation for an art which is practised in a continually changing environment. In the last 100 years, the growth in importance of the business corporation, the spread of private investment, the increase in taxation on incomes, and the fluctuations in the fortunes of business through wars and depressions, have brought under notice the need for some changes in accounting practices. The confidence even of practitioners was shaken, and attention began to be directed to the "principles" on which accounting was believed to be based.

The Search for Standards

One of the more obvious problems arose from the negotiability of security investments. The legislation which created the limited liability company recognized that investors needed information on the financial affairs of companies, by providing that public companies

---

* First published in *The Australian Accountant*, Vol. 25, No. 10, October 1955, pp. 428-34.

should publish financial statements annually. But of what use would this be if companies were to adopt different methods of computing income, or if they were to use technical terms indiscriminately in statements the recipients of which are mainly lay persons? Uniformity of method and terminology appeared to be such an important objective that many professional associations sponsored the publication of statements on these matters. Whether or not this legitimate and justifiable desire for uniformity led to the search for "accounting standards"—the foundations of "good" contemporary practice—is not clear. But there appears to be some ground for believing that the two movements had similar origins, or that one gave rise to the other, for both arose in the 'thirties in the United States.

Looking back, one is prompted to ask whether the search for accounting standards, and even the use of the term "accounting standards", was not premature. Paton and Littleton used the term in preference to "principles" for the latter "would generally suggest a universality and degree of permanence which cannot exist in a human-service institution such as accounting".[1] But it is doubtful whether such an impression is avoided by the use of "standards"; a standard may well be taken to be something established by authority, accepted, or generally approved, and the suggestion of authoritarian support is as much to be avoided as the suggestion of universality or permanence. The reason for asking whether the attempt to establish standards was premature, however, lies in the necessity for establishing foundations before worrying about standards. As yet it can scarcely be claimed that the foundations of accounting have been thoroughly examined; there are still large areas in which material differences of opinion exist. In fact, the whole process of conventional accounting should be considered as nothing more than the consequence of an hypothesis. In these circumstances it seems to have been unfortunate that attention was diverted from the development of a theory of the subject to the development of standards for practice.

The student of any other discipline may find it strange that the literature of accounting lacks the familiar signs of scientific discourse. Even though the subject has been rescued from declining into dogma, it is still difficult to trace the elements of logical and methodical inquiry through the writings of its exponents. The general treatment of the subject is lacking in rigour. There are many categorical statements which ought to be recognized as hypotheses only; there are some examples of inductive and deductive reasoning, but few examples of the systematic use of both to test or to support a hypothesis; there are many examples of value judgements masquerading as reasoned conclusions. Several general types of deficiency are worth noticing.

Adoption of Rules as Theory

It is paradoxical that the literature of a subject, the practical effect of which is to promote knowledge about other things, is lacking in

---

[1] *An Introduction to Corporate Accounting Standards*, 1940, p. 4.

evidence of appreciation of the ways of acquiring knowledge about itself. The labels attached to many propositions and concepts bear no similarity to the categories of scientific methodology. The commonly used classification of "basic" concepts into doctrines and conventions is ideally suited to give notice that the subject-matter is not amenable to the same treatment as other studies. The persistence of these terms through 16 years shows that notice was duly taken.

To be fair to Gilman, it should be pointed out that his *Accounting Concepts of Profit* is concerned with the practice of accounting. It was perhaps proper that he should describe as "doctrines" what were generally laid down as desirable practices, and as "conventions" what were commonly accepted practices, for he was not engaged in a study of the theory of the subject. If the latter had been his purpose, he would have had to take these observed practices as things needing inquiry and investigation. He was aware of the internal inconsistencies between some of the propositions he described, but he was not concerned with the construction of a self-consistent body of rules or principles. His followers have, unfortunately, borrowed his framework, adopted substantially the same concepts, and called the lot "accounting theory", regardless of the lack of precision of some of the concepts, and of the contradictions between them. There has been no attempt to link these concepts, or to set one against the other for the purpose of discovering more general concepts or fundamental propositions. In some cases the order in which the propositions are treated strongly suggests that the connexion between them is quite misunderstood. The study of the subject has not passed the stage of crude observation; it is a pity that rules are based on such an unsubstantial foundation.

Excessive Abstraction

The need for abstract thinking appears to have arisen before the art of meaningful abstraction has been mastered. If abstractions must be used, they should be used with care; to do otherwise is unfruitful and may be misleading.

"Accounting" is an abstraction. When it is used without qualification, it is reasonable to suppose that it is used with reference to the whole of a general class of processes, all of which are called "accounting"—single-entry accounting, double-entry accounting, business accounting, governmental accounting, etc. Many statements about accounting are invalid, because although they use the universal term they are asserted in contemplation of only one of its particular varieties. Professor Bray writes: "the familiar idea of double-entry is quite fundamental to all accounting theory".[2] There can be no doubt of the universality of the last three words. But is it true that there can be no theory of single-entry accounting? Professor Littleton calls his monograph *Structure of Accounting Theory*. But on examination it turns out to be concerned solely with double-entry accounting, on an accrual basis, for business enterprises—three distinct limits which

[2] *Four Essays in Accounting Theory*, O.U.P. 1953, p. 4.

make the use of the universal term inappropriate. It may be felt that to quarrel with such usages is splitting hairs, because the context in which the term is used clearly suggests the limitations which have been imposed, and any person is quite at liberty to limit his discourse in any way he pleases. But if the limitations are not explicit, abstraction can lead to confusion and to neglect of the part of the subject which is excluded.

This may be illustrated by reference to the entity concept. "Accounting entity" is an abstraction used to enable general statements to be made about accounting for different organizations with verbal economy. Without qualification the term can only be used validly in connexion with statements which are true of all accounting for whatever entity. There are very few such statements. It was pointed out in a previous paper[3] that organizations differ in material particulars, particulars which determine the type of accounting which is appropriate. These particulars may be derived from observation of different organizations; they do not arise within accounting, and no proposition in accounting can dispose of them.

Let it be assumed that there are four possible differences in entities:—

A, differences in expectation of existence:
- a_1, continuity;
- a_2, liquidation;

B, differences in expectation of income:
- b_1, profit objective;
- b_2, no profit objective;

C, differences in attitude towards capital:
- c_1, real capital to be maintained;
- c_2, money capital to be maintained;
- c_3, maintenance of capital not of prime importance;

D, differences in attitude towards participants:
- d_1, contractual rights enforceable and enforced;
- d_2, contractual rights not rigorously exercised.

The differences listed are not exhaustive, but they will suffice for the purpose of illustration. It will also be sufficient to consider two types of organization in order to suggest the differences in accounting method which may arise.

A business corporation may be defined in the above terms as $a_1b_1c_1d_1$; a professional association as $a_1b_2c_3d_2$. What proposition may be formulated for the recognition of gross income in each of these cases? For $a_1b_1c_1d_1$ the results of a year and the financial position at its end will be fairly represented if income is recognized when a claim arises. This, because a business corporation has legal rights to enforce such claims and has usually no hesitation in exercising them. But for $a_1b_2c_3d_2$, the results of a year and the financial position at its end will be fairly represented if income is recognized when cash is received. This, because a professional association usually prefers to remove

[3] "Blueprint for a Theory of Accounting", see p. 347, *ante*.

defaulters from its membership rather than to take legal action for the recovery of subscriptions.

Each feature of the accounting process would require a proposition, formulated in a similar way, and if necessary recognizing the differences of result arising from differences in entities. In some cases a proposition expressing a general idea would need to be supplemented with subsidiary propositions. The theory of accounting for each entity *abcd* would thus consist of a series of propositions related to one another and related to the observable or assumed characteristics of the entity.

The method of defining entities used above may appear to be cumbersome, but it is a certain way of ensuring that distinctive characteristics are not overlooked in the process of formulating hypotheses, procedures, rules or what-not. It is a safeguard against making general statements which purport to be universally true but which are valid only in a limited class of instances.

Unwarranted Limitation of the Field of Study

Errors and omissions appear also to have arisen from failure to look further afield than the processes of accounting. Attention will be confined to business accounting. If accounting is considered to be a service function, its methods and assumptions should be tested by reference to the needs of business and businessmen; and, except for the purpose of dealing with the history of business or accounting, the needs of the contemporary business and businessman. At major points in expositions of accounting this test is avoided.

An opportunity for a penetrating examination of the needs of businessmen seems to have been missed by Professor Littleton. He sets down[4] 23 "inductively derived principles". But his description of the inductive process is simply this: "Long ago the basic methods of double entry were worked out by trial and error . . . practices were presently verbalized into rules and procedures . . . . Methods devised by many different people were used and tested by many others. Over the years, and by common consent after tested use, the most suitable procedures became generally accepted practices. Teachers . . . found it necessary to supplement the accumulated rules and descriptions of procedure by explanations and justifications . . . . Hence it is appropriate to say that both the methods of practice and the explanations of theory were inductively derived out of experience." Clearly the study is limited to methods and procedures which have come to be accepted.

Further, the use of the term "inductively derived" appears to be inappropriate. It conveys the impression that the principles which follow have arisen simply from the observation of a number of specific instances, that they are statements of general truths which are demonstrated by particular cases. An inductive proposition is usually stated in a positive form; it can be so stated because it is a statement of fact. But none of Professor Littleton's principles is in the positive

[4] Op. cit., p. 185.

form; they are all imperatives! They begin with Define, Make, See that, Recognize, Ignore . . . statements of this kind cannot be derived by induction. They are rules; they may have some kind of inductive basis, but they necessarily incorporate a (frequently undisclosed) value judgement. They may be quite proper in a practical handbook, but they are not theory. What is more, it is apparent from the above quotation that there are some deductive elements in the derivation of the author's principles. "Trial and error" involves a deductive process, and "justification" is often entirely deductive. Nevertheless, it appears that Professor Littleton intended to limit the sources of his propositions to observable phenomena, and to avoid the use of the deductive method.

Besides, there are certainly some assumed limitations of the scope and function of accounting beyond which inquiry is not pursued. To impose limits within the subject seems to be at variance with the view that accounting is a "human-service institution", a view that is recognized by the author in his earlier work in collaboration with Professor Paton.

One other example of failure to extend inquiry backwards to business usage may be noted. Messrs. Yorston, Smyth and Brown observe: "Until recently it was held that a balance sheet showed the financial condition of a concern as at a given date. This view is now untenable."[5] These are reasonable enough observations. But the authors are not prompted to ask whether a statement of financial condition is, in fact, required by businessmen. The limitation of conventional accounting is accepted without question. This is legitimate in a work designed to teach the practice of accounting. But it is inappropriate to leave the matter in the air in a treatment of the theory of the subject; and the chapter from which the quotation is drawn is a chapter on "accounting theory".

Brief Outline of a Method of Acquiring Knowledge

The time seems to be ripe for a thorough re-examination of the nature of the propositions which would constitute a theory of accounting. It appears to be particularly important to recognize the distinction between the art and practice of accounting, and the body of knowledge about accounting. That is to say, the propositions which are put forward as instructions to accountants are to be distinguished clearly and unequivocally from the propositions put forward as a means of increasing knowledge of the accounting function. To confuse the two may lead, as it appears to have done in the past, to an unedifying mixture of theoretical propositions and practical rules.

Within the body of knowledge about accounting there will be no imperatives. This does not mean that writers about accounting are prevented from advocating certain practices or procedures. But when they do so they should be recognized as having, for the purpose in mind, abandoned the status of theorist for that of advocate. The

[5] *Advanced Accounting*, Vol. 1, p. 9.

difference is material. The only tests to which theoretical propositions may be subjected are tests of the validity of the premises and tests of the validity of the reasoning. The statements of an advocate may in addition, however, be subjected to tests of the value judgements which influence him to state his case in the imperative form. The importance of the distinction between these tests lies in the effects which criticism may have on the conclusions reached. One may effectively dispose of a defective theoretical conclusion by demonstrating its premises or its reasoning to be invalid. It is not nearly so easy to destroy a stated case, because value judgements are subjective and there is no certainty that one's own value system will be acceptable to or accepted by others. On the other hand, it is not usually difficult to identify a stated case; "must" and "should" are sufficient warning of the need to ask: what system of values is invoked here?

Within the body of knowledge about accounting there will be both positive and hypothetical propositions. A positive proposition arises from observation; it is a generalization about certain characteristics of the instances under observation. Such generalizations are true only of the cases observed, and only in respect of the qualities under observation. They may be interesting of themselves, but their primary function is to provide the foundation for further generalizations about the whole family of instances of which those observed are a part.

These deduced propositions may concern themselves with explanation of the observed facts; or they may use the observed facts for the purpose of deriving dependent propositions. Thus, for example, it is apparent that "accounting statements are a means of communication". This is an inductive generalization. It may be considered to represent the consequence of certain things—the complex nature of business, the remoteness of management from the points at which events occur, the legal and conventional pattern of relationships between an accounting entity and its supporters. Knowledge about accounting will be increased by discovery of the conditions which give rise to the use of accounting statements as means of communication. There may be many such conditions, all of which may not be identified at any time. The propositions which describe these conditions will therefore be under continuous scrutiny to ensure that none has been overlooked. This process of discovering the conditions underlying certain observed facts will be proceeded with to the point where the subject under study ends and some other science begins; for it is reasonable to take as premises the conclusions of another field of study. The underlying conditions, when discovered, may be taken as premises or assumptions for the development of ideas about—to pursue the example—accounting as a means of communication. It may transpire that these ideas represent quite a different kind of accounting from that about which the original observation was made. But note that these derived propositions are hypothetical. They will be true on the hypothesis that all the premises which have a bearing on the conclusions have been taken into consideration.

On the other hand, the same observation "accounting statements are a means of communication" may be taken as a premise, not as a consequence. It is a broad general idea which, of itself, provides no detail either of the particular kinds of information which may be communicated, or of the ways in which that information may be obtained. To provide this detail, subsidiary propositions will be enunciated; they will usually arise from relating different kinds of facts or from relating facts to prior deductions. Here again, it is necessary to keep the premises under constant scrutiny. The facts may change, new combinations of facts may arise; and even though they do not destroy the validity of the general idea they may necessitate restatement of the subsidiary propositions.

There may thus be developed a system of propositions, a theory of the subject, which will represent certain procedures. At this stage it is necessary to see whether the theory fits the facts as a whole. If the procedures indicated by the theory are found in practice, the premises and the reasoning may be considered to be valid. If the hypothetical procedures are at variance with practice, several kinds of inference may be drawn. The assumptions or premises may be inadequate; the reasoning may be illogical; or there may be temporarily operating factors which prevent the practice from conforming with the theoretical model. The former two possibilities would receive attention first, but if the theory is not inadequate on those grounds the third possibility would be considered. At this point it may be necessary to admit value judgements as hypothetical causes. But not for the purpose of adopting any particular scale of values; merely for the purpose of discovering what value system explains the adoption in practice of a method which does not conform with the method suggested by the theory. The identification of exogenous factors such as regulation, custom and inertia, and some knowledge of their importance is useful both to the theorist and to the advocate of changes in practice. It provides the one with an explanation, and the other with a point of departure.

A theory worked out on the above lines may be expected to have many advantages over the fragmentary and unconnected generalizations which are now current. Firstly, the development of rules for practice would be recognized as a pursuit distinct from the search for knowledge about accounting. Theory, as such, is not committed to the support of any specific technique, new or old. The theorist is free to ask any question in pursuit of knowledge about his subject, and as theorist, all practices, actual or hypothetical, and all phenomena which may be causes or consequences of accounting practices, are of equal interest to him. Secondly, the scientific method provides the means of linking ideas, of forming a network of ideas, in which each is necessarily related to the others as antecedent to consequent, or as premise to conclusion, or as cause to effect. And thirdly, this method is more likely than the prevailing notion of accounting theory to lead to an extension of knowledge about accounting; for the propositions which would be enunciated could be readily identified as assumptions, inductive generalizations or deductions, and the immanent necessity of testing hypothetical propositions by reference to the facts of the business world would prevent the assertion of unwarranted or unrealistic conclusions.

If the study of the subject proceeds in this way it should be possible to avoid what Roger Bacon described as "four stumbling blocks which hinder well-nigh every scholar: the example of frail and unworthy authority, long established custom, the sense of the ignorant crowd and the pretense of wisdom".

27

DETAIL FOR A BLUEPRINT*

Readers of the literature of accounting will often have been treated to a discussion of whether accounting is an art or a science or something else. The present writer has frequently felt that argument of this kind is pointless and that the way accounting is described has nothing to do with the effectiveness with which it is carried out. More recently, however, it has seemed that confusion among writers as to what accounting is has led to confused thinking about many of the commonest features of accounting, and may interfere with its development. An attempt is made here to draw some distinctions which may clear the ground for a more rigorous study of the subject.

Knowledge and Art

Analogy may serve as an introduction, but it is not to be taken as argument. Law is both a subject of study and a field of practice. So are surgery, engineering, chemistry. About each there is a body of knowledge, to the testing and development of which scholars and research workers devote themselves. In their inquiries these people are guided by a series of methods commonly known as scientific methods designed and proved to be methods of verifying the correctness of bold guesses or patiently worked out hypotheses, and thus of discovering new knowledge. One of these methods is reasoning, logical reasoning about the relationships between observed phenomena or concepts adopted to describe observed phenomena. Reasoning leads to generalizations, principles and laws, the general body of which constitutes the science.

All this is quite different from the field of practice which attaches to or is based on a science. The practising lawyer, surgeon, engineer or chemist is not concerned, as practitioner, with testing and developing knowledge; but rather with applying existing knowledge to specific cases or problems. In doing this he is not free to experiment; even if he has time he has no freedom from the restraints common in an organized profession. These restraints may be imposed by the profession itself or by the requirements of the general body of clients of the profession. But to the practitioner they are real and limiting. In short, the practitioner is working, on the basis of some underlying body of knowledge, but in a social environment; and, for his own protection as much as for the protection of his clients, he is obliged to

---

* First published in *The Accounting Review,* Vol. XXXII, No. 2, April 1957, pp. 206-15. The allusion of the title is to "Blueprint for a Theory of Accounting", see p. 347, *ante,* which was the subject of comment by Professor Littleton in "Choice Among Alternatives", *The Accounting Review,* July 1956.

conform with the standards, rules, codes or conventions imposed upon him.

The scientific study of any subject is not limited by the standards and conventions necessary in its dependent field of practice. The student is free to consider many possible modes of action, many possible combinations of facts and many hypothetical propositions in his search for knowledge. He is not constrained by the necessity of making any of his theoretical models work in practice; but if his observations are realistic and his reasoning is rigorous, his theoretical models often suggest to practitioners new and more useful practices than those they have been accustomed to follow.

The distinction between scientific propositions and rules of practice is evident from the form in which each is stated. Scientific propositions, i.e., the conclusions arising from observation and reasoning, are stated in the indicative mood[2]. On the other hand, rules of practice, standards and conventions, are stated in the form of directives or imperatives[3]. The distinction is not a mere verbal quibble; it represents two quite different approaches, one scientific, the other practical. It also has quite important consequences as far as the development of a science or an art is concerned. For, as I have argued elsewhere[4], the validity of a scientific proposition can be tested by reference to its premises and its reasoning, whereas the appropriateness of a rule is not subject to the same tests because a rule implies a value judgement, an opinion or a belief—none of which is susceptible to scientific testing.

It is emphasized that criticism is not offered here of standards, rules or conventions, as such. In practice they are essential. But they belong to practice (know how) not to science (knowledge about). A billiards player may learn the rules of the game: he then knows what to do. But unless he knows something about the second and third laws of motion and their corollaries, either by learning from books or from experience and careful observation, he is unlikely to be a player of great skill. There will always, of course, be the additional intangible something that makes the great player, the artist, but just what it is can neither be supplied by, nor be effective without, the rules and the knowledge of the underlying science.

Manifestly, although there is an important distinction between knowledge about a subject and knowledge about the practice of its dependent art, the two are not unrelated. Many critics of theorizing

---

[2] For example, the third law of motion: To every action there is an equal and opposite reaction.

[3] "Imperative" is used here in the practical sense, not in the grammatical sense. For examples, see the use of "should" in *A Tentative Statement of Accounting Principles* (American Accounting Association), in the *Recommendations on Accounting Principles* (Institute of Chartered Accountants in England and Wales), and in *An Introduction to Corporate Accounting Standards* (Paton and Littleton); and see the use of straight imperatives in the inductively derived principles of Professor Littleton in his *Structure of Accounting Theory*.

[4] "A Scientific Pattern for Accounting Theory", see p. 356, *ante*.

believe there is no such relationship; there are few more satisfying (but less effective) ways of condemning a proposal than to describe it as theoretical. Nevertheless, the principal qualification for entry to most professions is a demonstrable skill based on ample knowledge of the underlying science or sciences, i.e., an ample knowledge of the appropriate theory. This knowledge is expected to inform the judgement of the practitioner, enabling him to recognize particular cases as instances of significant large categories. Without the orderly array of connected generalizations of which the underlying sciences consist, the practitioner of a complex art would be reduced entirely to *ad hoc* solutions of his problems. Knowledge of the subject (theory) gives cohesion and consistency to practice. It cannot eliminate measures which have no other justification than expedience or custom, but as knowledge increases and becomes more widely accepted among practitioners, they may take steps to minimize the dependence of the art on rules and conventions which are inconsistent with reason.

Accounting Knowledge and Art

Accounting is in precisely the same position as any other practical art. The field of practice is apparent. The practitioner is expected to have certain skills. The standards, rules and conventions of practice are well known, and are admitted by the present writer to be essential to practice. It is not so apparent that accounting is also a subject of study and that its study can be pursued in exactly the same manner as other scientific inquiries. The reason why this is not apparent can only be guessed; it is possible that preoccupation with the art and a predilection to lay down rules has inhibited free inquiry: it is possible that the fact that scientific study and practice are two distinct disciplines has not been recognized; and it is possible that the course of preparation for entry to the profession has not included some study of a scientific nature which would awaken the curiosity or provide the logical tools for a rigorous study of the foundations of the art. This is, of course, simply speculation; but it is perhaps the same kind of speculation as caused Mr. Priestley to observe: "Nobody in his senses would expect a born seer to *do*. That much is generally acknowledged. But it is equally ridiculous to suppose that a dashing and triumphant doer can really *see*."[5]

What then is the body of propositions which may be said to be the subject underlying the practice of accounting? It has no name unless "accounting" is used (as it has been hitherto in this article) both of the subject and of practice. And what are its contents? Its contents will comprise a set of statements, in the indicative mood preferably, dealing with the relationships between concepts describing common accounting or business phenomena and operations. In seeking a point of departure it is reasonable to consider other subjects which bear reasonably close relationships with accounting. The closest and most obvious is economics. Some accountants, when confronted with this

---

[5] J. B. Priestley, "Thoughts in the Wilderness", *The New Statesman and Nation*, 12 March 1955.

suggestion, demur on the ground that economics is concerned with national aggregates and not with the individual undertakings with which accountants are concerned. This objection, however, can only arise from misunderstanding of the content of economics. Economists are concerned, it is true, to view economic events and phenomena from the viewpoint of whole communities; but as broad economic changes and major economic developments occur through the myriad contributing acts of individuals, business firms and other organizations, economists are equally interested in the ways in which persons, firms and other organizations act. A considerable part of the theory of economics is devoted to examination of such acts. Professor Robbins' definition[6] is indicative of the breadth of the subject: "Economics is the science which studies human behaviour as a relationship between ends and scarce means which have alternative uses."

It is not unreasonable to expect that economics may throw some light on, or provide some basic concepts which will be useful in the study of, accounting. But it is not the only subject to which accounting may be related. It may transpire that some of the conclusions of psychology, political science and jurisprudence are also necessary and useful. Further examples are not necessary. It is sufficient to stipulate that the scientific study of accounting, as a subject, requires the application of scientific methods to observable phenomena, and that, in carrying out such a study, the student (or theorist) is free to observe and to adopt the conclusions of any other scientific study as he requires them. The study would proceed from observations, from the conclusions of other sciences, or from assumptions, to build up by logical processes, a body of propositions which is self-consistent and consistent with reality. Whenever the deduced propositions lack self-consistency and consistency with reality, this lack will be regarded as indicative of flaws in the original observations or assumptions, or of flaws in the argument. Further study will be devoted to eliminating these flaws.

The article, "Blueprint for a Theory of Accounting", was an attempt to sketch the form which such a theory would take. It sets out four propositions as a basis from which to proceed:—

(a) Certain organized activities are carried out by entities which exist by the will or with the co-operation of contributing parties.

(b) These entities are managed rationally, that is, with a view to meeting the demands of the contributing parties efficiently.

(c) Statements in monetary terms of the transactions and relationships of the entity are one means of facilitating rational management.

(d) The derivation of such statements is a service function.

No claim is made that these propositions are themselves a sufficient basis; however, after considering some others, the conclusion was reached that these are perhaps the most general and the most fruitful.

---

[6] *The Nature and Significance of Economic Science,* London, Macmillan, p. 16.

The general form of these statements is deliberately selected in the belief that some conclusions of wide application could be reached. Two substantial uniformities, observable in the real world, provide the basis for the belief that the subject, accounting, includes a number of general propositions, i.e., some general theory. These uniformities are (i) the use of accounting information in organizations having vastly different purposes and legal or social forms, and (ii) the substantial similarity of method in all these cases. The general theory to which these observations point would consist of propositions applicable to all situations in which the art of accounting is found to be practised, propositions equally pertinent to accounting for private householders, unincorporated and corporate business firms, governments, nations, fiduciaries and eleemosynaries. Obviously these propositions would only be concerned with the broadest features of accounting, but the mere fact that diverse entities can be treated without distinction for some purposes is suggestive of similarities which would not otherwise be apparent. The general propositions in contemplation provide the foundation for all more specific or elaborative propositions.

The "Blueprint" article proceeded to suggest, however, that there are many critical differences between the organizations which use accounting information, differences so great as to require different sets of concepts and propositions (different theoretical models) for each distinct class of organizations or entities. There will thus be a theory of business accounting, a theory of governmental accounting, etc., each depending on the general theory or including the general propositions, but each dealing also with differences with which obviously no blanket generalization could cope. Further, even within the "entity" categories suggested in the last sentence, there may be alternative propositions to cope with materially different features, not of entities themselves, but of the real world in which entities operate.

Illustrative Theorem

Point may be given, to this very broad description of the way in which the subject may develop, by an example. Take as the proposition to be proved: "In the case of continuing ventures, periodical accounting is a necessary condition of rational action." The proposition is limited to continuing ventures; it therefore falls outside, though it depends on, the postulated general theory. And as it alludes to accounting, the kinds of action contemplated are those having measurable financial effects or consequences.

Proof. Let $p, q, r, \cdots$ represent different classes of acts having measurable financial effects or consequences; and let the subscripts $_{1, 2, 3, \ldots}$ indicate acts at different times.

Every continuing entity operates by means of successive acts

$$\begin{array}{llll} p_1 & p_2 & p_3 \cdots & \\ q_1 & q_2 & q_3 \cdots & \\ r_1 & r_2 & r_3 \cdots & \quad \text{(axiom)} \\ \cdots & \cdots & \cdots & \end{array}$$

Every such act is an action taken in the expectation of promoting the entity's objectives (basic proposition b, stated above).

Every such act changes the entity in some respect (axiom).

Acts of the subject entity and of all other entities change the environment of action (axiom).

Therefore, no act p_1 is necessarily identical with any subsequent act p_2, due to changes in the entity or in its environment or in the relationship between the entity and its environment, the objectives remaining constant.

Now rational action is also action taken with knowledge of the relationship between the entity and its environment at the time of action (by definition of rational action).

Part of this knowledge is knowledge of the financial relationship of the entity with its environment (axiom).

The financial relationship between the entity and its environment may be determined from statements in monetary terms, i.e., from its accounting records (basic proposition c).

Therefore it is a necessary condition of rationality in any act, $p, q, r, \cdots$ that such an act is taken with knowledge of the financial relationship of the entity with its environment at that time.

However, let it be assumed that no single act $p, q, r, \cdots$ is an act having a material effect on the entity, but that the cumulative effect of all acts $p, q, r, \cdots$ over the period y is material (assumption).

It follows that it is a necessary condition of rational action that the actor shall have knowledge of the financial relationship of the entity with its environment at a time not further distant from the time of action than the interval y.

Q.E.D.

A similar theorem may be devised to prove that periodical revenue accounts are also necessary.

This theorem is to be considered only as an illustration. The argument is set out fully and the nature of each statement is indicated in order that its quality may be examined. The conclusion is simply a consequence of the stipulated character of the entity and the observable facts of operation. There is only one assumption, and that appears to be a reasonable one. The conclusion is stated in the positive form. There are no imperatives or directives. The conclusion is thus a piece of knowledge. The scientist, or theorist, as such, is unconcerned whether practitioners use it or ignore it. Neither action on the part of the practitioners can prove or disprove it. But practitioners may well be expected to have learned it.

Now, it may seem that the example chosen is unfortunate. Some may say, "Everyone agrees that periodical accounting is necessary, so that the above demonstration adds nothing to practice." But for people to agree that something is necessary is one thing; to prove that the same thing is necessary is another. That people have agreed to prepare accounting summaries periodically is signified by the use of the term "convention" in respect of the period concept[7]. But once the necessity of periodical statements is proved, it is no longer necessary simply to agree. A principle is established; the practitioner may then know that his customary or conventional procedure is correct in principle (i.e., in theory), and that seems to the writer to be a clear gain to the practitioner. What he once did by convention, he can now go on doing with conviction.

There was another reason for selecting an accepted part of the practice of accounting as an illustration. The theorem demonstrates that one of the accepted notions can be supported by rigorous argument. Others, many others, may be supported by similar theorems. Using the same procedure, however, it is also possible to prove that some of the accepted practices are illogical, or without logical foundation. In the "Blueprint" article it was hinted that, given the fact that over time price levels change, it could be proved that for continuing business ventures, accounting statements which incorporate adjustments to reflect the change are a necessary condition of rational action[8]. This conclusion, again, is simply a piece of knowledge unless it can be demonstrated to be erroneous; and as a piece of knowledge it can neither be proved nor disproved by action on the part of practitioners as such. One who seeks to disprove it must have recourse to the same process of inquiry and argument by which the proof was derived.

It is the writer's view that a theory of accounting can be built up along these lines. Such a theory will be internally consistent, since it proceeds by logical steps to reasoned conclusions. It will also be consistent with the characteristics of the entities for which accounts are kept and with the environment in which those entities operate, since its premises will be realistic and its detail will be drawn from observation of the environment of action. . . .

---

[7] For example, Gilman, *Accounting Concepts of Profit,* Ch. 7; Paton and Littleton, *An Introduction to Corporate Accounting Standards*, p. 22.

[8] The proof is given in "The Formal Basis of Business Decisions", see p. 70, *ante,* though it is not set out as is the above theorem.

28

THE CONDITIONS OF RESEARCH IN ACCOUNTING*

There is a magic about the word "research" which makes it a prized appendage to the description of many kinds of activity. Its use even in the most trite or most obviously commercial connexion cannot be challenged for, like other words in the language, it has a wide range of possible meanings. But like any other currency, language is subject to Gresham's Law: bad usage drives out good. The consequence is that "research" may be used increasingly to dignify many inconsequential types of inquiry, the very ease and number of which may distract attention from the more fundamental types of inquiry for which it was once almost exclusively used. This is more likely to happen in fields in which there is no long tradition of research in the fundamental sense, and unless the possibility is kept constantly in mind there is little to prevent it from happening in accounting.

It is not intended by these observations to belittle inquiries which are narrow in extent or small in respect of the time and effort involved. Every general field of inquiry is made up of many smaller but related fields, any one of which may demand the time and attention of few or many workers, and knowledge in all these fields may be essential to the development of the general field. The history of all the sciences illustrates this. The need for caution arises rather from the possibility of inquiries being narrow in conception or lacking in relationships with contiguous fields.

The object of research is to promote knowledge. "Knowledge" may be used just as properly of know-how and of unconnected pieces of information as of the systematic statement of postulates, theorems and laws relating to broad aspects of human endeavor or experience. In research, "knowledge" is used in the latter sense; it has reference to knowledge about certain observable entities and relationships. To acquire knowledge about something is a process different from simply apprehending it. It requires the use of concepts denoting characteristics of events and things. The usefulness of a concept depends on the degree of completeness with which it denotes characteristics; to ensure its usefulness requires adequate and continued comparison of the concept with the apprehended thing. Thus, notwithstanding the frequently drawn distinction between theoretical and practical knowledge, all knowledge is necessarily connected to the apprehended ("real") facts of experience.

---

* First published in *The Journal of Accountancy,* Vol. 110, No. 6, December 1960, pp. 33-9.

The promotion of knowledge involves some or all of a series of operations; the stipulation of the limits of the field of inquiry; the statement of the fundamental irreducible postulates of the field; the observation of instances of the phenomena which fall within the field; the description of those phenomena in terms of their observable qualities; the postulation of concepts representing the phenomena and their qualities; the classification of phenomena; the deduction of relationships between postulates and derived concepts; the testing of such theorems by reference to the phenomena which the concepts represent; and, in respect of such conclusions as pass the test, the examination of alternative hypotheses for the purpose of demonstrating that the conclusion is the only one which is supported by the observable data. These operations embrace a number of methods of acquiring knowledge. They include the study, description and classification of observable things, an inductive or empirical process. They include the study of the implications of and relationships between the characteristics of observed things, a deductive process. They involve historical inquiry or examination of the sets of conditions under which particular ideas or methods were developed, used or rejected. Each method serves in its own way to fill out the knowledge of a subject. The feature that distinguishes all such inquiries as scientific is the attitude of doubt or scepticism with which they are pursued.

Fragmentary Nature of Present Knowledge

As a program for acquiring knowledge, this is a formidable prescription. Is it necessary to go to these lengths in accounting? It is imperative. Knowledge about accounting is altogether imperfect unless the whole range of phenomena (accounting entities, operations, etc.) and possible phenomena is systematically examined. It is only necessary to ask a limited number of questions to demonstrate how fragmentary is the content of present knowledge about accounting. Double-entry accounting is commonly taught and practised, but there are large groups of accounting entities which operate under different forms. Why? Accrual accounting is practised in many situations and is generally regarded as a norm; but cash accounting is used in some quite significant undertakings. What are the appropriate conditions, if any, for each? Depreciation is provided for on vastly different bases, for different undertakings in some countries and for all undertakings in different countries, and in some situations it is not provided for at all. What are the determining conditions for these varied practices? Cost is stated to be the proper basis for accounting for fixed assets, yet in some countries cost may be abandoned at the option of the undertaking, while in others blanket provisions permitting all companies to vary the base are made from time to time. How then, and in what circumstances, if any, is cost "proper"? Illustrations could be multiplied, but the point is that the literature of accounting does not provide unequivocal answers to such questions. It is not sufficient to say, in some cases, that the law so stipulates, or to say, in others, that a practice is generally accepted. Neither the law nor general acceptance proves or implies the validity, utility or relevance of a practice; these may only be ascertained by following the processes outlined in the previous paragraph.

Knowledge leads to economies in cerebration and in operation. Propositions from one area may be transferred to another area within the same field, without proceeding by the costly process of trial and error. But this can be done with skill only if the underlying conditions in each area and the relationship of the original propositions to those conditions are known. For example, from the utility of accrual accounting for business purposes it does not necessarily follow that for governmental purposes the same system is equally useful. Adequate knowledge also gives rise to the possibility of prediction. Changes in the conditions under which certain practices occur will suggest the appropriate modifications of practice, or given the same conditions it is possible to foresee and therefore to evaluate the probable consequences of a change in practice. Further, adequate knowledge gives a more assured basis for the control of an operation. Innovations may be tested, and accepted or rejected, in the light of established theory, whether they arise from the inventiveness of accountants, the evasiveness of administrators, or the resourcefulness of tax gatherers. It is impossible to present a solid front against any group seeking to make accounting serve special ends in the absence of a coherent and consistent body of ideas; it is even impossible to get accountants as a group to act consistently without a coherent and consistent framework.

The official statements and recommendations made by professional bodies in different countries have served and will continue to serve practitioners, inasmuch as they provide an official "norm" based on expert examination of specific difficulties. But the controversies some of these statements have generated indicate (and the need for occasional revision suggests, if it were not otherwise known) that there is no basic theoretical frame of reference. The superstructure is going up on a rather flimsy foundation. The American Institute of C.P.A.s' decision to sponsor research, at least in part of a fundamental nature, is timely. In a period in which the speed of processing information is rapidly increasing it is imperative that this should not be allowed to overshadow the importance of the quality of the product.

The Possibility of Scientific Study

The first condition of research in accounting is the belief that accounting can be studied scientifically. In what are commonly described as "the sciences" there is an accepted ideal attitude toward the subject-matter and there are established modes of operation. It is not generally believed that accounting can be studied in the same way, or that scientific modes are equally applicable. The barriers to such a belief are several.

In the first place, a distinction is sometimes drawn between the natural sciences in which the crude "facts" are natural phenomena independent of the persons studying them, and the social sciences in which the crude "facts" are the products of human invention in which the observers are inextricably implicated. But the subject-matter of natural science is not the group of things designated as electrons, atoms, molecules and organisms; it consists of ideas about, descriptions of, and concepts relating to physical things, and these concepts are dependent on the knowledge and insight of the researchers who put them forward. It is just as possible to have ideas about, descriptions of, and concepts relating to any product of human invention; sociologists may study society, political scientists may study government, accountants may study accounting—all scientifically.

Second, it is strongly believed that accounting, having been developed by practitioners out of practical problem situations, is different in essence from the sciences in which development has long been sought from the laboratories, far removed from practical problems. The implied difference rests on a further misconception. Most sciences had their inauspicious beginnings in the practical problems of field workers, and in their most highly developed and purest form they are still rooted in questions which arise out of the "real life" problems of the field to which they are related. The study of atoms and atomic structure may have seemed once to be pure research, but the product of this study is now of world-wide practical significance. The essential difference between practitioners and researchers lies not in the subjects they deal with, but in their methods of studying whatever they study.

Third, it is held that lack of precision in measuring, and in devising measures, in accounting makes the subject-matter intractable to the methods adopted in the natural sciences. This again rests on misconceptions—two of them. Astronomers, physicists and biologists have been confronted with a variety of phenomena which have at some stage seemed to be intractable to the methods of inquiry and analysis then known. In such difficulties, however, are found the very tests of the state of knowledge and the impetus to seek better understanding. Further, it is not the quantitative element, or the degree of precision in measuring phenomena which distinguishes science or scientific inquiry; rather, it is the rigor with which a knowledge of qualities, states and relationships is pursued that entitles a study to be called scientific. Though precision is necessary and desirable in formulating scientific concepts, the same precision is not expected in their adaptation to practice: Pharmacists, engineers, architects invariably incorporate safety or contingency factors in their applications of basic scientific knowledge.

In short, accounting differs in no material particular from other fields which are the subject of scientific study. Not all the methods of the natural sciences may be appropriate to the study of accounting, but the attitude toward the subject-matter can be essentially the same.

The Field of Inquiry

The first step is the stipulation of the limits of the field of inquiry. In accounting, the limits have been considered to be much narrower than is justified. For this the definitions of accounting have been responsible. Accounting is, fundamentally, a means of economic calculation, and accounting statements are used primarily by persons operating in markets ("market" being understood in the broad sense of a process by which goods, services and ideas are exchanged for an actual or constructive price).

Three things follow. First, study of the subject requires some knowledge of the ways in which people act, and some knowledge of the goals they pursue by means of their actions. Such knowledge is the special province of psychology or sociology. The research accountant does not have to be an expert in these or other fields, but he should recognize that they impinge on his own, and be prepared to look to them for the light they may throw on his own. Second, the study of accounting requires some knowledge of means of economic calculation in general, and of the nature of the markets through which people act. Lacking this basic economics it is possible to assume that all markets are the same and that any given form of calculation is equally relevant to all operators, and this may lead to extravagant claims about the universality of the application of the given method. Third, the study of accounting requires some knowledge of the function of language as a means of communication, of information processing systems and of communication theory. Lacking this it is quite possible to adopt concepts and devise systems which fail to serve the basic function; and it is possible to assume erroneously that the outputs of a system are uniquely determined by the objective inputs.

From these considerations emerges a second condition: The field shall not be limited to the ostensible products of the practice of accounting; it shall be considered as co-extensive with all human action in its economic aspects.

The Irreducible Postulates

It is commonly supposed that the irreducible postulates of the field will be few in number. They may be, but it is unwise to suppose at the outset that they will be.

The search for postulates extends to the boundaries of the field, where accounting affects action and is itself affected by economic and social conditions. The postulates put forward will depend on the insight and breadth of view of researchers. If one restricts his attention to accounting for corporate business in the United States of America, he is limiting inquiry in important respects, but even to describe fully the postulates of such an accounting may require more propositions than is supposed. To do the same for each different country and for each different kind of entity (merchants, fiduciaries, eleemosynaries, etc.) would require multiplication of such propositions. A critical question is whether the study of accounting should be limited geographically or institutionally. It may be convenient; one or few such areas may be as much as one person can handle. But unless the widest possible coverage of the subject-matter is obtained it will not be known whether the accepted postulates are simply incidents of the cases examined or whether they are irreducible. One may ask, are the postulates of accounting for sole traders and for business corporations the same, or likely to be the same? And one may pose the same questions for private business organizations and governments, for business organizations under capitalism and their counterparts under socialism. The superficial appearance of diversity may represent real differences and require different postulates, or may simply represent variations on a theme for which common postulates are sufficient.

Further, the "irreducible" postulates at any time may become intermediate concepts at a later time. In the light of further knowledge it may be possible to devise more satisfactory basic concepts. To recognize this is to forestall the expectation of a system of ideas which will be adequate for an indefinite future time. But any new theory must embrace and explain more satisfactorily what has been covered by previously accepted theory.

A third condition of research in accounting, therefore, is recognition of the varied sources of postulates and of the possibility that increased knowledge and insight may lead to the postulation of concepts of greater utility.

A fourth condition of research in accounting is that there shall be no limits to the types of accounting to be observed.

In haste to produce some results, some conclusions from a study, attention may be directed to the kind of accounting which seems to be common in the limited area being considered. But it is quite possible that different methods applied in another area may have features which also should be considered. For example, has the statement of affairs prepared in bankruptcy proceedings any relationship to the balance sheet prepared in the ordinary course of business? Or, has the method of calculating the feasibility of a contemplated operation any relevance for accounting once the decision has been made to undertake it? The researcher should be free of preconceived notions about the relevance or utility of any accepted or common procedures, free to consider all possible procedures on their merits. To do this requires an abundance of examples of actual and potential methods, methods used at different times, methods used in different places, methods used by different types of organization, methods proposed but not adopted—all properly related to the conditions and circumstances for which they were designed.

Further, the phenomena to be observed are not accounting methods only. They include the variety of entities for which accounts are kept, including entities of types which no longer exist; the varied transactions and events which affect entities; and the varied environmental conditions—economic, legal and political—and in particular the authorities (textbook writers, theorists, jurists, and organizations) which have or may have influenced the methods of accounting which have been adopted.

It will be apparent that accounting is being viewed as a body of knowledge without spatial restraints. And is not this proper? Other sciences are not confined by political boundaries, though their applications in different countries may take different directions.

Similarly, it is reasonable to conceive a general body of accounting knowledge, international in character, although its application in different places may be subject to specific conditions there operating.

Observation and description may seem to go hand in hand. But it is a commonplace that a given object has differing appearances according to the point of observation. Descriptions of the same thing (accounting operation, entity, relationship) may therefore differ as the point of view of the observer is more or less adequately informed. (How frequently do the uninformed say of a piece of property, "that is not an asset, it's a liability"!) It is necessary that descriptions be adequate: No description should be considered adequate unless it exhaustively denotes the characteristics of observed phenomena.

Observed phenomena are so rich in variety that there is always a temptation to reduce the variety by over-simplification. If description is incomplete, the range of possible concepts is correspondingly limited. Concepts representing actual things observed may include not only the qualities directly apprehended, but also qualities inferred or imagined. The latter are no less important than the former. They may be more so. A quality or relationship unobservable at one time may nevertheless later become observable, perhaps only because the fertile imagination can postulate more possible qualities and relationships than the limited powers of observation or the limited observable phenomena can yield. Chemistry, physics and astronomy provide well-known examples of the fruitfulness of hypotheses in filling gaps in the body of existing knowledge. Another condition of research, therefore, is that there shall be freedom for the mind to range over fancies as well as facts in seeking concepts which most effectively denote the qualities and relationships of the phenomena in the field.

The Hierarchical Structure of Knowledge

Adequate description makes possible the classification of observed things. Classification may, for certain purposes, or at certain stages in the growth of knowledge, be the terminal operation. Concepts derived from simple observation represent a low level of abstraction. Classes represent a higher level. The very discovery of classes suggests that there may be still more comprehensive concepts.

In every field it is possible to envisage a hierarchy of levels of abstraction, at its base the numerous observable entities and relationships, at its apex one or a few generalizations which comprehend all things appearing in the base. In between there are successive levels of generalization, each more inclusive than the one below but less general than the one above. The generalizations at any level provide the framework for specific propositions at the next lower level, and are in turn specific statements about which propositions at the next higher level may be formulated. The notion that a body of knowledge may be "structured" in this way may be challenged; one may say the operations designed to effect certain ends are so diverse that no formal classification or abstraction can be devised to meet the variety of experiences undergone or innovations developed in pursuit of those ends. It may be true that no satisfactory abstraction has been developed to cope with a given set of facts at any time; but to imply that none can be developed is to disregard the evidence of the history of science.

Although a comprehensive set of statements in any field may exhibit such a structure, there is no set pattern through which it may develop. In accounting, among the basic observable things are procedures and routines developed to meet economic needs. They may arise or have arisen independently as the solutions of many separate persons to similar problems. Only when a uniform basis for discussion or comparison is required may the many concurrent solutions be rationalized and a common method emerge. The common method arises from the (more fundamental) characteristics of transactions and events and their relationship to action. In other fields the postulation of general concepts may precede the discovery of basic phenomena; an example is the deduction of the nature and path of the planet Neptune from hypotheses relating to planetary motion. Progress toward a body of knowledge may thus proceed from less general to more general propositions, or in the opposite direction, or in both directions concurrently.

The importance of indicating these possibilities for the extension of knowledge lies in the fact that often, in accounting, general rules are developed at intermediate stages in the hierarchy without adequate exploration of the more general field into which they are to fit or of the range of specific cases to which they are intended to apply. Rules are developed in an *ad hoc* fashion; in the absence of a comprehensive set of self-consistent theoretical propositions to which novel situations can be referred, inconsistencies may arise. This may readily happen where the rule-making bodies are diverse, authoritarian, and technically inexpert (legislative and judicial authorities fall in this category), or where time does not permit exhaustive analysis of problems to be made before a course of action must be determined. Diverse provisions and notions relating to depreciation allowances, differences of opinion on cost or value as a basis of accounting, differences in allegiance to absorption and direct costing, and similar disagreements may continue to confuse until the general framework of accounting as a body of knowledge receives more attention.

In brief, the discussion of ways and means, and the discussion of general concepts to which basic entities and operations are related, are quite different levels of discourse. A further condition of research therefore is the recognition of a hierarchical structure of ideas, however imperfectly that structure may be discerned or described at any time.

Derived Concepts and Propositions

Beyond the empirical level of observation, description and classification, the subject of discourse becomes, exclusively, the concepts found to be useful and necessary for the theory or theories expounded. Those concepts have meaning only in their setting, though they necessarily have counterparts in the realities about which they are postulated. A deductive theory involves the relating of concepts in significant ways: The outcome is a logically connected set of propositions, a body of theorems.

Two things are required. Primarily, concepts need to be adequately defined. There is room for considerable improvement here. Though a number of terms expressive of certain general notions are employed in the theoretical literature, their exact denotations are often left to the imagination. Stewardship, continuity, objectivity, are examples of a numerous breed. Secondly, formal demonstration of the connexion between concepts is necessary. The many lacunas in stated cases will only become apparent when the laborious process of linking propositions is regarded as a basic task. Those who contend that "it is a condition of rational action that statements of financial position be expressed in terms of present values" or that "accrual accounting is the appropriate method of accounting for governmental undertakings" might be expected to demonstrate the procedure by which their conclusion is reached. Only if the procedure is laid bare can the validity of the conclusion or the propriety of the premises be examined by others or compared with the process by which contrary conclusions are reached. The importance of adequate definition and formal argument must be recognized.

Testing of Propositions

That a conclusion has been reached by careful argument from antecedent propositions (axiomatic or derived) is not enough; it must be tested by reference to the phenomena represented by the concepts it requires. Thus, for example, the proposition that "cost is the proper basis for accounting for fixed assets", must not only be shown to follow from antecedent propositions; it must also face the test of practice. Such testing is not always easy, for the facts of practice are complex, particularly where it is overlaid with laws and regulations designed for purposes other than the efficient administration of an organizational unit. The methods of scientific verification are well known. In the above case it would be useful to consider whether there were any times at which or places in which alternative bases were deemed to be proper and on what grounds. Every deviation from the cost basis, every expression of business opinion in criticism of that basis, every practice which serves to make good deficiencies of the cost basis, provides a test; and the test is not at the level of expert practice, but at the level of business operation. What is sought is not evidence of agreement on a formula by experts, but evidence of disagreement between the proposition and the real events and relationships its adoption is expected to influence. In short, after a proposition is established by argument from postulates, the next critical step is to attempt to disprove it.

Postulates and Testing of Alternatives

The process of comparison with other times, places and conditions is analogous to the laboratory testing of hypotheses in the natural sciences. Experimentation in the course of practice is difficult and costly, and is likely to be quite inconclusive. Accountants in any field of practice are under the constant necessity of producing some information in limited time; they can seldom afford the time to re-process the information in an alternative manner. Even if they do so, it is impossible to disentangle the effects on information users of the customary information and information in a new form or of a new quality; for a person informed by information of one kind has already become a different person (he has undergone an additional experience), and his reaction to information of another kind is conditioned by that prior knowledge. Further, since accounting is practised in a social matrix, the elements of which (habits, laws, regulations) cannot either be altered or held constant for the purpose of testing a new idea, the conclusions from any attempt to experiment with accounting ideas are likely to be vitiated by the numerous concurrent extraneous influences. And finally, the typical practitioner as practitioner is mentally geared to action, not to deliberate, critical, exploratory and tentative cerebration; he requires formulas and procedures which will work, however imperfect they may be on theoretical grounds; his tests are likely to be past experience rather than theoretical rigor.

These considerations indicate still another condition of research. Derived propositions shall be tested by reference to observable general characteristics of the field in which they are to be applied. In specific practical situations, the variables are too numerous for experimentation to be fruitful; hence, the necessity of proof by reference to general characteristics. The appropriate attitude for such testing is disbelief or at least doubt; the wish to prove a case is often father to a proof; the greatest possible freedom from any such wish is the appropriate frame of mind for testing propositions.

Beyond this point there is still room for doubt. Conclusive demonstration of the validity or propriety of a proposition depends on showing that no alternative proposition will serve equally well. Such alternatives may appear from cross comparisons of the accounting methods adopted in different places and circumstances; they may arise simply from exercises of the imagination; they may arise from reconsideration of the basic axioms or the impact of advances in associated fields of knowledge. The final step is, therefore, the postulation of alternatives and their examination by reference to the same tests.

In brief, the above prescriptions contemplate that, in an program of research, (a) there shall be no admitted authorities; (b) there shall be no temporal limits to inquiry; (c) there shall be no territorial limits to inquiry; (d) there shall be no limits to imaginative thinking; (e) there shall be no limits such as are implied in the necessity of action; and (f) there shall be no limits such as may be implied in allegiance to the policies (other than the policy of promoting knowledge) of organizations to which researchers are related.

Factual and Normative Problems

There are two general types of problem to which the methods of scientific inquiry might be directed. The first is: What is the present state of accounting and by what processes has it reached that state? A descriptive factual theory is necessary for this. Neither the description of accounting practice nor of the processes which have produced it is simple; practices are not uniform and development has taken place under the influence of an extensive and varied range of forces. But both are necessary to an understanding of present practice as such.

The second problem is: What form *should* accounting take? This appears to involve questions of value, whereas the first problem is limited to questions of fact. The question seems to require an answer from a particular point of view; is there then a multiplicity of answers, one for each possible point of view?

It may seem that, confronted with such questions, generalization is impossible. Nevertheless, it is quite possible, given a point of view, to apply the same kind of rigorous analysis to the factual content of the class of cases to which the point of view has reference, as is required to examine problems of fact where no problems of value arise. There may, of course, still be a number of competing or conflicting normative theories.

But is the appearance of a value question illusory? Admittedly the objectives, wants, tastes of persons and organizations differ; but given any set of objectives, wants, tastes (some such set is implicit in the adoption of any person or organization as a point of reference for accounting operations), the problem of accounting is to inform adequately (but subject to the limits of accounting) the actions by which objectives are pursued or wants and tastes are satisfied. Wherever there is an economic problem, there is an accounting problem. The problem of serving wants efficiently is the basis for the demand for information, of which accounting information is a significant class; but the problem of serving wants efficiently is not itself an accounting problem. The study of economic systems and the study of information processing systems are different in character, though the two are closely linked in their concern with economic events and transactions. The linking of accounting to economizing or optimizing may remove the subjective or value element from the question as to what form accounting should take. It should be possible to derive, in answer, a unique system of ideas of general application and validity.

The processes outlined above may have the appearance of remoteness from daily business problems—as proposals for a program of research in accounting, they may seem to be highfalutin' nonsense. Such a judgement would be mistaken. In so far as these processes demand an ample supply of facts, both for the purpose of suggesting fruitful propositions and for the purpose of testing conclusions, they are tied irrevocably to practical problem situations. In so far as they demand ample definition and thorough analysis, they would avoid the facile generalizations which now cloud instead of throwing light on real difficulties. To become more practical it is necessary to become more theoretical. There are still the problems of converting theoretically satisfactory systems of ideas to practically feasible systems of operation, but knowledge of what is required gives direction and significance to the task.

To stipulate that accounting may be studied the better by drawing on the methods of the sciences is not simply to propose for it a higher status; it is rather to indicate that extensiveness of view and rigor in analysis will yield more practically useful knowledge than *ad hoc* deliberation on the limited aspects of accounting which from time to time force themselves on public or professional consciousness.

29

WHY BOTHER WITH POSTULATES?*

Accounting has frequently been described as a body of practices which have been developed in response to practical needs rather than by deliberate and systematic thinking. Thus: "In one important respect book-keeping differs from other sciences, in that it is not in the least theoretical, but essentially and fundamentally practical. It is based upon expediency, and upon the actual needs and requirements of everyday life. It was invented because man wanted it, because he found that he could not get on without it. It is essentially utilitarian. It is not the result of the work of *dilletanti*, of men who conceived some theory and labored to prove the truth of it."[1] The view thus represented has persisted in various forms, such as: "Accounting is not formulated with reference to, nor does it stand on, general truths or the operation of natural or general laws."[2]

In one sense such statements convey an idea of the way in which accounting rules and procedures have been developed. There has been little regard for an orderly and systematic formulation. Multiple solutions have been put forward and adopted for many specific accounting problems. In another sense such statements are confused and confusing. For, if accounting is utilitarian there must have been some concept or some theory of the tests which must be applied in distinguishing utilitarian from non-utilitarian procedures. And, if rules are not formulated with reference to general laws or ideas of some kind then it is quite pointless to speak of rules and to write textbooks about them. It is largely because the tests of "utilitarian-ness" and the general ideas or laws which underlie accounting rules have not been made explicit that the body of accounting practices now employed contains so many divergent and inconsistent rules. Even rules which have been adopted, and recommendations which have been made, after considerable discussion over the past 30 years exhibit indeterminacies, divergencies and inconsistencies. The application of good intentions and long deliberations in an *ad hoc* setting cannot free practice of these features.

Recognition of this has given rise to the belief that some rigorous and extensive examination of accounting is necessary[3] and to demands

---

* First published in *Journal of Accounting Research*, Vol. 1, No. 1, Spring 1963, pp. 3-15.

[1] Arthur H. Woolf, *A Short History of Accountants and Accountancy*, London, Gee & Co., 1912, pp. xxix, xxx.

[2] C. A. Smith and J. G. Ashburne, *Financial and Administrative Accounting*, New York, McGraw Hill Book Company, Inc., 1955, p. 2.

[3] Leonard Spacek, "The Need for an Accounting Court", *The Accounting Review*, July 1958.

that such an examination should be undertaken[4]. The response of the Special Committee on Research Program of the American Institute of Certified Public Accountants to all this is singular in that it envisaged a program in which attention would be directed initially to the "postulates" of accounting[5]. Reactions to the product of such an inquiry are likely to be extremely diverse, for an examination of basic assumptions is not the kind of thing which falls within the common and regular experience of practitioners or teachers. Although there are some important differences, there are also some important similarities between an inquiry of this nature and the solution of practical day-to-day problems. It is the present purpose to explore some of these for the light that may be thrown on the close link between what appears to be a quite theoretical pursuit and the exigencies of professional practice.

Practice and Research: Similarities and Differences

An everyday problem, no matter how extensive, is circumscribed by a host of details which lead or confine the efforts of a practitioner. These include the specific characteristics of the firm considered at the time, and its specific problem at that time; the general standards of practice or methods available for solving similar problems at that time; and the amount of time available and its cost to the client. It is a matter of experience that different practitioners confronted with the same problem will offer different solutions—not invariably, perhaps, but often enough to suggest that any given solution is no more than a hypothesis. In effect each says: "That is my best advice; try it that way and see how it works out." If the proposed solution works satisfactorily no one says: "That was a sound hypothesis", nor even, "That was a lucky guess". The matter is closed. If the proposed solution does not work satisfactorily, some other solution is tried—another hypothesis. In fact, by virtue of the first trial the situation may have changed, and when further advice is sought by the client, the practitioner has a slightly different problem to solve. The first piece of advice is not then seen as an unsound hypothesis, or even as a hypothesis at all. In any event, the constant modification of advice and adaptation of practices and policies are the means by which business behavior is geared to circumstances.

Every new set of circumstances creates a new problem in a new setting, providing the opportunity to choose new assumptions and avoiding the need for consistency in those assumptions from one situation to the next; for what is required is a practicable and acceptable solution to one problem at a time. When a practitioner has a number of clients or has any one client over a long period, he should (and most do) take steps to see that there is a measure of uniformity, or that there are no gross inconsistencies, in the advice he gives and

---

[4] Alvin R. Jennings, "Present-Day Challenges in Financial Reporting", *The Journal of Accountancy,* January 1958.

[5] Report of the Special Committee, *The Journal of Accountancy,* December 1958.

the reports he gives on annual statements. But the range of clients of any practitioner is limited and every task he undertakes has a definite set of technical, temporal or institutional limits.

An inquiry into the postulates and principles of accounting has no such limits. From this, difficulties arise, both in carrying out the inquiry and in evaluating the products received. Ideally a statement of postulates or principles will be sufficiently comprehensive to provide the ground rules for solving problems in all specific situations in which people prepare or use accounting information. In other words, the person who seeks out postulates or principles is endeavouring to provide a general solution to the whole series of specific problems which may and do confront practitioners. To imagine or devise propositions which cover all conceivable situations is a difficult task because it is open-ended. It is possible to seek less comprehensive sets of postulates or principles, covering limited fields, such as, for example, corporate accounting, governmental accounting, fiduciary accounting. But even these are much more difficult to discover than is the framing of a solution to a particular problem. Once such a proposition has been put forward one or both of two things may befall it. It may be condemned "as a hypothesis" much more readily and by many more people than would condemn as a hypothesis a proposed solution to a practical problem. And it may be cause for considerable disappointment; for either it may appear to be so obvious that it is not worth stating, or it may appear to have no direct utility to the practitioner and give rise to irritation and impatience with the whole business.

These are natural reactions, even on the part of researchers, and more so on the part of practitioners. But a sense of history is some protection against disquiet. For all practical purposes, for over 2000 years men accepted the postulates of three-dimensional geometry; but the practical utility of non-Euclidean multi-dimensional geometries now extends through to the latest and most sophisticated and practical of scientific and business calculations. For 1300 years it seemed reasonable to postulate that animal and human anatomies are the same; it required the insight of Vesalius to question this assumption of Galen and to lay the foundation for scientific study of human anatomy. The number system using the base 10 has long been extolled for the economy it gives to calculation; but only by resort to the binary system has it been possible to do all the things which require the use of high-speed computers. There are literally thousands of examples of advances made in practically useful human knowledge by stating and questioning established hypotheses or their postulates, or by putting forward new hypotheses on the basis of postulates which appeared to be trivial or even ridiculous. There is no reason why accounting should be considered to be different in this respect from any other field of knowledge.

Analysis of Practices

As the last paragraph suggests, there are two ways of examining the foundations of accounting. By one of these, a statement is made descriptive of an operation; the description being full and complete, it is analyzed to dicover on what postulates the operation is based; finally these postulates are considered for the purpose of discovering whether they are reasonable by whatever criteria are deemed necessary to judge reasonableness. It will be useful to consider an example, say, the practice of setting down periodically the assets of a client or an employer, assigning dollar amounts derived by a diverse set of rules, and adding those amounts to arrive at a total. This is not all the accountant does periodically; but it is a full and complete description of one thing, one operation. The only objection that may be taken is in respect of the phrase "assigning dollar amounts derived by a diverse set of rules"; but a moment's thought will enable any accountant to recognize that different rules may be applied to different assets—to cash, the face amount; to receivables, the book value less a provision; to marketable securities, market value if less than cost; to inventories, cost on a L.I.F.O. basis; to fixed tangible assets other than land, cost less depreciation; to land, cost; to intangibles, a nominal sum—all these rules and many other variants of them are currently acceptable. Upon what postulates, then, is the above-mentioned operation based? There are at least two.

First. The assignment of money amounts, with the intention that they shall be added, is based on the assumption that there is a common quality which all items in the list possess and which may be represented by a money sum. That this is a reasonable postulate cannot be denied. But it is not the postulate appropriate to the above operation; for it has been shown that for seven types of asset there are at least seven methods, all different and all acceptable, of assigning money amounts; and by the description given to each of these methods, it is clear that the amounts assigned do not represent a common quality of the assets. The postulate underlying the use of a diverse set of rules is that the subject items do not have a common quality; or alternatively, if they have a common quality, it is not a quality with which accounting is concerned. Both of these possibilities lead in curious directions. Take the former—that assets do not have a common quality. The fact that they are called by a generic name—assets—signifies that they have some quality in common. This fact stands out above all the different methods of assigning money sums; assets have some quality in common. The first alternative postulate is therefore invalid. Take, now, the second that, if assets have a common quality, it is not a quality with which accounting is concerned. It may be observed here that this is the only postulate which can justify the use of a diverse set of rules for assigning money sums; but clearly it makes nonsense of all the discussion in accounting about common denominators. This matter will crop up again when the other postulate underlying the described practice is considered.

Second. The practice of summing the several money amounts assigned to specific assets postulates that such an addition can be performed legitimately. Legitimately means that the set of magnitudes can be added, and that when added they will give a total which has a definable meaning, and in particular a meaning of the same kind as the meanings of the individual magnitudes added. Now it is unlikely that anyone would propose, if he were asked to find the combined weight of two men, to add the weight of one man at sea level to the weight of an astronaut in orbit. If he did he would reach the nonsensical conclusion that the weight of two men is equal to the weight of one man. The sum of two weights means nothing unless they are measured by the same rule. Similarly, an uninformed person might easily take equal distances on a map drawn on Mercator's projection to represent equal longitudinal distances on the spherical surface of the earth; if he were to add two such distances and convert them on the scale given for distances at the equator, he too would obtain a meaningless result, for it would imply that the circumference of every circle obtained by cutting a sphere is the same as that of the circle obtained by cutting the sphere through its centre. What, then, about the procedure of adding the amount of cash held by a company today to the amount of cash paid 20 years ago for a piece of freehold land which the company still holds today? The practice is no less absurd than the other two examples. The two things cannot be added because they have not been converted to a common scale (unless a given amount of money can purchase the same amount of land as it could 20 years ago). And it follows that if they are added the result would be meaningless. As in the previous section the reasonable postulate stated at the outset is found to be inconsistent with the practice we are considering and we are forced to seek an alternative. The only alternative is this: that the process of addition can be applied to unlike things and that these may be added, regardless of their dissimilarity, to obtain a meaningful result. This, of course, is patently absurd.

In conclusion, of the only two postulates which are consistent with the described practice one makes nonsense of accounting and the other is absurd; therefore the practice is absurd; for there is no mental process by which two such propositions may yield a sensible result. It is quite useless to protest that this practice is "practical", or that it is time-honoured, or that it is a generally accepted practice; it has only become these things because men have not asked: upon what postulates is the practice based?

One of the purposes of this exercise was to show that every practice has certain postulates. Postulates are not some theoretical nonsense. They are the hard core of which practice is merely an expression. Every time a practitioner acts, in whatever capacity, he is acting on some postulates. He may not even know them; he may never have thought of them, for he may have accepted the weight of opinion or authority in place of personal conviction; but he cannot escape them. It is the great difference between a technician and a skilled craftsman that the latter knows the powers and limitations of his art. And these he knows because he has sought out the postulates underlying his operations; he has sought to discover the qualities of the materials through which his art is expressed and of the communities in which or about which he uses that art. The example of the previous section was selected because it is a widespread everyday practice, not simply a novel or ephemeral problem. It was analysed for the purpose of illustrating a method of inquiry into postulates or foundations which begins with known practices. It should not be supposed that every such analysis of a practice will reveal so starkly that there are flaws in the practice or its underlying ideas. But the consequence of proceeding this way is plain. No one likes his cherished habits to be lampooned, ridiculed or even criticized. What to one appears to be reasoned analysis appears to another to be an insolent, immoderate and irreverent attack on the establishment. A study which begins this way is likely to arouse animosity and resentment from the outset, and if it is more likely to be passionately rebuffed than dispassionately considered, the procedure is clearly impolitic. It will be dubbed "destructive criticism" and consigned to limbo or the waste basket.

But this procedure has also another flaw. If the inquirer is limited in his examination to practices which are already followed, the whole inquiry will be unnecessarily circumscribed. If "accounting" is the subject-matter, the scope of the inquiry should not be limited by present circumstances—one particular country, one particular decade, one particular class of organization. Nor indeed should it be limited to the practices of all countries, all historical times, or all classes of organization. For if the practices of one organization in one country at one time are circumscribed by traditional, legal or accidental factors, so is the sum of all practices of all organizations in all countries at all times. The inquirer should also be free to imagine forms of accounting which have not been tried, in exactly the same way as does a practitioner confronted with an entirely novel problem; in exactly the same way as people have "imagined" freely moving, self-powered road transport, synthetic fibres, telephonic communication, color T.V., before these things were used in practice. The only requirements or constraints should be that the outcome of a line of inquiry should be reached by logical steps, and that no patently absurd assumptions should be made. This leads to the second method of inquiring into the foundations of accounting, a method which begins, not by describing practices but, by discovering postulates which are useful.

Synthesis by Postulation and Reasoning

This method begins by selecting from the world of experience and reflection a set of ideas about things, which fall within the field of inquiry. If it is necessary these ideas are clarified by explicit definition, so that the correspondence between the ideas and the relevant aspects of the observable events and things they represent is established. Certain propositions are then set up which describe the relationships between the ideas or concepts thus derived, or rather the relationships which are postulated to exist. The implications of the ideas and the postulates are then worked out, the result being a set of theorems or conclusions about the events and things represented by the ideas and postulates. Postulates are thus propositions enunciated without proof —either because no proof can be given or because the assent of others to such propositions can be reasonably expected—and used in the derivation of other propositions. These latter propositions may culminate in a set of rules or prescriptions for doing something, such as keeping accounts and making summaries of results and position. If the set of rules and prescriptions is derived logically, reasonably, from the definitions and postulates, and if the result of applying those rules is something which is acknowledged to be useful, the postulates are confirmed, and the whole system of definitions, postulates, principles and rules will represent both a theory of and a method for producing the useful result. The proof of the pudding is in the eating, so to speak.

But what is a useful result? One may not judge the usefulness of a set of postulates, principles and rules by reference to the existing technical practices of practitioners or by generally accepted principles or procedures. Those practices themselves are the outcome of some judgements as to usefulness; but they may also be so hedged by conventions and expedients that usefulness has less than its share of influence. The existence of a practice is evidence that "it can be done"; it is not evidence of usefulness or of superiority over other possible practices, no matter how widely the practice may be found. The search for postulates is in the realm of the pursuit of useful knowledge, and, at every turn in the path to knowledge, history has proved generally accepted practices to be faulty, unreliable or incomplete and the ideas underlying them to be wrong, inadequate or inconsistent. That the earth is flat, that atoms are indivisible, that flying is only for the birds, that radio and television would reduce literacy, that pain is inevitable—all these are beliefs once widely held, beliefs which limited the practical pursuits of men until some individuals challenged their implicit assumptions and devised postulates which in due course gave men new knowledge and new practices.

The question of what is useful bedevils every inquiry, every science. And the typical answer of the scientist is: all knowledge is useful. By this he means that all propositions which put man in possession of more ideas about his environment or more ideas about his situation in that environment are useful. Now it may seem that the experimental sciences have the advantage of the social sciences here. For it is possible to test thoroughly the qualities of a new agricultural fertilizer, a new insecticide, a new paint, a new antibiotic, whereas it is not possible to test in any similar way the qualities of a new tax, a new form of city government or a new form of accounting. But the advantage is only an apparent advantage. Laboratory tests do not necessarily disclose all the consequences or even all the qualities of new products; they may have side effects which only become apparent over many years. Further, all knowledge, in the physical as well as the social sciences, is a matter of inference from statements put forward as descriptions of the phenomena under consideration, that is, from postulates.

Accounting, in common with other studies which relate to human behavior, has no recourse to experimental methods. Nevertheless there are two ways in which it is possible to determine whether any set of principles derived by logical processes from postulates are useful pieces of knowledge. It will appear that whichever of the two ways is adopted, practical experience and knowledge of acquaintance (i.e., knowledge of immediate perception and cognition as distinct from "book" knowledge) have much to do with any such determination.

The first way is to establish that the postulates are ample descriptions, for the purpose in hand, of the phenomena or events to which they relate. The process is simply an affirmation of the propriety of the postulates by skilled observers or by men of experience, preferably by both. It should be possible to reach agreement at this level. Given "the purpose in hand", the only room for difference of opinion arises from the word "ample". There is an enormous number of possible statements about the environment of accounting or about any aspect of it which can be affirmed. Not all of them will necessarily be useful in the sense that, taken together with others, they can be made to yield a conclusion. It is the particular problem of the researcher to ensure that he overlooks no possibly useful statement, and to select from all the statements about the environment those which will yield conclusions. Suppose one puts forward as a postulate the statement: Monetary calculation is concerned with market (or exchange) values. It should be possible to obtain agreement that this is or is not supported by observation and experience. If it is agreed that the statement is so supported, it is a potentially useful postulate. To give or withhold assent to such propositions is one of the functions of the voice of experience.

The next stage in deriving principles or rules is to draw out the implications of postulates, to link the bare statements in such a way that certain conclusions emerge. The process is the same, in kind, as men employ in the solution of any problem from a cross-word puzzle to the proof of an abstruse mathematical proposition. Given the same concern for care and rigor in reasoning, and the same level of skill, it should be possible for any person to assess the steps by which a conclusion is reached. Not necessarily the steps taken by the researcher in reaching the conclusion, because these involve initial insight, hesitation, subconscious reflection, re-examination of assumptions and eventual statement of the argument. By what personal processes is immaterial; at length he becomes able to state, step by step, an argument which can be assessed or tested by others. If it is agreed that the postulates are supported by observation and experience and if the steps in the argument are unobjectionable, the conclusion would appear to be unobjectionable.

The second point at which practical experience may bear on the whole process of deriving principles or methods from postulates is in testing the usefulness of the deduced result—in accounting this would mean testing the usefulness of the information flowing from a deduced method. This involves looking at the information from the point of view of all possible users for all possible purposes, but not from the point of view of the information processor, the accountant. For example, in the field of business accounting, if the current rate of return on invested funds is important to users, the product of a deduced method must be such that the rate can be derived, and that this derived rate is both a logical relationship and a mathematically valid relationship. If the expected rate of cash flow is important to users, the product of a deduced method should enable users to derive a useful idea of expected cash flow. If both rate of return and rate of cash flow are important to users, the product of a deduced method should enable both to be derived. If different classes of users are envisaged, and if any person may at a given time be simultaneously a member of several such classes, the product of a deduced method should be such that it meets the needs of all classes simultaneously. It is on the hypothetical part of each of the preceding sentences—the "if" clause—that professional men should be able to pass judgement, and, one would hope, uniform judgement.

Some Problems

In an examination of the propositions postulated by any person, or of the end result of argument from postulates, it is important to keep in mind that the purpose of deriving general statements is to cover situations in general. If it is postulated that "all men act reasonably" (whatever "reasonably" may mean), it is no criticism to assert that sometimes men act foolishly or without reason. Some men appear to do so, sometimes; but accounting is not for them at those times. If it is postulated that "privately owned business firms and corporations are motivated by the expectation of profit", it is no criticism to assert that some companies do not make profits. If it is postulated that "monetary calculation is concerned with market (or exchange) values", it is no criticism to assert that generally accepted accounting principles do not uniformly indicate market or exchange values; for it will be found that, for any operation intended in the market for money or goods, one calculates in terms of market or exchange values regardless of what his accounting system tells him. Generally, then no criticism of postulates or principles can be accepted simply because there are some cases in which they do not apply. In this respect there may be a difference between the natural and the social sciences. One instance may give rise to doubt about a theory in the natural sciences; but because the social sciences are concerned with classes of people rather than individuals, their postulates and conclusions have only to meet the general test: does this postulate or that conclusion amply describe or relate to this or that class of people or this or that group of people?

Two methods of inquiry into postulates have been considered. By one, the procedure is to discover the ideas which are implicit in an established practice and to consider whether those ideas appear to be consistent with the "facts of life" or the requirements of reason. By the other, the "facts of life" and human reason are used to build systems of ideas which are examined in the light of observation and experience to establish whether they yield something useful. Both methods should yield answers of the same kind, for it is impossible for reason to contradict reason. And ideally both methods are used as checks on the possibility of errors or omissions or plain bad argument. It should also be clear that the mental processes involved are the same as any intelligent person adopts if he deliberately attempts to solve any practical problem intelligently rather than by tossing a coin.

There is one further point to make. The method of defining one's terms, stating one's postulates and deducing a system from them does not suffer from the same disability as the method of seeking postulates from observable practices and submitting them to analysis. The latter, as we have said, may readily be dubbed "destructive criticism". The former is essentially constructive. One may, of course, say in a disparaging way that this is all pure theory. But to do so is simply to deny the power of human reason, including the reason of those who disparage reason.

From Postulates to Principles

There is no such thing as a set of postulates which is independent of a set of conclusions or principles or hypotheses. Postulates are only postulated for the purpose of reaching some conclusion. It is necessary in short to consider a whole system of postulates and a conclusion together. One may set down five or 50 or 500 potentially useful propositions as possible foundations for a conclusion; but if only three are necessary, all the rest are irrelevant to that specific conclusion; only three are postulates.

For any system of principles—say principles of accounting—there will be a series of separate sets of postulates, one set for each principle. Whether or not the system is internally consistent is of importance, for an internally inconsistent (i.e., contradictory) set of principles cannot be a clear guide to practice, nor is it satisfying to the intelligence. The whole system of principles may entail quite a large number of postulates, but if it is to be an internally consistent system, the postulates, however large in number, will necessarily be consistent (this is the test used above when dealing with the listing of assets). To repeat, neither postulates nor principles can be considered *in vacuo*. They are inevitably linked and they may only be evaluated as part of a system.

As an illustration the following is offered. A principle is stated: certain postulates necessary to establish it are set out and certain definitions of the terms used are given; by relating the postulates step by step the conclusion stated at the outset is reached.

Principle of Neutrality

The probability of optimal adaptation varies directly with the neutrality of accounting information.

1. Suppose a situation in which there is an actor and a processor of information on his behalf, so that acting and information processing are separate functions. (Postulate)
2. The state of satisfaction on the part of an actor, or action which procures it, will be called optimal adaptation. (Definition)
3. The independence of information with respect to any specific action will be called neutrality. (Definition)
4. Individuals have different systems of wants at any time. (Postulate)

5. The system of wants of any individual changes from time to time. (Postulate)
6. Satisfaction of an actor's system of wants at any time is the goal of and incentive to action. (Postulate)
7. The function of an information processor or processing system is to produce information relevant to action. (Postulate)
8. In the postulated situation 1 the processor will not know at any time what the present state of the actor's want-system is; or if he did know at some previous time, he will not know how far it has changed from that time to any other time. (From 4 and 5)
9. The processor is thus not able to anticipate what the next action of the actor will be. (From 8 and 6)
10. Therefore the greater the relevance of the information produced to all possible courses of action, the greater will be the possibility of optimal adaptation. (From 2, 7, 9)
11. Accounting information is one class of information available to an actor. (From 1)
12. From 8, 3 and 11 it follows that the probability of optimal adaptation on the part of an actor in the postulated situation 1 varies directly with the neutrality of accounting information.

Corollary: For even stronger reasons, the conclusion holds if the number of actors served by any financial statement is large and their interests are varied, for the information processor is removed from direct knowledge of the wants of any of them.

This principle is not to the writer's knowledge established at all in the literature of accounting; certainly not by the process adopted here. Yet it is an important and practical one. Apply for a moment the procedure of discovering the postulates underlying a stated operation, mentioned earlier in this paper. It is an established practice to publish one set of financial statements in respect of corporations in which it is known that the public and other institutions have equities, either as shareholders or as creditors. The only proposition which justifies this practice is: the information so published is equally useful to all parties in spite of their diverse interests. And this is simply a modified way of saying that the information is neutral with respect to the particular subsequent actions of all actors. The proposition is established from both directions! This should demolish the view, often asserted, but never found in practice, that companies should publish different financial statements for different classes of users (actors). The principle thus established in fact underlies a most important idea—the professional accountant's independence—an idea which has often been dogmatically stated, but the reason for which has never been proved by explicit argument. (It should be noted that the proposition discussed above has nothing whatever to say about the quality of the information contained in such statements; that is another matter altogether, requiring additional principles.)

What is a Postulate?

An attempt has been made to show by illustration what a postulate is. It will be seen on examination of all the statements described as postulates throughout this paper that none of them incorporates words or phrases which are peculiar to accounting. They are all descriptions of some thing, some event or some form of behavior found in the environment of accounting. Accounting has no justification whatever in itself. It has no rationale beyond the domain of men acting purposefully in monetary economies. All of its postulates must therefore be outside of it, must be descriptive of the world in which it plays a part. Of the thousands of statements it is possible to make about the environment in which we live, only those which deal with financial transactions or relationships or which have financial consequences or which deal with the problems of computation and communication can be related to accounting. That the same statements may at the same time be postulates or conclusions of other types of study is to be expected. In a sense it is to be welcomed, for it gives some assurance, if assurance be needed, that our concepts of the environment are not concepts we have invented for our own purposes. Those that are chosen as postulates are dictated by the function ascribed to accounting. Any proposition descriptive of the environment which is fundamentally necessary to support a conclusion, a principle or a practice in accounting is a postulate of accounting, however remote or trite it may appear to be.

Why Bother with Postulates?

Because every deliberate action of reasonable men, and every piece of advice proffered by practitioners, is based on some postulates, and reasonable men always want to be sure of their ground. Because it is common wisdom to re-examine the foundations of one's practices; practices may become so overlaid with habitual and conventional trappings that their avowed purposes are no longer well served. Because a man's postulates are the substance of his understanding of the world in which he acts; if his postulates are irrelevant or inconsistent, neither he nor his practices merit the esteem of his fellows. Because to examine one's postulates is the simplest and most effective way to discover the possibility and direction of improvements and innovations in practice. Because man's reasoned judgement is his only protection against self-delusion, cant and deceit.

30

THE MOONITZ AND SPROUSE STUDIES ON POSTULATES AND PRINCIPLES*

Background

Over an interval of 20 years the American Institute of Certified Public Accountants supported the publication of Accounting Research Bulletins on practical questions referred from time to time to its Committee on Accounting Procedures and Committee on Terminology. The first was published in September 1939; the last, No. 51, was published in August 1959. The full series, incorporating revisions made in 1953 to earlier Bulletins, was republished in 1961[1]. The series had covered diverse topics as they arose to the point meriting general attention. Meanwhile, the Study Group on Business Income had been jointly sponsored by the Institute and the Rockefeller Foundation, and in 1952 published the results of its deliberations[2]. Its conclusions included the proposition that accounting should produce integrated statements in which "the effects of changes in value of the monetary unit would be reflected separately" (p. 105). There was a host of dissents, and the direct effects of the study on the state of opinion was not noticeable.

These publications exhibited little of the orderly, systematic development or presentation of ideas which might have been expected to be associated with a more or less orderly art. Senior members of the profession had, by the latter 'fifties, become dissatisfied with this programme[3]. Following an inquiry by a special committee[4], the Institute set up an Accounting Research Division under a Director of Research with authority to circulate for discussion studies made by him and his staff, and an Accounting Principles Board which was to be the only agency of the Institute with power to make or approve public pronouncements on accounting principles. The first Director of Accounting Research, Dr. Maurice Moonitz, took up duty in mid-1960 on leave from the University of California at Berkeley, to which he returned in mid-1963.

---

* First published in *Proceedings* of Conference of the Australasian Association of University Teachers of Accounting, January 1964, pp. 34-54.

[1] *Accounting Research and Terminology Bulletins,* Final Edition.

[2] *Changing Concepts of Business Income,* New York, The Macmillan Company.

[3] For example, Marquis G. Eaton, *Financial Reporting in a Changing Society,* New York, A.I.C.P.A., 1957; Alvin R. Jennings, "Present-Day Challenges in Financial Reporting", *The Journal of Accountancy,* January 1958.

[4] Report to Council of the Special Committee on Research Program, *The Journal of Accountancy,* December 1958.

The Special Committee on Research Program had proposed that "an immediate project of the accounting research staff should be a study of the basic postulates underlying accounting principles generally". Postulates, the Committee said, "are few in number and are the basic assumptions on which principles rest. They necessarily are derived from the economic and political environment and from the modes of thought and customs of all segments of the community. The profession, however, should make clear their understanding and interpretation of what they are, to provide a meaningful foundation for the formulation of principles and the development of rules or other guides for the application of principles in specific situations."

Against this background *Accounting Research Study No.* 1, entitled "The Basic Postulates of Accounting", by Moonitz, was produced and published. It went through several drafts which were circulated for comments before publication in printed form in September 1961. Moonitz was joined by Dr. Robert Sprouse, also of the University of California at Berkeley, for the purpose of extending the studies of the Division to the development of a set of accounting principles. Moonitz and Sprouse collaborated in the production of *Accounting Research Study No.* 3. An earlier draft bore a title relating to "broad accounting principles". The printed version, published in April 1962 bears the title "A Tentative Set of Broad Accounting Principles for Business Enterprises".

The Special Committee's proposal referred to "the basic postulates underlying accounting principles generally". It seems reasonable to suppose that the Committee had in contemplation an extant body of accounting principles, for no reference is made to ideal or proper accounting principles. If the study of extant accounting principles were to be undertaken, the procedure would be to state clearly the principles of which the postulates are to be discovered, and then, one by one, to find the assumptions or statements of fact which entailed those principles. The process involves working backwards from observed rules to the underlying reasons[5]. Moonitz does not do this, nor does it appear that the possibility of proceeding in this way was considered. This in no way vitiates the study. But the point is made in case the similarity of some of Moonitz's conclusions to commonly accepted ideas may lead people to suppose that the study is a study of accepted principles. This it is not.

The Postulates Study

The method of inquiry selected by Moonitz is to examine the environment and to select from all possible statements about the economic and political environment those statements which relate "to the problems that accountants deal with" (p. 5). It is suggested that from these statements it is possible to deduce what accounting principles ought to be followed. In a general way this method of proceeding is unexceptionable. But there is the possibility that the problems which accountants deal with are, on the one hand, more extensive than any chosen definition of accounting; and are, on the

[5] The method is illustrated in "Why Bother with Postulates?", see p. 384, *ante*.

other hand, less extensive than the problems which the world at large requires to be solved and which fall within any chosen definition of accounting. In order to discover what principles ought to be followed in developing a contrivance—accounting is a human contrivance—one needs to know at the outset the purpose or function it is to serve, or at least to propose tentatively a purpose which will direct the kinds of question one should ask about the environment.

Moonitz defers stating the function of accounting (p. 23) until the five A postulates have been presented, so that we do not have at the beginning an indication of the grounds for including any given statement among the A postulates. Alternatively the "problems which accountants deal with" could have provided such grounds; but these problems are not specified.

After the presentation of the five postulates (which are the whole of A-1 and A-2 and the first sentences of A-3, A-4 and A-5, as they appear in the summary)[6], it is contended that the relationship between them and the field of accounting can be illustrated by means of a definition. The definition begins (p. 23) "The function of accounting is . . .". This definition is said to be compatible with other definitions of accounting. Indeed it is, for both Moonitz's definition of the function of accounting and the A.I.C.P.A. definition of accounting run in terms of operations. Now the function of an object and the object itself are two quite distinct conceptions—a "fry-pan" is not the "function of a fry pan"—and the functioning of an object is a different conception again. Moonitz's definition of the function of accounting is a description of the function of accounting, the series of operations which are performed in the name of accounting; it is not a statement of function in the sense of objective or purpose, and does not therefore meet the requirement stated above that the development of a contrivance depends on stating at the outset the function it is expected to perform.

To follow through Moonitz's selected method of inquiry requires that the operations to be performed be derived deductively from the postulates. It may appear as though the five A postulates find counterparts in the definition of the function of accounting: there is a one-to-one relation between the five postulates and the five specified operations. But the connexion is tenuous. Consider the first postulate and the first "function":—

> Postulate A-1: Quantitative data are helpful in making rational economic decisions, i.e., in making choices among alternatives so that actions are correctly related to consequences.
>
> Function (1): To measure the resources held by specific entities.

The "function" is not a derivative of the "postulate", for there is no unequivocal relationship between any of the terms used in the two

[6] Familiarity with the Moonitz and Sprouse Studies is assumed; the actual propositions are only reproduced here when necessary for illustration. "Summary" refers to the summaries in the Studies. Page numbers relate to the pagination of the Study being discussed.

propositions. A parallel reading of the remaining four "postulates" and four "functions" will reveal that they are all similar in this respect. Parallelism there is; but the processes are not inferences from the postulates as they stand. In fact, therefore, the proposed method of inquiry is not followed; for an operation presupposes a principle which, following the selected method, should be deducible from postulates.

The A Postulates

Consider now some of the characteristics of the A postulates. A-1 relates to quantitative data and rational economic decisions. It can as readily be said that qualitative data are helpful in making rational economic decisions; in fact both are helpful. If then we choose one proposition rather than the other, presumably there is a reason. If we seek the reason we will find that some properties of objects are quantifiable and some are not. We will then be obliged to limit the discussion to quantifiable properties, and to some particular quantifiable property. Postulate A-5 hints at such a property, "exchangeability", but this is not made a central feature of argument.

Again we are not told clearly what "rational" and "economic" mean in the phrase "rational, economic decisions". The phrase is equated with "making choices among alternatives so that actions are correctly related to consequences". But, at best, actions may only be chosen in the light of *expected* consequences. Unless, however, we are told what consequences men prefer, we have no indication of the basis of choice between any two or more possible actions. Any single action may be identified with certain expected consequences, but if there is only one possible action there can be no decision; and if there is more than one possible action, not all of them can be rational, economic actions, unless "rational" and "economic" are empty. In the treatment on p. 51, the whole question of choice is begged by reference to making allocations properly; properly necessarily has some referent, but there is no indication of what it is.

Postulate A-2 refers to most goods and services being the subject of exchange but makes no reference to goods not exchanged. Nor does it refer to prices and their function. The proposition is empirically verifiable but provides no limit to the sequel, such as would be provided by taking the position that only interpersonal exchanges provide a basis for quantifying in money terms. A-3 again is empirically verifiable provided that "economic activity" and "entities" are appropriately defined; but unless they are defined we have no ground for discovering what accounting information is relevant to whom, and to what activity or entity. Both activities and entities have so many forms that unless they are defined in terms of specific universal properties, generalizations relating to them may be invalid, unnecessarily restrictive or unwarrantably extensive.

Postulate A-4—economic activity is carried on during specifiable time periods—is of the same general kind. It is true but it scarcely helps. It does not hint at the difficulty which arises because some activities take place over a short time and some over many years, and many entities have activities with widely divergent time periods. The object of the postulate is to lay the foundation for periodical reporting; but the reason for periodical reporting lies elsewhere than in the stated postulate. It lies in the necessity for reviewing progress in a changing environment and for adapting behaviour to change.

Postulate A-5 likewise says too much to be useful. Money is not a common denominator; it is a medium of exchange. The monetary unit may be a common denominator, but only so long as its dimension is constant; that is to say, for all measurements made at a point of time, or for all measurements made so long as the purchasing power of money remains constant. The term "common denominator", borrowed from mathematics, needs to be explained in the context of economic activity. Failure to explain and develop its meaning leads to a situation in the Principles Study where monetary units of different dimension (denominating different things) may be assigned to objects, and added in financial statements without regard for denominators. Further the postulate relates to the measurement of exchangeability, but we are not told exactly what this property is, or how it is measured, or whether it is an invariant property or a variable property.

The second sentences of Postulates A-3, A-4 and A-5, as they appear in the summary, are not the same in kind as the five statements discussed above. They are imperative. They all contain "must", and are therefore subject to a criticism to be offered of the C postulates, namely that they are conclusions from unstated postulates. They are reminiscent of Mattessich's requirements[7], but they serve to pose questions rather than to provide grounds for the solution of questions.

The Function of Postulates

Before turning to the B and C "postulates", it will be helpful to clarify the function of postulates. The objective of inquiry is to discover the general rules which will serve as guides in the solution of problems of a certain kind. One first defines the problem, then imagines a solution, then proceeds to stipulate the conditions under which the proposed solution would be valid. If these conditions are found empirically to exist, the proposed solution is considered to be an acceptable solution. If the conditions include contradictories, or if they are not found empirically to exist, the proposed solution is rejected and an alternative solution is imagined—again as a hypothesis.

The formal demonstration to others of the conclusions one has reached proceeds from a statement of the conditions, which for the purpose of the demonstration are postulates or premises, from which the conclusions may be deductively derived. Thus, in a deductive system (and such a system is Moonitz's choice), a postulate is a statement in the indicative mood which is to be used in deriving some other statement. Of all statements which could possibly be postulates,

---

[7] Richard Mattessich, "Towards a General and Axiomatic Foundation of Accountancy", *Accounting Research,* October 1957, p. 346.

only those are required which are necessary in deriving some other statement or statements within the field of inquiry. It is therefore impossible to say that any statements are postulates unless one states the conclusions for which their postulation is necessary.

On the face of it, and to judge by its title, the Moonitz study does not purport to present conclusions, that is to say, accounting principles. It is therefore impossible to know why the "postulates" given in the study are selected and whether they are sufficient to support any conclusions the author may wish one to draw from them. There can be no such things as postulates *in vacuo*. And it will appear subsequently that the postulates given are inadequate to support the principles of *Accounting Research Study No.* 3.

We have said that a postulate is a statement in the indicative mood. The reason lies in the fact that any normative or imperative statement is in the nature of a conclusion from premises or postulates. The imperative "X should be done in manner Y" means "If the end E is to be attained, conditions A, B, C . . . indicate an action X, and a manner Y of doing X". The conditional clause, "if the end E is to be attained", represents an undisclosed premise or postulate. On this test, the latter sentences of A-3, A-4 and A-5 (as they appear in the summary) and all the C postulates are not postulates at all. As imperatives, they are all conclusions for which the premises are not identified.

The B Postulates

The statements in Group B are all in the indicative mood, but this does not mean they are postulates. Thus B-1 states: "The results of the accounting process are expressed in a set of fundamentally related financial statements which articulate with each other and rest upon the same underlying data." It is said that this is related to A-1, Quantification. But it is not logically derivable from A-1; A-1 does not mention accounting process, financial statements or articulation. If it were derivable, of course, it would be a theorem and not a postulate. But Moonitz uses a weaker term "related"; but how it is related is difficult to see when so many of the words and phrases used appear uniquely in A-1 and B-1. Statement B-1 describes what is commonly found; but it is commonly found only because there are some principles of design in accounting which make it so. Therefore B-1 is a conclusion or consequence and may not be considered as a postulate.

Again, B-2 asserts that accounting data are based on prices generated by past, present or future exchanges. The meaning of "based on" we are not given. Nor are we told what accounting data are, unless we resort to the definition of accounting; and the definition of accounting gives absolutely no warrant for including future exchanges. The definition says nothing about the future and it seems to be erroneous to speak of giving an account of something yet to happen or of measuring something yet to happen.

The inadequacy of the definition of "entity", referred to when dealing with A-3 above, affects B-3. Any person, for example, may be a consumer, and a businessman in his own right, and a trustee. There is a suggestion on p. 13 to the effect that the separation of business and personal affairs is recognized, but no ground is laid for this practice; there is no reason given that will enable us to discover whether and why the person mentioned above should be considered as two or three entities. The reason lies in the different considerations and thought processes appropriate to different roles, but the postulates make no reference to these.

The tentativeness postulate, B-4, is said to be related to A-4. As it stands, A-4 could mean that discrete intervals may be associated with a series of activities uniquely falling within those intervals; in which case there would be nothing tentative about the results. Clearly B-4 contemplates some other interpretation of A-4; there are some features of the activities of entities which extend over the boundaries of intervals. A statement to this effect would be a reasonable postulate, from which tentativeness could be deduced as a conclusion.

In general, the B postulates are all statements about the accounting process. They thus fail to meet the stipulation that postulates "are necessarily derived from the economic and political environment and from the modes of thought and customs of all segments of the business community". If anything the B statements are principles, resting on postulates which are not included in the body of postulates as published. Exactly the same comment applies to the C statements, but they will also be noticed critically[8].

The C Postulates

Postulate C-1, Continuity, in effect says A should be treated as A, and B should be treated as B. There seems to be no good reason for so stipulating, as this is a matter of common sense, unless there is an undisclosed reason why A *might* be treated as B; in which case the underlying reason is missing. In no sense can the proposition be considered a postulate of accounting generally. The continuity concept, we are told, includes the concept of limited life—discontinuity in fact. A word of such chameleon-like propensity can contribute little to clearer understanding.

The term "objectivity" as used in C-2 is given a special implicit meaning which does not accord with its usage generally. There are apparently some points of time at which a measure of an event cannot be obtained in "objective terms" (p. 41), and there is a later point of time when this is possible. But so to stipulate requires a clear definition of what "objective" means. The discussion is in contemplation, it seems, of recording the effects of shifts in prices; but in so far as depreciation is of exactly the same kind—something is happening but we cannot say how rapidly—statement C-2 would exclude conventional provisions for it as well. There seems to be no good reason for adopting an unusual meaning for objectivity which implies that we cannot measure the outflow from a tank until it is empty.

---

[8] An earlier draft of the Study bore the title "The Basic Propositions of Accounting". Many of the observations made here may have had less force if that title had been retained. The reason for the change is not known.

The notion of consistency, C-3, appeals to common sense. But the postulate as stated includes more than consistency. There are presumably some features of the environment which dictate the measurable features of the position and activities of an entity, and which indicate the meaning of "appropriate". It seems to be necessary to define these notions and to link them with the environment before it is possible to say what shall be produced consistently. And as we have said already, the imperative form clearly contemplates some undisclosed premises.

Similarly postulate C-4 requires definition of "stable measuring unit". The money unit is observably unstable. Over what period should accounting reports be based on a stable unit? It may be granted that all measurements in any report shall be measurements in a scale of the same dimension. But the postulate as stated asserts far more than this, and no indication is given of its effects on the usefulness of the results to those who must rely on them.

The disclosure postulate, C-5, is so broad that it entails the reporting of one knows not what. The double negative "not misleading" gives no positive indication of what should be disclosed; and we are not told whom we should avoid misleading.

General Comments on the Postulates Study

The Study seems to have been influenced by the Special Committee's suggestion that postulates are few in number. What the Committee meant by "few" one cannot know. Certainly, in a deductive system, one would like to have the smallest possible number; for the smaller the number the fewer the points at which initial objections could be raised. But small is relative. J. H. Woodger[9] has illustrated in detail the derivation of conclusions from postulates by logical operations by reference to biological cell theory. For the purpose of deriving one particular conclusion, 13 postulates are required, of which six are definitional. Any aspect of a theory of accounting seems likely to require a considerable number of postulates; and the basic postulates of accounting generally are likely to be numerous indeed. The actions and interactions of persons using and persons preparing accounting statements are numerous and complex. The things which are represented in accounting statements and the ways in which they are represented are varied and complex. Measurement, communication and interpretation, preliminary to action, are all complex, and not self-evident or self-descriptive operations. The technical names given to events and objects are numerous and require to be defined within the system they are to serve. For all these reasons it seems improbable that the number of postulates (including definitional postulates) will be small.

Whether or not the number of postulates offered was influenced by the Special Committee's suggestion, it is a small number; 14 in all if they be taken as presented, but only five if we exclude the B and C

---

[9] *The Technique of Theory Construction*, International Encyclopedia of Unified Science, Chicago, The University of Chicago Press, 1939, see p. 61.

statements on grounds already given. But the number of unspecified postulates underlying the B and C statements is, without doubt, considerable. Taking B-1 as an example, there is no (definitional) postulate which informs us of the ends or of the results of the accounting process; there is no definition of financial statements; there is no specified reason for the articulation of these statements, and no indication of the number of them; and there is no indication of the nature of the underlying data (because of the alternatives offered, B-2 does not help). It will be apparent that the "postulates" are really complex statements presuming a series of more fundamental statements which are not given.

Turn now to the nature of postulates. Langer has set down the characteristics of a postulate in a succinct manner. "All we ask of a postulate is, (1) it shall belong to the system, i.e., be expressible entirely in the language of the system; (2) that it shall imply further propositions of the system; (3) that it shall not *contradict* any other accepted postulate, or any proposition implied by such other postulate; and (4) that it shall not itself be implied by other accepted postulates, jointly or singly taken."[10] We shall not work through these requirements systematically. The following points are worth noting, however. In respect of requirement (2), we are given no indication of the implications of the postulates represented in the Study. The postulates singly or in various combinations may be expected to yield a variety of conclusions as Woodger shows in the work cited above. There is no comparable demonstration in the Postulates or Principles Studies. In respect of requirement (3), it may be observed that every proposition containing alternatives[11] implies contradictories of the form "A is B and A is not-B". Postulate B-2 within the context of both the Postulates and the Principles Studies is a proposition of this kind; in view of its importance in these studies, the defect is critical, for it strikes at the root of all proposals relating to measurement and aggregation. As for requirement (4), we have already shown that many of the postulates are in fact conclusions from unstated postulates.

By way of illustration of the variety of postulates on which any form of accounting similar to the existing form will be based, we pose a series of questions on which the Study is inadequate or silent:—

Why and how do men act? How do men choose? What are the criteria of choice? How is information related to choice? How are expectations related to choice? On what information are expectations based? Why is quantitative information useful? What is economic action? What things are the objects of economic action? What is money? Why exchange? By what right are things exchanged, and by what process? What is a price? How do prices arise? Do prices change and why? Why is the monetary unit used in calculating? Why is abstract information useful and desired? What abstract properties of what things are represented in monetary units? How is

[10] Suzanne K. Langer, *An Introduction to Symbolic Logic,* New York, Dover Publications, Inc., 1953, p. 185.

[11] This does not apply to the use of "or" signifying equivalence or identity.

the extent of these properties measured? What are accounts? Why keep accounts? Why double-entry? Why summarize accounts periodically? How often is periodically? What conditions make it possible to summarize accounts? What conditions make summaries comprehensible? What is financial position? What is its relation to action?

The list could be extended but it will suffice. The answers to all these questions are discoverable from the environment of accounting; at least, some usable answer, if not the whole answer, is discoverable in respect of each. And we believe that the answers to these and similar questions are all necessary as postulates of a theory of accounting. The giving of the above examples is not intended as an indication of the possibility of tackling the problem in a different way than was done. It is intended to indicate the gaps which exist, even if we accept the objectives and methods stated to be the basis of the Study.

The Principles Study

As with the postulates so with the principles: a study must begin with an explicit orientation. The Study begins with some observations on the dependence on accounting statements of various classes of person and institution having relationships with business enterprises. It asserts (p. 1) that the principles to be presented are designed to meet the needs of all groups. But there is no analysis of these needs, and no attempt to show that a particular design will meet the needs of all groups. Nor is there any discussion of what particular needs can be served by accounting statements, and how they are served, and what particular needs are served only by financial information not falling within the accounting framework. In these circumstances it is impossible to judge the resulting principles in the light of their presuppositions or their objectives.

A narrower ground for criticism, but one no less important, is the brief treatment of the balance sheet and income statement. Curiously, neither in the Postulates Study nor in the Principles Study is there a definition or a description of a balance sheet or an income statement[12]. Definition is not valued simply for itself: if we wish to understand their self-imposed constraints, we need to know exactly what the authors consider these statements and their functions to be.

One of the most common features of the Principles Study is its vagueness on many critical matters. Some of these may be indicated at the outset.

The study purports to rest on the Basic Postulates; and as we have seen the Special Committee contemplated that the postulates would "provide a meaningful foundation for the formulation of principles and the development of rules . . .". However, the references to the Basic Postulates are so few as to be negligible, and there is no

---

[12] They are briefly discussed in Chapter 2 of *The Basic Postulates of Accounting*, but nothing about them seems to have been regarded as sufficiently important to warrant specific definitions or postulates relating to them.

demonstration of the manner in which the principles are derived from the postulates. It will be shown in the sequel that the principles are only tenuously connected with the postulates.

One of the terms widely used throughout the Study is measure, or its substantive, measurement. "The principal task of accounting is to measure the history of the resources held by economic entities, to measure all of the resources and all of the changes" (pp. 11-12). "Accounting uses a wide range of measures..." (p. 12). "...the problem of measuring an asset is the problem of measuring the future services..." (p. 23). "The measurement of marketable securities at current market price..." (p. 25). "At the level of measurement, then, we are concerned primarily with the measurement of scarce services" (p. 33). "To measure a liability is to determine the 'weight' or 'burden' of the obligation on the balance sheet date" (p. 39). "...the revenue of an enterprise during a period of time represents a measurement of the exchange value of the products (goods or services) of that enterprise during that period" (p. 46).

The examples, with few exceptions, refer to the measurement of things (assets, services, liabilities, etc.). Now measurement is an abstractive operation. We do not measure a man, an engine, a plot of ground; we measure some stipulated property or properties of these things: height, weight, horse-power, area, etc. In the Principles Study measurement is used so often without specification of the property being or to be measured that one cannot avoid the impression that "measurement" is a loose, vague and therefore useless term.

Again, if we are to measure a stipulated property of a number of objects it is essential that the precise property be specified. It is pointless to take a number of measures of properties which look alike (e.g., because they are measured in money units) but which are not in fact alike. The weight of an engine (in pounds) is not the same as the "weight" of a liability (see reference to p. 39, above). This may be obvious, but it may not be so obvious that measuring future services and measuring exchange value (see references to pp. 23, 46, above) are not necessarily measuring the same property. Particularly is it necessary to specify the precise property if measurements of the possession of that property are subsequently to be added or otherwise related. The Principles Study makes no reference to such a requirement.

Further, measurement involves the application of a scale of specified unit dimension to existent objects at the time of measuring (which may, of course, include any past time of measuring). There are few, if any, circumstances in which it can be said that future events can be measured; future events are the subject of hypotheses, of calculation on the basis of hypotheses, but not of measurements. If it is desired to contend that accounting is a system for processing measurements, the measuring of future services (see reference to p. 23, above) is definitely excluded.

Other examples of vagueness occur in the definitions which are given early in the Study (p. 8). Financial statements are nominally defined so as to include every kind of accounting record—unless one adopts one's own restrictive connotations for all the schedules and statements named in the definition. Even more critical is the failure to define "financial position" and "results". Assets are said to *represent* something, but what they *are* the definition does not say. Cost is said to be measured by an exchange price, but at what point of time the definition does not say. Costs are incurred both at the point of acquisition and at the time of use (by business enterprises), and, as prices are variable, exchange prices at these two points of time are not necessarily the same. Depreciation accounting is said to be a process of allocating the cost or other basis of measurement of the services rendered—a doctrinaire assertion of which the validity should be demonstrated (if it is demonstrable at all) by reference to the kinds of information required. Profit, we are told, is attributable to the whole process of business activity, not just to the moment of sale. If this means that profit begins to accrue from the moment of commencing to provide a saleable good, it is false; otherwise every firm would make profits, none would make losses, even on a single line, and no firms would fail. Whether a profit arises depends absolutely on the price at the moment of sale (given a method of determining cost); the risk of loss exists until that moment.

Two other terms which are used in the statement of principles lack definition. Replacement cost we are told is a current exchange price. But replacement cost is not an unequivocal term; it may relate to replacement cost new, or to replacement cost in used condition. It is difficult to tell from its treatment on p. 23 which meaning is attributed to it. But we are told it is a cost method. It is certainly not a cost method in the conventional sense; and it is certainly not a cost method according to the definition of "cost" adopted by the authors. They say cost is a sacrifice; but the sacrifice involved in holding an asset is a sacrifice, not of its replacement price, but of its proceeds if sold, i.e., its net realizable price. Note that net realizable price is also a current exchange price, but that it is not mentioned as such on p. 23, and no reason is given for preferring replacement cost (current buying price) to net realizable price (current selling price).

Net realizable value (or price) is the other term for which adequate definition is lacking. On p. 27 it is identified with anticipated sales proceeds less costs of completion and disposal, and on p. 28 it is said to be a future exchange price. It may be asked how a future price can meet the test of objectivity, for a future price is hypothetical only. If net realizable value were based on current market selling price at the reporting date it would be free of this charge. And if current market selling price were reduced by costs of completion and disposal and by the current profit margin at the current selling price, the anticipation of earning a profit would be avoided (see the comment on "profit" above).

The Principles

We turn to consider the principles as they are presented in the summary. These are examined both for what they assert and for their dependence on the Postulates of *Accounting Research Study No.* 1.

A. The assertion that profit is attributable to the whole process of business activity has already been challenged. Profit is not a term it was considered necessary to define in presenting the postulates of accounting in general. When, as in *Accounting Research Study No.* 3, the argument is limited to a specific class of entities, one would presume the necessity of adding to the general postulates some specific postulates defining the character of business enterprises. As it is, we are left to infer the necessary postulates from general discussion, for the reference to changes in resources, claims and interests (third part of the function of accounting, *A.R.S. No.* 1) does not suggest accretions by way of profit or gain. Principle A is not therefore a derivative of the basic postulates.

B. The assertion is made that changes in resources should be classified as attributable to price level changes, changes in replacement costs, sale or recognition of net realizable value, and accretion or discovery. The description is obscure, but it seems as though none of these changes include changes in the nature of expiry, exhaustion or other form of downward change—a curious omission. If the environment had been adequately represented in the basic postulates, the variability of the level of prices and of relative prices would have been made explicit. The variability of the level of prices is implied in C-4, which as we have argued is not strictly a postulate. Part of Principle B could have been deduced from such postulates. But, again, the inadequacy of the treatment of the function of profits in the business sector prevents discovery of the reason for the suggested classification of changes.

C and E assert that all assets and liabilities of an enterprise should be recorded and reported. If financial position had been defined and if the function of a knowledge of it had been elucidated, these statements could have been derived. But no foundation is laid either in the basic postulates or by definition in the Principles Study. The telescopic form of these statements lays them open to further objection. Presumably only assets and liabilities at the terminal date of an accounting period should be reported; but in respect of recording and reporting, the statements make no distinction between assets and liabilities which have appeared and disappeared during an accounting period and those which remain at its end.

D. This statement on "measuring (pricing, valuing)" assets is one statement which clearly depends on one of the postulates (B-2): but it is vitiated by the same postulate. Measuring is an operation at a point of time; and if measurements at a point of time are to be aggregated they must be made in a scale with unit dimension effective at that time. In addition, to be interpretable at that time they require to be stated in units of contemporary dimension. The choice permitted by B-2 and carried through to Principle D violates these propositions.

The effect of the proposals of Principle D is a generally progressive one. Stripped down to essentials, they tend towards measurements in a contemporary scale. Thus, the prescriptions are:—

Money and money claims, nominal amount and present value; marketable securities at current market value.

Inventories, net realizable value or replacement cost.

Plant, cost adjusted for price level changes less amortization.

Intangibles, cost adjusted for price level changes.

But these prescriptions do not measure the same property in a contemporary scale. Thus for money, money claims and marketable securities, the measure obtained is a measure of the cash which could be made available immediately (for any proposed course of action). For some inventories a future price (net realizable value is so described, p. 28) is the proposed measure, but no indication is given as to the assumptions to be made about future changes in the level of prices. For other inventories replacement price is proposed. Neither of these proposals gives a measure of the cash which could be made available immediately for any proposed course of action. Similarly the proposals for plant and intangibles give no such measure. The measures obtained are thus measures of different properties and cannot be added; nor can their aggregate, if they are added, represent a particular property of a collection of assets. As Joseph Bertrand, French mathematician, is reported to have said: "The age of the captain, the number of the crew and the height of the mast can yield us no information about the position of the ship."[13]

On p. 25 the authors make a particularly significant point with respect to marketable securities. "The measurement of marketable securities at current market price eliminates the anomaly whereby otherwise identical and interchangeable securities are carried at different amounts merely because they were acquired at different prices." There is good reason in this, it seems, and its application to other assets seems to be quite proper. But the proposals for plant and intangibles—cost adjusted for price level changes—perpetuate the anomaly; they ignore shifts in relative prices which are of critical importance in stimulating shifts in economic activity (i.e., in decision-making).

While dealing with plant it may be observed that the authors appear to be somewhat uneasy or uncertain about the treatment they suggest. They speak of recording plant and intangibles at cost "with appropriate modification for the effect of the changing dollar either in the primary statements or in supplementary statements" (pp. 57, 58). Nothing is said about recording these modifications in the books of account: are we to understand then that their proposals relate to reporting only and not to the basic recording operations? And if so, what of the articulated statements resting on the same underlying data, which are the results of the accounting process (Postulate B-1)?

Again, why the alternative—primary statements or supplementary statements? The whole question of what statements may legitimately be regarded as the end products of the accounting process is avoided by the summary lumping together of a heterogeneous series of state-

---

[13] A d'Abro, *The Evolution of Scientific Thought,* New York, Dover Publications, Inc., 1950, p. 372.

ments and calling them financial statements (see Definitions, p. 8). If we proceed from B-1 and accept an articulated set of statements, either as a postulate or as a conclusion, it seems to be necessary to show what statements constitute an articulated set. It seems to be necessary to say whether or not supplementary statements are articulated in some way, and to specify in what way, if at all. The roles of the primary statements and of the supplementary statements, if they are admitted, need to be specified; if they are specified it should be possible to eliminate the alternative, "primary or supplementary statements".

The paragraph under discussion (para. 3 on p. 57) is confused by the introduction of a further differentiation. We are told: "In the external reports, plant and equipment should be restated in terms of current replacement cost whenever some significant event occurs, such as [reorganization, merger or acquisition by another company]." Are these external reports to be understood as something different from the primary and supplementary statements? If they are, what is the difference? And whether they are or not, why is it necessary to lay down "cost modified by the effect of the changing dollar" for primary and supplementary statements, and "current replacement costs" for external reports? Certainly the latter is proposed only whenever some significant event occurs, but the former is proposed without constraints. As the two procedures give different measures they are contradictories whenever some significant event occurs. But, again, what is a significant event? The examples given are surely only examples of one class of significant event. Is not a change in the relative prices of assets a significant event, whether or not there are reorganizations, mergers or acquisitions? As we have already said, changes in relative prices are the triggers to changes in the activities of firms—they are perennially significant.

The sentence which follows shows a further weakening. "Even in the absence of a significant event the accounts could be restated at periodic intervals, perhaps every five years." The "should" of the previous sentences is watered down to "could" and "perhaps" in this sentence, but no reason is offered for the permission given to vary the preceding imperatives. Note also that the attention is shifted from primary statements and supplementary statements and external reports —to the accounts!

It is difficult indeed to discover what this whole paragraph says, as a matter of "principle". Yet the treatment of plant items is of critical importance and the need for the utmost clarity is undeniable if these principles are to serve as guides to actual recording and reporting. Four types of record or report are mentioned and three distinct methods of treatment are offered. The idea of an articulated set of statements seems to have been disregarded and the potential effects of the proposals on reported income and financial position are not considered.

Two brief comments on F. Liabilities for such things as magazine subscriptions (p. 41) may well be subject to discounting in the same way as other liabilities; the prepaid term may be long enough to justify this treatment. Secondly there are three specified alternatives for the accruing of profit; performance, production and delivery. If these three are not different their specification is confusing; readers may imagine unintended differences. If they are different, there is surely some reason why one of them should be preferred to the others, not the least being that, if measurements are to be made, one will want to know when to make them.

G. The proposals relating to stockholders' equity are purely conventional: and we believe that the conventional treatment is open to modification. But attention is directed particularly to retained earnings. "Retained earnings should include the cumulative amount of net profits and net losses, less dividend declarations and less amounts transferred to invested capital." The definitions we are given distinguish net profit and net loss (revenue less expense) from gains and losses of a non-revenue nature. The import of the above quotation, then, is that retained earnings constitute net accretions of the "revenue" variety. The only other component of stockholders' equity is invested capital according to Principle G. Invested capital, we are told, should "be classified according to source, that is, according to the underlying nature of the transactions giving rise to invested capital". This is rather vague but we interpret it as saying that invested capital is the nominal amount of outstanding equities.

The authors have put themselves in a strange position. They have gone to some trouble to distinguish gains and losses; they have developed procedures for recognizing the effects of price level shifts and discount factors in the measurement of assets, and they have lost the other half of the necessary double entries! Each of these items has its counterpart among the equities, but the treatment of stockholders' equity makes no reference to them. Like the Arabs of Longfellow, these items have folded their tents and silently stolen away.

H. "A Statement of the results of operations should reveal the components of profit in sufficient detail to permit comparisons and interpretations to be made. To this end the data should be classified at least into revenues, expenses, gains and losses." No indication is given as to the kinds of comparison which users will want to make; "sufficient detail" is therefore incomprehensible. But more critical is the suggestion that the statement of operations, revealing the components of profit, shall include gains and losses of a non-revenue kind which have by definition been excluded from profit!

The authors are quite critical of the realization concept (p. 15); they "cannot accept it as an essential feature of accounting because the concept lacks analytical precision". But they seem to be in no doubt about its importance when illustrating the meaning of gains and losses. The sale of assets other than inventory at more (less) than book value is given as an example of gain (loss). Nothing is said under H about the price level adjustments dealt with under the treatment of plant and intangibles. But an entirely different treatment is accorded to inventory; increases (decreases) in the current value of inventory are examples of gain (loss), notwithstanding that sale has not occurred. Why these contradictory tests are used to identify gains and losses is unexplained; indeed it is inexplicable, for in a very real sense, all assets are part of "the inventory"[14].

But, further, although the authors note the distinction between changes in relative prices and changes in the general level of prices, the two are not treated as if they could both happen together. The result of holding inventories through a price rise is said to be a gain. It all depends upon what one means by a price rise. If the general level of prices rises 10 per cent and the price of a particular commodity rises 4 per cent, what has been the result of holding stocks of that commodity? Both general and specific prices have risen, so the Study maintains there has been a gain. But common sense tells us there has been a change in the measuring unit, and the price of the particular commodity has not kept pace with it; relatively it is worth less, and therefore there has been a loss.

There is no discussion of the nature of the "modification for the effect of the changing dollar", and the lack of analysis and definition seems to be the cause of the confusion illustrated at a number of points above. The definition of net profit excludes such effects; by implication the definitions of gains and losses include these effects. On p. 17 these effects are described as "a mere restatement"—to which the present writer would add "and is neither a gain nor a loss"—but Moonitz and Sprouse by their definitions contradict the implication of "a mere restatement". If at the same time there has been a change in relative prices the difference between the number of units representing current price and the number of units representing adjusted cost may be a gain or a loss. On this argument, the sale of assets other than inventory at more than book value may well result in a loss, whereas the Study categorically affirms that the result is a gain.

The Principles Study Generally

Although the intention generally was to develop principles for business enterprises on the foundation of the basic postulates there is scarcely any noticeable attempt to do this. The necessity of a system of measures in a common unit or denominator, suggested by A-5 and C-4, does not really find its expression in the principles, for the mixture of current prices, adjusted past prices and future prices in the proposed financial statements, cannot give an aggregate in terms of a contemporary common denominator. The description given omits to deal with one half of the effects of gains, losses and price-level changes, to which considerable importance seems to be attached, and the principles as stated cannot therefore be seen to yield an integrated set of statements. No attempt is made at the conclusion of the study to show that the relationships or ratios between the magnitudes derived by the proposed processes are in any way useful to all or any of the parties of interest, or to show that they are superior to information obtainable on alternative principles. Perhaps this last criticism

[14] See, for example, United States Steel Corporation's Annual Report for 1947; and consider the general meaning of inventory.

may be challenged on the ground that such testing or support was not considered to be essential to the exercise. But some such demonstration is essential to the establishment in the minds of others of the value of the conclusions.

General Comments

The task confronting Moonitz and Sprouse was a prodigious one. There was no precedent in the literature and relatively little guidance for an exercise of the kind proposed by the Special Committee. There sat upon their shoulders the incubus of well-established practices and procedures from which it is apparent they were not able entirely to free themselves. The general usages of many terms added to the burden; for general usages may predispose one to take meanings for granted, rather than to give definite meanings to the terms used.

It is not surprising then that the studies appear to be an attempt to find some compromise between different methods of inquiry, and some compromise between the ideas held by the authors and the established ideas about accounting. Compromise is essentially a political action, by which conflicting views are sought to be reconciled. The pursuit of knowledge is an entirely different operation. At the level of inquiry one does not want to reconcile conflicting views; one wants to find a way of understanding things. Conflicting and contradictory views may be held by others about those things, but this should not cloud or divert the attention of the searcher. The end of inquiry is explanation, not compromise.

In writing this critique the preliminary reading of other observations on the two studies[15] was avoided. This was done to avert the possibility of being immediately influenced by the opinions of others. The grounds for many of the comments in this paper have been laid by the present writer in work previously published or awaiting publication. It did seem desirable however to see, at the conclusion, to what extent the observations of others cover the same ground. As may have been expected, there are many points of similarity between the present comments and those already published. There are also many points of difference, both in the matters which are the subject of comment and in the grounds given for agreement and disagreement. It was surprising however to find no published comment on the matters raised in this paper under Principles G and H —matters which appear to be of critical concern to teachers, practitioners and business people, from all of which groups there were comments.

The present paper differs materially from other published comment. An attempt has been made to judge the studies in detail on the basis of their avowed intentions. The examination point by point may seem to be tedious and laboured, and it may give the impression that scant

[15] For example, the comments published at the end of the two Studies and the selected extracts from letters published in *The Journal of Accountancy*, for *A.R.S. No.* 1, the issue of January 1963, and for *A.R.S. No.* 3, the issue of April 1963. These were of course read at the time of publication.

regard is held for the studies. But it is necessary to give attention to details to discover the precise points at which difficulties arise and at which improvements may subsequently be made; and it is matter of self-discipline to attend to details, in order to avoid airy general criticisms. The criticisms are indeed numerous, and those treated are by no means exhaustive. But they are not offered unkindly. Rather they are offered with the greatest respect for the labours devoted assiduously by Moonitz and Sprouse to a task of great complexity, a task made difficult by the need to negotiate the Scylla of the practical world and the Charybdis of logical analysis, against the cold wind of pragmatic and sometimes visionless criticism. Only time will tell the impact of studies along the lines adopted on the theory and practice of accounting; but, as has happened in other fields which have developed from rules of thumb to sophisticated disciplines, one may feel reasonably confident that the work of Moonitz and Sprouse will appear, in time, to have been in the vanguard of progress.

31

CONVENTIONS, DOCTRINES AND COMMON SENSE*

It has become almost habitual in antipodean expositions of accounting to offer some treatment of the so-called conventions and doctrines of accounting, and to regard these as the foundations or the theory on which accounting rests. The formal treatment and amplification of conventions and doctrines appears to have been introduced to the non-periodical literature in Goldberg's *Accounting Principles*[1], published in 1946 as part of the post-war reconstruction training scheme. Subsequently they appeared in Fitzgerald's *Analysis and Interpretation of Financial and Operating Statements*[2], in Yorston, Smyth and Brown's *Advanced Accounting*[3], in Carter's *Advanced Accounts*[4], in Mathews' *Accounting for Economists*[5] and in Carrington and Battersby's *Accounting*[6].

In the first of these publications only four conventions (entity, continuity, accounting period and monetary conventions) and four doctrines (conservatism, consistency, disclosure and materiality) were presented. These were derived, as was the use of the terms "convention" and "doctrine" in respect of them, from Gilman's *Accounting Concepts of Profit*[7]. Fitzgerald did not produce the list completely, particularly in respect of doctrines. In his list of conventions he excluded the entity convention, substituted for the monetary convention as it was treated by Gilman and Goldberg a constant money-value convention, added an historical record convention and retained the continuity (going concern) and period conventions. Yorston, Smyth and Brown (1947) retained the original list of conventions and doctrines, but in 1949 added to the list of conventions. The entity, continuity and period conventions were retained: the monetary convention was interpreted in much the same way as Gilman and Goldberg had interpreted it, though there were references to changes in the significance of the monetary unit; the historical record convention was retained following Fitzgerald. Two

---

* First published in *The Accountants' Journal* (N.Z.), Vol. 43, No. 6, February 1964, pp. 182-7.

[1] Technical Publication No. 21, Department of Labour and National Service, Industrial Training Division, Melbourne.
[2] Butterworth & Co. (Australia) Ltd., 1947.
[3] Law Book Co. of Australasia Pty. Ltd., 1947.
[4] Curtis A. Reid, ed., Sir Isaac Pitman & Sons Ltd., 1956.
[5] F. W. Cheshire, Melbourne, 1962.
[6] Whitcomb and Tombs Limited, 1963.
[7] The Ronald Press Company, New York, 1939.

new items were added, the accounting equation convention and the recognition of law convention; but these were dropped in the 1963 edition. The new *Carter* presented the entity, continuity and period conventions following Gilman, the historical record and constant-money value conventions following the accounting equation convention of Yorston, Smyth and Brown, a new "arithmetic" convention, and omitted the recognition of law convention of the then current edition of Yorston, Smyth and Brown. The matching of costs with incomes was added to the list of doctrines.

Mathews noticed the entity, valuation, period, continuity and constant money-value conventions, all of which he described as assumptions, and the doctrines of conservatism, consistency and disclosure. Carrington and Battersby gave the largest list yet published: seven conventions—entity, valuation, period, continuity, constant money value, historical cost (following Fitzgerald of 1956), and recognition of law; and seven doctrines—conservatism, consistency, disclosure and materiality, all well established, and comparability, objectivity and economy, all introduced for the first time as doctrines. The 1963 edition of Fitzgerald appears to abandon the older structure altogether. It treats, as assumptions, the five imperatives of the "C" postulates of Moonitz[8], which, for the purpose of relating them to the established denotations, may be described as continuity, constant money value, consistency, disclosure and objectivity assumptions.

In all, the texts mentioned refer to 10 named conventions and eight named doctrines, and in quite a few cases the connotations differ as between texts.

The Emphasis on Practices

In the light of these differences it seems timely to inquire what is meant by conventions and doctrines and what we have in their substance. It is instructive to go back to Gilman who, after a brief consideration of the meanings ascribed in several standard dictionaries, conveys the sense in which he understands these words and the ways in which he is prepared to use them. The characteristics of conventions are that they are propositions which are "based upon general agreement" and are "more or less arbitrarily established" (op. cit., p. 184). From the illustrations he gives, these propositions are descriptive of practices. Fitzgerald speaks of conventions as practices in a similar manner: "a convention of accounting is a practice generally followed ... more often than not based on an implicit general understanding" (op. cit., 1956 edition, p. 8). As for doctrines, after considering these as propositions "taught by some persons" and as "a body or system of principles or tenets", Gilman concludes that a break with the implications of these dictionary phrases "would be a matter of considerable convenience"—a

[8] Maurice Moonitz, *The Basic Postulates of Accounting, Accounting Research Study* No. 1, American Institute of Certified Public Accountants, New York, 1961.

conclusion which is, to say the least, quite arbitrary. He chooses to use "doctrine" as "referring to a general statement of accounting or reporting policy" (op. cit., pp. 186, 187). Fitzgerald does not find it necessary to break so obviously with the common usage of the language: "an accounting doctrine is a belief that a given practice should be followed . . . a dogma inculcated by teachers of accounting, textbook writers or authoritative associations of accountants" (loc. cit.).

Now it is a matter of fact that systematic studies of the ideas implicit in accounting practices have not a very long history. Paton's explicit statements[9] of 40 years ago were not developed or even adopted by other writers, and it was not until the mid- and late-'thirties that interest re-awakened. One would not wish, therefore, in any way to minimize the difficulties of any person wishing to give a systematic account of accounting, accounting ideas and accounting practices. Nevertheless a few simple analogies will suggest that the form which has been taken by the texts cited, and in particular the emphasis on practices, is a form peculiar to accounting and should give rise to some doubts about its merits.

The practice of medicine involves such processes as diagnosis, prescription, surgery and therapeutic care. But there are principles of medicine which are in no way dependent on practice; they are embodied in knowledge of the human organism and of the organisms and inorganic substances which affect it. The practice of law involves such processes as pleading and the assessment of evidence. But there are principles of law which are in no way dependent on practice; they are embodied in knowledge of the legally recognized relationships between persons. The practice of engineering involves such processes as designing and construction. But there are principles of engineering which are in no way dependent on practice; they are embodied in knowledge of the stresses which develop in and which may be sustained by structural materials and of the way in which materials may be combined. Examples can be multiplied. But in each case the principles are independent of practice. One may know the principles without ever having in mind the operations of diagnosis, pleading or building. One may expound the principles without reference of any kind to these operations. Truly there may be conventions in the practice of diagnosis, pleading or building; but these are peripheral and incidental, as the mere fact that they vary from place to place suggests. The heart of the matter is always something more substantial than the conventional forms with which practice is embellished or restrained; it subsists in the realities with which a particular kind of practice is concerned.

It seems to be quite otherwise in accounting. It appears to have become accepted that the ideas embodied in the conventions and doctrines of accounting constitute the fundamental or basic ideas for

[9] W. A. Paton, "Assumptions of the Accountant", *Administration*, June 1921, pp. 1-17; and *Accounting Theory*, New York, Ronald Press Company, 1922. In the former, eleven assumptions are given only five of which appear among the conventions and doctrines of Australasian writers.

the field. The warrant for this inference is the fact that no other categories of ideas or of knowledge are put forward by the exponents of accounting as fundamental or basic to it. The conventions and doctrines are not peripheral or incidental elements of practice; they are all there is. All we have as fundamental or basic is thus a set of propositions which are more or less arbitrarily established, or which are plain dogmas. There is no body of ideas or knowledge by reference to which we can judge whether or not these propositions are preferable to others; we must simply accept them.

This position is surely offensive to any inquisitive mind. And in any case it conflicts with common sense. For if there is a set of bodily conditions and disturbances which exercise the mind of a physician quite independently of the "conventional" bedside manners he adopts, surely there is an analogous set of conditions which exercise the mind of an accountant (as accountant and not as business adviser) independently of conventions.

At this point the reader may interpose the suggestion that perhaps Gilman and his successors have simply made an unfortunate choice in the designations they have given to certain groups of ideas. But this choice was made quite deliberately, by Gilman at least. Nevertheless we will examine the suggestion. Examination is not easy, however, for in many of the expositions there is no clearly identifiable proposition which unequivocally states what the author(s) mean[10].

Some Conventions Examined

Consider first a convention which appears in all the quoted sources —the period convention. Yorston, Smyth and Brown assert that "necessity requires that in most cases [the] life [of the business enterprise] be divided into chapters known as accounting periods" (1963, p. 12). Now, in the first place, the everyday and common-sense usage of the term "convention" implies some kind of agreement, and in an earlier paragraph it was noted that Gilman and Fitzgerald countenance the notion of agreement. One might expect therefore that the statement of a convention would begin in some such manner as "Accountants are agreed that . . .". But the proposition quoted has not this form. It says "necessity requires that . . .". If we are told simply that accountants agree to do a certain thing, and if we know that accountants in fact agree, the proposition could not be further questioned. It would be a statement of fact and not a convention. When, however, the statement says "necessity requires that . . .", we are bound to ask the nature of necessity, and what there is in the nature of necessity which requires that accounting periods be recognized. Necessity is said to be the mother of invention. May we then read "The mother of invention requires that . . ."? The resulting proposition may seem ludicrous, but it tells us no less than the quoted proposition. If there is anything which requires periodical accounting,

[10] T. K. Cowan's exposition "Notes on Accounting Theory", *The Accountants' Journal*, June 1957, is a refreshing exception. Each of his propositions is clearly identified by the introductory "that . . . etc. . . ."

then periodical accounting is a consequence of that thing. And if there is such a thing, it is surely preferable to know it than simply to be assured that its consequence is a convention. The writer believes that the necessity of periodical accounting stems from a number of environmental factors, statements about which will lead to a conclusion of the form: "If such and such ends are to be served, accounting statements will be prepared periodically." The necessity of periodical accounting becomes a reasoned conclusion, a status which is much superior to that of a mere convention[11]. Furthermore, most of the texts cited refer to periods of equal or fixed length. Good reasons may be offered for periods of variable length in some cases; and indeed some firms summarize results and plan operations for unequal periods. A convention which refers to periods of equal length states too much to be considered as a general rule without qualification.

Consider next the accounting equation convention. Carter does not state this convention in any clearly discernible propositional form. But the treatment given to it (op. cit., pp. 4-5) has the form of an argument from certain premises and definitions. As we have just previously observed, the conclusion from a line of argument can in no sense be described as a convention. To do so simply results in the devaluation of it; for a conclusion based on argument from acceptable premises, that is from premises which conform with experience, is a far superior foundation of practice than something agreed upon more or less arbitrarily.

The recognition of law convention may be objected to, as a convention, on rather different grounds. We are told that "records and reports should give recognition to the legal position of the parties to whom the accounts refer (Carrington and Battersby, p. 44). Are we to understand that accountants simply agree to abide by this proposition and is it a more or less arbitrarily established proposition? Neither. Common sense suggests that the laws relating to the keeping of accounts are part of the environment of accounting. We do not consider all the elements of our environment to be simply conventions. We consider them as data, the facts of life. But, further, the authors go on to say that "it is frequently necessary to frame accounts in a manner that does not precisely display the legal position". And indeed every consolidated statement is a statement which does not display a legal position. Clearly, then, we are being told that accountants agree to give recognition to legal positions, and apparently they also agree not to recognize legal positions. What do they agree upon? If they agree upon both then neither can be considered as a convention.

This leads us to another curiosity. Carter includes, as we have noted, the constant money-value convention and the arithmetic convention. The former, we are told "assumes that the purchasing power of money remains constant, which is not, of course, a fact" (p. 4). In respect of the arithmetic convention we are told that "all the accountant's figure work is done by means of arithmetic;

---

[11] For a demonstration of the argument, see "Detail for a Blueprint", p. 369, *ante*.

it is an obvious fact, and so is entitled to be known as a Convention" (p. 5). Here we have two propositions designated conventions one of which is a statement of fact and the other of which is contrary to a statement of fact. Quite apart from our objections to describing any statement of fact as a convention, what useful meaning can be ascribed to the term "convention" when it is used to describe such obviously different statements?

But, consider more closely the constant money-value convention. The sense of it may be conveyed in the form: accountants agree that, in the accounting process, changes in the purchasing power of money shall be ignored. Now if accounting were no more than a recreation, an end in itself as far as accountants are concerned, one could not perhaps cavil at anything they agree to do. But, if it were not obvious, there are countless statements in the literature to the effect that accounting is not a mere game for the delectation of accountants, that it and its products are "utilitarian in character" and "indispensable to modern business and finance"[12]. As the usefulness of the information produced is a usefulness to other parties, it seems obvious that what accountants agree to do is not a matter of indifference—to themselves or to anyone else. Accountants are presumably no different from any other reasonable persons in attending to their own affairs. In budgeting their expenditures they do not think of the prices of bread, and cheese, and wine, in terms other than the prices they know to be relevant at the time. If they buy or sell a second-hand car they do not expect the sum initially paid for it to be relevant to themselves or to the seller or buyer. Yet, in respect of the information they supply to other people they agree, in effect, that other people do not need, or shall not have, the up-to-date information which they themselves would require. They themselves need to adjust their affairs to the immediate facts of life, but apparently other people need only to adjust themselves to the facts as they existed weeks, months or years ago. Ethically and logically, this is a most curious position to adopt. It requires more than mere convention to justify accounting on the basis of this notion. If there are reasons underlying the constant money-value proposition we are entitled to be told of them, in which case the proposition is a conclusion, not a convention. In fact, if usefulness is a criterion, common sense suggests that the reasons for accepting the proposition cannot be other than slight, if there are any reasons at all.

Sources of Confusion

It appears then that the term "convention" is applied to statements of fact, to statements contrary to fact, to conclusions from argument and to propositions of other kinds. Looseness of this kind can only mean that what is designated as a convention is itself quite arbitrarily determined. Without pure rote learning and indoctrination one cannot know what "accounting convention" means. For all its technical appearance, it apparently means nothing of a uniform kind which

[12] Yorston, Smyth and Brown, 1957 ed., p. 1, and Carter, p. 1.

common sense would suggest we might expect of a term used in a technical context, even if it is also a term in everyday usage.

The doctrines are no less confusing and confused. Consistency in accounting is strictly a quality deducible from features of the world at large: its necessity stems from the fact that all judging and choosing, and therefore all action, involves comparisons, and the fact that valid comparisons can be made only of statements which are consistent or are derived by consistent principles. Disclosure means nothing more than informing, and that is the very essence of accounting. To give an account is to disclose. Accounting implies disclosure; nothing more need be said. And generally nothing more is said except by way of giving illustrations. Materiality is nothing more than an informed sense of proportion. In everyday affairs we are quite accustomed to the kind of discrimination that is entailed. It therefore seems scarcely necessary to have an accounting doctrine to tell us to use our common sense. If the idea is extended to discrimination as between methods rather than as between results, it may acquire greater significance; Yorston, Smyth and Brown make brief allusion to such an extension (1963, p. 17) but generally the illustrations given of its application relate to formal features of aggregative statements rather than to the quality of the information they convey.

All of this may be confusing enough. But the failure to state what authors mean by the conventions and doctrines they treat leads to greater confusion in the treatment. Only a few examples will be given. Yorston, Smyth and Brown, dealing with the continuity convention, state: "From the accountant's point of view, since the enterprise is to be kept continuously alive for the greatest length of time, financial and accounting policies automatically dictate that everything done is to be directed towards maintaining such continuity of activity; in other words, a policy will be undertaken conducive to nourishing the business for as long as possible" (p. 12).

It is difficult to see by what line of reasoning such a conclusion can be reached. Surely it is the concern of managers or owners to keep a business going, or to decide whether it shall be continued or abandoned. The only role accounting and accountants can play subsists in supplying managers or owners with information on which they can decide. Financial and accounting policies automatically dictate nothing; they themselves are dictated by or chosen because of circumstance and managerial preference. The only conceivable accounting "policy" is a policy of providing comprehensive and relevant information.

Again, we are told that the accounting period convention "necessitates accruing and deferring items of income and expense" (idem, p. 13). There is no such implication. Entities which keep accounts on a cash basis also account periodically. It is true that if one does not account periodically the question of accruing and deferring items does not arise; but that is altogether different from the cited statement.

In a discussion of disclosure we are told: "If the basis of valuation of each asset is stated, persons reading the report are in a position to form their own opinions of the true meaning and significance of the report" (*Carter*, p. 7).

But what sort of a position are they in? This statement implies that the report has not, in and of itself, a true meaning and significance; or it implies that "true meaning and significance" is only a matter of opinion. Disclosure surely means very little that is useful if the true meaning and significance of reports are not apparent and are only matters of opinion. In any case how may the true meaning and significance be deduced from the stated figures and the stated valuation bases? Suppose that a company shows its commodity stocks at £10,000 and states that they are valued at "cost or lower", which is a very commonly stated basis. If the true meaning and significance of this valuation is not £10,000—and the quoted passage implies that this is so—how much better off is the reader for knowing that the valuation basis is "cost or lower"? No better off whatever. The value shown may be cost, £1 less than cost, or £1 million less than cost: but the user has no means whatever of knowing. How then can he form any opinion about the true meaning and significance of the statement or the report in which it appears? No skilled accountant could do it; yet accountants are quite prepared to assert that persons generally can do it. If the quoted example is a fair illustration of what the doctrine of disclosure means then it is an almost worthless doctrine.

Although no reference is made here to the periodical literature or to the English and American literature, it would be misleading not to point out that the kinds of confusion to which we refer occur also in that literature. Brief illustration may be given by reference to the continuity convention. Generally the meaning attributed to the idea is continuity of the accounting entity. But continuity is variously interpreted. Some speak of the enterprise remaining in operation indefinitely[13], some of it having "a life expectancy greater than that of any asset which it now owns"[14], some simply of it having a continuous life[15]. Gilman refers to continuity of proprietorship[16], and May refers to continuity of the accounting process[17]. Here is a series of quite diverse ideas masquerading as one; or at least having only one name. One wonders what respect would be accorded to physicians who had only one term for all diseases, or to lawyers who had only one term for crimes. To make one term serve for many concepts may be useful

---

[13] For example, Carman G. Blough, "Accounting Principles and their Application". *C.P.A. Handbook,* Vol. 2, New York, American Institute of Certified Public Accountants, 1956, p. 13.

[14] Smith and Ashburne, *Financial and Administrative Accounting*, New York, McGraw-Hill Book Company Inc., 1960, p. 50.

[15] Paton and Littleton, *An Introduction to Corporate Accounting Standards,* American Accounting Association, 1940, p. 9.

[16] op. cit., p. 81.

[17] G. O. May, *Financial Accounting*, New York, Macmillan Company, 1943, p. 49.

when all the separate concepts have been identified and labelled; but not when a general term is used sometimes to convey only one idea and sometimes to convey only one other idea. One other aspect of the matter is the explicit exclusion of the possibility that there may be any form of accounting for non-continuing entities. In many expositions the possibility is admitted, but it is brushed aside. Not even accountants treat continuing and non-continuing entities alike; so, if there is a convention to cover one type, in the interest of consistency and completeness there should also be a convention for the other type[18]. By implication a great deal of accounting is just ignored.

Oversights and Omissions

The conventions and doctrines, whatever they do assert, leave an enormous number of questions unanswered. They do not tell us why accounting exists at all. They do not say why it is necessary to conceive a business to be distinct from its owner(s). They do not give any rules or tests by which we may distinguish an accounting entity. They do not say why accounting is necessarily historical and not also anticipatory. They give no adequate reason for the preparation of two summaries, or for the form these take. They give no criteria by which the proper length of an accounting period may be determined in any particular circumstance. They do not tell us why some entities account on a cash basis and others account on an accrual basis. They do not tell us how to decide what is relevant information. They do not tell us how we may choose from among the multitude of valuation bases the basis which is appropriate in any particular undertaking.

In the whole range of discussions of conventions and doctrines generally, there is no body of factual knowledge which is put forward as the foundations upon which practices are to be based. There is much talk, in accounting as in other areas, about knowing why as well as knowing how. But it is no advance in a man's knowledge if he asks why accounting summaries are prepared periodically, and receives the reply that it is an accounting convention; nor, if he asks why follow the same methods from year to year, and is told that it is an accounting doctrine. If on the other hand one asks a surgeon why he makes an incision laterally or longitudinally he will explain his action in terms of the nature of the tissues, of the location of the blood vessels or the nerves and of the nature and location of the organ he seeks. If one asks an engineer why he goes to the trouble to get structural steel in special shapes rather than flat or round sections, he will explain his action in terms of the improved resistance to stresses which special shapes possess. The actions of these people are made understandable by reference to the qualities of the things they work with. Knowing why in accounting can rest on no other basis than the qualities of the things accountants work with.

---

[18] M. Moonitz (op. cit.) is the only author known to the writer who specifically provides for both possibilities.

Necessary Fundamental Knowledge

What are these things? They are all observable and it is a relatively easy matter to make sensible and useful statements about them. It is not so easy to weave those statements together so that they provide a comprehensive foundation for accounting rules[19]. We are content here to list some of them briefly.

It is an observable fact that people seek to have accounting information so that their actions are the better informed. Therefore we should understand the limitations of people which oblige them to seek such information. We should understand how people make choices and the part which habits, beliefs and verifiable knowledge play in the process. We should understand the part which valuation, estimation and measurement play, and the roles of experience and judgement in the selection of actions.

It is an observable fact that accounting is concerned with the economic aspects of actions. We should understand, therefore, something about the nature of the goods and services men seek to possess, of the processes by which they are transferred and of the media of exchange by which their transfer is facilitated. We should understand the different kinds of contexts in which actions are, or are to be, taken; and the different kinds of institutions for which accounting systems may be required.

It is an observable fact that accounting information bears on the actions of people in their relations with others. Therefore, we should understand the nature of co-operative systems, whether they are maintained voluntarily or contractually. We should understand something of the inducements and rewards of co-operation, of the nature of organizations and of the relationships between people in organizations, and between organizations themselves.

It is an observable fact that the processes of accounting involve the manipulation of numerical symbols. We should know, therefore, something of the ways in which such symbols may be arranged and related so that they do no violence to the real events and things they are used to represent. We should know something of the nature of information processing methods and the problems of minimizing losses of information in the translation of events to symbols and symbols to events.

It is an observable fact that accounting implies communicating. Therefore, we should know something of the nature of communication processes, of the interferences which may arise when human interests are affected by what is communicated, and of the rectifiers which it may be necessary to build into a communication system to overcome these interferences.

Sufficient examples have been given to suggest strongly that there is an extensive range of knowledge, of facts and principles, which underlie the practice of accounting. We can ignore them if we choose; we can be quite content with the vague notions which are described

---

[19] An attempt is made in "Towards a General Theory of Accounting", see p. 477, *post*.

as conventions and doctrines. But to do so is to ignore the observable facts to which we have drawn attention, or to deny that they have anything to do with the case. In the name of common sense we can do neither. Intelligent persons in their relationships with the external world do not seek to resolve their problems by insisting that the world conform with their own image of it. When they find that the world cannot be made to conform, they are obliged to adapt themselves to a world, of which they then have a better understanding. The brute facts of life cannot be met by conventionally accepted or arbitrarily adopted rules. If accountants are taught to think otherwise so much the worse will it be for their future.

One cannot help believing that accounting must shake itself free of the very terms "convention" and "doctrine". They have hindered and obfuscated inquiry long enough, and as long as they survive they can do nothing but create the impression that accounting is a maverick among the professions and among the fields of knowledge. There can be no reason but self-destruction behind persistence in accepting arbitrary and dogmatic and authoritarian propositions which are formulated without regard for the realities of experience in the world at large.

In the place of the customary framework we must seek to establish a body of propositions which represent the context or the environment of accounting and to deduce from these in a rigorous, common-sense manner, even in a scientific manner, the principles and rules to which accounting should conform. In their personal behaviour accountants act in just such a way, as do all reasonable people: in their professional behaviour and in formulating their own principles, they cannot surely be satisfied to do less.

32

EDWARDS AND BELL ON BUSINESS INCOME*

We wish to examine some elements of the proposals of Edwards and Bell for the measurement of business income[1]. Let it be said at the outset that we accept the general tenor of their scheme. In particular we accept the necessity of taking into account the effects of variations in specific prices and of variations in the price level in any computation of income which shall indicate improvement in well-offness. The points with which we shall be concerned are in part matters of principle and in part matters of effective communication, which in an important sense are matters of a different principle. The two will inevitably be intermingled. If any reader should suppose, when we begin to discuss particular terms or phrases, that we are engaging in mere verbal quibbles, we ask him to reflect at the outset on the fact that words and numbers are the stock in trade of all men who must trade ideas with others. This applies to the messages that accountants transmit to others every bit as much as it applies to those who discuss what messages should be transmitted and by what signs. It bears as much on the process of evaluating business behavior as on the process of assessing the merits of proposals for reform of accounting practices.

The Emphasis on the Income Account

We accept that Edwards and Bell have chosen to deal with income and with nothing else. They are certainly not primarily concerned with balance sheets or other financial statements; the treatment falls back on balance sheets for illustrative effects of the devices used only.

However, even accepting the emphasis, it is still a matter of direct concern to specify the function of a balance sheet or of the financial position it does or may disclose. At the very least, the balance sheet specifies the balances to be carried forward from one period to another, however those balances have been derived. The position represented must therefore have some meaning at the point of time as for which it is drawn. The financial position of a firm may be discovered quite independently of the records it may have kept; and indeed it should perhaps be so discovered from time to time, as a check against the distortions which may arise from the mere manipulation of figures as well as from deliberate misbehavior. Sprague seems to have been entirely correct when he suggested that a

---

* First published in *The Accounting Review*, Vol. XL, No. 4, October 1965, pp. 731-41.

[1] Edgar O. Edwards and Philip W. Bell, *The Theory and Measurement of Business Income*, University of California Press, 1961. References hereafter are given by page numbers in the text.

balance sheet could be obtained in two ways, by inspection and by inference from records, and that ideally the results from both methods would be identical[2]. In the intervening half century we seem to have forgotten that as between the figures appearing in balance sheets and income accounts only the former can be authenticated by reference to facts beyond the firm, and that such facts are the only facts relevant to its dealings with others. Figures in income accounts can only be authenticated by a less direct, inferential process, which in any case depends on the discovery of many matters not already in the books of account at the end of a period. We will return to this matter at a later point.

Evaluation

A great deal is made, and very properly, of the role of accounting information as a basis of evaluation. What is meant by evaluation is something akin to appraisal or judgement; it does not relate to putting a number representing a measure on any thing or class of things.

But evaluating what? Business decisions: "... a principal function of accounting data is to serve as a fundamental tool in the evaluation of past decisions. ..." (pp. 3-4). Now, if we contemplate the simple firm which economists often use in discussions of business behavior, it is not difficult to imagine that a single past decision can be appraised when its effects have worked themselves out. But there are few, if any, such simple firms making one homogeneous product, making one decision at a time, and waiting until its effects have become apparent before making the next. The typical firm has a whole series of specific acts, the consequences of specific decisions, in the course of execution at any and every point of time. And they are all in some respect interdependent. Which of all the past decisions can accounting "data" be used to evaluate? Which past decision, if any, can be said to have been in error, when so many past decisions are commingled? How are we to disentangle the effects of one decision from the effects of others? And even if there were only two choices open at the outset, how can we know, after the event and with the knowledge of its consequences, whether the consequences of the alternative would have been more advantageous? For, in experiencing the event we have modified our capacity for choice between the alternatives, and in bringing about the event we have changed the environment against which the assessment is made. "You maintain that you are free to take either the right- or the left-hand fork in the road. I defy you to set up a single objective criterion by which you can prove after you have made the turn that you might have made the other."[3]

There seems to be only one sense in which the evaluation of past decisions can have any meaning in the typical case. And that is evaluation of the complex of initial decisions and all intervening modifications (strictly new decisions) between the dates of initial

---

[2] Charles E. Sprague, *The Philosophy of Accounts,* New York, Ronald Press Company, 1907, p. 27.

[3] P. W. Bridgman, *The Nature of Physical Theory,* New York, John Wiley & Sons, Inc., 1964, first published 1936, p. 12.

decisions and the date of evaluation. But again, decisions are not made by any individual or small number of individuals constituting the "management" of a firm. Perhaps Edwards and Bell (p. 2) mean by "management" all the persons who have positions of authority. But decisions are also made by others who have no authority in the formal sense: by workers who may work more or less assiduously, by suppliers who may or may not deliver as and when required, by investors or creditors who may or may not influence the availability of funds, and so on. Of none of these possibilities, even for such a term as one year, can management have any exact foreknowledge. It is therefore difficult to see how "accurate" can be applied to expectations (p. 2).

The kinds of specific decision which Edwards and Bell use as illustrations represent the obvious major choices which confront many firms from time to time. But they leave aside all questions about methods of securing co-ordinated action, methods of adapting to changes in external circumstances, methods of inspiring the best efforts of all personnel, and a host of similar organizational questions. Every one of these has a bearing on the results which accounts show at the end of a period. The accounts simply do not show unequivocally whether an achieved degree of success was due to any singular decision or any limited number of distinctive major decisions. All they can show is the general effect of all decision-making and decision-changing behavior—in brief the quality of the adaptive behavior as a whole—of a firm in an interval. Edwards and Bell recognize this (p. 38), but in shifting from the evaluation of specific decisions to the evaluation of performance in general they fail to develop the full sense of general evaluation.

This becomes apparent in two ways. The first is the isolated nature of the test of success. "The test of success, and therefore the logical criterion for the evaluation of business decisions, is the extent to which the achieved increments in market value approximate the increases originally anticipated" (p. 48). This test of success is purely internal to the firm, and because one element of it is internally manufactured (the anticipated increases) the test is far from satisfactory. Suppose a firm sets out to earn, say, 30 per cent on its sales; and that a general rise in demand during the period for which the expectation was formed makes it possible to earn 50 per cent. Would the firm then have failed if it earned 50 per cent? Or would it have kept its margin to 30 per cent for the purpose of succeeding? The logical criterion for the evaluation of business decisions can only be how well they work out by comparison with other firms. Success, efficiency, and similar attributes are judged comparatively by outsiders, and therefore must also be so judged by insiders, with reference to other firms. This introduces the second point.

We are told that "accounting data must serve internal functions first" (p. 5). Perhaps first in time. But the relevance of accounting information to stockholders and creditors and its role in the allocative function of the securities market is very much played down; it receives brief mention on pp. 5, 59, 265, 279. Now the actual rate of return on capital, one would suppose, should be the prime test of those investing in business generally, so that it is not a mere sideline of the argument. The judgements of external users of accounting information have direct effects on the survival of firms. Stockholders and creditors may well wish to decide, and often do decide, that to liquidate a firm is preferable to its continuation. They cannot decide in an informed manner unless they know at least what could be obtained by disposal of the assets piecemeal (in a careful manner, not in a straight "knock-down" liquidation), for that is the minimum sum they could invest otherwise. Knowledge of financial position on this basis is a necessary factual premise of the choice; and the rate of return is a necessary factual premise of choice between alternative investments even if piecemeal disposal is not in contemplation.

One thing is left quite out of the picture of decision-making. We are told that "the successful management is one that acts upon expectations that are relatively accurate" (p. 2). We are not told anything about the facts that expectations are based on. One thing beyond doubt influences the expectations that come to be entertained and adopted. This is the relative advantage of one course over alternative courses employing given means. Decision-making is nothing more than choosing. At any point of time we must suppose that a firm has a given collection of resources and associations and potentials for making possible the attainment of the goals expected by its supporters. In particular, the collection of resources limits the alternatives; only some are feasible. Unless therefore the extent of the collection and the monetary equivalents of each item in the collection are known, it is impossible to compare the expectations entertained about alternatives and, therefore, impossible to choose. Contemporary knowledge of the given means is a prerequisite to choice. It provides the factual basis both of expectations and of future actions.

It should be apparent therefore that evaluation is only one of the functions which accounting may serve. A second is the continuous provision of statements of fact in contemporary terms, statements of the contemporary cash equivalent of the assets and equities; hence our earlier remark on the necessity of paying more than passing attention to the derivation of, and the meanings of the measures incorporated in, balance sheets.

Exit Prices or Entry Prices

The principal contribution of Edwards and Bell towards the elucidation of the problem appears to lie in Chapters 2 and 3. Chapter 2 sets up a scheme based on opportunity costs which is said to be apposite in the short run. Chapter 3 "extends" the analysis to the long run, choosing "current cost" as the basis of valuation.

To begin, we state the differences in the two bases. Opportunity costs are the "values [presumably prices] that could currently be realized if assets . . . were sold . . . outside the firm at the best prices immediately obtainable" (p. 79). Current cost is "the cost currently of acquiring the inputs which the firm used to produce the asset being valued" (p. 79). As the former is an "exit" price and the latter an "entry" price, it seems rather strained to call the long-run analysis an "extension" of the theory developed for short-run analysis. It is in fact an entirely different theory. We have therefore to inquire why quite a different basis is adopted for the so-called long-run analysis than that so strongly argued for the short run. The reason for the switch appears to lie in the manner in which the authors conceive the long run and the short run.

Now the short run and the long run are part of the same "run"; this includes all intervals from the time of choice to the effective horizon of expectations. Every such interval will in the course of time become a short-run interval on the expiry of its antecedent interval. Unless the long-run expectation is equal to the sum of all short-run expectations there would be a difference in expectations. No such difference is described, nor is there any discussion about the possibility of there being a difference. We therefore presume that the long-run expectation is equal to the sum of the short-run expectations. If, then, any course of action is taken in the short run which is less ambitious than would be taken if only a short run were in contemplation, the limitation would be predicated on the recovery of the short-run "sacrifice" in some period in the future when that period itself becomes the short run. Every short-run expectation is thus part of a long-run expectation; the two are not different things. We act here and now with the idea of being somewhere else later; if we wish to walk a mile we must first make steps; the one is part of the other. That we must do first things first is unchanged even if in the course of doing first things we change our goals. If we do not get through the short run, there will be no long run.

The distinction made by Edwards and Bell leads them to some curious assertions. Current operating profit, we are told, "is essentially the long-run profit associated with the existing process of production carried on under existing conditions" (p. 99). It is difficult to see what this short-run "long-run profit" is; at least it is difficult if the short run is regarded as part of the long run. Again current operating profit "does not indicate . . . the excess of what is obtained from one outflow of resources over what could be obtained from another outflow of resources" (p. 99). But if it does not do so, of what use is it in choosing between the present deployment of resources and alternative deployments? Of what use is it in decision-making?

Again, we are told that a positive realizable profit (based on opportunity cost) "indicates only that the firm should be operated in the short run" (p. 100). Of course it does no such thing. It indicates the surplus arising on the footing that the firm may do the same or other things in the succeeding period, and that the market prices of the goods and services available at the end of the period are necessary knowledge in making the choice between doing the same or other things. Again, we are told that "realizable operating profit has been constructed essentially on the basis of the theory of a single investment . . . and . . . on the assumption that the only alternative to operating the business in the way in which it is being operated is to discontinue the business" (pp. 100-101). We have not found any explicit adoption of the stated position. It is certainly not inconsistent with the conception of opportunity cost, as defined by the authors, to contemplate "replacement and chains of replacement" on an opportunity cost basis (p. 70). The definition says "if assets were sold"; it does not say "if *all* assets were sold and the business were discontinued". Replacement is in a very real sense no different from any other investment. With given resources, it is necessary to know what means are available for the acquisition of a new asset, whether it is a replacement or an innovation.

We are told that "realizable profit [i.e., on the opportunity cost base] may indicate when the assets themselves should be abandoned by the firm, but the abandonment of a particular use of those assets can better be determined on the basis of current operating profit. So long as there is some use to which the assets can be put within the firm and which will yield a positive current operating profit (in excess of interest), the measurement of realizable profit serves a secondary purpose " (p. 101). The entrepeneur in this case seems to be a rather short-sighted fellow. He is apparently quite unconcerned with any better use of the funds obtainable by abandoning their use, so long as the present return exceeds the rate of interest. He is clearly not a maximizer in any sense, except of ineptitude or inertia.

The additional justifications of current operating profit which occur in pages following those cited are of the same kind. They leave a clear impression that the authors have found themselves on the horns of a dilemma: ". . . it is our feeling that a strong case can be made for the incorporation of both sets of data [i.e., on opportunity cost and current cost bases] in the accounting records" (p. 97). In the end they say they have chosen on the basis of purposes with the highest priority and "upon certain practical considerations such as the wide acceptance of traditional accounting principles" (p. 98).

This dilemma goes to the very heart of the matter. At an early stage the authors after discussing internal and external users say: "It should not be surprising then if the same set of accounting principles can be used to develop data suitable to external as well as to internal users" (p. 5). Notice that this does not suggest that the two users require different data, and that the same set of principles can produce different data; the context of the passage is a discussion of similarity of evaluation processes, even though the evaluators may be different. At page 110, however, it appears that they countenance a number of concepts of profit. "The fact that accounting data can serve many purposes suggests that it may be a serious mistake to restrict accounts to the kind of data from which but one profit concept can be developed." And then at the end: "The information that real capital is or is not being maintained is perhaps good to have, but it is not relevant to profit-maximizing decisions" (pp. 264-5).

We cannot escape an uneasy feeling that several critical difficulties are being passed over. Suppose we wish to know the amount by which a tree has grown in height between two dates. This involves an exercise in lengths. We can imagine a number of different kinds of persons who might have use for the information in respect of any given tree; tree cultivators, foresters, lumber merchants. lumber carriers, and so on. Each of these has a set of premises specific to his own interests; each applies to his own set of specific premises the information relating to the growth of the tree; and each reaches his own set of conclusions. Notwithstanding that all the parties have different specific premises, the additional premise is common to all. None is free to say length or the increment in length is for him a concept different from what it is for the others. Nor does the surveyor, or whoever it is that measures the height of trees, know or care about the specific premises of potential users of the information that he produces.

The measurement of income is exactly the same in principle. If all kinds of users may have some use for the measurement, it seems a matter of the clearest moment that the concept shall be unequivocal. We may, if we wish, show the components, but that can in no way modify the concept. Now, as income is an increment, it is only necessary to decide of what it is an increment. It is an increment of residual equity. But if residual equity is measured according to different scales (units of different purchasing power), the original measurement in the earlier scale must first be converted to the prevailing scale at the date of income measurement. The difference between this converted measurement and the measurement of residual equity at the closing date is the measure of income.

To be quite unequivocal and quite objective in taking the measure of residual equity (by measuring the difference between assets and liabilities in a contemporary scale), it is necessary to disregard the fact that at one point of time the management of the firm committed the firm to a certain collection of assets with certain expectations in mind. On the discovery of the present position, any or all of those expectations may be revised. It would be circular or contradictory to allow the possibility of any such revision on the basis of figures which imply continuation without revision. We reach the conclusion that opportunity cost, and not the authors' current cost, is the appropriate asset measurement basis. Opportunity costs (market resale prices) are relevant to the firm always.

In stating this conclusion we are asserting a principle. If in any particular circumstance market resale prices are unobtainable, it seems not unreasonable to take an entry price as an approximation; it is the best available. But entry or replacement prices are not thereby elevated to the rank of principle. They are expedients only; necessary, but expedients only to be adopted when superior indications of opportunity cost are just not available.

Some Constraints

Edwards and Bell have adopted several explicit constraints in devising their solution. The first is that the system required is one which adheres closely to existing conventions and procedures. They leave the reader in little doubt that accounting profit is a meaningless or useless number; yet their solution is tied to methods which yield accounting profit. This can lead only to confusion. If the term "accounting profit" persists, readers will almost certainly try to attach some meaning to it; and if the methods of Edwards and Bell were to prevail as accepted accounting methods surely their "business profit" would become the "accounting profit" of the future. There seems to be no realistic grounds for the retention of the term if it denotes a meaningless quantity. Tax considerations are no criteria; a major reform can be expected to evoke some changes in tax laws; it is unlikely to occur if its supporting arguments are allowed to be whittled away by concessions to existing taxation rules.

Again, they adhere strongly to the notion of realization. More than anything else, the consequences of this contribute to the complexity of their solution. It gives rise to a whole crop of distinctions and new accounts—realizable, realized, and unrealized cost savings; realized and unrealized surpluses; realizable, realized, and unrealized fictional gains; and in Chapter 8, even more complicated terms. The whole demonstration has its logic, of course, and it is not beyond the comprehension of the patient and painstaking. But it gives rise to grave doubts about the communicability of the results. It is difficult to imagine what answer an accountant would give to an innocent question like "What is a fictional realizable cost saving?" put to him by a manager who thinks he understands business and the vernacular language.

Year-end Adjustments

Again, they appear to have adopted as one of the principal desiderata of their system that the necessary adjustments to traditional accounting statements shall be capable of being made in one set of operations at the end of each period. We wish now to challenge the propriety of this.

If year-end adjustments on the authors' pattern are to suffice, some quite heroic assumptions have to be made about uniformities of changes.

Consider first some physical changes. The example used when dealing with inventories shows an increase in physical inventories during a year (pp. 144-5). For the purpose of the exercise it is assumed that the growth in the inventory occurs at a constant rate (footnote 9, p. 144). Using the result, a certain sales pattern is deduced, purely formally, on the assumption that sales were on the dates of purchases and "were equal to 95 per cent of purchases on the dates when purchases were made" (p. 145). The process of deriving the dates and quantities of sales is quite unnecessary; in practice they would be data. These dates and quantities, based on the stated uniformity of growth in inventories, are then used to obtain the amount of the realized cost savings. But the assumption is quite unreal. The solution given is not the only solution to the question, "What sales and at what prices will aggregate 380 units and yield \$4000?" Quite different results can be obtained if this unreal assumption is not made. Indeed, if the units are indivisible, the authors' solution does not fit the facts; it yields halves of units. Some similar calculations occur on p. 241.

Consider, now, some price changes. When dealing with inventories, it is said that the current cost of materials used can be obtained by taking the weighted-average purchase price during the period in question (p. 144). Now, having already assumed that the increments to physical stock occur at the dates of purchases, spread through the whole year, it is assumed that the realizable cost savings on the increment may be computed by applying the difference between year-average and year-end prices to the physical increment in inventories. By implication the physical increment occurred in the second half of the year, whereas the figures given show that only half of the physical increment occurred in the second half. The two assumptions seem to be incompatible. This discrepancy may be regarded as a triviality; it may, however, also be regarded as a warning against multiplying hypotheses.

The real point of criticism is the gross assumption of uniformities and their treatment by averaging. In the simple example given it is quite possible to make easy assumptions about regularities. But the realities are much harder to live with. Suppose that inventories had in fact been run down and then up, or vice versa, during the year; suppose there were one hundred or one thousand items in the inventory moving at different rates and whose prices were moving at different rates and in different directions; suppose there were initially large mark ups followed by mark downs, or vice versa. What then would averages, supposed to fall mid-year, mean? Added to that, the calculations for a homogeneous inventory are complicated enough; a heterogeneous inventory would require a computer, putting the process beyond the reach of all but a small proportion of firms. Further, the reduction of opening and closing figures to average price figures, and the restoration of these eventually to closing price figures by the use of price indexes, increases the possibility of errors through the averaging process; for even if the calculations are done with impeccable accuracy, indexes are approximations only, to be used as sparingly as possible.

Edwards and Bell admit that their method contains and yields approximations. There can be no question that every such method includes and requires approximations. But it seems to be unnecessary to make approximations when the facts are available. They describe the accounting problem as "one of recording and relating to each other these particular price changes *as they occur*" (p. 17, emphasis added). They refer to the possibility of using the perpetual inventory as a vehicle for introducing inventory valuation adjustments as they occur, so that inventory is always carried on a contemporary price basis (for example, p. 144, note 9). But, notwithstanding this, they dismiss the suggestion in the belief that a single year-end adjustment will suffice. Such a view, however, overlooks the fact that contemporary information about costs and about the amount invested in holdings is always relevant to action. Action cannot be continuously informed if adjustment is deferred until the year's end. Deferring the adjustment is tantamount to saying that what is going on during the year is irrelevant during the year; it is as if one were to say, "We will not make up the accounts until the year's end." If some kind of adjustment is necessary, for evaluation of performance or any other purpose, at the year's end, it is no less necessary during the year; the year's end may well be too late.

An Alternative Solution

We have indicated elsewhere the basis of our own solution to the problem[4]. Simply as an exercise in comparison we use the figures of the Edwards and Bell examples without some modifications which our solution might require. (We omit 000's in each case.) We assume, for example:—

(a) a rise in the general level of prices to be indicated by the change in the index from 98 to 102. (E. and B., p. 237.)

(b) the contemporary cash equivalent of the inventory at the beginning to be \$515, and at the end to be \$690. (E. and B., Ch. 5.)

(c) the contemporary cash equivalent of the fixed assets at the beginning to be \$1650, and a rise to have occurred during the year in the index of fixed asset prices from 180 to 204. (E. and B., Ch. 6.) In our case this would give a gross balance at the end of the year of \$1870 (i.e., $1650 \times 204/180$) and a depreciation change of \$170 (i.e., one-eleventh of the gross amount, leaving ten-elevenths to be recovered over the next 10 years).

(d) the amount payable on the bonds to be \$600 at the end as at the beginning, no repayment having been made.

(e) the wages and miscellaneous costs (\$1536), interest (\$24), dividends and taxes (\$244) to be as given by Edwards and Bell.

(f) the timing of purchases and sales assumed by Edwards and Bell. Their adjustment of \$71 (p. 145, note 11) would be augmented under our method by \$6, the result of applying to 120 units the rise of 5 cents between 20 November and 31 December.

The balance sheets as they would appear on these assumptions would be stated in terms of the prices currently prevailing, at each year end, as follows:—

	1959	*1960*
Assets		
Net money claims	\$ 100	\$ 126
Securities	272	248
Inventories	515	690
Fixed assets (net)	1650	1700
	\$2537	\$2764
Equities		
Bonds payable	\$ 600	\$ 600
Capital (opening balance)	1937	1937
Capital maintenance adjustment		79
Retained income of year		148
	\$2537	\$2764

[4] "Measurement in Accounting", see p. 554, *post*. The argument is fully developed in *Accounting, Evaluation and Economic Behavior*.

The income statement for 1960 would be prepared along the following lines:—

Receipts from sales of goods		$4000
From sale of securities		30
Total revenues		$4030
Less:		
Contemporary costs of materials used or sold (opening stock, $515, plus purchases, $2200, less closing stock, $690, plus inventory price adjustment, $77)		$2102
Contemporary cost of securities sold		30
Wages		1536
Interest		24
Depreciation		170
		3862
		$ 168
Plus: Price adjustments		
Inventories	$ 77	
Plant	220	
Securities	6	303
		$ 471
Less: Capital maintenance adjustment (4/98 × 1937)		$ 79
Income of the year		392
Less: Dividends and taxes		244
Retained Income		$ 148

It would perhaps be odd if, in working from assumptions so similar, our own method should yield an income figure materially different from that of Edwards and Bell. And indeed it does not. Edwards and Bell, taking their figures to two decimal places, obtain a real business profit of $399.82; our own, omitting decimals, is $392. We have not attempted a reconciliation of the two; nor would it be profitable since the methods are materially different. But we may compare the two for interpretability.

The above method shows the revenues actually obtained and the cash outlays actually made. The final statement of Edwards and Bell shows neither (p. 254). It is difficult to see how the firm can be evaluated on the footing of sales at $4080 when actual sales were $4000. It is not difficult to foresee incipient confusion if a historical cost statement showing $4000 and a supplementary statement showing $4080 were tendered together—to anyone.

The above method shows, as well as the data can show, the origin of the various components of the income figure, the only explanations required being of the price adjustments and the capital maintenance adjustment. The statement of Edwards and Bell resorts to a variety of complicated terms in describing the components; and the meanings of the individual magnitudes are by no means easy to describe. The balance sheet of Edwards and Bell (p. 263) is even more complicated, with its notations, cost, adjusted historic cost, price-level adjustments, mixed dollars, current dollars, and fictional elements. (It is notable that, on returning to evaluation, Edwards and Bell make no attempt to carry out a little exercise or two in financial statement analysis to illustrate how their figures aid in the process of evaluation.)

The above method holds closely to the principle of recording nothing that is not observable or calculable from observation, and to the exclusion of any of the effects of events in other periods (a principle which Edwards and Bell avow). But Edwards and Bell require to assume a variety of "average" movements and changes, most of which would not be corroborated by observation; the results are therefore unlikely to be readily interpretable by any person who is himself an observer, especially if he were told how the figures were obtained.

Conclusion

There are other specific points of the exposition of Edwards and Bell to which attention could be drawn. But perhaps enough has been said to raise some questions. We set out some of our own views, without much in the way of argument, on just a few points not dealt with above.

We believe that the notion of realization should be applied more strictly—to revenues only. Income is the result of a calculation, an inference; it seems hardly correct to apply the term realized or realizable to it. In commercial usage generally, to realize means to convert into monetary assets; "realization" has a definite usefulness as describing this event, which it loses if it is also used in relation to income or profit.

We believe that it is unrealistic to attempt to find the specific impacts of price changes and price-level changes item by item, and then to add all the pieces together to get a total effect. The complex of assets and obligations is a complex in which changes, in respect of some items, in one direction are automatically accompanied by changes, in respect of other items, in another; it is not therefore reasonable to dissect the effects as if they were the consequences of quite separate decisions. It seems quite sufficient to discover the gross effects. Analysis of a continuously interacting set of variables can be expected to yield no more than this.

We believe that it is unnecessary, confusing, and potentially misleading completely to convert the figures of one period's statements into equivalents of the succeeding period's price level. Comparisons of specific magnitudes in successive periods yield little of help in the evaluation process. The only useful comparisons which can be made between successive periods are comparisons of ratios, and these of course can be derived without completely transforming the prior period's statements[5].

We believe that business investments are made for gain, or for avoidance of loss, of any and every kind, and sometimes for all kinds simultaneously. It therefore does not seem to be realistic to suppose that holding gains or cost savings are a class apart from sellers' margins. They all, if positive, make the firm better off, that is, able to command more goods and services than before.

In conclusion, we repeat our opening remarks. We do not disagree with the argument of Edwards and Bell in so far as it relates to the underlying incidents affecting the investments of firms and the necessity of bringing into account the effects of events other than transactions. We disagree in principle with the entry-price criterion; it is a concession to the historical-cost idea which Edwards and Bell disparage and it is at variance with the practical necessities of the users of financial statements. We reject the hypotheses of uniform change so lavishly built into their system. These are at odds with commercial experience, and can scarcely be useful in situations of the common kind. They are, as it seems, necessitated by the objective of year-end adjustment which is inconsistent with the premise of recording changes as they occur (p. 17). We regard changes in the prices and costs of non-monetary assets as perennially useful and necessary information. Their recognition during the course of any regular fiscal period is a prerequisite of informed action during that period.

---

[5] See "Measurement and Objectivity in Accounting", *The Accounting Review*, April 1964, p. 267.

33

A STUDY OF A PRICE LEVEL STUDY*

Though we turn our backs on it from time to time in the hope that it will go away, the price variation problem returns to plague accountants in one place or another every now and then. Severe inflation in South American countries, and actual or threatened rises in costs and prices in the United Kingdom, the United States, the Netherlands—to mention a few countries which have recently been concerned or affected—make the solution, in principle, of the accounting problem still a live professional issue; the more so as the practice of accounting becomes internationalized.

Accounting Research Study No. 6[1] presents a solution of one aspect of the price variation problem. It proposes the complete transformation or restatement of traditionally derived account balances to their equivalents in terms of contemporary dollars. In effect, this meets the whole problem only part way. Professor Mathews[2] has criticized it on this score. Although I have elsewhere[3] presented what I believe to be a solution of the problem as a whole, for present purposes I wish primarily to examine the Study for what it sets out to do. As the Study has been widely circulated it is quite likely to be the basis for experiments in practice if price or price level changes become critical. It is for this reason that, without prejudice to my own stated position, it seems worthwhile to consider some aspects of the solution it offers.

Rather than manufacture a new set of data it seems to be advantageous to use the data of the Study, especially for comparison with an alternative to be presented. Some of the components of the data, such as the large annual changes in the price level, are exaggerated, and the magnitudes of the adjustments may cause some readers to be uneasy; but the specific magnitudes are not of the essence of the problem. As illustration, the data of the Study will serve; no objection has been raised by others, and we raise none. We will, however, make one change to be mentioned presently. Most of the final figures presented in the Study are reproduced in the tables in the sequel; but knowledge of the assumptions of the example and the methods of working used in the Study will be presumed.

---

* First published in *Abacus,* Vol. 2, No. 2, December 1966, pp. 97-118.

[1] *Reporting the Effects of Price Level Changes,* Staff of the Accounting Research Division, American Intitute of Certified Public Accountants, 1963. Referred to hereafter as "the Study" or *A.R.S. No.* 6.

[2] R. L. Mathews, "Price Level Changes and Useless Information", *Journal of Accounting Research,* Spring 1965, pp. 133-55.

[3] R. J. Chambers, *Accounting, Evaluation and Economic Behavior,* Englewood Cliffs, N.J., Prentice-Hall, 1966.

Specifically, it is intended to show (a) that it is impossible unequivocally to separate losses or gains from trading, losses or gains from price variation effects, and losses or gains from price level variation effects; (b) that the presentation of financial statements on the traditional basis supplemented by statements on any contemporary basis will only increase, not diminish, confusion; (c) and that an alternative solution to that of the Study is more simple, more readily understandable, and less dependent upon questionable hypotheses.

A Preliminary Amendment

To clear the way it is necessary first to show fully the effects of the methods of the Study. One set of adjustments to the figures is required; one other possible set of adjustments will be mentioned:—

(i) The example states as one of its assumptions that "inventory is priced on a first-in, first-out basis". This entails that the inventory on hand at any time will be priced at a price quite close to the actual market price at that time, the more so the higher the inventory turnover rate. The example has an inventory turnover rate of about twice per annum in the first year, four times per annum in the second year. This at least means that the average price index for the whole year cannot be applied to the closing inventory to obtain a fair representation of the value of the inventory for balance sheet purposes or to obtain the cost of goods sold. Suppose one item of inventory was priced at $150 at the beginning (price index, 150) and $175 at the end of a year (price index, 175); and that one item of it was sold and one item was purchased during the year; and that the average price index was 160, as in the Study. After the adjustment is carried out as in *A.R.S. No.* 6, the value at the end of the year will be shown as $191 (= $175 × 175/160) instead of the $175 given by the F.I.F.O. basis. Alternatively, if we wished to show the cost of goods sold at average prices (to be consistent with the spread of sales through the year), the value should be $160 (= $175 × 160/175). But, of course, to do this is to abandon F.I.F.O., contrary to the stated assumption. In the reworking which follows, therefore, we follow the stated assumption exactly, using the original balance sheet data as giving an inventory value, on a F.I.F.O. basis, which is the best indication of the measure of the inventory in "current dollars" at the several stated dates. For convenience we shall designate these dates as t_0, t_1, and t_2.

It should be clear that the amount by which the net profit of the two years is overstated in the Study is the difference between the given F.I.F.O. value, $200,000, as at t_2; and the "adjusted" value, $210,526, given in the Study. In the reworking (Table 1, Column 6—to be written Table 1:6 hereafter—and Table 2:5), the net balance of losses from trading is shown as $29,949, which is, correspondingly, $10,526 greater than the balance, $19,423, given in *A.R.S. No.* 6.

(ii) Consider now the calculation of the net monetary losses on current monetary items. The telescoping of monetary assets and liabilities into "net monetary assets" seems to obscure some possibilities of gain or loss; at the very least, the treatment given in the Study is only one of the possible treatments in the absence of further

TABLE 1

FINANCIAL STATEMENTS BASED ON DATA OF A.R.S. No. 6

	Traditional Statements (basic data)			Restatements in t_2-dollars. Method of *A.R.S. No.* 6, but amended in respect of Inventory balances (see text)		
Column	1	2	3	4	5	6
Balance Sheets at	t_0	t_1	t_2	t_0	t_1	t_2
				Column 1 × 200/150	Column 2 × 200/175	
Monetary assets	200,000	195,000	235,000	266,667	222,857	235,000
Inventories	250,000	300,000	200,000	333,333	342,857	200,000
Plant	300,000	400,000	400,000	400,000	514,286	514,286
Depreciation		(30,000)	(70,000)		(40,000)	(91,429)
Total assets	750,000	865,000	765,000	1,000,000	1,040,000	857,857
Current liabilities	100,000	200,000	100,000	133,333	228,572	100,000
Long-term liabilities	350,000	350,000	—	466,667	400,000	—
Stockholders' equity	300,000	300,000	600,000	400,000	400,000	742,858
Retained earnings						
—Trading gain/loss		15,000	65,000		(36,190)	(29,949)
—Gain/loss on net monetary items					47,618	44,948
Total equities	750,000	865,000	765,000	1,000,000	1,040,000	857,857
Income Accounts						
Sales		800,000	1,000,000		1,000,000	1,052,632
Inventory—open		250,000	300,000		333,333	342,857
Purchases		520,000	500,000		650,000	526,316
		770,000	800,000		983,333	869,173
Inventory—close		300,000	200,000		342,857	200,000
Cost of goods sold		470,000	600,000		640,476	669,173
Depreciation		30,000	40,000		40,000	51,429
Other expenses and taxes		280,000	300,000		350,000	315,789
Total costs		780,000	940,000		1,030,476	1,036,391
Trading profit/loss		20,000	60,000		(30,476)	16,241
Gain/loss on						
—short-term monetary items					(19,047)	(2,670)
—long-term monetary items					66,667	
Dividends		(5,000)	(10,000)		(5,714)	(10,000)
Balance, to retained earnings						
—Trading gain/loss		15,000	50,000		(36,190)	6,241
—Gain/loss on net monetary items					47,620	(2,670)

specification of the assumptions. In the first year, for example, the firm ran into debt on current account to the extent of $100,000. If it did this at the beginning of the year, there seems to be every reason for bringing in a gain of $16,667 (= $100,000 × 175/150), in exactly the same way as there is brought in a gain of $58,333 up to t_1 in respect of the long-term liability (see Table 2:3). If the rise in current liabilities occurred right at the end of the year, of course, there would be neither gain nor loss. And if the rise occurred gradually, by deferring payment for purchases or other services as one might suppose, there would be a gain of some intermediate magnitude.

Consider now the second year. In this year the firm paid off current liabilities of $100,000. Again, when? If it was paid off at the beginning of the year, there should have been an entry in the calculations (say, in the lower half of p. 127 of the Study) showing an "adjusted" amount of $114,285 against an unadjustment amount of $100,000; and the purchasing power loss would have been greater by $14,285. Other pay-out dates, of course, other amounts for the loss. But, as far as gains or losses on monetary items affect a firm, it is surely indifferent to the source of its credit, and the retirement of long-term debt and short-term debt require equivalent treatment.

The point of these observations is not simply to show that some of the premises of the calculations are undisclosed. It is to show that a great deal of difference may arise in the amount of purchasing power gain or loss merely by shifting the dates at which the changes in monetary items are supposed to occur; for changing the dates changes the value of the "multiplier". The dates at which fixed loans are raised and repaid can admittedly be determined unequivocally. But not so readily the dates at which a company is significantly in debt or in cash, unless on a daily basis. This would entail an amount of labour which the Study does not contemplate. The alternative is to choose certain intervals shorter than one period in which, say, the firm is in debt or in cash to certain average extents. But such a choice is subjective, and the averaging process is much less accurate and much more open to abuse than may appear.

We shall return to this question at a later point. But to avoid too many specially introduced amendments to the calculations of *A.R.S. No.* 6 we adhere to the implicit assumptions with respect to the timing of changes in current liabilities, in the same way as the correction mentioned in (i) above simply expresses adherence to the stated assumptions of the Study. The only change made in the reworking, then, is in respect of inventories.

The Incidence, in Time, of Information

The first aspect to be considered, of the information resulting from the data and operations of *A.R.S. No.* 6, is the time at which the financial statements become available, for the time at which information is received has an intimate bearing on the response of recipients.

TABLE 2

SEQUENTIAL FINANCIAL STATEMENTS BASED ON DATA OF A.R.S. No 6 AMENDED IN RESPECT OF INVENTORY BALANCES

Column	1	2	3	4	5
Balance Sheets at	t_0	t_0	t_1	t_1	t_2
Purchasing power units of	t_0	t_1	t_1	t_2	t_2
		Column 1 × 175/150		Column 3 × 200/175	
Monetary assets	200,000	233,333	195,000	222,857	235,000
Inventories	250,000	291,666	300,000	342,857	200,000
Plant	300,000	350,000	450,000	514,286	514,286
Depreciation			(35,000)	(40,000)	(91,429)
Total assets	750,000	875,000	910,000	1,040,000	857,857
Current liabilities	100,000	116,667	200,000	228,572	100,000
Long-term liabilities	350,000	408,333	350,000	400,000	—
Stockholders' equity	300,000	350,000	350,000	400,000	742,858
Retained earnings					
—Trading gain/loss			(31,666)	(36,190)	(29,949)
—Gain/loss on net monetary items			41,666	47,618	44,948
Total equities	750,000	875,000	910,000	1,040,000	857,857
Income Accounts					
Sales			875,000		1,052,632
Inventory—open			291,666		342,857
Purchases			568,750		526,316
			860,416		869,173
Inventory—close			300,000		200,000
Cost of goods sold			560,416		669,173
Depreciation			35,000		51,429
Other expenses and taxes			306,250		315,789
Total costs			901,666		1,036,391
Trading profit/loss			(26,666)		16,241
Gain/loss on					
—short-term monetary items			(16,667)		(2,670)
—long-term monetary items			58,333		—
Dividends			(5,000)		(10,000)
Balance, to retained earnings					
—Trading gain/loss			(31,666)		6,241
—Gain/loss on net monetary items			41,666		(2,670)

A.R.S. No. 6 presents an illustration in which the point of disclosure or discovery of the financial position and results is taken as the end of the second year. It makes no reference to the statements which might have been produced at the end of the first year, except by way of a passing reference on p. 132. In Table 1 we have brought together the "historical" data, as derived by the application of traditional methods (cols. 1-3), and the set of statements which result from applying the methods of *A.R.S. No.* 6 subject to the inventory valuation treatment already mentioned (cols. 4-6). The restatement in this latter half of the Table is effected by transforming the historical data to their equivalents in terms of the purchasing power of t_2.

Now, in devising a scheme for the users of financial information, we must, as it seems, inevitably take account of the order in which those users will receive or will have received information. At t_0 they will have the information given in Table 1:1. At t_1 they will, or could, have the information given in Table 1:2. If the principles of *A.R.S. No.* 6 are to be applied at t_1, the users will also have a restatement of the information given in Table 1:1, 2 by transformation to equivalents in terms of the purchasing power of money at t_1. This restatement is not given in *A.R.S. No.* 6; it is given in Table 2:2, 3. Then, at t_2, the users will, or could, have the traditional information of Table 1:3; and, if the principles of the Study are to be followed, they will also have the information relating to t_1 transformed to equivalents in terms of the purchasing power of money at t_2 (Table 2:4) and the cumulative consequences of the second year's operations, as represented by the methods of the Study, up to t_2 (Table 2:5). The latter will necessarily agree with the final figures for t_2 obtained by following exactly the method of *A.R.S. No.* 6 (Table 1:6).

The object of transforming the "historical data" to statements in terms of t_2-dollars is to make comparisons legitimate, direct comparisons of measures in different units being logically invalid. But consider the situation of a user of information at t_1. What comparative statements should be given him? We could give the figures of Table 2:1, 3, for these represent the positions at t_0 and t_1 in terms of units of the purchasing powers prevailing at those dates; they represent the positions in which the firm stood at those dates. But, it will be argued, the two sets of figures are not comparable, being in terms of units of different purchasing power. The alternative, then, is to present the figures of Table 2:2, 3. However, to do this disregards the effects of the memories of users (or their access to previous reports) on the interpretation or understanding of the information. At least some of the users will recall that at t_0 the stockholders' equity was $300,000, not $350,000; that the long-term liabilities were $350,000, not $408,333, and so on. Some of the users will know that recorded sales were $800,000, not $875,000. In some of these cases the absolute magnitudes and changes in absolute magnitudes have an immediately apprehensible significance, and it would be difficult to convince others that comparisons of the restated magnitudes were the "proper" comparisons to make.

Consider some of the possible comparisons. Let us define net working capital turnover as sales divided by the average of opening and closing net working capitals. It will be found that approximately the same turnover rate will be obtained whether we use the original data or the adjusted data. No advantage. Take, next, the monetary assets, the magnitude of and movements in which are relevant to judgments on solvency. Comparisons of columns 1 and 3 of Table 2 will indicate that monetary assets have been run down about 2.5 per cent; columns 2 and 3 suggest they have run down about 16 per cent. Which is the "proper" comparison? For certainly the firm has only $5000 less in monetary assets than it had at t_0. Again, comparing columns 1 and 3, the net working capital appears to have fallen by $55,000 or about 16 per cent; whereas comparing columns 2 and 3 the fall is $113,333, or about 28 per cent. Which is the "proper" comparison to make? Or, again, comparing columns 1 and 3 it appears that nothing has been paid off the long-term liability; but comparing columns 2 and 3 it appears that $58,333 has been paid off. Which is the "proper" inference?

This suggests that there are certain magnitudes which cannot be changed as price levels change without misleading, or at the least confusing, an analyst of the statements. We may designate these as "key" magnitudes, meaning that they have a significance as absolute magnitudes, at least in the setting of one year's changes or operations, and are for that reason likely to be remembered or deliberately brought to attention from time to time. They include the amounts of monetary assets, of liabilities, of sales, of previously reported net profit and of dividends. Any subsequent "correction" or restatement of these, within and as part of the financial statements or any comparative table of financial statements, is likely to confuse, or to increase the difficulty of, lay understanding; and this, because monetary items are, of all items in the financial statements, believed to be the most reliable, and because sales, net income and dividends are, of all items in income statements, regarded as significant indicators of results or success. (No objection is taken, of course, to giving a purely statistical treatment to such an item as sales revenue, say, by reducing past sales revenues to a series having a contemporary price level base. The objection raised above relates only to the incorporation of modified sales figures in what purport to be financial statements at stated dates or for stated periods. We will presently argue that no general restatement of past financial statements is necessary or desirable.)

Supplementary Statements

It has long been held that it is necessary to present the financial statements as derived by traditional processes, and that if any other information is to be presented it must be presented by way of supplementary statements. This belief is reinforced by the stated "principles" of some professional bodies and by the appearance—in the companies acts in jurisdictions following the English pattern, and in Regulation S-X in the United States—of rules which imply the propriety of traditional processes. We will attempt to show that any combination of traditional and supplementary statements will only increase confusion; with what effect on the "reliability" of accounting, as reliability is judged by others, the reader can imagine.

The type of supplementary statements here considered is price-level adjusted statements supplementary to the traditional statements (which usually give the figures of two successive periods or balancing dates). Whatever is presented under such a proposal at any time t_n in respect of a previous time t_{n-1}, something different will have been presented at time t_{n-1}. The question is whether it is legitimate to restate the whole of what was presented at t_{n-1} in the light of events which occurred subsequently to t_{n-1}. The argument in support of so doing is that a complete transformation, by the use of a common multiplier or set of multipliers representing the shift in the purchasing power of money, does not change the relative magnitudes of the items as reported at t_{n-1}, and does not involve abandoning traditional rules; simply by virtue of the transformation or restatement, we may compare items as at t_{n-1} among themselves (because we can no longer conceive what a t_{n-1} dollar is), and compare items at t_{n-1} with similar items at t_n. But, in principle, the transformation violates a fundamental idea, that accounting statements are historical in character. Notwithstanding that we have shown in the previous section that confusion, if not downright error, may follow, it may be thought that to depend on the historical characteristic of accounting as an objection is footling. So we proceed.

Given that comparative statements are required for the current year and at least the previous year (a requirement which is not questioned here), there would be two sets of comparative statements, the traditional and the supplementary. Suppose that at t_1 there are presented the statements of Table 1:1, 2 and those of Table 2:2, 3, these being the traditional and the supplementary information respectively. The user of the statements is then free to make any comparisons or to compute any ratios he pleases. We will suppose that he makes comparisons only within the traditional or within the supplementary set of statements. But we cannot stipulate that he may calculate certain ratios only for one of those sets, and certain other ratios only for the other set; and if we were so to stipulate there is no way of preventing him from doing otherwise.

Suppose he calculates the rate of net profit on stockholders' equity, taking net profit as the algebraic sum of all gains and losses and the amount of the stockholders' equity as the amount given at the two dates. (As the stockholders' equity was materially increased at the beginning of the second year in the example, this choice is near enough to the average stockholders' equity for each year.) He will find the following:—

Net Profit Rates on Stockholders' Equity

Traditional statements	(t_0 - t_1) 6.35 per cent; (t_1 - t_2) 9.02 per cent
Supplementary statements	(t_0 - t_1) 4.17 per cent; (t_1 - t_2) 1.80 per cent

Notice that one set of statements shows a rise of over 2 percentage points and the other a fall of over 2 percentage points. Which is the user to believe when the figures do not even move in the same direction?

Suppose he calculates the net profit rate on total assets. The figures are similarly confusing. On the traditional statement basis the rate moves up from 2.31 per cent to 7.84 per cent; on the supplementary statement basis it moves down from 1.65 per cent to 1.58 per cent. Which set of statements is to be taken as indicative of the trend?

Suppose he looks more carefully at the statements in an attempt to trace the reasons for the differences. Using the traditional statements he will find that a 25 per cent increase in sales raised the net profit from operations from $20,000 to $60,000; and as the gross profit rate (sales minus cost of goods sold divided by sales) changed from 41 per cent to 40 per cent, the rise in net profit from operations is presumably due to the "fixed" element in depreciation and other expenses. Using the supplementary statements he will find that a rise of only 5 per cent in sales raised the net result of operations from a loss of $30,476 to a profit of $16,241. (Notice that the direction of movement is the same and order of magnitude of the change is approximately the same for both sets of statements.) The gross profit rate apparently changed from 36 per cent to 37 per cent, so apparently the change in the net profit from operations is again due to the "fixed" element in the other costs. But notice that the indicated change in the gross profit rate is in the direction opposite to the change indicated by the traditional statements. If the user of the statements happens to be the manager of the firm, which of these contradictory trends is he to use as a guide? Note, also, an additional implication. Clearly, from the traditional statements one would deduce that the break-even point is below the level of sales of the first year; while from the supplementary statements it will appear to be above the level of the sales of that year! And note, too, that whereas according to the supplementary statements there appears to have been a rise of only $52,632 in sales, this gave rise to an increase in net profit from operations of $46,717; which is at least odd.

The object so far has been to show that the presentation of both traditional and supplementary statements on the model of *A.R.S. No.* 6 can only put the user in a quandary, to the point where the interpretation of the statements is quite frustrated. And this position is far worse than supplying the traditional statements only; for if, upon acting on the traditional statements, a user finds that they have misled him, he may thereafter be cautious in trusting them; whereas he will not even know how to begin to act due to the contradictory premises of action with which he is confronted if both sets of statements are presented[4].

It is in the nature of the illustrations of the Study that the differences in the final results and statements will have arisen from the gains or losses on monetary items. We therefore turn to consider these.

Gains and Losses on Monetary Items

A.R.S. No. 6 purports to give a method which enables trading or operating profits to be separated from gains or losses on net monetary

[4] In case it is supposed that the emendation we have introduced by way of the change in inventory valuation adversely affects the assessment of the methods of *A.R.S. No.* 6, analysis of the statements actually given in the Study will reveal discrepancies and contradictions no less marked.

assets. It is intended to show that to do so is mistaken in principle, and that it is impossible to separate the two unequivocally.

It is mistaken to attempt the separation for several reasons[5]. First, the attempt depends on the view that the holding of monetary assets is a separable activity from the holding of other assets and their use in commerce and industry. This view is perhaps an outgrowth or an expression of the long-held distinction between "operating" and "non-operating" items in accounting statements. But we will deal here only with monetary assets. The above-stated view does not seem to be tenable. The whole of the assets of a business enterprise are devoted to earning income, in one way or another. Monetary assets are non-earning assets as such; for this reason firms may be expected to keep them at a minimum as long as prices are stable or rising; much better to make the profit on turning over inventories than just to have idle cash balances. But, if firms do have net monetary balances it will be because they believe they need them in order to carry on trading or any other operations which are expected to yield gains. The income, business, precautionary and speculative motives of Keynes may be conceptually distinguishable; but in the case of business firms they are simply different facets of the search for gains.

Second, the attempt is mistaken because there is no way of determining which of the several ways of becoming better off a firm or its managers had in mind when undertaking some financing or investment decision. These ways are (1) by obtaining pure sellers' margins, (2) by obtaining gains from expected rises in specific prices, (3) by obtaining gains on the fall in the purchasing power of money when in debt, (4) by using resources of any kind which are temporarily idle in ways which tend to reduce the costs of other operations. It is quite likely that all of these possibilities will enter into the evaluation of any course of action, and in varying degrees and combinations for every decision. The only conceivable way of treating gains from actions based on such mixed considerations is to treat them as mixed and inseparable.

It is, of course, wise when prices are stable or rising to have negative net monetary balances, to borrow. It may therefore be thought that a specific decision to borrow does not fall into the class of decisions just mentioned. But this too is mistaken. Borrowing is, in the general case, intimately connected with a firm's financial position, its capacity to borrow; and in general this entails that the firm shall have some stockholders' equity. If a firm borrows an amount equal to its stockholders' equity, and if it keeps its assets in cash, a rise in the general level of prices will only ensure that its stockholders' equity, in terms of the higher price level, is maintained. Net income, in the sense of increased command of resources, will be nil. At a more general level, regardless of the form in which a firm keeps its assets, any "gain" from debt must be offset to the extent of the fall in the purchasing power of the amount of the original stockholders' equity; and any decision to borrow must be supposed to be in

---

[5] See *Accounting, Evaluation and Economic Behavior,* pp. 117-9, 257-8.

contemplation of investing the proceeds in assets which, taken all together, will yield the best prospect of augmenting the stockholders' equity. Although, therefore, it may seem to be a simple matter to calculate a purchasing power gain on long-term debt, as in *A.R.S. No.* 6, its amount must be offset by the purchasing power loss on the original amount of the stockholders' equity. This, too, is a simple matter; but it would reduce the amount of "Inflation gains and losses" shown in the Study for the first year by $50,000 (i.e., $300,000 × 25/150).

But the problem of finding an unequivocal figure for gains or losses on short-term monetary items is much more involved. Although *A.R.S. No.* 6 purports to make the separation, it is demonstrable that the two figures—for trading gains and gains or losses on monetary holdings—are complementary, and are mutually entailed by the process of calculation adopted. This may be seen by following through the correction factors used in the Study; every correction which contributes to a purchasing power gain (loss) simultaneously increases (decreases) the charges against revenues.

Further, a difficulty arises over the selection of these correction factors or multipliers. In *A.R.S. No.* 6 the price indexes are given; for the first period (opening, average, closing) are given as (150-160-175), and for the second period (175-190-200). In practice these figures would have to be found. The opening and closing index numbers give no trouble; but what is the "average" change in the level of prices for a year? Clearly the Study implies some kind of weighted average, for the average figures given are not the arithmetical averages of opening and closing indexes. We are told: "In the usual case, in which numerous transactions take place during the period, grouping is required in order to facilitate the use of average indexes. Additions to monetary items and deductions from monetary items may be grouped, depending on the degree and rapidity of price change, on a monthly, quarterly or annual basis." (*A.R.S. No.* 6, p. 147.) Presumably transactions would also have to be grouped into periods in which net monetary balances were running up and running down. Presumably also, if we were given a time schedule of such shifts, and if the monthly price indexes suggested that the rate of change of prices itself varied through a period, we could choose the short intervals and the average indexes for those short intervals for which we would make the calculations. But every such choice involves a judgement of average conditions for each short interval, unless we calculate for every single change in the net monetary balances; the difficulty of doing the latter is just what the averaging method of the Study is intended to circumvent. The effect of such a choice is to give a "specific" weight to the average for the year as a whole; and doubtless that is why the average indexes used for illustrative purposes in the Study are not simple arithmetical averages.

Now every such weight will give a different distribution of total income between trading gains and gains or losses on net monetary items. Let us suppose that, in the second year of the example of *A.R.S. No.* 6, the judgement of the firm or its officers yielded an average index of 185. This is not a big deviation from the value of 190 used in *A.R.S. No.* 6, and where there are no finer rules a judgement could easily diverge by that amount. It is also below the arithmetical average (187.5) by as much as 190 is above it. It seems a reasonable value to use for testing the possible consequences of divergences of judgement in selecting the average index.

We apply the average index, 185, to the information given in respect of the second year, deriving final statements similar to those of Table 2:5. The use of a different average index will affect the adjusted sales figure and the figures for purchases, costs of goods sold, and other expenses and taxes. The consequences of using the different average indexes are as follows:—

Index Basis (second year)	175-190-200 (*A.R.S. No.* 6)	175-185-200
Sales	$1,052,632	$1,081,081
Net profit from operations	16,241	21,931
Gain (loss) on monetary items	(2,670)	(8,360)
Net profit and net inflation gain	13,571	13,571

Notice that the total gain is unchanged, the constituent parts are changed by material amounts, and the sales and other figures which entail cash movements are changed by material amounts: all through a comparatively small change in an index the choice of which is a matter of judgement. It should be clear that, if there were any suggestion that trading gains are in some sense "controllable" by management whereas gains or losses on net monetary balances are not within managerial discretion, there would be a tendency to choose an index which showed a high trading profit even if this were offset by a correspondingly high "inflation" loss. In other words, the necessity of choosing an average index would introduce into accounting another degree of indeterminacy[6].

Complexity of the Method

The method of *A.R.S. No.* 6 requires that a great number of calculations and adjustments be made to the amounts of the closing account balances to obtain the final statements, and that many of these adjustments be reversed immediately to show monetary item balances at their actual significances as at the end of each year. A complete reconciliation of the restated figures as given in *A.R.S. No.* 6 is presented in Table 3. The object of this Table is simply to show the complexity of the process. If error is to be avoided by any person doing the calculations in practice, he would have to prepare such a

[6] These objections to average indexes apply equally to Professor Mathews' alternative proposal in the article already cited. They have been aired in a different context in "Edwards and Bell on Business Income", see p. 426, *ante*.

complete reconciliation on double-entry principles, even if the adjustments are never incorporated in the accounts. The omission of such a reconciliation or of a *pro forma* series of journal entries from the Study tends to give an unwarranted impression of simplicity.

We wish to show that this complexity and the other difficulties and dilemmas previously mentioned are avoided by an alternative procedure.

An Alternative Proposal

The justification of the procedures of *A.R.S. No.* 6 lies in the proposition that the restated figures are simply the original figures of the traditional accounting transformed into contemporary measures by the use of indexes of the general level of prices. The traditional methods might appear thus not to be abandoned, even if at some future date (after people get accustomed to statements of the new style) the traditional statements are abandoned. But at least it will be noticed that the figures for plant and depreciation in the statements proposed in *A.R.S. No.* 6 are not the same as in the traditional statements; and, if the firm had used a L.I.F.O. basis for inventories in the traditional statements, the statements proposed in *A.R.S. No.* 6 would contain some other figures for inventories due to the need to express L.I.F.O. measures in terms of t_2 dollars. Only in respect of these two classes of assets and the stockholders' equity accounts are there differences between the traditional statements and those proposed in the Study. But the fact that there are these differences means that traditional methods and those of the Study are not logically equivalent. No amount of calculation and restating should be allowed to obscure this. The whole object of the exercise is "to make some difference" in what is presented.

There are some who believe that making adjustments for changes in the general level of prices is a first experimental step towards the realization of the preferable procedure of recognizing all price and price level changes. If we grant the merit of this (without prejudice, as we said at the beginning, to our own stated position[7]), we may adapt such elements of our own proposals are are applicable within the constraints of *A.R.S. No.* 6. This we have done in Table 4.

We draw attention to some of the contrasting features of Tables 2 and 4. The balance sheets as at the end of each year are the same, except for the designation of retained earnings, and this discrepancy is a definitional difference rather than a logical difference. The aggregate net profits for each of the years are the same. The two procedures are thus logically equivalent. But now notice the relative simplicity of method of Table 4, and contrast it with the complexity of Table 2, and the underlying detail shown in Table 3. Again, notice that Table 4 represents all transactions in their actually negotiated amounts; monetary item balances, sales, purchases, expenses are as in the traditional statements; and still it yields the same aggregate effects as the devious procedure of *A.R.S. No.* 6.

---

[7] See *Accounting, Evaluation and Economic Behavior.*

TABLE 3

RECONCILIATION OF FINANCIAL STATEMENTS OF A.R.S. No. 6

All amounts expressed in dollars of purchasing power at t_2
All data and assumptions *as in original*

		Balance Sheet at t_0	Transactions	Balance Sheet at t_1	Transactions	Balance Sheet at t_2
Monetary assets	Dr.	266,667	1,000,000A	222,857	1,052,632A	235,000
	Cr.		650,000B		526,316B	
	Cr.		350,000C		315,789C	
	Cr.		114,286D		57,143D	
	Cr.		(114,286)E		114,286E	
	Cr.		5,714J		10,000J	
	Cr.		38,096K		16,955K	
Inventories	Dr.	333,333	375,000G	375,000	210,526G	210,526
	Cr.		333,333F		375,000F	
Plant	Dr.	400,000	114,286D	514,286		514,286
Depreciation	Cr.		40,000H	40,000	51,429H	91,429
Total assets		1,000,000		1,072,143		868,383
Current liabilities	Cr.	133,333	114,286E	228,570	(114,286)E	100,000
	Dr.		19,049K		14,284K	
Long-term liabilities	Cr.	466,667		400,000		—
	Dr.		66,667L		342,857L	
	Dr.				57,143D	
Stockholders' equity	Cr.	400,000		400,000	342,857L	742,857
Retained earnings						
—Trading gain/loss	Dr.			4,047		19,423
—Gain/loss on net monetary items	Cr.			47,620		44,949
Total equities		1,000,000		1,072,143		868,383

Sales	Cr.	1,000,000A	1,052,632A
Inventory—open	Dr.	333,333F	375,000F
Purchases	Dr.	650,000B	526,316B
		983,333	901,316
Inventory—close	Cr.	375,000G	210,526G
Cost of goods sold	Dr.	608,333	690,790
Depreciation	Dr.	40,000H	51,429H
Other expenses and taxes	Dr.	350,000C	315,789C
Total costs	Dr.	998,333	1,058,008
Trading profit/loss	Cr.	1,667	(5,376)
Gain/loss on			
—short-term			
monetary items	Dr.	19,047K	2,671K
—long-term			
monetary items	Cr.	66,667L	
Dividends	Dr.	5,714J	10,000J
Balance to retained earnings			
—Trading gain/loss	Dr.	4,047	15,376
—Gain/loss on net			
monetary items	Cr.	47,620	(2,671)

TABLE 4

SEQUENTIAL FINANCIAL STATEMENTS — PROPOSED ALTERNATIVE

Column	1	2	3
Balance Sheets at	t_0	t_1	t_2
Purchasing power units of	t_0	t_1	t_2
Monetary assets	200,000	195,000	235,000
Inventories	250,000	300,000	200,000
Plant	300,000	450,000C	514,286C
Depreciation		(35,000)B	(91,429)B, D
Total assets	750,000	910,000	857,857
Current liabilities	100,000	200,000	100,000
Long-term liabilities	350,000	350,000	—
Stockholders' equity	300,000	350,000E	742,857E
Retained earnings		10,000	15,000
	750,000	910,000	857,857

Income Accounts		
Sales	800,000	1,000,000
Inventory—open (opening prices)	250,000	300,000
Inventory price-level adjustment	41,666A	42,857A
Purchases	520,000	500,000
	811,666	842,857
Inventory—close (closing prices)	300,000	200,000
	511,666	642,857
Depreciation	35,000B	51,429B
Other expenses and taxes	280,000	300,000
Total	826,666	994,286
Increment	(26,666)	5,714
Price-level adjustments		
—inventory	41,666A	42,857A
—plant	50,000C	64,286C
—depreciation		(5,000)D
Capital maintenance adjustment		
—capital stock	(50,000)E	(92,857)E
—retained earnings		(1,429)F
Net profit	15,000	13,571
Dividends	(5,000)	(10,000)
Retained earnings (Cr.)		(1,429)F
Balance to retained earnings	10,000	5,000

There are differences in the income statements. They are alphabetically keyed for ease of reference; we describe them briefly.

A. This is the amount required to bring the opening inventory, expressed in purchasing power units of the opening date of each period, to its equivalent measure in purchasing power units of the closing date of each period. The amount is brought openly into the account in Table 4, both as a charge to cost of goods sold and as an offsetting increment to this charge.

B. This is the amount charged for depreciation and the increment in the depreciation provision, being 10 per cent of the closing balance of the plant account, each year being taken by itself.

C. This is the amount required to bring the opening balance of the plant account each year to its equivalent in units of purchasing power of the closing date. The corresponding debit to the plant account is clear in the case of t_1. In the case of the period ended t_2, the amount is derived, as in *A.R.S. No.* 6, as follows:—

Increase in monetary units assigned to opening plant—

Original plant	350,000 × (200-175)/175	$50,000	Dr. Plant
New plant	100,000 × (200-175)/175	$14,286	Dr. Plant

D. This is the increase in the number of monetary units required to represent the opening balance of the depreciation provision in units of purchasing power of t_2.

E. The capital maintenance adjustment is what its name implies. It is the amount by which the measure of the whole of the opening net assets (= total stockholders' equity) must be augmented or restated as a consequence of the change in the purchasing power of the monetary unit during any year. Only if the net assets, measured at the current level of prices at the end of the year, exceed this restated amount of stockholders' equity is there any net betterment. In the first year the amount of the adjustment is $50,000 (= 300,000 × 25/150). Although retained earnings is part of the stockholders' equity, it has been convenient in the tables to separate the two. The amount shown as E in the income account of the second year is the adjustment in respect of the issued stock at the beginning of the year ($92,857 = 650,000 × 25/175); the corresponding credit is to the stockholders' equity account.

F. This part of the capital maintenance adjustment is in respect of the opening balance of retained earnings; it is analogous to and is calculated in the same way as the adjustment for issued stock. The corresponding credit to the retained earnings account is shown explicitly at the foot of the income statement to show the reconciliation with the cumulative balance in the balance sheet.

In practice it would be sufficient to give the aggregates C + D, and E + F; they have been given separately only for purposes of exposition.

We may now compare this alternative with the proposals of *A.R.S. No.* 6.

Some Possible Advantages of A.R.S. No. 6

1. It may be said that no calculation of income may properly be made unless all the magnitudes to be added or subtracted are expressed in units of the same purchasing power. The method of calculating the gain or loss on current monetary items in the Study (which, it will be remembered, simultaneously determines the trading profit) purports to avoid this error. But to obtain this gain or loss a "mixed" balance is subtracted from a "homogenized" balance (Study, p. 127). The principle upon which the complete transformation is based is thus violated at one of the most critical points. In fact, because monetary balances carry through time, the principle can never be strictly applied by reference to monetary items themselves. The proposed alternative circumvents this problem. To add and subtract magnitudes of the same dimension is logically equivalent to adding and subtracting magnitudes of different dimension plus or minus the numbers necessary to convert those magnitudes to a common dimension.[8] This the alternative proposal does by the device

[8] Some further observations on the point were prompted by a critique of this article by Maurice Moonitz, "Chambers on the Price Level Study", *Abacus*, August 1967, pp. 55-61. In reply I wrote:—

If we wish to obtain the length of an inch in centimetres we can state the following rules:—

(a) multiply the number of inches (one) by 2.54; call the result centimetres;
(b) add to the number of inches 1.54; call the result centimetres;
(c) add to the number of inches 1.54 per cent of the number of inches; call the result centimetres.

Notice first, we do not add inches or multiply inches; we add and multiply numbers of them. The numbers only carry a meaning, other than mere numerosity, when we call the result "a something". Note, second, that no one would make a mistake if he followed any one of the above rules; they are logically and practically identical.

Similarly, we deal with numbers of monetary units, not with monetary units themselves, when we transform some number which (with the added dollar sign) expresses a monetary property of some object into another number which (with the added dollar sign) expresses the same monetary property of the object at another time. We slip very easily into the habit of thinking we add like things when in fact we add numbers denoting the numerosity of like things; and the thinking comes out in the elisions we adopt in writing. In *Accounting, Evaluation and Economic Behavior,* at p. 95, I wrote: "It is . . . pointless . . . to add Belgian and French francs when they do not stand at parity." . . . Strictly I should have said "*numbers* of Belgian francs and *numbers* of French francs".

. . . Suppose we were given the following lengths of four objects: 2 feet, 3 inches, 10 centimetres and 1 metre. We could perform the operation of finding the combined length of those objects by any set of additions and transformations we please, provided that the transformation rules are appropriate. We could add 2 and 3 and 10 and 1 and then add the necessary numbers to bring all the measures to one denominator; if the denominator is inches we would add to the sum of the above numbers (16), 22, and zero, and minus 6.07, and 38.37, obtaining a total of 70.30 inches. There is thus nothing logically incorrect in setting out to present amounts in different scales in a single financial statement provided within the same statement there appear other amounts which have the effect of adjusting the measures in different scales to measures in a common scale. This should be clear from the fact that the balance sheet totals at t_2 under the methods of both *A.R.S. No.* 6 and my proposed alternative are identical. (From "A Study of a Study of a Price Level Study", *Abacus,* August 1967, p. 68.)

of the capital maintenance adjustment. If all measures at a given date are in units of contemporary purchasing power and the measure of the stockholders' equity at some prior date is converted to a measure in the same units, the difference between the two measures of stockholders' equity is the amount of the net profit in contemporary terms. If an intermediate magnitude such as trading profit were derived by inference from the record of transactions, the difference between the net profit and the trading profit would be the gain or loss on net monetary asset holdings and inventory holdings. But as these holdings fluctuate, and the application of "average" indexes to their amounts does not give unequivocal measures of those gains or losses, we have simply called the intermediate magnitude an increment. To call it anything else appears to give an unwarranted degree of precision to something we cannot ascertain without interposing an unquantifiable element of judgement.

2. It may be said that *intertemporal* comparisons cannot be made unless all the magnitudes of successive years are converted to similar terms, of contemporary purchasing power. Now, in the first place, this entails, for *A.R.S. No.* 6, a complete reworking of all the statements of past years presented in any comparative table, a reworking each year on a new purchasing power base. If this were necessary the task would have to be undertaken. But it is demonstrably unnecessary. For some purposes absolute differences between the amounts of items at successive dates are significant; it is necessary to know, for example, whether cash balances or liabilities are running up or down. Such inferences can be drawn from the traditional statements, and from the suggested alternative statements; they cannot be drawn from the uniform dollar statements of *A.R.S. No.* 6. For other purposes differences in absolute amounts are irrelevant, uninformative or misleading. In these cases ratios of successive periods are used; the current ratio, the debt to equity ratio, the net profit to capital ratio or rate are examples. If the numerator and denominator of any such ratio are expressed in units of the same purchasing power for a given date or period (as in the alternative but not in the traditional statements), multiplication throughout by a common multiplier (as in the Study) will not change the value of the ratio. Inter-period comparisons can be made without this step; the processes of the Study, in so far as such "homogenizing" is an objective, are unnecessary.

3. It may be said that intra-period comparisons cannot be made unless all magnitudes are converted to measures in units of the same purchasing power. In this respect the proposed alternative may appear to be at a disadvantage in some respects. Comparisons of balance sheet magnitudes will of course be valid, for those magnitudes are all expressed in units of contemporary purchasing power, given that the price level adjustments accomplish this. But comparisons of income statement magnitudes appear, at first, to be invalid because the components are not homogenized. Let us see what difference this makes.

The gross profit rates for the two periods are:—

		First period	Second period
A.R.S. No. 6	(Table 2:3, 5) ..	35.95	36.43
Alternative	(Table 4:2, 3) ..	36.04	35.71

The orders of magnitude are the same; the differences for both periods are small; but the trends are in the opposite directions, slightly. Which method is to be preferred? It will be recalled that the *A.R.S. No.* 6 figures depend on the validity of the correction factor for events occurring through the period; the above percentages for that method can never be unequivocal, therefore, because the choice of that factor is a matter of judgement. The figures of the alternative, however, are strict representations of the aggregates of transactions, except for the opening inventory price adjustment, which both methods share, and which involves an index at a point of time rather than an average through time. All such raw aggregates as sales, purchases, cost of goods sold and expenses are constituted from separate events spread through the year. There seems to be no invalidity in making ratio comparisons of any of them, certainly no invalidity, with respect to the choice of a common unit of measurement, which the adoption of an average correction factor based on judgement would remove.

In making comparisons between magnitudes from both the balance sheet and the income statement there also may appear to be difficulties unless the statements are fully homogenized. Consider the inventory turnover rate, sales divided by average inventory. The rates given by both methods are:—

		First period	Second period
A.R.S. No. 6	(Table 2:3, 5) ..	2.96	3.88
Alternative	(Table 4:2, 3) ..	2.91	4.00

The orders of magnitude are the same; the differences for each period are small; the trends are in the same direction though at slightly different rates. But, as the restated sales figure depends on the use of an average index, again it cannot be claimed that the method of *A.R.S. No.* 6 is superior, whatever may be the defects of the alternative. It should be clear that a valid net profit rate—the prime overall indicator of performance—can be obtained from the alternative.

4. It may be said that the method of *A.R.S. No.* 6 discloses the gain or loss on net monetary items, whereas the proposed alternative does not.[9] But consider this closely. The items at issue are, for the first year:—

A.R.S. No. 6, Table 2:3

Gain/loss on short-term monetary items ..	(16,667)
Gain/loss on long-term monetary items ..	58,333

[9] Moonitz, "Chambers on the Price Level Study", p. 57. This and the following two inserted paragraphs are from "A Study of a Study of a Price Level Study".

Proposed Alternative, Table 4:2

Price level adjustments—inventory	..	..	41,666
—plant	..	..	50,000
Capital maintenance adjustment	..	..	(50,000)

The net effects are the same. But the specific process of *A.R.S. No.* 6 in effect does four things:—

(a) it raises the face values of all opening balances of monetary items—Table 2:2

(b) it raises the face values of all opening balances of non-monetary items—Table 2:2

(c) it reduces the face value of all restated amounts of monetary items by the increments (a)—Table 2:1, 2, 3

(d) it sets off (b) and (c), bringing into the income account only the increments (a).

The set-off will not interfere with the magnitude of the final result because the net amount of all monetary items is necessarily equal to but of opposite sign to the net amount of all other items, and the same multiplier is used. But why set off (b) and (c), instead of (a) and (c)? Presumably to show up the monetary items effect and suppress the non-monetary items effect. Given the presumption of *A.R.S. No.* 6, namely that the monetary items effect can be ascertained independently and should be reported separately, this is understandable. But is it any less reasonable to offset (a) and (c) and bring into the income account the increments (b)?

The choice of a solution depends on what are judged to be the causal factors. The firm in the example is better or worse off because as the price level rose the prices of goods in which it invested rose (or are presumed to have risen) also. As prices are the independently discoverable magnitudes, as movements in prices are the signals on which movements in price levels are calculated, as prices are the data on which buying and selling is done or deferred, and as gains or losses due to the change in the purchasing power of money are inferences only and are thus dependent on the assumptions underlying the inferences, it seems reasonable to treat the price changes of non-monetary items as causal factors. The capital maintenance adjustment (as it is used both in this article and in *Accounting, Evaluation and Economic Behavior*) serves to reduce the gross gains due to price changes by the amount which is due simply to the shift in the purchasing power of money. The effect of the latter is thus not suppressed by the proposed alternative. Rather it is the method of *A.R.S. No.* 6 which suppresses the effect of changes in the measures of non-monetary items, by virtue of the two-step procedure represented in Table 2:2, 4 above; for non-transaction increments are made to appear in the balance sheets without any corresponding items in the income accounts.

On no score, therefore, do we find the alternative proposal deficient by comparison with the proposal of the Study. There are indeed additional points in favour of the alternative.

Advantages of the Alternative

1. By the method of *A.R.S. No.* 6 every figure in the original, traditional data is changed, either for the presentation of the balance sheet or for the calculation of income, and many of these changes are necessarily, and immediately, reversed for balance sheet purposes. The alternative requires few changes, and those are believed to be easily explicable and readily understandable.

2. The variations from the traditional form of accounting are few. Whatever view accountants may take of the representation of inventory, plant and equity at something approaching current significance, the financial statements, dated as they are, purport to represent them so, and they are commonly interpreted as being so. The few variations made explicit in the alternative would disclose the attempt to make them so.

3. If the proposed alternative statements were published as supplementary statements, the points of difference between them and the traditional statements would be few and understandable. However, we would reject the use of any combination of traditional and supplementary statements, as leading only to confusion through the simultaneous assertion of contradictory things about the same objects and relationships.

4. The statements of each year stand on their merits; the "key" items remain the same always; there is no "re-writing of history" in terms which, historically, were not so, as is the effect of *A.R.S. No.* 6.

5. Funds statements or cash flow statements can be derived directly from the alternative proposed. They could never be derived directly from the figures of Table 1:4, 5, 6, or Table 2:3, 5. If it were considered desirable to allow users to draw up funds statements themselves, it would be necessary always to give the traditional statements as well, with the consequence noted in 3, above; and if, instead, companies were obliged to give funds statements, these would not be reconcilable by outsiders with the allegedly superior statements of *A.R.S. No.* 6.

Comparisons—A Suggestion

A great deal of the argument of the Study and of this paper turns on the problem of comparing financial magnitudes. Our conclusion is that the transformation of past financial statements *in toto* is unnecessary. We have mentioned one magnitude, however, which may be misleading if attention is not drawn specifically to the current equivalent of past measures—sales volume. Dollar sales volume is frequently used, and emphasized, as evidence of growth. But the figure or series of figures thus presented is not then being used for a purely financial purpose, but for an auxiliary purpose. Nevertheless, to avoid misleading, even for subsidiary purposes, seems to be a sound objective of business reportage. In any digest of financial information for past periods, therefore, the dollar sales volume should be given adjusted to a common base, the level of prices as at the latest balancing date.

Further, the practice of giving "comparative" financial statements for long series of years, as is now not unusual, seems to have much less value than is supposed. It tends to comparison, across the long interval, of absolute magnitudes which are not comparable, and to serve as a substitute for the deliberate choice of those magnitudes and calculation of those ratios which, and which alone, are significant; even the very size and density of these tables has a soporific quality which may well interfere with the apprehension and the digestion of what is significant. Whether the practice of giving these extended tables is continued or not, it is believed that there should be given with the financial statements a table of significant measures, somewhat as follows (the illustrative figures are based on Table 4):—

Year	19x1	19x2 ..	.. t_1	t_2
Sales (actually recorded)			800,000	1,000,000
Price index (type and source given)			175	200
Sales (in dollars of purchasing power of latest date)			914,000	1,000,000
Net profit rate on (say, closing) Stockholders' equity (per cent p.a.)			4.02	1.79
Net profit percentage of sales ..			1.88	1.36
Net working capital (dollars) ..			295,000	335,000
Current ratio			2.48	4.35
Debt to equity ratio			1.53	.13

All of these measures are of general use in appraising the performance and position of the firm; there may also be others, but these are given by way of illustration. In transforming the sales to a common base, there need be no very strong feelings about the exactness of the index used, nor about the use of any end-of-year or mid-year index. No fine calculations depend on it; its object is simply to put the absolute magnitudes on a comparable footing. It does not seem wise to encourage a belief in greater precision than is reasonably attainable, or greater precision than is useful in indicating the trend.

Conclusion

We believe we have established the three conclusions which, as was stated in the first section of this paper, it was intended to establish. The only way in which one may judge the superiority of one method over another is by comparing both the inherent logic and the consequences of using both. This we have attempted to do. The outcome is only a determination of which is the better of the methods compared. As judgements about the usefulness or practicability of a method are always comparative, it seems that no exposition of a single method is complete unless it includes a demonstration of its superiority over other possible methods. The proposed alternative, although it is not the complete answer to the problem of accounting for changes in prices and price levels in our opinion, appears on the basis of the above experimentation to be superior to the method suggested in the Study.

34

ACCEPTED, BETTER OR BEST?—THE GOAL OF INQUIRY IN ACCOUNTING*

There seems to be a gap in the equipment with which many practical and theoretical problems in accounting and other business disciplines are approached. Every problem, by its nature, demands some answer. And whatever the answer, it is usually claimed by those who adopt it to be the best. Sometimes the concession is made "best—in the circumstances", but even where the claim is not so explicitly guarded it is generally safe to suppose that what is usually meant is "best in the circumstances". It is interesting to examine the foundation of such judgements as these.

What is Best?

We may suppose that the methods by which assets and equities are stated and the magnitudes by which they are represented in any audited balance sheet are the best in the circumstances, at least in the opinion of the accountants who prepared it and the auditors who reported on it. We must suppose this; otherwise we would be committed to a denial of the good faith of the accountants and auditors. This we do not deny. But we may well question the meaning of "best" and "circumstances".

There are many ways in which the amount shown for such assets as inventories or durable goods may be determined. We have dealt with them elsewhere[1]. The present question is: how is an accountant to determine in any particular case which of these many ways is the best, and which combination of ways is best for any given collection of assets? The question is not trivial, for it has been shown by different people that the combinations of methods used may, given the same data, yield materially different results.

We find it difficult to believe that every time the accountant of a given firm comes to prepare its annual financial statements he consciously and conscientiously makes the choice or choices anew, as for the circumstances then prevailing. If there were no other reason he would tend to use the same methods as in the previous year out of respect for the rule of consistency. And of course there are other reasons. Suppose a firm has three kinds of inventories and three classes of durable assets; and that for inventories there are three possible methods of valuation, and three possible methods of valuing

* First published in *The Singapore Accountant,* Vol. 3, 1968, pp. 27-33.

[1] See "Financial Information and the Securities Market", p. 174, *ante*; "A Matter of Principle", p. 242, *ante*.

durables. There is obviously a great number of possible combinations of these assets and methods, all yielding potentially different income and balance-sheet figures. It is at least highly improbable that any accountant would go through this list of possible combinations in order to choose the best. But if he were to do so, there remains the question of the criteria on which that best may be determined. There are, of course, no adequate discussions of possible criteria in the literature. We attempt to list some of them.

Some Criteria

What is judged to be "best" may be that combination of methods which:—

(a) yields the highest of all possible net incomes for a given year;

(b) yields the highest of all possible rates of return on shareholders' equity for a given year;

(c) yields the most realistic income figure, regardless of the effect of its calculation on the amounts of balance sheet items;

(d) yields the most conservative indication of results and position at any time;

(e) yields a net income figure which is consistent with some preconceived rate of growth in net income over a period of years;

(f) yields the least variable rate of net income to shareholders' equity over a period of years;

(g) yields the most realistic income statement and balance sheet at any time (and, therefore, also over a period of years);

(h) is the most widely accepted in general, or in the firm's line of business;

(i) is the least likely to give rise to objections or qualified reports on the part of auditors;

(j) is the easiest to justify (e.g., because it is the combination used previously).

There may be other criteria. But each of the above is a possible criterion; that is to say, there is in traditional literature and practice some warrant for each. Given the variety of methods available for valuing inventories, for charging for depreciation, for deferring and anticipating costs and revenues, for making adjustments to asset values directly rather than through the income account, and so on, every one of these criteria will yield a different set of financial statements. Some of these criteria will yield statements which show results in the most favourable way in the short run; some will show results which seem more favourable when taken in series; some will show results which are favourable to shareholders anxious to sell; some have nothing to do with how favourable the results appear to be, being based on other ideas altogether (e.g., (h), (i) and (j)).

The mere listing of these criteria should explain the absence of any analysis, in the literature, of the grounds on which an accountant may decide what is best. If there are so many possible aims, all potentially in conflict, nothing sensible could be said which would sharpen and focus the "judgement".

"Best in the Circumstances"

But we have not yet considered "the circumstances". Even if there is no "best", perhaps there is a rule for discovering what is "best in the circumstances".

Again we are at a loss. What circumstances? Whose circumstances? If a firm has reported a series of highly satisfactory profits in past years, do the circumstances warrant the choice of methods in any current year which will maintain the level, or the choice of methods which will serve to temper the expectations of shareholders? If a firm is approaching a position in which it may have to seek additional finance, do the circumstances warrant the choice of methods yielding results which will enhance the possibility of raising new funds? If a firm has had difficulties in convincing its auditors of the propriety of some valuation rules it adopted in the previous year, do the circumstances warrant the choice of methods which will cause no like trouble in the current year?

Perhaps we have construed "circumstances" too widely. We are told: "the major objective in selecting a method [of inventory pricing] should be to choose the one which, under the circumstances, most clearly reflects periodic income"[2]. This statement is followed by others which imply that the controlling circumstances may be the typical physical flows of inventories ("cost factors") of the firm and the common mark-up procedures of retailers. These two kinds of circumstances have nothing in common, nor do they seem in any way to be necessarily related to the "clearest reflection of periodic income". Indeed the latter phrase seems to imply that accountants (or perhaps managers) have some intuitive sense of what the income of a given period should be and are, in effect, being authorized to choose a method which will yield a result consistent with their intuitions.

The English recommendations are no more helpful. "Circumstances vary so widely that no one basis of arriving at the amount [of an inventory] is suitable for all types of business nor even for all undertakings within a particular trade or industry . . . The method [of allocating overhead expenditure to inventory] selected by the management . . . must have regard to the nature and circumstances of the business so as to ensure that the trend of the trading results will be shown fairly."[3]

By and large it seems that there is no discoverable content of the phrase "best in the circumstances"; or perhaps that its content is so diverse and extensive that it is meaningless as a guide to practice. There are two corollaries of this conclusion.

Comparison and Interpretation Thwarted

The first is that, notwithstanding the specificity of some rules, every one can be overridden by judgements about "the circumstances".

---

[2] American Institute of Certified Public Accountants, *Accounting Research and Terminology Bulletins*, Final edition, New York, 1961, p. 29.

[3] The Institute of Chartered Accountants in England and Wales. *Recommendations on Accounting Principles.* N22, 1960, paras. 1, 8.

The total effect is unreliable. We cannot read one set of financial statements and compare what we deduce from it with what we deduce from another set; for we have no knowledge of the contingent circumstances which may have rendered the two sets inconsistent. This observation we will only make, however, if we realize that the products of accounting processes become part of the pool of financial information available to all investors and financiers; that the statements of any one firm may be, and commonly will be, compared with those of another or others; and that the only legitimate foundation for such comparisons is that the statements were prepared according to common rules. The alternative, and unfortunately the prevalent, view is that each firm is permitted to represent itself in its own peculiar way, to give words and numbers its own peculiar meanings, as if its statements had nothing to do with other persons or institutions. Such a permissive accounting is at least banal, at the worst quite mischievous: for it denies the right to be informed, in understandable terms, which legislation and regulations for the protection of investors, creditors and financiers have sought to secure. Secret reserves have for some time been frowned upon. But the time is not yet present when users of accounting statements may take them as other than messages written in a private code.

The second corollary of our conclusion is that to perpetuate the use, the discussion and the teaching of diverse valuation rules, which may be taken up, or dropped according to "circumstances", is to deny that there is a reasoned basis for accounting at all. The justification of the dialectic of any field of practical consequence is that it yields practically useful devices or results. If the devices are linguistic, as accounting statements are, to be practically useful at any time the symbols used must have the same significances as equivalent symbols used in any other discourse at the same time. Thus $100,000 appearing opposite the caption "cash" in the balance sheet of A Company should mean the same thing as $100,000 appearing opposite the caption "plant" in the same balance sheet, the same as $100,000 appearing opposite the caption "marketable securities" in the balance sheet (prepared to the same date) of B Company, the same as $100,000 appearing as the balance of the account of any investor with his bank at the same time, and the same as $100,000 being the price of any parcel of shares or real estate at the same time. Accounting does not presently produce such results that those significances of the symbol "$100,000" are the same. Only in the first and the latter two examples may the numbers be properly matched; and then only because the numbers are not the product of rules which, through time, permit $100,000 to represent mixed and equivocal magnitudes, uninterpretable and therefore meaningless.

What is Better?

We are now able to return to the question which is our title. If accounting is at present undisciplined, what could with advantage be put in its place?

One clue to this has already been given. If, in the nature of things, accounting is a formal linguistic device, its main signs and symbols—the products of its operations—must all be equivalent in significance and freely interpretable by those who engage in commerce, at any given time. In ordinary discourse we do not use the same symbols, terms or descriptions for objects having a continuous existence through time. We speak of a three months old baby, a 10 year old boy, a 35 year old man, when at different times we speak of the same person. What at one time is a sapling, at another is a tree. Yet in accounting what is represented as the monetary equivalent of certain kinds of assets at the time of their purchase is quite commonly taken as the monetary equivalent for years afterwards, notwithstanding material changes in their monetary equivalents. The only monetary magnitudes which are significant for action at any time are the contemporary monetary equivalents of assets and equities at that time. There are, of course, some who regard balance sheets as synoptic histories of the firms they represent, and who therefore regard historical purchase prices as worth retaining. But, writing of history, Santayana observed: "There are many things which, as Aristotle says, it is better not to know than to know—namely, those things which do not count in controlling the mind's fortunes nor enter into its ideal expression."[4] Past prices, like other outdated symbols, and particularly mixtures of past prices paid at different dates, do not count in any present exercise directed to the amelioration of one's state, nor into any expression about one's present state.

We have therefore one constraint at least on the use of the imagination in formulating accounting rules. We may not accept any rule which is a clear violation of the notion that contemporary cash equivalents of assets and equities are alone significant indicators of a present financial state.

This principle subsumes another, which, if we were to argue from a different direction, could be shown to be a constraint in its own right. Firms commonly hold various kinds of assets at any time, subject to various kinds of equities. We need to aggregate some or all of these, either to discover their totals or to relate certain sub-totals (such as debt and equity, for example). The individual symbols for the monetary equivalents of assets and equities must therefore be additive; they must represent the monetary equivalents at a given time in monetary units of the same purchasing power dimension. As we have said, this is in fact secured if all monetary equivalents are contemporary monetary equivalents.

There is one further constraint. In all kinds of exercises involving growth or movement it is found to be useful to discover the rate of change between any two past points. As diverse examples, consider a driver on a racing circuit, and a man near or past middle age who is concerned with his weight for his health's sake. So, in business we are interested in the rate at which shareholders' equity has grown in the past period at any point of time. The commonest and simplest

[4] George Santayana, *Reason in Science*, New York, Collier Books, 1962, p. 40.

measure of this is obtained by taking the difference between the measures of shareholders' equity at the beginning and end of a period. If these measures are in units of the same purchasing power there is no problem; if not, the opening measure must be converted to the same dimension as the closing measure before taking the difference. This follows also from the principle stated in the last paragraph. We may not accept any rule, therefore, which interferes with the representation of the whole of the change between two points of time in the measures of shareholders' equity, as those measures are given in contemporary statements of financial position at each of those points. For, to the extent that we fail to represent the whole of the change in any one period the change in some subsequent period will be misrepresented.

There are here three primary principles, the contemporaneity of symbols, the additivity of measures, and the completeness of periodical representations. Their relationship to the usefulness of financial communications will be obvious. They require only modest elaboration, by reference to specified classes of financial characteristics of firms, of events and transactions, to provide a complete foundation for a rigorous accounting.

They are, of course, ideals. They do not, as stated, indicate the difficulties which may be experienced in discovering the magnitudes and devising the modes of representation which they hint at. If we set out to discover the contemporary cash equivalents (market resale prices) of assets, for example, we will find difficulties in many cases; for there are not markets in all goods in all states of use or stages of completion. We may have to seek approximations to or surrogates for such prices. We may feel that the use of these approximations and surrogates will so affect the results that the whole process is of doubtful value.

Grounds of Choice

But before dismissing what is already accepted or what is newly proposed we should be sure of the grounds on which we choose. It is apparent that countless thousands of accountants have accepted and do accept traditional modes of accounting as the best. "Best" means superior in all respects to any alternative system. (Perhaps it may be given some other meaning, but we rely on the common-sense meaning of what is "best".) However, unless we know the characteristics of more systems than one we cannot describe that system as the best. We can only describe it as the system; or perhaps we can call it the "accepted" system without any implication that it is the best. In any case, the use of "best" raises the whole question of how or whether we can make any absolute judgement of the kind "superior in all respects".

Our knowledge of "what is" is limited by our capacities for perception. Our sense of "what could be" is limited by our imaginations. In neither respect is our capacity so great that we can bring under observation or reflection all that does exist or all that could exist, for the purpose of judging what is superior in all respects.

We are limited to comparative judgements; to judgements as between the sets of ideas which we know of or which we can construct; and to judgements on the basis of those respects which we can bring to conscious attention and which seem at the time to be crucial. It is doubtful whether the analyst of any set of ideas or the champion of any cause has been able to marshal all the pertinent evidence or argument, for or against, at any one time. Although men are accustomed to rely on generalizations of the nature of scientific principles and laws for long periods of time, men of science are accustomed to the supercession of laws by more inclusive, and therefore better, laws. Science is said to advance by a process of successive approximations[5]. We may safely abandon the notion that we can judge which is best among accounting systems, in any ultimate sense.

That still leaves us with "accepted" and "better". Ideally, what is accepted at any time should be what is better than any alternative. We must however distinguish between what is logically better and what is psychologically better. What becomes accepted does not always become widely accepted on logical grounds. We have to reckon with habit, inertia, group solidarity and group indoctrination, if we are to discover why some practices persist and spread. Non-logical and illogical practices will persist to the extent that practitioners (and teachers) concern themselves more with personal-social questions than with logical or scientific questions. But whatever the grounds may have been for accepting one system, we are entitled to ask whether that system is logically better than any alternative; for whatever is logically the better we may expect will, in due course, come to be accepted and generally endorsed as the better.

Traditional Rules and Some Alternatives

How does traditional accounting compare, then, with the few principles on which we have said a preferable system should be based? It satisfies none of those principles except to a very modest extent. Cash, receivables and payables are the only balance-sheet items which are represented in contemporary symbols; the measures of the several assets are not additive; and the lagging of the effects of some transactions and events, and the disregard of changes in the purchasing power of money, result in incomplete representations of periodical changes.

In general, any change in any particular accounting or valuation practice which increases the conformity of the result with the stated principles will yield a better accounting. An obvious change of this kind would be the use of market selling price for marketable (quoted) securities held as assets, instead of the commonly used initial purchase price. Of a different kind would be the use, in respect of real estate, of valuations made, independently of particular asset-holders, for rating or taxing purposes. Objections to any such suggestion commonly take the form that these are not necessarily "true" values of

[5] A. d'Abro, *The Evolution of Scientific Thought,* New York, Dover Publications Inc., 1950, pp. 384-5.

the assets in question. This kind of objection is, however, purely defensive or escapist. What we need to know is something approaching a current market price. It is notable that those who refer to "true" values make no attempt to state what is "true" in the context. In practical affairs we accept as true those propositions on which we can place greater reliance than other propositions about the same objects. In the first place we would regard a price or value determined independently of the owner of the object as more reliable than any statement he himself makes about the value of the object. And, secondly, we would regard a price or value determined more recently than the date of initial purchase as more reliable at any subsequent date than the initial purchase price. The market prices or ratable values we have suggested may be approximations only; but they are approximations to something contemporary, and for all practical purposes they are better than exact but no longer relevant magnitudes.

The points we have sought to establish are that what is at any time generally accepted may be so accepted on grounds which have little to do with technical functions and constraints; that we can never know what is best in any ultimate sense; and that we can make progress only by choosing the better, as between any two or more competing generalizations or systems, and choosing on grounds which emerge from the character of the subject-matter rather than on grounds which are personal-social (i.e., mere preferences for "an easy life", for "status" or for any similar personal goal).

It should be clear that the style of thinking we have suggested and the end products we have sketched would eliminate almost all of the possible criteria of choice which we outlined in an earlier section. Only the criterion (g) remains. All the rest entail the exercise, as occasion arises, of particular judgements about peripheral circumstances; judgements which entail a knowledge of the diverse immediate psychological settings of managers, investors, auditors and the like which no accountant can seriously pretend to have. We just cannot anticipate what any recipient of any piece, or any collection, of information will do with it. The only sensible thing to do then is to give that information which is more readily interpretable and more pertinent to action at any time than any alternative information. We need not ask who in particular will use it, and how; it is pointless to ask these questions, for we can give no answers to them. If we seek contemporary information and seek to state it in understandable terms, a substantial part of the body of diverse rules now tolerated would be eliminated; and accounting would take on the appearance of a reasoned discipline, rather than its present appearance of unsystematic *ad-hoc-ery*.

In keeping with the general spirit of these observations, we do not hold that the three principles we have stated are the most crucial. We are content to say they are crucial; and that the system of accounting which shows the greater respect for them is to be preferred to all other actual or potential systems. There are other principles in addition to these, which we have tried to set down in *Accounting,*

Evaluation and Economic Behavior[6]. But we do not contend that even this more elaborate statement is exhaustive, or final. We are content to say that any system of accounting thought or practice is to be preferred if it satisfies a greater number of principles, or a given number to a greater extent, than any alternative system.

To Choose, or Not to Choose?

A professionally alert body of specialists may not, if it values integrity, persist in suspending judgement on matters which are within its competence. Professional bodies have shown that they sense this; otherwise we would not have at hand the attempts they have made to state what is permissible. But these statements and recommendations are still full of conflicting alternatives, each one of which is evidence of the suspension of judgement. If those whose responsibility it is to make judgements of what is better refuse to do so, they leave the outcome entirely in the hands of others who because they are technically untrained are technically incompetent to judge. As explanation of this suspension of judgement there are two possibilities.

The first is the belief that no judgement should be made until the "best" solution has been discovered. We have already made the point that what is ultimately the best can be of no help to us now if we have not yet discovered it. But there is a further point. In the history of science and technology it is a common place that only by the rigorous use of what at any time is better than alternatives does the next improvement in principle or technique become visible.[7] While ever accounting does not conform rigorously with a given set of ideas, however imperfect, while ever it permits the use of rules which are divergent in effect, it will not be able to throw up evidence of its defects; for the evidence of the need for improvement will be confused by the diversity of the rules and of their effects. It will be impossible to take advantage of the mode of growth which seems to be the common mode in other technologies.

The other possible explanation of the suspension of judgement is that comfort is taken in precedent, in what has been accepted in the past. If, of course, men had been content to live by this idea we would still be pedestrians; or, more recently, still drivers of horses and buggies. It is indeed curious what we are prepared to "accept". If a practice were generally accepted, we may still have the advantage mentioned in the previous paragraph. But, if the practices which are entitled to be called "generally accepted" are those which are catalogued in the series *Accounting Trends and Techniques*, published by the American Institute, it is clear that many practices which are adopted by only a few companies would qualify as generally accepted. Indeed, it seems that a company could adopt a procedure which was

---

[6] See also the next section of this volume, p. 473.
[7] Thomas S. Kuhn, *The Structure of Scientific Revolutions,* Chicago, University of Chicago Press, 1962, Ch. 6, 7.

"distinctly peculiar to itself" and still be said to be following "generally accepted accounting principles".[8]

This last cited instance may open ground for debate about whether, in fact, judgement has been suspended. Suppose we were to take as a generally accepted accounting principle that "depreciation is to be provided for". It may then be said that any method of making the provision would be consistent with this principle. But it is not permissible to say that any such method is consistent with generally accepted accounting principles if there are more principles than the one just mentioned. Any particular method must be consistent simultaneously with all the principles which bear on it, not just one. This is the point at which judgement is suspended. And largely, it may be supposed, because the principles to be satisfied are seen as isolated, not as a self-consistent system of requirements. In other words it has not been understood as necessary that accounting principles (the basic ideas) should be viewed as a network or screen through which no specific rule or procedure may pass to acceptance which does not meet all the tests which the body of principles imposes. Lacking this conception, much work on accounting has not even attempted the ordering of ideas so that they do in fact constitute a self-consistent system.

Perhaps progress to this point will be slow. But there is no good reason why reduction in the variety of "accepted" rules and methods should not proceed at a greater pace than is presently noticeable. For even on the basis of the few principles we have mentioned, there are some rules which are clearly better than others, and the "others" should yield to what are the better.

---

[8] The idea seems first to have been put forward in 1947 in *Generally Accepted Auditing Standards*, American Institute of Accountants; its persistence is evident from, for example, Paul Grady, *Inventory of Generally Accepted Accounting Principles for Business Enterprises*, New York, A.I.C.P.A., 1965, pp. 51-3.

TOWARDS A THEORY OF ACCOUNTING

35

"... A TIME TO BUILD ..."

Following the decision of 1954 (see p. 343 *ante*), it seemed necessary to undertake some work in a number of different directions. If a systematic set of ideas and their relationships were to be developed, it would have to satisfy simultaneously a variety of practical, theoretical and methodological requirements. Inquiries in these directions proceeded more or less simultaneously. Examples of empirical work, on accounting and financial practices, are *The Function and Design of Company Annual Reports* (1955: based on a study of the reports of companies in the United Kingdom, the United States and Australia); "The Implications of Asset Revaluations and Bonus Share Issues" (1957: a study of some practices of quoted Australian companies, see p. 95 *ante*) and other unpublished work of the kind used later in "Financial Information and the Securities Market" (see p. 174 *ante*). *Accounting and Action* (1957) was an attempt to illustrate the derivation and use of accounting information from the level of householder accounting through to the level of social accounting: the exercise of working through the practically related types of entity in this range confirmed the belief in the necessary homogeneity and contemporaneity of accounting information. Much of the remaining writing of the period to 1960 concerned itself with theoretical and methodological questions (see the chronological bibliography).

These different kinds of work seemed to converge. By late 1960 it seemed possible to build on the framework of "Blueprint for a Theory of Accounting"; and it seemed desirable to do so rather than to go on talking about how to construct a theory of accounting. The result was "Towards a General Theory of Accounting".

In early 1962 I was invited to give a lecture in the University of Tasmania. Relying, as before, on the convergence of evidence, it seemed worthwhile to attempt to show that the difficulties and contradictions encountered in the literature of accounting would be eliminated by adoption of the set of ideas developed in "Towards a General Theory of Accounting". The result was "The Resolution of Some Paradoxes in Accounting". Lectures based on it were given in the Universities of Tasmania, Malaya (Singapore) and British Columbia during 1962 and the paper was published by the University of British Columbia in 1963. Due to the separation of places of publication of the two papers, it is probable that their mutually supporting character was not apparent. This volume is the first occasion of their publication together.

When writing the two pieces abovementioned, I was still content to regard replacement price as the appropriate foundation for accounting in contemporary terms. But by early 1963 I had begun to think otherwise. The first draft of "Measurement in Accounting" contained the seeds of the idea that resale price was the appropriate basis. The published version of the paper (see p. 544, *post*) benefited from the writing of *Accounting, Evaluation and Economic Behavior* during 1963 and 1964.

The foundations of that book were laid in the "Blueprint" article (see p. 347 *ante*) and "Towards a General Theory". They seemed to provide satisfactory premises for the deduction of rules which would eliminate many of the widely-known defects in theory and practice. But some criticisms of the book indicated, at least by implication, that parts of the argument were less than convincing.

Some of the vaguenesses I tried to reduce, in "Accepted, Better or Best?—The Goal of Inquiry in Accounting" (p 462 *ante*), "Continuously Contemporary Accounting—Additivity and Action" (p. 612, *post*), and "Measures and Values" (p. 621, *post*). Further reflection on the consequences of my original assumptions led me to the answer to the question: "Are Consolidated Statements Really Necessary?" (p. 631, *post*), and to a more rigorous demonstration of the formal foundation of continuously contemporary accounting (p. 638, *post*). There will doubtless be need for more of these clarifications and modifications, but the core of the argument is as yet unassailed.

36

TOWARDS A GENERAL THEORY OF ACCOUNTING*

Introduction

1. The purpose of this paper is to explore the economic and social foundations of accounting in pursuit of a body of general ideas on which the practice of accounting is or may be based. The methods of accounting have been developed in response to a wide variety of impulses and under a variety of influences. Some have been dictated by the nature of the environment; others have been the invention of practitioners faced with technical problems for which the environment did not appear to offer clear direction. Development has been piecemeal; it could not have been otherwise; and it will no doubt continue to be so. It should not be surprising therefore that there are at present a number of concurrent accounting systems, different in some important senses even though similar in certain of their forms. It is not surprising either that the concepts by which some of these systems are described are contradictory. The variety of methods and the internal inconsistency of systems of concepts are the facts which force a reconsideration of underlying ideas and a search for a general theory.

2. This inquiry does not take the form of a survey of accounting practices nor of an appraisal of the lore of teachers and practitioners of accounting. There are eminent examples of such surveys and appraisals, and in the growth of a systematic body of knowledge their work has been invaluable. But confined as they were to accounting as it was taught or practised, these studies touched only tentatively or tangentially on fundamental ideas. What is now proposed is an examination of those ideas as such, without any attempt at the outset to relate them to any existing accounting system; the objective is to deduce from the nature of the environment of accounting the characteristics of a system which will serve the purposes for which it was or is designed.

3. The present exercise will have some defects and some limitations. It will be possible to consider at length only two classes of case—natural persons as producers and consumers; and simple trading enterprises. The generality of the argument may therefore be open to

* Prepared as a basis for the Annual Endowed Lecture of The Australian Society of Accountants in the University of Adelaide, 2 August 1961. The invitation of Professor R. L. Mathews to give this lecture provided the spur to set down these ideas even though they are only a first approach to a complete and systematic presentation.

doubt in some respects; the doubt can only be resolved by extending the demonstration to other cases, which will be done on other occasions. There may be defects of another less obvious kind. The foundations of accounting are varied; it will be necessary to draw on a number of seemingly unrelated disciplines; it is hoped that none of these is misconstrued, though that possibility is open. The treatment given to those disciplines is necessarily simplified, and simplification and the selection it involves may be challenged[1]. One thing specifically excluded is the effect of governmental levies or taxes on the form of accounting. The basis of such levies is a matter of governmental policy and administrative convenience; it has no necessary connexion with accounting concepts; it belongs to a different field of discourse.

4. The art of accounting is practised in a socio-economic setting. It concerns itself with representations to or for persons, singly, in groups or by classes, on the consequences of actions having financial characteristics. Its operations are designed, or expected, to add to the knowledge of persons for whom accounting statements are prepared. The study of it therefore requires and should be based on some knowledge of the ways in which people act, individually and collectively. Accounting represents transactions of persons in economic resources. Its study should therefore concern itself with that part of economics which deals with the characteristics of resources, their combination for the purposes of production and consumption, and the process of exchange. These processes are regulated by the laws and customs which prevail at the time; the legal and conventional framework cannot therefore be overlooked. Finally, accounting is a formal operation by which information is selected, processed and communicated; its study must therefore comprehend parts of the field of the communication sciences such as languages and of epistemology.

5. Out of this mixture of psychological, economic, legal, conventional and formal considerations must be spun a coherent network of ideas which will represent the source of all specific prescriptions for accounting practices.

6. It may be useful before beginning the analysis to indicate what it is expected to demonstrate. It will be suggested that conventional accounting procedures are illogical; that they lead to results which are irrelevant and misleading; that they are internally inconsistent and inconsistent with the realities they report on. It will be argued that a full historical record necessitates adjustments for shifts in value, that such a record is the closest approximation one can make to the representation of present reality for the purpose of future action. It will be argued that accounting to be useful will be oriented to

---

[1] Throughout this paper no references are made to the work of other authors in the field of accounting or in any other field of inquiry on the findings of which argument depends. The list would be extensive, and as the system of ideas presented has been built up over many years it is unlikely that such a list as would now occur to me would be exhaustive. I can therefore acknowledge only generally my debt to others, hoping that in some future restatement more specific acknowledgement can be made.

future behaviour and that it will concern itself always with values—not with costs in the sense of money outlays. It will be argued that many of the practical imperfections of existing methods arise from makeshift devices adopted in the absence of a consistent theory of accounting. The theory represented in embryo in this paper is not designed specifically to overcome these deficiencies: but it results in a system which is free of most of them.

Individuals as Actors

7. We begin by considering persons as actors. The human individual is a complex organism capable of perception, reflection and action. Perception, reflection and action have time dimensions; they are initiated at points of time and carried out over periods of time. But the total time available for these processes to any person is limited.

8. Perception is the observing or sensing in any way of characteristics of the environment or of the organism itself. At any time the environment and the organism itself offer for perception an extensive array of things and events. As the sensory devices are limited, the span of attention is limited; so that at any time only some of the perceivable things are in fact perceived; only some become the focus of attention.

9. Reflection includes all mental operations, such as relation, comparison, recollection and calculation. Relation is the apprehension of connexions between things perceived including causal connexions. Comparison is reflection on the similarities or differences between things. Recollection is bringing to immediate conscious attention things that have been perceived in the past. Calculation is the manipulation of qualities and quantities for the purpose of apprehending connexions, of making comparisons or contrasts. The operations of relation and comparison give rise to arrangement, classification and systematization. The capacity for recollection of specific things and events varies inversely with the number of specific unrelated things perceived, and directly with the extent of reflection on and systematization of things perceived.

10. Action includes, besides bodily action, such mental actions as choice and appropriation. Perception and reflection are always directed towards action in the future. Through time actions need not necessarily be consistent; for any individual may assume different roles—either during successive intervals or during a given interval. He may, for example, be at the same time father, breadwinner, worker, member or official of non-family groups; and some or all of these roles may be relinquished as time passes.

11. At any time an individual finds himself in a set of bodily and mental states. At the same time he has a set of preferred states. If the two sets are identical there is no incentive to change; but they are seldom identical. Perceived differences between existing and preferred states create strains or uneasiness. At any time there may be numerous strains; one may be hungry, thirsty, weary, elated and economically insecure simultaneously. Potentially the number of

concurrent strains is equal to the number of states postulated above. And as there are mental states appropriate to each role (10)[2] filled by any individual, the number and diversity of strains vary with the number of concurrent roles.

12. The intensity of a strain varies with the extent of the perceived difference between an existing and a preferred state (11). Intensity is a product of comparison; it is a matter of more or less. It is possible to imagine a scale of intensities for each different kind of strain, but the mind does not find explicit scales necessary. Even though there are many contemporary strains, all different in character, the mind proceeds to rank them in order of intensity. The ranking of strains (arrangement or ordering) is not simple; the difficulty of ranking varies with the number and diversity of strains. Ranking implies an order of urgency. As ranking involves an expenditure of mental effort over time and time is scarce (7), explicit ranking may be limited to the strains felt with greatest intensity; to all others the mind may, for the time being, be indifferent.

13. Strains are accompanied by wants; wants are desires to be relieved of strains. Wants are correlates of strains. Thus, there are diverse concurrent wants; wants are felt with different intensities and wants are ranked according to intensity. The relief of strain or the satisfaction of wants is the incentive to and goal of action. Goals are correlates of wants. There are diverse concurrent goals; goals at any time have different values and are ranked according to those values. The values assigned to specific goals are the values placed on the satisfaction of their associated wants. The values placed on the satisfaction of wants are personal and therefore subjective and intensive. The values assigned to goals determine the order in which they become the focus of attention.

14. The set of preferences of any person is variable. Attainment in whole or part of any goal will lead to a change in the ranking of goals. Or, of his own will a person may abandon one system of values for another, changing the whole structure of his wants and the values assigned to specific goals. Or he may recast his value system in response to characteristics of the environment. Any system of preferences may persist over a long time, but the possibility of change is ever present; its nature and extent are always unpredictable.

15. Because the span of attention is limited and the time for reflection may be short, the greater the extent of systematization the greater is the capacity to comprehend the variety of factors which are the environment of action, and the wants and values which direct action. The greater the number of sub-systems, the greater is the time and effort required to relate and co-ordinate them, and the greater is the possibility of lack of relation and co-ordination.

---

[2] The numbers appearing occasionally in the text are references to other paragraphs where the same ideas are dealt with.

Means

16. Goals are pursued by the appropriation of means. Means are all things other than free goods, believed to be serviceable in the attainment of goals or ends. Free goods are those which though useful involve no effort or sacrifice; they are part of the environment. Things with no perceived serviceability at any time are not then means; they are irrelevant. The value to a person of any means is derived from the values attached to the goals it serves. The expectation or belief that a means will be serviceable in satisfying a want is its utility.

17. Means are scarce relatively to wants; non-scarce means are excluded by the above definition. Means are varied in form; they include labour, natural things, artefacts and rights. With advances in knowledge and technology some things which were at one time considered as means cease to be so considered, and some things not previously considered to be means become means. Means vary in specificity, or in their appropriateness to the service of specific ends. Some means are said to be means of the first order; they are highly specific and have the capacity for directly satisfying wants, or direct utility. Other means are said to be goods of higher order; they have the capacity for yielding means of the first order. Means vary in durability; some may continue indefinitely to serve wants, some may lose over more or less long periods their capacity to serve wants, and some are exhausted immediately in serving wants. Means vary in divisibility; in some cases the minimum unit is large, in other cases it is small.

Environment

18. The environment is the complex of things, persons, relationships and events which surround and impinge on an individual. The environment in part determines the state in which an actor finds himself at any time. It provides some of the things which gives rise to strain; it also provides some of the means of relieving strain. Those things which tend to create states divergent from a preferred state or to create new preferred states will be called stimuli. Environmental stimuli include natural events and circumstances and social events, circumstances and customs.

19. Environmental stimuli may be fortuitous, recurrent or persistent; and their impact may be more or less severe. Knowledge and experience may enable people to distinguish stimuli which are expected to be fortuitous, recurrent and persistent. This is not certain knowledge; it is probabilistic only. Against recurrent and persistent sources of strain persons may make provision; but against fortuitous stimuli and against the possibility of any stimulus being more or less severe no specific planned provision can be made. In at least some respects, therefore, the environment is fluid and unpredictable. This is one source of personal uncertainty.

20. The environment includes laws, customs and other devices relating things, persons and events. The predictability of the environment increases with the stability and effectiveness of such laws,

customs and similar devices. But laws and customs themselves are responses to a given set of circumstances at a given level of knowledge and are therefore susceptible to change. The timing of such changes is not predictable. This is another source of uncertainty.

Categories of Action

21. The characteristic activities of men are production and consumption. Production is the combination of means for the creation of things having greater utility than the sum of the utilities of the means used. The process may be as simple as the expenditure of effort in performing a service; or it may be quite complex, involving many stages and the use of many intermediate goods. The state of technology and the methods of production change from time to time, introducing additional uncertainties to the environment of action. The purpose of production of final goods or intermediate goods is the satisfaction of wants. The incentive to production is the increase in utility or value expected to result. The amount by which the value of produced goods exceeds the value of goods used in production is the income from the process.

22. Consumption is the appropriation of means for the satisfaction of immediate wants. The difference between production and consumption is saving. Saving is the provision of means for the service of future wants; it involves the accumulation of a stock of means and depends therefore on there being some durable means. Individuals may save with the object of meeting unforeseen contingencies, or with the object of investing in productive operations. Prior saving is a condition of production by complex or roundabout processes. The incentive to invest is the expectation of increasing the income stream by improving the methods of production.

23. The accumulation of a stock of means, whether precautionary or for investment, is influenced by the predictability of the environment. Extreme uncertainty may dictate the immediate consumption of what one has. Short of extreme uncertainty, the greater the flexibility of one's goals and the less the predictability of the environment, the greater will be the tendency to accumulate non-specific means. Conversely, the greater the persistence or recurrence of wants and the more stable the environment, the greater will be the tendency to acquire specific and durable means. As, generally, the environment has some relatively stable elements (20) and personal goals have a measure of stability (14), persons will, if their means are above subsistence level, accumulate both specific and non-specific means. Some means are used alone, some are used in combinations dictated by technology and the planned scale of action, and some are substitutes for others. The proportions in which means of different kinds are accumulated depends on their complementarity and substitutability with respect to goals.

24. As there are concurrent competing wants, the greater the stock of a specific means the less is the desirability of adding to that stock; the utility of the n*th* unit is less than the utility of the (n-1)*th* unit. As action involves adding to or subtracting from stocks of means,

interest focuses on the unit last added or sacrificed, the marginal unit. The utility of the marginal unit diminishes as the stock of a given means increases. In pursuit of maximum total satisfaction (40) the aggregate stock of means will tend to be so arranged that the marginal utilities of all stocks are equal.

Action in a Market Economy

25. A society of individuals tends to arrange its productive processes so that the wants of its members may be satisfied in a greater measure than would be achieved by the efforts of each acting in isolation. All individuals have different innate and acquired capacities for action (individual differences). The greater the opportunities for specialization (the exercise of specific individual skills) the greater the aggregate product. But as individuals have diverse wants, the possibility of exchanging what one produces for what one wants is a condition of specialization. Exchange is the process by which each individual arranges that the marginal utilities of different stocks are equal.

26. Both consumption and exchange entail that individuals shall have control over, or the right to dispose of, means. These rights are secured by the framework of laws and customs (20). Control may take the form of possession or ownership. Possession is a matter of fact; but the conditions under which one has possession are matters of law and custom. Freedom to use and dispose of goods in possession may be limited by the role in which one has possession—for example, one may have possession as agent, trustee, lessee or owner. Ownership of (or property in) means is a legally enforceable right against all other persons to have, use and dispose of means. One may have ownership with possession, in which case the subject goods are entirely under the control of one person. One may have ownership without possession, in which case one's rights as owner are limited by the contract under which possession was transferred. And one may have possession without ownership in which case one's rights as possessor are only those which have been ceded by the owner. Both goods themselves and limited rights in them are means in terms of the above definition. Laws and customs establish the conditions under which ownership and possession may be transferred between persons. Generally ownership and possession may be transferred gratuitously or for consideration.

27. Except in the case of gratuitous transfers, the owner of means will only part with possession if he is assured that the transferee will at a future date perform his part of the contract. Performance is assured by legal rights of recovery and damages. But owners will frequently transfer means in the expectation of performance by the transferee without recourse to legal remedies. All transfers in advance of settlement by the transferee are credit transactions. The extent to which means are exchanged is increased by the use of credit.

28. In the absence of exchange one would only acquire means specific to one's goals. But the possibility of exchange increases the range of goods one may acquire so that it includes goods to be held

for exchange as well as for consumption. Goods may thus have a value in exchange as well as a value arising from the value attached to the ends they serve. Value in exchange is extensive and objective; it is independent of the private opinion of the owner or possessor for the time being of any good. Beyond the level of the stock of means necessary for planned consumption, no stock of goods may be considered irrevocably committed to any purpose. A change in the exchange value of a good or a change in the composition of wants will induce a change in the composition of one's stock, and as noted above many such changes are unpredictable (14). For any contemplated action involving a change in the composition of one's stock the values in exchange of the components of that stock are the relevant values to consider.

29. The rate at which goods are exchanged is the ratio of exchange. An exchange occurs when both parties expect to gain from the sacrifice of what they offer for what they receive. The sacrifice of the satisfaction which would have been obtained from the use and possession of the goods given is the cost of the goods received. As both parties have different wants the ratio of exchange is a function of their current preferences and current stocks; and as these change, so will the ratio of exchange alter.

30. The ratio of exchange involves specific units of goods. Direct exchange depends on the willingness of the parties to exchange goods in the units in which they are produced or in multiples of those units. But some goods are large in size (17), or high in exchange value by comparison with others. The possibility of exchange is increased by the availability of a generally accepted medium of exchange. A medium of exchange must be generally acceptable, otherwise it would not be worth taking in exchange for things having direct utility. It must be divisible, otherwise it could not serve as a means of settling transactions diverse in size. It must be durable, otherwise it could not be accumulated for the purchase of goods of high exchange value or for the purchase of things of low exchange value at a point of time remote from its acquisition.

31. Media of exchange are means in terms of the definition of means given above (16). They differ from other means in that they are demanded not for themselves but for the ease with which they are convertible into other means required for consumption or production; the utility of a medium of exchange is a derived utility, not a direct utility. Money is a medium of exchange. It is the most easily convertible means, or the most liquid means, and serves as a base for describing the degree of liquidity of other means. But in terms of exchange, money is not essentially different from other means.

32. The exchange of goods for goods through the intermediate step of money is indirect exchange. The ratio of exchange of other goods for money is the price. It is customary to speak of the price of other goods being such and such a sum of money; it is equally proper to speak of the price of money being such and such a quantity of goods. The purpose of this latter contrast is to draw attention to the fact that money and other goods are both wanted; in different amounts at

different times, it is true, but because both provide means of relieving wants. The marginal utility of money diminishes at a slower rate than that of other goods, but simply because it is convertible with ease into any of a great range of other goods. But like other means money does not have a fixed ratio of exchange with respect to any other goods (29).

33. Exchanges take place in markets. A market is simply a set of arrangements by which exchanges are facilitated. It need have neither specific location nor distinctive form. It is customary to consider markets as specializing in the exchange of a limited range of means, for example, the wool market, the share market, the money market. But each such market is only a part of the wider market in which all goods and services are bought and sold. The function of the market is to establish prices. Prices may be established directly by the higgling and bargaining of buyers and sellers, or indirectly by sellers making offers at what they expect the market will stand. But whether directly or indirectly established, the price of any good depends on the conditions of supply and demand (29), both actual and anticipated, for the good itself and for substitutable and complementary goods (23).

34. The market is also a device by which stocks of scarce means are rationed among potential users. Where prices are flexible and goods are mobile, goods will flow to the highest bidders, to those who, for consumption or production, place the highest value on them. In this way goods are employed in directions in which the aggregate product or satisfaction from their use is expected to be at the maximum. In this way too users are able to indicate, by the prices they offer, which goods shall be produced in greater or smaller quantities and which shall no longer be produced. It is unnecessary for present purposes to consider at length the specific features of different markets; it is necessary only to observe that prices and the distribution of goods and services are not determined unilaterally, but by the simultaneous choices of buyers and sellers.

35. Many things may be used for money. A special form of money is currency. Currency is the legally established medium of exchange in any given community. A currency has a prescribed denomination per unit. The monetary unit is the unit in which all bargains or claims arising from bargains are expressed. It is also the unit in which all derived forms of money, such as bank deposits and other debts, are expressed. Its general use in these ways has established the monetary unit as the unit of account, the unit in which costs, prices and values are expressed, in which economic calculations are made and in terms of which records dealing with such transactions are kept.

36. It may be useful to summarize the consequences of the use of money and money units. Monetary calculation relieves men of the task of comparing satisfactions with sacrifices in diverse ordinal scales (12). Values of diverse means are reduced to a common cardinal scale in which actual or expected gains or losses from alternative courses of action may be expressed. The strain on the span of attention is eased, as also is the problem of choice. Because most of the means

of satisfying wants are acquired at market prices in markets, it is possible to express goals in monetary terms, and to measure the rate, and extent at any time, of their attainment. As the effectiveness of action depends on the specificity of goals, the expression of goals in monetary terms increases the effectiveness of action. Again, reduction to a common scale enables values to be added, so that an aggregate value for a varied stock can be obtained. And if the scale is a monetary scale of present values, it is possible to set off money claims against the aggregate present value of a stock; both are brought into the framework of one system of calculation.

37. For all its convenience the monetary calculus has limitations. Reduction of the tangible and real characteristics of means to a monetary scale is an abstraction; a money value can represent only one characteristic—exchange value at some time. This is not the only characteristic which determines action; there are other relevant features of goods and services; but in its own field—actual or potential action in markets—monetary abstraction is a powerful aid. A second difficulty in using monetary calculations is that it may be assumed that all monetary representations are of equal significance. The very durability of units of currency and the fixed nature of money contracts nurture this idea; it is, nevertheless, false and misleading. Just as in the sale of merchandise different grades are distinguished, so also should the different qualities of money be distinguished. No five apples are thought to be equal to any other five apples; likewise monetary units may not without specific evidence be supposed to be identical in significance (32). Unless all monetary units in a given calculation are identical in significance—that is, in general purchasing power—the mere use of the conventional monetary unit does not provide a common denominator. A third difficulty is the ease with which people, seeing numbers, slip easily into the assumption that cardinal representation means precision. The monetary scale is not like a physical scale. It is always a scale with a significance for the moment, a significance depending on the actions of all buyers and sellers—and therefore quite lacking in stability through time. In spite of this its utility is enormous; but to disregard this limitation is to court confusion.

38. The extensive use of money and credit is one reason underlying the development of monetary accounting. Accounting is a systematic procedure by which the monetary or financial aspects of transactions and events are recorded, classified and summarized so that informed choices may be made. Its link with the problems of acting man specifies its character. It is an aid. It has no justification of itself. It provides a service only; its methods are dictated by the modes of action of those it serves. A prime characteristic which its results will be expected to have is relevance to action; its components will be selected and its methods devised so that the results are relevant. Relevance does not however imply giving direction. Relevance means pertinence to the behaviour appropriate to the role for which an account is given. It is the function of actors to decide and to assess; to decide and to assess one requires information that is neutral. An

actor sets his own goals; in pursuit of them he may err to his advantage or disadvantage; to decide whether in fact he did err is his prerogative. Neutrality with respect to any specific action is just as important as relevance with respect to a role in general. Accounting may influence choice; it has no criteria for determining choice. For, accounting is not to be understood as the sole source of information influencing choice. It presents a particular aspect of affairs only. For other aspects one must necessarily resort to other kinds of information. References to choice and action hereafter allude generally to financial criteria only; but the existence and importance of other criteria may never in practical situations be overlooked. Given the full range of financial and other criteria the mind can choose; lacking either, choice is in part blind.

Qualities of Action

39. Human action is purposive, aggressively adaptive, oriented to the relief of strains (13). Action may be spontaneous (habitual, instinctive) or deliberate. The more urgent the need for action (the greater the intensity of strain), the greater is the tendency towards spontaneous action. The success of spontaneous action (in relieving strain) depends on ready perception (9) of the relationship between stimuli, strains and means. But the greater the variety of stimuli, strains and means, the greater is the difficulty of perceiving their relationship, the more complex is the goal system and the greater is the need for deliberate action. This study concerns itself with deliberate action.

40. As means are scarce relatively to wants, deliberate action will be directed towards securing the greatest possible advantage for a given sacrifice. It is not implied that "the greatest possible advantage" is of a specific kind; the phrase does not mean the maximization of profit, for strains arise for other reasons than the mere scarcity of means; the phrase does not mean the maximization of money returns, for, firstly, money itself has no capacity for directly relieving strains and, secondly, money sums may have varying significance over time in terms of the power to purchase means having direct utility. "The greatest possible advantage" is to be understood with reference to the goal system as a whole (13). Nevertheless, the pursuit of the maximum profit or money return is part of the process of securing the greatest possible advantage. The goal system of an individual is beyond inquiry, but unless his overt actions are designed, in the framework of non-specific goals, to secure the maximization of economic goals, his capacity for achieving economic and other goals is needlessly sacrificed.

41. Further, in suggesting that action will be directed towards securing the greatest possible advantage, it is not implied that such an objective is attained. Nor it is a valid objection to this principle that people do not in fact maximize their gains. However carefully a course of action may be chosen, it is chosen at a point of time for a future period of time of which the actor has uncertain knowledge. As a point of reference it is useful to describe action which in fact

achieves the goal to which it is directed as optimal adaptation. The more deliberate the action the greater is the probability of optimal adaptation.

42. Deliberate action always involves choice of a course of action from among a series of possible courses. The outcome of choosing depends on (a) the goal system (set and ranking) at the time of action, (b) knowledge of the possible courses of action available in the given environment, (c) knowledge of the means available and (d) expectations of the consequences of each possible course of action.

43. Knowledge of the available courses depends in turn on several factors. It depends on the breadth of past experience and on the ability to recall (9) past experience. It depends on the propensity to search, that is on the freedom from inertia and habit. And it depends on the time available for search, that is, on the urgency of action (12).

44. Knowledge of the means available likewise depends on other factors. It depends on the ability to recall all means available and to marshal them in terms of their characteristics; in particular in terms of their specificity for the purpose in mind and of their liquidity if no specific good is available. It also depends on the ability to recall commitments of means or restraints on their use or disposal.

45. Expectations depend on knowledge of the consequences of past actions; not simply on past experience, but on the extent to which past experience has been the subject of reflection for the purpose of discerning cause and effect relationships (9). Expectations depend also on the predictability of the environment (20); expectations will be formed with greater precision and assurance if the environment is stable in significant respects. And the quality of expectations depends on the quality of judgement exercised in relating what has transpired in the past to the possible conditions of the future.

46. In the last three sections there have been persistent allusions to knowledge. All types of knowledge constitute information. But any actor may be informed—of his own affairs—or of conditions about him—poorly or adequately. The better informed the actor the greater is the probability of optimal adaptation.

Qualities of Information

47. Knowledge may be formal or informal. By informal is meant the accumulation of knowledge in the person, his memory and skill derived from past experiences. But the greater the variety of past experiences the greater is the difficulty of recalling any particular experience in the detail necessary to establish its relevance to a present problem. By formal knowledge is meant the knowledge accumulated by a recording process and stored independently of the person. The greater the variety of stimuli, means, experiences and available actions, the greater is the need for formal knowledge.

48. Human adaptation is a continuous process; or more strictly a continuous cycle of processes. Man acts; he observes, reflects on, and appraises the consequences of his action; he refers his new state to his goal system (which may have changed from the original system),

makes a new decision and acts again (7, 8, 9). The repetition of this cycle for every aspect of his behaviour is perhaps unnoticed; but it is constant, and by means of it he inches towards the satisfaction of his wants. As the process is continuous, the demand for knowledge is continuous. If his activities are limited in number and kind he may be able mentally to encompass the knowledge necessary for adapting his behaviour to his circumstances. But if his activities are varied so that it becomes necessary to augment his memory with a formal record (8), that record will necessarily be of a continuous kind.

49. A person may himself keep the records of his financial transactions and relationships. If he knows the technique and keeps the record he will know how relevant the result is to his purpose; and if it is not relevant the remedy lies in his own hands. On the other hand he may rely in the skill and knowledge of specialists in record keeping; the keeping of the record and the making of decisions are divorced. In this situation the actor does not know the method used, the skill with which it is used or the relevance of the resulting figures or statements to his purposes. He depends on the technical skill and probity of the record-keeper. Two kinds of problem arise; one because the design of recording and information processing systems becomes the concern of others than actors themselves; the other because the result of the recording and processing systems must be communicated to persons who must act on the result but are uninformed as to the method.

50. Formal or processed information is conveyed by signals which differ from the original observable events and things. Signals are necessarily abstractions (37). The probability of optimal adaptation varies with the correspondence of the signals to the observable realities to which they relate. Signals may convey more or less completely the characteristics of observable real events and things; they may be so conventionalized that they represent in one dimension what may only be described adequately in more than one dimension. Correspondence is critical where the actor has no possibility of confirming or testing the quality of the signals.

51. The probability of optimal adaptation varies with the processor's awareness of what is relevant to the actor (38). The processor acts as an extension of the actor's sensory and manipulative apparatus; what he observes he observes for the actor; the calculations he makes he makes for the actor. He can have no independent viewpoint.

52. The probability of optimal adaptation varies with the objectivity of the record and process. By objectivity is meant freedom from the influence of personal judgement or bias. As the future actions of an actor are with respect to other persons through markets, personal opinion and evaluation are irrelevant. An observation is objective if other persons reasonably well informed would concur with it—exchange value or market value is in this sense objective (28). It is not a fancy of the actor's imagination only. Further the same objectivity is necessary in processing as in initial observation. No procedure or criterion of the processor may be inconsistent with the procedure or criterion which an actor would ideally adopt for himself.

As to act deliberately requires that he shall know, without interposed distortion, states of affairs and rates of change, these are what the process should yield.

53. Distortion of information may take several forms. Distortion may be deliberate; deliberate distortion may be intentional (as, for example, to conceal fraud) or unintentional. The latter occurs when values or procedures continue to be used after they have ceased to be useful or to yield relevant information. Distortion may be due to the deficiencies of the signals used. Typically signals abstract—morse code cannot convey an inflexion, a gesture, or a facial expression. Distortion may also be inadvertent; errors may be made, attitudes or beliefs may be adopted which are inconsistent with the needs of a situation. Formal checks may be incorporated in an information processing system to eliminate or reduce some of these possible causes of distortion, but there can be no routine safeguard against attitudes inconsistent with the service functions of recording and communicating.

54. The probability of optimal adaptation varies with the perceived significance of signals on the part of the actor. Information processing is unlike many other forms of expert assistance; it accomplishes changes in mental equipment rather than in physical things. There are greater difficulties in conveying ideas than changing physical things; many persons can grasp the significance of a change in things, but the significance of ideas is not always self-evident. For this reason the terms of a communication, the words used, the measures involved, should be consistent where possible with general usage. The wider the range of recipients of a communication the greater is the necessity for consistency of its terms with general usage.

55. Processed information is accepted only subject to evaluation by the recipient. This evaluation is applied in part to the information yielded and in part to the processor. An actor will place greater confidence in processed information if it is found to be consistent with other knowledge, formal or informal, of the same matters. And, the greater the reliability of the process or the processor and the greater the prestige of the processor, the greater is the confidence with which processed information will be accepted. It follows that information prepared by experts (specialists) will tend to be accepted readily, even though it does not conform with the criteria of relevance, neutrality, correspondence and objectivity. Therefore, the greater the awareness among processors of these critical qualities of information, the greater is the probability of optimal adaptation.

The Entity

56. It has been observed that an individual may simultaneously fill several roles (10). He must of necessity reconcile the demands of different roles, but in order to do this it is necessary first to consider each role separately. It may appear that a given individual assuming the roles of householder (consumer) and employee (producer) would be content to regard the consumer-role as dominant and to gear his behaviour to that role alone. But two entirely different modes of

behaviour may readily be observed as his calculations shift from one role to the other; he may be shrewd and crafty in his business relationships, but open-handed and generous to a fault as a consumer. The goals of consumption and production are different in kind; one counts the cost far less carefully in the case of consumption than in the case of production, because the satisfactions obtained from consumption are personal and incommensurable (13), whereas the gain from production, in terms of additions to means, is measurable in the same scale as the sacrifices or costs incurred.

57. An information system can deal only with one role at a time if it is to enable the actor to discern and to distinguish the issues governing his actions. Roles are filled not only by natural persons but by groups of natural persons and by artificial persons. These roles are so varied that it is possible that no single information system will serve all role playing entities equally well. This is a matter for further development. But the point made here is that information systems are concerned each with a specific role. The role may coincide with or cut across legally distinguishable categories of persons; its prime characteristic is that it represents a limited potential set of goals.

Financial Position of an Individual Person

58. For any given role, the foundation of a plan of action involving a change in means is the existing state of one's affairs (24). As every such change takes place through bargains in which exchange values are expressed in monetary units, the state of one's affairs may be represented by a statement in monetary units.

59. Ability to engage in any exchange is represented by the means under the control of the entity expressed in terms of current exchange values. It is immaterial whether those means were acquired for a purpose other than exchange; a shift in relative prices may make it worthwhile to dispose of or replace any good in possession. Means in possession are described as assets of the entity.

60. All means are the property of some entity (26). By virtue of loans and other forms of credit some of the means in possession are not the property of the entity under discussion; so that the freedom to use or dispose of specific assets or of assets generally is restrained by the claims or equities of others (creditors). The equities of creditors (liabilities of the entity) are determined as to their character and amount, by contract. The present value of such equities is the amount of the liabilities of the entity.

61. The difference between the aggregate of the exchange values of assets and the aggregate of the present values of liabilities represents the present residual equity of the entity in the assets. The amount of the residual equity is significant for two reasons. Firstly, it represents the exchange value of unrestricted assets, providing assurance to creditors that their claims are more than "covered" by the assets of the entity. Secondly, it represents a basis on which further advances from creditors may be obtained. For an individual person, residual equity represents net worth or wealth or capital.

62. The financial position of an entity at any time is defined by the relationship:—

$$\begin{aligned} \text{Assets} &= \text{Equities} \\ &= \text{External equities} + \text{Residual equity} \\ \text{or}\quad A &= L + R \end{aligned}$$

each term being quantified in the manner described in the preceding paragraphs. This identity holds at successive instants of time; for whatever additions are made to assets a like addition must be made to equities (as all means are the property of some entity). It will in fact hold even if nonsensical values are given to assets and equities, provided only that the value assigned to a given asset corresponds to the value assigned to the equity by virtue of which it was acquired. However, whimsy is restrained by the requirement that the resulting information must be relevant to action (38).

63. In stating the financial position of an entity it is not sufficient to give the total amount of assets, liabilities and residual equity. The process of aggregation involves the loss of some information which may be important for any particular decision. On the other hand an indiscriminate listing of each asset and liability may present such an array that confusion results. The limited span of attention (8) dictates the classification of assets and liabilities into groups but the number of groups will be such that no serious information losses occur. It has been observed that stocks of means may be of varying durability, specificity and liquidity (17). Of these qualities the most significant in the adaptive process is liquidity. The utility of a statement of financial position is increased by ranking assets in order of liquidity. To some extent such a ranking will also be an inverse ranking according to specificity; for liquid assets are non-specific, and highly specific assets tend to be convertible only with difficulty ("specific" being related to goals, which may be shared by relatively few other entities). Similarly, the utility of a statement of financial position is increased by ranking equities in order of maturity, for in considering any change in the stock of assets, with or without any increase in external equities, one must first make provision for meeting existing commitments. These considerations relate to form rather than substance but form is significant in the sense that it determines in a measure the order in which things become the focus of attention.

Changes in Financial Position

64. The financial position of an entity will change over time. Consider a person who is a producer-consumer (say, a wage-earner) and suppose there are no lags between the initiation of any action and its consummation. In a given period he will earn a wage income, I, and receive cash, Mi, in the amount of it. He will incur expenditure, C, on consumption and pay out cash, Mc, in the amount of it. He will as a result have made savings, S, and there will be an increase in his cash holdings in the amount of it. In respect of each event there is an asset effect; resources are increased or decreased. But in each case, the increase or decrease is represented by a concept—

income, expenditure, savings. These concepts are the same in kind as the concept residual equity; they represent effects on the residual equity equal in amount to changes in the assets.

65. Thus, if we write $A_1 = L_1 + R_1$ to represent the financial position at time 1, and Mi — Mc = I — C to represent the events occurring between time 1 and time 2, the two equations may be added to obtain the financial position at time 2:—

$$A_1 + Mi - Mc = L_1 + R_1 + I - C \qquad [1]$$

or

$$A_2 = L_1 + (R_1 + S)$$

66. The demonstration may be extended by removing the assumption that there are no lags between the initiation and the consummation of any action. If the cash received is less in amount than the amount of I, the wage-earner will have a contractual claim, D, against his employer; A_1 will be increased by the amount of it and cash receipts will be less than Mi in an equal amount, Md. But the effect on the aggregate assets of earning I will be the same. Similarly, if the cash spent on consumption is less in amount than the amount C, the wage-earner will have incurred a liability, Lc, to another party; L_1 will be increased by the amount of it and cash payments will be less than Mc in an equal amount Ml. By inspection it can be seen that the identity [1] of para. 65 will take the form:—

$$A_1 + D + (Mi - Md) - (Mc - Ml) = L_1 + Lc + R_1 + I - C,$$
$$\text{or, } A_2 = L_2 + R_1 + S,$$

if allowance is made for both lags mentioned in this paragraph. Similarly again, if the wage-earner acquires assets by incurring liabilities—whether or not those assets are consumed or held—the identity will hold: A_2 and L_2 will simply be larger by equal amounts, but the residual equity will be as before.

67. The financial position at any time is the basis of action for the next ensuing period. But it offers no suggestion as to the mode of action. A person planning for a future period will find suggestive what happened in the last period. He will want to know his total income, its sources if there are more than one, and the regularity of the flow from each source. He will want to know his expenditure and the kinds of things for which it was incurred; in particular, he will find it useful to know which of his expenditures are periodically recurrent, which are occasional but predictable and which are unpredictable (19). He will want to know whether on balance he saved anything and how much, or whether he consumed part of his original wealth during the period. All of these have some bearing on expectations for the next period. Amounts representing income I, and consumption C, may be set down in a statement called an income statement, (I—C) being equal to savings, S, during the period. From para. 65, it will be clear that S also represents the change in the net assets (A—L) held; it could have been obtained by taking the difference between net assets at the beginning and end of the period. But in the absence of a continuous record linking two position statements, the systems for computing position from time to time are

sub-systems. To avoid the limitations of sub-systems (15) accounting resorts to a system of continuous records yielding from time to time completely articulated statements of position and change in position.

68. It will be recalled that income is the value of the net addition to utilities through production and that direct utility attaches only to non-monetary goods. A money income and a money stock are useful only in so far as they enable one to acquire non-monetary goods. The calculation of income proceeds therefore from a basic reference level—the amount of or the capacity to command non-monetary goods at the beginning of a period, or the initial capital or wealth. The phrase "the maintenance of capital" is used to indicate this criterion for the measurement of income. It does not imply that individuals will wish to maintain their capital in the above sense; to add to or to draw from their capital is their choice; but choice is uninformed unless the effects of operations are related to an initial stock of direct utilities and/or monetary equivalents.

69. A regular or contractual income, such as the income of a wage-earner, may be described as predictable income; expenditure on consumption may be considered as predictable expenditure. But in any interval, a residual equity may be increased and assets increased correspondingly by windfall gains such as the proceeds of a legacy or a gift; or it may be reduced with a corresponding reduction in assets by windfall losses such as the accidental loss or destruction of assets. These are unplanned incidents or events. One's reaction to windfall gains and losses will differ from one's attitude towards predictable income and expenditure. For this reason, it is necessary to distinguish between planned and windfall items. The assets arising from or dissipated by planned actions and by windfalls are, of course, the same in kind; the distinction is applied only to the conceptual designation of the source of the change.

70. As income and expenditure are concepts, they can be made to denote whatever is found to be useful or necessary for action. For example, income could be used to embrace windfall gains, but to do so would result in the loss of a significant piece of information (63). Our wage-earner, on the other hand could adopt as a guide and limit to his actions the amount of cash he receives and spends during any income period, notwithstanding that the lags of para. 66 occur. It is sufficient for his purposes only because of the regularities in his receipts and payments patterns. A small business firm may find the same basis sufficient where there are substantial regularities in receipts and payments patterns. An accounting system in which transactions are recognized when cash is received or paid is said to be conducted on a cash basis. Where transactions are brought into account when they become effective, even though cash is received or paid at other dates, the accounting system is said to be conducted on an accrual basis.

71. If changes occur in the composition of assets and liabilities and if the composition of assets and liabilities is critical for action, the income statement of itself will be insufficient to describe the change. The differences in the statements of position will need to be set out in

detail. This may be done by a summary statement showing the changes in the composition of assets and corresponding changes in the residual equity and in the composition of liabilities. The statement will be called a statement of the change in position, or a funds statement.

72. The formal framework outlined above may be restated as:—

$$A + C = L + R + I$$

From this identity may be derived the rules for recording all transactions of an entity in such a way as to yield articulated income and position statements. The method of describing transactions in terms both of changes in a stock and the corresponding changes in equities is double-entry accounting. It rests simply on the fact that all goods are the property of some entity (26). The demonstration of the preceding section has assumed that the monetary units, in terms of which the symbols used are expressed, are homogeneous or of equal significance throughout. This does not necessarily conform with reality (32). The argument could be extended here by relaxing this assumption, because shifts in the purchasing power of money are as important to wage-earners as to anyone else using money as a medium of exchange; but the extension is deferred to the treatment of the next class of case. The relaxation of the assumption of the constant purchasing power of money does not in any way affect the validity of the identity given above.

Simple Trading Ventures

73. Attention is now directed to trading ventures as such. Trading ventures include all ventures in which resources are converted, by combination or by holding against the future demands of consumers, into other means which are sold at a price per unit. A trading venture is a productive unit simply (21); its operations are not confused by the difficulties of evaluating satisfactions from consumption. It buys and sells. Its affairs may thus be regulated strictly according to economic sacrifices and gains. For the purposes of this paper, the trading venture contemplated has no investments or obligations unrelated to the production and sale of a line or lines of goods or services.

74. Trading ventures arise from decisions of persons to devote to or invest in (22) a productive activity part of their personal resources, in money or kind. The incentive to divest oneself of such resources is the expectation of gain—either in terms of a periodical division of the gains of the venture, or in terms of the proceeds from disposing of one's interest in it. No decision to invest is irrevocable (28); personal exigencies may at any time dictate the liquidation of an interest in a trading venture. Ease of withdrawal thus influences readiness to invest. The ease with which resources or the proceeds of their use may be withdrawn depends on the legal form and contractual capacity of the venture. Equities in a trading venture arise through loans or through capital contributions; the latter will be considered first.

75. A sole trader may contribute to his enterprise at will. He may withdraw resources in part or whole with ease as the matter is subject only to his discretion. He may, if he wish, disregard the equities of others in business assets. Legally, he and his business venture are indistinguishable, even though for the purpose of economic calculation it is useful to distinguish personal and business roles (57). However, he may shift the risks of his business by the sale of the whole of, or an interest in, it to others.

76. The limited liability business corporation differs in some significant respects. It is an independent creation of law arising in the first place from decisions of a group of people to devote part of their resources to a joint enterprise. That group, the members, acquire shares in the venture proportionate to their contributions; the corporation is thus a device for marshalling the savings of individuals for productive purposes (22). The corporation has an indeterminate life and an independent capacity to contract; its contracts may extend over long terms and some of the assets it acquires may not be reconverted to cash except over long periods. Individual members may, nevertheless, wish to convert their investments into cash for personal reasons in a much shorter time (63). To meet the unpredictable demand for cash on the part of members without disturbing long-term arrangements of the corporation, shares are transferable. A member, or shareholder, may thus shift the risks attaching to his interest by the sale of the whole or a part of his holding—in the same way as may a sole trader—but not by recourse to the corporation itself; he must sell in the securities market.

77. It will be clear that trading ventures are concerned with operations in three markets—the new money market, in which new securities are issued for new money contributions; the securities market, in which existing securities are exchanged; and the commodities market, in which goods and services are bought and sold. It will be useful to consider the nature of operations in each of these markets. But first a general view.

78. A trading enterprise is a co-operative system depending on the continued support of its participants. The participants may be grouped according to function—there are workers, suppliers, customers, financiers (lenders), and investors (risk bearers); and in so far as such ventures are restricted or authorized by law, it may be said that the public at large, through the instrumentality of government, is a participant. These groups participate in the expectation of receiving incomes or services appropriate to their functions. Workers, suppliers, customers and financiers may be described as freely contracting participants. Their rights are determined and secured by contract or the general law. In so far as they may offer their services to a wide range of enterprises they are able to obtain prices consistent with those obtainable in other enterprises. They may bargain in such a way that the inducements offered by the subject enterprise tend to be sufficient to maintain their consumption levels in real terms.

Risk, Information and Investment

79. But all trading enterprises are subject to risks—from changes in tastes (14), from technological changes (21), from competition (34). The risks fall on investors. Investors participate in the expectation of recovery of their contributions at some future time and of a periodical yield, appropriate to the risks assumed, in the interval between making and withdrawing their contributions. Although such expectations are held, the risks are acknowledged. No investor is of right entitled to the return of the whole of his contribution or to any determinate periodical yield. If the venture is successful he will obtain both; if it fails he may receive neither. But as investors are in another role consumers, it is reasonable to suppose that they envisage yield and contribution recovery in the same way as freely contracting participants, namely as providing the means for sustaining an expected level of consumption or a given amount of wealth in real terms.

80. In a manner analogous to the commodities markets, the new money market rations available new money among competing ventures (34). To those ventures money is a means of operating in the commodities markets; so that ventures compete in terms of the expectations they engender regarding the outcome of operations in the commodities markets. Funds flow most readily to the ventures in respect of which the expectation of gain is greatest—gain being understood to be the aggregate surplus above the investment, in real terms. Gain may take the form of periodical interest payments or dividends from the net proceeds of operations. In respect of residual equity holders it may take the additional form of increases in the market value of their securities. These values will increase as the aggregate value of assets is increased through the retention (re-investment) of part of the periodical surplus, for the increase in equity per share will be expected to lead to greater earnings—and dividends—per share.

81. To investors the new money market at any time offers a range of possible investments. In choosing between these investments, one consideration is the financial position of each venture—its solvency, the amounts and terms of its liabilities, the nature of its assets—for this represents its readiness to benefit from the opportunities the commodities markets offer. An equally important consideration is the rate of expected earnings on the residual equity of each, for residual equity earnings covers both the amounts available for distribution and the amounts available for reinvestment. The expected rate of residual equity earnings represents the capacity of a venture to benefit from the opportunities which the commodities markets offer. If an investor is to make valid comparisons between, and to form expectations relating to, investment opportunities, both capacity and readiness require expression in consistent terms; and because the choice is for immediately future operations in the commodities markets those terms will be current values (59), whether the venture is a new one or one with many years of operation behind it.

82. As investors invest at risk they are not indemnified against loss, however great may be their expectations. But if expectations change they may take their losses and shift their risks. The function of the securities market is to facilitate the realization of securities or the conversion of risks of one kind into risks of another kind. It effects a redistribution of risks; but it does not raise the income or wealth of the community generally. If some gain, others lose. No less than new investors in existing ventures, existing investors are dependent, for periodical re-assessment of risks, on statements of income and position in current terms.

83. Lenders are equally interested in the same information even though their risks are limited. Lending is geared to the residual equity and the periodical increment to it. These provide margins of security; but security is only significant if at any time it is represented by current evaluations. It is of no consequence that at the time of granting a loan expectations were of a high order; the probability that the service charges will be met as they fall due and that the loan itself will be discharged on maturity is a function of present capacity to exploit opportunities. Further, inasmuch as borrowing is limited by the residual equity and borrowing at a lower yield than the customary yield on risk investments increases the yield of the latter, opportunities for further borrowing can only be fully exploited, with due regard to the rights of lenders, by reference to present capacity and readiness.

84. One final line of argument for the expression of capacity and readiness in present terms may be developed from the point that the public at large may be considered as a participant in trading enterprises (78). The laws under which private institutions engage in trade for profit are public grants of power. As trading enterprises employ a large proportion of the capital goods of a community, and as the stock of capital goods is the means of maintaining or improving the income stream or potential living standard, the policies of trading ventures as to the division and distribution of surpluses are of social importance. It should be expected that the surplus available in any period for distribution and potentially available for consumption will be calculated on the basis of the capital employed at the opening of the period converted to present values at the time of calculation. A system of calculation, which does not proceed from such a basis may not prevent inadvertent consumption of capital (68). Given the maintenance of the community's stock as a desirable minimal objective, the information systems in use will be such that they clearly indicate whether or not a proposed division of business resources would result in consumption of capital. Further, the complex of markets serves to determine, through the allocative mechanism of prices, what enterprises shall have the support of the community, access to available savings and, through them, access to the resources of the community (34). For efficient allocation, the information systems in use will be such that the market is informed of the relative capacities of firms to add to the community's stock or supply of direct utilities. This capacity is represented by the relationship of the gain from trade to the capital employed, both being expressed in current terms.

85. It will be clear that new investors, existing security holders and lenders alike are dependent on information representing present capacity and readiness to exploit opportunities. It should also be clear that the objectives of the class of workers designated managers will include the preservation of the contractual equity of lenders and, at the minimum, the maintenance in real terms of the yield and capital contributions of investors. Managers direct the operations of firms in the commodities markets to which we now turn.

Trading Operations

86. All goods acquired, held and used in the process of manufacture or trade are, in those uses, producers' goods. Producers' goods are themselves manufactured and acquired in anticipation of their final conversion into and sale as consumers' goods. The exchange value or price of producers' goods is thus a function of the exchange values or prices of the consumers' goods to which their use gives rise (16).

87. More specifically, the exchange value or price of producers' goods at the time they are acquired is a function of the expected future proceeds of their product. The purchase of any asset is evidence that the present value of the expected future return from its sale is not less than its price. Whether or not a particular asset is acquired depends on the prices at which the output is expected to be sold; if the margin between expected input prices and expected output prices is not sufficient to satisfy all participants, the venture will not be undertaken.

88. But once a course of action is undertaken expectations may change. After the date of acquisition it may be found that an alternative use of the present exchange value of existing assets may have a higher expected yield than the use to which those assets are presently being put. This may occur either because the original expectations are themselves found to have been inappropriate, or because changes in the environment have presented opportunities for more economical (better-yielding) investment. In either case the initial cost of the assets will have no bearing whatever on future income from their continued use. The value of an asset in a given employment is neither more nor less than the present value of the future income expected to flow from its use. If there is an alternative employment expected to yield a greater income flow, it will be preferred (28); and however fixed the initial intention to use the asset for its initial purpose, it is economic wisdom to shift the investment from one asset to another. Adaptability, not constancy, is the characteristic of a going concern.

89. It should be pointed out that this does not entail constant revision of investments in specific durable assets. A plant built up of less specific items into an integrated and highly specific unit will tend to have a lower resale value—either as a whole or piecemeal—than the same items uncombined, because being highly specific there are few buyers whom it would serve equally well, or because of the

dismantling costs of individual pieces. The investment, once made, can therefore be justified on a relatively lower income than may initially have been expected.

90. As was stated above, the value of an asset in any employment is the present value of the future income expected to flow from its use. How is this present value to be assessed? Its assessment is implied in present market prices for equivalent assets, replacement prices. Replacement price (or replacement cost) does not mean some hypothetical future price to be paid on some hypothetical future replacement date. It means the price currently ruling for equivalent service potential. The price currently ruling for producers' goods is the market's assessment of the present value of expected income flows from their use at the present level of prices, for all potential users of such goods. It is therefore an objective valuation, and is equally relevant to decisions involving the continued use or abandonment of the use of any asset. Barring imperfections in the market, replacement cost and realizable value will be equal. If at a given purchase (or replacement) price an asset is able to earn a higher return in one employment than another it is not required that it be stated at a higher value than current price in the record of the more profitable venture. The higher earnings rate will simply result in funds flowing more readily to the one than to the other. Similarly, if the rate of return on the investment calculated at replacement prices is lower than it would be in alternative employments, a clear indication is given of the desirability of switching the investment. It should perhaps be mentioned that reference to replacement price in the above argument means always current replacement price for equivalent service potential; thus if an asset has already yielded half of its original service potential, current replacement price is equal to half the replacement price as new.

91. It may be suggested that, if prices are expected to change, the formation of income expectations (and hence decisions on investment in particular assets) must involve hypotheses or guesses about the degree and direction of such changes. But this is not so. One bases one's calculations (as distinct from one's speculations) on the present level of prices, that being the nearest one can get to the future. And such calculations are relevant. For if there is at the moment a certain functional relationship between present purchase prices of producers' goods and present selling prices of finished products, this relationship will be expected to continue. The prices of non-durable inventories and finished goods will go up or down the escalator together—both in fact and in the record; it is necessary to adjust the record to provide that the present value of the consumed services of durable inventories move in the same direction at the same rate. If changes in technology or in the relative prices of different producers' goods occur so that the functional relationship between purchase prices and selling prices is changed, the effect will show up in the rate of return, as suggested in para. 90, unless the consequential windfall loss or gain is taken into account immediately.

Continuity and Periodical Review

92. Business ventures may be undertaken for various lengths of time; some for specific functions over short periods, others for a potentially wide range of functions over an indefinite period. We will consider the latter as including the former. An indefinite "expectation of life" does not imply persistence in an originally chosen course of action. Adaptation is as important as it is to individuals; the extent to which a business venture adapts itself determines the extent to which it meets the expectations of its participants (78). For adaptation it is necessary to know the present financial position and its rate of change.

93. Continuous adaptation necessitates a continuous record except in the most modest ventures (48). The investors and managers of an undertaking may at the outset lay down specific objectives and specific methods of achieving those objectives. But the environment is unpredictable in a measure so that no plan may be expected to be carried out without deviation. Every small action in some way promotes or hinders the attainment of the objective; but because actions are so numerous and their individual effects so slight, it is not possible to review them all piecemeal. Nevertheless, the aggregate effects of many such actions may cause a deviation from the plan which is material; and the same actions or the environment itself may give rise to a change in the relationship of the venture to its environment which is material—i.e., sufficient to induce a change in actions. For review and replanning, a statement of the results of actions and of the position arising from actions is required at points of time no further apart than the interval in which material changes occur. This interval may be described as the accounting period.

94. The period contemplated is a function of the impact of actions and external events. If no actions having or expected to have material effects in themselves occur or are contemplated, the accounting period may be long; the greater the frequency of actions having, individually or collectively, material effects, the shorter will be the accounting period. The shorter the accounting period, the greater is the probability of optimal adaptation. Periodical summarization of results and position, however, adds to information processing costs; the accounting period is thus determined at the point where the marginal utility of information is equal to the marginal cost of producing it.

95. The assessment of the changes effected by action is made easier if the periods covered by summaries are equal in length. Planning for periods of equal length and reviewing operations over the same periods enables one to build up one's stock of comparable "period experiences", to improve one's judgement and capacity to plan (9). This advantage emerges for even greater reasons when the periods coincide with natural or social cycles—weeks, quarters, years.

96. These considerations have given rise to the customary procedure of summarizing the results and reporting on the position of business and other organizations yearly. Notwithstanding this custom, which, in terms of procedure and formality has its own justification, the predominant principle of periodical reporting lies in the materiality of

actual or expected change. The same principles apply whether the summaries are for the use of management or investors; reporting for equal periods is useful to investors, but further reporting on the occasion of material changes in operations or prospects is no less necessary.

97. Periodic recurrence of certain summarizing processes does not, of course, mean that events and transactions fit neatly into periodical compartments. There is a continual flow of goods, services and money; periodic assessment of the rate of change and of the position is a device for ordering that flow but it does not interrupt it. The continuity of the flow poses problems in measurement.

98. In the first place, measurement cannot be exact or precise: for three reasons. The flow is continuous; there is no point of inaction or period of inaction long enough to refine methods of identifying changes with accounting periods. Further, the measurement of changes necessitates the selection of a base for comparing magnitudes. Whether the base is the level of market prices or an indirect measure of present value these are inexact in themselves. Further still, there can be no exact knowledge of the period over which existing commitments or investments will be continued. These reasons are operative whatever system of accounting is adopted. Accounting summaries are at best approximations; the periodical problem is how to make the best approximations. Where unique values are unobtainable, the best approximation may be an average, as an average is a more representative value than any of the values from which it is derived.

99. In the second place, to secure comparability as between statements for successive periods requires that all changes shall be identified with the periods in which they occur. Operations which are consummated (i.e., which complete the cycle "cash-goods-cash") in any period create no problem of identification. Operations which straddle two or more consecutive periods involve allocation. The greater the consistency of use of methods of allocation the greater will be the comparability of successive statements. No possibility of alternatives at the discretion of the record keeper can be admitted (51). Nor can any procedure be admitted which is consistently biased in any direction (52). Nor can any external change which induces internal changes in a period or over successive periods be disregarded; for the impact of external changes will differ from period to period (the environment being fluid) destroying the comparability of successive statements. Comparability is not to be understood as similarity in size of results or effects; any device selected because this will be its effect operates to defeat the purpose of reporting and is inconsistent with the service function of the record (38). The very purpose of comparison is to discern the sizes of changes or deviations.

Recording Trading Operations

100. The framework considered in para. 64 needs to be restated for trading ventures. For consumption must be substituted expense; for savings, net profit. In all other respects the original terms will serve,

though they may be subdivided for some purposes. Assume that at the commencement of operations a trading venture has assets, liabilities and residual equity. Part of its assets and all its liabilities are fixed in money terms—they are either fixed amounts of money or claims to fixed amounts of money—monetary assets and liabilities. The remainder of its assets are real or non-monetary assets. Real assets embody services which are available for sale, or which by combination become available for sale, in different form. In the succeeding interval the venture will buy goods and services, combine them with the opening stock of real assets and purchases in the form of saleable products.

101. It is necessary to choose between the cash and accrual basis for recognizing transactions. As in the case of individuals (70), firms which have a regular income and regular expense and little change in the periodical level of claims may find the cash basis a sufficient approximation. But generally the pattern of business transactions presents few such uniformities; a firm is subject to arrays of influences from the expectations of its officers, of influences from the actions and pressures of its participants, and of influences arising from market changes in which it takes no direct part. Comparability can only be approached in these circumstances by adopting the accrual basis.

102. Given that transactions have been recognized in the record, it is necessary to devise some test by which transactions may be attributed to periods. Now, the risks of holding monetary assets (cash and claims) and non-monetary assets are different in kind. The risks of holding monetary assets and liabilities are risks that their purchasing power or redemption costs may vary in real terms. All persons may be assumed to be equally well informed of these risks, but no person may, on the basis of any present knowledge, quantify their future extent or their incidence in time. One may speculate on the probability that prices will rise or fall, and arrange one's stocks accordingly; but the outcome is not predictable. The risks of holding non-monetary assets are risks that the incomes they yield may vary due to changes in the commodities markets. As these incomes arise from the sale of commodities having direct utility, expectations and plans may be formed with a degree of confidence. Further, these are the specific risks which investors undertook, risks on which they could not be assumed to have knowledge but in respect of which they would wish to have some basis for future assessment of their investments. It appears that it is useful to determine periodically the gain from trade and that to do so the income side of the calculation will be based on the change in the character of risks which occurs at the point of sale. This may be described as the realization principle.

103. If there is no change during an accounting period in market conditions, prices or technology—that is if the environment is completely stable—money outlays and money receipts are of equal real significance, unit for unit, and costs may be set off against income to obtain the net increment to the residual equity. It is relatively easy to fix the amount of income by the realization principle. The costs attributable to that income are of two kinds. Some costs of a period

are not related directly to goods sold. They are general costs of being in business. They do not add to the value of inventories and are attributable directly to total income. Other costs are identifiable with inventories. The part of those costs attributable to the income of a period comprises—opening inventories plus purchases plus wage costs plus other service costs plus plant costs less closing inventories. All items except plant costs may be measured directly; the indivisibility of plant makes indirect measurement necessary. Plant cost for a period is that part which bears to the total cost of plant the same relationship as the services consumed during the period bear to the total expected service; this is the depreciation of the plant during the period. Income less total costs gives the net increment to residual equity or net profit. Note that under the assumptions of the first sentence of this paragraph, costs are equal to present values throughout the period and throughout the calculation. Opening and closing financial positions are stated in sums representing equivalent real things and the amount of net profit may logically be related to residual equity.

Recording and Restatement under Instability

104. If the assumption of complete stability is relaxed the problem increases in complexity. Prices are free to move and will move under the impact of changes in market conditions. Money receipts from sales of finished goods at the beginning of an accounting period will not be the same in amount as money receipts from sales of the same quantities at the end of the period; or to put it another way, equal amounts of money income at the beginning and end will have different significance in terms of goods. Initial outlays on commodity stocks and durables at the beginning of the period will not be the same in amount as outlays on similar stocks at the end of the period; nor will the values of stocks on hand at the end be the same as the money outlays per item at the time of acquisition. To match money outlays against money receipts in such a direct way that the money units paid out and received are of equal purchasing power is only possible if all goods acquired are completely disposed of before a change in purchasing power occurs; it is obviously impossible in the case of continuous trading ventures, for inventories must be carried, and no one can tell in advance when a change in purchasing power of the currency will occur or to what extent.

105. In these circumstances, money outlays are not equal to present values. The amounts paid for goods acquired represent values at the time of acquisition (28). The prices paid for goods by traders are derivatives of the expected values (prices expected to be charged) for final products, which are themselves a function of the then prevailing level of prices (87). If the level of prices shifts, purchase prices will shift but so also will the values of stocks on hand. Such shifts induced by price level movements are not productive of income. It is necessary to distinguish the gain from trade at current costs and prices from the induced shifts in value due to general price movements. The income from trade in terms of current values is

predictable in so far as demand is predictable. But changes in value due to general price movements are unpredictable in amount and incidence; and in any case they cannot be considered as increments to residual equity in any real sense. Unless the basic record is adjusted to take account of these shifts, income being represented by receipts of money or money claims at the contemporary price level would not be charged with the contemporary value of the services incorporated in goods sold. Such adjustment implies that the process of setting off costs against incomes is a process of assigning values rather than assigning parts of money outlays.

106. If the level of prices shifts, monetary assets and liabilities are affected as well as non-monetary items; if prices rise the value of monetary assets, in terms of goods, falls, and the cost, in terms of goods, of meeting liabilities falls, even though their monetary amounts remain the same. These changes, unlike changes in the valuation of non-monetary assets, do not enter into the costs of goods sold.

107. The consequences of a shift in price levels may be demonstrated as follows: Assume that a firm has monetary assets, M, non-monetary assets, N, liabilities, L, and residual equity, R, at the beginning of a period. Assume further that it engages in no transactions during a period in which the price level rises from 1 to $(1+p)$, p being the percentage rise in relation to a base 1. The position at the beginning then is:—

$$M + N = L + R \qquad [1]$$

Multiply throughout by $(1 + p)$:—

$$M(1 + p) + N(1 + p) = L(1 + p) + R(1 + p) \qquad [2]$$

Now, by hypothesis, at the end of the period, the firm has the same monetary assets and liabilities as at the beginning. Restore the terms representing these to their original amount by transposing and taking the differences to residual equity:—

$$M + N\,(1 + p) = L + [R\,(1 + p) + Lp - Mp] \qquad [3]$$

This represents the position at the end of the period restated in terms of the level of prices then ruling. Monetary assets and liabilities are in amount as at the beginning; non-monetary assets and initial residual equity are increased by the amount of the rise in the price level; and the residual equity is augmented by the "gain" on liabilities less monetary assets owing to the fall in the purchasing power of money.

108. The net adjustment to the residual equity may be obtained by a shorter process than by the adjustment of all items in the identity. For subtracting [1] from [3],

$$pN = pR + pL - pM \qquad [4]$$

The net adjustment to the residual equity, the right-hand side of [4], may thus be obtained by applying p to the initial value of N. Whether the adjustment is made by the process of the left-hand side of [4] or by the process of the right-hand side depends on the significance attached to the "gain" or "loss" on monetary items. In the first place, the decision to hold monetary assets and to have liabilities of given amounts is no different in kind from the decision to hold non-monetary assets of a given size; with given opportunities they are, in fact, mutually dependent decisions. The "loss" or "gain" from monetary items is the price of the advantage gained from or the sacrifice made by holding the consequential stock of non-monetary assets. This suggests that pN is an adequate adjustment. In the second place, one may consider whether the "gain" (if any) on holding monetary items is a divisible surplus. If the maintenance of the residual equity is adopted as the basis for measuring divisible surplus, no part of pR (= pN + pM — pL) is divisible. If, on the other hand, a policy is adopted of taking the maintenance of non-monetary assets as the basis for measuring divisible profits, on the ground that the maintenance of real assets is a condition of maintaining an income stream, then no part of pN (= pR + pL — pM) is divisible. In neither case is the separate calculation of pL and pM necessary. In the third place, one may look at the question from the viewpoint of the management of monetary balances. If the position given in [1] is an equilibrium position inasmuch as net monetary assets (M — L) are necessary to the employment of non-monetary assets N, then the position given in [2] would be the equilibrium position at the higher price level. It would be necessary therefore to have net monetary assets (M + Mp — L — Lp) or an increase of p(M — L). But net monetary balances are not independently determinable under fluid conditions, so that again the separate calculation of pM and pL seems to be unnecessary.

109. To take up the argument again from para. 105, it is now necessary to consider the combination of continuous basic recording and periodical restatement which will yield information relevant to action at the beginning of each successive accounting period. The difference between the positions at the beginning and the end of each period is to be accounted for completely. The conventional accounting procedures will serve as providing the basic record; it is necessary so to adjust the aggregates obtained that (a) only items relative to the period just ended are attributed to it and (b) classification of aggregates is adequate to distinguish restatements of value from gains from trade. A simplification is introduced to overcome the difficulties referred to in para. 104. Matching transactions at specific value levels will be assumed to take place uniformly during the accounting period, in order to avoid restating the values of every single transaction in terms of prices at the close of the period. Periodical restatement avoids the accumulation of errors of approximation in all but the residual equity balance. The error affects the distribution of the aggregate change in residual equity as between gain from trade and restatement. No further discussion of the possible error from such approximation is offered here.

110. Cash balances are readily determined. The present values of amounts owing under contractual interest obligations, discounted at the contract rate, are equal to their face value. For amounts owing and owed for short terms the present values may be taken as face values. For amounts owing and owed but not bearing interest the

present values are obtained by discounting face values at current interest rates, adjustments being made at the same time to interest paid or received during the period.

111. In respect of commodity stocks at the end of a period, current replacement cost is the principle to be adopted in all cases; for basic materials this means current prices, for partly or wholly processed stocks it means the present prices of material, labour and expense components. The opening inventory appearing in the income account will be the inventory as shown in the balance sheet of the previous period restated in terms of closing prices. Where direct calculation from closing market prices is not possible, an approximation may be made by applying a price index to the closing value of inventory of the last period. The amount of the restatement of inventory values would be credited to a residual equity adjustment account, the amount of which would not be available for dividend appropriation if the maintenance of capital were adopted as a policy (68). The value of commodity stocks to be charged against income from sales would then be the value of opening stocks at closing prices plus the value of goods and services purchased at actual prices plus the value of plant service calculated as below, less the value of closing stock at closing prices.

112. In the case of plant and other durables it is often not possible to obtain replacement cost quotations for the items in stock. An approximation may be made to replacement cost as new by applying a price index to initial money outlay. The differences between replacement costs as new at the ends of two consecutive periods would be entered in the record as adjustments to plant value and to the residual equity adjustment account mentioned in the previous paragraph. The value of plant service consumed in any period would then be approximated by applying to calculated replacement cost at the end of the period the ratio of service consumed to total expected service. Replacement cost at the end of the first period of use is replacement cost as new less the value of plant service consumed. At the end of the second period of use the replacement cost and the value of plant service consumed would fall short of the total value for plant service consumed if calculated as for the two periods combined. The amount of the shortfall would be equal to the percentage increase in the price level in the second year applied to the value of plant service consumed as computed at the end of the first year. The rise of the second year could not have been foreseen in the first year. To make good the total charge against replacement cost new at any time therefore requires a retrospective adjustment. This would be made out of past surplus, not out of current income, for to charge current income would be to charge an amount in excess (in the above circumstances) of the current value of plant service consumed.

113. The question may now be raised as to the appropriate index for making the adjustments referred to in the two preceding paragraphs. In the first place at each point it was stated that an approximation was being made. This is important; it is impossible to do precision work in a fluid environment with crude tools; all estimates, however well attested (including the estimates necessary in

conventional accounting), lack precision. In the second place, as the prices of each item in a non-monetary stock may change at different rates it may appear that an index for each type of stock would be required. However, there is no certainty that any given item of stock will be replaced; adaptation may involve quite different investments of the money proceeds of liquidating existing assets through the sale of their services. Furthermore, one of the purposes of the calculation is to determine the amount which can be divided and distributed without impairing the future potential income stream. This amount may be retained in part, and laid out in a variety of ways; and in part it may be distributed to residual equity holders, who likewise may lay it out in an even wider variety of ways. In these circumstances, a general index of the level of prices (or the reciprocal of an index of the purchasing power of money) seems to be indicated. But in so far as the prices of all producers' goods are based on the expected level of prices of consumers' goods—the ultimate product of and reason for production of all kinds (21)—a consumers' goods index is logically preferable.

114. The above adjustments will yield position statements and income statements which reflect financial position and its rate of change in comparable and relevant terms—as far as the imperfections of the methods of recording and restatement allow. If calculated adjustments are made, it may be necessary still from time to time to make *ad hoc* adjustments, for relative changes in demand and technology may cause the values of specific assets to diverge significantly from calculated values; but the magnitude of these adjustments will be of a much smaller order than those commonly occurring in quasi-reorganizations or asset revaluations within the conventional accounting framework.

Summary of Foundations, Assumptions or Postulates

115. The sequence of the above argument has something of the appearance of a layer cake; it has been dictated by the desire to proceed piece by piece to build up the case from a simple example to a more complex one, and gradually to introduce principles relating to accounting method and to relax simplifying assumptions. It will be useful to draw together at this point the characteristics of the world of action which have been used as foundations for the derived statements relating to accounting. These characteristics represent the way in which the environment of accounting is visualized; it is believed that they are realistic and verifiable by observation or introspection.

Para.

1.[3] *Individual differences.* Individual persons have different wants, different skills and different propensities for action . . . . 25[3]

[3] The numbers in the left hand margin identify each concept for subsequent reference; such references are designated subsequently by numbers in parenthesis ( ). The numbers in the right hand margin refer to relevant paragraphs in the body of the paper.

		Para.
2.	*Diversity of goals.* Persons have diverse concurrent and competing wants and corresponding goals	13
3.	*Diversity of roles.* Persons may fill varied roles concurrently or consecutively, and have sets of goals corresponding to each role	10
4.	*Variability of goals.* Wants and goals vary from time to time	14
5.	*Intensity of wants.* In any system of wants (2)[3] each will have a different ranking or intensity at any time; ranking will change from time to time (4)	13, 14
6.	*Orientation.* Deliberate action is oriented to the satisfaction of wants, individually and as a set. An action may satisfy a want or wants in one or more respects ..	39
7.	*Cerebration.* The choice of a course of action is the outcome of the processes of observation, recollection, calculation and comparison	8, 9
8.	*Incapacity.* For all persons there are limits to the capacity for observation, to the capacity for recollection and to the span of attention	8, 9
9.	*Choice.* For a given role choice depends on the intensity of wants (5), on present knowledge (7, 8) and on expectations of the outcomes of available courses of action (7)	16, 42
10.	*Revocability.* No choice is irrevocable	14
11.	*Abstraction.* Because there are various aspects of each actual or potential course of action (6), and because the span of attention is limited (8), each aspect of a series of possible actions is considered independently	37, 38
12.	*Means.* Wants are satisfied by the appropriation of means. Means are scarce resources which are believed to be serviceable in satisfying wants. The utility of a means subsists in the belief that it will be serviceable in satisfying a want	16
13.	*Diversity of means.* Means vary in specificity with respect to particular wants, in divisibility, in durability, and in convertibility to other means	17, 31
14.	*Valuation of means.* Means derive value from the value attached to the satisfaction of wants (5, 12). Any choice involving addition to, or sacrifice of part of, a homogeneous stock is based on the utility (12) of the marginal unit, i.e., on marginal utility	16, 24
15.	*Possession.* Appropriation of means (12) depends on possession	26
16.	*Equities.* Possession (15) may be unrestricted, in which case the equity in means vests in the possessor; or restricted, in which case the use of means is subject to the equities of other parties	26

Para.

17. *Legal framework.* The equity in and possession of means (16) are regulated by laws, rules and understandings relating to interpersonal relations, contracts and bargains: this framework lends predictability to the environment of action 26

18. *Uncertainty.* The environment of action is fluid. Many aspects of the environment of action are fortuitous; their incidence and severity are unpredictable. Every aspect of choice may be affected by changes in the environment of action 19, 20

19. *Accumulation.* The legal framework (17) makes possible and uncertainty (18) makes desirable the accumulation of means 23

20. *Optimization.* Because means are scarce (12) in relation to wants (2), deliberate actions are chosen according to their expected capacities for yielding the greatest aggregate satisfaction of a system of wants, e.g., the greatest gain for a given sacrifice (6, 9) 41

21. *Diminishing marginal utility.* Because of the diversity of competing wants (2) and the scarcity of means (12), every increase in the stock of a given means reduces the utility of further additions to it 24

22. *Combination.* A stock of heterogeneous means will tend to be so arranged that the marginal utilities of all types of means in the stock will be equal (14, 20, 21) . . 23, 24

23. *Specialization.* By making possible the exploitation of different individual capacities (1), specialization increases the potential supply of means 25

24. *Exchange.* Specialization of function (23) and the diversity of individual goals (2) require a mechanism for the exchange of means 25

25. *Markets.* A market is a process by which the interplay of the wants and preferences of different persons (1, 20, 21, 22) establishes ratios of exchange or prices. Exchange values or prices are the resultant of the choices of more than one person: for any person they are objective valuations 28, 33

26. *Money.* Money facilitates the exchange of goods which vary in divisibility (13). Money is a means of high convertibility (13) and low specificity (13). Because of the convertibility of money, monetary units are accepted units for expressing ratios of exchange (25), or prices, of non-monetary means 31

27. *Credit.* The existence of a legal framework (17) makes possible the exchange of goods and services (including

Para.

money) at one point of time for goods and services to be made available at a subsequent time. Credit gives rise to specific equities (16). The capacity to obtain credit depends on the extent to which the control of means is restricted or unrestricted (16) 27

28. *Price.* In the case of an actual exchange, the ratio of exchange or price expresses the value attached to expected service yields from the good acquired at the time. Prices are derivatives of marginal utilities (14). Prices are the only values relevant to actions in markets (25) 28, 29

29. *Variability of values.* Prices of goods and the purchasing power of money vary over time as the environment changes (18); the possibility of such changes subjects different parts of a stock of means to different risks .. 29, 102

30. *Monetary expression.* Every good or service acquired or to be acquired by exchange and every sacrifice made or to be made to acquire such goods or services may be represented by an actual or estimated price. Monetary expression enables the economic characteristics (see 11) of diverse goals (2), diverse means (13), and diverse equities (16, 27) to be brought within one framework of calculation (7), increasing the effectiveness of attention (8) and making easier the problem of choice (9) .. 36

31. *Monetary calculation.* Monetary calculation is concerned with market or exchange values, market values being measures of the sacrifices of means necessary to secure given ends (26, 28) 36

32. *Continuous adaptation.* Optimization (20) in the face of the variability of goals (4) and the variability of values (29) makes necessary continuous adaptation. Continuous adaptation depends on successive assessments of financial capacity for action and of the probable effectiveness of possible courses of action (9) 48

33. *Financial position.* Financial capacity for action is represented by the relationship between assets and equities at current valuations at a point of time 58, 62

34. *Change of position.* The probable effectiveness of possible courses of action may be deduced by reference to the result of past courses of action 67

35. *Complexity of organization.* Specialization (23) gives rise to complex organizations the existence of which depends on the actions of persons filling various roles (e.g., investors, financiers, managers, accountants, etc.). For each actor, action conforms with the propositions indicated above—see (9), (12), (20), (21), (22), for example 78

Para.

36. *Conflict of goals.* Specialization tends to result in the adoption of sectional or personal goals or points of view which may be inconsistent with the goals of an entity as a whole, either by reason of extra-organizational influence on specialists themselves or by reason of the conflict of personal goals with organizational goals .. 53, 78

37. *Balancing of interests.* The viability of a complex organization depends on the continued provision of incentives for participants which (a) are adequate as rewards for service and (b) are deemed to be fair by comparison with the rewards of other participants. To form opinions on these matters participants require information 78

38. *Specialization in information processing.* One form of specialization in complex organizations is specialization in information processing and the consequential separation of decision-making from direct apprehension of information 49

39. *Information systems.* The processing of information so that the results are relevant to choice situations requires systematization. The function of an information processing system is to provide a substitute for and a supplement to direct observation and a supplement to the memory of actors (7, 8) 9, 52

40. *Objectivity.* As individuals have different propensities for judgement and action (1), as individuals may simultaneously occupy several roles with respect to any complex entity (3) and as the viability of the entity depends on the satisfaction of parties occupying different roles (37), information will be so processed that the rewards and interests of all participants are objectively represented—it will represent the entity as such, not the viewpoint of any class of participant 52

These postulates are selected for their relevance to the framework of behaviour in which accounting plays a part. For the derivation of specific propositions relating to accounting a definition is also necessary:—

Definition. Accounting is a method of monetary calculation designed to provide a continuous source of financial information as a guide to future action in markets 38

Summary of Derived Principles

116. In this paragraph there are brought together and arranged the statements relating to the general nature of accounting which have emerged from the foundations just outlined. If a general description must be given to these statements they may be described as principles.

		Para.
(A)	*Accounting entities.* Accounting systems relate to specific entities defined by roles of natural or artificial persons or groups (3, 9)[4]	56[4], 57
(B)	*Relevance.* The probability of optimal adaptation varies directly with the relevance of accounting information to action (9, 20, 39)	38
(C)	*Neutrality.* The probability of optimal adaptation varies directly with the neutrality of accounting information (1, 4, 9, 20, 39)	38
(D)	*Correspondence.* The relevance of accounting information varies directly with its correspondence with realities (i.e., market conditions, contractual relations, etc.) at the time of action (9)	50
(E)	*Consistency.* Comparability and the legitimacy of inferences as to present position and expectations depend on consistency in the use of concepts and methods in accounting (7)	9, 52, 81, 99
(F)	*Communication.* The transferability of accounting information depends on the use of terms, concepts and measures having the same content and significance to all parties of interest (39, 40)	54
(G)	*Objectivity.* The relevance of accounting information depends on its freedom from the bias, influence or opinion of persons connected with an entity, whether as actors on its behalf or as information processors (35, 36, 40)	52
(H)	*Double-entry.* Transactions of and events affecting an entity are fully described for accounting purposes by simultaneous recording of the manner in which they affect the values of the assets of an entity and the equities by virtue of which those assets were acquired (28, 33)	62
(I)	*Accounting identity.* The aggregate values of the assets of, and the aggregate amount of the equities in, any entity are equal (16, 25)	62
(J)	*Basic record.* As a basis for any subsequent calculation or comparison, a continuous basic record is required which indicates the values attached to actions or events at designated points of time (7, 8, 9, 18)	93
(K)	*Summarization.* Because the span of attention is limited, summarization of entries representing varied transactions improves comprehensibility of the record and thus increases the probability of optimal adaptation (8, 9, 20)	8, 9, 93

[4] The numbers in parenthesis ( ) refer to points listed in paragraph 115. The numbers in the right hand margin refer to relevant paragraphs in the body of the paper. These references are rough indications of the grounds on which the statements depend and the places at which they are discussed.

Para.

(L) *Classification.* Summarization in accordance with the characteristics of assets and equities which are pertinent to action—utility, durability, convertibility, etc.—increases the probability of optimal adaptation (13, 16, 20) 63

(M) *Uniformity of valuation.* The operations of addition, subtraction and relation necessary in any form of summarization can only be performed validly if the separate items are valued on a uniform basis (7, 30, 31) 9, 81

(N) *Current valuation.* In so far as the monetary values assigned to events, things and transactions are at the date of assignment, the current valuation, the principles of relevance, objectivity and uniformity of valuation are satisfied (9, 28, 31) 28, 59

Corollary 1. At the date of purchase or sale, i.e., at the point of making the initial record, the prices at which bargains are made are the values to be assigned.

Corollary 2. At any other date (e.g., for the purpose of any subsequent calculation) the values to be assigned are replacement prices in respect of assets, present values in respect of specific equities.

(O) *Periodical interval.* The frequency of summarization depends on the frequency with which material deviations from planned objectives or operations have occurred or may occur (9, 10, 18) 93

(P) *Periodic identification.* Transactions and other changes are attributed to the periods in which they become effective by changing the character of risks and by changing or inducing changes in the characteristics or values of assets or equities (9, 29) 99

(Q) *Periodic restatement.* If changes in the value of any asset or equity occur, restatement of the values entered in the basic record is required (a) to validate arithmetical and relational operations after such change in value and (b) to conform with the principle of correspondence (9, 29) 105

(R) *Status representation.* Financial position may be derived by summarization of the basic record subject to restatement of values if changes in values have occurred. Such summaries enable decisions to be made with respect to combinations of assets (21, 22) and the use of credit (27) 58, 85

(S) *Change representation.* Changes in financial position during a period may be represented by a statement or statements describing completely the nature, magnitude and sources of the differences between the financial positions at opening and terminal dates. Income and funds statements serve this purpose in different but

Para.

complementary ways, assisting in the making of decisions having regard to the probable effectiveness of alternative courses of action (9, 34) 67, 71

(T) *Articulation.* The cause and effect relationship of transactions and events on financial position is reflected in an accounting system in which statements of financial position and changes in financial position are articulated by reason of their derivation from a basic record founded on market values (16, 24, 28) 67

(U) *Approximation.* Indivisibilities of assets, the fluidity of the environment, the flexibility of goals and the variability of values make statements of financial position and change approximations only (4, 13, 18) 98

117. The summaries given in the two preceding paragraphs seem to be sufficient as far as the demonstration has been taken. Until other cases than the two examined have been subjected to analysis, the "principles" derived may not be considered either sufficient or conclusive. It is believed, however, that they may be shown to be relevant over a wide field. It is repeated that a general theory or framework of concepts is sought by means of which accounting of varied kinds and for varied entities may be explained or described; it is believed that all the propositions of para. 116 are of this general kind. The method here adopted encompasses a range of ideas which conventional "theory" has taken for granted; for example, why account at all? why double-entry? why classify? Conventional "theory" has concerned itself with the areas which have provoked controversy, and without a general basic idea as a point of reference, the concepts adopted in those controversial areas have been special purpose concepts, often flying in the face of the brute facts of economic life.

Some Contrasts in Conclusion

118. In conclusion, some contrasts with the existing framework of conventional accounting may demonstrate the superiority of the framework set out in this paper:—

(a) One consistent principle is applied throughout—the relevance of information to human behaviour. Conventional accounting has no such explicit principle; it therefore disregards the need of men to know where they are in objective terms and the rate at which they are approaching real goals.

(b) As a corollary of relevance the proposed theory concerns itself with values—present market values. It avoids the melange which conventional accounting presents—with its different valuation bases for different things. It avoids the interminable arguments about the merits of H.I.F.O., L.I.F.O., F.I.F.O. and all the other F.O.'s. It avoids the contradictions of the conventional descriptions of the money valuation concept and the going concern concept; it has no special use for the notions of conservatism and disclosure and thus evades their inherent inconsistency. It substitutes for the false assumption that an investment is irrevocable the realistic assumption that adaptation is the essence of behaviour.

(c) By adhering to one set of values it permits of the logical application, over the whole array of entries in an accounting system, of the operations of addition, subtraction and relation. These operations cannot logically be applied to conventional accounts for, although all items are expressed in money units, those units lack similarity in substance.

(d) The proposed theory is disciplined by real circumstances. It does not resort to eclectic principles geared to the "uniformity" and "objectivity" conceived by protagonists of conventional accounting. It has its own uniformity and objectivity, based on the fact that all calculation in money is intended to guide action *vis-à-vis* the external world of men in markets.

(e) The proposed classification of assets into monetary and non-monetary groups is consistent with real differences. It cuts across the conventional current asset—non-current asset classification which has long stood in the way of clear understanding of the similarity of all commodity inventories and the application of consistent principles to both long-term and short-term commodity stocks.

(f) The proposed theory avoids the unrealistic assumption that money has a stable value. It treats the problem of shifts in purchasing power as an integral part of the problem of accounting, which indeed it is. Conventional accounting on the other hand persists in the delusion that only goods change in value, and treats the most obvious shifts in the purchasing power of money as occasional, pathological conditions from which the economy will soon recover.

(g) Adoption of the proposed model would do away with the many "grey" areas in which it is now considered that accountants may exercise discretion—areas which show up accounting as a vague and undisciplined product of circumstance and convention. Its adoption would sharpen the dim outlines of trends in results and position which rob investors of the means of review and criticism. Its adoption would provide accountants, businessmen and administrators with an unequivocal basis for determining the equity of the fiscal and regulatory policies of government. Its adoption would help remove the extensive opportunity for misallocation of resources which conventional accounting in inflationary periods provides. Its adoption would rationalize the merging of businesses which, under conventional accounting, makes every investor a speculator.

119. One final point. If conventional accounting has all the defects these contrasts suggest, how has it managed to survive so long? It has survived simply because of the enormous richness of the informal flows of information in and around business and other organizations. Cost accounts, budgets, *ad hoc* calculations, market prices, project successes and failures—countless pieces of information,

all from unintegrated sub-systems (para. 15), help men to manage in spite of the flaws in conventional accounting. Goethe had one of his characters describe double-entry book-keeping as one of the finest inventions of the human mind, because it enables one to see clearly the whole without becoming confused with details. Accounting, though it still has this original and basic function, today is frequently discounted, and relegated to the role of satisfying formal legal requirements. The hope of restoring it to consistency with reality and of restoring its internal consistency justifies the search for an accounting which is dynamic because it is related to the exigencies of human behaviour.

37

THE RESOLUTION OF SOME PARADOXES IN ACCOUNTING*

> "It may be said that in commercial or investment banking or any business extending credit, success depends on knowing what not to believe in accounting. Few concerns go into bankruptcy or reorganization whose books do not show them solvent, and often even profitable." Mr. Justice Jackson.[1]

Introduction

1. Consistency is not perhaps one of the outstanding characteristics of human behaviour. It is not difficult, if one wishes to be critical of another, to find examples of what may be alleged to be inconsistencies, and even to demonstrate that behaviour has been inconsistent. It is an entirely different matter to have the "accused" admit to inconsistency, or, if he does admit it, to think anything serious is involved. In some cases his indifference is quite legitimate. As a player, over any period, of several roles, he may be acting according to the requirements of each successively with due care but in a manner which appears to an observer, who does not appreciate the plurality of roles, to be inconsistent. On a more general level, few people want to think that living is such a perpetually serious business that inconsistency is inexcusable.

2. Those who assume the role of specialist or expert however can scarcely afford to indulge in such freedom from restraint when filling such a role. The "expert" is a phenomenon of social living; he is one deemed by others to be skilled and well informed in the field of his experience; and such a judgement on the part of others stems largely from the fact that he is of service to them. Few experts if any are expected by those who use their services to be expert opportunists; it is usually expected that they will show some evidence of consistency in their role as experts; that their knowledge will demonstrate such common understanding as will make their advice and skill reliable; and that where there is a body of such experts there will be evidence of mutual consistency in the actions and advice of individual members of that body. Mutual consistency depends in turn on there being a

---

* Occasional Paper No. 2, Faculty of Commerce and Business Administration, University of British Columbia, 1963. Written 1962 and used as a basis of lectures in the Universities of Tasmania, Malaya and British Columbia.

[1] Quoted by R. W. Pinger, "The Semantics of Accounting", *The Accounting Review,* October 1954, p. 652.

reasonably well-argued body of knowledge, consistent in itself. And in so far as the unskilled seek the advice of the expert, they usually expect that the advice and information they are given will be consistent with their purposes and with the real world with which they must contend. We shall be concerned with the extent to which these forms of consistency find expression in accounting. It should perhaps be pointed out that we are not concerned merely with uniformity. Uniformity may have quite different and less worthy justification than consistency. Uniformity may be adopted without serious thought, as a means of avoiding embarrassment. But consistency can only be achieved at the cost of deliberate and careful analysis of the circumstances with which the expert and his dependents are concerned.

3. In a paper entitled "Towards a General Theory of Accounting", an attempt was made to set down the foundations of a general theory of accounting. The line there followed proceeded from the characteristics of human behaviour and the characteristics of the economic environment, to a set of ideas which are mutually consistent, yielding a system of accounting which gives information relevant to action in markets. The present purpose is to demonstrate that, in so far as there is a common body of ideas among accountants today it is self-contradictory or internally inconsistent, and quite inconsistent with the needs of those whom accounting purports to serve. It will be argued that the resolution of those inconsistencies is of importance, and that they may be resolved by adopting the same framework of ideas as was presented in the earlier paper.

4. The procedure to be adopted will be as follows: at each of several points a paradoxical question will be set up. Each question relates to certain elements in the environment of accounting as they are understood among accountants. These questions will be explored by resorting to the literature of accounting. In each case a number of statements in the literature are referred to, in order to establish that the ideas under discussion are not isolated ideas of individuals or specific institutions, but are ideas which are widely and firmly held. The literature contains many statements which differ from and are more defensible than those examined here; but these statements do not form the basis of generally established practices whereas those to be discussed do. The quotations used may appear to be repetitious and for that reason tiresome: but it seems necessary adequately to authenticate the ideas under discussion to avoid the charge that they are minority views. It will transpire that some of these ideas are at odds with the facts of economic life, that some are inconsistent with other ideas on the same subject, and that some are so loosely expressed as to be useless. Care has been taken to avert the suspicion that any author or institution has been singled out for special mention. Such criticism as is offered is to be considered as general criticism of the present state of accounting theory; it is hoped that it will appear to be neither captious nor partisan. Towards the end of each section of the paper there is a paragraph setting out the ideas which seem to be pertinent to the section, ideas which are offered as alternative to the

ideas prevalent in the literature. Each of these ideas is given a numbered reference in [squared] brackets (see e.g., para. 9, *post*), which is the number under which it appears in paragraph 115 of "Towards a General Theory of Accounting" (pp. 508-15, *ante*). It is intended to show that the set of ideas which emerged from the direct argument of that paper would, if adopted, obviate the ambiguities and contradictions noticed in the course of the present analysis.

When is a Service Function not a Service Function?

5. There is perhaps no better point to begin than with the picture of accounting as a function. How do accountants regard their art? One might expect to find the answer in definitions of accounting. Perhaps the most widely quoted definition is that offered by the A.I.C.P.A. Committee on Terminology[2]. This takes the form of listing the types of operation which comprise accounting; no attempt is made in the definition to indicate the purpose of those operations. There is, no doubt, an implicit purpose, for the appendage "and interpreting the results thereof" involves a recipient of the interpretation. Sanders, Hatfield and Moore[3] assert that "accounting should make available all material information of a financial nature relating to (a) the financial condition or status of the business, (b) its progress in earning income". No statement of these kinds is in itself objectionable. But all such statements are sterile. They provide no explicit clue to the precise manner in which accounting serves or may serve human purposes. Implicit functions or purposes can be anything the reader chooses.

6. Some assert a purpose which is described as reporting on stewardship. "The primary purpose of the annual accounts of a business is to present information to the proprietors, showing how their funds have been utilized and the profits derived from such use"[4]. "Corporate financial statements are usually prepared as an accounting by the management for its stewardship of the stockholders' property . . ."[5]. ". . . financial stewardship is the paramount objective and rests at the base of accounting . . . . The whole process of accounting is geared to record funds entrusted and their subsequent disposal."[6] An explicit statement of purpose is worth having, but any statement alluding to stewardship of this kind has several defects. Firstly, it seriously oversimplifies things. For unincorporated businesses it is quite proper to speak of the funds and property of the proprietor or proprietors. But it is an error of fact to speak of the

---

[2] American Institute of Accountants, *Accounting Research Bulletin No.* 9, Report of the Committee on Terminology, 1941, p. 67.

[3] A *Statement of Accounting Principles,* 1938, p. 113 (Reprint, 1959, by American Accounting Association).

[4] The Institute of Chartered Accountants in England and Wales, *Recommendation* 15, Accounting in relation to changes in the purchasing power of money, 1952.

[5] Samuel J. Broad, "Recent Developments in Accounting and Auditing", *The Journal of Accountancy,* September 1944, p. 190.

[6] R. A. Irish, "Fundamental Concepts of Corporate Accounting", *The Australian Accountant,* June 1950, pp. 216-7.

funds or property of proprietors in the above context in the case of corporate business. An investor who divests himself of funds in exchange for a paper title to a share in a business can no longer speak of "his" funds. Further, the "funds" which he exchanged for his paper title may not have gone to the business in which he holds a share, but to a previous shareholder; there is no necessary connection between "his" funds and the funds available to the business. Secondly, the stewardship view of accounting implicitly represents managers as custodians rather than as businessmen. There is no particular point in knowing what has been done with the funds of the business unless one adopts the view that managers are fiduciaries—and this view is false. Investors may want to know how efficiently funds have been utilized—but not simply how they have been utilized; and they want to know this because they are buyers of managerial talent. It is in any case pretending too much to speak of the annual accounts as showing how funds have been utilized, for all sorts of things are quite legitimately eliminated in the process of drawing up the annual accounts. The accounts may show the net effect of utilizing funds—but this is a very different thing. And even if investors did have a comprehensive statement showing how funds have been utilized, would they be able to make any use of it? It is quite improbable, for seldom are they able, as are managers, to assess the merits of a given deployment of funds or to know of alternative deployments and their prospects.

7. Statements such as those considered in the previous two paragraphs are still current; but there are more explicit and more useful statements. It is many years since Paton stated the setting of accounting in the following terms: "The conception of the manager must be exactly that of the business entity as an economic unit; and if, as is repeatedly said, the most important purpose which modern accounting can serve lies in the rationalization of business administration, the accountant must of necessity adopt the viewpoint of the manager in large measure."[7] If the managerial function is fully described it will embrace both the problems of investment in and use of a body of assets and the problems of maintaining the rights and interests of the various equity holders who make possible the use of that body of assets. Paton's view may legitimately be extended to include investors as "economic units"; but by the late 'thirties the investor was beginning to be specifically mentioned in descriptions of the accounting function. Sanders, Hatfield and Moore[8] wrote of "satisfying the need for information of all the parties of interest, especially of (a) the management of the business, (b) outside groups, such as investors and creditors, (c) government, in such matters as taxation and regulation". Paton and Littleton[9] commenced their monograph thus: "The purpose of accounting is to furnish financial

---

[7] William A. Paton, *Accounting Theory,* New York, The Ronald Press Co., 1922, p. 478.

[8] *A Statement of Accounting Principles,* p. 4.

[9] Paton and Littleton, *An Introduction to Corporate Accounting Standards,* American Accounting Association, Urbana, 1940, p. 1.

data concerning a business enterprise, compiled and presented to meet the needs of management, investors and the public." Others have stated in general terms the governing idea, without alluding to any special class of users, "... the fundamental principle of accounting is usefulness ... this principle ... provides a basis for accounting outside itself".[10] "... fundamentally the objective (of accounting) is to make enterprise activities understandable."[11] More recent statements make specific allusions to "communication" which is another way of indicating the needs of users; thus, "Effective measurement and communication of economic data on a business enterprise ... represents the accounting function".[12] And, "Accounting's purposes are to serve as a language for communicating the financial facts about an enterprise to those who have an interest in interpreting and using those facts, and to provide a useful tool for analyzing, controlling and planning enterprise operations".[13]

8. There is sufficient evidence here to indicate that the notion of service to one or more groups of persons associated with business has long been a part of the general impression its exponents have had of the accounting function. But it is easy to use the appropriate words while having a confused and inadequate view of what the words mean in an operational context. Few objections can be taken to any of the above forms of words; but in so many cases they gloss over the implicit but essential meanings of component phrases. For example, what do Sanders, Hatfield and Moore mean by "the need for information"? What do Paton and Littleton mean by "financial data" and "meeting the needs of management ..."? What does Littleton mean by making enterprise activities "understandable"? What do Black and Champion mean by "financial facts"? It seems generally to be supposed that such words or phrases have an unequivocal and uniform meaning, or that they are self-explanatory. But this is far from the case as will be shown.

9. It is necessary, if the above types of description are to have any content which will be of use in formulating an accounting system, that the precise character of the service to be given be delineated. It is necessary to have a clear idea of the manner in which accounting fits into the framework of individual and business behaviour. Businessmen do not simply want to "understand" enterprise activities; they want to understand so that they can "control" and "plan"; but even these words do not say specifically what they want to do. Businessmen, in fact all men, must act and every act involves a choice between available courses of action[6]. What determines these choices and hence the actions which follow? Any group of persons

---

[10] Wilcox and Hassler, "A Foundation for Accounting Principles", *The Journal of Accountancy*, October 1941, p. 309.

[11] A. C. Littleton, *Structure of Accounting Theory,* American Accounting Association, Urbana, 1953, p. 77.

[12] Bedford, Perry and Wyatt, *Advanced Accounting,* New York, John Wiley & Sons, Inc., 1961, p. 6.

[13] Black and Champion, *Accounting in Business Decisions,* Englewood Cliffs, Prentice-Hall Inc., 1961, p. v.

will display individual differences; different wants, skills and propensities for action[1]. At any time each will have a series of diverse goals which compete for attainment, because each will feel uneasiness or strain in a variety of directions simultaneously[2]. These goals will depend on the diverse roles which an individual fills during the period in which each moment of action falls[3]. But wants and goals will vary from time to time[4]. To use time and other scarce resources with the greatest effect at any time goals will be ranked in order according to the intensity of wants, and because degrees of uneasiness will vary from time to time so will the order in which goals are ranked vary[5]. At any time action will be directed towards the most urgent goal. But for thinking men, action will not be random; it will be deliberate, involving the mental processes of observation, recollection, calculation and comparison[7], and, in respect of each of these, every individual has limited capacity—both absolutely and with reference to the amount of time during which choices must be made[8]. Choice is thus influenced by the intensity of wants, the amount of present knowledge and one's expectations of the consequences of various possible actions, the latter also being a consequence of present knowledge[9]. But every course of action may have several aspects and bear on more than one goal; each of these aspects must be considered independently, the emergent action being finally the consequence of mentally synthesizing the various abstracted implications of each available course of action[11]. Above all, the whole purpose of choice is that some person or persons may obtain satisfaction of wants, in terms of what can be consumed—sooner or later[6]. The orientation of action is towards things or control over things, never towards money as such. It is believed that, unless such characteristics of behaviour as these are explicity taken into account, it is impossible to stipulate the kind of service accounting can or should render. The portmanteau term "service function" may be good enough in everyday parlance; but it is far from enough for technical rigour, for it may equally connote things of incidental or questionable use as well as things of the utmost importance. If incidental, implicit or questionable functions steal the limelight, a service function may in fact give very little service.

10. When is a service function not a service function? When the modes of action of the entities it is supposed to serve are so poorly defined that no specific basis is provided for designing the service or for testing whether any task performed by a service unit is in fact a service; and when the service function itself is so poorly defined that no link is established with the entity served and its mode of action. In these circumstances its practitioners can quite blandly assert that they are giving service even though the service is trifling and inconsequential.

When is Information not Information?

11. It is an easy and comforting belief that all statements convey information. It is just as easy to show that this belief is mistaken.

Logicians are partial to the invention of nonsense statements to demonstrate the error. Some lines from Lewis Carroll's *Through the Looking Glass* will serve:—

> "'Twas brillig and the slithy toves
> Did gyre and gimble in the wabe;
> All mimsy were the borogoves,
> And the mome raths outgrabe."

This is a useful example because it has sufficient recognizable words —'twas . . . and . . . the . . . did . . . and . . . in the . . . etc.—to give it the form of a statement in the vernacular without conveying anything. Many political and ceremonial speeches are of the same kind. Carroll's lines may of course well convey some information, but only if the terms used are translated into terms which are generally understood by the reader. Likewise a code or cipher is a device for conveying nonsense to the unauthorized or misinformed, but conveying very much in the vernacular to the person who has the key. It is also easy to show that although some statements convey information, the information is not worth having, and the statement is not worth making. To fill up the silence, as a conversation piece, one may say "Ughrr. It's cold", when it is apparent to every shivering one of the audience that it is cold. Questions relating to the content and significance of statements will occupy this section.

12. Accounting records and reports consist of sets of statements. At early stages in the development of accounting, each entry in the record was in fact a detailed and sometimes lengthy statement of the facts behind it[14]. The forms and formal conventions since adopted enable events and transactions to be recorded in abbreviated ways, but every entry is still a statement. "Cash, 1000 money units", "Plant, 10,000 money units", are statements. But they are statements in code. Plant and money units are not the same in kind. "Plant, 10,000 money units" is a statement relating "plant", "10,000" and "money units". To understand the relationship one must have knowledge of the symbols used and the rules for putting symbols together in statement form. These are precisely the problems of language, and the similarity has not been overlooked by some accountants. Montgomery described accounting as "the language of finance"[15]. Goldberg[16] deals briefly with the "lingual" aspect of accounting. And a number of the extracts quoted in paragraph 7 imply that accounting serves as a form of language.

13. To be a little more precise, accounting is a form of language which concerns itself with quantities and magnitudes. The form of its statements is not the same as the form of some statements in economics; for example, it is not concerned simply with tendencies,

---

[14] Edward Peragallo, *Origin and Evolution of Double Entry Bookkeeping*, New York, American Institute Publishing Co., 1938 4ff.

[15] Foreword to Peragallo's *Origin and Evolution of Double Entry Bookkeeping*.

[16] *An Outline of Accounting*, Sydney, The Law Book Co. of Australasia Pty. Ltd., 1957, p. 13.

with higher or lower, with more or less. A businessman does not simply want to know that his assets today are more than they were yesterday; he wants to know how much more. He does not simply want to know that last year's income was less than that of the year before; he wants to know how much less. He does not simply want to know that a new product will increase his profit; he wants to know by how much. Thus if accounting is to be the means by which he is informed, accounting will involve measurement and the propositions which appear in accounts will be expressive of measurements made.

14. This aspect of accounting is noticed far more frequently than reference is made to language. Paton says, "accounting strives to measure economic forces in financial terms and to communicate the results of such measurement to interested parties"[17], and in another place speaks of accounting as "*measuring* and arraying economic data"[18] (emphasis in original). Paton and Littleton say: "The primary purpose of accounting . . . is the measurement of periodical income by means of a systematic process of matching costs and revenues"[19]; and they use "measured consideration" of costs and revenues (pp. 11-12). Canning styles one of his chapters "The Measurement of Income"; he speaks more commonly of valuation when he refers to assets, but is impelled (p. 199) to offer some general rules which describe the characteristics which measures must possess if they are to be "merged"[20]. He does not however establish general principles of accounting which conform with the general rules relating to measurement. Kester repeatedly refers to measurement. His second chapter is styled "Measurement in Accounting", and he applies the term to specific items throughout the text. Of the significance of the measurement problem he writes: "Regardless of what the items are which are given a place in the balance sheet . . . it is their measured amounts which give them their real significance when used to show financial position."[21]

15. But, in spite of the implied importance of measurement, the only type of measurement contemplated by Kester is measurement in terms of cash outlay or its equivalent, and the only justification offered is the "primary need of management" for "information as to the status of invested funds" (p. 30). He writes of the need for "remeasurement" of balance sheet items "at successive fiscal periods", but this turns out to be nothing more than an introduction to the usual conventional going concern methods of valuation: "going-concern measurement is not so much a distinct type of measurement as it is a term descriptive of the kinds of dollar measurements suitable for a going business" (p. 33). In these respects most accountants follow the same road.

---

[17] *Recent and Prospective Developments in Accountancy Theory,* Dickinson Lectures, 1939-40, Cambridge, Mass., Harvard University Press, 1943, p. 87.

[18] William A. Paton, *Essentials of Accounting,* New York, The Macmillan Co., 1955, p. 1.

[19] *An Introduction to Corporate Accounting Standards,* p. 123.

[20] *The Economics of Accountancy,* New York, The Ronald Press Co., 1929.

[21] *Advanced Accounting,* New York, The Ronald Press Co., 1946, p. 29.

Canning, as an observer, is disillusioned about accountants' measurements: "What is set out as a measure of net income can never be supposed to be a fact in any sense at all except that it is the figure that results when the accountant has finished applying the procedure he adopts" (pp. 98-9). He notes six types of commonly accepted valuations for different classes of assets, and comments: "These diverse values of things are added ['merged'?] to find an asset total that, dollar for dollar, cannot possibly have a common significance" (p. 319), . . . "No competent student of the joint field of economics and accounting can doubt that the measurements in accountants' reports are of diverse statistical orders" (p. 320). If this is the state of affairs, can the resulting information be informative? Who can interpret such mixed aggregates?

16. All this is rather disappointing. One might be pardoned for supposing that measurement would entail a conscious, deliberate and skilled attempt to assign quantities to things by reference to a scale which applies equally to all the things to be measured. For such a scale to be applied equally, consistently, to all things measured, it must be applied to one and only one of the characteristics common to those things. Further one might be pardoned for supposing that any remeasurement would involve more than a simple mechanical adjustment to the original measurement. The reasons why these suppositions and expectations are disappointed may lie in the attitude accountants adopt towards the signs and symbols they use and towards their processes of assigning symbols.

17. Notwithstanding all references to communicating facts and information the accountant has reserved the right to dictate what information shall be communicated. What, for example, does Kester imply when he speaks of "the dollar amount of an item as measured *for the accounting records*" (p. 29; emphasis added)? He seems to imply that there is a distinction between "for the accounting records" and "for business purposes". What does Gilman imply when he speaks of "*the accounting viewpoint*" which "has caused some difficulty to those who use accounting figures"[22]? He seems to imply a viewpoint which is different from that of users of accounting figures. What does Littleton imply when he refers to "objective reality in *the accounting sense*"[23] (emphasis added)? He seems to imply that there is an objective reality for accountants which is different from the objective reality for anyone else; but what can "objective" mean if this is so? Scores of such adjectival usages of "accounting" imply that there is a clear difference between the way accountants see things and the way businessmen and users of accounts see the same things. Montgomery speaks of this as a "tendency to expect business to conform to an accounting pattern rather than the reverse"[24]. This tendency is a bias which accountants perhaps do not find in themselves, but it is a bias

---

[22] *Accounting Concepts of Profit,* New York, The Ronald Press Co., 1939, p. 609.

[23] *Structure of Accounting Theory,* p. 182.

[24] Foreword to Peragallo's *Origin and Evolution of Double Entry Bookkeeping.*

which is well known to psychologists and logicians. It finds occasional mention in the literature relating to business problems; thus: "There is a widespread notion that an adult person can always discern facts that are exposed to observation.... This belief is illusory because a mental bias can operate to prevent a person from either ascertaining the relevant facts or from appropriately interrelating facts and drawing logical conclusions therefrom"[25]. If accounting statements are to convey information, accountants must first see things as the users would see them if they were able; there is no room for a special accounting viewpoint interposed between the facts and those who must act upon them.

18. The recording of events, transactions and "facts" generally, can only be done in terms of symbols—words, numbers, positions and so on. Attention will be confined here to the numbers assigned to descriptive words. What do the numbers in accounts represent and what information do they communicate? The assignment of numbers is described by Gilman[26] as the valuation convention. "By this convention non-homogeneous assets and claims to assets are translated into financial equivalents or money values." At another point he says that valuation in the sense in which he uses it "is no more than a convenient method of symbolizing" (p. 56). And at another point still, "If it be conceded that dollar valuations are no more than symbols, then it follows, in theory at least, that consistency results from leaving the symbols unchanged. Thus, if the symbol $5 is used to represent one ton of fuel, as long as that ton of fuel remains intact, the symbol itself should theoretically remain unchanged.... Essentially all that the convention of valuation really accomplishes is substitution.... Instead of calling a ton of coal $5, it might be called X. Just so long as the ton of coal remained, it would be symbolized as X, but as soon as half of it was consumed, it would be symbolized as X/2" (p. 247). Though Gilman is the source of this particular demonstration, something of the same kind underlies all statements which sanction the assignment of numbers, other than numbers representing market values, to items in accounts. What is the character of Gilman's statement? If the numbers assigned are symbols, what are they symbols of?—for Gilman does not make this clear. If all that the assignment of numbers "accomplishes is substitution", what is substituted for what? Suppose a merchant has three trucks, one that is so old that it is held together with wire and Scotch tape, but is still usable, one that is three years old and rather battered, and one that is quite new. He can see the condition they are in, he knows what they can do and he can even estimate how long they will last. But, suppose his accountant gives him the following information—Trucks, 10,000 money units, less depreciation 6,000 money units, net 4,000 money units; now what does he know? According to Gilman, he knows that

---

[25] William L. Campfield, "Re-examination of Bases and Opportunities for Applying Accounting Judgment", *The Accounting Review*, October 1959, p. 556.

[26] *Accounting Concepts of Profit*, p. 26.

someone has substituted a money symbol for trucks and another for depreciation—no more than that. And that piece of information is not information worth having. Further, if Gilman offers his coal example seriously, the merchant can have no means of showing anything less than, say, Y, for a truck, for there is no such thing as half a truck—accounting is not concerned simply with quantities. Again, if a ton of coal were denoted by X presumably one would have to denote a truck by something not-X, say Y, so that a merchant having a truck and a ton of coal would have X + Y, and the "translation" of "non-homogeneous assets" into common terms would not have been accomplished.

19. It is not generally enough realized that every translation of facts and events into symbols involves a loss of some information. Whatever information his accountant gives the truck-owner mentioned above, it is less than all the facts about his trucks. But for specific purposes one may be prepared to forgo much information in order to see clearly in its context some specific piece of information: the necessity of abstraction has been referred to in para. 9. It is the particular advantage of the use of money symbols in the formal framework of accounting that it *can* provide a specific class of information of which the parts may be related and from which inferences may be drawn with respect to the actual and potential flows of money—the only common means, in a monetary economy, which gives access to control over other means. Generally an information system may use symbols which simply denote items, for example, a catalogue, a chart of accounts. But if a system is to use symbols of such a kind that a common characteristic of all items is represented, and if the magnitudes of those characteristics are to be capable of summation or relation, any given symbol will necessarily have the same connotation wherever it appears in a list of items: thus "500" assigned to "plant" will mean the same thing as "500" assigned to "cash" or "500" assigned to "creditors". The intention to add, subtract and relate symbols will discipline the whole process of measurement and of determining what will be measured.

20. If we are to design an information system which conveys information, it is necessary to start with the service notion dealt with in the preceding section[39]. It is necessary to admit explicitly that where, as a consequence of specialization[38], the processing of information and the choice of actions are divorced, processors and actors may see things differently; but it is necessary at the same time to demand, as a corollary of the service function, that accountants make every effort to convey relevant information in a manner free of their individual predilections[40]. This is a critical aspect of the objectivity of information. Accountants have ostensibly feared that, without restraints, managers would report affairs in a manner favourable to themselves, but have disregarded the equally possible bias on their own part. If the symbols used are strictly relatable and contemporary it is possible to conceive that summary statements may be derived which are relevant to action—summaries representing

financial position or the financial capacity for action[33], and changes in position, the results of past actions and a guide to future action[34]. If symbolization is artificial and the results must be re-translated to be useful, then one of two undesirable things will follow: there will be unavoidable losses of information both at the point of symbolization and at the point of interpretation, and the resulting information will be less useful than it could be; or the re-translation will not be made and what appears to be information will in fact be useless, or if used will be misleading.

21. When is information not information? When the information generating system has a low degree of selectivity due to inadequate definition of its purpose: when the transmitting system is subject to interference; and when the signals transmitted lack precise meaning to the receiver because the same symbols at any time have quite different significances. The conventional accounting model has all three defects. Though it has the appearance of an information system, the information units it produces and transmits are of mixed character, due in part to lack of definition of the function of the system and in part to bias in processing; and, as for the utility of its signals to receivers, the exponents and practitioners of conventional accounting alike freely admit that on many matters more precise and more relevant information is required than their system yields.

When is a Going Concern not a Going Concern?

22. The notion of the going concern has a well-established place in the literature of accounting. But there is no consistency in the interpretation of its purpose or its implications. "[Following the convention of the going business] no attempt is made [at the end of each period] to value all the assets of a company on a realizable basis. Rather the emphasis is shifted to the amortizing of initial costs . . . the resulting asset figures are not influenced by market price fluctuations ascribable to the law of supply and demand."[27] "Business in general does not consist of an array of sporadic, short-term ventures and its accomplishments are not normally subject to the test of complete liquidation. Liquidation is not the normal expectation; continuity is."[28] "The business is viewed as established and as expecting to operate continuously. Capital has become tied up in equipment essential to the undertaking, in the sense that to dispose of it in its entirety would mean a break-up of the business. It cannot therefore be freed or put to other uses without a reconstruction of the present enterprise".[29] "The 'going concern' concept assumes the continuance of the general enterprise situation . . . the assets of the enterprise are expected to have continuing usefulness for the general purpose for which they were

---

[27] Stephen Gilman, *Accounting Concepts of Profit,* p. 81.

[28] Paton and Littleton, *An Introduction to Corporate Accounting Standards,* p. 9.

[29] Roy B. Kester, *Advanced Accounting,* p. 306.

acquired, and its liabilities are expected to be paid at maturity."[30] "... it is assumed that the business entity has continuity of life.... Properties used by the entity are deemed to have been irrevocably dedicated to the carrying on of its purposes and will remain in use as long as they serve those purposes".[31]

23. Several threads run through every such series of statements. The first is most concisely expressed by Owen, the irrevocable dedication of properties to purposes. This concept of the character of a going concern is quite inconsistent with business behaviour. There are admittedly countless examples of firms which have acquired assets which they have held continuously over long periods for their original purposes. But there are probably no less numerous examples of assets which have been disposed of piecemeal before their full service potential was exhausted, of assets which have become technologically and economically valueless to one firm for its purposes but which are quite useful and valuable to other firms for their purposes. In a very real sense business does "consist of an array of short-term ventures" for each of which the test is liquidation. Every purchase of an asset is potentially a short-term purchase, and businessmen are quite concerned about the interval over which such investments may be liquidated. For the essence of the business enterprise is that it is surrounded by the ceaseless ebb and flow of technical and economic change. A vehicle, a machine, a security investment may for this reason be considered as a worthwhile investment only so long as the present value of the expected services it will yield exceeds the present value of the yield from investing its present resale price in an alternative manner. If the alternative yield is greater it is sheer folly not to take it—liquidating the earlier investment in the process. The fact that certain assets are complementary in character is not overlooked; complementarity simply requires that in any re-examination of investment possibilities complementary assets must be considered together, as a unit. There is no more likely way of making a going concern defunct than to force it to dedicate its properties to one purpose as long as they will last.

24. Another thread running through such arguments as are quoted above seems to be the notion that the alternatives available to any business are continuation as it is or complete break-up. Kester makes the clearest statement of this view but it occurs also in the statement from Paton and Littleton, and in many similar statements by others. Quite apart from the possibility of alternative investment mentioned in the previous paragraph, liquidation at some time of the investment in any business asset is always and inevitably in contemplation; but not liquidation in the sense of forced sale as seems to be implied in most statements relating to the going concern which refer by antithesis to

[30] American Accounting Association, *Accounting and Reporting Standards for Corporate Financial Statements*, 1957 Revision (pamphlet), p. 2.

[31] James N. Owen, "A Review of the Basic Concepts of Financial Accounting", *N.A.A. Bulletin*, June 1958, p. 70.

liquidation. Gradual liquidation is one of the most obvious characteristics of a going concern; if a business is not liquidating some of its assets, by sale of their services, it is not going. Every advocate of the importance of cash flows in business calculations attests the importance of liquidation as a feature of a going concern. And even those who deny the relevance of liquidation have to fall back on it in the long run: for example, "the complete picture [*sic*] of an enterprise is never discernible prior to final liquidation"[32]. But, of what use is the "complete picture" then, when the business is gone? Surely it is important while the business is a going concern to consider each part of it as undergoing liquidation in a planned and orderly fashion! For this is the commonest way by which firms adapt to new conditions.

25. The thing represented by the phrase "going concern" is not merely an abstraction. We may use abstract words to denote it, but any tendency to think of it as an abstraction will mislead. A going concern is a collection of live persons using tangible things and enforceable rights to change the form or the location of other tangible things and to create other enforceable rights. To keep going it is obliged to do these things in a manner consistent with its purposes and the environment at the time: its actions must be planned. It is misleading to assert that "the entity does not plan—it only acts"[33]; acting can only be dissociated from planning in the case of instinctive action, but a business entity can have no instincts. It is misleading to dissociate the accounting viewpoint from the trading viewpoint as does Gilman[34], when after stipulating that the accounting viewpoint requires unchanged symbols for assets he adds: "As soon as the trading viewpoint is adopted, it is inevitable that consideration will be given to changes in the market value (of an asset)". Going concerns are traders; the only viewpoint they can have is a trading viewpoint. It is also misleading to stipulate other "viewpoints" as if all were unrelated either to accounting or trade. "Only when (the) question of valuation is approached from the ownership, credit or legal viewpoints does a non-cost basis become of serious import. It is only when the task of interpreting accounting figures is faced that the convention of dollar (cost) valuation causes trouble. Such interpretation is always from the ownership, legal or credit viewpoint, never from that of the entity", says Gilman (p. 56). Ownership, credit and legality are not viewpoints separable from a trading entity; they describe some of its inseparable characteristics. If accounting statements must be translated from their conventional form into the form appropriate to actions affecting or affected by ownership, credit or legal considerations, then apparently they were pointlessly translated into the conventional form in the first place. A going concern is intimately involved in a network of ownership, credit and legal restraints, conditions or relationships.

---

[32] Paton and Littleton, *An Introduction to Corporate Accounting Standards,* p. 10.

[33] Wm. L. Raby, "The Two Faces of Accounting", *The Accounting Review,* July 1959, p. 460.

[34] *Accounting Concepts of Profit,* pp. 247-8.

It cannot avoid them, nor can any accounting legitimately be devised which is so abstract that it ignores them.

26. There is little doubt about the utility of the idea of a going concern. It does set up a way of approaching the problems of recording, processing and restating the significances of events and transactions. But its implications need to be specified, otherwise an entirely amorphous entity will be imagined and there will be no definite characteristics which will point to the style of recording and reporting suited to it. These implications apply to a very large extent to individuals and business entities alike. A going concern, like an individual has a goal system[2]; it and its goal system are both products of specialization[23], and the exploitation of individual differences. Its method of functioning is complex, for it operates in every market which provides means of attaining its goals, whether the market provides services in exchange for money or money in exchange for services[35]. Its method of functioning involves giving satisfaction to every class of person associated with it. If any one class (customers, workers, financiers, etc.) ceases to be associated with it, because there is a conflict of goals[36] it ceases to be a going concern. To give satisfaction to all classes entails a balancing of interests[37], a balancing of the rewards and incentives flowing to participants; in some cases to assure participants of the equity of their respective shares in the product, a statement of the results and their division is made available. The management group of participants is expected not only to balance conflicting claims but also to operate efficiently, so that the amount against which all claims can be made is the optimum[20]. As the going concern operates through time in which the environment changes, optimization involves continuous adaptation of policies, physical equipment and other arrangements to take advantage of the new circumstances[32]. Continuous adaptation is possible only if no past action or choice is regarded as irrevocably binding; revocability of choice is a condition of survival[10]. Changes in tastes and in the environment generally are in many respects unpredictable, so that there is an element of uncertainty as to the outcome of all actions or proposed actions[18]. The legal framework[17] makes possible, uncertainty makes desirable and indivisibility of means makes necessary the accumulation of means[19], but the accumulation of any class of means is necessarily related to the continuously changing nature of operations. A going concern is not an inert or passive thing; it takes an active part in changing or meeting changes in its environment—this is its dominant feature.

27. When is a going concern not a going concern? One cannot change the nature of a going concern by attributing to it characteristics which it does not have and by denying it characteristics which it does have. But if it is envisaged in terms which disregard the very nature of going—of constantly acting on and reacting to the environment—it is quite improbable that any worthwhile aid to its continuation will emerge. It may continue to go—but in spite of the actions of those who conceive it as a venture irrevocably committed to

its past choices and unconcerned about the shifts of preferences and group pressures which surround it. The conventional going concern concept can only lead to its dissolution.

When is a Going Concern Value not a Going Concern Value?

28. The whole apparatus of accounting is concerned with the individual resources in which entities deal. The very reason for keeping separate accounts for different assets is so that each item may be considered on its merits from time to time, rather than that all assets shall be considered as an indivisible complex. There are of course occasions when an enterprise as a whole changes hands, lock, stock and barrel; but this may be assumed to occur only when the proceeds of selling the individual assets would fall short of the proceeds of the sale of the enterprise. In any case the frequency with which individual assets change hands is much greater than the frequency with which businesses change hands. All of which raises the question: When "going concern value" is used, is it used of the value of a business as a going concern, or is it used of the values of assets to a going concern?

29. There is some confusion on this point. Consider for example the following: "The fallacy of attempting to establish present values through the medium of the balance sheet is twofold. In the first place it is frequently impossible to establish satisfactory present values for various items in the balance sheet. More important, a significant present value of an enterprise can be established only by dealing with all balance-sheet items as an entirety: 'enterprise value' is only rarely equal to the sum of the present values of its component parts".[35] This represents a positive answer to both parts of the question posed in the previous paragraph. Somewhat earlier George O. May asserted that present values of fixed assets "if ascertained would be irrelevant. What the investor is interested in is the value of the enterprise in which he is acquiring an interest as a whole . . . . If the enterprise is profitable its value will be determined mainly by consideration of its earning capacity".[36] This represents a positive answer to the first part of the question, as also the following appears to do: "Earning power —not cost price, not replacement price, not sale or liquidation price— is the significant basis of enterprise value. The income statement, therefore, is the most important accounting report."[37]

30. These statements slip from one focus of attention to another without explanation; for example, the parenthetical section of the extract from Paton and Littleton appears clearly to refer to prices of individual assets, for in the context no reference is made to the price of a going concern, but the remainder of the statement refers to the

---

[35] James L. Dohr, "Reflections on the Development of Accounting Procedures", *The Journal of Accountancy*, July 1942, p. 44.

[36] "Valuation or Historical Cost: Some Recent Developments", *The Journal of Accountancy*, January 1940, pp. 19-20.

[37] Paton and Littleton, *An Introduction to Corporate Accounting Standards*, p. 10.

whole enterprise. Now it is quite true that enterprise value is significant to investors. But this gives no warrant for disregarding the individual assets and their individual earning powers. Every single investment in plant or other assets will, if efficient or rational management is assumed, be required to be justified in terms of its expected earnings. If the expected earnings of any asset fall it is proper to consider whether its use should continue. If the expected earnings of any asset become less than the expected earnings of an alternative asset, it is proper to consider whether the former should be replaced. If the expected earnings of any asset would be greater in the hands of another user than in those of its present user, it will pay the latter to sell if any alternative investment is expected to yield more than this asset to its present user. In all these cases the test is the present market price of the asset in question; for the present market price, on the one hand, is the amount which will be available for re-investment in the event of sale, and the amount which determines the scale of the expected yield from re-investment: and on the other hand, present market price is the market's assessment of the capitalized value of future yields from the asset in question itself.

31. The legitimacy of this argument may be challenged in respect of those assets which have no market. Why, for example, should a steel manufacturer be interested in the present value of a blast furnace or a rolling mill, for which break-up is the only alternative to continued use? He may not be an operator in the blast furnace market, but he is an operator in the market for his products. And if he wishes to remain in the business of making steel he will at any time expect his customers to pay the going rate for the output of a steel plant not only as a whole, but also piece by piece—the going rate for ore, coal, coke ovens, blast furnaces, steel furnaces and rolling mills, individually. In so far as the market permits, he will make sure that his prices allow him at least to maintain his physical capacity. His prices may remain steady while other prices rise if he can cut his costs; but once he reaches the limit of cost-cutting as he then sees it, he will raise his prices to ensure that they yield at least the present value of the plant service consumed.

32. It is sometimes suggested that an important attribute of a going concern is its attitude towards "the long run", and that short-run (market) values are not therefore pertinent. Paton and Littleton aver that "accounting and business can follow a scientific pattern only by adapting themselves to the long run" (p. 20). But what is the long run? Does it fall short of liquidation, when a business has become an "unneeded industry" and capital cannot be used by it "effectively" (p. 3)? And if it falls short, how far short? It is quite unscientific to believe that businessmen only adapt themselves to the long run. They do not ignore the long run. But they want returns in the short run rather than the long run—the longer the run the less is the present value of their returns. And they want returns in the short run, for only by meeting the expectations of supporters in the short run will their businesses survive in the long run. They will not calculate their prices and formulate other policies on the basis of last year's outdated

costs or conditions. They will not keep their prices down because they bought assets at a lower price than a more recent entrant to their industries. They will not gear their prices to initial money costs of plant for years and then, on replacement, raise prices by the whole of the difference between the appropriate parts of initial plant outlays and outlays on new plant. They will not assume that when an old piece of equipment comes to be sold its scrap value will make up the difference between the sum of all depreciation charges on the basis of initial outlay and the cost of a new piece of equipment of the same capacity. They will not adopt the equivocal position of expecting customers to pay the current price for labour service embodied in their products but not to pay the current value of plant service embodied in the same products.

33. Accounting is concerned with value in only one sense—the values of individual assets and claims. It is not concerned with the value of a going concern *in toto*. The securities market is, on the other hand, concerned with the values of enterprises as units *in toto*. The price it puts on securities is an expression of this. The market value or price of securities is known to investors and prospective investors independently of the accounts; it may arise in part from what investors think of what appears in the income accounts of companies, but only in part; and, however it arises, knowledge of it is readily available. The other side of the picture however is the values—the present prices —of individual assets. It is quite misleading to assert that: "In a well-managed and profitable business, the current worth of assets is really only of academic importance."[38] Dohr's statement is much more realistic: "the present value of property is generally speaking the factor of outstanding importance"[39]. If the aggregate of the present prices of assets exceeds by a significant amount the aggregate market value of the outstanding securities, investors are given an indication that they should consider whether to liquidate the assets, to change the management, or to cut their losses. If the aggregate of the present prices of assets falls short, by a significant amount, of the aggregate market value of the outstanding securities, investors are warned that they should consider part of their incomes as a premium for the risk they run, either of inadequate cover for their investment or of the entry of new firms wishing to take advantage of apparently high returns. Similar types of argument may be adduced to cover the uses management may make of accounting which reports present values. No such series of tests can be made however if, by going concern valuation of assets, one means valuation on a cost basis. No such series of tests is even contemplated by those who, acknowledging the irrelevance of balance sheets prepared on a cost basis, assert the overriding importance of the income statement.

---

[38] R. A. Irish, "Fundamental Concepts of Corporate Accounting", *The Australian Accountant,* June 1950, p. 219.
[39] James L. Dohr, "Cost and Value", *The Journal of Accountancy,* March 1944, p. 193.

34. To summarize, "going concern value" in accounting has reference to the values of specific assets and claims of a going concern. Accountants in the ordinary course of accounting are not required to produce market assessments of the value of a going concern *in toto* or of particular shares in it. The market does this. But the right of investors and managers to have some comparable independent information on the values of assets and claims cannot be denied; comparison is essential to informed judgement, and comparison of security prices with balance sheet values is useless unless both are in current terms. As a going concern is constantly changing in every respect—financial supporters, customers, suppliers, workers, stocks, obligations, market conditions—the variability of values is an ever-present reality[29]. Financial position at any time can only have a useful meaning if it relates to the position a going concern occupies in the market situation then prevailing[33]; and because of the severability of every asset, every claim and every specific relationship, the present value of every marketable thing or right is a necessary aspect of going concern value. It is pointless to consider the skill, acumen and foresight of management and the organized arrangement of its facilities as assets; they will both be reflected in earnings and hence in market evaluations of securities. It is unnecessary and incompetent for accounting to recognize them, for the skill of management may be lost or withdrawn and any given arrangement of facilities may be altered.

35. When is a going concern value not a going concern value? Investors are not simply concerned with the income which they receive as dividends—their probable receipts from dividends, from the sale of their securities and from the proceeds of liquidation are all significant to them. Accounting should aid them in making calculations in all these directions; and it can if present prices are what it reports; the prices investors offer or demand will only then be informed indications of the going concern value of an enterprise as a whole. But accounting can only give the financial data behind investors' calculations. In its limited field, going concern values can only relate to the present prices of items piece by piece, for a going concern treats them piece by piece for all investment or re-investment purposes. A going concern value which is rooted in the past is a contradiction; a going concern value which incorporates imponderables is, for accounting, an impossibility.

When is a Cost not a Cost?

36. One of the most strongly entrenched ideas in accounting is that cost is the proper basis for entries in accounts. If cost is to be made the cornerstone of accounting one would expect to find the notion of cost defined. On recourse to the literature it will be found that cost has at least as many variants or expressions as value has (see for example, Greer, quoted in para. 56). But in spite of the alleged importance of cost it is difficult to find any reasonable discussion of its meaning in relation to human action. If one were inclined to accept operational definitions, that is, to assert that cost is only definable in

terms of what can be measured, one may be content with some of the descriptions given: "... cost is measured by cash outlay or by the fair market value of property acquired in exchange for securities"[40]; "Historical cost is cost measured by actual cash payments or their equivalent at the time of outlay"[41]; "The price at the time of an exchange is 'cost'. Thus the cost of an item to a business is the cash outlay necessary to acquire the item. If property other than cash is given up in the exchange, then the cost of the item acquired is the cash equivalent of the property given up"[42]; "Cost, or the amount of cash or its equivalent paid to acquire an asset, is the dollar amount to be accounted for"[43]. But what has all this to do with human action?

37. It seems to be necessary to clarify the notion. Firstly, there is no such thing as cost unless it relates to some thing; only things or services cost. Secondly, the cost of things or services falls on some person or persons. And thirdly, the cost of any thing to any person is, regardless of the state of the market, potentially different at different times. The first two points may be obvious, but the third is apparently not so obvious for it is completely disregarded in accounting. At any time the cost of a thing to a person is what he must sacrifice or forgo to acquire that thing. Thus, if a person has very little of a certain good but wants much of it, he will be prepared to pay much for an addition to his stock, provided he has the means of adding to it. On the other hand, if he has a large stock of a given good and wants little, if any, more than he has, he will only be prepared to pay little for an addition to it. One may test this by introspection. But a clear example can be obtained by trying to induce a retailer who believes he is adequately stocked to take in additional quantities; if the retailer is at all sensible he will only do so, if at all, at a reduced cost to himself. If, at another time, the retailer does not believe he is adequately stocked, he will be prepared to take additional quantities at the same cost as before. In other words the cost of acquiring a thing at any time to any person is a function of what he then has and what his other wants are at that time. The sacrifice he is prepared to make is an evaluation of the relative advantages of having more or less of some things and less or more of others.

38. The example may be extended. At any time a business firm has a certain combination of assets and obligations by reason of which it is able to exploit the demand for what it sells at that time. But as time passes, the combination of assets and obligations changes, not only in amount but also in quality and variety; and the demand for what it sells changes both by reason of changes in buyers' preferences and by

---

[40] American Accounting Association, "A Tentative Statement of Accounting Principles", *The Accounting Review*, June 1936 (Reprinted in pamphlet cited in footnote 30).

[41] American Accounting Association, "Report of the Committee on Cost Concepts and Standards", *The Accounting Review*, April 1952, p. 176.

[42] Rufus Wixon (Editor), *Accountants' Handbook*, New York, The Ronald Press Co., 1956, ch. 1, p. 16.

[43] Smith and Ashburne, *Financial and Administrative Accounting*, New York, McGraw-Hill Book Co. Inc., 1960, p. 49.

reason of the actions of competitors through advertising or the provision of substitutes. At any time, therefore, the firm is in a different position than it was at a previous time or will be at a subsequent time. The sacrifices it will make or demand of others (its customers) will not at any of these times be the same unless every feature of the firm and its environment is the same, and this proviso is patently inconsistent with reality. As costs are sacrifices made in the course of exchange, the cost of anything acquired or used for any purpose is always a dated cost.

39. It is a common practice to justify the initial cost basis of accounting on the ground that accounting records and statements give an historical record of activities. "... the balance-sheet is historical in character"[44]. "Financial accounting is now generally recognized as being primarily historical in character"[45]. "... it is a fundamental convention that accounting is purely an historical record ..."[46]. "... a balance sheet is ... an historical record ..."[47]. "From the viewpoint of the entity, accounting is historical only"[48]. "Accounting is a historical record ... a balance sheet is an historical document ..."[49]. Few writers link "history" directly with "action" and hence may overlook the connexion. Not so Hill and Gordon[50]: "... accounting may be viewed as a special type of history, a history of the capital committed to a business venture. ... it is of much interest only in so far as it provides bases for action, particularly as it increases our ability to predict and plan the future course of events." This implies that there are at any time open alternatives, and at that time various possible costs of those alternatives. The minimum cost of every alternative is the sacrifice made in the pursuit of it, and the minimum cost of every alternative depends on the structure of financial and operating conditions at the time of action and at no other time. It is quite inconsistent therefore to add to the above statement: "the raw material of accounting is history, and hence unchanging regardless of end use" (p. 12).

40. What is the "history" to which allusion is so commonly made? Or, to use the form of the paradoxical question, when is history not history? The amount paid for a good or service at a time in the past is an undeniable fact; it is history. It is also undeniable that the amount

---

[44] Sanders, Hatfield and Moore, *A Statement of Accounting Principles*, p. 56.

[45] George O. May, *Financial Accounting*, New York, The Macmillan Co., 1943, p. vii.

[46] Yorston, Smyth and Brown, *Advanced Accounting*, Sydney, The Law Book Co. of Australasia Pty. Ltd., 1957, Vol. 1, p. 5.

[47] The Institute of Chartered Accountants in England and Wales, *Recommendation* 15, Accounting in relation to changes in the purchasing power of money, 1952.

[48] Wm. L. Raby, "The Two Faces of Accounting", *The Accounting Review*, July 1959, p. 460.

[49] E. B. Ross, "Notes on Accounting Theory", *The Accountant's Journal* (New Zealand), June 1960, p. 386.

[50] *Accounting: A Management Approach*, Homewood Ill., Richard D. Irwin, Inc., 1959, p. 5.

paid represents the buyer's sacrifice for the good at that time; that too is history. It is also undeniable that after the date of acquisition the holding- or user-value of a good may vary; if such a variation takes place, and accountants admit that it may and does (see para. 48), that too is history. It is also undeniable that, if, for example, the user-value of a good has risen, the sacrifice made by using it then is greater than the sacrifice made by using it at the time of acquisition. It follows that unless one shows that the unit sacrifice made is greater at the later date than the unit sacrifice made at the earlier date, one does not write history. One in fact falsifies the history by disregarding critical determinants of the scale of revenues. History ceases to be history. Balance sheets become agglomerations of snippets of history—organically unrelated in spite of the appearance of relatedness which accounting processes give them.

41. Accountants who adhere to the cost doctrine as history and the service notion are caught on the horns of a dilemma. The cost doctrine has the consequence of showing assets at figures relevant at the time of acquisition (subject to subsequent adjustments formally based on the same figures). If the "raw material of accounting" is money cost at the time of acquisition and cost is "unchanging regardless of end use", how would one explain the facts that businessmen frequently discard assets before their "usefulness" is at an end, and as frequently go on using assets after they have been completely written out of the accounts? This behaviour is only explicable on the ground that the value of the subject assets is, in the first case, lower than the value of having the cash proceeds, and, in the second case, higher than the value of an equivalent new asset. But accounting systems and statements based on cost will give none of the relevant figures; in short they will be of no service in solving any such problem. And inasmuch as the whole of business is a matter of exchanging one thing for another, such accounting throws no direct light on business transactions at all.

42. It is possible to hold to "cost" and the "historical record" in a vital sense. But only if cost means value means price at the time of action, not only at the time of acquisition but for every subsequent use or disposal of a good—in other words, if cost always means current cost. And only if history is understood to include the history of changes in values as current costs represent them. Under conventional accounting, "cost" as used is irrelevant and "history" is a misnomer. If accounting is based on current market values, the costs it represents will be of service, the history it represents will be complete, and the two ideas will be quite compatible.

43. Cost only has significance in terms of the sacrifice of means[14], that is, of things which are believed by someone to be serviceable in satisfying wants of some kind[12]. But means may only be sacrificed if one possesses them[15], whether one has the unrestricted right to dispose of them, or whether disposal is subject to the equities of others[16]. These rights are governed by the legal framework[17]. But neither an individual nor a business firm will consciously sacrifice more to achieve a given end than is necessary; each will strive to make

the greatest gain for a given sacrifice, to optimize the result of acting[20]. The more one has of a given means, the smaller will be the sacrifice one will make to add another unit to it; in other words, additions to the stock of any given means are subject to diminishing marginal utility[21]. There are considerable diversities in means—differences in specificity to a given purpose, in divisibility, convertibility and so on[13]; so that if one is able to accumulate a stock of means the optimum combination will be such that the marginal utilities of all types of means will be equal; that is to say, the total sacrifices or costs of having that combination will be at a mimimum[22]. Sacrifices may be made in the course of consumption and conversion of means, or in the course of exchanges with others[24] in the market[25]. In so far as any means is bought and sold in a market place, the sacrifice one makes to acquire it or in consuming it or in converting it is measurable by the price at the time of acquiring, consuming it or converting it. The price at the appropriate time is what one forgoes; that is its cost[31].

44. When is a cost not a cost? When accountants compute and set down, as cost, figures which have no relationship to present values presently sacrificed. The acquisition of anything in advance of the time of its use is an act of investment, not of use. One may speak of the cost of the investment, but every investment may increase or decrease in value, as time passes, without use. Cost is the loss in value of an investment through use; unless this loss in value, this sacrifice at the point of use, is measured, cost is not measured. Accounting of the conventional sort confuses loss in value with cost; its "costs" are not costs in any precise sense which is pertinent to action.

When is a Value not a Value?

45. Many attempts have been made to eradicate "value" from the accountant's vocabulary. Following Bonbright[50a], many have attempted to argue that value has no precise meaning and is therefore useless as a guide to the numbers or symbols to be assigned to things described in accounts. Many others have stated directly or implied that accounting is not concerned with values. An oft-quoted nutshell dictum runs "The purpose of accounting is to account—not to present opinions of value"[51]. George O. May[52] averred, "We accountants . . . know, or can find out something about prices; we are less able to determine values. . . . a price is the amount of money for which something can be bought or sold. It may be a buying price or a selling price; it may or may not coincide with value." The American Institute attempted to remove from the word every vestige of its everyday connotation: "Value as used in accounts signifies the amount at which

[50a] J. C. Bonbright, *The Valuation of Property*, New York, McGraw-Hill Book Co. Inc., 1937.

[51] R. E. Healy, "The Next Step in Accounting", *The Accounting Review*, March 1938, p. 6.

[52] "Valuation or Historical Cost; Some Recent Developments", *The Journal of Accountancy*, January 1940.

an item is stated, in accordance with the accounting rules or principles relating to that item"[53]. Kohler[54] says that under standard accounting procedures, "going value . . . is synonymous with book value", which is the same in effect as the A.I.C.P.A. statement just quoted. Paton and Littleton[55] seek to avoid the cost-or-value dilemma by suggesting the use of the term "price-aggregate". Irish[56] asserts that "accounting . . . has no interest in value of any kind". Littleton[57] asserts that "accounting . . . deals with prices rather than values". Of the same genre are such statements as, "accounting is essentially the allocation of historical costs and revenues to the current and succeeding fiscal periods"[58]. The Institute of Chartered Accountants in England and Wales includes the following in its recommendations: "Assets are normally shown at cost less (amortization) . . . . A balance sheet is mainly an historical document which does not purport to show the realizable value of assets such as goodwill, land, buildings, plant and machinery; nor does it normally purport to show the realizable value of assets such as stock in trade. Thus a balance sheet is not a statement of the net worth of the undertaking and this is normally so even where there has been a revaluation of assets and the balance sheet amounts are based on the revaluation instead of on cost"[59]. Cost and value are explicitly or implicitly set up as alternatives and the obvious weight of sentiment lies against value.

46. But all these attempts to eliminate "value" have failed. Try as they may, writers have been unable to avoid the use of "value" or "valuation". A bracket of examples from recent texts which otherwise adhere to the so-called "cost principle" will serve to show that the term is ineradicable. MacFarland, Ayars and Stone[60] say that the statement of financial position "must show clearly the respective values of the assets, liabilities and owner's equity". Paton and Dixon[61] require the notion of value as a test for identifying assets: ". . . things and rights . . . which have . . . value to the enterprise". Husband[62] describing transactions, says "an item of value must have been

---

[53] American Institute of Accountants, *Accounting Research Bulletin No.* 9, Report of the Committee on Terminology, 1941, p. 76.

[54] *A Dictionary for Accountants*, Englewood Cliffs, Prentice-Hall Inc., 1957, p. 237.

[55] *An Introduction to Corporate Accounting Standards*, p. 25.

[56] "Fundamental Concepts of Corporate Accounting", *The Australian Accountant*, June 1950, p. 228.

[57] *Structure of Accounting Theory*, p. 12.

[58] Gilbert R. Byrne, "To What Extent can the Practice of Accounting be reduced to Rules and Standards?", *The Journal of Accountancy*, November 1937, p. 372.

[59] The Institute of Chartered Accountants in England and Wales, *Recommendation* 18, Presentation of balance sheet and profit and loss account, 1958.

[60] *Accounting Fundamentals*, New York, McGraw-Hill Book Co. Inc., 1957, p. 21.

[61] *Essentials of Accounting*, New York, The Macmillan Co., 1959, p. 16.

[62] *Accounting: Administrative and Financial*, Philadelphia, Chilton Co., 1960, p. 8.

received and another item given up", and speaks of "the value flow" on certain conversions of assets. Though Smith and Ashburne[63] sedulously avoid the use of value and valuation in their table of contents and in their detailed index, they cannot avoid them in the text. They speak of current assets being reported "at realizable value" and of "accounting valuation" (p. 77), and of the use of "appraised values as a substitute" for cost where a mixed parcel of assets changes hands for a single price (p. 217). Even the more obviously theoretical work of Paton and Littleton[64] has use for the term and the notion of valuation: "The price aggregate that emerges at the moment a bargaining exchange is consummated is a mutually acceptable 'valuation'" (p. 26). They clearly visualize an act of valuation when they regard as a legitimate procedure the use of "the amount of money which would unquestionably be necessary to acquire the resources in its established commercial status" when "resources are discovered or developed which have an immediate economic significance far in excess of the actual outlay required for their acquisition" (p. 28). The Institute of Chartered Accountants in England and Wales unashamedly uses valuation in respect of stock in trade[65]; the permissibility of a valuation of assets is implied in its statement on accountants' reports for prospectuses[66]. When dealing with appreciation in values of security investments held by trading companies, lengthy circumlocution is adopted to avoid any suggestion that revaluation is condoned: "Exceptional circumstances may arise in which an undertaking, wherein an important trade investment is held, has retained and accumulated profits on such a scale that the income which reaches the investor company and the amount at which the investment is carried in the accounts are a wholly inadequate reflection of the value of the investment, although this fact is not apparent from the trade investments item in the balance sheet or from the accounts as a whole. In such circumstances consideration should be given to the question whether the relative importance of the matter is such that without some explanation in the accounts they would fail to show a fair view"[67]. Not a word here about revaluation, but there can scarcely be any doubt that the statement implies a value other than cost.

47. Examples such as these can be multiplied. But the point emerges clearly enough that there must be something so crucial about "value" and "valuation" that no formula can be devised to eliminate them. What is this crucial thing? Looking back to the references

[63] *Financial and Administrative Accounting*, New York, McGraw-Hill Book Co. Inc., 1960.

[64] *An Introduction to Corporate Accounting Standards.*

[65] *Recommendation* 10, The valuation of stock-in-trade, 1945.

[66] *Recommendation* 13, Accountant's reports for prospectus: fixed assets and depreciation, 1949.

[67] *Recommendation* 20, Treatment of investments in the balance sheets of trading companies, 1958.

cited in para. 45, it is noticeable that May and Paton and Littleton explicitly or implicitly are contrasting value and price to the disadvantage of value. But a price is a value! It is pointless to argue as May does, that a buying or a selling price may or may not coincide with value. A price is the only value of "economic significance", to use a test which Paton and Littleton have found useful[68]. Price is the only value contemplated in market economics. May's usage of "value" can only have legitimate reference to some form of non-market evaluation; and non-market evaluations, being a matter of private knowledge, can have no usefulness of themselves in determining the course of actions in markets. Value in this sense can have no relationship to accounting. Although he does not follow its implications, Kester[69] at one point states what, in a relevant sense, value is: "The value of anything is its worth in exchange or in use at a given time and is determined normally by the acts of buyers and sellers."

48. There is some evidence of the recognition of value in this sense even on the part of writers who would not be regarded as supporters of the value basis of accounting. Paton[70] says, "The accountant... assumes that *cost gives* actual value for purposes of initial statement" (italics in original). The idea recurs in Paton and Littleton (p. 122): "Under normal conditions cost incurred may be assumed to represent the market value of the factor involved at the date of acquisition; at the outset, in other words, cost and value are substantially identical in the typical case." Owen's review[71] includes it: "When acquisitions of properties (or services) take place, ... value in the usual economic sense and cost in the accounting sense are one and the same." All these statements refer to value in connexion either with initial acquisition or initial entry of the transaction by which goods or services are acquired. Now, if value is not the concern of accountants, why bother to make a point of the fact that at some time value and cost coincide? Why?—because it is necessary to establish that the first entry in the record is "objectively determined, inasmuch as it is, in most cases, the result of bargaining between two parties with opposing interests"[71]. The point made in para. 37—that a bargain represents an evaluation—does not seem to be appreciated. But once it is admitted that market value is the figure which determined whether or not the two parties did business together, it is impossible to deny that for any and every acquisition or contemplated acquisition (or sale, too) the market value determines whether things will change hands, and it is impossible to deny that "values" meet the needs of interested parties. Logically, if one admits "values" into the accounting system one should proceed to show how, after initial acquisition, one continues to represent values. But the logical consequence of the fact that price equals value is disregarded. Paton and Littleton state the conditions

---

[68] *An Introduction to Corporate Accounting Standards*, pp. 28, 123.

[69] *Advanced Accounting*, p. 29.

[70] *Accounting Theory*, p. 489.

[71] "A Review of the Basic Concept of Financial Accounting", *N.A.A. Bulletin*, June 1958, p. 72.

quite clearly: "With the passing of time . . . the value of the particular productive factor . . . is subject to change in either direction, and when a change occurs it becomes clear that the actual cost . . . is not fully acceptable as a measure of immediate economic significance" (pp. 122-3). But, they ask, "would accounting meet . . . the . . . needs of the various parties concerned if . . . current values were regularly substituted for recorded costs incurred? There seem to be no convincing reasons for an affirmative answer". In short, the whole reference to value at the time of acquisition is pointless!

49. Some appear to appreciate the link between value and expected service potential but do not appear to appreciate the link between value and market price. "The value of an asset is the money equivalent of its service potentials. Conceptually, this is the sum of the future market prices of all streams of service to be derived, discounted by probability and interest factors to their present worths"[72]. This is precisely what the market price of any producers' good represents, so that there is a clear indication of a method of measuring value, namely, by using market price. But the A.A.A. statement continues: "However, this conception of value is an abstraction which yields but little practical basis for quantification. Consequently, the measurement of assets is commonly made by other more feasible methods." This is a rationalization for switching right away from the groundwork laid in the previous passage. The switch is evidenced by the use of "quantification" and "measurement" in the second part of the passage quoted, instead of continuing the use of "value", as in the first part. Far from offering "little practical basis" for valuation, in so far as the discounted value of all expected service flows from an asset is represented by its market price, the aggregate discounted flow concept offers the only practical basis for valuation. And what is offered as more feasible? For monetary assets, the discounted expected cash flow; for non-monetary assets, acquisition cost. In short two methods are offered; both represent quite different things; the second is in no way related to the notion of value as described at the outset, and therefore cannot be a "more feasible" method of measuring value.

50. But these are not the only inconsistencies. If it is contended that a balance sheet in which assets are represented by "unexpired costs" meets the needs of parties of interest, there can be no need for any other information than is yielded by the orthodox matching process. It would be quite unnecessary to use any other basis than cost for inventories; the cost-or-market rule would be abandoned; L.I.F.O., F.I.F.O. and other similar hypotheses would be superfluous. There would be no need to state market values of marketable securities. There would be no such thing as revaluing assets—up or down. And there could be no grounds for recommending the use of supplementary statements as a solution to the problem of accounting under conditions of price instability. But not one of the supporters of

[72] American Accounting Association, *Accounting and Reporting Standards for Corporate Financial Statements,* 1957 Revision (pamphlet), p. 4.

cost against value will go this far!! It follows that they do not really believe in the "unexpired cost" theory of the nature of the balance sheet or the "cost" theory of accounting; or, if they do believe, they have not analysed the grounds for belief; or they have a double or multiple standard in which a wide range of mutually inconsistent behaviours is quite permissible—truly "Wonderland" material.

51. Value may be based on the importance a person attaches to an object or purpose. This value is knowable only to the person. One may manage to rank things as one values them, but there is no scale in which such private evaluations may be measured. Other persons can only know that one values something by his actions with respect to it; and others can only know how much one values something by what he will sacrifice to acquire it or what will induce him to part with it. The only values we can communicate to others and expect them to understand are the values which become explicit through exchanges[24]. Values in exchange are significant to all actual and potential operators in markets[25]; in an economy in which money[26] and credit[27] are used to facilitate exchanges, price is the measure of value in exchange[25]. And because all means and equities are acquired or arise through exchanges the values of them all may be given monetary expression[30]; and monetary calculations may be made in terms of these values at any time as guides to action[31]. There can be no gainsaying the importance of value in exchange when contemplating actions which change the composition of the resources of persons or firms[28]. No amount of evasion or circumlocution can destroy it. The only reasonable thing to do is face it and to design accounting systems which conform with it.

52. When is a value not a value? No money sum attributed to an asset is a value in an operative sense unless at some point its basis is an actual or possible evaluation by a person faced with a choice involving that asset. Such an evaluation is necessarily related to some market operations—so that it is not a personal evaluation only. If cost is taken as value after a shift in the level of prices, such a "value" is a non-market evaluation, specific to a person or an enterprise and is therefore subjective. It is not a value which is of any use or consequence once the particular pattern of prices and markets shifts from the form it had at the time of acquisition. A value is not a value whenever the method of evaluation disregards the ineluctable fact that values change as the conditions of the valuer and of his environment change.

When is a Principle not a Principle?

53. A series of questions of this kind may be posed—about theories, postulates, conventions, doctrines and like terms. It will suffice to deal with a few only of such questions. In spite of the extensive literature on, and the enormous amount of time devoted to, accounting principles and theory, the whole area is confused. "Principles" has long been used of common ideas in accounting though many of the so-called principles were not stated with any precision. The term "standards" was adopted in American literature and practice during

the 1930's, to avoid the implication, supposed to inhere in "principles", that universal rules could be laid down; but there is just as much haziness about "standards" as there was about "principles". The same ideas have been variously described—the going concern idea, for example, has been described as a concept[73], a point of view[74], an assumption[75], a convention[76] and a hypothesis[77]. Generally, in designating ideas, guidance has been sought from dictionary "definitions"; but this is not always helpful. A dictionary is a general purpose device designed to inform users of the customary usages and meanings of words. If we are to converse with lay people it is necessary to converse in terms that are generally understood; common sense or customary usages are highly desirable if not obligatory. Thus, in published financial statements, the users of which may be very sophisticated or quite unsophisticated, it might be expected that everyday usages would prevail; but it has been shown that precisely in this area, accountants tend to flee from everyday usages and to invent highly specialized meanings for such everyday notions as cost and value. Yet, in the highly specialized and technical field of concept and theory formation the tendency to run to dictionary meanings is quite marked!

54. If we are concerned to discover the character of an art, a science, or an operation, it may well be found necessary to devise special notions for the purpose, notions specifically relevant to our inquiries. For example, "true" has in general usage a connotation of reliability, universality and even immutability; but in the usage of the logician and the philosopher it has no such meaning. When a logician says a statement is true he may mean that it is logically irrefutable. A philosopher may assign the label, "true", to certain statements which meet stated tests. It is not a matter of indifference what general designations are given to groups of ideas. Designations should convey some idea of the way in which concepts are regarded; they should indicate which ideas are primitive and which derived. The model adopted in conceptualizing is thus not necessarily that suggested by dictionary descriptions except in so far as those descriptions include scientific usages; for the process of discovering the character of a set of ideas or operations is essentially scientific and there are established scientific procedures for going about it. Purification of the character of discourse in accounting is unlikely if the rigorous modes of scientific inquiry and exposition continue to be disregarded. But this is no place for an extended discussion of methodology.

---

[73] For example, Roy B. Kester, *Advanced Accounting*, p. 306.

[74] For example, Paton and Paton, *Asset Accounting*, New York, The Macmillan Co., 1952, p. 504; Smith and Ashburne, *Financial and Administrative Accounting*, p. 50.

[75] For example, William A. Paton, *Accounting Theory*, p. 478.

[76] For example, Sanders, Hatfield and Moore, *A Statement of Accounting Principles*, p. 3.

[77] For example, Carman G. Blough, "Accounting Principles and their Application", *C.P.A. Handbook*, New York, American Institute of Certified Public Accountants, 1957, Vol. 2, Ch. 17, p. 13.

55. The prevailing attitude of accountants towards their principles, however designated, may be explored, as before, by reference to the literature. "In the opinion of accountants generally, accounting principles are not principles of nature but rules of human behavior. They are not inherent in nature to be discovered by man but are developed by man. They are, therefore, not immutable and they need to be changed to meet changing needs"[78]. Again, "Action in accounting clearly does not rest on immutable laws"[79]. Now statements of this kind are acceptable but not for the reasons usually given. No statement—and every principle, every law is a statement—is immutable. For a statement expresses how some person at a given time and place visualizes the thing or the relationship which is the subject of the statement. Many persons may agree with any such statement at a given time, but this does not prevent other persons at other times from formulating quite different statements about the same thing. The thing itself may not have changed one whit; but people may picture it quite differently, and the statements—principles or laws—which express the picture will therefore be different from the statements made in a different environment of knowledge. There are thus not even any immutable laws of nature that man can describe. Differences of other kinds between fields of study there may be—in the nature of the subject matter and of the evidence obtainable in respect of it. But the contrast made or implied in the above quotations is pointless, and no distinction can be drawn between the natural sciences and accounting to the latter's disadvantage, so far as the formulation of principles is concerned.

56. Just as the formulation of statements in the natural sciences will vary with changes in the state of knowledge so also will the statements in the field of accounting. One can agree with Blough that "principles . . . need to be changed to meet changing needs" and with the statement "Accounting rules or principles must be flexible and in continuous process of evolution"[80]. But this does not mean that at any time any given principle, as then understood and stated, may have a variety of mutually exclusive meanings. The cost-or-market rule for inventory valuation is a well-established "principle"—using principle in a loose sense. But it is not one principle; it is a combination of two conflicting, mutually exclusive principles which, taken separately, can yield results which diverge by material amounts. Or, to take a more extensive recommendation on the same problem, consider the following: "The portion of the original cost of each class of product, materials, and supplies inventories to be carried forward as applicable to future operations, should be not more than the least of the following: (a) actual cost, determined on a first-in first-out basis, with substitution of standard for actual cost components where appropriate, (b) current replacement cost, similarly computed,

[78] Blough, loc. cit.
[79] A. C. Littleton, *Structure of Accounting Theory,* p. 170.
[80] Editorial, *The Journal of Accountancy,* February 1938.

(c) current net realizable value. Alternative valuation bases, permissible as a measure of conservatism, include (a) original cost, determined on a last-in first-out basis, (b) initial cost of a normal base stock plus actual cost of subsequent additions, (c) prospective realization value less expenses remaining to be incurred, including a normal profit margin, (d) other procedures appropriate to the conditions of individual industries and enterprises, when consistently and reasonably applied"[81]. According to my calculations there are seven specific "principles" and one completely open-ended "principle" in this statement; (d) in the last sentence virtually permits any basis of valuation! It is no defence to point out that "the least of the following" unifies the statement. It does not. In any given series of situations any one of these bases may become the "appropriate" basis; so that the statement as a whole sanctions them all individually. The above statement could in effect be condensed into a three-word principle: "Anything will do."

57. Let it be noted that the Greer quotation is not an isolated example. It expresses the sense of many other statements of the same kind by individual writers and professional organizations. The general attitude towards principles is evident in many statements relating to uniformity and the exercise of judgement. "To the extent that personal judgment is involved, standards are subjective; to the extent that standards are formulated by authoritative bodies, standards are objective. It follows that objective standards narrow the spheres of individual judgment and personal opinion as to what the standards are; but it does not follow that they restrict the reasonably free play of judgment and individual opinion as to the propriety of applications of generally accepted principles"[82]. "An accounting principle is not a principle in the sense that it admits of no variation, nor in the sense that it cannot conflict with other principles"[83]. "There . . . remains ample scope for the exercise of professional judgment in determining for example, what principle or standard applies in particular circumstances where a choice is possible; or in deciding the manner or extent to which it is to be applied"[84]. "Uniformity of accounting method is neither expected nor necessarily desirable"[85]. The trouble about the latitude which these views allow is that they serve as a licence for disregarding any discipline or stricture such as one usually means by "a matter of principle"—to turn a phrase, accounting as a result is "unprincipled". It should be no cause for wonder that "today it is difficult to decide just what significance may be attached to the annual

---

[81] Howard C. Greer, "Benchmarks and Beacons", *The Accounting Review,* January 1956, p. 12.

[82] Victor H. Stempf, "Critique of 'Accounting Principles Underlying Corporate Financial Statements' ", *The Journal of Accountancy,* August 1941, p. 106.

[83] American Institute of Accountants, *Accounting Research Bulletin No.* 7, Report of the Committee on Terminology, 1940, p. 60.

[84] Samuel J. Broad, "Recent Developments in Accounting and Auditing", *The Journal of Accountancy,* September 1944, p. 186.

[85] American Accounting Association, *Accounting and Reporting Standards for Corporate Financial Statements,* 1957 Revision (pamphlet), p. 9.

accounts of a corporation"[86]. Nor should one be surprised that "there remains a widespread belief that published financial statements still leave too much to imagination and guess-work, and that the variety and inconsistency of corporate accounting practice bring needless confusion and uncertainty into the study of business affairs"[87].

58. In what sense, if any, may it be said a principle may be varied? that uniformity is not necessarily desirable? that choice of principles is possible? Only in one sense; namely, that as knowledge increases, as new points of view are put forward, the whole of the previously accepted body of ideas is seen in a new light and an entirely new set, or a set related in new ways, emerges. Or, to put it another way, when one set of principles, accepted as a working hypothesis, is found to be invalid a superior hypothesis is set up in its place. This, of course, is counsel of perfection. It is not pretended that in other sciences mutually inconsistent theories are unheard of. They do occur; but their appearance is not considered to be an occasion for accepting both. It is a spur to efforts to resolve the inconsistency, by seeking out the flaws in one or the other or both. One may act according to one or the other, while the problem is unresolved; but one may not legitimately take bits and pieces of both and hope to act consistently. All talk of flexibility and expedience is simply an excuse for evading the discipline of rigorous analysis. One may be permitted a fictional allusion, to a passage in Ayn Rand's *Atlas Shrugged* (The New American Library, New York, 1959, p. 343):—

> "You know, Mr. Rearden, there are no absolute standards. We can't go by rigid principles, we've got to be flexible, we've got to adjust to the reality of the day and act on the expediency of the moment."
>
> "Run along, punk. Go and try to pour a ton of steel without rigid principles on the expediency of the moment."

59. If accounting were concerned with physical things the futility of attempting to hold simultaneously two or more inconsistent principles would become apparent. It is equally possible to drive a car on either side of a road; but let a driver attempt to drive on both sides, or on the left-hand side in North America, or on the right-hand side in Britain; he will soon discover that there is no middle ground, and that there are no subtle verbal devices he can adopt to escape disaster. Why should such behaviour be permissible in accounting? Gilman[88] long ago pointed out the inconsistency of certain generally held ideas; but their existence has bothered little his successors. Some scarcely seem to notice them. Dohr[89], for example, states categorically that "the present value of property is generally speaking the factor of

[86] George O. May, "Talk with George O. May on his 80th Birthday", *The Journal of Accountancy,* June 1955, p. 43.

[87] Howard C. Greer, "Benchmarks and Beacons", *The Accounting Review,* January 1956, p. 9.

[88] *Accounting Concepts of Profit,* for example, p. 235.

[89] "Cost and Value", *The Journal of Accountancy,* March 1944, p. 193.

outstanding importance", but later in the same article reaches the conclusion "that accounting is generally on a cost basis and that there is and should be a strong presumption in favor of statement in terms of cost" (p. 195)—a conclusion which appears in italics as if cost were of greater importance than "the factor of outstanding importance". Others attempt to argue inconsistencies out of existence[90], but they have to resort to the use of ideas which are inconsistent with reality or with the service function of accounting. Others admit them without a blush. None of these reactions is likely to clear the air.

60. One might expect of a rule or a principle that it should state an ideal procedure or notion in unequivocal terms. If there is a key concept or set of concepts to which it is geared this should not be difficult. There may well be ways of interpreting a specific rule or principle so that some discretion is allowed, but the statement of the key concept should circumscribe this discretion. Further if a key concept were formulated and incorporated in the definition of accounting, all elaborations of rules and principles which would follow it would be freed of loose expressions and readers would have some clear guidance. But statements of or on accounting principles are noticeably deficient in this direction. For example, the Recommendations of the Institute of Chartered Accountants in England and Wales include no such statement. It is believed to be a consequence of this that the recommendations give clear and unequivocal direction on very few things; categorical statements are almost invariably qualified, suggesting that two or more principles are involved; "normally" appears frequently, carrying the implication that the principle will not stand up in all circumstances other than undefined "normal" circumstances; "preferably", "where practicable" and similar qualifications are employed, so that one is apparently allowed a discretion in respect of what is stated to be "preferable", and one is given a clear sanction for ignoring the rules if one deems that in a given case the recommended procedure is impracticable.

61. It is not for one moment suggested that the authorities have been in error in prescribing the characteristics which a theory or statement of principles should possess. Thus "... a corporation's periodic financial statements should be continuously in accord with a single co-ordinated body of accounting theory"[91]. "... accounting standards should be orderly, systematic, coherent; they should be in harmony with observable, objective conditions; they should be impersonal and impartial"[92]. "Theory [should have] clarity... orderliness... pattern; [it] should be in harmony with observable, objective factors and conditions... [and have] impartiality...

---

[90] For example, Carman G. Blough, "Accounting Principles and their Applications", *C.P.A. Handbook*, New York, American Institute of Certified Public Accountants, 1957, Vol. 2, Ch. 17, p. 14.

[91] American Accounting Association, "A Tentative Statement of Accounting Principles", *The Accounting Review*, June 1936 (reprinted in pamphlet cited in footnote 30, at p. 61).

[92] Paton and Littleton, *An Introduction to Corporate Accounting Standards*, p. 6.

consistency"[93]. "A fairly broad set of co-ordinated accounting principles should be formulated on the basis of the postulates"[94]. All these descriptive words and phrases one would have no hesitation in endorsing. But the whole purpose of this paper is to demonstrate that the requirements of these statements are not in fact met. Nor can they be met while practitioners and writers adopt multiple standards, conflicting principles and inconsistent rules. No "principle" which has these consequences is worth designating by the term principle.

A Proposed Set of Postulates and Principles

62. This paper may appear to be a wordy wrangle about words. It is not. It is concerned with meanings. Its purpose has been to show that many words have a chameleon-like character which poorly serves the demand for precision which rigorous discourse requires. Terms such as service function, information, going concern, cost, value, very often do not mean what they appear to mean. Consequently their users, and more so their readers, frequently jump to conclusions for which no foundation is laid and which are at variance with realities and with one another. A rich and varied language is the principal feature which differentiates man from other creatures. Users of the language assume the obligations of being precise, of defining their terms and of submitting to the discipline of their definitions. This is not a plea for definitions for their own sake: nothing is so sterile as arguments over terminology as such. But no proponent of a concept, a principle or a theory is thereby absolved from defining his terms adequately for his purposes if he wishes his propositions to be understood by others. If he fails to do so, both he and his readers may unwittingly fall into the trap of assuming more than is intended; every such interpretation is then privy to the interpreter and is not a matter of public knowledge nor of ascertainable reliability. This possibility falls with multiplied severity on accounting, for it affects both knowledge about accounting and the knowledge which accounting processes and statements yield. Inconsistency in both directions is tolerated because none of the ideas put forward is considered to be part of a systematic set of ideas, each of which is as necessarily related to the others as are the pieces of a mosaic or a jig-saw puzzle. It might be argued that accounting has its system builders. Does not Gilman[95] provide a system? A categorization of ideas, maybe, but certainly not a set of interlinked ideas. Does not Stead[96] provide a system? Certainly a categorization of over 20 ideas,

---

[93] William A. Paton, *Recent and Prospective Developments in Accounting Theory, Dickinson Lectures,* 1939-40, Cambridge, Mass., Harvard University Press, 1943.

[94] American Institute of Certified Public Accountants, Report to Council of the Special Committee on Research Program, *The Journal of Accountancy,* December 1958, p. 63.

[95] *Accounting Concepts of Profit.*

[96] "Toward a Synthesis of Accounting Doctrine", *The Accounting Review,* October 1948, p. 355.

but none of them is described in sufficient detail to demonstrate that the system is coherent in substance. Can such a set of ideas be devised? It is believed to be possible.

63. At the conclusion of each of the preceding sections of this paper there is a paragraph which states what are believed to be pertinent concepts denoting conditions which govern the type of accounting which will be of use to adaptive entities in a changing environment. They apply in fact to all organizations and persons, for all seek to adapt themselves aggressively or passively to their environments. These paragraphs are numbered 9, 20, 26, 34, 43 and 51. Some 40 specific ideas are emphasized. In the following paragraph they are described and rearranged in the same manner as they were presented in the earlier paper, "Towards a General Theory of Accounting". It is believed that every one of these ideas is directly or indirectly apposite to accounting and that their separate identification is necessary to provide an adequate and realistic foundation for accounting. They represent the way in which the environment of accounting is visualized. It is believed that they are all verifiable by observation or introspection.

64-65. [In the original publication these forty basic ideas and the principles derived from them were set out exactly as they appear in paras. 115 and 116 of "Towards a General Theory of Accounting". The reader should refer to pp. 508-15, *ante,* before proceeding.]

66. The two sets of statements, of assumptions and derived principles, constitute a body of ideas which are believed to be self-consistent and consistent with the environment of accounting, the world of economic action. The references linking the numbered postulates to the derived principles indicate the coherence of the system; it will be apparent that the whole system is closely interwoven. Every postulate is necessary directly or indirectly to provide a basis for one or more of the derived principles, and no principle is stated which is independent of one or more of the postulates. The number of postulates and principles identified may appear to be large but it is no larger than is necessary to eliminate ambiguity and to avoid the paradoxes which a paucity of concepts forces on exponents of accounting. The complex interrelationships of thinking, acting, recording and reporting in a market economy cannot be described in terms of a smaller number. This system leaves no ground for doubt about the kind of information required for intelligent action; it states clearly the character of a going concern and the meaning of value to a going concern; it links cost and value to current price, for current price is the only objective evidence of value and the only measure of cost which is relevant to action. The whole system is based on one general idea, namely that the function of accounting is to provide a continuous objective representation of the transactions of and events financially affecting an entity so that its participants are assisted to act in a rational and informed manner.

67. It will soon be 1984. The persistence of anomalies and contradictions in accounting over the last 22 years makes one wonder whether they will survive the next 22 years. No doubt they will if

accountants continue to follow the philosophy of doublethink so well described in George Orwell's *Nineteen Eighty-Four*: "Doublethink means the power of holding two contradictory beliefs in one's mind simultaneously, and accepting both of them . . . . The process has to be conscious, or it would not be carried out with sufficient precision, but it also has to be unconscious, or it would bring with it a feeling of falsity and hence of guilt . . . . To forget any fact that has become inconvenient, and then, when it becomes necessary again, to draw it back from oblivion for just so long as it is needed, to deny the existence of objective reality and all the while to take account of the reality which one denies—all this is indispensably necessary." Doublethink and doubletalk will not resolve the paradoxes of accounting. If it were not for doublethink and doubletalk there would be no paradoxes.

38

MEASUREMENT IN ACCOUNTING*

This paper is an extension of earlier work which was given expression in "Towards a General Theory of Accounting" (1961) and "The Resolution of Some Paradoxes in Accounting" (1962). The former paper made only brief allusion to a general rule of measurement. It appears as the principle of uniformity of valuation; namely, the operations of addition, subtraction and relation necessary in any form of summarization can only be performed validly if the separate items are valued on a uniform basis. At that time the view was taken that it is necessary to specify the ideas and things with which accounting is concerned before considering how they shall be quantified and whether any possible quantification rules will constitute a measurement system.

In this paper we turn to the latter questions. It transpires that the assumption of adaptive behavior in a changing environment necessitates a set of quantification rules which shall be a measurement system. It transpires also that the straight application of the principles of measurement entails a set of periodical summaries which are expressed in contemporary monetary terms. The general conclusions of the earlier papers, and their implied criticism of traditional procedures, are thus reinforced. The proposals for the measurement of income, however, differ in some material particulars from those of the 1961 paper.

It may appear that at some points the argument is at variance with the line of argument in the earlier papers. For example, the terms "value" and "valuation" appear not infrequently in the other papers, but it has been found to be possible to do without them, except for brief references, in this exposition. In part their elimination is a deliberate attempt to remove words which have repeatedly given rise to misunderstanding; but it seems also that greater clarity of argument is possible if the distinction is made between acts of valuation which always have reference to the future, and acts of measurement which have reference to the past and present. The term "current cash equivalent" has been used in this paper with the same connotation as was intended by earlier uses of "present value" or "present exchange value". Again, as a matter of consistency in argument, the idea of replacement cost has been abandoned; replacement cost implies a

---

* First published in *Journal of Accounting Research,* Vol. 3, No. 1, Spring 1965, pp. 32-62. The first draft of this paper was written in January 1963, and given a small circulation in mimeographed form. Some unnecessary complications have been eliminated and some variations in the argument and conclusions have been introduced.

replacement decision which, it is contended, cannot be made until all present facts are brought to attention. The idea roughly conveyed by "replacement cost" is approximately the same as that now intended by the use of present or current cash equivalent. There may be other such deviations; they have arisen through more rigorous analysis of matters previously treated briefly.

This paper takes uncompromisingly the position that accounting is concerned strictly with the past and present, but so that it is always relevant to the future. To mix measurements with expectations is to confuse an already complicated present. To make measurements is the business of the accountant as such; to form expectations is the business of actors. Only if the two functions are carefully distinguished will actors be able to pursue their goals with informed skill.

* * *

Does accounting measure anything? Should accounting measure anything? Can accounting measure anything? If the answers to these questions are affirmative, what does, what should, or what can accounting measure? If the answers are negative, of what other use is accounting? And why are accountants so concerned with definitions of terms and discussions of ways of quantifying things? These and similar questions pose themselves when one thinks of the processes of accounting and the uses that are, or may be, made of accounting information. Do investors, credit grantors, analysts imagine that accounting aggregates or ratios derived from them measure anything? It is not unreasonable to suppose that they do; clearly they perform operations on the results of the accounting process which are similar to the operations commonly performed in other fields where there are established measurement systems.

The presumption that accounting measures something is supported by references to measurement of one aspect or another of business in a considerable number of textbooks and articles on accounting in recent years. However it was not always thus. Early in the present century it was far more common to speak of accounting and accounting operations in rather different terms. Dicksee (1905; 371)[1] wrote of a revenue account *showing* net profit or loss and of a balance sheet *showing* the position of affairs. Dickinson (1914; 31) wrote of the objective of keeping books on sound principles as to enable the actual financial condition to be *ascertained* at any time. Esquerre (1914; 406) stated that the balance sheet *exhibits* the balances of the real accounts open on the books after the closing of the nominal accounts. Paton and Stevenson (1917; 214) stated that the function of the accounts is to *record* the status of the complex economic equipment used in production. The italicized words and words like them were common and have continued to be commonly used; for example, the American Institute definition of accounting makes use of a variety of similar words but makes no reference to measurement (A.I.C.P.A., 1953; 32). There were early references to accuracy and approximation (e.g., Dickinson, 1914; 32), terms which are proper to the theory of

[1] References are given at the end of the article, see pp. 581-2.

measurement, but it was not until the third decade of the century that explicit references to measurement appeared in any quantity. Kester (1933; passim) made repeated references to measurement but without careful analysis of the function of measurements. Canning (1929; 199-200) came closest to laying an adequate foundation for a theory of measurement in accounting, in stipulating the conditions under which measures could be merged, by summation or otherwise. But he did not proceed to apply these conditions, and no writer has since taken the matter up on the basis of the lead he gave. In spite of the increasing frequency of usage of the terms measure and measurement, there has been scarcely any examination, in the literature of accounting, of what the measurement process entails and of its specific features in the field of accounting.

The Purpose of Classification

Acting man is confronted with a wide and varied environment. Its incidents are so numerous and heterogeneous that the mind is unable to comprehend them all as individuals at one time. The mind is also unable to hold them all simultaneously, as individuals, for the purpose of making comparisons of them or judgements with respect to them. In seeking to reduce the diversity of things experienced or observed to manageable order, men resort to classification, and to the formation of general ideas about groups of things.

Events and things—the content of experience—are ordered or classified according to properties they possess in common, and which are significant for some purpose. The purpose may be a gross purpose—for example, one may wish to distinguish between men and animals in order to know what to expect in response to speech—in which case the classes may be distinguished on the basis of one or several broad or vague properties. For his own information, one person may use one set of properties whereas another person may, in the same context of potential behavior, use another set and both may behave appropriately; both may satisfactorily distinguish between men and animals. There are no natural classes. Classification is a purposive mental action. Its object is to economize future cogitation. It is useful, it accomplishes its purpose, if it provides a satisfactory short cut in future thinking. Any element of experience may, therefore, be classified in many ways, according to the number of properties it is seen to possess and according to the purposes to be served by classification. But the effect of every classification is to emphasize an abstraction, to concentrate the attention on the specific properties recognized by the classification system and to disregard all other properties.

One may find it necessary to classify events and things multidimensionally; that is, there may be several properties which a population of events and things has in common and it may be useful to set up classes which describe the population in a number of quite different ways. But if each of these ways relates to an independent property (e.g., color, size and shape) there is no way of scaling one property in terms of another. Where purely personal behavior is involved and where no formal representation of a variety of independent properties is necessary, men find no insuperable difficulties in making choices, say, as between a number of objects of varied color, size and shape; the choice is based on a direct personal evaluation or preference which is incontestable by any other party and the grounds for such choice are often not communicable to other parties. But in a social context in which some persons are required to make representations in respect of certain properties of a class of objects for the information of others—and this is the situation of accounting—the general proposition (stated above) holds: there is no way of equating or relating property *a* with property *b* if *a* and *b* are independent properties. For any given purpose, therefore, it is necessary specifically to stipulate the property on the basis of which the classification is, or will be, made. That property will be dictated by the use which is expected to be made of the knowledge which the classification yields of the class of events and things which possess it in common.

The Purpose and Nature of Measurement

The taking of reasoned action in many situations requires more than simply the knowledge that varied events and things have or have not certain properties. Some things may possess some properties in greater or less degree. In respect of any property, beside the question, whether or not, the question may be asked, if so, more or less? There is a number of kinds of answer to this question; the answer that can be given depends on the property by which we are to choose between things and the existence of a scaling or measurement system in respect of that property. A triangle can have no more "triangularity" than another triangle; but one may have a greater or smaller area than another. Area can be measured and areas can be arranged in order; triangularity cannot be so measured. Now if there is a property which a series of objects have in common but to a different degree, they can be ranked in order. If the occasion for such a ranking occurs seldom, it is sufficient to rank them by inspection when necessary. If ranking is a recurrent necessity, and particularly if the ranking is to be communicated to others or done by others for some mutual purpose, ranking may be standardized. The several "ranks" may be described and to each may be assigned a symbol from some ordered system of symbols such as the alphabetical or numerical systems. Such a scale is an ordinal scale.

Again it may be possible in respect of some properties to establish ranks or classes which have equal class intervals along some necessarily numerical scale. Whether a given object possesses more or less of a property of this kind can be indicated by identifying its class interval, whether or not the scale has a meaningful zero point. Such a scale is an interval scale. And again it is possible, in respect of some properties, to rank objects according to an interval scale in which zero has a definite meaning. The scale of natural numbers is such a scale. The characteristic of every such scale is that the ratio of the numbers designating the classes in which any two objects fall remains constant whatever the size of the class interval or unit selected. Such a scale is a ratio scale.

Ratio scales have particular advantages. If a unit of convenient size is selected, it is possible to classify uniquely all objects possessing the property in question. (If a unit of convenient size does not give the discriminatory possibilities desired, the inclusion of fractions will not affect the general characteristics of the scale.) As between any two objects, judgements of the kind "more-or-less" may then be made with greater precision than by using interval or ordinal scales. It is also possible to add the numbers designating the possession of the property by any two or more objects to obtain the number which designates the possession of the property by these objects taken together; likewise it is possible to subtract, and to relate in the form of a ratio, the numbers designating the possession of the property by two or more objects. And it is possible, if a change in the unit becomes necessary, to transform these numbers into corresponding numbers in a different scale, by using the transformation rule which describes the relationship between the original and the required units.

All these properties of ratio scales are of importance in the measurement of monetary properties of objects. It is necessary for some purposes to add numbers of units; in others to obtain differences; in others to obtain ratios of numbers of units; and in others, as we shall show, to transform numbers of units in one scale to numbers of units in another scale. We shall use "measurement" of the assignment of numbers of monetary units to represent monetary properties of objects and collections of objects[2]. It is by virtue of the assignment of such numbers that it is possible to judge whether an object has "more or less" of a certain monetary property. And as in any place there is commonly a conventional money unit, the measurement of monetary properties in the scale of numbers of monetary units enables the result to be used in a wide variety of contexts at any given time (see Churchman, 1961; 102).

Measurement has been described as the "process of assigning numbers to represent qualities" (Campbell, 1920; 267). The general definition permits the use of many sets of rules for the assignment of numbers to objects. Classes of objects possessing properties which may not be measured in the scale of positive, rational numbers may yet have numbers assigned to them according to rules such that an orderly sequence of objects having some quality in common is represented by an orderly sequence of numbered classes. Charts of accounts, library and inventory catalogue numbers, are examples. We are not concerned with assignments of numbers to classes of this kind; nor are we concerned with properties for which no scale can be devised. There is no scale for measuring the subtlety of a perfume, the bouquet of a wine, or the flavor of a cheese. These qualities are

---

[2] Extended treatments of the conditions of measurement and of scales of measurement are given in Campbell, 1920; Cohen and Nagel, 1934; Nagel, 1932; Stevens, 1946; Hempel, 1952; and Ackoff, 1962.

esteemed not because of their component properties (sweetness, sharpness, mildness, etc.) but because of the aggregate effect of, or the relationship between, those components. Such classes of properties are mentioned simply to emphasize that it is only worthwhile endeavoring to establish measurement scales and rules in respect of properties which are significant individually, properties for which there can be established a measurement system which will provide more information than a qualitative description.

Definition of Accounting

With this general background we turn to the question of measurement in accounting. Accounting is defined as a method of monetary calculation designed to provide a continuous source of financial information as a guide to future action in markets[3]. Definitions are matters of choice. Others may put forward definitions implying quite different purposes or objects. It is necessary, therefore, to establish the propriety of this definition and to specify the context in which such an accounting is supposed to function.

We postulate a community of actors (or entities) who are economically interdependent; that is to say, the community has developed a degree of specialization of function so that each member has a specific role or set of roles which determine the bounds of his relationships with others at any time, but which may change at his discretion from time to time. The community will be supposed to have a code of laws, understandings, or rules which govern interpersonal relationships, and which, in particular, establish contractual and property rights. These will be assumed to be of the kind common in societies which have modified capitalistic economies. The aggregate supply of goods available to the community will be supposed to be insufficient to satisfy all the wants of members. The specific demands of members will be supposed to be satisfied by exchanges between them, the process being facilitated by a medium of exchange—a money which is freely acceptable in exchange for goods and services in their several markets. To perform this function money itself will necessarily be a scarce, or economic, good. We suppose that all individual behavior is purposive and adaptive and that its objective is the relief of uneasiness or strain (see Dewey, 1939; 33; von Mises, 1949; 13). The goals of actors will vary from time to time as changes in the environment and in their preferences give rise to changes in their states of uneasiness. Adaptation in a fluid environment entails that no actor shall be considered to be irrevocably committed to any past choice or decision. His future choices are, nevertheless, influenced by the consequences of those decisions. It may be observed that these assumptions reasonably represent the state of affairs in the type of community with which we are familiar.

It is proposed to discuss the accounting function, not the varied tasks which accountants perform, many of which lie outside the

[3] The definition and the postulates which follow were suggested in "Towards a General Theory of Accounting", p. 477, *ante*.

accounting function. Actors may themselves prepare their own accounts. But for the purposes the definition envisages, the ideas which underlie the function and its execution are the same whether an actor prepares his own accounts or an accountant prepares them for him. We shall postulate that the function is performed by a person other than the actor himself. Not only does this enable the discussion to cover the whole range of possibilities, it also conforms with the commonly observable situation in most businesses of moderate or large size.

Now the definition makes reference to the guidance of future action in markets. Some assert that accounting has a historical function as well as a function in respect of future action; some assert that it has a historical function only—as a report on stewardship or as a report on the disposal of the entity's funds. These views are limiting and even misleading. Information has no meaning other than with reference to future actions. In a world of scarce resources it is pointless to incur the costs of collecting information unless the possibility of making wiser decisions in the future justifies it. The financial statements published by companies to stockholders are not simply reports of what has transpired in the past; they are the means by which stockholders' judgements, either in the market for managerial talent or in the securities market, are aided and informed. It is true that accounting information is not the only information an actor will want or will have in making choices. But it will be shown that the type of information an accounting system can supply is a necessary condition of informed choice in markets.

Next, the definition alludes to monetary calculation and financial information. By these terms we mean monetary calculation and financial information in respect of events which have transpired in the past. In this respect the definition does not depart from many other definitions. But it is necessary to dispose of some possible objections. It may be suggested that accounting is concerned with physical units. But it is only so concerned for the purpose of making correct monetary calculations. The very reason for the persistence of accounting as a specialty lies in the fact that money is the medium of exchange. People do not want money for itself. They want it because it is ordinarily the one and only good which can be freely used to acquire other goods. "Money is the thing which serves as the generally accepted and commonly used medium of exchange. This is its only function" (von Mises, 1949; 398). Its usefulness as a medium of exchange is the only reason why individuals, business firms, governments and other entities reckon, or account, in terms of money. Reckoning in terms of money is not done because money is a common denominator. It is not a common denominator except under severely limited restrictions as to time and place. The only circumstances in which money is a common denominator are those in which the significance of the monetary units assigned to things they "denominate" is the same for all such assignments. Money is a good, like any other good. Its price in terms of goods varies as does the price of goods in terms of money. This is known to all users of money. Hence it is not for the reason that money is used as a store of value or a common denominator that it is the basis of reckoning: it is so used because, and only as long as, it is known to be convertible, with greater ease than other goods, into the goods of one's choice.

Another type of objection should be noticed. Some say that preoccupation with monetary calculation is in fact a distortion of the goals which men seek; that it is necessary also to have measures of other aspects of men's goal systems. The mere use of money terms as a basis of calculation makes no assumption as to men's goals. Money units are a device only. No one suggests that in taking a census the authorities are concerned with numbers only. Money units are counters in the same way as are numbers. Their use does not imply a concern with purely "materialistic" aims; even institutions which have philanthropic, cultural, or charitable roles, none of which are purely or even partially materialistic, find it useful and necessary for some purposes to reckon in terms of money. Accounting does not concern itself with specific personal goals, except to note that goals are varied and may vary for any person from time to time. Only an actor himself can state what his goals are at any time and assess the extent to which any course of action has attained or may attain his goals.

The limitation of accounting to calculations in respect of the past may give rise to objections. In making choices an actor may make calculations with respect to future events, but all such calculations are hypothetical. He uses his past experience and present knowledge as a guide; but these issue in a series of expectations—the expected costs of and yields from persisting in an existing course of action are compared with the expected costs of and yields from alternative courses, with or without discounting at a hypothetical rate—none of which is, at the time, capable of verification. Reasoned choice cannot be made otherwise. But the necessity for these calculations does not make calculations relating to the past of no consequence. If anything, calculations relating to events in the past, provided they result in full and complete representation of the position at the time of choice, are the more important, for whatever a man's position is at a point of time determines and limits his range of choices at that time. He may make the shoddiest or the most elaborate calculations about the future, that is his prerogative. It is his resources that are to be committed and his expectations that are to be achieved or disappointed, but, if he is uninformed or inadequately informed about his present position, only by chance will he make decisions appropriate to it. By limiting accounting to calculations in respect of the past, there is specified a field of events and things all of which are capable of observation or testing with reference to existing pieces of evidence. The results of those calculations can be objective whereas every calculation about the future can be no better than subjective. What is more, the results of such accounting calculations can be neutral with respect to future actions whereas every calculation about the future is linked in some way to the actor's personal fancies and preferences.

Now we must ask, what are the objects of these monetary calculations? What events and things are to be taken into account?

Accounting has traditionally concerned itself with things which are, or are capable of being, traded in markets and with the legal or equitable relationships between actors which arise from trading in markets. By market is meant any process by which goods or services are transferred from the control of one person or entity to the control of another. The limitation of the objects of accounting to things which are capable of being traded in markets is important. Only in so far as rights or property are transferable is accounting concerned with them. The personal qualities of people are not so transferable; they cannot be severed, nor can they therefore be subject to the monetary calculus. But the services arising from those qualities are transferable, and accounting can and does concern itself with such transfers. Similarly, no possession of an actor of which he has no intention of parting (trading) can usefully be an object of accounting. The accounting system of any actor will thus be concerned with the stock of things he possesses, under legal or equitable title, which are capable of being traded in markets, with his and other equities in that stock and with changes in that stock and those equities from time to time.

If accounting is concerned with monetary aspects of marketable things it is necessary to identify the events which bear on them. Changes in the composition of an actor's stock may take place in two ways. The first is by a transaction by which we mean any exchange of goods or services to which the parties are the actor himself and one or more other parties. Such a transaction involves the conscious choices of two or more persons, at least one of whom has not the same wants and point of view as the actor. The price at which such an exchange takes place expresses the willingness of one party to forgo the possession of goods, and the willingness of the other party or parties to forgo the possession of money. It does not express the valuation placed on the goods or the money; it implies that the vendor prefers money to goods without implying the minimum amount of money he would be willing to accept, and it implies that the purchaser prefers goods to money without implying the maximum amount of money he would be prepared to pay. Only in this sense may it be said that the price represents the value of the goods to both parties.

The second way in which a change in the composition of an actor's stock may take place is by conversion of things he already holds, by combining things acquired by virtue of transactions. Conversions are at the discretion of the actor or his agents; they express the expectation that the result will produce more money, on sale, than the things originally acquired by transactions would produce on resale. They do not necessarily express the expectation that the result will produce more money, on sale, than the money originally laid out on their purchase. A purchase transaction and a conversion are not necessarily linked; they involve distinct decisions separated in time and therefore in a different context.

Both types of change have bearing on the monetary aspects of an actor's stock; for the conversions of money into goods, and of goods of one kind into goods of another kind, influence the availability to the actor of means of exchange. There is also a third class of event which influences this. These are changes which occur due to the actions of persons or organizations other than the actor, and in respect of which he has no choice. An unconditional gift is an example. A more common and more important example is a change in the economic or technological environment which falls on the actor, for good or ill, without any choice on his part. If goods of a given class held by the actor fall in price, so that his command over resources falls, the event has a bearing on his financial position and he needs to know the effect. If these effects are disregarded on the ground that only arm's-length bargains between an actor and another are appropriate objects of accounting, the consequence can only be to deprive actors of information necessary to informed choice.

Monetary or Financial Aspects of Choice

Hitherto we have spoken only in a general way, as is the custom in most definitions of accounting, of "monetary aspects" and "financial position". But it is necessary to discover what particular monetary aspect of events and things is the concern of accounting. To do this we must examine the kinds of information which people require as a basis for decisions having consequences which involve money or money's worth. The following list is not exhaustive but it covers the greater part of the day-to-day business of entities engaged in commercial activities. Such entities cover a wider range of separate transactions than individual actors; decisions of the latter and of non-commercial entities will therefore fall within the range to be considered.

It is necessary to know or to be able to discover at any time the amount of money (i) on hand, (ii) which would become immediately available if any asset or any collection of assets were to be disposed of because a switch in holdings is desired, (iii) which will have to be paid to discharge any liability which is due immediately or the existence of which constrains in an inconvenient way the immediate choice of actions. As we have supposed no choice to be irrevocable, it is also necessary to know the present measure of the residual equity, based on present measures of assets and liabilities, so that choice as between the existing investment and any alternative may be exercised, and as knowledge of the equity on which relationships with creditors are based. To be relevant to the spending of money, the alternative investment of money, the borrowing of money, and the discharge of debts at any time, all these measures will necessarily be contemporary measures.

We will describe this contemporary property of all assets and equities, the amount of money for which each can be currently exchanged, as the current cash equivalent. No other monetary property of any asset or obligation is relevant to the classes of action indicated and these classes embrace all possible actions in the market place. The information referred to is not the only information relevant to choice, and some additional useful or necessary information will be treated presently, but there can be no question that, at least, the information indicated above is necessary. The several assets and equities of an entity with their current cash equivalents may be so arranged as to give a balance sheet; as all assets are subject to the equities of some party, the aggregate measures of the assets and equities will be equal. This balance sheet would represent the "financial position" of an entity, its position with respect to the wide range of possible choices dealt with. This position indicates the limits of all possible actions in the market place where, it will be recalled, the medium of exchange is money. It is relevant to all actions.

Clearly, as all items are denominated in terms of a common unit at a given point of time, the addition, subtraction and relation of any measures of any items are valid. The possibility of aggregation at least is of importance. For a given alternative to his present course of action, an actor may wish to add the money units assigned to any collection of things short of all things in possession—to cash, to holdings of some commodity stocks, and to holdings of some units of durable producers goods. This can only be done with ease if all things are represented in common terms; neither the actor nor his accountant can know which such collection, of all possible collections, to aggregate unless all items in each class of things are set down in a way so that substitutions of one item for another in any class or as between classes of things can be considered in making up the collection. Again for reasons to be given later, it is necessary to have some way of discovering the aggregate of the money sums assigned to all things in possession.

Goals, Valuations and Choices

Some consideration should be given at this point to the mode of action of the actors or entities under consideration. We have already postulated that the goals of any actor may vary from time to time. It is a matter of experience that many people have much less of the community's scarce resources than they need, that many others have much less than they want, and that even those who seem to others to have an abundance can always find ways of using more than they have. The generalization seems warranted that all actors prefer to have more rather than less of the community's scarce resources. But which scarce resources? It is impossible to obtain an answer to this question which has any relevance in accounting.

For, in the first place, although it is undeniable that the direct personal evaluations of things by actors influence their choices, these evaluations vary from time to time as the goals of each actor vary and as the degrees of satisfaction of each want vary. There is no such thing as an inherent or intrinsic value; goods have values to persons in specific states at specific times. Valuation is an act of preferring. A person may at one time prefer to possess *a* rather than *b*, and quite reasonably at another time prefer to possess *b* rather than *a*. Valuations invariably have reference to present expectations of the future. They are subjective, and there is no invariant scale in which the values of even one actor may be expressed. Further, the valuations of a given thing by different persons differ; if this were not so there would be no exchanges. So there is no scale of valuations which may be considered to be equally relevant to a community of actors and which may therefore be used as a means of "codetermining purposive decisions" (Churchman, 1961, 102). We may say that a given person prefers *a* to *b* and adduce as evidence the fact that he possesses *a* not *b*, or the fact that he has just exchanged *b* for *a*. But we have no measure of his direct personal valuations of *a* or *b*. He may in fact prefer *c* to *a* but in the absence of *c* is obliged to make do with *a*. An exchange results in part from a valuation, but a price does not represent a valuation.

In the second place, the choices of actors as between alternatives are inextricably bound up with the costs of those alternatives. The cost of an alternative is the sacrifice or the value forgone by the actor which its choice entails; where resources are scarce there are limits to the costs which any reasonable actor will incur for a specific end (see Dewey, 1939; 40 ff.). The ends he chooses are thus in part determined by the expected costs of attaining them. For both the above reasons, therefore, it is only possible to speak in a general way of the goals of actors, of their preference for more rather than less.

Not only is it impossible to obtain a specific answer to the question, which scarce resources are preferred by an actor at a point of time; it is unnecessary in a market economy having a monetary medium of exchange. All scarce resources have a market price. If one has more of some goods than he wants, he may dispose of the surplus at the market price and acquire, at the market price, other goods for which his want is greater. The expression of market price in terms of units of money permits the expression of all goods in possession in terms of units of money. The preference for more rather than less is then translatable into the general form, more rather than less command over resources generally, more rather than less purchasing power. In so far as any part of a collection of goods in possession is not money, it is necessary to discover what money it commands, for only in this way can the extent of one's command over an alternative collection be ascertained, and only thus can the objects of one's future actions be chosen.

The immediately preceding discussion has been carried out in terms of persons having preferences and acting on their own behalf. The going business concern has some features which may make the predominant role of monetary calculation clearer. A business concern as such has no wants like those of persons. For obvious reasons therefore the goods in its possession have no intrinsic value; their significance subsists only in their expected power to generate cash for the satisfaction of equity-holders, junior and senior. If an existing collection is expected to generate less cash than an alternative collection (after allowance for time discounting), the alternative collection will be chosen. It is of no consequence that certain goods, often described as "fixed" assets, were initially purchased with the intention that they would be held and used over a more or less determinate future period. The investment in those goods may be less readily convertible to cash, so long as the intention persists, but the intention may be abandoned in the light of the position as indicated in the accounts and the state of the market at any moment of assessment. Much the same considerations apply to the possessions of individuals, except those irrevocably committed to consumption.

The judgement "more or less" entails knowledge of how much one has now. For cash this is simply a matter of counting. But for other items this knowledge is not readily available. It involves the assignment of numbers of money units to non-monetary things and the addition of the numbers of money units so assigned. This is a process of measurement. The proposal that the rule for assigning numbers of money units shall be the number of money units currently exchangeable for non-monetary things meets the general principle of measurement that all items shall be represented by numbers indicating the degree to which each item possesses one specific property. It also meets the requirement of relevance, for the units as assigned are those appropriate to appraisal and choice at the moment of assignment.

Accuracy and Relevance of Measurements

The argument so far suggests a form of accounting which is relevant to every possible future action in markets and which conforms with the characteristics of a system of measurements. But it may be said that the current cash equivalent of many things is indeterminate, and, that for many other purposes than those discussed, it is irrelevant. These objections must be answered.

The current cash equivalent of many things may not be determinable with the degree of accuracy which some would like to expect of accounting. But those who have had such expectations are surely overlooking the imperfections inherent in every kind of accounting. The enormous variety of methods of assigning numbers of monetary units to inventory and durable goods under traditional accounting methods must surely mean that accuracy has no meaning when it comes to comparisons between firms such as those that creditors and investors make. If, in a given industry, one firm uses the L.I.F.O. method and another F.I.F.O. for short-term inventories, it matters not how carefully these principles are applied, no external party may usefully compare the measures of the two inventories or any aggregate or ratio which includes them. Such a comparison would be equivalent to using different scales of measurement and expecting the results to be comparable. But the challenge of accuracy may be taken up more directly. Those who raise this objection appear generally to have in mind the type of accuracy they imagine the so-called exact sciences to possess. The presumption that the exact sciences provide measurements which are paragons of accuracy is false (see, e.g., Schrödinger, 1931). Even the exact sciences are not concerned with accuracy as an absolute. They are concerned with degrees of accuracy, and the degree of accuracy is always a function of the quality and precision of the instruments (including the hand, the eye and the brain) used (Ackoff, 1962; 205-214). Not only that; the degree of accuracy sought is the degree necessary for practical purposes. "The problem of accuracy is the problem of defining the allowable limits [in the construction of measurements]. These allowable limits must be defined in part in terms of the uses to which the measurement is to be put" (Churchman, 1961; 127). In essence then, the problem of accuracy of measurements in accounting is simply the problem of finding a degree of accuracy which is useful for practical purposes—for making choices. This is not, perhaps, simple of solution in all cases, but for practical purposes, given the property to be measured and a scale of measurement, the process of measurement to any required degree of accuracy is a technical one only.

The charge that the current cash equivalent of the varied objects of accounting is irrelevant is commonly based on the ground that in a going concern there is no intention to dispose immediately of many assets or to meet immediately many obligations. In the first place this assumes that accountants can know the specific intentions of the actors to whom they provide information, and we have already concluded that this knowledge is not available. In the second place a system of measurement is quite unconcerned with the intentions of those it serves. Its purpose is to enable people to *form* intentions. In the light of the variability of roles and specific goals, it is improper to assume that past intentions will persist. Intentions are irrelevant and the objection cannot be sustained.

One final objection may be raised. The suggested basis places emphasis on the short run, the position from which action in the immediate future will be taken. But it may be said, businessmen concern themselves with the intermediate and the long run as well. Do they not require to know values in the long run? Long-run considerations certainly enter into the formation of expectations and hence of decisions. But they are entirely hypothetical and subjective and are capable of being changed in large or small measure as time passes, and as what was once the long run becomes the short run. These changes arise in part from the financial position as it develops over time. So that whether planning concerns itself with the short or the long run, knowledge of the immediate financial position is always relevant to action. The definition given of accounting refers to a continuous source of information for this very reason. Financial position may not be formally assessed with each change in it, but the means of assessing it at any necessary time inhere in the type of accounting here proposed.

Further Financial Aspects of Choice

We turn to some other kinds of information which are required as a basis for making choices which involve money or the money equivalent of goods and equities. The ends and the pecuniary capacity for attaining the ends of individuals and other entities change from time to time. It is therefore useful to know the time rate of change in the measure of the residual equity. This is the periodic income of the entity. It is the sum out of which individuals make consumption and other expenditures and out of which trading ventures make divisions among holders of the residual equity and expenditures on new investments. Its magnitude, as discovered from time to time, indicates whether, and to what extent, levels of consumption or distribution to equityholders may be raised or lowered; it enables estimates to be made of the time which must elapse before a desired project beyond present means may be undertaken; and, as it indicates the outcome of a given past course of action, knowledge of it may be used in estimating the expected consequence of pursuing the same course for comparison with the expected consequence of alternative courses of action.

The change in the residual equity for a selected interval may be ascertained by taking the difference between the residual equities at opening and closing dates as shown by the statements of financial position at those dates, provided both statements are in units of the same dimension. Alternatively, if unequivocal measures of revenues and costs can be obtained, the measure of income may be obtained from the difference. The results from proceeding in both ways will, necessarily, be identical. In fact, in most cases it is necessary to discover some of the costs of a period by inference from measures of assets at opening and closing dates. The measure of depreciation is one such cost. The common process of continually relying on an allocation decision taken when an asset is first acquired relies on estimates unsupported by subsequently discoverable facts of the market; in no way is it a process designed to measure a cost or to give the current cash equivalent of the asset from time to time. One further point worth making: pure windfall elements of income require to be separately identified if the estimation of the probable future consequences of pursuing a past course of action is to be based on past income.

If choice is predicated on the preference for more rather than less for a given sacrifice, and if the opportunity exists for actions which involve larger or smaller sacrifices and larger or smaller commitments of one's resources, it is necessary to know the relationship between the outcome of discretionary operations in a given period and the sum committed to obtain this outcome. For any past period this relationship can be computed provided the measurements of both the resources employed and of the outcome are expressed in units having the same significance. For the immediately past period this "rate of return" will provide an indication of what may be expected from the same complex of actions in the immediately future period if it can be assumed that other things will remain constant. This may be compared (subject to adjustment, if the assumption of constancy cannot be made) with the probable rates of return from alternative complexes of action, subject to appropriate discounting for time. This rate of return is also a measure of efficiency which may be compared with rates of return of other firms, when choosing between investments in alternative firms if all firms adopt the same measurement principles.

It is a matter of experience that other types of information are used in making assessments, comparisons and calculations with respect to money magnitudes. In addition to having measures which relate to the operations of an entity as a whole, specific facets of those operations throw light on the availability and advisability of future courses of action. Thus, for some purposes or on some occasions, it is necessary to compute such ratios as the current ratio, the leverage ratio, merchandise turnover rates. On such information relating to the past, one may base calculations indicative of efficiency of operation and decisions relating to specific future operations. In choosing future courses of action one may also wish to act in such a way that ratios of a preferred size result. These ratios, like rates of return, may only be validly computed if the units employed in numerators and denominators have the same significance.

Measurement in Accounting

It will be useful at this point to summarize the types of information dealt with and to indicate the types of measurement they entail. The initial recording of a transaction is a recording of a measurement of the number of money units traded against a good or a claim. It represents the current cash equivalent of the good or claim. It does not express the valuation placed on the thing given or the thing received by either party except in the above special sense. It implies that, in the positions of the parties at the time, both were willing to and did participate in an exchange. The transaction has no more significance than this. From that time both parties must make the best of it, and making the best of it may mean using the money or the good acquired in the way intended at the time of the transaction or in some entirely different way.

Measurements become more obviously necessary when one wishes to compare two or more things or to obtain aggregates or differences between things for the purpose of comparison. Thus one may wish to compare an amount of cash on hand with the amount demanded by the vendor of a good one wants. Or, one may wish to discover a combination of goods in possession which if presently sold will enable one to pay a debt. The assistance it renders in making choices in the future is the justification for measurement, but it is an operation which can be applied only to things which are now accessible for comparison with the same scale or some related scale. Now, from the stipulation that the future actions with which accounting is concerned are actions in markets in which the means of exchange is money, it follows that the unit of measurement is the monetary unit of the time and place in which the measuring is done. Every monetary system has a unit of currency so that the scale of measurement is the scale of numbers of monetary units corresponding to the scale of natural numbers. From the stipulation that future actions are only determinable in the light of present command over resources, the rule emerges for assigning numbers of monetary units to the financial aspects of events and things; such numbers shall be assigned on the basis that they represent present command over resources generally, or current cash equivalents. If numbers are assigned according to this rule, it will be possible to add and subtract numbers representing this common property of assets and obligation so that the aggregates or differences have the same significance as the significance of the numbers assigned to each item separately.

The range of events and things with which an entity is concerned may extend beyond the area in which a given monetary unit is the medium of exchange. But different media of exchange are themselves exchangeable at market prices. As it is impossible to add and subtract numbers of different monetary units, transformations of the measures of foreign events and things into measures in terms of the domestic monetary unit are necessary if aggregations representing all operations of the entity are required. The domestic monetary unit is in general the unit of the area in which the entity is domiciled. The transformation rule will be the rate of exchange prevailing at the date at which any aggregation for the purposes of comparison is to be made. Similarly, any entity may endure over a period of time in which a given monetary unit has changing significance as a medium of exchange. As a consequence the number of monetary units which expresses the current cash equivalent of any non-monetary good in possession through such a period will change. If at any time it becomes necessary to aggregate or compare the monetary aspects of non-monetary goods in terms relevant at that time, it is necessary to transform earlier measures to the number of current units having the same significance in terms of command over resources; the number of units currently assigned will thus be the number of units assigned earlier, adjusted by the change in the purchasing power of the monetary unit.

We have specified the property to be measured, the unit of measurement, and the scale of measurement. It may be asked, what is the dimension to be measured by this scale? The dimension of the monetary unit is its purchasing power at any time. All operations in markets are based, on the monetary side, on the adequacy of a buyer's pool of monetary units to meet the number of monetary units demanded by a seller. Similarly all expectations, except those which are beyond the market, are formed on the basis of monetary aggregates the components of which are assumed to be or are adjusted to be of equivalent significance. Like is being related to like—monetary units to monetary units; and the test is only more or less—monetary units. But the control of monetary units is sought only because it gives control over other things in general. Control of more or less monetary units is sought according as more or less such units are required to command other things in general. If we resort to use of the terms value and valuation, we do so only as a convenient way of saying we require the market's assessment of current monetary equivalents. We do not intend to imply that the scale of measurement measures values or that we are concerned with direct valuations by the person or entity for which the accounts are kept. A man's own direct valuations are fleeting, subject to change, even whimsical, and this is so whether he is considered as an individual or as an agent of a corporation or other entity.

The mere stipulation of a unit of measurement may give the impression that it is a unit in the same sense as the units of measurement of the physical sciences. In those fields, units are generally understood to be invariant units whereas we have suggested that the unit we have adopted is not of this kind. However, physical units of measurement only have a fixed practical significance if the conditions stipulated or implied in their definition are satisfied. Just as it is possible and necessary to make corrections for atmospheric pressure and temperature when using measures of mass and length under conditions which differ from those stated in definitions of the standard units, so it is possible and necessary to make adjustments from point of time to point of time in the significance attributed to monetary units. Measurement at a point of time requires only that the unit shall be the same in significance for all items measured. There is no stable monetary unit through time in any sense which is relevant in market places. This being the case, the only way of solving the problems of comparison and of measuring changes through time is by finding a basis for performing transformations on measures taken under different conditions.

Within the above system all measurements derived from any set of financial statements will be mathematically valid measurements simply because their constituent numerators and denominators are measured in units having the same significance throughout the measuring process. But what is the meaning of the number derived by relating one measure to another? Of themselves, ratios and rates mean nothing. They derive their meanings from comparisons either with expected ratios, or ratios of the same firm at different times, or ratios of different firms at the same time. Expected ratios are the product of anticipatory calculations, and they are, therefore, subjective. Each user of actually derived ratios may make what he wishes of deviations from his expected ratios. Deviations may suggest in a general way some change in the user's course of actions simply because actual results or performance did not match expectations. But expected ratios are in no sense a norm which is invariant through time.

Inter-temporal comparisons of original measurements of the monetary equivalents of particular things are meaningless if the unit of measurement has a variant dimension and if the periods or dates which are compared hold different potentials for action. In view of the shifting goals of actors, the shifting character of the environment, and the changes in financial position as investments are switched and the aggregate resources controlled increase or decrease, every period is unique in respect of the potential for action. Comparisons of cash holdings, inventory holdings, or durable goods holdings as between two or more dates and comparisons of amounts of net income as between two or more periods are, of themselves, pointless and potentially misleading. The only measures which may be validly related are either (a) ratios of successive dates, the numerators and denominators of which are measured in units of equal significance, or (b) pairs of absolute measurements one of which is a transformation of an original measurement. But comparisons of pairs of the latter kind (say, sales revenue for two periods) may be confusing, because the consequence of a transformation is to show a different magnitude than the magnitude previously reported. On the other hand, comparisons of ratios of the kind mentioned need not give rise to this kind of confusion. Ratios or rates are pure numbers, having no dimension. Whatever the dimension of the unit in consecutive periods, ratios for each separate period are comparable as between periods. It follows that tables of comparative figures should give far less prominence, if any at all, to absolute measurements made at antecedent points of time, and far more, if not exclusive, prominence to ratios.

Measurements as Language

Hitherto we have concerned ourselves primarily with one actor in the community of actors initially postulated. It is necessary now to consider an actor whose affairs are interwoven with those of others. Consider the case of a corporation as actor through its agent, a manager. The corporation depends for its initial and subsequent financing and operation on the contributions of investors, creditors, customers, suppliers, and employees. Each individual in each of these classes is an actor in his own right; each will be assumed to act according to his judgement of what will yield him more rather than less. As before, we shall not be concerned with more or less of what; every actor has some demands on the community's supply of scarce resources which he can only satisfy by having media of exchange. In his relations with the corporation, he will want to know whether continuation of his connexion with it appears to promise more than an association with some other entity. One of the tests of this is whether the corporation is sufficiently profitable to meet the demands, as they change from time to time, of the several classes of contributor—whether these demands take the form of higher dividends, better products, or better wages and working conditions, they all depend on the corporation having ample control of, or the ability to acquire ample control of, resources. Another test is whether the corporation's relationships with its creditors are such that it will be able to continue to offer such prospects of meeting the demands of other contributors. These two features, profitability and solvency, are critical, and information about them can only be obtained from accounting statements.

We are thus confronted with a situation in which the results and position of an actor require to be appraised by other actors who may be technically incompetent in respect of accounting but whose need for information is none the less legitimate. Strictly, the corporation itself has no ends such as the consumer satisfactions of individuals; it exists solely to promote the ends of those who participate in its operations. How are these participants to judge how well they are served so that, in choosing their associations, they may compare their present association with alternatives? They may do so by the comparison of rates and ratios for different firms, but only if all corporations adopt the same principles of measurement and reporting.

That accounting is a system of measurement has been demonstrated at least for the varied possible actions of a given actor. But if, as we have supposed, an actor does not keep his accounts personally but engages an accountant to do so, the system is also a language communicating information to the actor. For obviously greater reasons, if other parties need or use similar information to guide them in their relationships with a given actor, the system of measurement required is one which communicates information to an extensive range of potential users. This is, in fact, the feature of all widely used measurement systems. The units of length, of mass, of time, are units which are not peculiar to certain users. They mean the same thing to all persons in the community which adopts them. It is of no consequence that one user requires a measurement of length for reasons different from those of another. The unit of length informs them all; it matters not how varied their ends or how intimate and complex their relations. It is neutral with respect to the purposes for which individuals may use it; its neutrality is an essential element in its utility.

The same applies to accounting. If a property of income or assets is represented by units having current significance in terms of their purchasing power, each user of statements which contain measures in terms of those units will be equally well informed, for each user has himself the means of knowing what the current significance of the units is. Under traditional accounting no user can possibly know what the significance of reported income or assets is, for both are represented in mixed units having no common significance. It is not unreasonable to suppose that readers of accounting statements now assume that the significance of the units is the present significance of money units—at least accountants enter no caveat in this respect—and if the supposition is valid even in respect of some users, they are being seriously misled particularly if they engage in comparisons of the results and positions of different corporations.

There are some who claim that different parties having relations with a given actor, and in particular with a corporation, require different information as guide to their actions. If this only means information differing in detail, no objection can be taken. But it seems to be implied that the information should differ in quality. This position is taken explicitly for example in A.I.C.P.A. *Accounting Research Bulletin*, No. 5, Depreciation on Appreciation, paras. 2 and 8. In this case clearly, the possibility of accounting being the language of finance is denied for it entails that the same events and states can be represented by quite different symbols. Now the cost of developing a measurement system or a language system is considerable as, indeed, is the cost of developing the kinds of specific messages to be conveyed by either system. In a world of scarce resources it seems reasonable to expect that such systems would be so designed that they serve the greatest possible number of users or potential users. This suggests that systems should yield information which is of the one quality which serves equally all users (see Chambers, 1955).

Further, suggestions such as that cited in the previous paragraph imply that the participant-corporation relationship is bipartite only;

in other words, it is implied that each class of participant takes no cognizance of the relationships of other classes of participant with the corporation. This is an over-simplification. These relationships are all multipartite. The commonest form of complaint is that one group of participants is doing better than another (whatever that means), no reference being made to the corporation which is the focus of attention of all specific interests. It is only possible for one class of participant to judge his own prospects if he has the means of knowing the position and results of the corporation and how other classes of participants are faring. As cross comparisons of the yields to different classes are potentially numerous, and as any person may be simultaneously a member of several classes, it follows that a system in which the symbols have a common meaning to all parties is a condition of intelligent participation. For the same reasons, only such a system will be above suspicion. In order that an accounting system may be considered as a measurement system and as a language system, it is necessary that its products describe an entity as such and are not geared to the demands of any particular party. If this condition is fulfilled, each party is free to make his own judgements with respect to his own ends. If this condition is not fulfilled, the actions of any party may unwittingly be such as to defeat his own ends. The present section suggests, in short, that accounting information should be of the nature of public knowledge, knowledge ascertainable independently by persons other than the processors of it or the actors who publish it. Valuations and feelings are private knowledge only, closed to the inspection of others. One cannot expect others to act upon one's own set of valuations. Valuations of assets otherwise than by reference to markets, and freedom to choose as between different accounting procedures, make traditional accounting a hodge-podge of private valuations or private facts. Only a communication system which expresses public facts—facts which other parties could test and to which they would give assent as facts—can serve to produce the interplay of informed actions which is the essence of an efficient market mechanism.

Implementation Problems

The argument has been carried forward in terms of a current monetary expression of the command over resources. It has therefore disregarded so far some of the difficulties of finding ways of obtaining such an expression. These difficulties will be exposed in an attempt to produce a method, and a rationale for it, of obtaining the numbers of monetary units to be assigned to specific classes of things.

For monetary balances (cash, receivables, and payables) the task is easy. For cash, mere counting will suffice. For receivables and payables, the monetary amount of these claims and obligations discounted to the date of the summary statement at current bank interest rate or the contractual interest rate (where this is applicable) will suffice. The traditional procedure of making provisions against doubtful receivables should be abandoned; instead, debts judged to be bad will be written off as they are so judged. One reason for this is the view taken that only past events and present knowledge are capable of being subjected to the test of supporting evidence. A second reason is that such provisions are formal and subjective and are, therefore, liable to be used to equalize reported profits by augmenting or drawing upon them, as profits, otherwise determined, appear high or low. This possibility deprives users of financial statements of fair representations of annual profits and of trends in profit rates.

The non-monetary items create greater problems. Current cash equivalent has been regarded as the sum of money which would be currently available if a switch from investment in one combination of assets to investment in another were to be considered. This entails measuring command over resources in terms of what the market would presently pay for non-monetary assets as they are. For finished goods inventories this would mean selling price. It does not mean, however, the selling price of one unit multiplied by the number of units in stock, unless the good in question can be sold in any quantity at the one price (e.g., gold, where the price is determined otherwise than by the play of the market). Except in such cases the selling price would be the price for the full parcel at the time. This may be less than the selling price per unit multiplied by the number of units for several reasons. If the full parcel could be sold to another firm, the latter would assume the risks of carrying the inventory until sale to users and would therefore pay less than the full proceeds of sale to users. If the full parcel could be sold to users, its release would tend to force down the price per unit to an extent which is indeterminable otherwise than by actual sale. Again as the sale of the whole parcel is likely to be spread over an unknown future period in which the operations of competitors may influence prices in either direction, it is impossible to know, even by discounting prices for possible future selling dates, what the present cash value of the inventory is. Work in progress inventories pose a problem of a different kind. It is often said that the market price of work in progress may well be very small, even zero, and perhaps a negative sum. To assign money units on this basis may give as serious an understatement as using selling price multiplied by units on hand may give an overstatement for finished goods inventory.

In view of these difficulties we take an alternative position, but holding nevertheless to the same principle. We may suppose that the measurement of command over resources will be given by the sum of money which would currently have to be paid to obtain possession of the goods at present on hand. This may appear to have some similarity to replacement price as it is generally understood. But this appearance must be dispelled; replacement price is avoided for a number of reasons. First, it is not intended to give replacement price status as an alternative; the provision of alternatives tends to remove clarity and precision from all rules. Second, although replacement price of specific goods is a factor which enters into choice, so does the price of all alternatives; the use of replacement price presupposes a choice yet to be made and thus introduces circularity to the process of choice. For action, replacement price is an *ex ante* consideration, whereas the position taken here is that accounting deals with events and things *ex post*. Third, the very nature of things precludes the determination of replacement prices in any but a subjective manner. For most work in progress there is no market in which such a price is made; the same applies to finished goods which are in any way differentiated from substitutes.

By contrast, the proposal indicated has none of these defects. Its use would result in the representation of stocks of finished and unfinished goods by the sum of money which the entity would presently have if it had not these inventories in possession. In determining this current cash equivalent, present market prices of the materials and services embodied in inventories would be used; in so far as these are prices for undifferentiated goods or services, market prices are more readily available. Consequently, rises and falls in the buying prices of materials and labor service will be reflected in the sums assigned, and these sums will therefore more closely approximate the capacity to generate cash than sums assigned on the basis of original unadjusted buying prices which have varied historical significance but no contemporary significance. The current price proposal is not without some defects. If all markets for the goods which appear in financial statements were perfect, that is to say, if there were many buyers and many sellers for all goods including those partly used and those partly processed, market prices would be obtainable. In fact, of course, not all such markets are perfect, so that a variety of quotations may be obtained. It is for the reason that markets for undifferentiated goods and services are more nearly perfect that their use in determining the present cash equivalent of inventories was suggested above. Even then recourse to averaging may be necessary. An alternative would be to adjust original money cost of the inventories by the change in the level of prices appropriate to the inventory. It may be noted that these are alternative methods of approximating the same quantity, not alternative principles such as market price and replacement price are. For both methods the necessary money costs and market prices are ascertainable—they are past or present facts at the time of calculation. No hypothetical future elements enter into the calculation. The possible error in calculation is no greater than the possible error in every set of facts relating to the market upon which action may be based; the process will therefore yield measurements which are as accurate as they can or need be for practical purposes.

Further difficulties arise in the case of such potentially long-term inventories as plant and equipment which are subject to wear, tear, and obsolescence. Wear, tear, and obsolescence are incidents of a technical nature. They are not financial facts. There is no way of measuring technical facts on a monetary scale. Nevertheless these technical facts bear on the monetary equivalent of things subject to them. It is common to consider that the use of durable goods entails a flow of services from those goods to the products of their use, and that the effect is a diminution of the service potential of those goods.

Now, by our definition, accounting does not measure assets or their services or service potentials; it measures the monetary aspects of them. In the present context therefore this flow is to be understood as a change in the monetary equivalent of assets. Now the only way of measuring an irregular flow is to take readings before and after it occurs. The only way therefore of measuring a change in the monetary equivalent of these assets is by taking the difference between market prices at successive points of time. But this is complicated by two factors.

The first is obsolescence. The conventional methods of providing for depreciation are strictly methods of providing for the element of wear and tear. They postulate a useful life, a scrap value and the validity of a selected plan of amortization. The rate of future obsolescence is unknowable; estimates of it, if they are made, are entirely subjective. Not uncommonly it is ignored. Yet, as time passes the effect of obsolescence on financial position is compounded. There is thus good reason for recognizing it in the accounting system. The only way in which this may be done is by taking the aggregate effect of wear and tear and obsolescence as it is represented by differences in market prices. For financial accounting this does no damage to the facts. Any attempt to separate the two effects would involve an arbitrary distinction which it is unnecessary to make; for there is no probability that rates of usage or rates of obsolescence of the past can be extrapolated into the future in the process of forming expectations.

The second complicating factor is the possibility of continued use of a durable good over periods in which the purchasing power of money varies. It is possible that the effects of wear, tear and obsolescence on the monetary equivalent of an asset may be completely offset, more than offset, or augmented by shifts in the level of prices. The difference between market values at successive dates thus will include the effect of the shift in the level of prices. Although the market price at the latest date of assessment includes this effect—and it is proper that it should do so in order to represent financial position—the effect requires to be isolated in measuring periodic income. The problem is taken up presently.

In the determination of the current cash equivalent of a stock of durables the treatment parallels that given for short-term inventories. But here, as there, the problem of finding a contemporary market price, preferably a resale price, arises. Now each item of durables is in a more or less vendible condition. If we posit periodical or programmed reconsideration of existing investments in plant—and we may do so on the assumption of adaptive behavior—a user will from time to time have to obtain some estimate of resale price. Where there is some used goods market it is thus possible by inquiry to obtain an estimate, or a series of approximations reducible to an estimate, of current cash equivalent. For goods not capable of treatment in this way because of greater imperfections of the market, the current cash equivalent at closing date may be approximated thus:—

(a) Apply to the opening cash equivalent a price index of the class of durable goods in question: let the result of the operation be a.

(b) Obtain a current estimate of the expected remaining life of the asset (in, say, years) in the light of current economic and technical knowledge; suppose this is n years.

(c) The depreciation charge for the past year may be regarded as $a/(n+1)$; and the approximation to the current cash equivalent of the asset as $na/(n+1)$.

Repeated estimation of the remaining expected service life prevents the cumulation of error which occurs when an initial expectation is persistently applied; and the attempt to bring the measure of the current cash equivalent to contemporary terms has a like effect. The introduction of expectations at all should be avoided if possible; the suggested solution is forced by the imperfection of the market and the consequent imperfection of the available knowledge of current cash equivalent based on actual market prices.

We have dealt with short-term inventories and durables. There remain the residual equity account and the net monetary assets (or cash and receivables less payables). The monetary assets are always expressed in current cash equivalents. But holdings of net monetary assets give rise to changes in the current cash equivalent of residual equity if the dimension of the monetary unit changes through time. If opening balances of non-monetary assets are in current cash equivalents of the opening date the residual equity will then be expressed in terms of units of the dimension then prevailing. The maintenance of opening capital at the closing date will be brought into account, in determining the change in the residual equity, if the measure of the opening residual equity is transformed by a general index of prices (i.e., of the purchasing power of money) to its equivalent in units of the dimension prevailing at the closing date. The difference in the number of units is neither profit nor loss; it is simply a restatement in terms of a different unit. The opening balance (the actual number of units of opening dimension) is augmented by the amount of this difference (which may be styled a capital maintenance adjustment), the result being the opening balance in units of closing dimension.

Now if the closing balances of the non-monetary assets are expressed in units of closing dimension, by whatever methods are necessary to approximate their current cash equivalents; if the opening residual equity is restated in units of closing dimension; and as net monetary assets are always expressed in units of contemporary dimension; then the difference between the measure of total assets less liabilities and the measure of residual equity will represent the amount, in units of closing dimension, by which the firm is better off. This will be the amount of profit or income of the past period in units of closing dimension. The financial summaries, balance sheet and income account, will then consist of a series of particular statements in units of closing dimension. All arithmetical operations may be legitimately performed on the result; and all inferences from the result will be contemporarily relevant.

It will be of interest to indicate the method of deriving an income statement which will yield the same result as the taking of the difference between opening and closing residual equities. As contemporary prices alone, of all past and present prices, are relevant to choices at any time, inventories and durables accounts will be continually adjusted to present prices. The adjustments, both for short-term and durables inventories, will be carried to an inventory price adjustment account, a credit entry being made for each debit entry in the inventory account itself. To the income account will be credited all sales at actual prices; it will be debited the direct costs of all goods sold at the contemporary cost at time of sale, i.e., the latest price shown in the inventory account. All costs other than direct costs will be debited at actual prices paid except depreciation which will be calculated in the light of all available information indicative of the change in the cash equivalent of durables. The inventory price adjustment account will be closed by transfer of its balance to the income account (a credit entry if prices have risen), and the amount of the capital maintenance adjustment will be debited. A corresponding credit balance of the same amount will appear separately among the residual equity accounts in the balance sheet. The balance of the income account after the above operations will be the income of the period. Note that the inventory price adjustments include the effects of changes in the general level of prices and of relative changes in prices. The entity is better off by upwards movements in relative prices but worse off by upwards movements of the general level of prices, *ceteris paribus* in both cases. The general effect of the latter on holdings of monetary assets and the elimination of its effect on the inventory price adjustments are brought into account by way of the capital maintenance adjustment. Note also that in so far as price indexes are used, specific indexes are used for inventory price adjustments and a general index (e.g., a consumers' goods index) is used for the capital maintenance adjustment.[3]

Summary

(a) The accounting systems of adaptive entities can conform with the characteristics of a measurement system; only if they so conform is it possible to make valid comparisons and inferences from the information they produce.

(b) The unit of measurement is the unit of currency of stipulated denomination but of no fixed dimension. A unit of fixed dimension is inconsistent with the characteristics of money as a medium of exchange in a fluid economic environment.

(c) Original measurements have a time dimension which is generally implicit. Such measurements are relevant at that time only.

---

[3] The argument for, and a fuller description of, the process here outlined is given at length in *Accounting, Evaluation and Economic Behavior.*

(d) Measurements which represent current cash equivalents yield statements which express financial capacity to engage in market operations; such statements are a necessary condition of reasoned action. They predict, or express the numerical laws which form the basis of, the limits of future operations.

(e) Derived measurements which are rates or ratios eliminate the time-bound dimension of the monetary unit and are thus comparable as of different intervals or dates for a given entity.

(f) Derived measurements are comparable as between entities only if the same measurement rules are generally adopted by all entities.

(g) Derived measurements are, for the reasons implied in (e) and (f), the most general and most useful type of information, expressive of trends and indicative of expectations, yielded by an accounting system.

Conclusion

The properties of an accounting system, it appears, should be those of measurement systems generally. Notwithstanding that the unit of measurement has not an invariant dimension, means are available for making the necessary transformations which constitute the resulting set of specific statements a homogeneous set at any time. The products of such a system would have the qualities of relevance, neutrality, correspondence, communicability, and objectivity; and we have shown elsewhere (Chambers, 1961) that possession of these qualities by accounting information is an essential condition, though not the only condition, of adaptive economic behavior.

A measurement system is the product of deliberate design as to the property to be measured, the specification of the unit to be used, and the rules for assigning numbers of units to things possessing the measurable property. The literature of accounting is at best vague and in general contradictory on these points. Traditional rules for assigning money sums to assets and obligations allow such wide latitude that they permit gross violation of the principles of measurement and communication. Traditional accounting is, thus, in no sense a measurement system. People who use its results in the form of ratios, percentages and other comparisons, assume that it is a measurement system. But in this they are misguided for traditional methods have not been deliberately selected with the properties of such a system as constraints.

The above analysis strips the cost-or-value controversy and the price-level problem of much of their mystery and empty verbosity. In the market-place there is no invariant standard of value, so that no transaction in it acquires a measurement which is standard for any length of time, long or short. There is only a medium of exchange with a variable value in exchange. This fact must be taken into account by every actor in deciding every course of action. Initial money cost means literally nothing to him. He is the steward of what he has, not of what he spent to acquire what he has. The only way in which he can manage the things he has to suit his ends is by making bargains which give him more of the means for serving those ends. And the only way in which he can make such bargains is on the basis of knowledge of his present position.

There has been a tendency in recent years to pay greater attention to the analysis of past results for the purpose of assessing the propriety of past decisions. If behavior is adaptive, such analysis can only give a general idea of the efficacy of the decision-making function as a whole. No specific decision can come under close scrutiny, for its effects are inevitably intertwined with the effects of others. In fact to expect light to be thrown on the propriety of specific decisions is to expect what is logically impossible. Foresight is not a quality which is capable of precise assessment by hindsight; specific anticipations are bedeviled by the vagaries of a changing world. Nevertheless it is possible to test the efficacy of the adaptive processes as a whole; men may make specific errors in spite of foresight, but, over a range of problem situations and adjustments to them, it is reasonable to expect acuity of vision and prevision to reveal itself. But only if the measurement system is equal to the task.

There has also been a tendency in recent years to give a forward-looking emphasis to accounting, and to suggest the inclusion in accounting statements of all kinds of future estimates. The view advanced here may seem to be retrogressive by comparison with this tendency. Such a conclusion, however, would be mistaken. The greatest service accounting can give in relation to future actions is knowledge of present financial positions for this is universally necessary knowledge. Calculations relating to the future involve hosts of evaluations and speculative anticipations which are not knowledge in the sense of ascertainable and verifiable facts; they are calculations purely and simply, not measurements. We have no objection to people trained as accountants making such calculations, but the product is not accounting. There is no such thing as accounting for the future. It is the very confusion of past, present and future which has given rise to inconsistent, self-contradictory rules. One of the principal purposes of this study has been to distinguish sharply the characteristic differences between measurement and forms of anticipatory calculation so that accounting may be seen as essentially a measurement and communication system. If it is seen in this way its rules may be freed of the varied discretionary elements which defeat analysis and comparison on the part of those for whose benefit accounting is done.

REFERENCES

The dates given in the text are dates of original publication. Intermediate sources used are indicated below.

Ackoff, Russell L., *Scientific Method*, New York, John Wiley & Sons, Inc., 1962.

American Institute of Accountants, *Accounting Research Bulletin, No.* 5, Depreciation on Appreciation, 1940.

Accounting Terminology Bulletin, No. 1, 1953.

Campbell, Norman R., *Physics, The Elements*, Cambridge, England, 1920. References to reprint, *Foundations of Science*, New York, Dover Publications Inc., 1957.

Canning, John B., *The Economics of Accountancy,* New York, The Ronald Press Co., 1929.

Chambers, R. J., *The Function and Design of Company Annual Reports,* Part 1, Sydney, The Law Book Co. of Australasia Pty. Ltd., 1955.

"Towards a General Theory of Accounting", The Australian Society of Accountants, Adelaide, mimeo. 1961; printed 1962.

"The Resolution of Some Paradoxes in Accounting", mimeo. 1962; printed, University of British Columbia, 1963.

Churchman, C. West, *Prediction and Optimal Decision,* Englewood Cliffs, N.J., Prentice-Hall Inc., 1961.

Cohen, Morris R., and Nagel, Ernest, *An Introduction to Logic and Scientific Method,* London, Routledge & Kegan Paul Ltd., 1934. References to 1957 reprint.

Dewey, John, *Theory of Valuation,* Vol. 2, No. 4, International Encyclopaedia of Unified Science, Chicago, The University of Chicago Press, 1939. References to 1960 reprint.

Dickinson, Arthur Lowes, *Accounting Practice and Procedure,* New York, The Ronald Press Co., 1914.

Dicksee, Lawrence R., *Advanced Accounting,* 3rd ed., London, Gee & Co., 1905.

Esquerre, Paul-Joseph, *The Applied Theory of Accounts,* New York, The Ronald Press Co., 1914.

Hempel, Carl G., *Fundamentals of Concept Formation in Empirical Science,* Vol. 2, No. 7, International Encyclopedia of Unified Science, Chicago, The University of Chicago Press, 1952. References to 1962 reprint.

Kester, Roy B., *Advanced Accounting,* 3rd rev. ed., New York, The Ronald Press Co., 1933.

Nagel, Ernest, Measurement, *Erkenntnis,* 2, 1932. References to reprint in Danto and Morgenbesser, *Philosophy of Science,* Cleveland, The World Publishing Co., 1960.

Paton, William A., and Stevenson, Russell A., *Principles of Accounting,* Ann Arbor, George Wahr, 1917.

Schrödinger, Erwin, Indeterminism in Physics, 1931, in *Science Theory and Man,* New York, Dover Publications Inc., 1957.

Stevens, S. S., "On the Theory of Scales of Measurement", *Science,* Vol. 103, 1946.

von Mises, Ludwig, *Human Action,* London, William Hodge and Co. Ltd., 1949.

39

THE COMPLEMENTARITY OF ACCOUNTING AND ECONOMICS*

There is a modest literature on the relationship between accounting and economics. It is to some extent surprising that it is not of greater volume, for the entities about which accounts are kept are the entities of which economics studies the behaviour. That the analytical study of business entities from both directions should have overlapped is to be expected; that from the overlap some integration of the ideas of economics and accounting may have emerged could be expected. But neither has happened on any significant scale.

True, there have been some treatments of the similarity of the subject of study in both fields[1]; there have been attempts to elucidate the concepts in each field which bear common names, such as cost, income, capital[2]; it has been noticed that some economists have come to champion practices commonly employed by accountants[3]; and some accountants have come to accept concepts well established in economics[4]. But none of this represents a general view of the attitudes of accountants towards economics, or of economists towards accounting. Indeed, although there have been some instances of economists recognizing accounting as part of the apparatus of business, they have seldom considered its role in business; generally their remarks have been confined to simple description or to mild criticism. And although some accountants have recognized that there is a relationship between accounting and decision-making, they have commonly either slipped into what may properly be regarded as economics, or have paid only token regard to the implications of the relationship.

We take the position here that there is a positive relationship between the products of the two disciplines and between the practical

---

* First published in *Calculator Annual*, Singapore Polytechnic Society of Commerce, 1965, pp. 78-86.

[1] For example, Richard Mattessich, "The Constellation of Accountancy and Economics", *The Accounting Review*, October 1956.

[2] For example, Report of a Joint Exploratory Committee appointed by The Institute of Chartered Accountants in England and Wales and by The National Institute of Economic and Social Research, *Some Accounting Terms and Concepts*, Cambridge University Press, 1951.

[3] For example, full average cost pricing; see R. L. Hall and C. J. Hitch, "Price Theory and Business Behaviour", *Oxford Economic Papers*, May 1939.

[4] For example, the emergence of interest in marginalism and differentials; see James S. Earley, "Recent Developments in Cost Accounting and the 'Marginal Analysis' ", *The Journal of Political Economy*, June 1955.

outcomes of their application. The two meet in the person of economic actors, individuals or businessmen; and at such a meeting point they are complementary. It will appear, then, that it is pointless to remake accounting in the image of economics, or economics in the image of accounting; for both have a function, each its own.

Scarcity

Economists, as to a considerable part of economics, consider the ways in which men organize and interact in the pursuit of satisfaction or the means of satisfaction when goods, generally and specifically, are in short supply relatively to the demand for them and when they can be used in alternative employments. In the absence of scarcity there would be no occasion for economizing, no occasion for calculating, no point in keeping accounts of the past as guides to the future. Economics also recognizes the scarcity of goods in the control of individual persons or firms which arises from legal rights in goods, as well as the scarcity of goods collectively in relation to the collective demands of a society.

The orientation of accounting is towards the specific entities which, by virtue of property laws, have determinable rights in scarce goods as against other entities. The specific rights of such entities which have been the basis of accounting are rights of possession, not of ownership. The law recognizes qualified rights of possession which fall short of outright ownership; but, however qualified, rights of possession give rise generally to rights of use consistent with the legally defined role in which an entity has possession. Accountants thus concern themselves with the scarce goods in possession of singular persons or groups (in general, entities), having defined or implied legal roles and rights, and the claims of other entities to satisfaction out of those goods. In so far as the law confers on some entities rights against persons or other entities, these rights are generally satisfied or satisfiable out of the scarce goods of those entities: for it is no longer possible for private entities to attach or impound the persons of defaulters. Double-entry accounting, then, expresses these two facets of the affairs of entities; the economic facet and the legal facet, scarce goods in possession, designated assets, and enforceable claims against those goods, designated equities.

That scarcity is a common foundation of economics and accounting, however, does not make its implications the same in both fields. This may be illustrated by considering the determinants of some kinds of choice. Suppose that in a community at large there is a demand for a producers' good sufficient to induce some producer to manufacture it for sale. The conditions required to be satisfied are that the proceeds of manufacture and sale to some producer are expected to exceed the cost of production by a margin greater than the proceeds of an alternative employment of the same resources, and that this expected sum will in any case exceed the proceeds of a riskless investment. For continued production of the good, the cost of production, the replacement cost, must continue to yield such a superior margin.

A user of the good however is not in the same position. He operates in a different market for his product. He will operate under the same general conditions already mentioned, but once he has acquired such a good he is not committed to its continued use. He will go on using it as long as the proceeds from its use are expected to exceed the proceeds from an alternative employment of the amount he could obtain by selling it. A user may from time to time consider replacing a producers' good; but the cost to him of replacing it is then no different in principle from the cost of any investment alternative to his existing investment. The one thing that is therefore of continuous significance to a user of producers' goods is not its replacement cost to him but its market selling price; for assuming his command over resources in general to be limited (scarce in relation to his wants), the amount of the resale price determines the alternatives open to him.

Thus although replacement price has much to do *ex ante*, and continuously, with the production for sale of any good, the market resale price has much to do, and continuously, with the use of any producers' good by a user. It seems reasonable to expect that replacement cost would therefore be of greater significance in economics; and that market resale price would be of greater significance in accounting as providing the factual premise for all choices of a user of producers' goods.

It is true that there are many instances of reference to the use of market resale price in ascertaining the monetary sum to be assigned to some assets for balance sheet purposes. However, most of these apply to only limited classes of assets, and they do not occur in the context of acceptance of the balance sheet as a statement of financial position. On the other hand there are many more instances of reference to the use of replacement prices for the same purpose[5]. It is not at all certain, but it seems more probable that the usage is borrowed directly from economics and the context of exploratory calculation, than that it is used as an approximation to an element of a dated financial position. If so, and it appears to be so, its proponents overlook the necessity of providing factual premises of action from which all exploratory calculations must proceed if ends are to be likely of achievement. The processes of choice are confused with the discovery of the factual premises, which latter we regard as the distinctive function of accounting.

The Maximization Principle

The economic theory of the firm has, by most of its exponents, been based on the maximization principle. This principle stems from the scarcity of means available to and the plurality of unsatisfied wants of men. If a man makes any sacrifice to obtain something in

[5] Dating from at least as far back as 1929 and embodied more recently in Edgar O. Edwards and Philip W. Bell, *The Theory and Measurement of Business Income*, Berkeley and Los Angeles, University of California Press, 1961.

return, he is supposed to prefer to have more rather than less of what he gets in return. He prefers to strike the more favourable bargain, for the more favourable bargain enables him to satisfy the want to which the good received is specific to a greater extent than a less favourable bargain. And, of course, the satisfaction expected to be gained is preferred to the expected satisfaction forgone by the sacrifice he makes. This is what the maximization principle seems to mean. It is a motivational premise: that is its function in economics. It is not a generalization about what happens as a result of action. It is a generalization about the tests men use when choosing between alternative actions. Not only is it a corollary of scarcity; it is an empirically defensible generalization.

It may be noticed that the preceding paragraph makes no reference to profit-maximization. The maximization of satisfactions may seem to entail the maximization of profits, for in general it may be supposed that the divisions of profit in the form of dividend payments provide the means of satisfaction. But satisfactions and profits are incommensurable; the one is psychic, the other monetary. The entailment mentioned is therefore impossible. It seems indeed that the interposition of a medium of exchange alone enables us to speak of profit maximization; and that the use of profit maximization as a motivational premise is permissible strictly only if the firm is viewed as an abstract entity which has no capacity for satisfaction out of its operations or out of their proceeds. If any criticism may be offered of this view of the firm, it is on the ground that it omits to consider the firm as itself the focus of a coalition of persons some of whom are able to take satisfactions in the course of the firm's operations. The satisfactions which may be taken out in the course of operations are not available to those whose participation in a firm is wholly pecuniary. But whatever psychic satisfactions and monetary compensations are taken out, by others as well as by those having pecuniary interests, maximization may (if not must) be supposed to underlie the choice of participation in one firm rather than another. The firm must be regarded on this view as a power-complex, in which each participant seeks to maximize his own satisfaction *vis-à-vis* other participants; and each firm is also part of a greater power-complex, consisting of all firms competing for the participation of persons who may choose among alternative participations on the maximization principle. The acceptance of the maximization of satisfactions as a premise of action is thus entirely justifiable on this view. The view itself suggests that the notion of "satisficing"[6], put forward as an alternative to maximization, is not an alternative but a description of the consequence of the pursuit of maximization by the individual persons or groups which at the time are the coalition we describe as the participants in the firm.

What then has all this to do with accounting?

---

[6] See, for example, Herbert A. Simon, *Models of Man*, New York, John Wiley & Sons, Inc., 1957, Ch. 14, "A Behavioral Model of Rational Choice".

On the one hand, very little. Its *ex ante* character entitles it to a place in the theory of choice. But it cannot be itself a theory about the choice of accounting methods, except perhaps in the sense that accountants may choose the easiest. On the other hand, accounting may provide some of the informational premises of maximizing behaviour. If the next succeeding action of any person or firm is to be an action which reduces the gap between the present position and a desired position, a necessary premise of choice is knowledge of the present position. For clearly, if the present position is not known one cannot know the extent of the gap and therefore cannot choose in an informed way that course which is expected to reduce the gap by the greatest amount. If behaviour is adaptive, continuously, it is apparent that the discovery of the contemporary position, or the best possible approximation to it, is continuously necessary. And this is the reason why a continuous record of its financial affairs is of importance to firms and other economic entities. As we shall presently point out the record will necessarily be continuously in accord with the circumstances of the entity in relation to the economic environment.

There is an additional point. One of the informational premises of choice is the ascertained consequence of past choices. We are not concerned with the premises of past choices, but with the consequences. The premises of past choices may have included a range of mental conditions—more or less certainty, more or less optimism—quite different from those of any present time. But we refer to the informational premises, not the psychological premises. Now if certain actions did in fact procure certain consequences we may assess subjectively the probability that similar actions will in the future procure similar consequences. Generally we presume that at least to some extent past experience may be extrapolated to the immediate future. But the consequences subsist in the change wrought between two points of time, and the measure of the consequences subsists in the measure of the difference between positions at two points of time. Only if there is a system by which the positions may be ascertained reliably and from which inferences may be drawn as to the rate of change of position is it possible to bring one's own past experiences into account in choosing. And in so far as one's own skills (subject to modification by learning from experience) are to be employed in the following interval, such information is a psychologically as well as an informationally valuable premise of action.

Value and Valuation

In market economics, value theory is concerned with the influences which determine exchange values or prices. Value is commonly used of market price, and those accustomed to or engaged in expositions of price formation processes mean and understand by value the market price or market value of a good. Value, when so used, means the number (mathematical value) of money units of a certain kind bid or offered in exchange for the good. It does not mean the valuation attributed to the good either by the buyer or seller. When a person directly values a good, he prefers it to some other good[7]. If, acting on such a preference, he exchanges a sum of money for a wanted good, we can say no more than that he preferred having the good to having the money. We cannot say what maximum sum he would have been prepared to pay: indeed it is unlikely that he himself would be able to say what that maximum is in many cases. Nor can we say what minimum sum the vendor would have accepted. Nor can we say that the price is the value either of the money or of the goods exchanged to both parties at the time; for if price is equal to value, what is the point of an exchange? The parties do not expect to be just as well off afterwards as before; both expect to be better off.

Acts of evaluation are always antecedent to choice; they are always anticipatory, either of a decision to carry on as before or of a decision to carry on in a different way. Economics explores the evaluation and choice making processes of businessmen. The cost and revenue diagrams of hypothetical firms purport to indicate which of the possible price and output combinations is to be preferred, all other things being constant. But acts of evaluation are not the only acts antecedent to choice. As we have said, there are also acts of discovery. Thus, in the simple cases represented by the diagrams of economics, an acting businessman must first find the costs of the alternatives before him: and typically in simple cases he will find them in the market place at the time of choice. But where a firm has been in existence prior to some moment of choice it will have some things already on hand. What they are is to be discovered, and the then cost of using them is also to be discovered. This situation differs partially from the simple situation where the businessman has only a stock of money awaiting use in some preferred way. The difference lies in the fact that a going concern has a stock of goods; perhaps money as well, but certainly a stock of goods. This stock, the resultant of past investment, is a constraint on choice because the freedom to choose is limited by the vendibility and the proceeds of sales of this stock if it were to be sold. As alternatives may only be compared with ease by reference to the costs they entail, the proceeds or market resale price of goods on hand gives the monetary equivalent of the cost of use at the time of choice. The complex case of the continuing entity with a stock of goods on hand is thus reduced to the same situation as the simple case where there is a stock of money only on hand.

The point is that without some such act of discovery the businessman is unable to make his valuations; for in so far as every possible alternative involves a cost he must first know what he has to sacrifice before he can decide what alternatives are open to him. This act of discovery may be performed by inspection; but in complex cases

[7] "Every valuation *is* a comparison; we have no conception of an absolute utility or an absolute standard of utility. The notion of value is meaningless except in relation to alternatives of choice". Frank H. Knight, *Risk, Uncertainty and Profit,* Boston and New York, Houghton Mifflin Company, 1921, p. 63.

where the stock is large, varied or remote, it is aided by the continuing process of accounting. No other functionary in business performs just this task.

The complementarity of the processes of discovery and evaluation should be apparent. To act we must know first of all what we have now to sacrifice; to choose between the possibilities open by virtue of what we have now we must evaluate, compare and rank those possibilities on the basis of hypothetical expected outcomes. On the one hand we require knowledge; but to this we must add expectations. We cannot choose without both. It is therefore difficult to understand the sense in which "potentialities are . . . more important than the actualities [in the making of decisions]". And it is, to say the least, confusing to speak of what the accountant does as "evaluation . . . on the basis of knowledge about the future which he cannot possibly have"[8]. The things to which accountants assign monetary magnitudes are present things, capable of being observed and having more or less determinate monetary properties. The task of discovery is the accountant's: the task of evaluation, of choosing, is the actor's, the businessman's, for only the businessman knows his specific goals at any time, and it is only in the light of specific goals that choice has meaning.

The matter has been greatly confused by the simple alternative, "cost or value", in terms of which the materials and objectives of accounting have been discussed. Neither of the terms has an unequivocal meaning. But we may briefly consider the consequence of using the terms with their more common meanings.

(*a*) *Cost*

There are some who interpret cost as purchase price and contend that costs in this sense are the magnitudes with which accounting is concerned. Now there can be little doubt that "cost gives actual value for purposes of initial statement"[9] if cost is interpreted as an actual sacrifice and actual value is interpreted as purchase price. The statement is not true, however, if it is interpreted as saying that the evaluation of the sacrifice made is equal to the evaluation of what is received, for as we have already indicated exchanges only occur when both parties expect to be better off as a result. But the principal element of the above statement at the moment is "for purposes of initial statement". What, then of subsequent statement? Those who hold the view we are here considering hold that cost is also pertinent for subsequent statements; that is to say, for continuing entities, initial purchase price is continuously relevant in some sense. But whose sense? "When the balance sheet is prepared on the basis of cost or investment no one who understands accounts will expect a statement

[8] K. E. Boulding, "Economics and Accounting: the Uncongenial Twins", W. T. Baxter and S. Davidson (eds.) *Studies in Accounting Theory*, London, Sweet & Maxwell Ltd., 1962, pp. 52-3.

[9] William A. Paton, *Accounting Theory*, New York, The Ronald Press Co., 1922, p. 489.

which is correct and valid on the basis of economic conditions at any given point of time."[10] But if such a statement is not correct and valid "on the basis of economic conditions" at any given present point of time, it cannot serve as an aid to action in the economic conditions at that point of time, whether one understands accounts or not. Such a view gives accounting no informative role at all; and if accounting has no such role, those who have to act have clearly to find out for themselves what their present positions are from time to time.

The case for an initial price base is supported by some on the ground that the acquisition of a good in fact determines the future course of action and constrains the behaviour of the firm. In one sense this is so; the payment of the purchase price removes a determinate amount of cash from the firm. But in two other senses it is not so. What the firm obtains at a price may subsequently come to command a much higher or a much lower price; notwithstanding the cash payment, the change is a material fact which would and should be taken into account in any subsequent reckoning if it were not for the cost doctrine. Secondly the future actions of the firm are by no means severely constrained. There are few goods if any and probably no sets of producers' goods which may not be turned to producing variant products or mixes of products; and there are relatively few goods, though there are some, which may not be resold if the resale will enable a more profitable investment to be made. It is apparent that initial purchase prices only determine who shall buy the goods, not how they shall subsequently be used; once acquired, their employment and their resale is determined by reference both to their resale prices and the prices of the products they yield.

The cost basis is also defended on the ground that the prices actually paid are unquestionably the experience of the firm which paid them. They are peculiar to it; and it would be a mistake to regard the experience of other firms, before, at the same time, or since, as being pertinent to that firm[11]. This, of course, is the error of solipsism, the belief that there is only one's self and that all other selves are merely one's own constructs. It seems curious that such a view should survive, since the whole business of buying and selling is done in the light of the things experienced by others as well as by one's self. The attribution of such an attitude to firms or their managers can only have arisen by divorcing the whole apparatus of business from the keeping of records about it.

It should be clear that the view that initial purchase prices are the magnitudes with which a continuous accounting system is continuously concerned robs accounting of any link with the process of discovery and with the process of evaluation. It cuts accounting off completely from the dynamic economic process. We attribute its

---

[10] Maurice E. Peloubet, "Is Value an Accounting Concept?" *The Journal of Accountancy*, March 1935.

[11] For example, Roy B. Kester, *Advanced Accounting*, New York, The Ronald Press Co., 1933. "From the viewpoint of accounting, determination of cost value . . . has reference always to the individual business concerned." (pp. 100-101.)

adoption to the facile interpretation of cost as a sum paid out, a usage quite different from the economists' usage, as the measure of a sacrifice made.

(*b*) *Value*

There are some who interpret value in the sense of valuation for a specific future purpose peculiar to a firm temporarily in possession of a good, and who contend that accounting is, or should be, concerned with such valuations. Value in this sense is related to its usage in economics. And it is precisely on the ground that such a value is related to a future purpose and therefore involves the estimation of future magnitudes that supporters of the cost doctrine rebut it.

The magnitudes which such valuations yield are the sums of the future flows from the use of goods, discounted to the present. The gross inflows, the gross outlays, their timing and the discount rate are all hypothetical. The attempt to make them realistic in no way robs them of their hypothetical character. The necessity or desirability of making such calculations to throw light on alternatives open to choice is not in dispute. But they rank only as expectations. They are not facts: they are entirely subjective: they cannot be independently authenticated: they cannot be audited. To be pertinent to future action they will of necessity be based on a presently known set of facts at the time of calculation; but they are not themselves the facts of the present at the time of calculation.

Indeed if such valuations are to be made there is already presumed some knowledge of the present facts. But the supporters of value in this sense give no indication of the instrument by which such knowledge is made available. In the nature of things, as we have shown, purchase prices are less than the valuations placed on goods by buyers. In the same way the present position of a holder of goods, that is to say, the present prices of those goods taken in the aggregate, will be less than the valuation obtained in the manner described above, for otherwise the holder would be foolish to go on holding them.

(*c*) *Current Cash Equivalent*

The two kinds of views considered in the previous sections lean heavily in opposite directions, the cost basis towards the past, the value basis towards the future. But what of the ever insistent present, from which alone action can be taken? Explicit recognition of the relevance of contemporary information is not given, although economists presume such information is available and accountants imply that what the traditional processes yield is relevant. What the situation of firms and businessmen requires is a form of accounting which is as free as possible of hypothetical magnitudes, which is objective and thus pertinent to operations in market places, and which is continuously indicative of the contemporary position of the firm in its economic environment. The magnitudes which appear in periodical summaries of this kind would in general be contemporary market resale prices, subject to provisos where the processes of bringing goods to the point of realization are uncompleted. In principle the magnitudes are neither costs nor values, but what we choose to call current cash equivalents[12]. Such a system would fill the gap in the knowledge of users of financial information which is left under both the cost and the value hypotheses. And such a system would be complementary to the choosing or decision-making which is the business of actors and the concern of economists.

Marginal Analysis

The typical form of economic analysis of the behaviour of individuals and of firms is marginal analysis. Every action is directed towards the procurement of some effect which is incremental to a given state, and calculations with respect to all such possible actions are deemed to be made as from that state. There can scarcely be any objection to this view of anticipatory calculation and reasoned action. It will be confirmed by conscious self-observation as well as by observation of others. It is by the operation of many such choices at the margin, on both the buyer's and the seller's sides, that prices are formed and the prices of given goods are moved up and down from time to time. For any producer, therefore, the valuations he places both on goods in use and on goods for sale are dependent on prices ruling or expected to rule when he places his goods on the market. They do not depend on what he paid to acquire those goods. The difference between purchase price and selling price will determine whether he stays in business or in a given line of business. But the purchase price does not of itself determine the selling price; if this were so no good would be sold at a loss and no firm would fail. The implication of this is clearly that a mere record of purchase prices, however precise and however imaginatively allocated, apportioned and aggregated, has no direct bearing on the subsequent market price except in the purest of monopolistic conditions.

Consider also the kind of adaptive behaviour appropriate to a hardening of market conditions. If selling prices move against a seller, he will search for the smallest number of changes which can be expected at least to reinstate his position. He will seek for the smallest number of changes because (a) there are costs of retraining or redirecting staff and, or, (b) there are costs of changing the physical composition of his asset holdings, both of which he would prefer to keep to a minimum, and (c) the greater the number of changes the greater is the difficulty of envisaging their repercussions. Adaptation to an unfavourable change in market conditions thus requires knowledge of the contemporary costs of operations singly. A complex calculation of the costs of products, based on acquisition prices and including all or a large number of essential and ancillary operations, is of no help. Adaptation to a favourable change is no less dependent on contemporary and particularistic calculations.

---

[12] It is impossible here to deal fully with this notion which is one of the essential elements of, *Accounting, Evaluation and Economic Behavior.*

Marginal analysis has had its clearest exposition in the context of the highly simplified, single product, illustrations of the economics texts. For this reason some have held that it is inappropriate in the highly complex undertakings which make and sell many commodities in a host of different ways. But, on the contrary, marginal analysis is the most economical, if not the only, way of dealing with complexity. For suppose that a firm manufactures many lines and that the question of increasing or decreasing the output of any one of them arises for consideration. (The question of increasing or decreasing the output of all or a large number at once does not seem to be a typical question; changes in the nature of stimuli occur consecutively not simultaneously.) And suppose that the firm has computed the average total cost of each product. The average total cost of any product will, by reason of the allocation of common costs, be a function of the average total cost of every other product. The effect of changing the output of any one product on the cost of that product will therefore not be discoverable without completely recalculating the costs of all products for the new hypothetical mix. We have never heard that such recalculations are made. It is probable rather that the question of changing the output of one product is resolved by disregarding the effects of the change on the costs of all other products, simply because of the difficulties of complete recalculation.

If, on the other hand, the direct costs of each product and each operation were computed, without any attempt to allocate common costs, the prospective additional or avoidable costs of any and every change in operations singly would be ascertainable with ease, and with greater precision. In short, if the accounts were kept so that all items were approximations to current cash equivalents, and if the cost accounts were kept so that the direct or avoidable costs of every operation could be ascertained, these latter would give the closest approximation to the (*ex ante*) marginal cost of making a change given the existing complex of other operations and the existing equipment and materials. This businessmen need to know in order to compare it with the marginal costs of alternatives, which are only discoverable from the market at the time and which are therefore in terms of contemporary prices.

Summary

We have attempted to show that in respect of economic behaviour accounting and anticipatory analysis serve two distinctive functions, complementary functions. There can be no deliberate behaviour without anticipatory calculation; the economics of the firm concerns itself with this. But there can be no valid anticipatory calculation without a foundation in the contemporary facts of the firm, its financial position at a point of time which it is the business of accounting to discover; for without this knowledge it cannot be decided what alternatives are financially feasible. Specifically we have argued that although replacement cost has a function in economics, market resale price is the concept appropriate to the discovery of financial position; that as maximization in some sense is a necessary assumption for the analysis of alternatives, the discovery of contemporary financial position is a condition precedent to informed choice; that neither original costs of acquisition nor anticipatory values are relevant to the discovery of financial position, and that current cash equivalents alone provide the factual premises of choice; and that direct costs in contemporary terms are indicative of the marginal costs of changes within a given organization of factors of production, and are comparable with the marginal costs of alternatives.

Any attempt simply to translate the terms of economics into accounting analogues is therefore beside the point and misleading. The processes of choice and of discovery require different concepts and different viewpoints. But the processes and concepts of the two must be at least compatible, for the one depends on the other. In this lies the complementarity of accounting and economics.

The direction in which advances in the theory and practice of accounting may be made are indicated by the analysis of the relationship of accounting to economic action. Advance will be obstructed if the relationship is conceived as one of identity rather than of complementarity. Equally it will be obstructed if the complementarity of economics and accounting is not taken as a premise, for accounting will then have no function as a source of knowledge essential to informed economic behaviour.

40

THE FOUNDATIONS OF FINANCIAL ACCOUNTING*

The widespread contemporary concern with the quality of the products of financial accounting prompts me to take the view that we should be, and are, engaged in a discussion of an aspect of practical affairs which is a matter of some urgency. I take it that this is not the occasion for a mere academic excursion, and I do not propose to consider, except by way of illustration, the merits of antecedent academic excursions. There is ample evidence of belief in the inadequacies of the present mode of financial reporting. There is also ample evidence to the effect that the existence of these beliefs is not taken lightly by the appropriate professional and regulatory authorities. These are concerned with practical matters. And, as it seems to me, the foundations of financial accounting are to be found by contemplation of the practical contexts in which its products are used, not by contemplation of the justifications and rationalizations by which any existing body of accounting rules is sustained.

I shall take the position that we are concerned with accounting in the economic and commercial context of the present. There is a widespread phobia about being positive or definite or unequivocal about statements of principle and rules. It purports to be founded on the idea that accounting should evolve as the economic context changes, and that to be positive or definite or unequivocal now will foreclose the possibility of further development. But this is mere temporizing, procrastination. There will be no better financial accounting or reporting in the future, in a different context the style of which we cannot possibly envisage, unless, by resolute inquiry and willingness to act upon its reasoned outcome, we are prepared to learn from the circumstances and context of the present. Some say that accounting should be allowed to "evolve". But, just as there was no such thing as the evolution of power-driven vehicles from horse-drawn vehicles, there is no evolution in accounting. There have been and should be changes. But to use the metaphor of evolution in respect of a matter which properly is the outcome of deliberation and choice is to confuse. Likewise, to suppose that the alternative to evolution is revolution is to confuse. To label necessary or conceivable changes is not to bring them about. The invention of the phrase "generally accepted accounting principles" has not brought about the general acceptance of any principle, not even of any rule, as a glance at *Accounting Trends and Techniques* will show.

---

* First published in *Berkeley Symposium on the Foundations of Financial Accounting*, January 1967, University of California, Berkeley, pp. 26-44.

For strong practical reasons we are concerned with general acceptance, with the general acceptance of some principles and the concomitant or consequential rejection of others. The basic matters with which we deal are interrelated elements of the concrete world in respect of which some persons expect to be informed. Toleration of conflicting principles and vacillation between principles can only lead to confusion on the part of those who expect enlightenment, to distrust of issuers by the users of financial information or distrust of the specialism which provokes misunderstanding. On the other hand, as long as conflicts of principle and vacillation persist they rob the practicing expert of the sense of direction which is the foundation of a professional ethic. The only sense in which general acceptance can have a valid and useful meaning among experts, however, is with reference to acceptance by conviction and on the incontestable evidence of the observable world. Experts naturally, as experts, tend to expect their views to be respected by others, even by other brother-experts. But comprehension of the foundations of an expertise is not so much a matter of having "views" as of grappling with the events and things to which it is related. It is a matter of being impressed by what one observes, not of pressing what one observes into an already fixed mould. The sooner and the further we fly from the world of events and things to the ethereal world of third, fourth and fifth level abstractions, the sooner we reach the point where nothing we say can be tested and much we say is mere gobbledegook. There is abundant evidence in the literature of the tendency to run in the direction of the higher abstractions and to shun the attempt to seek the order which pertains among the observable events and things.

In the following outline I have attempted to keep to the commonly observable events and things—to goods and money and transactions; to people having and people wanting money; to what they want and what they can know and what they can only expect. The propositions to be presented commend themselves to me as yielding a financial accounting which is superior in demonstrable usefulness to the financial accounting now in use, and as foundations they seem to be demonstrably superior to the foundations of many present practices.

Following a common custom, reference will be made primarily to corporations, but the argument is quite general in application. Where it is used, "firm" will generally mean corporation.

1. Financial Accounting

Financial accounting is concerned with the representation of the monetary consequences of the transactions of single entities (firms) and the monetary consequences of non-transaction events which effect the economic or commercial characteristics of those entities.

Every such entity is conceived to be a going concern engaged in continuous adaptation to the markets in which it operates, adaptation stimulated by the prices of goods and services as these are disclosed in those markets. The decisions of its managers may, and generally will, be based in part on expectations of future prices, but the capacity of the firm to give effect to those decisions depends on the relationship between the firm's holdings of cash (and the equivalent of cash) and the prices of required goods and services at the time.

By transaction we mean any wholly completed or partially completed engagement between the firm and other entities, already settled by the giving or receiving of money, or giving rise to a right to such a settlement in money at a future time. Transactions thus include purchases, sales, loans, subscriptions to security issues.

By non-transaction event we mean any event which bears on the monetary measures (or cash equivalents) of goods or rights held or obligations owed by the firm during the holding or owing. Non-transaction events include gifts, losses by theft or other such causes, changes in prices and changes in price levels.

By monetary consequences we mean actual effects on the cash holdings and monetary equivalents of goods held and obligations owed. The purport of the definition of financial accounting, or rather, of its scope, is to require the representation of all such actual effects in the accounts. The monetary measures of the consequences of all transactions are given by prices expressed in monetary units at the time of such transactions. The monetary consequences of all non-transaction events are given by prices if those events occur at identifiable points of time, and by differences in prices if those events occur through an interval of time during which goods or money are held or obligations are owed.

The definition of the scope of financial accounting and the other necessary definitions are framed in contemplation of the usual understanding of finance, namely, money and money's worth and the provision of money and money's worth. Financial accounting is concerned with these matters alone. Other characteristics of goods, transactions and so on may not be disregarded by managers and other officers of firms, but the monetary calculus has a capacity for representing only monetary aspects of rights, goods, transactions and events. Its significance is not to be disparaged on the ground that its scope is limited, for all specialized devices are limited in scope. Its significance lies in the fact that in a monetary economy the provision and the continual renewal of the provision of money is a condition of survival.

2. Money, Cash Equivalents and Financial Position

The possession of money (currency or bank deposits) confers the right to demand any and all goods having prices equal in the aggregate to the amount of money held. The usefulness of money and of calculations in terms of the monetary unit depends on this freedom to demand any goods up to the limit of the money held. As it is said, money and money holdings are valued by reason of their general command over goods and services.

If a holder of money has also holdings of other goods and rights, he may be deemed to hold a number of money units equal to the sum of the actual money units held and the number of money units which represent the several resale prices of those other goods and rights. As in the simpler case, this sum represents the holder's command over goods and services in general at any given point of time, and the extent to which the holder is able to liquidate any debt or make any other payment in money at that time.

The quantity of money necessary to buy a given quantity of goods and services in general changes from time to time; the purchasing power of money changes. If the purchasing power of money falls (rises), a firm will be able to buy less (more) in general than previously. A change in the purchasing power of money is clearly a non-transaction event having a monetary consequence; as allowance must be made for the depreciation of durable goods (one type of non-transaction event), so also must allowance be made for the depreciation of the purchasing power of money—but each in its own way.

Although a firm may hold specific goods and trade in specific lines of goods, the prices of those goods are all and always expressed in units of the same general currency at any given time. It might appear that a firm in a particular class of business or industry is concerned only with the purchasing power of money in that industry. But any such idea does violence to the idea of money as a common medium of exchange, and to the idea of the monetary unit being a common denominator at a point of time. A businessman in a specific industry cannot pay his workers, his creditors, his suppliers and his taxes in units of purchasing power, peculiar to his industry. What he is concerned with is the relationship between units of general purchasing power and the specific prices of particular goods. His wisdom expresses itself in the use to which he puts common monetary units in his industry, as, for example, when he purchases goods whose prices move upwards at no less a rate than any rise in the general level of prices. It seems entirely proper that the consequence of such exercises should be made known to managers and to investors; not separately, but as part of the net result of the period or periods in which the advantage becomes apparent. The treatment of asset holdings which we propose would secure this.

The relationship between the monetary measures of the holdings of money, claims to money and goods (collectively the assets) of a firm and the monetary measures of the obligations (equities) of the firm is its financial position. A statement of financial position at a point of time is significant only in so far as it represents the monetary measures of assets and equities in terms of the monetary unit of prevailing purchasing power at that time, and only in so far as the monetary measures of assets are, or are approximations to, resale prices ruling at that time.

The evidence for this view is extensive. The granting of credit by or to a firm may be determined in part by its current ratio; the use of this ratio is misleading unless the numerator approximates the current monetary equivalent of the current assets. The granting of loans for medium and long terms may be determined in part by the borrower's debt to equity ratio; the use of this ratio is misleading unless its denominator represents (through the representation of assets at contemporary cash equivalents) the then current measure of the stockholders' equity. The magnitude of loans against specific collateral is always a function of the contemporary prices of the assets charged, and it may be increased or decreased by the lender as the prices of those assets change. Prior consideration by management of the possibility of obtaining finance in any of these ways would involve resort to the same criteria. In any of these cases, as in all choices, other factors, such as the reputation of the borrower or its managers, may enter into the lender's considerations; but in so far as the lender is guided by the financial facts of the borrower, only the contemporary financial facts are relevant. Furthermore, any calculation of future cash inflows or outflows will be closer approximations if based on contemporary prices than if based on any other prices.

It follows that every transaction shall be recorded at the amount of the price paid, for this is the amount of the actual cash outflow or inflow consequent upon each transaction. It follows also that changes in prices of goods held shall be brought into the accounts for such goods, so that those accounts will always approximate the contemporary cash equivalents of holdings at any time and the financial position of the firm at that time. The different treatments of accounts for cash balances and goods account balances are due to the fact that the representation of money (and other monetary asset) holdings in terms of money involves a one-to-one relationship, whereas the monetary measurements of goods, their prices, are variable relationships.

The traditional objections to the modification of the account balances of non-monetary assets are without logical or practical foundation. It is said, for example, that increases in the prices of goods held should not be brought into the accounts because they are not objectively determined. But every market price is an objectively determinable price; a firm may or may not buy or sell at that price, but this in no way bears on the objectivity of the price. It is said that increases should not be brought in because they may only be temporary; but the same reason is not invoked against bringing into the accounts decreases in prices. It is said that increases in the monetary measures of goods held should not be brought into account until the point of sale, when the amount of the increase in assets is unequivocally determined; by the same reasoning no allowance for depreciation should be brought into the accounts until the amount is unequivocally determined when the asset is finally put out of use; the one event, final sale, determines the magnitude in both cases, yet the accrual principle is applied to one and not to the other. None of the objections is sustained or sustainable on grounds consistent with principles accepted in traditional accounting even now. They can only be sustained by invoking principles which contradict the accrual principle, and which defeat the practically significant object of providing presently relevant and useful information.

3. Expectations of Investors and Financiers

The time-preferences of different persons and firms for the immediate use of money for transaction purposes differ. Those having preferences for the immediate use of money are able to bid for the use of the limited supply available from those who have immediate possession but have preferences for the direct use of money themselves at a later date. The suppliers of money are investors and financiers (creditors); bids are made by virtue of the type of securities offered and the issue prices and other terms at which they are offered.

The outcome expected of an investment in securities is subjective for each investor or financier. But the several kinds of expected outcome may be specified. (1) In general, investors and financiers expect to be able to convert their securities into money when their time preferences for having money become immediate; hence the transferability of securities, and the differing maturities of some classes of security. (2) They expect to be able to convert when alternative opportunities occur for which the prospective gain (loss) appears to them to be greater (less). (3) They expect to be better off by making the investments they in fact make than by making no investment at all. By "being better off" is meant having a greater capacity to command goods and services in general; whether they are or become better off in any other sense depends on how they use this capacity. This greater capacity may arise through periodical dividend or interest payments and through differences between purchase prices and resale prices of securities. (4) They may be presumed to expect to be better off by a greater margin, as a result of their choice of securities, than they would be by the choice of any alternative investment; this because the greater the margin the greater the capacity to satisfy their wants by the direct use of money, and because in general wants exceed means.

The expectations may be described briefly as the time preference for money, the safety of the investment in terms of purchasing power, and the yield in terms of purchasing power. Safety and yield are in no case absolutes; relative safety and relative yield, by comparison with other opportunities, are the criteria. No issuer of securities can know what combination of these three criteria any buyer will prefer. Nor can any buyer be supposed always to give the same weight to each of them, for buyers may make up their portfolios from securities of which they expect quite different outcomes in terms of the three factors. But issuers may be presumed, for their part, to issue securities having features which they expect will be sufficiently attractive, again in terms of these criteria, to ensure that their issues will be taken up in the conditions of the securities market at the time. The reference to safety of investment and yield "in terms of purchasing power" is justified not only on the logical ground that purchasing power rather than numbers of monetary units determines the recipients' capacity for satisfying wants. There is also the evidence of preference for common stocks on the practical ground that appreciation in market prices, rights issues, and rises in dividends are believed to offset diminutions in the purchasing power of money. It may not be argued that holders of preferred stocks and bonds do not conform with the set of expectations we have suggested. Their preferences must be supposed to give less weight to yield and more to safety than the preferences of investors in common stocks.

The characteristics of securities and the nature of the institutions for dealing in securities are predicated on the idea that all holders of securities may at any time want to dispose of them. All holders are potentially short-term holders, either by virtue of the uncertainty of personal exigencies or by virtue of the emergence of opportunities for which superior expectations are entertained. This does not preclude the possibility of some holders turning out to be long-term holders; but even long-term holders may sell and there is no way of foretelling when any holder will want to sell. In order that there shall always be a fair and informed market in securities, a periodical supply of information on financial position and results is necessary. There can be no justification for taking the view, in accounting, that "in the long run total profits will equal the sum of periodical profits however much the profits of particular periods may be influenced by conservatism or other elements of judgement". Conservative representation robs the holder of securities who is obliged to sell during the period in which conservatism is applied of the advantage of knowledge of the actual rights then attaching to his securities, and confers an equivalent advantage of an unrequited and windfall nature on holders during periods in which conservative representation is relaxed. In so far as accounting is expected to provide certain kinds of knowledge it is no part of its function to withhold knowledge of those kinds, whether the withholding is described as conservatism, prudence or by any other name.

4. Financial Information and Financial Supporters

All choices, including all choices of investors and financiers, depend upon both information and expectations. In particular, information on security prices influences choices, for security prices constitute the amounts of money to be invested in securities to obtain the gains expected; expected dividend yields vary as prices vary, inducing some to buy and others to sell as yields move into or out of the preferred range of yields of buyers and sellers as these stand from time to time. Further, information on earnings yields and earnings per share influences the expectations of dividend yields. Further still, information on the present composition of a firm's investment in business assets and the composition of its liabilities influences the expectation of safety of investment and the expectation of gains by way of dividends, interest and shifts in security prices. For example, other things being equal, a firm with a high debt to equity ratio and a low current ratio will be considered to be a more risky investment, requiring a higher dividend yield, than a firm with a low debt to equity ratio; it will be considered to be more risky both because the fixed interest charges take up a large proportion of gross earnings, making net income volatile under shifts in the amount of gross earnings, and because the firm's capacity to adapt its operations to shifts in business is restricted by the extent of its borrowings and the poverty of its net working capital. These considerations apply equally to investors in common stocks and to lenders, for the priorities of lenders are affected as firms shift towards the limits at which the safety of investment and the regularity of interest receipts by lenders become questionable.

At the lower limit, choice depends on the relative advantage of an investment in company securities by comparison with a pure monetary contract with minimal risk, such as an investment in governmental or semi-governmental bonds backed by taxing powers. Much less doubt attends the assessment of the probable monetary outcome of a pure monetary contract than the outcome of a business investment. As the investment of business firms is an investment at varying risks as business conditions change and firms attempt to meet those changes, it is necessary that investors and financiers shall be able to choose whether any given firm shall remain in business or shall be liquidated or sold as a going concern. As long as a firm remains a going business, the several amounts of the present resale prices of its assets determines its capacity to adapt itself, and the total amount of net assets (measured severally at resale prices) is the basis for determining the rate of return—current earnings as a percentage per annum of the current measure of the capital employed. If the liquidation or sale of the business *in toto* is contemplated, it may be possible by inquiry and bargaining to obtain a higher price for the business *in toto* than the aggregate amount of its net assets. But, in the first place, it is the drift in the rate of return which triggers this type of inquiry, and in the second place it is necessary to know the amount of the net assets in order to know whether it is preferable to liquidate than to sell the business *in toto* at any price obtainable from a prospective buyer.

Above this lower limit investors' choices depend on the relative advantage of investments in the securities of different companies. But the calculation of rates of return on the same footing is the only valid way to obtain comparable foundations for expectations.

It will be clear that even though investors and financiers may inform themselves of the general state and trend of business conditions and the general state and trend of particular industries, this itself is insufficient to inform the choice of particular firms as investment opportunities. It should also be clear that to invest merely on the basis of security price movements—for example, by buying when security prices begin to rise, in expectation of further rises—is to commit oneself at least in part to the judgements and expectations of other investors, rather than to the substantive capacities of firms. The securities market in such circumstances is merely a device for shifting wealth from one person to another (through outguessing others) rather than an auxiliary device in the augmentation of general wealth through the selection of the more efficient and the rejection of the less efficient firms.

5. Alternative Bases of Accounting

A number of bases of accounting are in use or have been proposed, the implications of which are that present resale prices of assets are irrelevant to going concerns and irrelevant as information to investors in them. In keeping with the proposition that choice is based on comparison, some brief comparative observations on these are made.

First, there is the position that the prices relevant to going concerns are the original purchase prices of assets, modified by such things as depreciation allowances. This position disregards the perennial flux of prices and the bearing which contemporary prices have on business behavior. If the prices of goods held by a firm rise the firm has a broader equity base for additional borrowing. The firm also has expectations of a greater cash flow than would be indicated by original purchase prices. Present prices are, on both scores, more pertinent to managers', investors' and financiers' judgements and expectations than original purchase prices. Again, original purchase prices represent the consequences of expectations held at the time of purchase; but expectations, like prices, are continually changing, and investors need to have some indication of expectations at a more recent date than the dates at which assets were bought. The resale price at the latest balancing date gives an indication of more recent expectations; for, in so far as a firm still holds an asset, at the prevailing market resale price, the expectation entertained by the management is that the proceeds of continuing to hold and use the asset exceed the expected proceeds of any alternative investment of the amount of the resale price.

It is also said that the original purchase prices provide a foundation for judgements of stewardship, of fiduciary responsibility, in so far as they represent what has been done with the funds subscribed to the firm. If this means only that investors need assurance from time to time that no unwarranted loss or misappropriation of assets has occurred at the hands of or through the negligence of managers, then elementary periodical audit processes should provide that assurance, even without the publication of financial statements. In any case, once the assurance has been given in respect of any year, it is not necessary to give the same assurance about that year in the following year, and the next, and the next . . . as reporting in successive years on the basis of initial cost implies. Further, in so far as financial statements are summaries of the net consequences of past transactions and events, they do not give an account of all the resources which may have come under the control of managers and all the dispositions made of those resources. Nor is it necessary that they should do so. The responsibility of managers is to use the resources under their control from time to time in the most efficient manner they can devise. Whether they have succeeded in this as well as others have succeeded can only be judged by reference to the express consequences of their actions as these are represented by the prices prevailing through the periods reported upon and at the dates of reporting. Indeed, perpetuation of the use of original purchase prices enables better rates of return to be shown the older a firm is (granted a secular tendency for prices to rise), interfering with the possibility of comparing performances of older and more recently established firms on the same footing of contemporary prices.

Second, there is the position that what investors and others need to know is what the future earnings of firms are likely to be; and that the relevant magnitudes are not the purchase prices nor the present market prices but the future yields of assets. However much investors and managers would like to know this, it is of course impossible to know. Like the initial price basis, this basis entails that the future course of events is already given and definite and unalterable, for one can only calculate the probable flows in the future from one single hypothesis of the complex of future operations if one statement of present value is to be presented. Adaptation is brushed aside. Further, there is abundant evidence in the failures of firms, in the failures of managers and in the failures of particular projects to the effect that all such future calculations are hazardous. Further, inasmuch as they represent present position in terms which are the product of calculations upon hypothetical outcomes, they do not represent the magnitude of the resources by which the firm may attempt to secure those outcomes; a hoped for end, but no knowledge of the means of reaching it. These calculations may be made, indeed must be made, to discover whether the commitment of present resources to a given course of action is likely to be worthwhile; but they do not tell us what the magnitudes of the present resources are. The making of these calculations may enable managers to avoid gross errors, but, being entirely subjective and hypothetical, they may also lead into error. The information they yield is complementary to the information yielded by financial accounting; but, being expressions of expectations only, they do not constitute any part of financial accounting which, as we see it, is concerned with expressions of fact.

There can be no legitimate ground, in our opinion, for supposing that investors should be as well-informed as to the detailed operations of firms as managers, nor as understanding of the various specific alternatives open to firms, nor as capable of judging for themselves the expectations of managers. The phenomenon which has become widely and popularly known as the separation of ownership and control is, in fact, nothing more than an example of the specialization of functions, the object of which has always been to make possible the doing of things more efficiently than before. In effect, investors choose those firms and managers which shall have the use of money; managers choose those projects which seem to promise the better returns; both operate in different markets, but they are linked by the fact that operations in the goods and services market provide the prices (i.e., profits, hence dividends and rises in share prices) at which money is made available in the securities markets. Thus, while general knowledge of particular trades is pertinent to investors, no particular knowledge can be expected of them (the alternative is to expect them to be encyclopedists, having particular knowledge of all industries), and no technical explanations of business or accounting methods are likely to be comprehensible to them. They may, however, be presumed to be able to understand the monetary outcomes of business, for safety and yield are matters of common experience to all who have ever had the most elementary form of savings account or bond investment. Managers, on the other hand, are expected to have or to have access to detailed technical knowledge of their own trades, and general knowledge of the effects on firms of evaluations made in the securities market. The focal points of interest of the two classes are different but complementary.

The belief that great detail should be given to investors, including, as some have suggested, statements of divisional profits, and even budgets of future operations, has arisen from too great a preoccupation with the minutiae of particular firms, and too little regard for the fact that investors and financiers must choose between firms. It is well known that too great a supply of signals can lead to vacillation and complete breakdown of the processes of thought as one signal jams another; over-elaboration of detail is likely to produce just this effect, for in matters of detail all firms differ and publication of such details increases exponentially the difficulties of comparing firms. Perhaps the suggestions and demands for the publication of greater amounts of detail arise from perceived shortcomings of financial accounting, but they are no substitute for uniformity and contemporaneity in financial accounting; for monetary measurement and representation constitute the one respect in which diversity of business activities is reducible to common denominators and the one respect which bears on the common interest of all investors and financiers, managers and others, namely monetary returns.

A third position, intermediate to the original purchase price and the present value positions, holds that the monetary measures which are relevant in accounting are replacement prices. This certainly comes closer to a representation in contemporary terms, and one conceivably based on ascertainable prices. But it suffers from the defect that the replacement price of a good does not give an indication of the firm's capacity to meet future conditions, its capacity for adaptation; and from the defect that it presumes replacement of specific assets with identical assets to be among the regular *modi operandi* of firms; by implication it disregards the continuous changes in tastes and technique which modify the operations of firms, making replacement sometimes impossible and sometimes uneconomic.

6. Individual and Aggregate Measures

The preceding argument has been limited to the establishment of the importance of obtaining aggregates in terms of contemporary prices at each balancing date. We wish to stress that the obtaining of aggregates or aggregate measures is the necessary end of financial accounting. It has been objected that to take the several assets of a firm and to add their present resale prices does not give the expected proceeds of any possible grouping of those assets. This we freely admit, as we admit that the present resale price may well be more or less than the firm does subsequently obtain by use or sale. Resale prices, and indeed current purchase prices in some cases are, however, surrogates for the general property, current monetary equivalent. The object of accounting seems to be, from our examination of the uses to which its products may be put, to discover positions and changes in position, expressed in monetary equivalents from time to time. It is not to assert that any precise given sum will be realized on the sale of any asset or combination of assets; it is rather to give the best possible indication of position and results, so that actions thereafter may be taken in the light of this knowledge. Only when investors and others obtain a representation of the financial position and results is it possible to decide whether past policies have been as effective as the policies of other firms or as effective as they were expected to be; and only then does it become apparent to managers whether they should aim for greater liquidity of assets, whether greater investments in assets of different liquidities is possible, whether efforts to make profits should be intensified, and so on. In short, it is the discovered aggregate result which influences behavior in the following period, not some possible future action which influences discovery of the results of the past period.

The mechanism by which these responses to a financial position and result are put into effect is the series of directives given by management, directives which, of course, may be changed from time to time during any accounting period as the firm interacts with the commodities and securities markets. Buying and selling operations and the concomitant bargaining are not done with reference to balance sheet or other account balances; they are done within the framework of managerial directives and the present potentialities of the market. But because at the year's end, or more frequently, the results come under review by investors and creditors, managers themselves must try to ensure that the rate of return, solvency and other aspects of the firm will continue to justify the support of stockholders and creditors.

It is not expected, nor can it be expected, that managers will not make mistakes of judgement. Inasmuch as decisions and choices are made for an unknown future, expectations are always likely to be at variance with subsequent attainments. What is expected, however, is that on balance there will be a favorable aggregate outcome in any period. It is the business of managers to change their directives when the outcomes are or are expected to be unfavorable. And if, in their judgement, it is impossible to change from one directive or policy to another, or possible only at an uneconomic cost, it is their business to find additional ways of offsetting unfavorable outcomes. These steps are all part of the adaptive process.

It follows that to break down operations and results may do injustice to managers and may misrepresent the adaptability and performance of them and of the firm. It seems reasonable to treat the whole complex of activities and effects of decisions as integrally related to one another, for they are so related. It cannot be known, independently of the subjective assertions of managers, whether a course of action was taken entirely on its own merits or for its side-effects, or to what extent for both reasons. Gains in command of purchasing power from traders' margins, from borrowing in anticipation of a fall in the purchasing power of money, from buying in anticipation of rises in particular prices of inventories or durable assets, from so-called non-operating activities, are all gains to be sought; none is intrinsically more desirable than another, and a gain of one kind may necessarily entail a loss of some other kind. Gain in the aggregate is what matters; the only kind of gain (or loss) which it seems to be legitimate to isolate is a pure windfall, the consequence of an event which was in principle unforeseeable.

Now, although all buying and selling is done in the context of the day-to-day state of markets, of buying and selling prices, the periodical determination of aggregate gains must take account of the drift in the purchasing power of money. There is no simple way of doing this except on an aggregate basis. The monetary measures of all bargains during a period are in units of the purchasing power prevailing from time to time during the period; the sum of the measures of all transactions will be a sum expressed in units of various purchasing powers. This applies alike to sales, purchases, common costs of production and administration and to specific price adjustments made during the holding of goods. It is necessary to set off against the resultant of these transactions the effect of the drift in purchasing power, indicators of which only become available periodically. The double-entry process gives a ready method of periodical reduction or augmentation as the case may be. If the opening (closing) stock of assets is represented at then current prices, the amount of the stockholders' equity will be in monetary units of the then current purchasing power. But if the purchasing powers of the monetary unit at the two dates differ, the opening measure of stockholders' equity must be augmented (reduced) by a sufficient number of monetary units, if purchasing power of the unit has fallen (risen), to secure the maintenance of capital in purchasing power terms. This number is obtained by applying to the opening measure of the opening stockholders' equity the proportionate change in the index of the purchasing power of money. The amount does not represent an increase in command over resources in general (when prices have risen), and the amount of the total surpluses of the year must be reduced by it to obtain net income (before tax). Thus, even though the component items of an income account may be expressed in monetary units of mixed purchasing power, this method of adjustment gives the net income of the year in monetary units of the purchasing power prevailing at the end of the year. It is logically permissible, then, to relate this amount to the adjusted opening amount or to the closing amount of stockholders' equity to obtain a rate of return, for both numerator and denominator will be in units of the same purchasing power.

In further defense of this procedure we make a comparison with a fourth proposed method of accounting, a method of adjusting original purchase prices of assets by the use of indexes of changes in the price level, price-level accounting. This process results in the representation of assets in monetary amounts which may differ materially from the contemporary prices of specific goods held by a firm; the emergent representation of financial position may diverge from the actual position of the firm in relation to the rest of the environment, and the net income will be affected correspondingly. Suppose, for example, that a firm is running down, its products are suffering a decline in demand and its plant and machinery are therefore falling in value; and suppose that the general level of prices is rising. These are all eminently possible; firms fail even in boom years. Price-level accounting would in these circumstances show rising amounts for specific assets the values of which were falling, a rising stockholders' equity when in fact it was falling, a falling debt to equity ratio when in fact the effective ratio is rising. It would also show lower net profits than in fact were being made, because of the higher depreciation charges on fictitiously higher asset values. These divergences between the substantive facts and the representations work at cross purposes to some extent; but, in so far as decisions are made on the basis of the rate of return, they both conspire to interfere with the rehabilitation of the firm and to hasten its demise. In conditions of the reverse kind, in which the rate of growth of a firm exceeds that of firms in general, financial position would be understated relatively to the prevailing prices of the firm's assets, and income would be overstated to the extent of the difference between depreciation charges based on price-level adjusted values and charges based on prevailing prices.

Furthermore, price-level accounting appears to involve the implication that, say, a rise in the general level of prices automatically leads to a rise in well-offness, inasmuch as assets come to be represented by greater monetary amounts and the stockholders' equity is equally augmented. But, in fact, the effect of a rise in the general level of prices of itself is to diminish well-offness; only if the actual prices of specific assets rise at the same rate is well-offness maintained. The disregard of the counteracting effects of changes in specific prices and changes in the purchasing power of the monetary unit constitutes what may be described as a logical solecism of price-level accounting. The procedure we proposed earlier in this section gives explicit recognition to these separate and counteracting effects.

7. Accounting as Feedback and Foundation

The conclusion to which we are led is that, to serve managers, investors and financiers, accounting on a continuously contemporary basis is required; and that such an accounting will serve them all equally well in the only way accounting can serve, namely by aggregate representation of the financial consequences of what has transpired.

As informational feedback, financial accounting serves a function which is not otherwise served. The consequences of small, localized, specific acts can be observed by those on the spot; they can modify their actions (decisions, policies) in the light of what they observe, from observational feedback. But at the level of general administration and of the financial supporters of the firm, organizational and spatial distance, and the complexity of internal relationships and effects, prevent direct observation of consequences. The pertinent consequences are, of course, the changes in the firm's financial position in relation to the rest of the community in which it operates; changes in other than financial respects must be observed in other ways. If we assume the necessity of adaptive behavior, neither the management nor the financial supporters of firms can wait for the long-run consummation of the stream of events which constitute the life of the firm; they require periodical reports of what has transpired in the recent past from time to time, of all that has transpired in the immediately past period, whether by action or inaction on the part of the management. Informational feedback, descriptive of the change in the firm's position in relation to its economic environment is the only way they have of knowing whether, in general, the firm's operations and the policies of its managers are as effective, in terms of financial outcome, as the operations and policies of other firms in the same economic environment. There are no absolute tests of effectiveness; these tests are all relative. And this entails that all firms shall do their accounting on uniform principles, regardless of diversity in specific business operations.

As informational foundation for expectations of the future, again accounting serves a function which is not otherwise served. Businessmen and investors must formulate their own expectations of firms; but expectations which have no basis in the financial facts of a firm's operations and position from time to time are nothing more than vague guessing; the frustration and the satisfaction of such expectations are equiprobable. It is, however, a function of accounting to increase the probability of favorable choices; it will only do so if the financial position represented from time to time coincides with the position as prevailing prices establish it.

On these grounds we hold that continuously contemporary accounting is logically and practically imperative, and that the following principles constitute the foundations of financial accounting:—

(a) The users of financial statements have varied points of view and entertain varied expectations. These require to be informed from time to time by statements of fact, as well and reliably as the facts of the time can be ascertained and stated.

(b) Buyers, sellers and holders of securities may variously interpret the facts, giving different weight to the facts in the light of information from other sources and their general expectations; but no worthwhile expectation may be formed of any specific investment at any specific time without knowledge of the facts.

(c) Present facts are ascertainable; the facts of a company's financial position at a point of time are ascertainable by reference to the market prices of assets and the amounts of its equities or by deliberately selected approximations to prices, but independently of wishes or expectations.

(d) Only if financial position is ascertained, independently of expectations, at successive dates is it possible to deduce the incomes of the periods denoted by those dates.

(e) Only if all measures appearing in financial statements are measures as of the point of time or the period to which the statements relate can valid inferences be drawn from ratios of different aggregates.

(f) As investors choose between alternative security investments on the basis of expected financial outcomes (capital safety, dividends and other gains), and as choice involves comparison of the factual basis of expectations, uniformity of principles and practices (yielding information of uniform quality) for all firms is indicated.

APPENDIX.

At the beginning of the paper it was suggested that a choice must be made between alternative systems of accounting if vacillation and recurrent exposure to recrimination are to be avoided, and indeed if accounting is to perform a specialized function well. An attempt is made here to present an evaluation of the main types of system used or suggested.

The main differences between the systems relate to methods of asset valuation and the five systems compared differ primarily in this respect; the names used reflect the general principles of asset valuation employed; variants are disregarded in all cases. The systems are:—

Initial price accounting (I.P.A.): the general basis of asset valuation is the initial purchase price of each asset in possession at balance date.

Price level accounting (P.L.A.): the general basis is the original cost modified by application of a general index of changes in prices. Because of its link with original cost, this system has many of the characteristics of O.C.A.

Discounted value accounting (D.V.A.): the general basis is the discounted expected net product of each asset. In essence all such values are based on sets of hypotheses about the future, including the primary hypothesis that the firm's operations will remain substantially the same.

Replacement price accounting (R.P.A.): the general basis is the replacement cost of assets. This entails that replacement is intended and feasible, and is thus akin to D.V.A. in the assumption that the firm's operations will remain substantially the same.

Continuously contemporary accounting (C.C.A.): the general basis is the measure given by prices of assets held as they are evidenced, at balance dates, in the resale markets of those assets. The system is the system alluded to in the paper, and developed at length in the writer's *Accounting, Evaluation and Economic Behavior.*

In the following table the criteria are of two classes: A, technical accounting questions, and B, questions on the practical utility of the products of the systems. The questions in each group and in the set as a whole are not mutually exclusive, so that the mere number of "yes" and "no" entries is not to be taken as giving the weight of evidence conclusively. These numbers do, however, indicate the relative positions of the systems in such an evaluation scheme. There may be other criteria, and the reader may not agree with the scores given in every case. But, if a choice is to be made, some such scheme must be employed, and must include at least these questions.

Comparison of Five Accounting Systems

		I.P.A.	P.L.A.	D.V.A.	R.P.A.	C.C.A.
A1	Is it, in principle, a double-entry system?	Yes	Yes	Yes	Yes	Yes
A2	Are its transaction inputs, in principle, facts?	Yes	Yes	Yes	Yes	Yes
A3	Are its transformations (depreciation, inventory valuations, etc.), in principle, facts?	No	No	No	Yes	Yes
A4	Are its transformed magnitudes measures?	No	No	No	Yes	Yes
A5	Are its transformed magnitudes contemporary?	No	No	Yes	Yes	Yes
A6	Do its transformations give prompt effect to relative price changes?	No	No	No	Yes	Yes
A7	Does it give a comprehensive history of the relationships and transactions of the firm? (Is it isomorphic?)	No	No	No	No	Yes
A8	Is aggregation of measures of items logically possible?	No	Yes	Yes	Yes	Yes
A9	Is it a representation of facts, or, alternatively, does its theory provide for other ways of getting contemporary facts?	No	No	No	No	Yes
B1	Are the results neutral as to specific future actions?	Yes	Yes	No	No	Yes
B2	Are individual measures relevant at stated dates to choice or adaptation?	No	No	No	No	Yes
B3	Is income a measure of general command of goods and services?	No	No	No	No	Yes
B4	Do magnitudes provides a basis for comparison of present operations with future potential variants?	No	No	No	No	Yes
B5	Is a valid current ratio given?	No	No	No	No	Yes
B6	Is a valid debt to equity ratio given?	No	No	No	No	Yes
B7	Is a valid rate of return given? (Is rate of return comparable with rates of return on pure money contracts and other opportunities?)	No	No	No	No	Yes
B8	Are interfirm comparisons of ratios valid?	No	No	No	Yes	Yes
B9	Do balance sheets and income accounts fairly present positions at stated dates and changes between those dates?	No	No	No	No	Yes

41

CONTINUOUSLY CONTEMPORARY ACCOUNTING—ADDITIVITY AND ACTION*

This note is prompted by criticisms of some elements of the theory of accounting presented in *Accounting Evaluation and Economic Behavior*[1]. No short name was given to the theory in that place. At other times subsequently the phrase "continuously contemporary accounting" has been used as the theory is directed towards the provision of continuously contemporary financial information. I will continue to use it, hoping to avoid the possibility that the theory may be dubbed a CCE theory, alluding to the use of current cash equivalents, whereas the implications of the theory are much broader than the particular concepts it employs.

The differences of Professors Larson and Schattke appear to lie in their concept of "financial action". The alleged refutation of the additivity of current cash equivalents, it will be found, turns on argument relating to mercantile action, rather than to financial action or even metrological action. Such mixtures of considerations have provided the justification for many rules and practices in accounting that are inconsistent with other rules. Thus, for example, though it is said to be one of the functions of accounting to disclose what has taken place, it is also held to be legitimate that accounting statements should not overstate (but, by implication, may understate) what has taken place. And in case it may be contended that conservatism is not now an avowed principle, the fact remains that the lower of cost and market rule and the last in first out rule for inventories (both tending to the understatement of the monetary measures of inventories) are still endorsed and used. This inconsistency between disclosure and conservatism only arises if we regard the accounting function as appropriating part of the managerial function. It may well be a safe rule of business behavior to be conservative in some respects; but I find it impossible to accept any justification for an accounting procedure which, by being "conservative", fails to disclose or discloses in a distorted manner the consequences of what has happened. "Distorted" is used quite deliberately, for it is known, even by those who practice it, that the effect of the rules mentioned is to represent inventory measures by smaller monetary amounts than more recent and therefore more relevant purchase prices would justify.

---

* First published in *The Accounting Review,* Vol. XLII, No. 4, October 1967 pp. 751-57.

[1] Kermit Larson and R. W. Schattke, "Current Cash Equivalent, Additivity and Financial Action", *The Accounting Review*, October 1966, pp. 634-41.

It has been one of my aims to avoid the confusion to which the mixing of ascribed functions gives rise. The emphasis on the specialization of functions and on the consequent differentiation of orientations of specialists within firms is an important element of my position. Larson and Schattke's criticism shows that my explication has been less than convincing, at least to some, and I welcome the opportunity of attempting to clarify the issues.

Macroscopic and Microscopic Considerations

It is beyond dispute that financial statements have reference, in some sense, to the financial outcomes of past actions: to the net change in the residual equity and to the change in the composition of assets and equities. They relate only to financial consequences and characteristics. They say nothing about purely technical or purely mercantile outcomes of possibilities or positions. They do not indicate the age, the technical capacity, the spatial distribution or any similar characteristic of assets; they say nothing about the numbers and types of customers, suppliers, or workers of firms. For information on all such matters as these, business managers turn to other sources. The capacity of accounting to represent the aggregative consequences of actions taken in terms of the current monetary unit, and the value of aggregative statements of results and positions from time to time as indicators of possibilities and constraints (for the present command of resources constitutes the constraints of future actions), are the reasons for the widespread use of financial statements and the sources of the usefulness of accounting. Accounting may serve other functions. But because aggregate consequences are the financial measure of success, and because aggregate positions from time are determinants of future actions, the importance of the function of providing aggregative statements cannot be gainsaid. No process other than accounting serves this function.

It is both convenient and consistent with the way in which business is done to distinguish two types of action and two types of consideration antecedent to action. To these two types different contrasting designations may be given; we will use the terms "macroscopic" and "microscopic" as having some allusion to the scope or breadth of view required for the two types. A macroscopic action (or consideration) is one which has or contemplates effects of a substantial kind on the position of the firm, one which entails a series of consequences ramifying through several or many divisions or functions of the firm. A microscopic action (or consideration) is one which has or contemplates effects of a localized kind.

Thus, by way of contrast, a liquidity crisis is a macroscopic consideration; an excessive investment or overstocking of any given line of inventory is generally a microscopic consideration. The effects of many microscopic actions are in the aggregate a macroscopic consequence; a macroscopic consequence of a series of past actions may become a macroscopic consideration leading to a change in the criteria for subsequent microscopic actions. For example, a liquidity crisis may lead to reductions of individual purchases, to sales at reduced prices, to limitations of the credit given to particular customers. But no single microscopic action can influence future macroscopic considerations or actions. The distinction is consistent with the fact that all minor decisions are expected to be taken within the framework of, and subject to, the constraints of major decisions.

Financial statements relate only to macroscopic effects and considerations. Accounting embraces the recording of the financial effects of all specific transactions and events, it is true, and with an object—the protection of an entity's specific resources—that has merit of its own. There are strong grounds on which it can be argued that the protective function is served only by accounts dealing with minutiae, and never by aggregative statements. Yet aggregative statements are prepared periodically, for an additional purpose, namely, to give the aggregative effects of some sub-classes of transactions or events. Business income, business capital are macroscopic concepts; rates of return and measures of solvency are macroscopic concepts. All are necessary in the process of appraising the performances, positions, and prospects of firms. The requirement of additivity is not only "vitally important" in the system I described; it is an unavoidable requirement under any circumstances in which the magnitudes of the variables just mentioned and others like them are informational premises of choice.

Larson and Schattke observe that "additivity of course occupies an important place in traditional accounting". But this is patently false. Addition, not additivity, occupies an important place; but whether the magnitudes added are in fact addable is a question which is not explicitly raised, and is implicitly disregarded, in traditional accounting. Magnitudes measured in different scales and under different environmental conditions are added as if the differences were of no consequence whatever. Such a form of accounting cannot represent the macroscopic outcome of past events and transactions, nor, therefore, the macroscopic considerations pertinent to future actions.

The *ex post* relationship between the macroscopic and the microscopic is merely a matter of faithful recording and of careful transformation of recorded measures to units of common dimension and common temporal significance for the purpose of aggregation. The *ex ante* relationship between macroscopic facts, macroscopic financial objectives, and microscopic future actions is a matter of managerial choice. Given the position of a firm at a point of time (its solvency, the composition of its assets and equities) and the expectations and aspirations of its managers, there will be established such things as gross-profit rates and mark-up rates, the volume of credit business permissible, the expected collection period, all for the guidance of the buyers and sales personnel of the firm. These are all macroscopic constraints, not microscopic constraints.

The discretion given to the firm's officers is usually a discretion to sell particular goods above, at, or below, the target rates, but so that the aggregate consequence is the result and position which the macroscopic constraints entail. Some goods may be sold at losses, some at high profit rates, and so on; but the maintenance of solvency and the earning of an income consistent with continued financial support condition the particular (microscopic) bargains which the sales and purchasing officers strike. The target rates may be changed by senior management from time to time, even during any accounting period, as the cumulative effects of a period's transactions and conditions become known through the accounting system. But the targets that stand at any time are what buyers and salesmen must take into account in making bargains. They are engaged in mercantile operations subject to specified financial constraints.

The Larson and Schattke Example

The Larson and Schattke interpretation has no place for such constraints, no way of ascertaining the macroscopic conditions that influence particular mercantile transactions. They object to the determination of financial position by reference to the current cash equivalents of assets individually, on the ground that a firm may be able to sell a group of assets for a greater or smaller sum than could be obtained by selling assets singly. They cite as an example a firm having goods x and y whose separate resale prices are \$10 and \$15 at a given balance sheet date. The resale price of x and y together may be greater than, equal to, or less than \$25. We consider the case before indicating its inconsistency with the system we proposed. If the resale price of x and y together is less than \$25, the firm would not sell the combination at such a smaller price at the time. If the resale price of x and y together exceeds \$25, the excess is a potential profit which buyers may, in the event, not pay and which the firm, in any case, may not anticipate. Whether or not a buyer will take x and y will be determined by many things; whether or not he wants both at the time of any offer; whether the vendor wants to part with both rather than the one only at any time; and so on. We do not know the answers to these questions. The object of finding resale prices is not to discover what is expected of any future transaction; it is simply to assign a contemporary measure to an asset. If therefore there are any reasons why \$25 is a less satisfactory measure of the current cash equivalent than any other measure, I do not as yet apprehend them; and Larson and Schattke do not provide any circumstance in which it is obviously appropriate to take some other measure.

But further, the Larson and Schattke criticism disregards at least three principles (specialization, ignorance of the future, and the temporal sequence of information and choice) which are part of the theory of continuously contemporary accounting—and this in spite of their repeated insistence that they are taking all elements of the theory, other than the additivity of current cash equivalents, for granted. Their example presumes that the accountant knows what goods will be sold and in what combinations and at what prices before the point of sale is reached. The theory of continuously contemporary accounting depends on no such presumption. It recognizes the impossibility of knowing future events and their outcomes in the present. By virtue of the principles of the specialization of functions it grants the superior knowledge of sales personnel as to what goods can be sold and in what combinations; and it grants the possibility that buying and selling personnel may influence the price of every bargain struck on behalf of the firm. And it recognizes knowledge of past events and present position as temporally antecedent to the determination of profit objectives and hence of prices for the period in which goods on hand are expected to be sold. The theory has a defined logical and temporal structure for the steps which different officers of a firm take in the course of setting financial constraints, buying and selling; the Larson and Schattke example appears instead to assume, simply, an all-knowing accountant which to say the least is quite unrealistic.

The theory of continuously contemporary accounting does not represent a system giving certain knowledge of present position and past events, much less certain knowledge of the future. In specifying CCE as the property to be measured and resale prices as the ideal measures of CCE, it is concerned with obtaining the most probable monetary measures of assets and equities at a point of time; it says nothing of what the future may bring, of what package deals marketing divisions may find possible. It is concerned only with providing financial information.

Additivity

In dealing with additivity I made frequent use of the words "combine" and "combination". The context of the discussion indicates that these terms have reference to monetary measures; to the combining of monetary measures, not to the combining of goods or rights, nor to the monetary measures of any specific combination of goods and/or rights as such. The discussion is directed to the resolution of the problem of aggregating differing measures through time, measures taken in a scale which itself varies through time. In contemplating a future action which appears to require a sum of money larger than the proceeds of any particular asset, managers will wish to consider the various combinations of assets whose sale will yield the necessary sum, so that they may choose the combination which is expected to have the optimum effect on future earnings. Only if they may make alternative hypothetical combinations of the present measures of assets can they discover which combinations to examine further for their effects on future earnings. And only if the measures themselves are in the same contemporary scale may they make alternative hypothetical combinations of the measures of assets at a given time[2]. Larson and Schattke say nothing whatever about the problem of reducing diverse measures to units of homogeneous dimension; clearly they miss the whole point of this part of the argument.

---

[2] See *Accounting, Evaluation and Economic Behavior*, pp. 92-3.

But we consider their views. They say "we may argue . . . that CCE and numerosity are separate and distinct properties, and that, while measurements of each may be attempted, it is not appropriate to attribute characteristics of the latter to measurements of the former". I am at a loss to understand this. Consider an analogous example. A rod has a given length; to obtain the measure of its length we apply it to a scale calibrated in inches. The function of such a scale is to give the number of inches (the numerosity of the units of length) in the length of the rod (and all other such objects). It cannot be said that the measure of the length of the rod and the numerosity of inches corresponding to that length are "separate and distinct properties". Rather, the choice of a certain unit is necessary in order to enable us to quantify the property, length, of the rod. So also with current cash equivalent and the numerosity of monetary units by which it is denoted.

Larson and Schattke appeal to Hempel on additivity, but they make no attempt to apply Hempel's terms to the theory they criticize. We make good the omission. Hempel's definition is as follows: A quantity s is additive relatively to a combining operation o if $s\ (x \circ y) = s(x) + s(y)$ whenever x, y and $x \circ y$ belong to the domain in which s is defined[3].

Let x and y be two parcels of money of a given currency, and let o be the operation of putting the two parcels together. Let s be the scale of units of money of the given currency. There is an "operational interpretation for the numerical addition of the s values of the two different objects" x and y, as Hempel requires. And x, y and $x \circ y$ belong to the same domain in which s is defined; they are all sums of money. There is nothing "artificial" about the operation o; an operational interpretation can be given for the numerical addition of the s values of the two objects x and y even if x consists entirely of metallic tokens and y entirely of currency bills. Likewise there is an operational interpretation for the numerical addition of the s values of x and y if x is entirely in currency and y is entirely in things for which the monetary equivalent is discoverable, for monetary equivalent is simply the s value of such things as such value is given by market prices. The theory of continuously contemporary accounting meets the Hempel test exactly.

A Fruitful Theory

Larson and Schattke are equally reticent about the grounds for their assertion that the theory of continuously contemporary accounting does not lead to a "simple and fruitful theory". Again we will make good the deficiency; we give only some of the considerations.

The summation of current cash equivalents of assets gives the firm's present command of purchasing power, for any and every

[3] Carl G. Hempel, *Fundamentals of Concept Formation in Empirical Science*, International Encyclopedia of Unified Science, Chicago, The University of Chicago, 1952, Vol. 2, No. 7, p. 75.

possible action for which it may need purchasing power, and without any special presumptions about the firm's possibilities of taking a long time to dispose of any assets in order to obtain the best possible prices, or about the strains it may be under to dispose of assets in minimal time. If we assume informed choice, special presumptions about future behavior must be avoided in the course of finding the facts on which future behavior will be decided. The total or some sub-total of the current cash equivalents of assets is relevant:—

(i) to any consideration of the solvency of the firm;

(ii) to any consideration of the settlement of any obligations of the firm;

(iii) to any consideration of the capacity of the firm to buy any good or goods it does not at the time possess, the possession of which is expected to be more advantageous than the least advantageous of the goods presently in possession and whose aggregate current cash equivalent would furnish the price of the more advantageous goods;

(iv) to any consideration of the capacity of the firm to borrow on the collateral security of goods in possession, for current cash equivalents are the only objectively determinable basis for the security of creditors' advances;

(v) to any consideration of ways and means of increasing profitability (by seeking out markets which will pay higher prices, a time-consuming process not available to firms under liquidity strains) or of increasing liquidity if this appears to be necessary for survival (survival being the preferable alternative to allowing creditors to interfere with the firm's independence);

(vi) to any consideration of the merits of the whole undertaking relative to alternative investment of the proceeds of liquidation. (If switching to an alternative investment comes to be preferred, the net assets or the firm sold as a going concern may realize more or less (not necessarily either) than the current cash equivalents, but this cannot be discovered until bargains are actually driven.)

These examples will suffice. Note that (i), (ii) and (iv) relate to the money or securities market; (iii), (iv) and (vi) relate to the firm's factor markets; and (iv) and (v) relate to the firm's product markets. In short, then, we have one concept which is relevant to considerations in all classes of market in which firms operate. In each of the examples, of course, current cash equivalents of assets are not the only considerations, for every choice involves contrasting one set of considerations with another or others. But current cash equivalents are the only considerations common to all. A concept the quantification of which enters into so many problem situations surely has the merit of simplifying the theory of choice in response to financial information. As for the fruitfulness of the theory, let it be demonstrated that any other theory yields a homogeneous magnitude or set of magnitudes which can enter so freely into combination or comparison with other magnitudes in the contemplation of financial aspects of business problems. The theory surely is fruitful in so far as it entails a form of accounting in which individual measures are additive because they are, in principle, taken in the same context in units of the same dimension. If it is to be deposed, let it be shown that some other theory is equally fruitful.

Some Other Matters

Larson and Schattke's attempt to introduce intangibles into the counterargument is, of course, a departure from the "other aspects of the theory" which they proposed to accept. But it puts them in a position of asserting some things which appear to lack support. "... individually nonseverable, intangible factors ... are of great importance ... in setting the limits of financial action in markets", they say. If this is so, why, then, do companies eliminate intangibles from their balance sheets? And why do analysts disregard the magnitudes shown for intangibles in balance sheets? And why do accountants protest that non-purchased goodwill should never be written into balance sheets?

Again: "As assets are combined into various collections, the CCE of the collection, due to positive or negative goodwill, may be greater or less than the summation of the CCE's of all constituent assets. These intangible factors become 'embodied' only in asset collections ...". Now if intangible factors become "embodied" we should first be told how, but we are not told. And if the measure of their embodiment may be positive or negative we must know in advance what the measure of goodwill is. But of course we cannot say a firm has a goodwill (or its opposite) until by its actions it proves to have earned superior profits (that is, if we follow the traditional ideas on goodwill), which means that in order to measure the monetary property of the assets at the end of a year, and hence to discover its profits, we have to know a magnitude which we cannot discover until we have calculated its profits. It should be obvious that this is an untenable position, a position which the theory under criticism escapes altogether.

Larson and Schattke have whetted my anxiety to clarify. Perhaps they will reveal the "many points" it is possible to criticize—their disagreement with the "basic assumptions about human behavior", the faults they pick with basic definitions adopted for economic terms, the "certain factors" which are left out, the technical faults in the deductive approach. Perhaps they will say in what sense I excluded discounted cash flows from "the accounting discipline" when I did no such thing; nowhere did I discuss "the accounting discipline" to the best of my recollection. Perhaps they will explain how the importance of CCE is asserted and the role of discounted net cash proceeds is de-emphasized, when in fact the roles of both in the process of choice is a fundamental point in the theory of continuously contemporary accounting. Perhaps they will answer the "interesting question—should accounting be a valuation system, rather than a measurement system?", a question which I thought I had taken pains to answer.

As for their conclusions, they do not, as they assert, demonstrate that CCE is a non-additive property, because they do not discuss the criteria for addition. They only disagree with the manner in which the singular measures are taken and that is a very different matter. But then, of course, they did not take cognizance of the fact that exactly the same problem must arise in the case of any inventory valuation method in traditional accounting which has reference to "market", and indeed to "cost"; and presumably there is some evidence to the effect that it is solved in some manner. If two theories have some point in common there seems little point in attacking only one of them, for what we need from criticism is a demonstration of relative superiority or inferiority.

42

MEASURES AND VALUES*

More than one kind of financial information is necessary to every choice; monetary magnitudes of quite different types are necessary. At the risk of being tedious they may be mentioned. First, there are the monetary magnitudes (measures) of the assets and equities a firm has at any time. Second, there are the monetary magnitudes (valuations, as distinct from measures) obtained by discounting the expected cash inflows and outflows from proceeding in the same way as up to the point of choice, and from every alternative course which seems to be feasible at the point of choice. There is no problem of dealing in money and goods in a deliberate and informed manner for which both types of magnitudes are not necessary.

A Managerial Problem

Consider first a managerial problem—the switching of the holding of one asset (A) for the holding of another (B). The requirements for a solution of this problem are as follows:—

Let $CCE(A)$ be the current cash equivalent of A.

$P(B)$ be the purchase price of B.

$V(A)$ be the net present value of continuing to use A up to some specified time, exclusive of $CCE(A)$.

$V(B)$ be the net present value of using B, assuming for convenience the same time horizon, but exclusive of $P(B)$.

Assume, in the first instance, that $CCE(A) = P(B)$, so that no other change in the use of funds occurs.

Then, all other things being equal, the firm will choose A if

$$V(A) - CCE(A) > V(B) - P(B) \qquad (1)$$

and B if

$$V(A) - CCE(A) < V(B) - P(B) \qquad (2)$$

which under the assumption abovementioned makes the resolution of the problem depend on whether $V(A)$ is greater than or less than $V(B)$. But notice particularly that it is first necessary to discover that $CCE(A) = P(B)$.

Assume in the second instance that $CCE(A) < P(B)$, and that the deficit must be made up by borrowing, at a cost, the present value of

* First published in *The Accounting Review,* Vol. XLIII, No. 2, April 1968, pp. 239-47. This is a reply to George J. Staubus, "Current Cash Equivalent for Assets: A Dissent," *The Accounting Review,* October 1967.

which is I for the stipulated time of the project; and let $V(B)$ be exclusive of I.

Then, all other things being equal, the firm will choose (A) if

$$V(A) - CCE(A) > V(B) - P(B) - I \tag{3}$$

Notice in this case that it is first necessary to discover $CCE(A)$ in order to discover the amount to be borrowed, for on this depends the value of I.

The demonstration applies to all combinations of the elements, including cases where the time horizons differ, for the discounting entailed in $V(A)$, $V(B)$ and I allows for this. In all cases knowledge of $CCE(A)$ is necessary to choice; I have not claimed that it is both necessary and sufficient. It should be clear from the above expressions that no single magnitude ever can be both necessary and sufficient.

Professor Staubus contends that decision makers want to know the present value of an "asset's contribution to future cash flows", or as they are maximizers, the "maximum time-adjusted cash potential". Presumably in both cases the terms are to be understood as net of costs of continuing to use an asset, for maximizers would not be interested in gross inflows. Before going further it should be pointed out that no decision makers can ever know the present value of an asset's contribution to future cash flows. All they can know is what some specific person thinks may be the contribution to future cash flows. Now, there is no way in which "what any person thinks may be the contribution" may be challenged (for no two persons have equal degrees of optimism, pessimism, pugnacity, and so on). It must follow that any statement purporting to say something about what someone thinks may say more about the person than about the firm and its assets. And as one of the objects of reading the accounts is to assess "the accomplishments of the company", it seems, at least to me, patently improper to judge past accomplishments on the basis of what some person (a manager, in particular) may think about the future. This is mixing two quite distinct things. One cannot assess how far he has travelled in the last hour by taking account of where he expects to be an hour hence. He may take account of both in making the whole of a journey, but progress to date and what lies ahead are in no sense the same; neither is part of the other.

But to return to the substance of the argument: what is the meaning of maximum time-adjusted cash potential? This surely is the same as $V(A)$ in the example instanced above, on the assumption that managers are maximizers. At the very least, Staubus' proposal comes no closer to giving all the monetary magnitudes necessary for choice than does current cash equivalent; it supplies no more than one of the four (at least) necessary magnitudes. But notice the defects of $V(A)$. Its magnitude depends on someone's assessment or stipulation of the particular receipts and particular outlays, period by period, which are expected to ensue from the continued use of A; on someone's stipulation of the discount rate; on the assumption that A will be used to the stipulated future date—all of which are speculative and in no sense factual as at the date of any balance sheet or choice.

Further $V(A)$ or MATACAP, to use Staubus' acronym, will never tell what is available as asset-backing for a loan management may seek, and never help in obtaining an indication of the financial capacity of a firm at a point of time to switch from one asset to another, with or without upsetting the investment in other assets. Only current cash equivalent will help; and even it will give no more than an approximation for it takes no account of hard bargaining or bargaining from weakness.

An Investor's Problem

Consider, now, an investor's problem—the switching of the holding of one security (E) for a holding of another security (F). We could consider the case of switching a holding of cash for securities or securities for cash; but the case we choose to consider is inclusive of more of the variables than these simpler cases. The requirements for the solution of this problem are substantially similar to those for a switching of business assets. But we have to take account of the particular part the financial statements of the two companies may play in the decision.

At the moment of choice, $CCE(E)$ and $P(F)$ are given; they are prices of the securities. For the investor at the time, the contents of the companies' financial statements do not affect these. The contents of financial statements can only affect $V(E)$ and $V(F)$. In very few cases can an investor know the specific consequences of the choices which managers have in fact made; this would be possible, for example, where the specific security investments of the firm and the dividend or interest income received from these were matters of public knowledge; but the circumstance is rare. All that investors can know is the general effect of all the choices or decisions of management taken together. If we were to expect them to be able to judge whether or not the specific choices of management were good, bad, or indifferent, for every one of the firms in which a given investor may invest, we would be expecting the impossible. We would be expecting that investors could know and would know more about more firms than any manager could know—which, at least to me, seems absurd.

Among the things an investor might expect to know are the rates of return earned by the two companies, their liquidities or degrees of solvency, and their leverages. The general significance of these was argued in *Accounting, Evaluation and Economic Behavior*. In forming expectations, every investor and every manager may place different weights on these characteristics of the firms, in the light of his more general knowledge of their markets and expectations of the future of those markets.

Consider the firm issuing securities E; call it the E Company. Let the characteristics of the state of the company at a given time be represented by S; S includes all aspects of financial position at the time, including degree of solvency and leverage which are entailed in its statement of financial position. Let there be a certain amount of public knowledge, K, about the industry of the E Company.

Let Q_m, Q_n be the expectational quotients of the manager and of an investor in *E* Company respectively; by analogy with the concept of intelligence quotient, we posit a complex of attitudes which affect the way in which a person views prospects, personal factors which affect expectations. Let *R* be the rate of return of the *E* Company as obtained from its financial statements, and *D* the dividend paid by the company.

Using current cash equivalents, *S* will be a close approximation to the factual state of the company at any time and *R* will be a close approximation to the rate of change in the factual state in the immediately past period. There will be two values of the company's enterprise:—

the managerial valuation

$$MV(E) = f(S, R, K, Q_m) \tag{4}$$

and

the investor's valuation

$$NV(E) = f(S, R, D, K, Q_n) \tag{5}$$

The valuations will be different not only because Q_m and Q_n will differ but also because the manager may have some influence on future values of *D* which investors cannot anticipate; investors will tend therefore to be influenced by past values of *D*.

The values *S*, *R*, *D* and *K* will form the basis on which investors may estimate the future cash flows they can expect. It is common to represent the expected proceeds of an investment, exclusive of the initial amount of the investment as above, by

$$NV(E) = \sum_{t=1}^{n} PV(D_t)' + CCE(E)_n' \tag{6}$$

where the first term is the sum of the present values of the expected dividends through to time *n*, and the second term is the expected resale price at *n*, the primes signifying expected values in each case. But this expression does not indicate the foundations of the dividend and price expectations. A little reflection will show that *S*, *R*, *D* and *K* or various components of these are necessary for the formation of dividend and price expectations. To lay these bare has been the object of the expression in the previous paragraph.

Using the MATACAP concept will entail different concepts of *S* and *R*; let them be denoted by *S′* and *R′*. *S′* and *R′* will not be close approximations to *S* and *R*, for their values will have been obtained by the operation of Q_m on some data, which, in the nature of the case, are not available to the investor. The *Q* of any individual cannot be known to any other. We may try to assess it, but we can only do so if we have factual expressions of its consequences from time to time. But as the factual results of business operations are the consequences of many other causes, besides the *Q*s of the managers, we cannot assess the *Q*s even if we have factual expressions of business results.

Now *S* and *R* will not be known to investors in the present case; they will have *S′* and *R′* which are based on some data or estimates, which we may designate as U (unknown to investors); S' and R' are functions of (U, K, Q_m); we will write them as $s(U, K, Q_m)$ and $r(U, K, Q_m)$.

Making the appropriate substitutions in the expression for the investor's valuation, (5), above, we have:—

$$NV(E) = f(S', R', D, K, Q_n) \quad (7)$$
$$= f[s(U, K, Q_m), r(U, K, Q_m), D, K, Q_n] \quad (8)$$

Notice that S' and R' are not independent values. Both depend on the use made by the manager of the knowledge K; they are the result of the operation of Q_m on K and other data or estimates. Suppose K is suggestive of some growth to any member of the public, although the expectations of different persons differ in degree. Instead of K operating once only on an investor's valuation, it will have operated in some sense exponentially; first, through the determination of the values reported to investors by the manager, and second, through the response of the investor to what is reported. It is hard to say what the consequences could be of the operation of Q_n on values which have already been affected by the operation of Q_m; but the exponential effect suggests serious overvaluation by investors in the growth case, and serious undervaluation in the opposite case. (The demonstration seems to suggest a hypothesis explanatory of at least some of the marked swings in market prices: for even under traditional accounting there is an element of some Q or Qs in the magnitudes assigned to the constituents of S' and R'.)

In rebuttal of the above, it may be contended that investors should accept the operation of Q_m and make no attempt to interpose their own expectational quotients; but I know of no serious contention in this direction. It may also be contended that an investor should ignore S' and R' and apply his Q_n only to (D, K); but this would entail that financial statements serve or should serve no function, and I know of no serious contention in this direction.

So far we have dealt with the investor as though there were no alternative investment; we now take up again the securities F. We work through the case using current cash equivalent first. Putting together the expressions developed for the managerial problem (1, 2 above) and the investor in E, the choice of holding E or switching to F will turn on whether

$$NV(E) - CCE(E) \gtrless NV(F) - P(F) \quad (9)$$

In the simple case in which a straight switch can be made without cash deficit or surplus, this reduces to

$$NV(E) \gtrless NV(F)$$

Using current cash equivalents for the derivation of the S and R for both E and F Companies we obtain sets of magnitudes which are themselves comparable, for they are all in principle prices from the interdependent set of all prices ruling in the community at any time. Q_n is therefore being applied to two sets of facts, one for E and one for F, which are in principle the same in kind. The same applies however great the number and variety of alternative opportunities to E, provided all firms derive S and R in the same way.

Using the MATACAP concept the problem is much more, if not completely, confused. Suppose, for simplicity that K is some public knowledge which has implications for the future of both E and F. As before (8 above)

$$NV(E) = f[s(U_e, K, Q_{m1}), r(U_e, K, Q_{m1}), D_e, K, Q_n] \quad (10)$$

and

$$NV(F) = f[s(U_f, K, Q_{m2}), r(U_f, K, Q_{m2}), D_f, K, Q_n] \quad (11)$$

The two sets of facts U_e and U_f on which the managers $m1$ and $m2$ based their financial statements, are unknown to the investor; Q_{m1} and Q_{m2}, the expectational quotients of the two managers, are different but unknown to the investor; S_e', R_e', S_f' and R_f' are sets of magnitudes which are not factual, and the investor does not know the extent to which Q_{m1} and Q_{m2} have entered into the determination of them. D_e, D_f and K are all known to the investor, but the application of Q_n to the collections of non-factual and factual statements in respect of each company cannot possibly provide comparable values for $NV(E)$ and $NV(F)$. The investor is unable to make an informed choice—informed about the facts of the companies—in such circumstances. And as an investor may have many opportunities alternative to investing in E, for each of which there is an unknown but unique Q_m, the possibilities of him being mistaken or misled are legion.

That the operation of Q_m on the opportunities, and with the resources, of a company contributes to its profits or losses, its growth or failure, is not questioned. But we will not learn of its profits or losses if we allow Q_m to influence the measures of these. It is widely acknowledged that managers seek personal aims in the management of companies—power, prestige, continuity of tenure and so on. We may consider Q_m, in its actual effect in any instance, to be a composite of pure expectations and consciously or unconsciously self-protective predilections. Even if we could absolutely trust that in some cases Q_m is pure expectation, we cannot so trust in all cases. Where we have any doubt we would like to have evidence on which trust could be based. But Q_m, being entirely subjective, is not open to inspection; we can never have any such evidence. If wishes were horses, beggars would ride, they say; it seems a poor service to give investors a wish when they want a horse.

Some Conclusions

The conclusions from the above demonstrations are two:—

(a) For any choice between holding an asset and acquiring another, whether by managers or investors, current cash equivalents of the assets held enter into the statement of conditions for informed choice.

(b) For any valuation of a future project, aggregative statements based on current cash equivalents (i.e., indicative of factual states at specific times) provide certain of the materials.

None of the argument denies the necessity of valuations, however varied and tenuous the grounds for making those valuations may be. In a certain world valuations would be less tenuous, for there would be no use for expectations in making valuations; but we live in an uncertain world which necessitates the forming of expectations as a first step in setting up valuations; and there are personal, and therefore unique elements in both, elements which are matters of private knowledge only.

As was argued, both in *Accounting, Evaluation and Economic Behavior* and above, choice requires both factual information about the firm's holdings and valuations of its prospects on the basis of those holdings. To provide the former is the function of accounting as we see it; we leave the valuing to be done by whomsoever wishes, for we accept the impossibility of knowing the personal components of valuations. The MATACAP proposal, on the other hand, provides only valuations. It implies the existence of some facts, but denies these to the users of financial statements; or it implies that valuations can be made without facts, a proposition it is impossible to swallow; it certainly entails, if accounting is to give the valuation Staubus requires, that some function other than accounting must supply the facts—some accountant to fill the gap left by some quasi-accountant, no doubt.

Counterarguments?

Some particular observations of Staubus may be noticed as they occur commonly in discussions on the use of financial information. It should be clear that in no sense are they counterarguments to the position I have taken.

"Readers of financial statements are interested in information that will help them choose among alternative future courses of action". But what is help? help in what way? We have tried to show specifically the way in which information helps; and it seems that current cash equivalents or aggregations of these invariably help. Staubus sets up no demonstration to the contrary.

"The dates and amounts of cash inflows from debtors are crucial to the planning and control of liquidity". Doubtless. But so also is knowledge from time to time of actual holdings of cash and receivables—both current cash equivalents; and the actual amounts are the only basis on which steps can be taken, and the only indication whether or not steps should be taken, to tighten or relax the rules which influence liquidity.

"Short-term lenders . . . must predict the firm's ability to pay at a near future date". Why must they? and what does predict mean? Lenders have contractual rights against borrowers; this is some protection even if they never predicted, and most short-term lenders rely on their legal rights. But they would, of course, want to have "some idea" that the debtor will pay. Predict in any very definite sense they cannot.

"The making of the contract is a part of management's overall performance so we must surely take its effect, for better or for worse, into account as soon as possible". There's many a slip 'twixt cup and lip. If we are to take the making of contracts into account (before their execution), must we not also take account of all the possible variations, revocations, novations and so on in respect of every contract—for the right to these also arises out of the contract.

Where goods are "difficult to sell", the accountant "is forced to assume that the goods will eventually be sold for at least a break-even price vis-à-vis production costs at the time of sale". Why is he forced so to assume? If the assumption were valid, surely no firm would ever find the production of any good unprofitable.

"As of any given balance sheet date the accountant should provide the . . . maximum net proceeds (of existing stocks of goods) indicated by the objective evidence at hand". How can he do this? Maximum net proceeds he cannot know; it is a future sum, and he is not an operator in the market himself—on both scores he can only have subjective evidence.

"The investor wants to learn as much as he can about what will happen or at least what could happen under existing conditions . . . , not what could happen under quite different conditions". This is an odd investor; surely he wants to know what might happen under future, not existing, conditions. But however much he wants, he also wants to know what the company has now, so that he can form an opinion about the company's present capacity to face those conditions.

One of the most common provisos through Staubus' article has reference to objectivity—"acceptable objectivity", "objective evidence", "if objectively ascertainable", "standard of objectivity", "lack of objectivity", "objectivity", "evidence of future contributions to company cash flows that is objectively ascertainable". The use of the term in the course of an argument supporting statements colored by expectations of the future seems quite improper. It is incontrovertible that no statement embodying beliefs or expectations about the future can be objective; beliefs and expectations are always personal, not open to inspection by others, and therefore subjective.

In contrasting the uses of CCE and MATACAP, Staubus asserts "CCE is most commonly associated with 'What we could sell our assets for if we did not go ahead and use them in the ordinary course of business' ". But this description does not entail that the firm shall or shall not go ahead and use them. It is not a notion that has sale in contemplation at all. It is a concept which yields an indication of the resources presently under control so that managers and others can choose one way or the other. MATACAP entails that the choosing has been done; there is no factual foundation of choice; and there is no possibility of change up to the horizon of expectations on which MATACAP values are based, for MATACAP gives the "net contribution our assets *will make* to cash flows in their *most likely future course*"; note the finality of the italicized words.

Points of View

Much of the debate about the magnitudes accounting should deal in is due to failure to apprehend the necessity, in all choice situations, of having knowledge of the immediate facts. This failure is never complete; but the adoption of some specific point of view tends to push the significance of the immediate facts aside. And it is so in the course of Staubus' argument. "The appraisal of overall management performance depends on measuring the accomplishments of management and the sacrifice made to achieve them . . . measurement of the net assets . . . at the end of the appraisal period . . . and similar measurements at the beginning of the period" (p. 657). We agree. But we disagree with the concept of measurement adopted by Staubus, and others. The word is very loosely used. No one would think of measuring a man's weight at age 30 with reference to what he expects to weigh at age 40. We would measure his weight at age 30, simply. No one has yet demonstrated that the measurements relating to business from time to time must be based on any other rule than the best possible observations of things as they are at a given time. No calculation indicating where a firm may be at some future time can contribute to a statement of where it is now. If I say that I expect to be in New York in eight hours' time, no person receiving that statement can tell where I am now. I may be in Honolulu or London or Rio de Janeiro or Atlantic City. It is the same with the financial positions of firms. To measure the performance of management on the basis of what has been done plus what is still undone (i.e., what is expected) entails a curious meaning of performance.

It is the lack of conception of the importance of the state of a firm in any immediate present, both for assessing performance and as a basis of expectations, which causes much foot-shuffling. Dealing with depreciable assets Staubus asserts: "We are forced to fall back on the assumption inherent in any use of entry prices, viz., that management's judgement when it decided to acquire the asset was a good one." Why we are forced to accept such an assumption is not clear. One of the objects of accounting surely is to show up whether management's judgements have been good or bad. We cannot do this if in the very process we are forced to assume that management's judgements have been good. In a similar way every "futuristic" statement, and all MATACAP statements are of this class, presumes that we can rely on management's judgements. But a very large slice of human experience shows that this is foolish—otherwise there would be no loss companies, no liquidations, many fewer decisions than there now are. The whole argument for reporting other than what is rests on some vague deterministic notions which ill consort with the experience we have of business. The sooner we give up being believers in or apologists for managerial omniscience, and concentrate on showing what has occurred, the better for managers, investors and the rest of us.

One of the traps in campaigning for a particular form of accounting is the tendency to feel that one has the best solution to problems which cannot be resolved without the aid of things beyond accounting. Thus Staubus says "CCE represents a second best value". As I have expounded its use, of course, CCE is not a method of valuation but a concept used in measuring. In the places cited by Staubus, I have readily admitted the necessity both of measures and valuations. The preceding demonstration is perhaps a more succinct way of expressing the necessity. It does not imply that some such notion as MATACAP is unnecessary. I have simply rejected it as part of accounting because the values it yields and the beliefs on which they are based are matters beyond the competence and judgement of accountants.

Staubus derides our emphasis on the sell-or-hold decision. "Need we be so concerned with the sell-or-hold decision? It frequently is not a difficult one." To sell-or-hold is simply the most common form of all choices; all choices are in contemplation of some switch in holdings or uses. Choice and decision mean nothing other than switching. What "broader view of the uses of accounting information is more appropriate" than a view which concentrates on choices I cannot conceive.

I lay no claim to perfection of argument or exposition. I strove to minimize laxity in thought and to propose a scheme which would minimize looseness in practice. I tried to offer argument rather than assertion or mere belief. I also tried to construct a tight set of basic notions, and then to relax some of them just sufficiently to make the system workable. That, of course, is what any engineer, chemist or other practical specialist does. Perhaps I did not make this double-edged intention clear enough; for it is precisely at such points that others have found what they describe as "inconsistencies". But "inconsistencies" of this kind are no different from the incompatibility of the straight line in geometry and the non-existence of any such straight line in practical affairs which are based on geometry.

Perhaps the attempt to produce something theoretically tighter than alternatives, and at the same time to propose something which approached the ideal but was workable, was over-ambitious. But I believe so strongly that a theory should aid in the resolution of practical problems that I cannot regret trying to meet practical difficulties without too great a sacrifice of principle. There is no principle known to men which is not relaxed somewhat in application.

43

CONSOLIDATED STATEMENTS ARE NOT REALLY NECESSARY*

The question, to which the title of this note is the answer, has long since ceased to be asked. Consolidated statements have become part of the paraphernalia of accounting and reporting. But they seem to be the wrong solution to the problem from which they arose.

The problem is this. A company, A, which controls another, B, may direct B to buy from A or sell to A any goods at any prices it fixes. A may oblige B to lend to or borrow from A any sums it wishes on any terms it wishes. A may secure that B declares dividends in any amounts it wishes, or that it declares no dividends (within the constraints of the general law on dividends and of contracts with outsiders). In consequence of these things the financial position of B at any time and its results for any preceding intervals are at the discretion of A. Further A could have paid to original owners of B any consideration it deemed fit, either greater or less, by large or small amounts, than the market prices of the net assets acquired; and after the acquisition of B it could acquire new shares of B for any consideration it deemed fit.

The legal balance sheet of a holding company would show among the assets its shares in subsidiaries, but this would give no clue as to the nature of the assets of subsidiaries, whatever the basis used for valuing those assets. Any person relying on the legal balance sheet would not know whether the assets represented by the investment in the subsidiaries were real estate, or cash, or intangibles or what combination of these. It seemed reasonable, therefore, to give to shareholders in holding companies some idea of the ultimate investments of the subsidiaries in legal rights and tangible goods; and we accept the merit of this.

One solution, still legally available, is to give the separate balance sheets and profit and loss accounts of the subsidiaries as annexures to the financial statements of the holding company as such. But this is cumbersome, particularly for a company with many subsidiaries. It also imposes severe burdens on the patience and ingenuity of any person who wishes to trace the assets which in some sense are represented by the shareholdings of the holding company in the subsidiaries.

The solution perferred by many is the preparation of consolidated statements which eliminate inter-company security holdings and

---

* First published in *The Australian Accountant,* Vol. 38, No. 2, February 1968, pp. 89-92.

inter-company transactions and the profits therefrom. We contend that this is a solution which confuses some things and does not elucidate others.

First, assets and equities (liabilities and shareholders' rights in assets) can only have a sensible meaning in relation to some legal entity which can own properties and incur obligations. The only entities of this kind are natural persons and corporations. A holding company and its subsidiaries, as a complex, is not an entity of this kind. To suppose it is, is to depend on a fiction; and to depend on a fiction seems to invite confusion.

Second, for the above reason consolidated balance sheets and consolidated profit and loss accounts are not balance sheets and profit and loss accounts in any ordinary sense of those terms. To use the same words of the two different kinds of statements—of a legal entity and of a non-legal entity—is again to invite confusion. The use of the same words predisposes readers to make the same kinds of inferences from consolidated statements as from the proper statements of a legally competent entity; but such inferences are strictly illegitimate.

These two points have to do with the basic nature of the entity reported upon and the general significance of any statements embodied in such reports. But the greatest difficulties have to do with the specific significances of statements embodied in balance sheets and profit and loss accounts.

We have argued at length elsewhere that only if financial statements are in contemporary terms are they of any use to shareholders and creditors, either as indicators of past performance, or of present financial position, or of the possibilities of future growth or adaptation[1]. By statements in contemporary terms we mean statements in which assets are represented at current prices or the best possible approximation thereto. The case for doing this is not argued here. We will merely assert what seems to be self-evident: that rates of return, measures of solvency and measures of the relative interests of shareholders and creditors in the assets of a firm, are useless as guides unless they are based on prices ruling at or about the time at which financial statements are prepared.

Suppose that such a system of continuously contemporary accounting were in general use. Whatever assets were represented as those of a subsidiary company in its own accounts would be represented at their contemporary prices. Liabilities would be of known amount. The difference between the aggregate of the measures of the assets and the aggregate amount of the liabilities would be the measure of the shareholders' equity in the assets. (For simplicity we assume wholly-owned subsidiaries having only one class of shares.) Only if this difference—the measure of net assets—is used in calculations relating to the financial position and results of the company will the results of the calculations be significant. No calculation

---

[1] *Accounting Evaluation and Economic Behavior.* The proposals of this article differ from and are superior to the treatment of consolidated statements at pp. 288-9 of the work cited.

using par values of the shares or the prices paid for them in the past will yield significant figures. Clearly, then, in the balance sheet of the holding company, the amount to be shown as the amount then invested in the shares of subsidiaries will be the amount of the net assets of the subsidiaries, which will be the same as the sum of the net assets shown on the faces of the balance sheets of the subsidiaries.

Now we have already accepted the merit of giving shareholders in holding companies some idea of the composition of the assets and equities of subsidiaries. This is readily achieved by giving, as annexures to the financial statements of the holding company, simple aggregative statements of the assets and liabilities and profit and loss account items of all the subsidiaries. These statements would be in the same general form as those of the holding company; and, for the purpose of disclosing what the statutes regard as necessary, they would contain aggregates of the specific items required by the statutes to be disclosed by holding companies as companies.

Where for any good reason it is deemed desirable to distinguish subsidiaries which are to some extent dissimilar, separate aggregate figures for the two classes could be given in the same form in separate columns. The two classes of subsidiaries referred to would generally be (i) those operating in the same country and under the same disclosure rules as the holding company, and (ii) those operating in other countries which permit the use of different accounting principles and those operating in countries whose fiscal policies or economic conditions may interfere with the holding company's rights to repatriate dividends or capital.

In the annexures, the aggregate equities would be subdivided into equities of the holding company and of outsiders, and these would be further broken down into obligations on current account, long-term liabilities, and equities arising from shareholdings. To the extent that any of these are assets of the holding company they would appear, identical in amount, in the balance sheet of the holding company. If, for any reason peculiar to class (ii) subsidiaries of the previous paragraph, the figures carried into the holding company's balance sheet were different from those shown in the annexures, the difference would require to be explained. Where some subsidiaries earned profits and other made losses, the aggregate amounts of profits and losses would be shown, for the annexures are simply summarizations of the several statements of subsidiaries without any set-offs.

In the above brief outline we have omitted reference to many of the problems which the consolidation solution raises. Some of them simply disappear under the proposed alternative. But some indication of the reason for their disappearance may be warranted.

There is no necessity to eliminate inter-company profits. If assets are valued at a year's end at contemporary market prices, any over- or under-pricing (by reference to market prices) of inter-company sales will simply inflate the profits of one and deflate the profits of another company. However biased the inter-company pricing, its effects wash out at the end of the period; the valuation rule, current market prices, itself washes out intra-group profits. If, of course, the inter-company transactions have left one company better off than it might have been but for an "artificial" transfer price, that is merely the consequence of the transaction. It would be false to the facts to say or imply afterwards (as is implied by elimination on consolidation) that the actual transfer price was not the price.

There is no problem of splitting transactions to eliminate that part of the profit on an inter-company transaction which constitutes the holding company's proportion where there is a minority interest in a subsidiary. In consolidation accounting this is a highly artificial exercise, and its effect is false to the legal consequences of such transactions.

There is no problem of the continuous inflation of values as one company sells merchandise to another down a line of subsidiaries or as one company sells securities to another up the line. Assets are always brought to contemporary market prices at a year's end; and as the measure of equities is the measure of net assets, the measure of equities is also reduced at the year's end, if during any year shares have been issued for greater nominal amounts than the market prices of the assets acquired.

The consolidation solution has given rise to debate about the possibility of showing which subsidiaries have made profits and which have made losses. The debate is almost pointless as long as it is permissible to carry assets (of any company in a complex) at cost; for as between any two companies in a complex the amount charged by one to another may be quite arbitrary. But if current market prices are used at the year's end and the contents of the annexures are simple aggregations of the figures of subsidiaries, the amounts of profits and losses will be shown. This seems to be quite sufficient. For at the least it puts readers of the statements on notice of these amounts so that they can demand any elucidation they require; and to insist upon greater detail, as a matter of course, may well lead to obscuring the vision of readers rather than to their enlightenment.

It must be apparent that, as long as companies are permitted to use any one of the vast range of asset valuation methods now current, and in so far as companies within a complex employ different methods, the exercise of consolidation is a purely arithmetical one. There is, for example, no clear meaning that can be given to the sum of amounts for inventories for one company on an average-cost basis and for another on a lower-of-cost-and-market basis; the addition of such amounts is illegitimate. Whether or not any accountant or auditor confronted with such aggregates feels any uneasiness, or the obligation to make any adjustment or notation to bring such diverse magnitudes to a common footing, is not known. But the question is not raised as a significant issue in the literature.

The problem does not arise in the suggested alternative. For its basis is the valuation of assets at something approaching contemporary prices; and in principle contemporary prices are always aggregable and a clear meaning can be assigned to the aggregate. This problem is at least one of the problems which should exercise the judgement of auditors of parent companies and consolidated statements. But if accounting were required to yield statements embodying contemporary prices of assets, all auditors could be expected to exercise similar kinds of judgement on the extent to which the figures represented the contemporary facts. One of the difficulties, and quite possibly most of the difficulties, which are commonly discussed under the caption, the auditor and the group concept, would disappear.

The suggestion that consolidated statements be abandoned in favour of aggregative annexures in the nature of explanatory notes may not be easy to accept. Consolidated statements have been accepted for about 60 years, notwithstanding the fact that their justification has required quite a deal of verbal gymnastics. In the same way so many other devices which are now questioned have arisen. The present writer has been as guilty as anyone else in perpetuating the acceptance of the consolidation solution. But it now seems that the alternative is much more easy to defend on logical and practical grounds, and that the result is far more comprehensible and realistic than the product of the consolidation process.

44

PRICE VARIATION ACCOUNTING—A GENERAL NOTATION*

In the course of many years' discussion of the effects of variations in prices and price levels, many numerical examples have been used in the literature. These have ranged from treatments of single classes of assets to full-scale treatments of financial statements. There are difficulties associated with the use of numerical examples. They may fall under the suspicion that the author has used numerical values of a kind which support his case, whereas there may be counter-examples of a kind which do not. The very figures used may lead to conclusions which are peculiar to the chosen hypothetical case, even though it was developed in good faith and without initial bias in favour of a particular set of conclusions. The figures may be judged to be unrealistic or exaggerated for effect; the illustration may, therefore, fall under censure on the ground that the demonstrated consequences are not in fact experienced. Numerical examples which extend through a hypothetical series of years may be questioned on the ground that the actions supposed to be taken would not be the same as actions taken in response to the resulting information in a real-world context.

To avoid challenges and objections of these kinds, it seemed to be worthwhile to try to devise a means of representing the effects in a pure symbolic form. Some early attempts showed that, if the demonstration were to embrace the whole range of events and transactions which are usually dealt with in accounts, the result would be enormously complex and difficult to follow, on my own part as well as on the part of readers. The number of symbols required, and the number of changes in the symbols—as assets changed their form, for example—were such that concise demonstration would be impossible.

* The object of this note is to clarify and amplify a form of notation first used in "Towards a General Theory of Accounting". The necessity of refinement became obvious in the course of some interchanges with Professor R. L. Mathews in *Journal of Accounting Research* (see Mathews, "Price Level Changes and Useless Information", Spring 1965; Chambers, "The Price Level Problem and Some Intellectual Grooves", Autumn 1965; Mathews, "The Price Level Controversy: A Reply", Spring 1967; Chambers, "Price Variation—An Improved Representation", Autumn 1967.) Some subsequent work (see, for example, "New Pathways in Accounting Thought and Action", at p. 704, *post*) necessitated a notation which was more versatile, which could be extended to demonstrations in which monetary units of diverse purchasing powers could be distinctively represented. The present note synthesises the relevant parts of the articles mentioned.

However, periodical summarization involves an actual or constructive determination of the assets and equities of firms, even if only for the purpose of correcting for errors, omissions, losses and gains, not already incorporated in the record. It would be sufficient therefore to construct an example for a single year, and to regard the accounting for a series of years as successive applications of the same ideas. And if the number of categories was reduced to a minimum which was typical, the symbolic representation would be of general use in exploring varied kinds of change. The problem could be cut down to manageable size by adopting a four-category balance sheet (monetary assets, non-monetary assets, liabilities and residual equity), and a transactionless interval in which there were changes only in prices or price-levels. The result was the demonstration given in paras. 107, 108 of "Towards a General Theory of Accounting".

The construction of a symbolic system and the inferences drawn from it are, of course, no less subject to one's general apprehension of the problem than in the case of a numerical example. In 1961 my view of the kinds of change in accounting which variations in prices might necessitate was not greatly different from the views of many others. In the preparation of statements of results and position replacement costs should be used instead of historical costs. The use of the word "costs" in both cases, tends to force attention on the adjustment of amounts originally paid, by the use of a price index. I held that the index to be used is an index of the general level of prices, on several grounds. First, as firms hold many different types of asset, such an index would provide an adequate adjustment over all assets. Second, as money and money income are non-specific and may be applied by firms or dividend recipients to the purchase of any goods or services whatever, a general index would provide an adequate correction for changes in the purchasing power of money. Third, as money is generally regarded as a common denominator, there could be no ground for supposing that the effects of changes in the purchasing power of money would fall unevenly on the members (or other entities) of a community; and as any holder of money was at liberty to hold other things, it was sufficient that the accounting system used in a community should show up the relative consequences, as between members (and other entities) of whatever their holdings happened to be. Each of these reasons has some element of truth, but we will presently show that each also has elements which are misleading. For the moment they are set down to explain the mode of argument of 1961.

The possibility of a further simplification of the demonstration became clear in 1963. By transposing the item "liabilities", merging it with "monetary assets", and dealing only with "net monetary assets", "non-monetary assets" and "residual equity", a three-category balance sheet, which would still be typical, could be obtained. As liabilities and monetary assets are affected equally, dollar for dollar, but in opposite directions by a change in the general level of prices, no damage is done to the demonstration. This form will be used in the following explanation of the 1961 demonstration.

Now, assume a firm has net monetary assets (cash and receivables less payables) in the amount M; non-monetary assets in the amount N; and residual equity in the amount R; all at t_0. Assume the firm engages in no transactions between t_0 and t_1. Assume also that in that interval there is a proportionate change in the general level of prices represented by p; so that if the general level of prices is represented by unity at t_0, it is represented by $(1+p)$ at t_1.

At t_0

$$M + N = R \qquad [1]$$

Multiply throughout by $(1+p)$

$$M(1+p) + N(1+p) = R(1+p)$$

Because the *amount* of the net monetary assets is the same at t_1 as at t_0, transpose Mp:

$$M + N(1+p) = R(1+p) - Mp \qquad [2]$$

This expresses the position of the firm at t_1.

The 1961 argument proceeded as follows. As, by the subtraction of [1] from [2], $Np = Rp - Mp$, to discover the increment in the residual equity through the period it is only necessary to find Np. The conclusion was supported on three grounds:—

(a) One may hold monetary assets (or borrow) for gain, just as readily as one may invest in non-monetary assets for gain; and for given total resources the gain or loss Np entails the loss or gain Mp.

(b) If, for the purpose of calculating income, one uses the maintenance of residual equity as a base, no part of Rp $(= Mp + Np)$ is income; for $(R + Rp)$ is the amount of the original equity expressed in terms of the purchasing power of the monetary unit at t_1.

(c) If the preferred combination of assets at t_0 was given by the ratio $M:N$ at t_0, the corresponding preferred combination at t_1 would be given by the ratio $M(1+p):N(1+p)$. But the mere calculation of Mp does not put additional monetary units in the hands of the firm, so that the calculation of Mp is pointless.

Each of these grounds seemed plausible. In each case the premises are true, but the inferences are beside the point or incorrect. Consider (b). It is true that no part of Rp is income. But the total amount of the residual equity at t_1 is $R(1+p) - Mp$; and of this $(-Mp)$ is income, a positive amount if the signs of M or p are negative, a negative amount otherwise. Similarly with (c); it is true that the mere calculation of Mp does not put additional monetary units in the hands of the firm, but the calculation of Mp is not pointless if, as in the circumstances chosen, $(-Mp)$ is the income of the firm. Though I had written "for the purpose of calculating income", I had not asked "what is the amount of income?".

It should be pointed out that the terms used in the demonstration were generalized but the assumed event is highly specific, namely a rise in the level of the prices of non-monetary assets at exactly the same rate as the rise in the general level of prices. I had pointed out ("Towards a General Theory", para. 104) that "prices are free to move and will move under the impact of market conditions", but I had not followed this up with an example which really illustrated the particular movements of which a price index is only an average. This was to wait until 1963 and to be published only in 1965.

The demonstration lends itself to the support of "price level accounting" of the kind which proceeds by adjusting original purchase prices of non-monetary assets. It has been cited both by those who would use a general index[1] and those who would use a specific price index for the purpose[2]. These two kinds of price level accounting depend on different conceptions of income and the maintenance of capital; but their expositors could accommodate these differences of definition by distinguishing parts of the increment in the residual equity as income and parts as capital gain or inflation gain. If one seeks, by reasoning, to reduce the scope for differences of opinion, there was yet some work to be done.

I had for several years been urged by Ernest Weinwurm to direct attention to the metrological elements in accounting. I declined to do this until I felt that I had formulated a description of the context of accounting which was reasonably satisfactory to myself. "Towards a General Theory" seemed to be a sufficient basis for the time being. During 1962 and 1963 therefore I considered more closely the characteristics of accounting processes and statements as measurement processes and reports of measurements.

Although the words "contemporary information" or words to like effect had been used in many antecedent articles, I had not clearly seen the process of deriving it otherwise than by transformations of historical costs by the use of index numbers. But this does not give a contemporary measurement except in the improbable circumstance that particular prices of the assets specific to a firm changed at exactly the same rate as the index used. Generally, therefore, contemporary measurements must be taken independently of historical costs and price index movements. Contemporary monetary measurements would be given by the product of contemporary unit prices and physical quantities. The thought of "prices" suggested that what has widely been described as historical costs are strictly initial purchase prices. But what prices should be used at the close of each period? The object of accounting is to show results. But purchase prices (even those ruling at the end of a period) only account for inputs, not for results. It followed that selling prices were the proper basis of an accounting for results. By these steps the habit of thinking in terms of "costs" was broken; the sources of information on contemporary measures became clear; and a way of representing the whole accounting process as a measurement system was discovered. Whatever practical difficulties there may be, it was at least possible to set up a scheme for dealing, in principle, with a variety of possibilities.

---

[1] E.g., Staff of the Accounting Research Division, A.I.C.P.A., *Reporting the Financial Effects of Price-Level Changes,* Accounting Research Study No. 6, 1963, pp. 12-13.

[2] E.g., R. S. Gynther, *Accounting for Price-Level Changes,* Oxford, Pergamon Press, 1966, pp. 138-9.

In late 1963 and early 1964, while preparing the manuscript of *Accounting, Evaluation and Economic Behavior*, the form of the analysis of 1961 was applied to three possible sets of circumstances: (i) the case where the general level of prices and the prices of the non-monetary assets of a firm changed at the same rate during a period; (ii) the case where the general level of prices remained constant while the prices of non-monetary assets changed; and (iii) the case where both the general level of prices and the prices of non-monetary assets changed at different rates. The first two cases are unrealistic, but they isolate different effects and make easier the development of the third case. The third case is the general case for all firms in all circumstances. Using the same notation as before, together with q representing the proportionate change in a period in the prices of non-monetary assets, it was shown that, in the third case, the position at t_1 is given by

$$M + N(1+q) = R(1+p) + N(q-p) - Mp \qquad [3]$$

all in terms of the purchasing power of the monetary unit at t_1.

In this equation p is derived from the general price index numbers of t_0 and t_1. However q is not so derived; it is calculated from the actually discovered prices of non-monetary assets at t_0 and t_1, i.e., from contemporary measurements at t_0 and t_1. The result seemed intuitively sensible. $R(1+p)$ is the original equity, R in terms of the purchasing power of t_0, transformed into the number of units which at t_1 have the same purchasing power. $N(q-p)$ represents the improvement in the equity due to changes in the actual prices of non-monetary assets, less the effect of the change in the purchasing power of the monetary unit in terms of which those assets are represented. Mp is the effect of the change in the purchasing power of the monetary unit on the holdings of monetary assets. Every one of the magnitudes is discoverable, in principle, at any date; and being in terms of the same units the individual measures may be added or related as in any other collection of measurements proper.

However, the demonstration did not seem to others to be as conclusive as it did to me. On reflection the reason seemed to lie in the omission from the algebraic treatment of a symbol indicating the differences in the purchasing power of the monetary units at t_0 and t_1. I developed a tighter form of demonstration using \$ and \$ to distinguish the units. Some subsequent work suggested that a slightly different notation is of more general use, particularly for examples extending beyond one period. I would now set up the general case as follows, all symbols used before having the same interpretation.

Let $\$_0$ and $\$_1$ represent the purchasing power of the monetary unit at t_0 and t_1 respectively. Then $\$_0 = \$_1(1+p)$.

At t_0

$$\$_0M + \$_0N = \$_0R \qquad [4]$$

Because $\$_0 = \$_1(1+p)$, the position at t_0 may be represented in $\$_1$ thus:—

$$\$_1M(1+p) + \$_1N(1+p) = \$_1R(1+p) \qquad [5]$$

By observation at t_1

$$\$_1M + \$_1N\ (1 + q) = \$_1R_1 \qquad [6]$$

Now the change in the magnitude of the terms on the right-hand sides of equations [5] and [6] is the income of the period; and it is equal to the change in the aggregates of the terms on the left-hand sides. Let $\triangle R$ be the income. Subtract the left-hand side of [5] from the left-hand side of [6]:—

$$\$_1 \triangle R = \$_1N\ (q - p) - \$_1Mp \qquad [7]$$

The similarities of the equations to those of earlier demonstrations will be apparent. But the notation now used makes it clearer that there are no arithmetical solecisms, by way of adding or subtracting amounts expressed in units of unlike dimension.

It should also be clear that price level accounting, of the kinds which entail the use only of a general price index or only of a specific price index, is a solution of an extremely limited set of problems; strictly only those cases in which the general price level and the prices of the specific collection of assets of each firm move in the same direction and at the same rate. It should also be clear that the effect of the change in the general level of prices (or the purchasing power of money, its reciprocal) cannot be obtained merely by reference to the amount of net monetary assets; for, in [7] above, p appears in both terms on the right-hand side.

The form of the analysis may be applied to periods of any length, and to changes of any kind. It may be extended to the case where there are numerous transactions. The right-hand sides of equations [4] and [6] are, in principle, obtained by actual observation at the respective dates. Whatever the magnitude of $\$_1R_1$ turns out to be as the result of all events and transactions, it is necessary only to subtract $\$_1R\ (1 + p)$ from it to obtain the amount of the income of the period.

It may seem that the conclusion is the consequence of simply merging the proposals for using general indexes and specific indexes. But this is not so, if for no other reason than that the above process cuts loose the discovery of the position at any time from the prices paid at some other time. But there is a more fundamental difference which disposes of the case for the use of specific indexes. A rise in the general level of prices (a fall in the purchasing power of the monetary unit) works in the opposite direction from a rise in specific prices, on a given initial position. This is shown clearly in [7] where p and q have opposite signs. It should be noted also that the only point at which p enters into the calculations at t_1 is in the term $\$_1R\ (1 + p)$. This represents the amount of the original equity expressed in $\$_1$, and therefore secures that the purchasing power of the capital at t_0 is the basis for calculating income of the period in $\$_1$. Income is calculated by reference to the maintenance of capital, whatever form the assets may take from time to time.

The analysis suggests some possible refinements in verbal usage and some possible causes of past confusion. There has long been debated the question whether accounting is concerned with costs or values, meaning past prices or present prices in most contexts. The words "costs" and "values" relate to assets, and some choice must be made certainly. But income is a difference which is affected not only by differences in prices, but also by differences in the purchasing power of the unit in which "costs" or "values" are expressed. "Costs or values?" does not therefore fully state the character of the dilemma. If nothing else, the problem is a trilemma; its representation as a dilemma could with advantage be abandoned.

The analysis, in using the notion of a general level of prices and its reciprocal the general purchasing power of money, is consistent with the general usage of economists at one extreme and men in the street at the other. There persists a view that firms are concerned with particular collections of assets and therefore with the level of prices of such collections; hence the specific index proposals. But, as in the case mentioned in the previous paragraph, this view confuses particular prices with the units in which they are denominated. And it confuses business policy with the facts on which policy may be based. A steel manufacturer does not receive or spend "steel money"; a food manufacturer does not pay its dividends in "food money"; a brewery does not pay wages in "beer money". If a plastic goods manufacturer wants to purchase a new machine, he cannot calculate how much "plastic money" he must pay to acquire a machine the price of which is expressed in "machinery money". Money is money to all and sundry. What they do with it is their own affair. What they do will certainly be influenced by the prices of different things—but prices expressed in the one unit common alike at any time to all buyers and sellers from housewives to tycoons.

For all these reasons it seems that what has long been described as the price level problem is in fact a price variation problem for it involves the consideration of variations in particular prices and the effect of all such variations on the general purchasing power of money.

DESSERT AND COFFEE

45

NON-COMMENTS ON NON-ACCOUNTING*

You may be familiar with the iconoclastic or anti-classical movement in art, literature and music; with nonsense sculpture, which tells nothing; with non-poetic verse and unartfully composed prose; with non-musical muzak, to the point of John Cage's composition "4 minutes and 33 seconds", in which the pianist is required to sit at the instrument, noteless, while the named time ticks away and then with full dignity quit the platform. I have no objection to these caperings and posturings as such. People may, for their own amusement or for the amusement of others, engage in whatever fanciful or undisciplined nonsense they please. But I do object when the same type of thing is taken seriously and finds its way into the world of the intellect, particularly into the part of that world which concerns me.

This is the reason why my title has the form it has. By non-comments I intend to leave myself free. Comments often have no direction; but I wish to be free to pontificate, to tilt, and as well as I can to point in one direction. And by non-accounting, I imply a wish not to talk about specific issues or special problems, but rather to concern myself with the mental or intellectual climate of accounting and its study. I ask these two degrees of freedom; beyond that I intend to be quite disciplined.

I can admire a clown on a slack rope. But I cannot admire an accountant on a slack principle. I can admire the virtuosity of, and perhaps enjoy the spectacle of, an artist dragging a nude woman across a wet paint covered canvas—the process could be interesting even though the result is meaningless. But I cannot admire an accountant dragging his pen or his hi-fi computer across a page and putting meaningless numbers at its foot. I can admire the idea of individual freedom. But because freedom means respect, on the part of those who claim it, for the rights and interests of others, I cannot admire the unbridled freedom which is implicit in the open-ended rules which masquerade under the name of generally accepted accounting principles.

These distinctions can be drawn only because the pleasure from entertainment or diversion and the substance of freedom are ends in themselves. Accounting is not an end in itself. People do not want accounting statements because they are pretty, or because they provide something on which one may allow the imagination free rein. They want accounting statements rather because they need something to discipline the imagination, something from which to commence a

---

* An address before the North Eastern Division of the American Accounting Association Meeting, Boston, October 6, 1962.

deliberate process of thought. And as this process of thought has to do with the world about them at any point of time, accounting should in an equal degree tell them something of their precise relationship—financially—with the world at that time. Reference has been made to slack principles, meaningless numbers and open-ended rules; some explanation is in order.

It is not intended to attack any particular slack principle. Every principle or rule which incorporates "either . . . or", "normally", "preferably", and other such face-saving devices is a slack principle. It is not difficult to find scores of statements of principle which include words of this kind. In every case it is possible, I might even say certain, that the use of such words is evidence of failure to discover a principle; the task has been abandoned half way. And I make bold to suggest that this failure has been due to putting the ease of mind of accountants before the value of the result to the mind of the user.

Few accountants seem to know to what specific area of human endeavor accounting belongs. There are, for example, many statements about accounting which link it with economics. But generally the linkage is only superficially made; it occurs in the first few pages of a text or the first few lines of an article, and is thereafter forgotten. Nevertheless these statements are themselves interesting in so far as they indicate some limit to the field which concerns accountants. Accountants concern themselves with rights and interests in economic goods—scarce resources. But so do businessmen, lawyers, economists, to name just a few classes of non-accountants. Businessmen make decisions about the disposal of economic goods; attorneys take measures to protect the rights and interests of people in economic goods; economists study the processes by which the command over goods is exercised and changes from time to time. Does accounting embrace all of these groups or none of them?

My answer is, none of them. Accounting is a process by which people become informed of some of the economic aspects of their affairs. It is a process as a result of which people expect to be able to act with greater knowledge than is yielded by their otherwise unaided senses. The field of accounting is thus part of the field of "getting knowledge"; accounting is properly a form of empirical inquiry. It may well be said that this statement is nothing novel; and it is true that many texts and articles, of older as well as more recent vintage, make statements to the effect that the function of accounting is to inform this or that class of people. But here again the linkage is only superficially made. You will, I think, look in vain for a systematic treatment of accounting as a means of acquiring knowledge and a development of the implications of this idea. And yet this is the very heart of the matter.

Whatever its past and whatever the deficiencies it has at present, accounting is one systematic means by which people having properties and transactions may be kept constantly informed of their affairs. To turn the provisional "may" into a positive statement requires some analysis of any existing or proposed accounting system for two purposes—one, to ensure that it bears on the kinds of matters on which people want information; and two, to ensure that the system itself is free of deliberate or accidental bias. On each of these points I am here only able to make brief comments.

By "the kinds of matters on which people want information" I do not mean the things one might discover by taking an opinion poll. Nor do I believe that these "matters" are dependent on the specific people we may nominate as interested parties. An entity operating in markets is what accounting is concerned with. Accounting is not concerned with the guesses and opinions of those (managers, investors, or others) associated with such entities, but with providing a substantial, factual basis on which opinions may be formed and by which projections may be disciplined. If accounting would only represent the financial capacity of the entity to go on operating in markets and the clear results of operating in markets, every interested party would be free to judge for himself the relationship of the entity to his particular market, and, if he wishes (and he often does), to speculate about the possible effects of the actions of other interested parties in their dealings with the entity.

By "free of deliberate or accidental bias" I mean that an accounting system should be so designed that the information it yields is such as each interested party could acquire by means of his senses if only he could be there to see for himself. To devise systems which are free from distortion is a matter requiring great skill—optical experts and communication engineers are constantly striving at enormous cost to do the same in their fields. But accountants seem to have little care or concern for eliminating the distortion of appearances which accounting methods presently produce. Skill in eliminating or reducing distortion is, in my view, the most important skill of all. It is the idea which lies at the back of objectivity and independence; but we seem to prefer to pay lip service to these notions rather than to be constrained by them. In a sense we prefer to be non-objective and non-independent. Now you may think I am just bandying words about. But I want to follow through.

It is necessary clearly to distinguish the kinds of knowledge we may have. A distinction may be drawn between private and public knowledge. Private knowledge is personal to its possessor. Useful as it may be to him, it can be of no use, except unilaterally, in his dealings with others. It may influence his behavior; but he cannot expect the behavior of others to be influenced by it. Public knowledge on the other hand is knowledge which is the common property of many men, and can be the property of all men. This being its character all men in their mutual behavior towards one another may be expected to be able and ready to act upon it. What then is the character of the knowledge which accountants may be expected to give?

Men are prepared to pay the salaries and fees of accountants because they must know how the entities they manage fare in, and stand in relation to, the market place. And the market place is a public place in which many groups of people trade with any given entity. For the purpose of trade no private knowledge is of any use whatever. [Private knowledge does not mean privileged knowledge.] The only knowledge useful to one group of people having common commercial intercourse with others is knowledge which is equally useful to all other groups. For one cannot expect others to assent blandly to one's private evaluations in the course of trade; to be in any way useful in trade, one's monetary evaluations of present things and relationships must be of such a kind that they approximate the monetary evaluations of one's counterparts in trade. Further, as one's next transaction may be with any one of a number of different types of "others", one's monetary evaluations of present things and relationships must be of such a kind that they command the assent of many types of one's counterparts in trade; and simultaneously! In short, the kind of financial information men want must have something of the character of public knowledge.

But what does conventional accounting offer? We are told emphatically and repeatedly that only the "costs" incurred by a given entity through an arm's length bargain are worthy of entry in accounts and that these remain the proper basis of accounting. In other words, the private experience of one firm at one point of time shall thereafter be, for that firm, the source of all knowledge about the good which is the subject of the transaction in question, regardless of what the evaluations of other people happen subsequently to be. This can only result in the delusion of those who must act in market places, or in the abandonment of accounting as a basis from which to plan their future actions. For this is private knowledge only. Transactions in varied markets can only be contemplated in an informed manner if one is armed with facts to which at least a large part of the other operators in those markets would give assent—i.e., with public knowledge.

Now some may say that the cost basis of accounting yields results which are in the nature of public knowledge; for the prices paid for particular assets were the prices known to prevail at the time of purchase. Following this line, it has been held in an English Court that, if shareholders are given the aggregate of prices paid in the past, they could if they wished, discover the present worth of assets still held. This could only possibly (but not necessarily) be true in respect of single assets specified individually, and then only if the dates of purchase of those assets were given. But balance sheets do not list individual assets, and they certainly do not list dates of purchase. Even if they did the task of interpreting them would be difficult for even the technically skilful person with access to voluminous price data. For shareholders the task would be impossible. For, if we imagine an investor with a choice of one of three stocks in contemplation, he would have to know the price movement and present price data for all the different assets held and used by the three companies —as I said, an impossible task; but it is only a beginning.

Against the aggregate of prices paid are set off allowances for depreciation and other valuation provisions. These are not public knowledge. They are the products of the particular applications of particular formulae chosen by particular firms at particular points of time in contemplation of particular future events. Their present significance is just not discoverable by outsiders, no matter how skilled.

It is a poor service to those who only need information in the nature of present public knowledge to give them a "do-it-yourself kit" with most of the pieces missing. If we are asked for an indication of our present state, and we say merely what we did at various, singular times in the past, we evade the question. We give a non-answer. We practise non-disclosure.

We are also told that apportionments and allocations of initial costs provide information which helps to build up useful aggregates and differences. But apportionments and allocations also are privy to each individual firm, and can only yield private knowledge. They may be useful (we will not debate the question here); but they can only be useful if they are continuously corrected in the light of new knowledge of a public sort, that is from the market place. Norbert Wiener has pointed out the tendency of information continuously to break down, to become disorganized (and therefore useless) unless it is consciously and continuously kept related to environmental facts. Conventional accounting is a system which connives at the continuous breaking down of the informational content of its messages; which is just the opposite of what an information system should be.

There is a further side to the matter. How often does one read, from the pens of accountants, phrases such as "from the accountant's point of view"? Much too often. For, "an accounting point of view", in the contexts in which it occurs, means that a special noise is being inserted between the facts and the recipients of the message. How then, can the message come through loud and clear? The phrase "accounting point of view" is, in fact, a signal that the message contains or is to contain private knowledge only; for though all accountants may agree that the message is according to "generally accepted principles", that message is often astronomically remote from the public knowledge of the market place—and is therefore useless in relation to operations in the market place.

The search for public knowledge, knowledge which will be useful in any possible situation entailing a choice, is essentially no different from the search which scientists of every variety are engaged in. The physical scientist, for example, wants to know the character of light or of electromagnetic force—not in a specific situation, but so that knowledge of this "character" may be used in any and every situation in which light or electromagnetic force plays any part. The process of discovering the character of any such phenomenon is called *research*—searching carefully, meticulously, searching again and again. But in *applied* research laboratories you will find scientists making particular "discoveries", about the properties of particular things, the spectra of light from particular sources, the tensile strengths of particular materials, the boiling points of particular liquids. The numbers and descriptions they assign to these properties of particular objects have meaning in the context of the general scientific laws and theories. They are not derived in contemplation of what may suit scientists personally ("a scientist's point of view") or what may suit the clients or employers of scientists ("a user's point of view"). Once the specific properties of an object or substance is known, this knowledge constitutes the "laws" which determine the use of the object or substance, by anyone whatever.

In the same sense, accounting is applied research. There is a real-world framework in which the financial characteristics of the entities it deals with have significance. There should be a theory adequate to describe and explain these. Given this theory, the particular descriptions and numbers assigned to the objects of accounts by any accountants in any firm will have meanings in the context of the theory. If the theory is a realistic representation of the real-world framework, the particular descriptions and numbers assigned will be realistic. They will not be statements from "an accounting point of view" or from "a user's point of view". They will be representations of what *is* at a given point of time, able to be used by any person to whose judgements a knowledge of "what *is*" is relevant—managers, stockholders, financiers and others. In this sense accounting *is* research, the continual "rediscovery" of the state and consequences of relationships which are themselves continually changing. Accounting statements should be the same in kind as the statements of research scientists generally.

The financial statements should ideally embody the "laws" which for the moment define and constrain the operations which are possible —financially. They should be such that they predict the limits—the financial limits—of immediately future actions. They may not predict the precise form which any such actions may take. But they should predict the financial limits of any and every immediately future set of actions. This being the character of accounting ideally, its procedures should follow the same procedures as any other form of research or scientific inquiry. It must be rigorous, working with the only things it is competent to work with, limiting itself to the discipline of its own subject-matter, concentrating on the one thing it is capable of doing—discovering the relationships which constitute the financial constraints of future actions. It is only because those constraints are continually changing that accounting is a continuous process: otherwise it differs no whit from other kinds of research which from time to time congeal in "fixed" laws.

Now there are many who think that accounting is so intimately linked with decision-making that the link is indissoluble. Such phrases as "accounting for the future" are so freely used that the impression exists that the area of decision-making is fair and proper game for accountants. Much of the talk about more mathematics in the accounting curriculum is, I believe, sired by the idea that accountants are or should be in the decision-making business. But it does not matter into what non-accounting business accountants go; what they *do* is no indication of what accounting *is*. Decision-making and all that it implies is non-accounting. No one can account for something that has not yet happened—it is plain abuse of the language to talk about accounting for the future. It is also plain abuse of common sense to talk about decision-making on the basis of any other facts than those which define exactly where we are now. And yet accountants want to get into this bewildering and murky business of figuring about the future when they have not yet resolved the problem of representing the state of a business as it stands in the market place at any point of time!

This insistence on the limits of accounting as a subject may seem petty, peevish and pedantic. But it rests on what seem to be sound principles. Everything that has gone before is now a matter of record, or can be made a matter of record. It can be made into a representation of how things stand now. Unless this occurs in accounting, accountants should forever give up talking about accounting for decision-making. The production of the statement of how things stand now may be difficult—but no more difficult than the discovery of how to isolate oxygen or mercury; and these steps were necessary before anyone could make use of those elements. But whatever the difficulties, this problem must be resolved—if you grant that the function of accounting is to provide useful information. For this purpose, what any body or bodies do with the information once it is compiled is immaterial. If in compiling such information accountants have in mind any *specific* future use of it, the result is inevitably biased and such statements cannot be said to be objective or independent. In fact it leads to absurdities. For if one prepares accounts from a particular viewpoint (rather than accounts which represent an entity to all beholders), and if one admits that there are many interested groups with different viewpoints (and this is freely admitted in the literature), it follows that there must be different accounting statements for every such group. And, as every such group has individually different component members, each with his own viewpoint, it follows that there should be different accounting statements for every single interested party. Now, can you imagine American Telephone and Telegraph preparing over two million individually tailored financial statements—just to mention its stockholders alone? To fly from the difficulties of representing the entity as it stands, so that each class of persons may assess its status in the knowledge that all others can get an equally useful impression of it, is to choose the fire rather than the frying-pan.

Perhaps the greatest of all the deficiences in the discussion of accounting is deficiency in definition. We much prefer non-definition. Where, for example, does one find a worthwhile description of the function, the objective, of accounting, by reference to which one could determine how to go about it? There are descriptions in terms of the specific operations which are performed in the process of accounting, but these give no orientation or sense of direction. Where does one find a description of any specific class of accounting entities sufficiently clear to suggest the type of accounting appropriate to it? There are many bold assertions and many more implicit propositions in treatments of this or that variety of accounting; but one cannot begin to design a system of appropriate ideas unless one first discovers the features of the entity for which the system must be appropriate.

There are even examples of definitions in the literature which clearly imply that accountants may play fast and loose with the established usages of the language. One could not, of course, complain about this if there were a tightly knit set of definitions and other propositions which required that everyday terms should, for accounting purposes, have special connotations. But there is no such set of definitions and propositions and whether it is necessary to give everyday words special meanings has not been the subject of even the most tentative inquiry. Inadequate description and non-definition lead to woolliness in thinking. Instead of accepting the rigor of the intellect, we labor under the threat of intellectual rigor mortis.

This has perhaps been a rambling kind of non-discourse, a collage of blacks and whites when the world is really full of other colors. But in case you disagree with me, may I restate a few of my points so that you will be quite sure what you disagree with?

1. Accounting is of the same genre as scientific research. There must therefore be for it the same kind of discipline as pertains to any serious process of getting knowledge—a determination on the part of its executants to discover the possibilities and constraints of action from time to time and to represent those possibilities and constraints so faithfully that the information is useful to whomsoever it is given and for what purposes soever it is used.

2. Accounting is not decision-making, nor should its information-product contemplate any specific decision. All reasonable decision-making is based on what is known of the here and now. The choice of a course of action involves consideration of many hypothetical factors in hypothetical combinations with hypothetical probabilities of achieving hypothetical results. Many quite untrained and intellectually undisciplined people can size up prospects surprisingly well. But this morass of hypotheticals is confined by reliable knowledge of where one is, financially, at the time. It requires perceptiveness, discriminating skill and discipline to do the work of sifting out the momentarily relevant facts. This is the pre-eminent task of accounting—the one task which makes it a genuine specialism.

3. Contemporary routines do not enable accounting to give the service of which it is capable. And largely because of lack of definition, the sort of definition which ties together the formal procedures of accounting with the observable realities of the contemporary financial and commercial world. In a vague way ancient history illuminates the present, but one does not attempt to explain World War II by starting with the Greeks. Accountants should, I believe, forswear an analogous sort of vagueness and irrelevancy.

4. Accounting needs no apologetics. In a monetary economy it has a clear and significant function. It needs to build no empires in non-monetary and non-quantifiable areas. It certainly needs overhauling so that its function may be more competently performed; and in this direction there is ample opportunity for the exercise of constructive imagination. Those who possess the vision and competence to grasp this opportunity will find no need to venture into the everyman's land of non-accounting.

46

LOOKING AT ECONOMISTS LOOKING AT ACCOUNTING*

There are good reasons why economists should look at accounting. They are concerned, at least to some extent, with the process of economic choice and the only justification for the process of accounting is that its products bear on economic choices. Economists may, if they choose, ignore the detailed features of accounting, just as they ignore the psychological factors which underlie choices: but to the extent that they do so their models can only be the less characteristic of the domain of economic behaviour they are intended to represent. In any event some economists have found it desirable and useful to include in their expositions some references to accounting. We shall look at three examples of treatments of accounting by economists.

P. W. S. Andrews devoted the second chapter of his *Manufacturing Business* to a description of the reckoning of business income, "consistent with what accountants actually do". At a later point (p. 160) he observes that cost accounting "makes a careful allocation of all the costs of operation so that a businessman can use his accounting records as a valuable guide to his control of his business". Clearly Andrews supposes that accounting provides useful information. But control of a business means adapting its operations to the realities of the environment. What then, if accounting fails to represent the business in a manner other than is relevant to control or adaptation? If this is so then it is clearly false that accounting records—the product of what accountants actually do—may be used as a valuable guide to control.

Now it is demonstrable that accounting does not represent businesses in a manner relevant to adaptation. After describing the balance sheet Andrews concludes (p. 67) that the only items in it of any general significance are the statements of "the values of floating assets on the one side and of the current liabilities on the other. The other items will have analytical importance only in so far as they result in revenues, or give rise to charges which affect the revenue accounts, and they are directly taken into account there". It seems to be overlooked that a revenue account is a set of inferences from two balance sheets. Now if, as Andrews notes (p. 54), the values at which plant assets appear in accounts are their money costs less previous charges against income, and as those money costs are costs at different

* First published in *The Economic Review* (Sydney University Economics Society), 1964, pp. 36-7.

times, and if money outlays procure different amounts of plant capacity at successive times, no balance sheet containing them can be relevant to any specific point of time, and no inference from two successive balance sheets can be relevant. How then can cost accounts, which are a further analysis of revenue accounts, provide a valuable guide?

Andrews was aware that the cost basis of accounting was under dispute and that a change to replacement cost as a basis had been proposed, but it seemed to him that "those accountants who resist the change . . . are correct" (footnote, p. 35). It is hard indeed to reconcile this with the adaptive process he subsequently describes. At bottom many of the procedures of accountants in practice are habitual. It is therefore quite insufficient to rely on accounting information as a basis in a description of adaptive behaviour. We are told that "a businessman is notoriously interested in flexible minds" (p. 98). It seems to be reasonable to expect some theory of the manner in which the results of inflexible rules are corrected by flexible minds in the process of control and policy-making. It is difficult to resist the conclusion that Andrews takes too much for granted in accepting the products of the formal accounting process, as it is actually carried out, without reference to their deficiencies and the other sources of information which in some respects compensate for those deficiencies.

Samuelson (*Economics*) offers an appendix, entitled "Elements of Accounting", to his chapter on business organization and income. This is entirely descriptive: there is no noticeable attempt to link it with the ideas developed elsewhere. It would seem to be obvious that the varied methods of accounting for inventories and depreciation of durable assets (Samuelson gives examples of both) will result in varied representations of the income of any business firm. If then there is no unequivocal meaning of income, it would seem to be pointless to go on to present a theory of income. Dealing with money and interest rates, Samuelson observes in a footnote that "a widow who keeps her money in a stocking when inflation is wiping out the value of her wealth [thinks she] is holding her own: when, actually, she is frittering away her inheritance". This same "fallacious reasoning" underlies the kind of accounting he describes; it is difficult to understand why this fact, obviously of greater importance than the case of the witless widow, escaped mention. Treating the possible alternatives to holding cash balances, Samuelson resorts to the beliefs or expectations people entertain in respect of future incomes. But if business incomes, as they are represented in accounts, depend on artificial rules which are unrelated to market situations, potential investors in business securities can have little guidance, if any, from business accounts in forming their expectations.

As with Andrews, the treatment of accounting seems to be an excrescence; recognized because it has some "practical" form, but handled gingerly, if not in a cavalier manner, because the consequences of its processes are only vaguely perceived.

Our third and last example will be Boulding's article "Economics and Accounting: the Uncongenial Twins"[1]. Boulding has a good deal to say that is pertinent in any discussion of accounting as a guide to economic choices. But he also says some rather curious things. He notes that the valuation of assets as "discounted future net receipts" is "the truly significant figure", but adds immediately, "The accountant is wise to take the past accounts as the basis for his evaluations". If one piece of information is truly significant, what is the wisdom in deriving a quite different piece of information? If the accountant were to take all past changes in market prices into account, Boulding's observation would not be inappropriate. But at another point he says, "I am particularly suspicious of attempts to improve accounting by building into it an explicit recognition of the fact that the price level changes". It is difficult to imagine how one can be suspicious of a device which attempts to give explicit recognition to a pertinent fact.

The real sting lies in the penultimate paragraph of the article. "There is something to be said . . . for a certain naiveté and simplicity in accounting practice. If accounts are bound to be untruths anyhow, as I have argued, there is much to be said for the simple untruth as against a complicated untruth, for if the untruth is simple, it seems to me that we have a fair chance of knowing what kind of an untruth it is. A known untruth is much better than a lie, and provided that the accounting rituals are well known and understood, accounting may be untrue but it is not lies; it does not deceive because we know that it does not tell the truth, and we are able to make our own adjustments in each individual case, using the results of the accountant as evidence rather than as definitive information."

This is a devilish broth of apologetics. Why are accounts bound to be untruths? Is it not possible to devise an accounting which yields something better than untruths? Are accounting untruths as "simple" as Boulding supposes? In what way is an untruth better than or different from a lie? How can untruths be used as evidence of anything? And how can anyone make adjustments in individual cases from a basis of untruths? These questions apart, accountants will scarcely be induced to improve their art if they find it possible to excuse themselves from trying on grounds such as those given by Boulding. Those who find no comfort in Boulding's view will find even less comfort in the fact that it is the view of an economist.

To give Boulding his due, however, he does visualize something better. "Nobody, to my mind, has yet developed an adequate theory of information collecting and processing from the point of view of the decision-making process. When this is done, we may find that both accounting and economics may each lose their life in a larger science and a larger process."

That, perhaps, is a sufficiently challenging point at which to conclude.

---

[1] See W. T. Baxter and S. Davidson (eds.), *Studies in Accounting Theory*, London, Sweet & Maxwell Ltd., 1962, pp. 44-55.

47

PROFESSSIONAL EDUCATION AND THE VATTER REPORT*

Introduction

A major product of the Vatter inquiry is the collection of the statistical and descriptive material which makes up the greater part of the report. Few people who have been concerned with the teaching of accounting or with the examination of candidates for professional bodies will be unaware of the shortcomings of the present state of affairs. Some would be able to compare the Australian system with the systems of professional preparation used in other countries, not always to the disadvantage of the Australian system. None however would have known much of the way in which various groups of qualified accountants occupy themselves, of their educational backgrounds or of a variety of other matters on which Professor Vatter has gathered information. To have this information may be convenient for many people: it will perhaps be used as evidence for all kinds of claims, in one context or another. But our principal concern, and no doubt the object of its collection, is the light it might throw on the requisite standard of professional training and education in the future.

Major assessments of this kind occur infrequently. It might be supposed therefore that the prescriptions which emerge would be pertinent to accountancy education over the next 10, 20 or 30 years. This supposition does not seem unreasonable, for changes particularly of a major kind take many years to implement and their effects are not noticeable until years still later, when those educated under a new system at last acquire positions of professional and commercial influence. Now, on the demands which will be made on the profession 10, 20 or 30 years hence, the collection of descriptive information on the present state of affairs can hardly be expected to throw much light for several reasons.

If the inquiry were made of a stable or mature profession, with a uniform mode of entry there is at least the possibility that the present position and the recent past may provide a basis for some kind of extrapolation to the future. But this stability or maturity is not a feature of the profession, as represented by the respondents, today. The survey revealed that 13 per cent of the Australian Society of Accountants sample were university graduates; no comparable figures are given for the Institute of Chartered Accountants in Australia

---

* First published in Proceedings of Conference of the Australasian Association of University Teachers of Accounting, May 1965. The Report discussed is William J. Vatter, *Survey of Accountancy Education in Australia,* 1964.

sample. No age distribution of this 13 per cent is given, so that we do not know from the report whether there is a tendency one way or the other for entrants to the profession to come by way of the universities. If there is any such tendency, the findings of 1964 may well be quite irrelevant not many years hence. Further the heterogeneity of the sample tends to vitiate conclusions about the adequacy of educational experience and the specific deficiencies mentioned by respondents (pp. 46-47).

For a second reason the survey method is not illuminating. It is notorious that advances in technology and pedagogy emerge from the relatively small number of practitioners of both kinds who have devoted assiduous attention to the possibility of advances being made. Surveys of a general cross section or of a whole population will, because of the averaging effect, be less relevant and less pointed than the informed and carefully formed opinion of a minority. There could have been no objection to an intensive examination of the views of at least a selection of people critically concerned with the problems of advancement, for the independent position of Professor Vatter could have ensured a fair weighing of those views. The responses to a question on the kind and duration of education thought to be desirable indicate the incapacity of respondents to give a considered answer to a question on educational requirements. Indeed Professor Vatter himself was forced to accept the role of sole expert, for none of the tabulated statistics lead directly to the kind of programme of study he recommends.

Thirdly, there is no evidence that the survey or any part of it attempted to assess the adequacy of present arrangements, of the competence of present practitioners or of the propriety of present practices, by reference to the non-accounting users of the services of accountants or the users of accounting information. This seems to be a critical omission. It is a common propensity to value ourselves more highly than others value us; in an undertaking of this kind it seems very proper to take notice of some quite independent views—say of company managers, directors, lawyers, stockbrokers—both in respect of competence and specific practices.

Fourthly, there is a noticeable generality about the information sought which leaves open the credibility or the comparability of opinions expressed. From our own acquaintance we are led to wonder how well informed the respondents are—practitioners or teachers. We do not know whether the opinions expressed are based on mere hearsay, on special interest or on balanced judgement. In particular, for example, much was asked of the teacher group; but every respondent will have been more or less biased by his own experiences, his reading, his unconsidered intellectual commitments, as well as by his well-considered commitments. The differences in reading lists from university to university and as between universities and colleges suggest some material differences in viewpoint which are concealed, or at least not mentioned, in the treatment of responses.

There are many other matters germane to the objectives of the inquiry, such as, for example, the bases of correspondence courses, which rank quite heavily as suppliers to the profession. Had the survey been carried out over a longer time, no doubt information on some of these matters may have become available. But the general tenor of our present observations is that relatively little light is thrown on educational objectives and requirements by the devices adopted.

The Goal of Professional Education

Before examining the specific proposals of the report, we consider, as did Professor Vatter, the objectives of a programme of professional education. "Professional competence", says the report, "comes from the possession of knowledge . . . about the professional field. Thus the accountant's competence is based on his knowledge of business situations and business measurements and in his ability to apply this accumulated experience to problems in any particular business" (p. 2). Perhaps elision is permissible in a document addressed to the informed, and perhaps therefore one should not expect this statement by way of orientation to embrace what will be obvious as soon as it is mentioned. But it is curious that "business situations and business measurements" are mentioned as if they constitute the "professional field" and no reference is made to the very feature which distinguishes accounting, namely *monetary* aspects of business situations and *monetary* measurements.

The omission may be trivial if it were not for the fact that the less precise and the more abstract the definition of the field, the more diffuse and the less pointed will be the efforts to promote professional competence. It is not easy to point to any specific part of the Findings and Recommendations to demonstrate this, because most of the "right" words occur in the suggested programme. But the very vagueness of the descriptions at many points leaves the impression that the financial or economic aspects of business situations are a rather fuzzy core of the programme.

We would like to amplify the objectives of a programme of professional education in a way that provides a justification for "wider" studies than studies of technical detail, and that suggests how wide they should be. We seek broadly a good professional man. The first requirement shall be that he is technically expert in a limited field. By expert we mean that he shall be fully aware of all the purely technical elements of the general practice and the specific application of the existing level of technical knowledge in his chosen field. We do not expect him to be master of the technical elements of *specialized* practice in his field. Only some will aspire, and only some will be competent, to practice as specialists within the limited field of a profession. The second requirement shall be that his conception of his professional task is tempered by an understanding of and a sympathy with the environment of that task. At its simplest, this means an understanding of the place of the expert and the function of his task in the immediate environment. At its broadest, it means a wide understanding of the elements of the culture of his society, and an open-mindedness which will admit the influence, on his outlook and his practice, of shifts in the customs, institutions and general values of his society. If there is any ethical element in the practice of a profession it rests on this understanding and sympathy, not on technical competence alone. We do not believe that this "tempering" is achieved, at the basic educational stage, by the mere addition of some seasoning to the educational mix. A profession, limited though its task, is practised in an environment whole. The professional requires, then, not an introduction to other professions to broaden his understanding and engage his sympathy, but an orientation to the environment whole as an integral part of the introduction to his own profession.

Given these requirements it will be clear why we said the Vatter report uses the "right" words. Specialized knowledge within a limited field is part of the immediate environment of practice; a prescription of any kind could scarcely omit reference to special topics of a highly technical kind. And the subject-matters of psychology, sociology, political science, economics and so on are elements of the wider environment of practice; reference to them likewise can scarcely be omitted. What we challenge is the method by which these topics or cognate fields shall be introduced, and the extent to which they shall be introduced, into a programme of professional education.

The Proposed Programme

There are a number of difficulties about attempting to appraise the proposed programme of study. The first is the lack of any indication as to the manner in which it may be implemented. If we disregard many of the realities and constraints it is possible to devise and perhaps to justify almost any programme of study. Part II of the report has a deal to say about the role of universities and technical colleges in professional education; but there is no comment to the effect that preparation by way of correspondence courses should be abandoned, an oddity in view of the large proportion of the sample which proceeded to qualification in this way. The proposed programme differs to such an extent from the existing professional syllabi that some uniformity would be expected by the professional organizations; and it differs so much from the existing style of courses in universities and colleges that it would be beyond implementation in the foreseeable future even if its desirability were granted. To mention only the problems of the universities, their objectives have always exceeded mere preparation for professional practice and within the limits of their existing regulations and educational philosophies the introduction of the additional material suggested in the report would be impossible—at least in some places. The flexibility of the American undergraduate credit system is not generally available within the Australian system; nor in some quarters is it believed that it should be.

A second difficulty is the absence of any indication of the extent of the material to be covered in each phase of the programme. One element of this is the time which it is considered should be devoted to each section. The outline is laid out in years. But what is meant by a year of, say, social science? One hour per week, or five, or what, and for how many weeks? If this were known it would be possible to think for ourselves just how much ground could be covered; it would provide some idea of the intensity or variety which the proposal contemplates. Again, are we to suppose that each of the subdivisions in any year should share equally the time involved in a year's work? Are the social science, economic analysis and basic accounting units of the first year to be equivalent in study hours or work load? And again, are we to suppose that a year's work involves the same time or work load in successive years? Are the accounting units in each year, for example, to be considered as equal burdens? These may all seem to be trivial questions. But as we are given no idea, by reference to a list of topics or a set of texts for example, of what is implied by the outline, we are forced to ask for some other indication of the dimensions of the programme.

Suppose, for the purpose of discussion, that the plan is something akin to the university undergraduate course (see report, p. 22); and that to each division of the programme for any year there is allotted three to four hours of class work and twice that amount of reading, learning and exercising time. One is given seriously to wonder how much Psychology-Sociology-Political Science can be done in that time (as one of three first-year units), and with what effect, in the light of the fact that relatively little of any one of these fields can be covered in a *full* first-year course for each subject singly in university programmes at present. The same applies to the tripartite Economic Analysis (a second of three first-year units) and to other divisions. Truly, subjects can be cut down or blown up to any size one wishes; but the miniscule proportions to which the programme reduces wide ranging fields of study is likely to do little to encourage the respect of candidates for disciplined thinking, intensive or extensive. It is more likely to produce dilettantes than professionals; in others it may well induce ridicule rather than respect.

When one comes to details there are grave difficulties still. To take the Social Science unit, one would like to know what materials are contemplated which would give "an understanding of how these fields relate to business activities" (p. 24). For even if, in the end, different educational institutions choose to use different materials, in the beginning it would help to know in which direction to turn. It is demonstrable that, even in the universities, the concurrent study of economics and accounting has done little to establish in the minds of students the character of the relationship between the two. The present writer knows of nothing in the social science field which will serve the stipulated function of giving an understanding of relationships at the *first stage* level of study. This is not to say it cannot be done. But it is not done; for the very reason that most of the writers in other fields write, as do accountants, for their professional fellows, as an introduction to their own professions, not to establish relationships with other fields. Some acquaintance with the literatures of related areas leaves no doubt that conclusions which may be quite significant for students of accounting may be drawn; but they have not been explicitly drawn and they leave no clear ideas, for beginners, about the manner in which accounting methods "relate to the economic and statistical notions of analysis, and what implications [sic] there are between accounting and the social sciences generally" (p. 25).

Why a four-year programme to qualification has been chosen is not easy to understand, unless it is somehow analogous to the American undergraduate programme; or perhaps, allowing for the difference between Australian and American secondary education, it is analogous to the undergraduate plus professional programmes offered in some American colleges. Again, if for comparison we take the present professional syllabi, the switch to such a large proportion—one-half—of non-accounting units requires to be supported by argument. And again, the relegation of some matters to the advanced stage seems to require more support than is given; it may well be supposed, for example, that public auditing, system design and such matters have more bearing on professional competence of a general kind than studies in marketing and production problems.

Looking at the four-year qualification programme as a whole, it seems to have been designed specifically with the processes of management in mind. But this seems to be an unfortunate bias in view of the important function accounting plays in influencing the relationships between owners and managers, lenders and borrowers, buyers and sellers of securities. Over-emphasis on management and internal accountability may well mean under-emphasis or neglect of external accountability; the result may be intellectual dependence on the views of management instead of the intellectual independence which may be expected of the professional expert. Because of the rapidity of change in the affairs of any firm, the role of the auditor is of particular importance as assuring the reliability of information not open to inspection by others. Little enough attention is paid as it is to this authenticating function; but to relegate its study to the post-qualification stage removes a significant element of the general apparatus of discovery and the general practice of the profession.

Scope of the Programme

But turn, now, to the scope of the programme; if we telescope the description in the report, we have the following list of specific things to be studied over a four-year period: psychology, sociology, political science (all to an extent not indicated); statistical and mathematical analysis, through to time series, index numbers, regression and correlation, probability and statistical estimation, tests of hypotheses and statistical inference; micro- and macro-economics to a level beyond the "typical" first course in economics; measurement and communications (concepts and their application) in accounting; machine and computer work; business institutions and business decisions (an intensive view); business law and finance and financial institutions; business organization and management; quality and price policies, channels and methods of distribution; plant location and layout;

inventory control, quality control; operations research, linear pro-programming and mathematical models (some preliminary ideas); taxation and financial mathematics; organization theory "in relation to the overall management area"; financial management; and the ordinary basic accounting material plus "the conceptual and logical basis of financial statements" and "adjustments for changing price level" (to mention just two additions to the present curriculum). And all this in two full-time years and two part-time years of study! There must be serious doubt whether the world will ever see the product of putting a matriculant through this programme in the stipulated time.

At the risk of digressing, but because it has some features in common with the Vatter proposals, we mention another set of observations on the future training and education of accountants. As you may know, there is at present in progress in the United States an inquiry into the common body of knowledge necessary for certified public accountants. One of the submissions to the inquiry has already been given publicity[1]. Its authors make the following suggestions. "... the accountant's education ... certainly should include economics, history, political science, psychology, natural science, physical science and a foreign language .... The accountant's formal university-level education must include such courses as psychology, anthropology, sociology, political science, and organization theory ... 'operations research' must become the concern of accountants ... the accountant [should] be thoroughly grounded in linear algebra, with special emphasis on the theory of matrices and determinants ... a working facility with the fundamentals of integral and differential calculus is desirable ... the accountant of the future must be thoroughly grounded in [electronic data processing] techniques .... Accountants need a background in statistics that emphasizes the mathematical theory of probability and sampling theory .... He needs to be intimately acquainted with the finance function, the production function and the marketing function. The accountant must concern himself with all problems of management. He must comprehend the total environment of the business, including the legal, regulatory, cultural, political and social environments in which it operates, as well as the internal forces in the organization."

One wonders how seriously readers are expected to take this pre-scription, and how such a paragon could be produced (if at all) in anything like the six years of undergraduate and graduate work which the submission stipulates.

Rather than analyze these detailed proposals, we will in the sequel look at the whole problem from another angle which appears to offer an alternative solution to the basic problem of what should be taught and learned.

---

[1] Submission to the Commission on the Common Body of Knowledge for C.P.A.s, by the Committee on the Education of an Accountant, of the College of Measurements of The Institute of Management Sciences, *The Journal of Accountancy*, December 1964, pp. 79-83.

Some General Views of Professional Education

There can be no question that the growth in knowledge and the growth in the complexity of social organization impose increasing burdens on us all. We cannot be adequately equipped to deal with our environment unless we know something of what is going on out there, and something of a more or less contemporary kind. It follows that educational programmes will necessarily be different from those of a less complex age. And as new knowledge reaches the point where it is not simply the "heresy" of its discoverer, but has become part of the general framework of knowledge, educational programmes should take cognizance of the fact. However, this does not entail that educational programmes designed to produce the experts in any one field should be crammed with what is the proper business of other kinds of experts. One cannot turn back the clock. Specialization has always been the way in which men have sought to cope with complexity; it is folly to suppose that the process can be halted by attempts to annexe incipient new specialisms; the more one imposes on an entrant to an expert profession the less expert will he become.

Many proposals for giving a new look to curricula appear to overlook these points. The age of the encyclopaedist is past in any event, and there never was an educational programme for producing an encyclopaedist. The type of educational programme we have been considering we do not believe to be the type which will produce at once the competent expert and the sympathetic and comprehending professional. Instead of an infusion such programmes are mixes. They take so much of so many ingredients, ingredients often specially prepared for other purposes, and mix them in a selected order, in the expectation that the result is digestible and wholesome. There is a danger that it may produce what Pope described as:—

> "The bookful blockhead ignorantly read
> With loads of learned lumber in his head."

It seems curious that little notice has been taken of some of the observations of a number of people who have concerned themselves with the broad problems arising from the vast expansion of knowledge and the growing complexity of affairs of this century.

Some 40 years ago Whitehead[2] was already concerned with the rate of progress in knowledge and the professionalization of knowledge. He granted that "effective knowledge is professionalized knowledge, supported by a restricted acquaintance with useful subjects subservient to it". But professionalism in knowledge "produces minds in a groove. Each profession makes progress, but it is progress in its own groove. Now to be mentally in a groove is to live in contemplating a given set of abstractions . . . . But there is no groove of abstractions which is adequate for the comprehension of human life". Whitehead sees the tendency to professionalism in knowledge as a great danger in society at large; ". . . the specialized functions of the community are

[2] *Science and the Modern World* (1926). The quotations are from Chapter 13, "Requisites for Social Progress", of the 1938 Pelican edition.

performed better and more progressively, but the generalized direction lacks vision. The progressiveness in detail only adds to the danger by the feebleness of co-ordination". Wisdom being "the fruit of balanced development . . . the make-weight which balances the thoroughness of the specialist intellectual training should be of a radically different kind from purely intellectual analytical knowledge . . . [it should] strengthen habits of concrete appreciation of the individual facts in their full interplay of [diverse] emergent values . . . . There should be some analysis even here, but only just enough to illustrate the way of thinking in diverse spheres".

The dilemma—specialization only or specialization plus balanced development—is a difficult one to face. Specialization is a relatively easy way for those who practise it, as teachers or as professional experts. It is inevitable, but its dangers may only be mitigated by a different device than the mere accretion of additional specialisms or specialist abstractions to those of any professionalized field.

Ortega y Gasset approaches much the same problem from a different direction, from an examination of the function of the university in a world of professional specialization[3]. Ortega concludes that the university's teaching comprises three functions, the transmission of culture, the teaching of the professions, and scientific research and the training of new scientists (p. 48). It is the combination of the first and second which gives the good professional man, of competence and sympathy as we suggested earlier. It is the combination of the first and third which produces the good professional teacher as we shall consider him later.

Ortega is impatient with the "fabulous profusion" of studies characteristic of university programmes. "It is impossible even for the better than ordinary student to come anywhere near real success in learning what the university professes to teach him" (p. 49). "Instead of teaching what *ought* to be taught, according to some Utopian desire, we must teach only what *can* be taught; that is *what can be learned.*" What is suggested is that we are too prone to believe that the capacity of students is more or less infinite, or perfectly plastic, that we can cram any quantity of subject-matter into a programme and that it will *ipso facto* produce a better graduate than a smaller quantity. Ortega protests. We must rather take the limitations of students consciously as a datum. We must then select from all existent knowledge what appears "strictly necessary for the life of the man who is now a student", and this must be pruned to "what the student can really learn with thoroughness and understanding". Only thus can we can avoid the cant, the humbug, the pretentiousness, the delusions of grandeur, which would strike at the integrity of educational institutions.

This is not to be understood as setting a low standard upon what can be taught and what can be learned. It is natural that really novel discoveries must pass through a stage in which although their merit as

[3] Jose Ortega y Gasset, *Mission of the University*, London, Lund Humphries, 1946.

new knowledge is recognized by the vanguard of scientists, their application to professional life and their incorporation in programmes of study is delayed. Ways of teaching must be modified, new ways must be learned; but the delay between discovery and exposure of students to new discoveries should be as short as possible. But of that more later.

It will be important for the sequel to understand what Ortega means by culture. He means the "repertory of the active convictions" of an age as to the nature of the natural and the social environments and as to the prevailing hierarchy of the values of the age. Explaining this, he says: "Naturally any age presents very disparate systems of convictions. Some are a drossy residue of other times. But there is always a system of live ideas which represents the superior level of the age, a system which is essentially characteristic of its times; and this system is the culture of the age. He who lives at a lower level, on archaic ideas, condemns himself to a lower life, more difficult, toilsome, unrefined . . . . The man who lives on a plane beneath the enlightened level of his time is condemned, relatively, to the life of an infra-man . . . . It is a life crippled, wrecked, false . . . he is swindling himself out of his own life" (pp. 65-67).

If we accept Ortega's tri-functional idea of the university and the natural limitations of men, as students or teachers, we are more or less bound to his view that science must be distinguished from practice, that the university does not, except in few cases, produce scientists (in any field), and that curricula of the general kind should not be geared to the requirements of the scientist as such (in any field). The design of such a curriculum calls for clear apprehension of the core of a professional specialism and a capacity for syntheses and systematizations which contribute to the general understanding of the relationship of specialisms to life beyond the "groove". This requires "a kind of scientific genius which hitherto has existed only as an observation; the genius for integration" (p. 72).

Jacques Barzun[4] more recently finds cause for disquiet in the tendency for the mystique of science to invade, even to overwhelm, the common understanding. Like Whitehead and Ortega he recognizes the productivity of specialization and the pervading scientific component of contemporary culture. But, like them, he deplores the disparity between the veneration for science of the common man and his lack of understanding of what science is. He attributes this in part to the increasing divergence between technical and vernacular vocabularies. Even specialists in related fields "decline to speak the same language even when they can" (p. 11). Specialization leads to esotericism; science moves further and further from the possibility of it being an "object of contemplation" to laymen. And as we are all laymen beyond the limits of our own specialism, we are increasingly unable to bring to bear on our many-valued and many-sided actions the fruits of the processes of science. "The rampant specialism, an arbitrary and purely social evil, is not recognized for the crabbed

[4] *Science The Glorious Entertainment,* London, Secker & Warburg, 1964.

guild spirit that it is, and few are bold enough to say that carving out a small domain and exhausting its soil affords as much chance for protected irresponsibility as for scientific thoroughness" (p. 27). The solution to the problem of recognizing specialization and tempering its effects does not lie in exposing men to a variety of specialisms as such, but in cultivating an understanding of the many facets of living as a whole at the same time as professional competence is developing. If, because of his wide influence and his involvement in problems having many of the elements of living as a whole, we regard the ideal professional as a "universal man", we may take up Barzun's prescription: "A universal man should approach within himself the universality of all men. Though he cannot take in all possible conclusions, his mind should be open, at least temporarily, to all modes of use, from the analysis of the scientist to the synthesis of the historian, from the art of the poet or musician to the study of primitive man's superstitions, and thence upward to the intuitions of mystics and religious men" (p. 299); or as he puts it succinctly "one mind in many modes".

Education for Professional Accounting

Now what has all this to do with a professional programme in accounting? Very much, we believe.

In the first place the importance of deciding the scope of the specialism itself is undeniable. Without such a decision it is impossible to know what must be regarded as bearing on professional competence as an expert; and what may therefore be regarded as tempering the judgement. In the second place, as a principle of economy, we may select from the field of practice those elements which can best be learned in the course of an educational programme, leaving aside those elements which, because of their specificity to particular environments of individual experience and practice, can best be learned through experience. Those elements which can best be learned are general in character; for the object of the educational process is to fit a man for meeting many situations which are not replicates of the particular past experiences of teachers, book-writers or practitioners or their clients. In the third place, as a principle emerging from the objective of training professional men, we may select from the field of knowledge, those elements which are of general importance for all professional specialists in accounting. There will thus be excluded such highly specialized elements as are of interest, or of application, in narrow fields, however important they may be in those fields. Techniques and ideas peculiarly relevant to the research workers and "scientists" of the specialism would thus be excluded; for the object is to give students the best of the product of scientific inquiry, not to make of them scientists as such.

What is the residue from this filtering process? The first filter removes matters which are not strictly of the same class. If, for example, we decide that accounting has a function which relates to economic behaviour, the decision commits us to concern with economic concepts and magnitudes; if by force of circumstance physical concepts and magnitudes must be resorted to, it will be only because they have some bearing on economic concepts and magnitudes. The point should be emphasized that the scope of the function is a matter for decision, and if necessary from time to time a change in the decision. The example just given is given as example only, not as a full description of the function. But whatever decision is reached it will of necessity be conditioned by, if not absolutely determined by, the carefully considered needs of users of the products of accounting. The second filter excludes all purely mechanical operations, the form and style of which are matters of taste and vary from place to place. It lets pass all matters of general principle; such for example, as the implications of the separation of the producer from the user of the products of accounting, or the implications of the differences between discovery and evaluation of what is discovered, or the implications of the specialist, and therefore necessarily, abstract nature of the product. Matters of this kind have hitherto attracted little attention, but we believe they are very much at the heart of general practice. The third filter excludes advanced technical specialisms whether they be of the highly mathematical, or methodological or highly legalistic kind.

The filtrate is the necessary common body of specialist knowledge relevant to the general practice of accounting as a specialism. But already the illustrations of the previous paragraph suggest the direction in which educational processes for the profession should move. They should move, it seems, in the direction of intensified study of facets of accounting which are already acknowledged, but the implications of which are not so readily acknowledged. To clarify the view we hold, we list the components of what seems to be the necessary foundation of specialist practice.

(*a*) *A knowledge of the methods of empirical inquiry generally, and some familiarity with their application in some of the sciences.*

The practice of accounting consists in "finding out" some of the facts of one's environment; it is thus essentially a method of empirical inquiry. There is a descriptive literature of many of the sciences which expounds their methods and illustrates the results of the applications of those methods. It is not necessary to study these methods (including the mathematical and statistical devices employed) intensively. But some descriptive study of the ways in which some men go about the business of "finding out" has long been the habit of others who wish to engage in the same business; it is no less appropriate in accounting. At the same time such study may contribute to sympathy, in the environment of practice, with other specialists whose modes of thought are conditioned by the sciences. And lastly it contributes to the awareness of fields beyond one's specialism, fields which have contributed materially to the general culture of one's time.

(*b*) *A knowledge of the history of the development of science, with particular reference to the methods of discovery used and to changes in concepts and beliefs through time.*

This is a necessary antidote to fixity of beliefs in set ways of solving problems, and of beliefs as to matters of "fact". If, as is commonly said, accounting records and statements in series represent financial history, then apprehension of the variability of knowledge and of the variability of the present significance of past facts is a necessary qualification. Some study of the development of accounting in parallel with developments in other fields would be instructive. In any case, a sense of history also contributes to an understanding of the culture of one's time.

(*c*) *A knowledge of the perceptual, cognitive and affective limitations of individuals; of their ends and modes of pursuing ends.*

We do not require a general study of individual psychology, but sufficient insight to comprehend the advantages of co-operation, the gains and losses from conflict, and the role of the division of labour (or specialization) in human affairs. All of these matters are directly pertinent to the practice of accounting and to the design of accounting systems and statements which are to serve as interpersonal messages, for accounting as it is commonly practised is a form of the division of labour and its products have a bearing on co-operation and conflict between those it serves.

(*d*) *A knowledge of the relationship of knowledge as experience, knowledge as new information, and of expectations, to action.*

It is necessary to distinguish the knowable from the unknown and unknowable; to distinguish information from hypothesis; to consider the nature of evidence and the dependability of statements. All this as part of the process of sharpening the powers of discrimination; but more specifically because, as expert, the accountant is caught in the midst of such diverse kinds of proposition in the course of his duties. Failure to distinguish the objective from the subjective, the knowable from the unknowable, fact from prediction, puts his technical task beyond discovery and prevents understanding of the way in which these contraries influence action.

(*e*) *A knowledge of the legal and social processes by which interpersonal relationships are established and maintained and modified.*

We do not mean a lawyer's knowledge of law, a sociologist's knowledge of sociology, nor any other such thing. We mean rather a sufficient insight into the appropriate special fields to regard legal, social, organizational, economic and other processes as ways in which living is structured under interdependence. This would include some knowledge of the roles of groups; of individuals in groups; of associations, corporations and government; of experts. And its value lies in the fact that the accountant is involved both in micro-social processes as an expert, and in macro-social processes as a citizen.

(*f*) *A knowledge of the nature of systems and of the role of communication in systems.*

Firms, organizations generally, economies as wholes, are examples of systems. Some systems are externally regulated; some are self-regulating; some are exceedingly simple; some exceedingly complex. In some systems the linkages or means of communication are physical; in others verbal and numerical. Accountants are involved both as parts of systems and as operators of sub-systems. They have no role otherwise and their role is only discoverable and understandable in the context of some system. The contents of accounting records and statements constitute systems which are linked to and descriptive of the systems which are accounting entities. The notion is pervasive and its use enables the interconnections between the elements to be readily apprehended.

(*g*) *A knowledge of market and price formation processes and of the nature and role of money in those processes.*

Again a specialist knowledge is not requisite; but a reasonably satisfactory working knowledge is. For, on the one hand, accounting is intimately concerned with money prices; and on the other hand, those who use its products are intimately involved in adaptive processes carried on through the medium of money in markets. If the accountant fails to understand that pricing and production and financial policies are not unilaterally determinable, he is unable to discriminate between the relevant and the irrelevant.

(*h*) *A knowledge of the theory and methods of classification, measurement and calculation.*

This is perhaps a subdivision of (*d*); it is distinguished here for its quantitative element. Of what is knowable, only some things are measurable. It is of importance to distinguish what is measurable, to know the conditions under which measurement is possible and calculation is necessary, both in general and in relation to monetary magnitudes specifically. This involves logical rather than mathematical exercise. For general practice of the specialism it seems unnecessary to proceed to advanced mathematics, not the least reason being the crudity of anticipatory magnitudes and the imperfections of markets as sources of measures.

It will be apparent that this list has two features. Every item has a specific relation to the actual practice of accounting as a general expertise. And every item has also a wider aspect which contributes to awareness of or sensitivity to the general characteristics of living, in large or small groups as occasion demands, to the "height of the times", to use Ortega's phrase. The variety of subject-matters included in the Vatter prescription and others occurs here too; but in integrated fashion, not as a mere mixture; and in a limited but perceptibly relevant way.

But there is a further point. Being integrated with what we believe to be necessary professional education, the treatment does not depend on the availability of general texts in the related fields or on the "servicing" of studies by experts in those fields. It depends rather on the actual interweaving of the appropriate propositions or findings of experts in other fields with the technical features of accounting as and when they become necessary. The task is entirely in the hands of the teachers of accounting as such. They alone have the particular orientation necessary to select from the findings of logicians, scientists, psychologists, economists and others, those which are pertinent to accounting. They have it in their hands to make the study of accounting a routine, clerical, technical exercise or a rich experience, full of the verisimilitude of practical living in a complex, differentiated society.

Yet another point. Studies organized on this pattern do not fall back on the seemingly lame notion that there is a thing called liberal arts to which a certain percentage of time should be devoted, for "broadening" or "cultural" purposes. These effects are built in. We believe it is as possible to make the study of accounting a liberal study as it is to make the study of philosophy or history or literature a narrow and technical and limiting experience. But not without some costs.

The costs, it seems, are the paid labours of teachers and researchers. The problem of giving a professional education to the general practitioners of a specialism is linked closely with the problem of producing the teachers and researchers behind such an education; but they are not the same problem. The link subsists in the fact that, if teaching is to be at the topmost level available at the time and within what is capable of being learned, teachers have a necessarily discriminatory role. They must know more than they can teach. It is their business ideally to know what is the utmost level of presently available knowledge in their fields; otherwise there is no way of considering what at any time can be learned. And it is their business to translate the findings of the researchers into forms which are relevant to the world in which general practitioners will practice, which are assimilable into the existing framework of doctrine but advance its level, and forms in which those findings are capable of being learned. Teachers are the organizers, the integrators of the new and the old, the matchers of the essentially technical with the necessary elements of adjoining fields of study. If there is any distinction between teaching and research it subsists in this: that the researcher's role is analytical, exploratory, critical, destructive and constructive, whereas the teacher's role is discriminatory and integrative, pedagogical, illuminative and in a sense emotive.

It is fashionable these days to speak of interdisciplinary studies, to feel that the narrow boundaries of subject-matters should not be too highly respected; and to believe that the way out of the dilemma of producing either the generally informed non-expert or the narrowly informed expert is to require some study by students of things beyond their lines of specialism. That is the source of the suggestions which involve mere additions to the curriculum. It entails the belief that somehow or other students will be able to see as a whole the several things served to them in discrete parcels. We believe this is a baseless and forlorn expectation. There is abundant evidence to the effect that what does not become an integral part of one's educational experience and of one's practical expertness is soon forgotten; and that the integration of diverse matter is beyond many teachers, and *a fortiori* beyond students. What the situation demands is interdisciplinary work by teachers, leading to a richly interconnected curriculum tightly related to a professional objective, however diverse its contents may seem superficially. Against "the mental dryrot" of "inert ideas", Whitehead enunciated two educational commandments: "Do not teach too many subjects" and "What you teach, teach thoroughly." "The result of teaching small parts of a large number of subjects is the passive reception of disconnected ideas, not illumined by any spark of vitality. Let the main ideas . . . be few and important, and let them be thrown into every combination possible."[5]

These observations are perhaps rambling. Their purport however is simple enough to state. A new philosophy of education in accounting is called for by the recognition of the complexity of modern commercial affairs, the vast growth in technical knowledge, and the necessity of producing experts who are technically proficient and who have a wide-ranging sense of the realities within the framework of which they practice. Major changes have occurred in the teaching of English and mathematics in our time, in response to major appraisals of the available knowledge and of the functions of educational experience in these fields. A similar change is necessary in respect of accounting. To attempt to cover in a curriculum the diverse applications of accounting method found in practice seems simple in the abstract, but its effect is to limit the understanding and to place precedent above reason. It goes no distance towards meeting the objective of producing practitioners who will confront the unusual and the novel with the utmost understanding of broad principles and of the conditioning forces which will or should influence the choices made under circumstances not previously experienced.

For too long accounting has been cut off from the stream of advancing ideas in other fields of inquiry. But the deficiencies of present programmes will not be made good merely by adding here and there an annexe from other disciplines. The relevant findings of those disciplines must be absorbed into contemporary ways of thinking about and teaching accounting. The vague belief that other disciplines have "some" relation to accounting or "some" usefulness is not enough.

We have been concerned here primarily with the task and the general content of a professional education programme. We believe that the basic ideas which we have suggested may be made the framework on which technical features of accounting may be superimposed progressively; and that the whole may be taught and learned effectively, because it is linked systematically to understandable elements of the environment, in a three-year university programme.

---

[5] Alfred North Whitehead, "The Aims of Education" (1916), in *The Aims of Education,* Mentor Books, 1957.

Whatever may be the divisions and subdivisions of the material in any given programme, the development of professional skill, understanding and responsibility will be impeded unless the study of the subject is loosed from the shackles of long-standing habit and geared to the demonstrable features of other forms of empirical inquiry. The myths, the fictions, the unsystematic nature of present doctrines, we have gone on accepting, largely we believe because of the long divorcement of accounting from other fields. Ill-considered accretions will only compound the present confusion; a major reconstruction one could hope would do much to eliminate the illogical, the patently irrelevant, and the obfuscating features of doctrine and practice.

48

UNIVERSITY EDUCATION IN ACCOUNTING

DEVELOPMENTS IN AN AUSTRALIAN UNIVERSITY*

Some recent comments[1] on professional examinations and examinations of the universities operating under the Institute-Universities joint scheme, and illustrations from both, suggest there may be some interest in the programme of a university operating under rather different conditions. For many years the universities in Australia have offered courses in accounting as part of Economics or Commerce degrees. They were served principally by part-time teachers and their contents were influenced substantially by the published examination syllabi of the professional bodies. The latter, in recognition of the similarity, gave varied exemptions to graduates from larger or smaller parts of their own examinations. The extent of these exemptions differed and still differs as between universities, for each has developed its own degree structure and its own style of accounting curriculum.

We do not intend to elaborate upon Australian developments generally but to describe the underlying ideas of, and the growth in, the curriculum in the University of Sydney. The first full-time appointment to the accounting teaching staff was made at the beginning of 1953; there was then already established a full three years' curriculum in accounting as part of the work leading to a Bachelor of Economics degree; and two years in law and five courses in economics were required of all students as part of the twelve-course degree programme. Gradually the staffing was changed from an almost wholly part-time staff to the present position of an establishment of eight full-time teachers in accounting and two in law.

Objectives

The principal objective of the accounting school from the beginning of 1953 was the development of a programme which was at the same time an adequate technical introduction to accounting and an adequate educational experience of university standard. The appropriate analogies seemed in the first place to be such degree programmes as those in medicine, engineering, agriculture, veterinary science and others leading to professional standards of knowledge and skill. We shortly came to the conclusion that exactly the same kind of analogy could be drawn for every university programme. The

---

* First published in *Accountancy*, Vol. LXXVIII, July 1967, pp. 469-74. Written in 1965.

[1] A. M. Bourn, "A Question of Degree", *Accountancy*, January and February 1965.

objectives of teachers, or some of them, may well have been to expose students to the joys of discovery and to develop in them a love of learning (for its own sake, as it is often phrased). The objectives of students are almost always, unashamedly and indeed quite realistically, to prepare themselves for the vocational opportunities which the community offers to the better educated. A university programme, or any part of it, was therefore not to be considered as an esoteric discipline or a strictly practical exercise; we wished to combine the two elements of rigorous, exploratory thought and practical relevance, with the object of developing competent entrants to professional life having a thorough understanding of the real foundations of responsible practice.

Such an objective seemed rather remote. The customary texts then available were quite unimaginative. They could cope with the technicalities but not with the broader aims. At the time (the early 'fifties) the problems of rising prices, high taxation and industrial renovation and development were bringing some alleged defects of traditional accounting practices into notice. There was little on the subject in the contemporary texts, but there was a considerable amount in periodicals. Part-time teachers could scarcely be expected to keep abreast of this and to modify full programmes in the light of it. But we could develop some additional optional course work, experimentally, without interfering with the requirements of the professional bodies which secured students' exemptions. This we did; over the next few years such a course was offered; it did not attract large numbers, but that was an advantage, the available staff and reading materials being what they were. The previous practice of granting "pass with credit" for superior work in the regular courses was abandoned and credits were granted to those succeeding in distinguishing themselves in both the regular and the additional courses.

Experiments in the Integration of Subject-Matter

We ourselves had had experience of studying accounting as part of an economics degree programme. It had long been and still was the case that students taking accounting and economics courses concurrently regarded the two as subsisting in watertight compartments, largely perhaps because their teachers did so. If there was any merit in concurrent study, and indeed if accounting were to be developed as a university study, it seemed that the link between the two must be made explicit; even if teachers of economics were otherwise engaged, we could perhaps, for students of accounting, establish more clearly the relationship between the economic behaviour studied in economics courses and the factual premises of that behaviour which could be supplied by accounting. We set out to do so.

This entailed a complete switch in methods of teaching. The traditional texts had proceeded (and still do proceed) either from simple book-keeping to more complex kinds of book-keeping, or from a presentation of the income account or balance sheet to describe in detail the procedures by which each item is accounted for. Then, when all the technicalities have been explored, they offer a chapter or chapters (commonly the last in the book) on financial statement analysis. The student is confronted with a *fait accompli*, and he has been so indoctrinated by concentration on how to do it that he does not stop to ask why do it at all. This seemed pedagogically unsound. A much more effective process is to ask what information is required by people having dealings in money and goods in a market economy of the kind we know, and to proceed from this to develop a kind of accounting which will yield that information. This would give a sense of the logic of accounting and its processes, a sense of discovery as the matter is developed and a position from which existing practices could be appraised.

The upshot was emphasis upon economic action, on the financial information which managers of and investors in firms require to know, and on financial statement analysis as a guide to action—all at the beginning of the course rather than at the end. This entailed weaving together the elements of law, business finance, economics and accounting, an exercise which differs from the common treatments of accounting in textbooks and professional syllabi. At the same time we introduced some brief analytical studies of governmental accounting and finance and of social accounts.

Our experimental attempts towards a synthesis of the ideas and concepts of the different disciplines mentioned made obvious the necessity of definition and explication. The literature was, and still is, notably deficient in systematic treatment of the underlying problems of measurement and communication, which are the fundamental and universal functions of accounting. We began to see that, although the matters with which accounting deals are economic, its own tasks are more in the nature of the tasks of metrology and language. We gave considerable attention to the main theoretical works available (such as Canning's *The Economics of Accountancy*[2] and Gilman's *Accounting Concepts of Profit*[3]) and we used the price level problem, as it was an immediate, practical issue in the early 'fifties, as an empirical test of the various formulations of accounting principles. By this test we found the expositions of traditional views gravely defective and those views themselves quite out of touch with the function of accounting as we saw it. We were much more in sympathy with Sweeney's *Stabilized Accounting*[4], the Report of the Study Group on Business Income (*Changing Concepts of Business Income*[5]) and the publications of The Association of Certified and Corporate Accountants (*Accounting for Inflation*[6]) and The Institute of Cost and Works Accountants (*The Accountancy of Changing Price Levels*[7])—and of course the periodical literature which contested the propriety of the traditional rules.

---

[2] New York, Ronald Press Co., 1929.
[3] New York, Ronald Press Co., 1939.
[4] New York, Harper & Bros., 1936.
[5] New York, The Macmillan Co., 1952.
[6] London, Gee & Co. (Publishers) Ltd., 1952.
[7] London, I.C.W.A., 1952.

This was heady wine. We dispensed it to a limited class—to those seeking pass with credit, as has been said. But it was considerable compensation to have a group of final year students say, after three years of conventional accounting teaching, that at last they had found there was something in accounting which titillated the intellectual palate.

A by-product of these exercises was the initiation, by invitation, of a short course for all students in the first stage of the economics programme. In Sydney, unlike many other Australian economics and commerce courses, no compulsory course in accounting was required; students could choose to major in government, economic history, economic statistics, or accounting (besides in all cases the compulsory courses in economics). The object of the new short course was to provide all students with some knowledge of the methods of quantifying such concepts as capital, income, cost and so on; for they would encounter them frequently in economics and other studies, but generally unquantified. *Accounting and Action*[8] was written out of experience with, and for, this course.

Search for a Synthesis

We sought to give some indication of the direction we were taking in a short piece, "Blueprint for a Theory of Accounting"[9], in 1955. By the end of 1955 we were ready to propose that accounting be established as an honours school, entailing three years of distinction work concurrently with and in addition to pass work. This meant for honours candidates an additional seminar each week, with the attendant reading and preparation of papers, additional essays and examinations.

The honours school was established. The 1957 *Handbook* gave the following outlines for the distinction courses:—

> *Accounting I*—Financial information and choice in economic matters. Rational choice; knowledge, judgement and expectation. The evaluation of alternative courses of action. Accounting as a means of accumulating and communicating information. The abstract nature of accounting information; its limitations.
>
> Financial criteria. Relevant concepts; income, profit, yield; capital, maintenance of capital, financial position, liquidity, solvency. The financial structure of firms; capitalization, gearing, reorganization. The influence of accounting on the flow of investible funds, on the non-financial relationships of firms and on the domestic policies of firms.
>
> The theory of accounting. Types of accounting entity; liquidating and continuous ventures; commercial and non-commercial organizations. Periodical income; concepts adopted for its determination; outlays, costs, imputed costs; receipts,

---

[8] R. J. Chambers, *Accounting and Action,* Law Book Co., Sydney (Sweet and Maxwell, London), 1957. Revised edition, 1965.

[9] *Accounting Research,* January 1955; see p. 347, *ante.*

acquisition of claims. The assumptions underlying these concepts and their effects on the presentation of income and capital.

Accounting II—Concepts of income in accounting and economics; accounting income, real income; taxable income, distributable income. Objectivity, measurability, and relevance, as criteria. Fluctuating price levels and income measurement. The effects of alternative measures of income on business decisions, on the intensity of economic fluctuations, on the distribution of industrial capital. Stock valuation and depreciation problems.

Governmental accounting. Criteria of performance of administrative and commercial agencies contrasted. Receipts and payments versus income and expenditure. Effects of alternative methods on rate-fixing, the measurement of performance and the allocation of resources.

Social accounting analogous to private accounting. National income, consumption, saving and investment. Inter-relationships of the major sectors of an economy. Measurement and estimation of the relevant magnitudes. Private accounts as a basis for social accounts; problems arising from differences in concepts. Input-output tables.

Accounting III—Cost analysis. The relationship between costs and business decisions; price, volume, product-mix, investment decisions. Concepts and types of cost. The assumptions and methods of cost analysis; absorption cost analysis; marginal cost analysis. The meaning of cost under conditions of monetary instability.

The development of accounting practices and accounting theory. Origins. The impact of changes in the social and economic environment of business; the corporation, public investment, commercial legislation, professional associations, the stock exchanges, taxation. The emergence of a critical and theoretical literature. The structure of a theory of accounting.

The foundations of the programme were in such books as von Mises's *Human Action*[10], Weber's *The Theory of Social and Economic Organisation*[11], Barnard's *The Functions of the Executive*[12], Simon's *Administrative Behavior*[13]. We were thoroughly convinced that no adequate explanation of accounting, an entirely human invention, could be obtained, and no attempt to design a functional accounting system could be realistic, unless we began with the basic properties of behaviour. On this was superimposed a wide range of materials on accounting terminology, theory and history, economic thought and language, business economics and finance, costing and cost analysis: English, American and Australian sources were drawn on. The objective of all this was not to study these things exhaustively as such,

---

[10] London, William Hodge and Co., 1949.
[11] London, William Hodge and Co., 1947.
[12] Cambridge, Mass., Harvard University Press, 1947.
[13] New York, The Macmillan Co., 1949.

but to bring every contiguous field to yield its share of widening influence on the comprehension of the accounting function and process.

In 1960 new by-laws were adopted as a consequence of which the honours programme was extended. Distinction work was required to be taken in the second and third stages of the course (not in the first, as hitherto), and a final honours year was superimposed. In the latter, three seminars per week, an honours essay of 20 - 30,000 words, and three or four final examination papers constituted the regimen. The process of cutting out older materials and adding new was continuous. The study of social accounts was dropped when the economics department introduced a substantial treatment of the subject. Less time was devoted to governmental accounts when their study was introduced in 1958 to the pass course in accounting.

Meanwhile the search for foundations had been widening and deepening. The historical study of the origins of contemporary thought and practice was extended; the growth of business, the impact of the industrial revolution, the emergence and efflorescence of the corporation, the spread of investment in securities, the regulation of utilities, monopolies and securities exchanges, the growth and influence of professional accounting associations, were explored for explanation of the specific observable elements of current practice and doctrine. At the same time inquiries into the behavioural premises of an ideal system of accounting were extended. In this the pattern of the natural sciences was adopted as the appropriate mode of proceeding. We would ask what elements of the observable behaviour of men, singly and in groups (for example, partnerships, corporations, whole societies), in the kind of society and social and economic organization now prevalent, necessitated the device of accounting at all; and from those elements we would build up by inference the rules which observable facts and behaviour indicated to be necessary[14]. We hoped that by seeking the explanation of existent practices and doctrines we would discover how much and for what reasons they differed from the ideal derived by inference from observable and well-established facts of economic behaviour. The two-pronged attack on the matter—by the historical method on the one hand and the hypothetico-deductive on the other—was expected to yield a synthesis, a broad experience for students giving perspective and insight of the kind a university education should provide.

There was a reasonable amount of historical material available, but it had not been arranged or interpreted with a view to the explanation of the apparent deviation of contemporary practices from what seemed to be contemporarily necessary. There was evidence in the commercial history of the nineteenth and twentieth centuries of the inadequacy of contemporary practices. The price level controversies

---

[14] Indications of the point of view were given in "Blueprint for a Theory of Accounting", see p. 347, *ante*; "A Scientific Pattern for Accounting Theory", see p. 356, *ante*; "Detail for a Blueprint", see p. 365, *ante*; and "The Conditions of Research in Accounting", see p. 372, *ante*.

after two world wars, the revaluation practices of many companies, the frauds and failures both of modest and of spectacular dimensions —all served to suggest the need for a revision of practices. Empirical studies of some of these[15] focused the attention of students on the idea that the "ideal" system being developed was not simply a figment of the imagination of teachers but was plainly necessitated by experienced anomalies. Students were obliged to undertake some such studies themselves[16], to inculcate a respect for facts above authorities, whether the authorities were their teachers, the dicta of judges, the prevailing state of relevant legislation, the writers of textbooks, or any others.

Broadening the Base

In seeking the factually based and logically justifiable "ideal", inquiries ranged over a number of disciplines—individual and social psychology, administrative and organizational theory and practice, law, mathematics, physical science and its history, economics, language, information and communication theory including cybernetics, logic and philosophy. In nearly all these fields we were rank amateurs; but we were curious and wanted our students to be curious, for every one of these specialisms has its justification in its relevance to human action of the reflective or of the affective kind.

The programme developed gradually. By 1964 the five units of additional work for the honours degree comprised: at the second stage, a study of economic, financial, psychological and metrological ideas culminating in a theory for the construction of a system of corporate accounting; at the third stage, a study of the generally held beliefs, doctrines and rules of the conventional kind and of the numerous partial solutions of the price variation problem, the latter as a test of the validity of the former; at the honours year stage, three units—one on the development of accounting practices; one on twentieth century developments in accounting thought based on English, American and Australian material; and one on methodological questions including an examination of the general theory[17] which had emerged from our own experiments and observations.

During the 12 years over which these developments took place there were several changes in the pass courses; by 1964 these courses included all the usual material on financial accounting, cost

[15] For example, "The Implications of Asset Revaluations and Bonus Share Issues", see p. 95, *ante*; and "Financial Information and the Securities Market", see p. 174, *ante*.

[16] Set assignments required intensive work on the developments of ideas as represented in sequences of company and other statutes; work with official and other publications on the growth of companies generally, classes of companies and specific companies; international comparisons of rules and practices; changes in methods of financing and methods of reporting, and so on.

[17] A pilot statement was given of this in "Towards a General Theory of Accounting", see p. 477, *ante*. A more comprehensive development is given in *Accounting, Evaluation and Economic Behavior*, Englewood Cliffs, Prentice-Hall Inc., 1966.

accounting, budgeting and investment analysis, governmental accounting and auditing. But from the outset we had envisaged that many of the ideas introduced first to honours candidates would find their way into pass courses. The opportunity arose at the beginning of 1965 (the Australian academic year corresponds with the calendar year). The whole of the honours work had assumed an integrated pattern; it seemed that, if the subject were developed logically so that it had an obvious appeal to the discriminating common sense of pass students, it would be possible to teach much more and much more rigorously than by older and widely used methods (as represented in the modern texts). The proposal to redesign the first year pass course along these lines came, in the event, not from the head of the department but from the staff, whose interest and enthusiasm had been fired by the prospect of a challenging and exciting enterprise beyond the narrow confines of book-keeping and the available text-books. This enterprise was to be an exacting one, because in one year pass students would be required to work through fundamental and theoretical matters well outside the range of usual texts and to cover an appropriate one year's share of the technical and procedural aspects of accounting at the same time. The response from students has been so encouraging that lecturers have felt well satisfied, despite the increased burdens they have assumed.

The Prospect

In the next few years this change in style and content of the courses will spread throughout the whole pass and honours programme. It would be foolish to anticipate the form of these changes, but, as we view the whole as a pedagogical and intellectual adventure, on both sides of the rostrum, changes there will be. In graduate work we take the same view; the course work offered is an intensive study of significant theoretical, financial, information processing and commercial concepts and developments, in the hope that candidates for higher degrees will be kept mentally alert and agile while in the process of preparing their theses.

The idea underlying the whole of these developments has been the conjoint study of practical issues and methods and the theoretical foundations of practice. We have carefully avoided the temptation to concentrate on "academic" questions (whatever they may be), in the belief that the competent professional requires to have both technical competence and the widest possible understanding of the context of practice, which is indeed a large proportion of the business of living in a modern society. We have mingled the technical, the empirical and the theoretical, to the point where the student may be critical and may understand of what he is critical and the reasons why he is critical. And in dealing with the historical development and institutional setting of practice we have hoped that his impatience with what he criticises may be tempered by sympathy with the difficulties practitioners face. Such a programme may produce some rebels, but better that than a crop of uninformed conformists.

In the foregoing we have passed rather easily over some questions which those with traditional views of the function of a university might think we have disregarded. These may be more satisfactorily treated at another time.

APPENDIX

Mr. Bourn's article gives a selection of questions from examination papers of the universities. A selection from the Sydney papers may be of interest. No examples are given of questions on analysis and interpretation of accounts, amalgamations, consolidated accounts, costing and budgeting questions of the manipulative kind. These have long been part of the regular examinations at pass level. The symbols indicate the stage in the programme at which questions were set (that is, I, II, III, Hons.), the grade of award obtainable (C = Credit, D = Distinction), and the year. The questions are taken from special papers for awards above the pass level, but the changes mentioned in the article may lead to many questions of the kind illustrated appearing in future pass papers. The classification of examples is less specific than Mr. Bourn's: the items are numbered straight through.

Accounting Generally

1. Is the maintenance of capital a purpose of accounting or an issue in accounting theory? (I, C, 1954)
2. Consider the relative merits of "historical accuracy" and "present relevance" as bases for a system of accounts. (I, C, 1954)
3. Discuss the reasons for the demand for accounting standards. Is the search for accounting standards premature? (III, Hons., 1958)
4. "The real functions of accounting are to a large extent intermingled with and obscured by the apparent functions." Discuss. (III, Hons., 1959)
5. "Accounting may more properly be considered as a language than as a branch of economics." Discuss. (Hons. 1963)
6. State a case for there being only one true and fair view of the financial position of a firm at a given time. (Hons. 1963)
7. "Whereas the function of information is to reduce doubt, the effect of many features of published financial information is to increase doubt." Discuss, giving illustrations. (Hons. 1963)

Accounting Theory

8. "Imperative propositions involve value-judgements and thus have no place in theory." Discuss. (I, C, 1955)
9. Outline a proof of the proposition: Periodical accounting is a necessary condition of rational action in the case of continuing organizations. (I, C, 1956)
10. "The case for incorporating the effects of price level changes in accounts can only be *illustrated* by empirical studies of past operations; it can only be *proved* by argument from realistic premises." Discuss. (III, D, 1962)
11. "Accounting conventions and doctrines describe, they do not explain." Comment. (III, C, 1956)

12. Write a critical note on the Moonitz and Spouse studies on postulates and principles. (Hons. 1964)

13. "[It is a fallacy to assert] that things and services exchanged are of equal value . . . . Values and valuations are intensive quantities and not extensive quantities. They are not susceptible to mental grasp by the application of cardinal numbers" (von Mises). Is accounting concerned with the measurement of values, notwithstanding the above view, or is it concerned with the measurement of something other than values? (Hons. 1963)

14. "Accounting has no justification whatever in itself . . . . All of its postulates must therefore be outside of it, must be descriptive of the world in which it plays a part" (Chambers). Discuss. (Hons. 1963)

15. "In economics, . . . the ultimate constituents of our fundamental generalizations are known to us by immediate acquaintance. In the natural sciences they are known only inferentially" (Robbins). By what process are the fundamental generalizations of accounting discoverable? (Hons. 1964)

Systems Design

16. Consider three features of organizations, differences in which many influence the kind of accounting system which is appropriate. (I, C, 1955)

17. Write a note on the problems of designing an information communication system. (III, Hons., 1961)

18. "Science has been characterized as a search for system (order, constancy) amidst diversity and change. The idea of isomorphism is the clearest expression of what such a system means" (Cohen and Nagel). Has this any bearing (*a*) on accounting theory, (*b*) on accounting practice? (Hons. 1963)

19. "Most human decision-making, whether individual or organizational, is concerned with the discovery and selection of satisfactory alternatives; only in exceptional cases is it concerned with the discovery and selection of optimal alternatives" (March and Simon, *Organizations*). Examine this view of economic action and its adequacy as an assumption for accounting. (II, D, 1963)

20. "Unless accounting is a measurement system its products can have no useful relationship to the making of business decisions." Discuss. (Hons. 1963).

21. ". . . the evidence indicates that accounting has never been consciously directed towards serving the needs of investors" (Staubus). Discuss this criticism, and suggest broadly what needs investors have for financial information. (Hons. 1963)

Business Finance

22. "New emphasis on debenture and note financing has caused concern as to whether the financial structure of Australian companies has been weakened" (Press Comment). Consider the issues involved. (I, C, 1958)

23. Has the quality of accounting information any bearing on the allocation of economic resources? (I, C, 1958)

24. A considerable number of companies have revalued their fixed assets, especially freehold property, in recent years, both to bring book values into line with market values and to protect their independent positions. Discuss this matter in relation to generally accepted accounting conventions. (III, Pass, 1958)

25. "Taxation of business incomes on the basis of conventional accounting procedures involves undisclosed discrimination." Discuss. (III, D, 1961)

26. Examine the cases for and against par value shares. (Hons. 1963)

27. Are there any general factors which govern (*a*) gearing of every type of business; (*b*) gearing of specific types of business? (Hons. 1963)

28. To what extent, if at all, is it true that in spite of the best endeavours of the legislature ordinary shareholders are, of necessity in many cases, little more than unsecured lenders of money at an uncertain rate of interest? (Hons. 1964)

Costing, Budgeting, Pricing

29. Using whatever classifications of cost are required, state and justify the cost aggregations appropriate to the following decisions: (*a*) whether to establish a new manufacturing enterprise, (*b*) whether to make or buy, in the case of an established firm, (*c*) whether from time to time the efficiency of a manufacturing department is changing, (*d*) whether to add a new line requiring additional capital expenditure. (III, Hons., 1958)

30. "Nowhere in all the domain of business does cost make its direct mathematical way in price" (Hamilton). Discuss. (III, Hons., 1959)

31. "Cost accountants have spent too much effort in trying to arrive at total cost by building up complicated and delicate structures which depend on arbitrary assumptions" (Edwards). Discuss these assumptions. (III, Hons., 1960)

32. "Practically every industrial firm is so structured that its divisions must be in conflict with one another" (Churchman). Discuss, with illustrations. In these circumstances what is the function of a budgetary control system? (III, Hons., 1961)

33. Indicate the possible uses, and examine the assumptions, of break-even analysis. (III, C, 1954)

34. "The net profit per product is a meaningless figure if a firm manufactures or trades in a variety of products." Discuss. (III, C, 1955)

35. Is direct cost a useful approximation to marginal cost? (III, C, 1957)

36. "It is to the curious rigidity of the accounting conventions of modern industry that we owe the survival into the twentieth century of the full cost principle" (Wiles). Comment. (III, C, 1957)

37. Is "standard cost" a contradiction in terms? (Hons. 1963)

History

38. "The principal discursive treatments of accounting over the last twenty years cannot be described as theory." Discuss with illustrations. (I, C, 1956)

39. Compare the "Inventory" of Pacioli with the modern balance sheet. (I, Pass, 1961)

40. Discuss the influence of the corporation on the development of accounting technique. (III, C, 1954)

41. Discuss the change in the relative importance attached to the balance sheet and the profit and loss account since the seventeenth century. (III, C, 1954)

42. Consider the impact of law and judicial decisions on the development of concepts of income. (III, C, 1955)

43. Examine the influence of professional organizations on the practice of accounting during the last century. (III, C, 1956)

44. "The accounting profession in Britain in the mid-nineteenth century was ill-equipped to shoulder the burdens of the financial publicity provisions of the Companies Acts." Discuss. (Hons. 1963)

45. Discuss the development of American professional opinion as evidenced by the Accounting Research Bulletins, the Report of the Study Group on Business Income and the Accounting Research Study series. (Hons. 1963)

49

PROSPECTIVE ADVENTURES IN ACCOUNTING IDEAS*

I owe my title in part to Alfred North Whitehead's *Adventures of Ideas* of some 30 years ago; indeed I owe more than the title. But the switch in its form is significant. Whitehead recounted the vicissitudes of some of the great ideas that have modified the course of man's knowledge and thought, which, indeed, have modified his whole history. I am more concerned with our personal involvements in the process. The adventures I allude to are the intellectual opportunities that lie open to us, rather than what happens to our ideas. The two, of course, are not wholly separable. "A great society", said Whitehead, "is a society in which its men of business think greatly of their functions." If we think greatly of our functions our ideas will themselves persist or contain the seeds of even greater ideas of the future.

We cannot profitably look back over the thousands of years which Whitehead spanned. Almost the whole of the development of accounting ideas as they are today relevant has occurred within the lifetime of the Association; and in that development members of the Association have played a prominent and honored part. Without belittling the record or the massive endeavors of many we cannot here name, we can usefully look at a few ideas, a few cases in which men have thought greatly of accounting.

Looking Backwards

These 50 years have seen quite a few potentially fruitful ideas, with wide implications, brought to notice, noticed scarcely at all and almost abandoned. In 1922 Paton set down what he saw as the accountant's postulates or assumptions. This was an adventurous exercise, novel in the literature. At the same time he roundly criticized some of them. This too was rather bold. But though the intervening years have provided outstanding illustrations of the inadequacy of these assumptions, substantially the same assumptions underlie today's accounting. Sweeney, impelled as it seems by respect for some obvious facts of experience and for some of the basic mathematical verities, and MacNeal, impelled as it seems by a strong sense of the ethos of accounting, launched spirited attacks on some of the inherent illogicalities of extant practices. But although there has been abundant evidence of the validity of their criticisms, there has been little response. The enterprise of Paton and Littleton on accounting

---

* First published in *The Accounting Review,* Vol. XLII, No. 2, April 1967, pp. 241-53. Presented at the American Accounting Association Convention, Miami, August 1966.

standards foreshadowed a great possibility, that accounting could become a real language of business finance instead of a mass of only vaguely understood and only vaguely understandable symbols. But the shadow has since been taken for the substance and 25 years later we still have the confusion of tongues which plagued the construction of the Tower of Babel.

At the heart of each of these ventures lies a seminal idea, waiting to be taken up, worked over, polished, applied, tested. We cannot know why we do what we do unless we are aware of our assumptions; we know scarcely more about them than when Paton first essayed to state them; indeed I think we understand them less clearly. We cannot improve our technique unless our professional "nerves" are sensitive to the observations of such as Sweeney and MacNeal; they seem to have touched quite different nerves. We cannot talk to one another, let alone talk to the business world in the manner entailed by that magnificent word "disclosure", unless we have a standardized vocabulary and syntax. But Paton and Littleton's exercise was followed by no serious polishing, application, or testing; and even to speak of uniformity in accounting is today still anathema to many.

These men were opening the casements on some new vistas. They were on the brink of something new, something uncertain and therefore something exciting to the adventurous. I do not know whether they felt the excitement or exhilaration of say Balboa when he gazed on the Pacific, or of Archimedes as he raced towel-clad down the street, or of Roentgen as he pored over his apparatus and X-ray pictures for days without thought of food. But certain it is that there was not much excitement about the possibilities they hinted at—the possibility of an increasingly useful accounting on the one hand, and the possibility of increasingly mature study of it on the other.

It may appear to be unseemly to talk of the subjective feelings, the emotions, of men whose labors are in the realm of ideas; a kind of abstract, bloodless and bodiless realm, as it is commonly thought. But the extent to which we feel there is something transcendental about what we do or could do, something universal or path breaking or elemental or liberating, determines the success with which we do it. Excitement, exhilaration heightens our capacities for apprehension, so that we see things we would not otherwise see—possibilities and difficulties both. The more we see the more extensive and intensive does our understanding become. The more we see the more we are able to see. We see old things in new settings. Because we see the world differently, we see a new world. But new worlds are only for the adventurous.

From Symbol to Myth

Accountants, as such, necessarily lead symbolic lives. They receive symbolic messages, digest them in a symbolism of their own, and transmit other symbolic messages. Some accountants, those who write about or talk about or teach accounting (this includes a great number of practitioners as well as teachers and theorists), are drawn even further into the morass of symbolism. They talk about what accounting is, what accountants do, and to whom and why—all in symbolic terms.

Now like the use of fire, the use of symbols can give us greatly increased power to do things, things in the real world. But like the misuse of fire, the misuse of symbols is fraught with the danger of losing what we have. We face the gravest danger of taking the symbol for the substance, of losing our apprehension of what is real, the advanced form of which, of course, is psychosis. Professional psychosis! A rather shocking thought. But I use no idle metaphor, for this elevation of the symbolic above the real has happened on an alarming scale.

We frequently tell ourselves that market prices at any time are unrepresentative, unreliable guides to "true values" or "real values" (whatever those symbols may mean), when in the hard cold world of business, in which our symbols are somehow supposed to be useful, market prices are the very things that influence the behaviors of the firms about which we account. We have told ourselves that movements in prices and in the purchasing power of money are irrelevant in accounting, when in fact they are so relevant in business that businessmen spend much time and ingenuity taking steps to profit by or to avoid losing by them. Some of us talk about firms replacing assets with identical assets, and on that ground argue for the use of replacement costs; but replacing durable assets with identical assets is a thing firms never do. Some of us talk about going concerns as going on doing what they are doing; but no firm ever does just that. We talk about money being a common denominator, but then promptly disregard the fact that money amounts held or spent at different times denominate nothing in common that is of any present use.

We say that "historical cost" data are relevant to present behavior and serve up the result of manipulating them to managers and investors, when we wouldn't dare give our wives household expense checks adequate for 1956 prices. Many of us say that the value of an object to its owner is its cost (meaning its price); which is patently false, for otherwise the owner would surely have preferred to have the money which gives him greater freedom of choice. You well know that the literature and practice of accounting abound with such statements and operations as these. And you well know that the stated antithesis in each case holds in the world of business and commerce. How we can expect the rational businessman or investor, of whom we often speak, to act sensibly on the basis of reports derived on such plainly unreal principles is difficult to understand.

If we must lead symbolic lives, and if we make any pretensions to produce useful information, our symbols must have some immediate and apprehensible connexion with the things symbolized. Rather than struggle to do this, we seem to have contemplated our umbilicus, to have invented entities of a kind which do not exist, performing operations in a world we have invented of a kind that does not exist. We have then told ourselves, and sometimes others, that in accounting this or that is the proper, or appropriate, or useful, or meaningful, or satisfactory, or best thing to do—and almost always with a host of caveats which nullify what we have said. We make these epithets serve as reasons because there are no reasons or none we care to expose. (Have you ever noticed how many useless and unnecessary adjectives and adverbs befog the literature? If they were excised there would be room for quite a few more articles in the journals. The Preface to recent editions of Kohler's *Dictionary* should be prescribed reading.)

In effect we have built a wall around ourselves. Inside the wall we do what is proper in accounting. When in Rome we do what Rome does. The erection of any wall is, of course, the way to security, personal security. Wall-building is after the manner of fearful people, those who want to hold what they have. Some, like the Romans, have built physical walls. Some, like the psychotics, have built walls of ideas. Some build intellectual walls. But all wall-building spells the end of adventure. Protected by walls, people have no longer to use their wits; their wits get rusty, for they think they have solved the problem of security. One of two things, however, may bring about a change. People beyond the walls may be anxious to conquer them, to breach them—think of Rome, think of the Maginot Line. The once walled-in are then the losers. Alternatively there may still be a few adventurous souls within the walls who will not be constrained. They are prepared to take the risk for the sake of the new possibilities they envisage. Columbus was one such adventurer; and Spain, once walled in by beliefs about the Atlantic, became much the richer. History forgets the unadventurous; it remembers the adventurous, and the course of history is changed by them. The questions confronting us today are whether we are going to isolate ourselves to the point where we become flabby, to use Hatfield's epithet, and open to destruction, or whether from within we are to encourage and undertake adventure.

What walls, then, have we built, and with what materials? What impediments are there now to adventures in accounting ideas? But before I attempt to answer these questions I would like to assure you that wall-building is not peculiar to accounting. It has occurred over and over again in the history of ideas, even in what we now call the exact sciences. Its origin lies in something basic in human nature, perhaps the desire for security, the wish to enjoy the good life, a life made good by what seems to be the very efficacy of the ideas held at any time. There is absolutely no good reason to be shamefaced about accounting if for long periods we observe no major transformation in its theory or practice; for accountants are also people. They are just as desirous of the good life as others, and just as prone to seek freedom from doubt by belief in the perfection of present modes and belief in the wisdom of their intellectual forbears. Nevertheless, we may well be made to look foolish yet, if the walls are breached from outside because we have trusted in them too blindly. What walls, then?

Exclusivism

The first I shall describe as exclusivism. Many of us believe that accounting is not like other subjects of inquiry and fields of practice; that it is not capable of being analyzed by the same methods as other fields of knowledge; that it is not a science and cannot be brought under laws and principles of the kind which give order and intelligibility to other fields of knowledge. Every such notion limits our vision; it makes our field of interest an isolated field. It cuts us off from the very experiences of business that alone give meaning to our professional existences. And it cuts us off from the benefits we might have from contemplating other modes of inquiry.

If we were conscious of these effects, we would ask on what authority this notion of exclusiveness is asserted—for it is only asserted, never proved. Is it true, or reasonable to suppose, that there can be a form of mentality, of intellection, peculiar to accounting? If the answer is yes, we must accept the consequences—namely that anything accountants do, the product of that intellection, cannot ever be grasped by the ordinary run of intelligent people. In saying "cannot ever be grasped" I am merely stating the logical consequence of the assertion of different forms of mentality. Now, of course, there are some who assert that accountants must educate the rest of the world to understand what their statements say. But it is also a logical consequence of the assertion of different forms of mentality that we cannot ever teach others to understand; for to teach others we must begin with the assumption that our modes of thinking are the same. In short, if we hold this view we are bound forever to talk only to ourselves about our own mental constructions—and clearly clients do not pay accountants to do just that. We become nothing but mystics.

If the answer is no, there is not a peculiar form of intellection, we must accept the consequences of that—namely that the same mental procedures, for the generation of broad principles and general laws, apply equally in accounting and in every other field of human inquiry; and that the statements we produce should be understandable to intelligent people without any indoctrination on our part.

In case you suppose I overpaint this exclusivism consider just a few examples. We have almost fled from the use of the term "principle" in the sense in which it is used in other fields of rigorous discourse. We have cut the meaning of "objectivity" down to a size that suits us, regardless of its meaning in other fields of discourse and in the ordinary everyday world. We speak of "measurement" and produce measurements in ways that are quite inconsistent with other usages and forms of careful measurement. We speak of "financial position" with reference to something no ordinary intelligent person would think of as his financial position. We include as assets and liabilities things which no ordinary intelligent person would think of as assets and liabilities. And, on a more general level, hardly ever do we find in the literature any reference to analogous procedures in other fields of thought and practice. And this, in spite of the fact that analogies have produced many of the great leaps in human thought; and in spite of the fact that we argue freely from what we call "models", which are after all only invented analogies. So much for exclusivism.

Mistaken Identification

A second type of wall-building material or principle I shall describe as the principle of mistaken identification. The basis of this principle is in flat contradiction of the principle of exclusivism: nevertheless we seem to be able to hold these two contradictory positions at the same time—and this is an indication of professional schizophrenia. Let me develop the idea by several examples.

There is a great tendency to identify theory and practice. The tendency finds expression in many ways. It is said explicitly by some that theory is the rationalization of practice, that theory must be based on practice. A great deal of what is called research—and research is properly the handmaiden of theory—consists in looking at what is done by accountants, disregarding the actual or potential consequences in the outside world of what is done. A great deal of the textbook literature presents what is called theory, but what is really no more than descriptions of practice.

Now, in the normal practice of a profession in any age, there is necessarily a great deal which must be taken as accepted or acceptable among practitioners. If it were not so there could be no common understandings among them on professional matters and no basis for contractual arrangements among their principals or clients. However, notwithstanding this stability, there has been, in all fields marked by clear signs of technical progress, a concurrent questioning of the nature of things among those who may properly be described as theorists. These people are not concerned with making better things today. That is a technician's job. They are concerned with reaching better understandings of the nature of things. It is a happy circumstance when they reach this better understanding, for it paves the way for practitioners and technicians to produce better everyday commodities or services. The theorists see a new world, the practitioners exploit it. Both have their adventures.

But if theory and practice are closely identified—by theorists or practitioners—it is very unlikely that any such happy circumstance will occur. Something else will occur however. Both will identify themselves with the same causes, the same doctrines. As against the rest of the world (given, for example, the tendency to exclusivism) they will reinforce one another's beliefs in those doctrines. They will build defenses against opposing doctrines. These are well-known features of group behavior. They will together build bigger walls. But if the foundations are shaky, and no one is paying any attention to the foundations, the bigger the wall the more resounding the crash.

Instead of making any such identification, it should be recognized that practitioners and theorists have complementary functions. Both are concerned with the same materials, the same devices, the same end products; but in different ways, against different frameworks. The practitioner's framework is the immediate urgency of a single client's problems, which he must resolve in the manner commonly accepted in his field given the state of the art. The theorist's or researcher's problem is to see the field whole, without regard for immediate clients, but with high regard for the relationship of the field to all contiguous fields and to the whole enterprise of human discovery. If theorists adopt the same reference framework as practitioners, the immediate solution of immediate problems, they no longer act as theorists. But if theorists assert, as some do assert, that they are unconcerned with immediate problems or practical problems, they forfeit the right to be considered as theorists—dreamers perhaps, but not theorists. The challenges lie out there in the real world in the first place, not in our heads.

Another illustration of the principle of mistaken identification is the identification of teaching and learning. These appear to occur at the same place and time, but the appearance is deceptive. The practicing profession wants recruits; it wants them in a hurry and in many cases it wants them already equipped to earn an honest dollar. That is to say they must be equipped to carry on the normal practices of the profession at the time. This is an understandable expectation in some ways. But no one ever expects a new automobile, a new secretary, or a new wife to perform up to expectations without a running-in period. On the other hand, the teachers often have quite varied notions of their task. Some go along wholeheartedly with the idea that they should produce graduates fully equipped for normal practice, and that is all they try to do. Some on the other hand think practice is less important than "a sound theoretical foundation" for practice. They justify this on the ground that they are educating, not training; a quite legitimate justification in most people's minds. What very often happens, of course, is that their students get just another kind of indoctrination, in somebody's theory. There are others who think an educational process is different; it means throwing a whole lot of theories and practices at students and saying: "Take your pick." This at least has the effect of not closing the mind; it also has the effect of not helping the emergent intellect to discriminate.

But it seems to me that students graduating under the hands of any of these types of programs are handicapped in one way or another from the start. They are being sent out into a world where they will be leaders in 20 years more or less; but in that time it will be a different world. How are they equipped to meet that? Those who have learned normal practice will be badly equipped unless they have managed to hold back the advancement of their profession to the level it had reached when they graduated. Those indoctrinated with someone's theory will be no better off unless that theory has stood the test of intervening changes in the world outside. Those who were thrown the lot are likely to flounder and vacillate until they find thinking too hard, then settle down to the conventional wisdom—which, as you may remember, Galbraith pictured as always being behind the times.

There is an alternative to all these policies which lays a foundation alike for good researchers, good teachers and good practitioners, 10,

20, 30 years from now. That method is to inculcate the idea that the world of experience, not just accounting experience, is the perennial source of useful insights, indeed the only source of tests of our mere beliefs and opinions; and to show how observation of that world will lead to thoroughly valid sets of accounting ideas now, and as long through his life as the graduate takes with him the idea that the observable world is the matrix of his life. The graduate then will go on learning as the changes in the world teach him. He will never be out of date. He will not "learn by experience" as this phrase is commonly used in contrast to academic learning. He will learn by the "intellectual content of experience", as Dewey in *Experience and Education* described it:

"... experiences in order to be educative must lead out into an expanding world of subject-matter, a subject-matter of facts or information and ideas. This condition is satisfied only as the educator views teaching and learning as a continuous process of reconstruction of experience. This condition in turn can be satisfied only as the educator has a long look ahead and views every present experience as a moving force in influencing what future experiences will be." This type of teaching is teaching-for-learning.

I wonder how many students have gone out without an atom of sense of the adventures they may have in continually reconstructing experience as the facts of the real world impinge on them and their art. Many, I fear, have been walled in, from graduation; with no sense of where their foundations lie, but knowing only the current dogma of their time.

But the point I am making here is that it is a mistake to identify teaching with learning a curriculum. Teach techniques we must, otherwise students will not even know what we are talking about if we question those techniques. But the teacher should also, as it seems to me, be the bridge between what is past and present and what is to come. At the very least he should know and present the very best of what is being done in the laboratories and the studies of the researchers, for there is a distinct probability that some of it, heresy today, will become orthodox and accepted in practice in the students' lifetimes. Failure to do this only promotes wall-building.

I would like to give further examples—of the identification at important points of accounting with management, of accounting with economics, of accounting with anticipatory calculation. In all these cases some have failed to see that the two things are neither in conflict nor identical, but complementary. If we fail in apprehension we move further from the real into the symbolic world we have substituted for the real.

Premature Dismissal

The third material or principle in wall-building I shall describe as the principle of premature dismissal. We all tend to simplify our problems in some respects: the only way we can cope with complex problems is to cut them down to a size we can manage. The trouble is we often do this all too thoughtlessly, so that we cut out of the picture we have of the world and our part in it some quite vital elements. And this is a grave distortion of reality. Again some examples.

In the mid-twenties Hatfield, a very adventurous soul who many times championed the cause of direct observation, straight thinking, and exact expression, observed that everyone would agree with the importance of the balance sheet as a product of accounting. I wonder what Hatfield would say today. In the last 30 years the balance sheet has been so run down in the eyes of accountants that it can be described merely as "a footnote to the income account". How is the mighty fallen! There is no time here to trace the downfall of the balance sheet. But it began when accountants realized that the balance sheets and income statements they were drawing up didn't make sense in the outside world. They chose to have "better" income statements and to give up worrying about the balance sheet. Yet in the world outside it is as demonstrable as ever that statements of financial position are necessary to the users of financial information. Instead of seeing the two statements as complementary, and facing the challenge of really making them consistent, one of them was just dismissed, regardless of the needs of the outside world.

At the same time as this was happening it appeared that some practices, by which it was attempted to show assets at something like current values, had been used wantonly. Instead of seeing how wanton misuse could be curbed without doing violence to the quite proper use of the same idea, the whole notion of asset revaluation upwards was banished, and we took in its place the cost doctrine. Now presumably one of the uses of accounting information is to help people and business firms to be better off than they are now. But the application of the historical cost doctrine will never tell us how well off we are now; nor for the same reason could it tell us how well off we were last year; and for the same reason it could not allow us to discover how much better off we are as a result of last year's business, which in the case of business firms is income! Instead of seeing that both original prices and intervening changes in prices are complementary pieces of information in the derivation of the present actual position, we just dismissed one of them outright. Again that is cutting the world's business back to a size which is the "proper" size in accounting.

My third example of premature dismissal is quite different. There are many practitioners who conscientiously believe that research can only properly be done by those actively engaged, or who have long been actively engaged, in practice. There are also very many academics who believe that properly to carry out research one must keep intimate contact with practices. Both dismiss the possibility that "outsiders", those who are not so intimately familiar, can see what the problems of accounting are. The history of many ideas of course proves this to be quite a false position, quite apart from the necessary subjectivity of the views of anyone closely involved in a thing he is also observing. If we take the more or less traditional origins of some famous physical discoveries, we will note that Archimedes did not discover his displacement principle as a professional bather; nor Newton the gravitational principle as a professional dropping-apple watcher. Nor was Galileo a professional rubbish dropper from the tower of Pisa, nor Einstein a professional time-keeper or clock-watcher. And to take some examples of the opposite sort from chemistry, Priestley and Dalton, two of the founders of modern chemistry were, respectively, a cleric and a meteorologist professionally. None of this proves that professional practitioners cannot conduct research, or should not. All it does is serve as warning against the dismissal of other kinds of experience, and particularly of independent observations, as qualifications for research activity. In a very real sense, the independent observer can be the auditor of professional practice, and just as valuable to the professional practitioner as the professional auditor should be to the manager and the investor. As in the other examples, what are so often seen as alternatives may be much more realistically seen as complementaries.

There are other examples of this principle of premature dismissal. But I turn now to the mortar that binds the bricks together in this wall which encompasses accounting.

Dogmatism

If two things are complementary it is highly probable that their methods and styles should be different. I have contended that accounting practice and accounting theory are complementary in as much as they take place, or should take place, against different settings. I am now to propose that dogmatism is necessary in the one, but thoroughly stifling in the other.

There can be no objection to the dogmatic statement by practitioners, or their official exponents of the professional view, that inventories should be valued in such and such a way; that marketable securities should be valued in such and such a way; and so on. (There are, of course, grave objections to statements which are both dogmatic and self-contradictory, as when more ways than one of doing a specific thing are promulgated. I have dealt elsewhere with this, and am not concerned with it here.) The continual assertion of such statements is one way in which younger practitioners come to learn the present state of normal practice at any time. It also has the effect of holding practitioners, who might otherwise deviate under pressure from clients, to a firm line (if, that is to say, there is a firm line). It also makes clear to observers, such as theorists and other users of financial statements, what the rules are supposed to be.

But there is the strongest objection to value-loaded, dogmatic expression in a theoretical literature. Like all dogmas, statements in the imperative mood have the effect of stifling discussion, of closing an issue by making a judgement. This is quite inconsistent with the ethics of inquiry, of research, and of the reporting of conclusions in other fields. Not only that; history demonstrates repeatedly that dogmatic systems will survive only if they are supported by authoritative measures that effectively cut off their subjects from intercourse with the world at large. Indeed it is one of the objects of dogma to make adherents independent of the facts of the world at large, to close their eyes to the facts. The ideology of Nazism could only be sustained by the constant assertion of statements that were demonstrably false and by the elimination of all who could make contrary assertions and of all whose very existence was evidence of the truth of contrary assertions.

Notice that dogma can only survive if it is backed up by force. Now theorists, of course, have no political power to back up dogmatic assertions, to make them effective in practice. They have, at least they can have, only the power which their apprehension of the facts of the world and the rigor of their logic gives them. But if theorists, upon whom the world depends for the discovery of error and the testing of ideas, become so debilitated that they see no logical errors, see no divergences between dogma and common-sense observation, they will make no contribution to the advancement of understanding or of practice.

Take a small cluster of illustrations involving two notions, the cost doctrine and the accrual principle. Suppose a firm buys two identical machines from two different suppliers at the same time but at different prices, $400 and $500. In practice the accounts for these two machines will open with these two money magnitudes, and the charges for their use will forever afterwards be different. Now an independent observer, say a theorist, will surely apprehend that for every practical purpose the two machines are the same; the contribution each makes to end products is the same, and if both produce the same end products the prices of those products will be the same. Yet accounting practices imply that the contribution each machine makes to end products is different! Isn't there ground for some uneasiness in this contradiction? Now suppose there is subsequently a rise in the price of such machines due to an increased demand for their products. Every unit of service output of those machines will then produce a greater inflow of cash than previously; as we say colloquially, every unit of service output is more valuable to the firm. But we will find in practice that the charge for each unit of service output is no different from the charge before the rise in the price of the machines. Another contradiction. Now under the accrual principle we take notice of changes in the machines through use long before the amounts of those changes become finally discovered, long before we get their scrap value in cash. But under the cost principle we refuse to take notice of the rise in prices of the machines on the ground that the distance to discovery of the effects, which again is the point where we get the scrap value in cash, is remote. Put briefly, there is one event in the future which determines both things; its futurity stops us from taking account of one change, but doesn't stop us from taking account of the other. The conclusion of an independent observer of all this must surely be that the cost doctrine yields numbers which do not, subsequently to purchase, tally with the facts as they are pertinent to managers; that the accrual principle is both held and denied at the same time and that the two principles are mutually contradictory or inconsistent.

I am well aware that some people are relaxing their allegiance to the cost doctrine. But they are still hanging on to it as even the latest official statements attest; witness the idea of supplementary statements. But as someone has said, "To move forward clinging to the past is like dragging a ball and chain."

As I have said, the role of the theorist is not just to observe practices, to rationalize them, and to parrot the conventional wisdom; it is to observe their effects in the world at large, to collect evidence of their effects, and to judge them on the weight of evidence. But he will not do this as long as he is walled in by what is done in accounting. The proof of a pudding is not in the cooking, but in the eating. If he gets out beyond the wall, he will find that many things dogmatically asserted and passionately believed are just not so. And that, of course, is the beginning of pure adventure, for he cannot just push the facts aside, and yet he runs the risk of appearing foolish, of being described as heretical and a lot of other things besides. If, however, he thinks greatly of his subject, he will enjoy the risk for the improvement his observations promise.

The Way Ahead

Once we grasp the futility of accepting dogmatic statements a whole new universe opens for exploration. As long as men accepted the dogma of the sanctity of the human skin, they were unable to benefit from the knowledge which enlivened the anatomical work of Vesalius and the art of Leonardo and Michelangelo. As long as men conceived the objects about them as being of the essences of earth, air, fire, and water, after the manner of Aristotle, they were unable to benefit from the knowledge to which the dawn of the age of empiricism gave birth. As long as men accepted the postulates of Euclidean geometry they were unable to benefit from the insights which the geometries of Bolyai, Lobatchevsky, and Riemann have given the world. These examples are mixed: some relate to the consequences of patient observation; some relate to sheer invention; but none of them would have emerged from mere observation of normal practice at the time.

But besides the possibility of new ideas emerging from observation of the practice and the consequences of the practice of an art, is the fact that only observation of the consequences provides any test of the usefulness or failings of the art. Who, then, sits off, independently, and examines the consequences of accounting as it is practiced? Not managers, nor investors, nor creditors. None of them is independent. Neither are practitioners independent of their practices, for they practice them. In fact no one does this independent assessing if theorists and researchers do not do it. No one marshals the evidence for or against any practice by reference to its actual consequences if theorists and researchers do not. Compared with the volume of mere opinion and dogma which fill the so-called theoretical literature of the past 50 years, the amount of actual evidence, the empirical evidence, is pitifully small. Yet the amount of evidence there is, in those

50 years of commercial history, of the inadequacy of many accounting practices I believe to be enormous and much of it is a matter of publicly accessible record.

Let me illustrate the method of observation by reference to astronomy. Astronomy has many things in common with the study of accounting. The observables of astronomy are remote and not manipulable by astronomers in the way chemicals are manipulable by chemists. The observables in the study of the consequences of accounting practices are remote; they are the actions and interactions of business people, and these are not manipulable by theorists; we can only observe. Both astronomy and accounting are concerned with problems of measurement, and in both cases because measurements are or are believed to be of guidance to others than astronomers or accountants themselves. How then are astronomers, or accountants, to test the beliefs that are held, by reference to the observable facts of experience? For to do so is the only assurance that those beliefs are not merely myths. The only way is by working out the logical consequences of those beliefs and seeing whether over time the consequences turn out to be as they were expected. Time is the crucible—and perhaps in accounting also space. Time is necessary because it takes some time for the consequences of fallacious devices to become apparent. As for space, we can test the consequences of beliefs if we find them held also in other countries that otherwise have different conditions.

By observing and testing, however, I do not mean taking the actual financial statements of firms and demonstrating what they would have looked like if they had been prepared on some different basis. That only proves that some alternative can be used; it does not prove that a hypothetical alternative would be more efficacious in the practical world of business. The proof I would seek is proof from the actual devices used and the actual observed consequences. It is the same in kind as Copernicus accepted as evidence of the defects in the Ptolemaic system of astronomy—the divergence over time of what was expected from what was actually experienced.

Observation is also the beginning of the construction of a set of ideas which shall be a firm foundation for a practically useful system of accounting. In this case we are not looking for tests of an existing rule, but for uniformities which might yield useful generalizations. The theorists' conclusions are thus not of the form, "I believe . . ." or "I recommend . . ." or "We should do this or that." They are of the form, "If *A*, then *B*." The whole fraternity of researchers and theorists is then able to see clearly the assumptions, presuppositions, and data on which the conclusion rests. They can then themselves test every step of the argument, every piece of factual evidence, every generalization. Attempts may be made to test the concurrence of *A* and *B*. Inquiries may be made to discover whether the conditional proposition is consistent with other propositions so far accepted within the literature, or accepted in the associated field of experience, or accepted in the literature or practice of any analogous field. If and as the evidence mounts, the validity of the conclusion becomes accepted, the more so if the evidence is shown to be "real world" evidence.

There is enough evidence of this kind ready to hand to demonstrate the folly of many things now asserted as practical rules and used in practice; I am convinced that one of the major reasons why fallacious rules persist is that the theorists of the game have not known how to marshal it; for practical men, the practitioners, cannot long hold to rules which on "real world" evidence are shown to be inconsistent with their ethos, the reason for their existence.

Whitehead reminds us that "The history of ideas is a history of mistakes. But through all mistakes it is also the history of the gradual purification of conduct." The instrument of this purification he speaks of as a "noble discontent" which is provoked by "the gradual emergence into prominence of a sense of criticism founded upon appreciations of beauty, and of intellectual distinction, and of duty." If we value dogma above duty, rationalization above reality, bovine placidity above intellectual distinction, we shall never experience that noble discontent, the sense of the possibility of intellectual adventure.

I have been striking out in many directions, looking at the past and present to see into the future. I would like to stress, that all my suggestions have a common source: a passionate belief in the value of knowledge, in the capacity of knowledge to free us from the influence of dogma, in the capacity of knowledge to free us from the conceits and deceits of others. And when I say us, I do not mean just theorists, or just practitioners; I mean us as ordinary intelligent men in the street as well, and all other ordinary intelligent men in the street.

One of the basic tenets of free societies is that every man shall be able to choose for himself what he shall do within the law with the things secured to him by the law. This is a great and valuable freedom; its possession is one of the things in which free societies take great pride. To choose for himself knowledgeably is what the laws governing the sales of goods and the sales of securities try to ensure to every individual. There is not a law for the wise and a law for fools. The law requires the facts to be stated as they are known at the time any statement is made about goods or securities, leaving the consumer free, knowledgeably free, to make his choices. The law has imposed a great responsibility on accountants to assist in this process—to free the millions of investors in corporate securities from being misled by the wishful thinking, and even in some cases the twisted thinking, of those who have the use of investors' money. Quite apart from the legal situation there is a similar responsibility that accountants assume as specialists, even in the ordinary course of business—to free the hundreds of thousands of managers from being misled by their underlings and from being misled by their own optimisms. The basic question we must ask of ourselves is, therefore, whether we are going to help all these parties to be knowledgeably free. If the statements we prepare or publish or permit to be published contain old elements of the past that have no present relevance, or if they embody expectations of the future that are always and inevitably subjective, or if they are prepared on the basis of dogma we impose, the managers and investors of this world will never be knowledgeably free. As long as our practices have these elements, they prevent the users of financial information from having the constitutional right to choose knowledgeably, which the institutions of a free society are expected to uphold and enforce. It is our business to discover the facts as they unfold themselves, to report them as they are, not to confuse the picture by telling only part of the facts (as when we use historical costs) or by including things which are not facts (as when we use our own estimates of future things which may never happen).

At a meeting of this Association (under its earlier style) some 43 years ago, Hatfield said: "Let us boldly raise the question whether accounting, the late claimant for recognition as a profession, is not entitled to some respect, or must it consort with crystal-gazing . . . and palmreading?" I wonder what Hatfield would think today, to see how far some would have us go in the direction of crystal-gazing. I leave you to think about what I am referring to.

There are some among us who think little of Hatfield's "houn' dog". His coat has been allowed to become shabby; he has become a psychotic. Some seers sound as though they await his early demise. But count me not among them. I am only anxious to prevent this psychosis from developing to the point where he must be "put away" in the public interest.

50

NEW PATHWAYS IN ACCOUNTING THOUGHT AND ACTION*

To many it may seem that there is little new that can be said about accounting. In the past such a view has been held in respect of other arts and sciences. But no sooner have men come to the conclusion that at last they knew all than some new idea or ideas have opened up entirely new ways of looking at things; and the reorganization of old knowledge and the alignment with it of new knowledge have begun all over again. There is no reason to suppose that accounting may not undergo changes such as the change in mechanics which resulted in Newton's mechanics becoming regarded as a special case of Einstein's mechanics, or such as the changes in biological science which followed the discovery of micro-organisms.

We hold that there is much that is new to be said about accounting. Many seem to think that the foundations of accounting are well established. We hold, on the contrary, that they are yet to be established. Many seem certain that present accounting practices, being the product of long use and experience, yield quite satisfactory and useful information. We hold, on the contrary, that they yield information which is far from satisfactory and which, in many important respects, is useless. Many seem to think that new levels of sophistication have been reached by the association of accounting with managerial decision-making. We hold, on the contrary, that the association is as yet merely verbal and that much of what is described as accounting for decision-making is quite unlinked with any decision process. Many seem to think that the computer is the most significant thing that has happened to accounting for a long time. We hold, on the contrary that the computer is a moron, and that it has little to do with the kernel of accounting.

These views may seem presumptuous. But they are not idle. They may seem to imply that our professional ancestors have done very little. They imply no such thing. At different stages in the history of other arts and sciences men have avowed that they were only able to see so far because they have stood on the shoulders of giants. It is not likely to be otherwise in accounting. But we have fewer ancestors in accounting. After all, the only history of accounting ideas that has counted towards what we now know and use is no longer than five generations, and in many respects no longer than two generations.

---

* First published in *The Accountants' Journal* (N.Z.), Vol. 46, No. 11, July 1968, pp. 434-41. This is the text of an address delivered to the 16th Advanced Accountancy Seminar in the Victoria University of Wellington in August 1967.

Contrast this with some facets of the history of science. For 2000 years, until Lavoisier, men of science believed that water was the generator or source of all matter. For almost the same interval, until Copernicus, the earth was believed to be the immobile centre of the universe. For 1400 years, until Kepler, the motions of the planets were believed to be basically circular. The history of science is full of such examples. But the men of science were neither dullards, nor idle, during these long intervals. They observed, they thought, they experimented—all three perhaps rather crudely by modern standards. But then they did not have the advantages of modern standards. And indeed, without the accumulation of their observations, without the benefit of their inconsistencies and failures, modern standards would not be what they are. Those who propounded what is now believed could not have done so.

There are good reasons why for a long time accounting ideas and practices have lacked a systematic foundation. Workers with metals have used heat for thousands of years without having any systematic knowledge of heat as such. They have handed down processes which were known to produce specific effects because the effects were apparent. Accounting, however, is not something which produces observable and nearly consistent effects. The commercial environment is volatile, so that it is never possible to conduct controlled experiments which would show up the advantages or deficiences of different modes of accounting. The knowledge produced by any actual accounting system becomes combined with all kinds of other knowledge of those who may be supposed to act upon it, and with mere beliefs and hopes as well. It is impossible then to tell whether the consequences of any action, based on such a mixture, are due to factual knowledge, or beliefs, or hopes, or chance. Opinions about alternative methods of accounting likewise are the product of factual knowledge, beliefs and hopes, even though they are given the appearance of being based on factual knowledge more often, and to a greater extent, than they deserve. It is a difficult task to unravel the threads of fact, hope and unsupported belief, particularly when men, all men, tend to cling tenaciously to the hand-me-down recipes of their instructors, in business, profession or college. It is more difficult still if we fail to take advantage of the hindsight we may have from the failures and successes of men in other fields of disciplined intellectual endeavour.

If we seek new pathways in accounting thought and action, we have much to learn from other fields. The newness which concerns me is not a complete novelty in ways of thinking. It is the application of tested ways of thinking about other things, ways which, until recently, have not been tried in the field of accounting. This is where the newness lies. Doubtless many currently held ideas about accounting are legitimate and fruitful ideas. But many other such views are inconsistent and some are demonstrably false. To make progress we need to examine them systematically; to eliminate the false, the self-contradictory and the anomalous; to endeavour to set up a system of ideas which is observably realistic and logically coherent.

Evolution or Conscious Construction?

We may take either of two views of the development of accounting thought and practice. We may suppose that there is some evolutionary process by which what now is done is best because it has survived. Or we may suppose that what now is done is a consequence of a mixture of insight, precedent and dogma.

If we take the former view we will be little concerned with systematic analysis. No amount of analysis will upset our conviction that incompetent methods, ideas, principles will have been cast off in the process of growth.

This view has notable defects. The advancement of knoweldge is not an evolutionary process. Unquestionably each generation, each century, each millenium is the inheritor of the products of preceding periods. But mere inheritance proves nothing about the quality of the knowledge transmitted. Taking a long view of the growth of knowledge in most fields, we will find that some novel ideas survive for long periods eventually to be discarded; that some after being discarded are later reinstated, if not in the field in which they originated then in some other field; that some ideas which engage their promoters for lifetimes of work yield nothing enduring; that others are extraordinarily fruitful. We find that ideas sometimes lie dormant, almost forgotten, often completely forgotten, until some fortuitous set of circumstances makes their exploitation possible. We find that many ideas arise from the mere chance that some person is confronted with what then seems to him an anomaly worth further investigation. The strong accidental element—the coincidence of persons and circumstances—in the history of thought casts grave doubt over the notion of evolutionary development[1].

Again, if we take a long view, how are we to know whether the ideas we now hold will not shortly become the dinosaurs and the brontosauruses of thought and practice, swept away without progeny because they are unfitted to the environment of the moment? There is no virtue in holding on to rules which the accidents of history have thrust upon us.

The alternative view is to regard the development of the subject as something which may have occurred in accidental fashion, and to apply to each phase of it the critical analysis of informed common sense. Consider an example. We all take stock of our personal finances now and then, when we are thinking of buying a new house or a share in a business or of taking an extended vacation. When we do this we would not dream of adding up the initial purchase prices of the house and land, the shares or bonds and the car we already own. We would try to find out their market prices. Yet when we take stock of the position of a business we merely add up the initial purchase prices of assets (less some formally calculated depreciation,

[1] See, for example, W. I. B. Beveridge, *The Art of Scientific Investigation*, New York, Random House, 1957. Ch. 3 and Appendix; R. Taton, *Reason and Chance in Scientific Discovery*, New York, Science Editions, 1962.

in some cases) and resolutely refuse to take notice of market prices. What we find quite sensible for ourselves we find quite ridiculous for business. Why? Some will say, because business firms are to be treated as going concerns. But when we make such calculations for our personal affairs it is not because we contemplate bankruptcy. We view ourselves as going concerns, going to do the same as before or something we judge to be better, depending on what we find out our positions to be. The only difference between persons and business firms is that business firms must take stock of their positions more often, because changes in customers' preferences, technical processes and the degree of competition force them to consider changes in their asset holdings more frequently. This makes up-to-date knowledge of their positions even more crucial than for persons. Yet the historical cost basis of traditional accounting ignores this, in defiance of common sense. We shall look at the matter again presently from another angle. Even at this point, however, it should be apparent that there is something curious if not absurd about the processes we adopt or the way they have come down to us, something needing conscious analysis and reconstruction.

Verbal Analysis or Observation?

There have been ages in which the pursuit of knowledge has been hampered by metaphysical beliefs about what is good or proper or permissible. Until the time of Leonardo da Vinci and Michelangelo, for example, dissection of human corpses was forbidden by the church, and these men, who wished to know more of the structure of the body for the advancement of their arts, were forced to be grave-robbers and dissectors, illicitly and nocturnally. When factual knowledge is either forbidden or believed to be unattainable, men turn their ingenuity to purely verbal and logical analysis of the views of their masters, those they esteem to have been the intellectual giants of their fields. This was the mode of medieval scholasticism. Learned men spent lifetimes in disputation, interpretation and comment on the works of wisdom of "authorities".

But these are, and were found to be, sterile exercises. As Leonardo said: "All our knowledge has its origin in our perceptions." He had scant respect for authorities as such, preferring the full and complete observation of nature. Since his time, observation has been regarded as the prerequisite of scientific inquiry and the test of scientific conclusions.

There can be little doubt that accounting at present is closer to the mode of the scholastics than to the mode of inference from observation. For years the touchstone of accounting propositions and practices has been the dicta of authorities. Sometimes they have been legal authorities, as in the case of the distinctive rules for valuing current and fixed assets; sometimes they have been accounting authorities whose names have been lost but whose dicta have survived. In recent years we have come to accept statements by professional bodies or their committees as authorities. But it is noticeable that hardly ever is any "authoritative" statement backed up by a demonstration of its consequences and by argument to the effect that these consequences conform with what is required of accounting.

Consider again the traditional practice of recording assets and representing them thereafter at cost less depreciation. Suppose a firm buys three pieces of machinery: A for \$1000 in 1955; B for \$1000 in 1960 and C for \$1000 in 1964. The total of these outlays would appear in the balance sheet of 1965 as the cost of these assets. There will be shown as deductions from this total (assuming each piece has an expected life of 20 years) the sum of \$500 (A), \$250 (B), and \$50 (C); in all \$800. The balance will be \$2200. Superficially this seems sensible. But a closer examination will surely show it to be rather absurd. It is well known that \$1000 in 1955 and \$1000 in 1964 did not mean the same thing. None of us personally would think that \$1000 was the same for any personal purpose in those two years. The New Zealand consumers' goods price index (base 1958 = 100) rose from 91 to 115 in that interval. If over any period of years we are to add different sums of money spent in different years we should at least recognize that equal sums have not equal meanings.

We may give them subscripts to distinguish them. The total outlays would then appear to be $\$(1000_{55} + 1000_{60} + 1000_{64})$. Once this is done it is clear that the sum is not $\$3000_{65}$. It is not 3000 dollars of any particular year; and in representing the total as \$3000 the cardinal error of adding unlike things will have been made. If, at the end of 1965, the firm had also \$1000 in cash, this amount is strictly $\$1000_{65}$. But it makes no sense to add $\$1000_{65}$ to \$2200 of unknown but mixed vintage; a second example of adding unlike things. Further there will have been deducted (in respect of asset A, for example) $\$50_{56}$, $\$50_{57}$, $\$50_{58} \ldots \$50_{65}$ from $\$1000_{55}$, so that the depreciated value, \$500, means nothing that we can readily grasp. This is a third example of the same kind of error, this time subtracting unlike things. It is impossible to conceive that a balance sheet which is the resultant of such repeated fallacious addition and subtraction can mean anything sensible in 1965.

It may seem that this misrepresents the traditional and authoritatively endorsed accounting for such items. It is said that accounting for fixed assets subsists in writing off a proportionate part of the cost each year. Taking this view, in each year, in respect of asset A, the amounts written off through the income account were: in 1956, $\$50_{55}$; in 1957, $\$50_{55} \ldots$ in 1965, $\$50_{55}$. In this case the asset balance will be $\$500_{55}$ in 1965. But then the charges made in the income accounts of successive years will have committed the same error as before. For the current revenues and outlays of 1965 will be in $\$_{65}$, while the depreciation charges will be $\$50_{55}$, $\$50_{60}$ and $\$50_{64}$. Further, the balances in the balance sheet will include cash $\$1000_{65}$, asset A (net) $\$500_{55}$, asset B $\$750_{60}$ and asset C $\$950_{64}$; and to add these, as is done in balance sheets, is an example of the same fallacy.

It is thus demonstrated that the traditional practice, however simple and sensible it may seem on the surface, involves arithmetical fallacies at numerous points. These fallacies will never become apparent if we merely take the dogma of authorities for granted. The advancement of knowledge depends on finding out what is observed and observable as matters which have a clear impact on human action. In accounting it is useless merely to observe what accountants do; it is necessary to show that the results of what they do have a clear connexion with the kinds of action people take and with the attainment of the ends they pursue. It is easy to say people do act upon financial statements; but if it is shown that the very processes used in deriving those statements are fallacious, then it follows that the actions of users are misdirected by the information given in the statements.

Accounting and its products can be of little use unless all of the changes which take place in the financial position or condition of a firm are fully represented as they occur, so that the contemporary position at any time, in terms of current prices, is continuously discoverable. Only such a continuously contemporary accounting can arm managers and investors to meet the possibilities they foresee or the exigencies which external circumstances impose on them[2].

Facts, Opinions and Judgements

Some things are matters of opinion, others are matters of fact. Whether a face, a figure, or a flower is beautiful, is a matter of opinion. As it is said, "Beauty is in the eye of the beholder". But before any opinion can be expressed there must be some face, figure or flower in contemplation; a present or recollected fact or set of factual configurations which give rise to the opinion. If, however, an opinion is to be formed about something which cannot be brought directly to the inspection, there is the possibility that a representation made by some intermediary may serve. There is also the possibility that the intermediary may distort the original by the way in which he represents it. The tricks of perspective used by cameramen can make what is naturally beautiful in the eye of a direct beholder seem ludicrous or abhorrent to the beholder of a photograph.

The relation of accounting to the users of accounting statements is the relation of a representation of the financial characteristics of a firm to persons who must form an opinion about those characteristics of the firm. No manager of or investor in a firm can have the whole of the firm before him for direct observation. He must rely on a representation of it, or a series of successive representations. The opinions to be formed of the firm will be of no avail to managers or investors unless the representations are factual. And if they are factual they will be of equal value to all who must form opinions of the firm—managers, investors, creditors, trustees for secured creditors, potential investors and creditors and all.

The necessity of such a factual foundation for opinions seems to have been quite lost to sight by accountants. Of this there are several clear strands of evidence.

---

[2] The grounds for such an accounting and the method of deriving such accounting statements are dealt with at length in *Accounting, Evaluation and Economic Behavior.*

First, there is a relatively recently developed notion to the effect that different users of information need different kinds of information, for they have different points of view. Certainly different persons may have different points of view. But this applies as between different shareholders just as much as between, say, a shareholder and a creditor. Some shareholders may become disposed to sell, others to hold, when they become aware of a company's results and position. No accountant can possibly tell which shareholders will do which. Clearly a seller, if he had any say in the matter, would want the best possible "face" presented by the company, while a buyer (who is a shareholder already) would want the worst possible "face" presented, if each is to make the best of his bargains. If the accountant has any latitude in the "view" he will present, there is no way in which he can determine which shareholders to favour at any time. The same applies to the juxtaposition of, say, shareholders and creditors. Suppose there were published a "shareholders' financial statement" and a "creditors' financial statement", both on different principles, for that surely is what "different kinds of information" must mean. A shareholder who was also a debenture-holder would be in a quandary. He would not know which to believe, particularly if both statements have an auditor's report to the effect that a true and fair view was given. The problems raised by the notion in question are insoluble. They do not even arise if it is understood that users of financial statements want factual statements. They are pseudo-problems and should be seen to be absurdities.

Second, there is the view that accountants, and auditors, are entitled to accept the opinions of management on the values placed on various classes of assets. Now it may be a fact that managers hold the opinions that they say they hold. Notice, however, that the audit report appended to financial statements does not say anything in affirmation of the managers' holding of such opinions. It purports to assert something about the representation of the results and position of the company, not something about the managers' opinions about the results and position of the company. The opinions managers hold are personal to them. They may be optimistic or pessimistic. But optimism and pessimism alike are attitudes towards the future and should have no bearing whatever on what has passed nor on the representation of what has passed. No one would take seriously the claim by a manager that his firm had sold $100,000 worth of goods when in fact he got only $70,000 for them. There is equally no good reason for taking a manager's opinion on the value of inventories and other assets unless, of course, his opinion coincides with some independently ascertained values or prices. It is the accountant's and auditor's business to find out whether or not there are such coincidences. If there are, if the representations are based directly or indirectly on present market prices, then it is reasonable to regard them as facts, and not manager's opinions. There is another side to this question. The financial statements are indications of how the management of a firm has been able to make out against the market places in which the firm operated. To allow managers to influence the score-keeping process is surely curious when their performance against the firm's markets is one of the things on which the users of financial statements would like to have facts on which to form their own opinions.

Third, there is the view that the audit report is after all only an opinion, and that all the auditor is required to do is to assert whether the view given of the results and the state of affairs of the company is a true and fair view in his opinion. There seems to have arisen some confusion over the significance of the audit requirement. The auditor is not called upon to say anything about his opinion of the company. He is required only to say something about the relationship of the representations to the facts. Users of financial statements want an assurance that the representations are fair representations of facts. Given the facts they will form their opinions. The emphasis given to opinion either has stemmed from, or has lent weight to, the view that the individual monetary representations of specific items in accounting statement are only opinions. On this matter many have spoken simultaneously with two voices. While asserting the influence of opinion and judgement they have, at the same time upheld the notions of objectivity and of independence on the auditor's part. But worse still, we are now being told by many that financial statements should have more components of the nature of opinions and less in the nature of objective statements of fact. Nearly all proposals which involve taking account of the possibilities of the future rather than of the actualities of the past are of this kind.

The counting of cash, the custody of negotiable documents, the physical counting of inventories, the inspection of plant, the examination of title deeds, and so on, are all steps designed to secure that at least some elements of the components of financial statements are matters of fact and not of opinion. No one supposes that, if a check of physical inventories disagrees with the perpetual inventory, one or both of the figures is a matter of opinion; an attempt is made to discover which is factual. Yet, when it comes to putting a monetary measure on such inventories the same recourse to what is factual at the time is generally forgone. The most obvious case is the use of initial purchase price for marketable securities when there is a discoverable market price. Accountants and auditors are in no doubt at all that the goods physically possessed at one time are not necessarily those physically possessed at another. Why they are not equally sure that the prices of goods possessed at one time are not necessarily the prices which should be applied to the same goods at another time is hard to see; especially when their real knowledge and expertise is supposed to lie in the direction of monetary, not physical, calculation and representation.

In saying all this I am not saying there is no place for opinion or judgement. I am only saying that the accountant—like the artist, the pianist, the engineer, the surgeon—can have opinions in the practice of his art only within limits. The limits are imposed by knowledge of the media with which he works and the ideal function his product performs. If he disregards these he is no more skilful, for all his opinions, than a mere layman. He must know that people need factual statements as indicators of progress; and when the facts are hard to get he must perforce exercise his judgement about what he will consider as best approximations.

If he is an auditor he must exercise his judgement about the steps others have taken to get at the facts. He is not called upon to say whether the results and the position of a firm are true and fair; he is required to say whether they are truly and fairly represented by the statements. He will never see this as his task if he supposes there are many true and fair views, all matters of opinion.

Wholes and Their Parts

In the ordinary course of living we deal with most things as wholes. We deal with automobiles, business firms, accounting systems as wholes. For most purposes this concern with wholes is sufficient. However, if we hold out to be expert in any matter we need a much more exact knowledge, otherwise we are prone to take superficial appearances for substantial reality. For about 2000 years men classified the inert substances with which they were familiar on the basis of appearances—as earths, liquids and airs, or as metals, salts, acids and bases. Modern chemistry differs from pre-eighteenth century chemistry because the practice of thinking of things only as wholes was abandoned, and wholes were understood in terms of their constituents and the ways in which they combined. There seems good reason to suppose that accounting may make similar distinctive advances if attention were directed to the understanding of wholes in terms of the constituents.

We have all heard of going concerns, and the valuation of assets on a going concern basis. But hardly anywhere is there a discussion of what "going" means. We think generally of a going concern as a whole, but without consideration of its processes. We distinguish going concern values from values under forced liquidation, but without considering the processes by which forced liquidation is avoided.

Consider this. We are told that durable assets should be valued on a going concern basis, and that that basis is cost, or initial purchase price. Now from time to time a going concern must change its asset holdings. To think of the possibilities managers must know what its holdings are in cash or the equivalent of cash, that is to say cash and the resale prices of its non-cash holdings. Initial price is quite irrelevant. A going concern may borrow on the collateral security of its assets. To think of the possible extent of such borrowings managers must know the resale prices of its assets. Initial price is quite irrelevant. A going concern will seek to insure itself against the loss or destruction of its assets. The direct amount of any such loss is the resale price of the asset. Initial price is quite irrelevant. A going concern will seek to secure itself against illiquidity; but if illiquidity threatens, it will keep the resale prices of its several assets under notice so that any necessary sale of assets involves the least expected sacrifice. Initial price is quite irrelevant. Instances of these component elements of "going" could be multiplied. In no case is the initial purchase price or cost basis of valuation relevant. The view that it is relevant can be upheld only if we think of "going" as a whole process and disregard the constituent elements of it.

Consider an example from quite a different phase of accounting. For a long time accountants have been accustomed to regard unit product cost as a significant figure. Again, notice it is a whole. But how significant is it? Its components are a measured and priced amount of labour and materials (suppose they are directly measured). They include a proportionate part of direct supervisory costs (what part depends on the total of all other actual or expected operations under the same supervisory unit, so that it is not unique to the product). In addition there is a proportionate part of an amount spent, perhaps long ago, on the plant or machinery used (what part depends on the depreciation period and formula adopted, so that it is not unique to the product). Also included is a proportionate part of indirect supervisory and managerial costs (what part depends on the total of all operations of the firm and the formula adopted for allocating these costs, so that it is not unique to the product). Moreover, there may be other allocations or subdivisions of those mentioned. The addition of these several components cannot possibly give a figure which is significant for the product or any decision in respect of it. The view that a total unit cost is relevant can be upheld only if we fail to consider the dubious quality of its constituents.

For a third example we allude to decision-making. The phrase is so commonly used without elaboration that there can be little doubt that its users think of it as a whole. But no one "just decides". Deciding is difficult; we often prefer to avoid it. There are several distinct components of a decision. First, there are at least two possible courses from which a choice is to be made. Second, there are different expected pay-offs, to be calculated for each course by time intervals and discounted to present values. Third, there are different judgements about the relationship between the present values and the timing of pay-offs. One may prefer a lower present value if there are other valued elements in the timing of pay-offs. Fourth, there is a stake, either common to the possible courses of action, or different as between them, in which case there will be further judgements about the source or the employment of the difference between the stakes. There may be other such elements. We can understand the process and the role of accounting in it only if we spell out its constituents. Every reference to choice, expectation and judgement in the preceding sentences implies managerial choice, expectation or judgement. Apart from the mere arithmetical processes of formally calculating pay-offs, the major role of accounting is to provide contemporary measures of the cash equivalents of assets, so that the choice of assets making up any particular stake in any actual situation requiring decision or choice is simplified.

The purport of these examples is simply to suggest that close analysis will yield insights which the superficial recognition of wholes will never give. We have scarcely begun the task of examining analytically the concepts and processes we employ or could employ.

Experience, Education and Research

Some may say, in response to the points that have been made, that a long-tried and accepted form of accounting must have proved its worth in the world of business. But of course some said the same of the horse and buggy, which only goes to show that our experiences may confirm our prejudices. But we can also learn from experience, or rather from reflecting on our experiences. We learn from our experiences if, on reflection, we find confirmation or contradiction of the views we hold in the consequences of holding them.

Now all of our experiences of getting and spending money converge on two simple ideas. We can always acquire things we want but do not have up to the full extent of the sum of money we have and the prices we can get for the non-monetary things we have. And, the extent to which we judge ourselves to be better off financially from time to time is given by the changes in the purchasing power of the sum of the money we hold and the contemporary prices of the non-monetary things we hold as between two points of time. There is nothing in all our experience of getting and handling money and goods which contradicts these propositions. Yet, the accounting that is presently done for firms large and small contradicts them both. There is nothing in all our experience which leads us to believe that by adding quantities of unlike things we can get a total which has a sensible meaning. Yet accounting makes no attempt to reduce the unlike dollars spent over years by firms to a common and contemporary likeness.

We cannot pause here to inquire why practices which are contrary to all experience of a commercial or financial kind should have persisted[3]. We see their persistence merely as a roadblock in the path of progress, and are more concerned with their removal than their explanation. Their removal and the substitution of practices which accord more closely with experience may be expedited if we each will critically question the propriety of the rules we employ, and submit them to the test of our own personal experiences. After all, some other person or persons will use the results. If we, too, are persons, and not automata, what is common sense to us in our own dealings is very likely to appear to be common sense to others in theirs. No doubt many are afraid to use their common sense, otherwise we would have had changes before this. This suggests a second way of expediting improvement.

You may know that it has become a habit in recent years to present in the early stages of textbooks, college and university courses, what are called the conventions of accounting. These conventions are almost entirely inconsistent with the facts of financial and commercial dealings and many of them are self-contradictory[4]. Perhaps it is because they are so incomprehensible that they have some mystic hold

[3] A brief survey is given in *Accounting, Evaluation and Economic Behavior*, Ch. 14.

[4] An examination of some of them was made in "Conventions, Doctrines and Common Sense", see p. 415, *ante*.

over their expositors, and hence over the students to whom they are expounded and who subsequently become practitioners. We could well do with less of this mysticism and with more of the realities instead; less servility in the face of doctrinaire teaching and more courageous common sense.

There seems to be a view abroad that advanced education should be directed to giving a greater number of snippets of knowledge—a course in psychology, a course in mathematics, a course in statistics, a course in high-speed morons—in the hope that this will "broaden" the outlook and comprehension of accountants. But snippets of knowledge will not advance understanding and wisdom. What is much more to the point is an intensive analysis of the bits and pieces of accounting on the one hand and a careful study of how, in intimate detail, these and their products fit into the deliberative processes of those who use them. Students, and practitioners too, need to consider the immediate and less immediate effects of following out the rules on managers, bankers, investors, trustees, other accountants, and, in a wider framework still, their effects on the distribution of the command of the community's resources between the more efficient and the less efficient users of capital. There have been quite a few "new looks" at accounting education in recent years. But almost all seem to be directed to the production of starry-eyed encyclopedists rather than to the production of well-disciplined experts able to spot logical and practical flaws because of their intensive study of what has been done and is being done, and their comprehension of the effects of these things on individuals, industries and the economy as a whole.

The only comprehensive way in which the managers and investors and public men of a community may keep under observation the shifts in efficiency of firms is by recourse to financial statements which represent, with the least possible fuzziness, the results and standing of firms. Accounting done on the varied and often irrelevant bases described in most textbooks will not yield financial statements which are comparable as between firms. We would not tolerate clocks and watches, speedometers, foot rules and similar devices which yield inconsistent indications. There is equally no reason why we should tolerate accounting rules or systems which produce figures which are not comparable. There seems to be good ground for believing that the inadequacies of accounting in this respect have much to do with the general efficiency of industry. Educational programmes which have no provision for analysing these consequences in depth are unlikely to produce the consciousness of defects which is the precursor to progress.

There is a third direction in which improvement may be expedited: by research. Research is a relatively new thing to accounting, and there can be little doubt that its character is poorly understood. I take but one example of this. It has become the thing to establish research committees. Numerous associations in different countries have done this, and I would not wish to belittle the good intentions of the promoters of these committees nor the labours, often prodigious, of those who compose them. Nevertheless by the standards of other fields of enquiry, much, if not most, of the work of these people is misdirected. You have never heard of the committee to discover the laws of gravitation, or of the committee to develop the periodic table of the elements, or of the committee to establish the circulation of the blood, or of the committee to transmute nitrogen into oxygen. But you have heard of Newton and Mendeleev and Harvey and, perhaps especially, of Rutherford. You could name scores of such names, honoured in the annals of human inquiry for their researches. Why individual names? Because research is a painstaking and individual affair. Researchers are men who see anomalies—real world events and things which do not fit into the accepted frameworks of thinking of their time. They are puzzled, individually puzzled. They are impelled to ask why the facts do not fit the ideas men hold. They are not concerned to brush anomalies aside, not content to go along with generally accepted principles. They are concerned to inquire diligently into the characteristics of the anomalies they observe, to assure themselves that their apprehensions are not in error, and if necessary to propose reconstructions of the ideas men hold. Only individuals can bring to bear the concentrated attention over long periods, on the facts they observe and on the then accepted ideas of their peers—attention which yields new insights, new knowledge. In our time you will hear of committees to finance research of one kind or another; but the individualistic character of research remains. Committees may evaluate; it has never been shown that they can originate.

There is no reason to believe that accounting is different in this respect from anything else. The expert accounting community may do much to help in the direction of encouraging individual initiative. But it will do so only if it is realized that the pursuit of knowledge is an open-ended exercise, and that the fruits of research are, in their nature, likely to be disruptive of established ways of thinking. If we take seriously, instead of trying to rationalize, the observable defects of traditional modes of accounting and of thinking about accounting, we shall welcome this disruption, for it is the sign of vitality in any field.

To Progress or to Dream?

There have not been lacking, in the history of accounting, people who exposed what they believed to be errors in conception and practice. It is just one month short of 40 years since Hatfield pointed out to the American Institute of Accountants that in argument and practice accountants are "illogical, inconsistent and vacillating"; that they "rely on reiteration in lieu of argument"; that the vagrant usage of different terms for significant conceptions constitutes "the chief defect in accounting". Much the same could be said today. In 1929, Canning pointed out that accountants have no clear concept of income, or of financial position. Much the same could be said today. In 1936, after some 10 or so years of study of the problem, Sweeney pointed out the folly of treating all dollars as the same through time.

The practice persists. In 1939, MacNeal treated at length the misleading character of the products of traditional accounting practices. The same practices are still with us. And there have been other critics before and since.

There have also been dreamers. Some are convinced that all accounting is good accounting; that if there are faults they are due to the naughtiness of some accountants (or some managers), not to flaws in accounting. Some are convinced that there's nothing wrong with accounting; that there is only something wrong with what people expect of it; and that this can be cured by re-educating the commercial community. However, it is noticeable that they have never been able to get such a re-education process started. Some do not worry about present defects; they look into their crystal balls and see the "accountant of the future" all decked out with knowledge of computers, linear programming, communication theory, higher mathematics and total information systems to his fingertips.

But flights of fancy are only escapist. What the dreamers fail to see is that ostensible defects will be removed only by assiduous re-examination of present thought and practice, by taking them apart and reshaping their component ideas so that they conform with the way in which business is done and the need for factual information of those who do business. It is possible to delimit the accounting process, and to define asset, equity, financial position, income, cost and so on in a much more rigorous way than is generally done. It is possible to link into a coherent system the many concepts necessary for the full development of the subject—to link financial accounting, cost accounting, auditing as between themselves and to link them with the processes of appraisal, evaluation and choice of managers and financial supporters of firms. Nevertheless, at almost every step the traditional definitions and the vague ideas of linkages must be abandoned or substantially modified. There is nothing new in this. Many advances in other fields have necessitated the development of a whole set of new meanings for old terms, a new language in effect. The result may seem strange. However, its test will lie in whether or not the resulting system of ideas is more fruitful in practical terms, and logically more coherent (more understandable) than the system it purports to replace.

The reconstruction of ideas on the basis of our unfolding experiences, the reconstruction of ideas through modifications in educational patterns, and the reconstruction of ideas through the work of researchers—all may converge on the improvement of thought and practice. By this stage in the twentieth century there have been enough disturbing experiences, and there is enough consciousness of the necessity of better education, and enough recognition of the need for research, to provide an excellent springboard for diving into the 'seventies. Only timidity or overriding respect for the habits of the past stand in the way of notable advances. The looseness, illogicality and irrelevance of much accounting is obvious to many, and is on the way to becoming notorious. The only question is whether the profession wishes to take a positive part in the advancement of practice and thought, or whether it prefers to wait until circumstances and pressures from beyond its ranks force improvement on it. That is a question the profession will have to ask and answer for itself in the near future, and almost certainly before the end of the next decade.

51

THE MATHEMATICS OF ACCOUNTING AND ESTIMATING*

The emergence of a rather intense interest in mathematical processes and computations among some accountants is a recent phenomenon. But already the periodical literature is beginning to reach the stage where the general run of readers must either brush up their mathematics or find themselves debarred from participation. There can be little question that mathematics and statistics have given rise to methods of demonstration which are rigorous in form and economical of words. But, like other tools of great sophistication or refinement, they require to be used with matching discernment and discrimination.

This discernment and discrimination is of two kinds. One of these comes from the expert mathematician's knowledge of the limitation of his field. As a master of mathematical concepts and devices he knows that his tools will take him only so far. He knows the assumptions which underlie his theorems and strategies, assumptions which those with more modest foundations may overlook. The other kind of discrimination is of the non-mathematical kind; it is the familiarity with the characteristics of a field of inquiry other than mathematics to which some mathematical processes may conceivably be applied. It is just as important that workers in such fields shall be familiar with the characteristics of their fields as it is that mathematicians shall be competent in mathematics. For unless they well know the relationships between things, the relationships between concepts and what they denote, and the relationships between concepts themselves, they will not be able to set up mathematical expressions of the relationships which will elucidate the matters they discuss.

The New Interest in Mathematics

To what extent the surge of interest in mathematics derived its momentum from the references in the Gordon and Howell and the Pierson reports is a matter of speculation. These reports allude to opinions held in many places to the effect that mathematical competence is inadequate. But the question is, "inadequate for what?" It may well be inadequate for the specialized courses which some schools conduct. If it is, then those schools whose curricula demand substantial mathematical knowledge have the remedy in their own hands. They can refuse to admit those with inadequacies. But it does not follow from the demands of schools with specialized programmes

* First published in *Abacus*, Vol. 3, No. 2, December 1967, pp. 163-80.

that all students in business schools should have undertaken or should undertakes studies in mathematics beyond the secondary school level. The Pierson report raises doubt on this point: "Whether some kind of advanced mathematics should be required of all undergraduate business students is perhaps debatable."[1] But the Gordon and Howell report, after some observations on the sample of curricula considered, concludes that "The standards of mathematical competence implied by these requirements are inadequate for the kind of world in which tomorrow's businessman will work and live."[2] It may well be true that the business world of tomorrow will require more mathematical skill—and more logical, technological, scientific and linguistic skills. But there seems to be no reason to believe that these will not be provided, as in the past, by specialists. It would be folly to suppose that business school undergraduates or graduate students should all be crammed with the variety of specialized knowledges which the business world may wish to draw upon.

It will be recalled that these two reports were concerned with business school curricula generally. If we take any cognizance of the "exponential" rate of the growth of knowledge, and if this growth is supposed to extend to the field of business studies, these reports, it would seem, should be read as indicating that there is a place for advanced work requiring advanced mathematics in the business school curricula, and that the opportunity for undertaking such work should be available in some schools. But the matter has been taken further than this in subsequent reports on education, specifically in the field of accounting.

Nearly 40 years ago Canning judged that the mathematical competences of accountants were then inadequate for the tasks he imagined to fall within their functions[3]. He offered no specific prescriptions for extensions of their studies, however. No doubt there have been others of similar persuasion in the interval. Of more direct significance at present are the suggestions which have been made in the recent past for changes in the curricula. It will be sufficient to mention three sets of proposals in the order of their appearance.

The Vatter Report[4] proposes that an extended curriculum should include statistical and mathematical analysis, through to time series, index numbers, regression and correlation, probability and statistical estimation, tests of hypotheses and statistical inference, operations research, linear programming and mathematical models (some preliminary ideas) and financial mathematics.

The establishment of the Commission on the Common Body of Knowledge for C.P.A.s prompted a submission by a committee of the

[1] Frank C. Pierson and others, *The Education of American Businessmen*, New York, McGraw-Hill Book Co. Inc., 1959, p. 188.

[2] Robert Aaron Gordon and James Edwin Howell, *Higher Education for Business*, New York, Columbia University Press, 1959, p. 161.

[3] John B. Canning, *The Economics of Accountancy*, New York, The Ronald Press Co., 1929, pp. 308, 329.

[4] William J. Vatter, *Survey of Accountancy Education in Australia*, n.p., 1964.

College of Measurements of The Institute of Management Sciences[5]. Like the Vatter Report it envisaged a greatly extended curriculum, of which the parts of interest are as follow: "Operations research must become the concern of accountants . . . the accountant [should] be thoroughly grounded in linear algebra, with special emphasis on the theory of matrices and determinants . . . a working facility with the fundamentals of integral and differential calculus is desirable . . . . Accountants need a background in statistics that emphasizes the mathematical theory of probability and sampling theory."

To what extent the authors of the above proposals were depending on the advices of others or on their own beliefs is not clear. The Directors of the Commission on the Common Body of Knowledge however made an attempt to obtain an indication of opinions on the ranking of 53 "subjects" which they presumably believed would exhaust the possibilities. Their report[6] gives the composite rankings, by 1890 respondents, of subjects in descending order of importance. The median rankings of the mathematical "subjects" were:—

10 Algebra
12 Business Math
19 Statistics and Probability—introductory
34 Geometry, Trigonometry
36 Operations Research—introductory
39 Statistics and Probability—advanced
47 Operations Research—advanced
48 Actuarial Math
49 Finite Math
51 Calculus, Differential and Integral
52 Differential Equations

There are many curiosities about this so-called "card-deck" experiment. One would like to know why 11 of the 53 "subjects" were of a mathematical kind, when Humanities (surely a very broad field capable of some subdivision) could be ranked only twice, introductory and advanced; when the same could be said of Social Science; when Philosophy-Logic-Ethics appeared as one subject only; and when only 11 of the 53 were accounting or auditing subjects.

Opening the chapter on mathematics, statistics and probability, the authors remark that "no other theme has had such recurrent emphasis [presumably in the preceding pages of the report] as the topics to be discussed in this chapter" (p. 245). They note that the consensus of the respondents "did not place emphasis upon these mathematical subjects to the degree which will be called for here". In the light of the discrepancy between the authors' "beliefs" and the evidence of the individual respondents and the reported evidence of the work done by C.P.A. firms, they deny "neither the possibility of [their] own bias, nor even the possibility of preconception" (p. 246). They admit also

---

[5] *The Journal of Accountancy,* December 1964, pp. 79-83.

[6] Robert H. Roy and James H. MacNeill, *Horizons for a Profession,* New York, American Institute of Certified Public Accountants Inc., 1967.

to having "been affected by the contagious enthusiasm of an enlightened and aspiring profession" (p. 246): though, to say the least, the rankings of subjects show very little enthusiasm for the topics they recommend. The case for greater mathematical sophistication on the part of the general body of accountants can hardly be said to be established when it rests only on beliefs and an infection of enthusiasm from the few. If there is a case, it should surely rest on the common body of problems which the performance of the accounting function requires to be resolved. But this report, like others, makes no reference to the observable debate among professionals and the observable objections and open criticisms of accounting on the part of those who use its products. These observables surely suggest that there are some inadequacies in the common doctrine and practice of accounting, inadequacies which will not be overcome by turning our eyes in the direction of mathematics and blandly ignoring the uncomfortable facts of experience.

The Social and Physical Sciences

There are some ways in which work in the field of social interaction is quite different from work in the natural or experimental sciences, and these have much to do with the possibility of transferring to the one mathematical and statistical methods which have been found serviceable in the other.

The history of the natural sciences may be divided into two phases. The early phase was marked by the use of a physiological model to explain (to make plain or understandable) the characteristics of what we describe now as inert matter. Natural objects and substances were deemed all to have the propensity for growth and improvement which living things were seen to have. When men began to realize that the imputation of purposes was an invention, they sought to eliminate the subjective, anthropomorphic elements from their explanations of non-human phenomena. They concentrated on observing, refined the process by adding measurements to their descriptions, and developed an objective language. This second phase of the history of the natural sciences covers a relatively modest period of time, not substantially more than 400 years[7]. And it is only in this period that emphasis has been given to the mathematical treatment of observables.

When dealing with naturally occurring phenomena (making counts or measurements of specific properties) it is reasonable enough to make use of such devices as measures of central tendency and of dispersion, probability theorems, the normal curve of error, and the differential and integral calculus. It is reasonable because, or rather if, we can assume that the observed instances are part of a large population the measurements of which vary continuously through some range of values, or if we have taken enough observations to establish the range and pattern of variation.

---

[7] For a brief but lucid and entertaining account see Stephen Toulmin, *Foresight and Understanding*, New York, Harper & Row, 1963.

But when dealing with social phenomena the observed population of instances is commonly much smaller. If it has been selected as representing some property of interest it is not easy to escape the possibility of bias in selection, for there must be some ground for supposing that the instances have some similarity. And if the instances are taken from different time intervals, there is the possibility that exogenous factors have changed, changing the incidence of the property under observation. In the case of business phenomena (as distinct from purely technical phenomena of the kind encountered in quality control problems), the population of instances is generally smaller still, and their magnitudes are more subject to variation by intention or choice. "The mathematical error of applying a continuous curve to a discrete number of observations produces ludicrous results. It is vain to expect that the crudeness of our observation and the vagueness of our fundamental categories will be cured by manipulation of the paraphernalia of statistical methods."[8]

Lest it be supposed that these observations are biased one may take the testimony of an eminent mathematician, Norbert Wiener. "... I have found ... that one of the chief duties of the mathematician in acting as an adviser to scientists in less precise fields is to discourage them from expecting too much of mathematics. They must learn that there is no intellectual virtue (and that there is, in fact, a severe intellectual vice) in using a number of three digits when our available accuracy runs to one digit. [In one case where many specialists were involved] it was the mathematicians rather than the physiologists and sociologists who had most to throw cold water on an overestimation of the detailed possibilities of mathematics in these other fields."[9]

The two observations cited have reference to the computational aspect of mathematics. But the cautions they express seem to apply equally to the construction of models in the physical and social sciences. In ordinary usage, a model is a scaled-down, simplified analogue of an object or system. We may scale down or simplify without recourse to mathematics, as when we postulate motion without friction in mechanics or perfect competition in economics. The model enables us to analyse "something like" an experienced phenomenon when we find it impossible to analyse the totality of the elements of any actual occurrence of it. In describing the model we are specifying the postulates of the theory we intend to derive from it.

The model chosen is commonly something of which we already know at least some of the rules which govern its behaviour. In certain branches of physics the objects considered are observably like geometrical solids; and the paths traced by objects under specified conditions are like the lines derived by taking some plane section of some such solid. The geometrical properties of the idealizations of

[8] Morris Raphael Cohen, *Reason and Nature,* New York, The Free Press of Glencoe, 1964, p. 353.

[9] Norbert Wiener, *I am a Mathematician,* Cambridge, Mass., The M.I.T. Press, 1964, pp. 285-6.

such solids and sections (the rules governing their behaviours) are well known; they can be represented graphically or in algebraic form. But this, though it suggests a reason for adopting a mathematical model, is not sufficient reason. Such models persist and the recourse to them persists because they are found to be serviceable in attempts to understand experienced phenomena, or in bringing to light phenomena not yet experienced, or in "visualizing" phenomena which cannot be known otherwise than by observing their effects. In the latter case, indeed, the conception of the phenomenon in question is almost entirely, if not entirely, mathematical.

In the case of social phenomena we may proceed in a similar way. We may conceive models which are abstractions of some observable thing or system. But in all operations involving human volition there are elements which are interdependent. Training and experience, potentially every singular experience, change the ways in which individual men react to problem situations; preference (or value) systems change, not only on the initiative of individuals but under the influence of their neighbours: initiative, inertia, the propensities to do this or that and the capacities for doing this or that differ between individuals. And although we may know or discover under specific experimental conditions that some people possess skills and propensities in different degrees, we have no way of quantifying these properties, no assurance that they operate beyond the experimental circumstances, and no way of knowing what combinations of them will produce any particular result. If we apply heat continuously to a copper bar we know specifically what will happen as the heating continues; but if we supply money or leisure continuously to an individual we cannot tell specifically what will happen as the amount supplied increases.

These difficulties do not prevent us from making some observations of the kind qualified by "generally", "on the average", and so on. But the qualifiers do not mean the same thing as they may mean in other fields. And because of the interdependencies of the properties of individuals, and the interdependencies of individuals themselves, we do not observe behaviours similar to the mathematical patterns of the behaviours of physical phenomena. Indeed, it is possible that by moving away from what is observable to the higher abstractions of mathematical models we run the risk of "saving the mathematics" rather than of "saving the appearances".

With these preliminaries we turn to some examples.

The Accuracy of Point Measurements

Among the applications of mathematical and statistical ideas is the determination of the accuracy of measurements, and other statements of magnitudes.

One of the tasks of accounting is to represent financial positions of firms at points of time. It matters little, for the moment, which of several theories we consider as a framework for the derivation of the numbers of dollars assigned to particular assets. If we take the market prices of assets as a basis, some will question the "accuracy" of any given price or average of prices. If we take the traditional cost basis, less depreciation where appropriate, some will question the "accuracy" of one or more of the magnitudes represented in the balance sheet. The question is whether there is any mathematical or statistical procedure by the use of which magnitudes to a greater degree of accuracy can be derived.

The degree of accuracy is the obverse of the degree of error. It is contended by some that a greater amount of information will be provided if a measure of error is given with each of the magnitudes stated in the balance sheet. Consider the proposal of Morgenstern: ". . . a balance sheet is the attempt to state the conditions of a firm at a given moment of time. The different component parts, shown in so many dollars have, however, different probabilities of being realized and in that sense 'true'."[10] Notice, first, that there is a switch in timing here. A given moment of time is some present moment. It may turn out at some future moment that a different amount will be realized. And it may be true that at the present moment the firm's managers expect that a certain sum will be realized at some future moment. But given the above statement of what a balance sheet is, neither of these two propositions (both entailed in the second quoted sentence) is relevant.

But suppose that a balance sheet is to represent the amounts expected to be realized. The argument continues: "If we take 'cash on hand', the probability of this cash being convertible into cash of the stated amount at the date of the balance sheet (or at least immediately thereafter) may be considered to be one. [If 'Government securities' is represented by] a certain amount of dollars, the probability of realizing this amount or more will be high, but less than one, since the market may not produce that much money when sold. Say, it will be .98." For accounts receivable the probability may be "say, .85, or depending on the state of business and the nature of the firm, even lower". For inventory the probability "will fall even more, say to .75 . . . for each item a 'true' dollar value should be shown besides the given value. Such a dollar figure will have a probability distribution attached to it, the amount being obtained by adding (integrating) the various possible dollar values multiplied by their respective probabilities" (p. 76).

There seem to be two difficulties in any such programme. The first is the determination of the probabilities. If the probability distribution is obtained on the basis of experience, there will be an implicit assumption of unchanged behaviour of the population represented by the distribution. Suppose, for example, that the information available to the member firms of an industry were pooled and it was found that 85 per cent of accounts receivable were in fact collected. This would not justify the use of a probability of .85 by a given firm unless it were also assumed that the credit and collection policies of all firms had no bearing on the result; which is equivalent to saying that the

---

[10] Oskar Morgenstern, *On the Accuracy of Economic Observations,* 2nd ed., Princeton, Princeton University Press, 1965, p. 76.

formation of any such policy is pointless. Suppose on the other hand that from its own experience the firm found that it collected 85 per cent of its receivables. Neither would this of itself justify a probability of .85 for accounts receivable at any date, unless it were assumed that there were no secular effects on collections and no change in policy—both sweeping assumptions. Suppose further that it was expected that a change in policy would produce a probability of .90. We have now exhausted the use of experience and are confronted with a pure subjective probability—a guess, for which no mathematical technique can provide a more refined substitute.

This brings us to the second difficulty in the programme. One of the functions of a representation of the conditions of a firm is to prompt investigation of the possibility of improving its performance or preventing the deterioration of its performance. But these possibilities are sheer inventions. There may be certain limits to them, limits given by the present state of an industry, a society and its institutions and conventions; but none of these is inviolable. And even within the limits, every choice of a different course of action changes the probability, as it may be assessed before the choice, of realizing so much from this or that; that is the chooser's purpose.

If we say, in a rather loose way, that the present monetary measures of assets are what we expect to realize, the statement should be taken, it seems, as it stands, with the degree of latitude which ignorance of the future imposes on us. If it is so taken, we will take steps to inform ourselves approximately, but as well as we can, of the magnitudes in question. We will not seek a degree of accuracy which we suppose is obtainable with an "adequate" sample. The attempt to increase the size of the sample may well take us beyond the point where the measures are independent. And even if we could attain such a degree of accuracy we would be forced, by ignorance of the future, to make only the crudest use of it.

There is more than a trace of determinism in proposals to augment present measures or future estimates with indications of probabilities or probable errors. It is as if we knew the form of the distribution of numerous observed or estimated values, at a given time and in similar circumstances, of the magnitude of each thing or class of things we represent numerically; and as if managers lacked the power, by making a choice, of influencing the values or their distribution. (In the latter case we do not mean merely the choice by managers of a magnitude or of a method of deriving a magnitude; we mean rather the choice by managers of a course of action which is expected to yield a greater magnitude than some alternative.)

But suppose we were to seek a measure of the presently realizable price of a parcel of securities. We could take the latest price at which a parcel of the securities changed hands. This is a determinate price. But, some will say, it is not a typical price. However, apart from the common knowledge that security prices may differ from transaction to transaction, there is no ground for saying that the latest selling price is not typical. There is no better ground for saying that the average of the selling prices for the whole of the day in question is more typical than there is for saying that the latest price is more typical. Indeed, every transaction in the securities in the given day changes the state of the market, so that the average would be an average of prices obtained under continuously changing conditions. It would not in fact be an average in any strict sense of the term and no measure of the standard error based on actual prices could help us to escape the fact that the observed prices were not independent of one another. We cannot even say that the size of the parcel we hold precludes us from using a price quoted for a larger or a smaller parcel. For although a large parcel may in some circumstances be saleable only at a lower average price than a small parcel, there are also circumstances in which it may command no less; and lacking perfect knowledge of other operators in the market we do not know into which category the securities we hold then fall.

Even greater difficulties supervene if we seek an estimate of the realizable price of the securities at a future date. We can have no knowledge of the shape of an array of prices at some future date, hence no means of making any estimate "more informative" by appending the estimate of the standard error.

We have taken as illustration the prices of a holding of securities because there is, in respect of many securities, a fairly ready market. But even in this case we can claim to know no more than the last quoted price. We cannot suppose either that it is indicative or that it is not indicative of what we could realize if we were to try to sell a parcel we hold. We cannot say it is typical or it is not typical. All we can say is that it is a discovered price. And we cannot add to our knowledge by any trick of probability or any measure of error for we have only a unique price. For other kinds of assets we are in an even worse case to judge whether a quoted price is a realizable price, for there are fewer transactions in many kinds of goods than there are in securities.

The laws of supply and demand and of diminishing marginal utility entail that, for a very extensive range of goods and services, dated prices are unique prices. And the known differences in individual propensities to estimate and to judge entail that all expected values are unique to the valuers. In neither case therefore does it seem feasible to adopt a statistical correction or estimate of error, for these depend on distributions of observations of which we can have no knowledge. The only strategy which is feasible in the circumstances is to make such unique observations and unique evaluations as are possible at any time, and to take notice of all changes from time to time in the magnitude of the observed property as they emerge from the interactions of the market-place. This demands, not mathematical or statistical competence, but simply an attempt to make the most careful observations of contemporary facts as they unfold.

These remarks are not to be construed as arguments against the theoretical explication of the processes of substantive choice. The problem we have been considering is the problem of point measurements. Some such measures are essential premises of choice; for whatever choice is made, the chooser must know what he has available to stake upon it. The discovery of the stake is a problem which much discussion of decision-making tends to bypass. We are told, for example, that the characteristic elements of a problem situation are (a) that there are various possible states of nature (or of the environment); (b) that there are alternative actions available to the chooser; and (c) that there are varying payoffs as between the available actions[11]. The stake is, of course, implicit in (b), and demonstrations of the process of choosing stipulate some stake. But the discovery of the stake is not disclosed to be a problem in itself by such steps.

Nor is the payoff determinable in any particular instance unless one knows the amount of the stake in the first place; this problem is bypassed by the relative simplicity of the examples chosen to illustrate the process. Examples which suppose that the chooser has so much money, or a building "worth" so much, and in which the payoffs are stipulated (and usually of one kind only), are greatly simplified instances of the kind of case which confronts business men and investors. The data relating to the stake are not directly observable in such complex cases; they must be derived. The omission of this problem from the formulation of the elements of decision processes results in an inadequate model; the reparation of the inadequacy may lead to some quite different conclusions in the theory of choice. At the very least it would allow that accounting has some explicitly describable bearing on choice, a matter which has hitherto received quite inadequate attention.

Empirical-Statistical Exercises

In some schools it is now almost obligatory for candidates for higher degrees to have demonstrated competence in mathematical and statistical computation. This competence seems to be expected to be demonstrated by the collection of some empirical data and their treatment by some form of regression analysis or correlation. There is more than a little danger in this, particularly if it is believed that it is possible to isolate causal factors by the study of data which are the resultants of numerous possible causes, many of which are related.

Take a specific instance. Suppose we were to attempt to discover whether shareholders did in fact make better judgements when inventory was reported on a F.I.F.O. basis than when it was reported on a L.I.F.O. basis. The example may seem trivial, but it is a proper matter for accountants to attempt to discover.

One method of tackling this problem would be to collect instances of companies which used the two bases. If there are many companies we could introduce some refinement such as random selection or

---

[11] For example John C. G. Boot, *Mathematical Reasoning in Economics and Management Science,* Englewood Cliffs, Prentice-Hall Inc., 1967, p. 76; Yuji Ijiri, *The Foundations of Accounting Measurement,* Englewood Cliffs, Prentice-Hall Inc., 1967, p. 151; William Fellner, *Probability and Profit,* Homewood, Richard D. Irwin Inc., 1965, pp. 11-13.

stratified sampling. We could then attempt to discover whether one of the two classes showed a superior performance to the other over some period, using as the measure of performance, say, the dividends paid plus the change in share prices through the period. We could test the results, again by statistical devices, to see whether the difference, if any, between the two classes was significant. Suppose it were found to be. The exercise is empirical in some sense. It involves the use of mathematical or statistical devices. But the operation is pointless and its results misleading.

In the first place the superior performance of one class may be due to a variety of factors of which the method of valuing inventories is but a trivial one; those factors may occur in differing combinations and in differing degrees, but still so that in their specific combinations they gave a superior result in general for the companies of the class. In the second place, the suggested measure of performance may seem to be a valid measure; but if it is granted that reported results could influence share prices (a belief which is implicit in the statement of the problem), then the mere fact that the two classes of companies reported results on different bases would invalidate the exercise. The suggested method also presupposes that there is no reason to believe that the amounts and timing of the dividends declared by the several companies in the period reviewed were declared for any specific reason in contemplation by the boards of those companies. It also makes no allowance for the effect of the supply of and the demand for the shares of the companies on the prices of those shares. The reader may like to add other inadequacies.

Another method of tackling the problem would be to construct two sets of financial statements for a hypothetical company, one on a F.I.F.O. and one on a L.I.F.O. basis and to submit the two sets to, say, equal numbers of different respondents. The questions one may ask might be of the kind, what price would you pay for a share in the company? and, to what extent is your answer influenced by the method of inventory valuation used? Now, as to the first question, no bidding or offering price in reality is as completely free of context as the case of a hypothetical company: the respondents will almost certainly supply an implicit and personal context, so that their answers will not be answers to the same question. And if any attempt is made by the inquirer to supply a context this will vitiate the generality of the conclusion. As to the second question, there is an implied assumption that respondents will know the effects of using one basis or the other on expected dividends and share prices; merely to state the assumption is to indicate how unrealistic it must be.

Alternatively one could supply all respondents with the two sets of statements, asking which they would prefer as investors. But the implicit assumption just mentioned remains. Or, to retain a closer resemblance to reality, one could supply the financial statements of an actual company, using both bases of valuation and asking the same question. But in this case again the implicit assumption remains, and there is also the problem of securing that non-specified elements of the case, which are known in different degrees and combinations by the respondents, are eliminated from their consideration.

There are published examples of inquiries of these kinds, and if mathematical and statistical expertise is required to be shown we may well expect more of them. But the fact remains that pure empirical materials, actual observables, are the consequences of so many joint and often interacting causes, and are so likely to be unique, that mathematical treatment of them is unwarranted, if not dangerous. This is not to suggest that we can obtain no answer to the kind of question posed in the example: nor to suggest that no mathematical or statistical devices are useful in accounting or its periphery. There are other ways of finding such answers; and if we find some we may be in a better position so to structure inquiries that mathematical devices will be useful. But we are a long way from that position yet; and if there are any strategic priorities it does not yet seem to be proved that sophistication in computation ranks highly among them[12].

Mathematical Reasoning

There is a sense in which mathematical training and expertise may be of great value to some accountants. This is the logical rather than the computational sense. And the accountants to whom we refer are those who concern themselves with the structuring or restructuring of systems of ideas, the textbook writers and the theorists of accounting.

Whether they are concerned to expound an existent body of technique or to propound a novel system, all who deal in exposition deal in ideas. Ideas are manipulable only by reflective and connective processes. If ideas are vague, reflections on them are vague to the point of being fruitless; and postulated relations between such ideas can at best be tenuous, and at worst be misleading. Demonstrations in mathematical form are potential devices for eliminating some of the errors or possibilities of error in argument. They require first that the symbols to be used be uniquely defined, at least for the purposes of a given exercise. The requirement is a mathematical or logical requirement: but the defining itself is not a mathematical or logical task. Defining is the devising of a form of words which will stand for some concept or object of perception with minimal possibility of confusion and with maximum fertility. This demands the application of the non-mathematical discrimination we mentioned at the outset.

As an example, consider one of the commonest statements in mathematical form employed in expositions of accounting: assets = equities. No one supposes that this constitutes a definition of assets. Whatever the statement means, therefore, we need a definition of assets. Whatever definition we adopt of assets and equities it will be clear that no asset is identical with or equal to any equity as such. The statement therefore cannot be a legitimate statement about assets and

[12] For some sobering remarks on the "success" of the use of mathematical statistics in an adjacent field see Gerhard Tintner, "Some Thoughts About the State of Econometrics", in Sherman Roy Krupp (ed.), *The Structure of Economic Science*, Englewood Cliffs, Prentice-Hall Inc., 1966, pp. 114-28.

equities. If now we skip to the "apparent" practical consequences of the above statement we find that equal numbers of dollars are shown at the foot of balance sheets under the captions assets and equities. Evidently the statement "assets = equities" does not mean what it says; and no inference from it or mathematical or quasi-mathematical operation on it can yield a sensible result. If it is intended to assert the equality of certain properties of assets and equities—and that is what seems to be intended—it is necessary first to say what assets are and, second, to specify the property in question. There is little doubt that much of the confusion over the nature and function of balance sheets, and indeed of accounting, is traceable to failure in specifying these things.

Demonstrations in mathematical form require, secondly, that the relational terms shall be defined. We need, for instance, to know what "=" means in the example just used. And if the totals at the foot of the balance sheet are the sums of individual items, we need to know what "+" means, what operation the reader may presume to underlie the summation, if we are to know what the totals mean.

Variant description

The difficulties which arise from failure to be specific and explicit about the terms of a demonstration may be illustrated by a few examples. Consider first the consequences of variant description with reference to the following passage:—

"It is only too obvious that the layman has made a distinction between accounting on the one hand and facts on the other . . . the distinction has been brought about to some extent as a result of the accountant's failure to indicate the *most significant facts* in a variety of situations. In presenting fixed assets, for instance, the fact of *cost* is unquestionably important, but if a holding company has investments which cost $40,000,000 and which have a present market value of $1,000,000, obviously the latter fact is highly significant. To show the assets at a valuation of $40,000,000 is to ignore the most significant fact in the situation. And it is to be noted that such a showing is due not to improper accounting rules but to a failure to apply existing rules intelligently. If the general rule of valuation is cost, it should be understood that the capital so valued is *recoverable* in the conduct of business; if it is not so recoverable, cost loses much of its significance. On the other hand, if the investments have a cost of $1,000,000 and their present market value is $40,000,000 the latter fact may not be ignored. One may be misled by understatement as well as overstatement . . . no wedge may properly be driven between accounting entries and financial facts."[13]

The object of the argument seems to be to show what it is most important to represent about an asset in a balance sheet. "Most important" is of itself empty: there is an implied person to whom a

[13] James L. Dohr, "On the Understanding of Accounting", *The Journal of Accountancy,* March 1941, p. 205.

given piece of information is most important. The gist of the quotation may be represented by four statements:—

> cost is unquestionably important to the user;
> market price is highly significant to the user;
> market price is most significant to the user;
> market price may not be ignored by the user.

We do not wish to discover the conclusion of the author at the moment. All we wish to indicate is that four statements are made in which four quite different statements of relation are made and that no rule is provided by which one may be converted into or related to another. The superficial similarity of the statements of relation, and the fact that cost and market price are mutually exclusive, suggest that the passage asserts two contradictories; and from two contradictories no conclusion can be drawn. The use of variant forms of expression is common in exposition. Indeed it may be justified on stylistic grounds. But the possibility of variants being misleading can only be avoided if there is, at least in the back of the mind and preferably on the face of the page, a set of well-defined concepts linked by operators or connectives which have an unequivocal meaning.

Non-coherence

The example just given illustrates a form of exposition which relies on the use of terms denoting varying degrees of this or that when the meaning of these degrees is indefinite. Repeated assertion takes the place of logical development. The individual statements stand more or less on their own; they are not a series of coherent statements leading, as does a mathematical or logical demonstration, from some position to another.

Consider the treatment of standards for accounting information given by the A.A.A. Committee to Prepare a Statement of Basic Accounting Theory[14]. The Committee recommends four basic standards for accounting information: relevance, verifiability, freedom from bias and quantifiability. We will not concern ourselves with what these terms mean at this point. We will attempt merely to see what relationships hold between them in the view of the Committee.

We are told that "these standards provide criteria to be used in evaluating potential accounting information" (p. 8). This seems to mean that, given the standards, we could devise a satisfactory set of accounting rules which would exclude certain kinds of statements from the category "accounting information". We will use the initial letters R, V, F, Q to represent the standards. We are told that there are different degrees of adherence to each standard (p. 10). We will represent this proposition by assigning to the standards the values w, x, y, z respectively, where these values may range from 1 to some positive value greater than zero. (We suppose that, as they are standards, a degree of adherence of zero is impermissible.) We will

[14] A *Statement of Basic Accounting Theory,* Evanston, American Accounting Association, 1966.

use the sign "+" to signify that each of the standards is to be satisfied to some extent, and "=" to signify that there is a relationship between "useful information" (I) and some combination of the values of R, V, F and Q. We may then write:—

$$I = Rw + Vx + Fy + Qz$$

We have an expression in four unknowns.

We are told that "the required degree of adherence to each standard is conditioned by the degree to which the other standards are met (p. 10). This may be represented by $w = f(x,y,z)$, $x = f(w,y,z)$, $y = f(w,x,z)$, $z = f(w,x,y)$ where f means "some function of". There is no way of breaking out of this circle of dependencies for the purpose of solving the original equation.

We are told, however, that "the minimum conformity required with any one of the standards and rates of substitution (trade-off) among the four standards are conditioned by the circumstances" (p. 10). These "rates of substitution" may enable us to reduce the four unknowns to some smaller number. It is said that "the standard of relevance is primary among the four recommended standards" (p. 9). In the absence of any other indication, this may be interpreted as $w \rightarrow 1$ and $w > x, y, z$. But, if this is any indication at all, it is the only indication of the possible "rates of substitution", and it does not help to reduce the unknowns or to break the circle. Indeed if the minimum conformity and the rates of substitution "are conditioned by the circumstances", w, x, y and z have no theoretical meaning; and the notions of degrees of adherence and rates of substitution are much less precise than the terms themselves seem to suggest.

But apart from this, it is clear that the Committee does not find the framework of standards which it sets up to be useful as "a basis for inclusion or exclusion of data as accounting information" (p. 8). It concludes that two sets of rules, those of historical-cost accounting and those of replacement-cost accounting, both yield information which satisfies the criteria; and that the results of applying both sets should be derived (p. 31). Indeed the use of the term "multi-valued" suggests that even more diverse rules may be acceptable. This seems a far distance from the aim of the exercise. The standards turn out quite literally to be non-standard. The ideal of coherence (p. 2) is not approached.

The cause of this result seems to lie in the lack of clear conceptions of the population of statements from which permissible accounting statements may be drawn and of the manner in which the mode of drawing such statements may be specified categorically. A little mathematical or logical ordering would help. The elementary notions for the treatment of classes include "inclusion" and "exclusion". We wish to draw a smaller from a larger population of statements. We need exclusion rules. We can employ successive dichotomies if we order the criteria in a fruitful manner.

Let the total population of statements include all possible singular statements about a firm, statements about its past, present and future.

Make the first cut on the basis of quantified statements. Make the second cut on the basis of statements quantified in money; only such statements are "economic" (pp. 2, 5) in character. Make the third cut on the basis of verifiability; this cuts out all statements about the future, a cut which the authors do not appear to relish. Make the fourth cut on the basis of whether or not the statements are in fact verified; this achieves what is meant by freedom from bias. Make the final cut on the basis of what is contemporary, for only the contemporary can be relevant at any present moment.

It will be noted that much the same criteria occur as in the Committee's statement. But there are no trade-offs and the resultant information is clearly describable because of the explicit statement of what is excluded. (Whether or not one disagrees with the particular dichotomies used in the preceding paragraph is immaterial for present purposes; we are considering method only.) The exercise and its results are coherent in the sense that each step involves an operation of known effect and each is related to its precursor and its successor. And given some other elements of the theory in which the concepts employed are embedded, we can test the propriety of the hypothesis underlying each cut. It seems extremely doubtful that any such test could be devised for the set of ideas embodied in the exposition we set out to examine.

Addition

The most serious departure from rigour occurs in respect of one of the simplest and most commonly used operations, addition. Accountants have tended to accept addition as an operation with self-evident meaning, perhaps because of its apparent simplicity reinforced by disregard for the definition of what is added. It has become routine, and of routine Whitehead has observed: "Routine is the god of every social system: it is the seventh heaven of business . . . . But when the adequate routine is established, intelligence vanishes, and the system is maintained by a co-ordination of conditioned reflexes."[15] Accounting is not, of course, peculiar in this respect. The practice of normal science, as well as business, is largely a matter of routine, of habit. But it is proper to question routines and habits now and then.

It is quite possible to add any set of cardinal numbers, however derived, provided we are indifferent to the meanings of the numbers. But if the sum is expected to have any particular significance only numbers having the same kind of significance can be added. The problem may appear to be overcome by such observations as the following: ". . . it is impossible to add railroad tracks, buildings, bridges, etc., without reducing all these items to a common denom-

---

[15] Alfred North Whitehead, *Adventures of Ideas,* Penguin Books, 1942, pp. 110-11. To put it another way, addition has become a habit, of which it has been said "habit-formation is accompanied by a gradual dimming and darkening of the lights of awareness". Arthur Koestler, *The Act of Creation,* London, Pan Books Ltd., 1966, p. 155.

inator"[16]. But there is no common denominator of railroad tracks, buildings and bridges other than the term "assets". If we allow that the reference is not to railroads, etc., as such but rather to some common property of them which is expressible in dollars, the problem is still not overcome, in the accounting context. Given a firm with an extended life there is no way in which the dollars spent for railroad tracks 50 years ago, for buildings 40 years ago and the dollars remaining in its treasury now can be added to obtain any sensible aggregate now. There is nothing novel about this observation; equivalent observations have been made by numerous authors in the past. But somehow it has failed to find its way into the expositions of the usual texts and into practice. No cognizance is taken of the impossibility of adding numbers taken from different sets of numbers (prices at particular times), which sets are different in significance. It is little wonder, if the exponents of accounting give the matter no attention, that the practice of accounting is so open to assault.

These few examples are sufficient to demonstrate the opportunities which lie open for the application of the rigorous procedures of mathematical reasoning to reasoning about accounting. The condition of fruitful discourse is that the things to be discussed and the rules to be accepted in discussion shall be made clear at the outset and that the rules shall be followed wherever they lead.

It is for this reason that things to be discussed are often reduced to symbols. If income is to be denoted by Y and expected income by, say, Y′, it is much more difficult in a symbolic demonstration to slip from one to the other than it is by the use of words; for it is very easy indeed to omit the word "expected", either by oversight or in the expectation that the reader will supply the word which makes "income" and "expected income" two different concepts. But whether we use words, as in discourse, or abstract symbols, as in quasi-mathematical demonstrations, or numbers, as in computations, it is of paramount importance that the conceptions they represent be specified with the utmost clarity and that the words or symbols themselves be used consistently, if we are to avoid unwittingly giving assent or seeking assent to contradictory propositions.

Relatively little use has been made in accounting of the logical processes of which mathematics provide the archetype. The possibility that the use of such processes may be fruitful is not infrequently brushed aside with assertions to the effect that accounting is practical or pragmatic, as if the same were not also true of other forms of expertise which are based on rigorous reasoning. The consequence is that the literature is crammed with non-definitions and non-arguments and non-conclusions.

This is ground enough for disenchantment on the part of the discriminating. It may explain, in some measure, the shift of interest towards mathematics in the computational sense. For, if in other

---

[16] William A. Paton and Russell A. Stevenson, *Principles of Accounting,* Ann Arbor, George Wahr, 1917, p. 2. The quotation is a random instance of a wide variety of similar statements in the literature.

fields the development of applications of mathematical and statistical devices has promoted knowledge, there may seem to be good reason to believe that the same may occur in accounting. But it is important to remember that concepts, categories and classes have always had to be distinguished before it became possible to apply numerical or quantitative methods to their description or to the description of their relationships. Until we know what kinds of things we are talking about, numbering and measuring are merely groping in the dark.

Conclusion

These remarks are not intended to discourage the belief that greater possibilities of measurement and mathematical manipulation may lie ahead in the field of social science, or in the study of finance and accounting. But if they do, we will only progress towards them by the greater application of mathematical reasoning. The tolerance with which there have been absorbed into the corpus of accounting discourse terms having diverse meanings, and into the corpus of accounting doctrine rules which have diverse effects, is explicable largely in terms of the lack of a common logical discipline. It is vain to expect mathematical computations to make good, or to serve as a substitute for, our ineptness in observing what is observable or in devising constructs which are fruitful because they are linked in a demonstrable way with observables.

Mathematics, we are told, is "the subject in which we never know what we are talking about, nor whether what we are saying is true"[17]. "... mathematics studies nothing but hypotheses, and is the only science which never inquires what the actual facts are."[18] "Mathematics is thought moving in the sphere of complete abstraction from any particular instance of what it is talking about . . . . The certainty of mathematics depends on its complete abstract generality."[19] For the refinement of thought, particularly deductive thought, the value of mathematics is unquestionable. For if we have set up the symbols aright we are able to give undivided attention to the derivation of the logical consequences of the postulated relationships among them.

But in these characteristics of mathematics lies also the greatest danger; namely, that the propriety of the postulates, when they have any reference to experienced events, may be inadequately established; or that the model of reality on which the postulates are based may be so imperfect that the inferences, however carefully drawn, will be misleading. If we seek a richer understanding of the facts of experience, the finest acquaintance with computational technique is no

---

[17] Bertrand Russell, "Mathematics and the Metaphysicians" (1901), in Robert W. Marks (ed.), *The Growth of Mathematics,* New York, Bantam Books, 1964, p. 26.

[18] C. S. Peirce, "Logic of Mathematics in Relation to Education", in *Values in a Universe of Chance,* Philip P. Wiener (ed.), Garden City, N.Y., Doubleday & Co. Inc., 1958, p. 341.

[19] A. N. Whitehead, *Science and the Modern World,* Penguin Books, 1938, p. 34.

substitute for discernment and discrimination in the field of experience which we study.

If this is understood we may encourage some to apply themselves to the advanced types of analysis and computation which they believe may be fruitful. But we will not expect such advanced competences of those who are concerned to learn the skills necessary in the normal practice of a profession. I do not believe that a case has yet been made for the inclusion in the general accounting and business curricula of the advanced mathematics which some have thought to be necessary.

52

THE LINKED LOGICS OF PRACTICE AND PEDAGOGY*

I am concerned with the dissonance amongst accountants. It may be detected from the utterances of practitioners on teachers and teaching; from the utterances of teachers on practitioners and practice; and from the utterances of practitioners *as* practitioners and of teachers *as* teachers. Both classes, as it seems to me, have paid inadequate attention to some of the ineluctable circumstances and demands of their callings. Certainly some members of both classes are presently anxious about the prevailing relationship between teaching and practice. But anxiety is not enough. Without some deliberate analysis of the situation, anxiety will demand relief: and it may take the form, as it has done in the past, of diffuse effort in unrelated directions, leaving confusion worse confounded.

There are superficial signs of an entente between educational and professional people and organizations. The inhabitants of the city's towers are looking more than ever before for the products of the ivied towers. At least some teaching institutions, if not most, have felt they should give the city what it seems to want; in general, more of its own kind. But, in both cases, it is doubtful whether the wants are well-grounded. And, notwithstanding these superficial signs, there is still evidence of an uneasiness on both sides, amounting almost to disdain, which will, if it continues, establish nothing more than an artificial or transient bond; as if the product of the universities, graduates or ideas, were merely articles of commerce.

Prevailing Dissonance

The impression of dissonance and disdain must be substantiated, if I am not to be put off by allegations to the effect that trifling differences are being overemphasized.

Anyone who has paid attention to the writing of professional accountants will have noticed the almost total absence of references to the work of teachers and scholars. The subjects on which practitioners write are dealt with, often repeatedly and at length, by teachers, sometimes in professional journals themselves, but more often in books and academic journals. But to read the articles of practitioners one would suppose either that there is not an academic literature at all, or that it is beneath notice. There is not much difference between disregard and contempt. If you are observant, you

---

* First published in *Proceedings* of the Annual Conference of the Australasian Association of University Teachers of Accounting, Newcastle, August 1968.

will find that few, if any, practitioners are aware of the books and articles you and your colleagues have written, even in the recent past; or if some are aware, it is only vaguely; few are moved.

Practitioners are not entirely to blame for this; which brings me to the attitudes of academics. The same kind of example, the literary kind, can be given. Very few academics write about the kinds of things practitioners do. They may write much about what they think practitioners do or ought to do, or about what practitioners individually or "by sample" say they do. But there are very few studies of what practitioners actually do, notwithstanding the wealth of material available. On the other hand the number of articles loaded with polysyllabic persiflage and pedantry is large. On both counts practitioners are unlikely to find the work of academics interesting or instructive even if they know of its existence.

Another kind of indicator of the leaning of teachers away from practice and practices lies in the descriptions given by some of their task as they see it. It is not at all odd to hear: "We are not concerned with the details of practice; we are concerned to teach basic concepts and principles, with training the mind, with broadening the outlook" —and other such noble sentiments. It is held that this view is "in the interest of the intellectual development of the individual and the good of society"—whatever this means, for seldom is any attempt made to show how teaching in the manner so vaguely described will lead to the end envisaged. There is no avowed interest here in producing skilled and competent persons, able to assume leadership in a specified profession. The attitude shows no concern, indeed it shows some disdain, for the anxieties of a profession which, by the very actions of its members, shows that it wants the most competent people the teaching institutions can produce.

There is a contrasting type of attitude which may attract the passive disdain of practitioners. Teachers may be so anxious to please practitioners or so anxious to avoid criticism that they write and teach only the "conventional wisdom" which, as Galbraith observed, is always long out of date. Practitioners would certainly find the products of this formula comfortable, easy to live with—recruits who could parrot the words, phrases and rules which are familiar to eye and ear; addresses and articles which have a pure ritualistic function, to confirm beliefs in the rightness of what was learned 10, 20, 30 years before. But neither the recruits nor the speeches and articles of their teachers would be worth any other notice by practitioners, certainly not the notice which presages leadership; for there is nothing in what the one learns and the other teaches that is not already old hat to the practitioner.

But I have said nothing yet about dissonance among teachers. I venture to say that there are few subjects on which teachers have so many divergent views as accounting. There are some who, misunderstanding the nature of the academic enterprise, see in this diversity a sign of vitality. There are others who see it as the effervescence of immaturity—not yet worth bottling. This is unfortunate; for while practitioners judge it thus they are unlikely to accept academic work as a guide to the advancement of the profession. But even if teachers contemplate their own bailiwick diversity is unfortunate. If there is a common subject-matter and if there is a common respect for the modes of discovery, demonstration and argument which workers in other disciplines respect, it is just not possible that there could be so many divergent doctrines as there now are.

The Course of Learning

It is commonly said that learning is a lifelong process. There would be less agreement about what "learning" means in this context. To some, no doubt, it means the accumulation of factual knowledge; to others it may mean increasing the systematic understanding of the relationships between things; to some it may mean growth in general wisdom; some may think of learning as all of these things.

A child learns many things before school age: the names of persons and things—elementary exercises in the art of discriminating and classifying; the relationships between some persons, between some things and between some events—elementary exercises in causal and sequential relations. Primarily he wants to know what things are and how they can be used, in some sense or another. It would be foolish to try to tell him he was learning to discriminate, to classify and to sense causal and other relationships. But it is important that teachers recognize that this is, in fact, what is occurring.

In school some of this learning is formalized and extended. The child learns many more facts. If the teaching is well done the facts will be systematically arranged, so that the grasp of some will make easier the grasp of others. He learns something of the symbolic arts, language and arithmetic; something of the social arts, getting along with superiors, equals and inferiors; something of the use of tools and instruments. These are learned not merely from the descriptions of his teachers; they are learned the better by observing and doing himself—writing, computation, play and team sports, manual and experimental work. He learns that doing things in some ways will and in other ways will not produce results he expected or has been led to expect. He learns that there are easier, harder and useless ways of going about some things, particularly those things which have to do with physical objects. But at the same time he learns that some things can be done in many ways, no one of which can be said to be right or wrong because "tastes" differ. This applies to such things as literary expression, music, and the graphic arts, to forms of human interaction generally. We may distinguish the two differently structured kinds of learning we have just juxtaposed as formal-scientific and social-dramatic.

The general learning of elementary school continues into higher school. The child learns more facts, more of the art of discriminating and classifying, and more of causal relations. He learns how to draw conclusions himself from facts he is given or observes. He learns even by making mistakes. The effect of all of this school learning is to overlay the natural or instructive capacities and drives with something of the culture of the society in which he is to live. We speak of intellectual and social discipline; we mean that the child learns of the constraints he is expected to live within or work within if he is to live amicably among his fellows or work knowledgeably at a chosen task.

In technical school and university, studies become specialized. There are still facts to learn and skills to acquire and relationships to apprehend. But the student is approaching the age when he will have to face the world of affairs, where there are many more things related in much more complex ways than he has so far understood. The tasks and problems which he faces in his tertiary education begin to approach, in style and scope, the tasks and problems he will face as a technologist, a specialist, a professional in just a few years. From the tertiary stage he will emerge either as a specialist, skilful in a chosen, restricted art; or as an analyst and constructor, knowing a particular art and what it has to do with the world's affairs, and skilful in moulding that art to the complexities of scientific, economic, social or cultural realities. The tertiary educational institutions are expected to provide the kinds of learning experience which will serve these two kinds of person. There seems to be little doubt that that is what students expect; and little doubt that the institutions attempt to provide it.

But no school or university can hope to cope with the variety of experiences which a man will meet in his commercial or professional life. Whatever his understanding when he graduates, it is generally expected that it will grow as his knowledge and skill are confronted with more varied and more complex situations. However, growth in understanding is not inevitable. We must distinguish between advanced understanding and adroitness in problem-solving.

Because in the world of affairs there are no clear divisions similar to those of academic "subjects", there are few problems which may be resolved solely on the grounds of one kind of academic specialism. There are more compromise solutions than uniquely determinate solutions. We are always to some extent free to exercise tastes, free to weigh up or evaluate differently the several features of any problem or any solution to it. We are commonly short of time to find out all the facts pertinent to a problem, and to work out all the relationships between them. We are not even competent to deal with matters of which we have no specialist knowledge; we must choose whether to seek specialist advice or to try to get along with our lay knowledge. There are at least three kinds of reaction to complexity.

One may choose the role of problem-solver, simply. Even though he understands only moderately the field of knowledge he professes, he may be highly regarded among his associates. His reputation may depend much more on his apprehension of the state of the "polygon of personal forces and strategies" in problem situations, than on his understanding of his specialism and its function. A person adept at making "political" decisions, which will please or appease most people, or rock fewest boats, is not likely to acquire greater understanding of his professed specialism; for, by compromise at an early stage of any dispute, he will avoid placing his professional ideals and principles under rigorous test. He is unable to distinguish between what is a matter of principle and what is merely expedient.

A second kind of reaction is to fall back on the learned doctrine, or to avoid complexities by formulating rules which ignore them. The effect of both is to cut off the opportunity of learning from experience. For to learn by experience means to reconstruct one's knowledge in the light of new events, to see things differently as newly experienced events shift the weight of evidence from favouring old beliefs to the support of new beliefs.

A third kind of reaction is to attempt to face complexity, to use it to advance one's understanding. But a man will only advance his understanding of his technical or professional field, on passing from the hands of his teachers, if he has been shown clearly how his teachers and others have distinguished what is right from what is wrong, what is relevant from what is irrelevant, what is necessarily true from what is contingently true. He will only be able to carry on, in business life, the reshaping of his knowledge, if in his university years he has been shown clearly how the things he has been taught depend on things he can observe himself. In short, he must learn how to learn. Learning for himself entails the same kind of discriminating and classifying as he began to learn at an early age. But unless his higher education has brought explicitly to his notice the way in which generally useful notions emerge from particular instances, and the way in which choices are made between any two or more notions about the same object or event, his subsequent acts of discrimination and classification are likely to be short-sighted, or pedantic, and in both cases restrictive.

Certainly in university and in professional life he will (or should) meet problems which are more complex than in junior schooling. And he will (or should) find that specific problems are solved by the weighing up of many different kinds of potential consequence. But the necessity of compromise in specific situations does not mean that there is less need for sharp distinctions and clear apprehensions at the prior stage of reflection. We use our understanding to reflect upon problem situations before we turn our hands to meeting them. The more complex they are the greater the need for a clear sense of the principles their solutions depend on. And the greater the need for sufficient self-consistent principles to cover systematically the range of phenomena which do or may constitute such situations. For the grasp of complexity, only the most discriminating analysis of the diverse forms of experience will suffice.

Discriminating analysis does not mean footloose fantasy. To dream, to make believe, to suppose things to be otherwise than they are, is the fashion of children at play. The discipline of practical affairs leaves us much less freedom; we must take the world as we find it and do with it what we can. Intellectual discipline is not less constrained but more so. Whereas in any practical circumstance we may adopt what is or seems expedient, in the course of disciplined reflection expedience is the last resort. We seek to understand generalized situations, to derive general principles which will serve, as major premises, in any chain of reasoning about specific instances of a given class of situations. The incidental or contingent elements of specific instances are set aside. If in subsequent experience we meet particular circumstances, it is open to us to join major premises (the general rules of recurrent behaviour) with minor premises (the specific elements of those circumstances) and to deduce the action which, while conforming with general principles, is appropriate to the particular circumstances we are in.

Given the understanding of this relationship of the general principle to the specific act, one may hope, throughout his professional life, to go on learning whether or not the general principles he has espoused conform with the general character of experience, and to react positively to this learning rather than, in the manner of children at play, to brush aside the realities. Learning from experience can mean nothing more nor less fundamental than this. We must work within two kinds of boundary—the factual and the intellectually satisfying, or the logical. The exercise of the mature imagination is thus properly directed, not to the circumvention of problems by inventing a world in which they do not exist, but to the discovery of complete and consistent ways of resolving them.

This brief outline of the course of learning suggests several things.

The Object of Learning

To begin at the end, the object of advanced learning and of professional experience is surely the one object: to advance the world's work by bringing to it, as well as technical expertise, a more intensive and sympathetic understanding of the relationship between one thing and others. Formal learning experiences should telescope the period which it takes to absorb a basic understanding of those relationships, thus extending the amount of time, out of a man's lifetime, which he can devote to the application of his learned skill and understanding, and to the advancement of both in the interest of his profession. There is no conflict between academia and the city in terms of ends.

Even this proposition, which seems innocuous enough, may give rise to dissent. Some will say that no amount of classroom tuition can be a substitute for real-world experience. This is confusing the part with the whole—on two scores. We did not suggest that the classroom can provide the distillate of all experience; only that it can provide the essence of some experiences, in concentrated form because it excludes in greater or lesser degree the contingent and peripheral components of those experiences. The classroom and the world are, in terms of ends, complementaries not substitutes. On the other hand the observation in question seems to presume that the real-world experience of any one man is superior to what can be conveyed in a classroom. Certainly in its totality a man's experience is richer than a classroom diet can be. But in respect of any particular subject-matter the classroom diet can be far richer than one man's lifetime experiences. For it is the proper function of the teacher to garner and digest the best part of the experiences and ideas of many men. That some may do the garnering and digesting inefficiently is no argument against the principle.

Some will say that the function of the university is not to serve as a substitute for some part of practical experience, but to develop the mind by submitting it to an academic discipline or disciplines. This is an example of unnecessary discrimination, pedantry, hair-splitting. If "developing the mind" is anything but a cliché it means developing the capacity to identify the connexions between the substances of experience, the better to be able to choose wisely and deal swiftly. One who knows, or knows how to discover, the relationship between antecedents and consequents, between causes and effects, is the better able to choose wisely and to deal swiftly. If "discipline" means anything but jargon, it means the disciplined study of some objects or events, some real-world things. Certainly in the disciplined study of objects and events it may be necessary to resort to simplified examples. It may be necessary to contrive or to imagine that other things remain constant while one thing is examined. But observer, student and teacher alike are deluded if the simple or simplified instance is made or appears to be unreal. We study one thing at a time intensely the better to understand the real-world occurrence of it in varied forms and combinations. This is an eminently practical end, quite consistent, as we have said, with the ends of practitioners.

A second point which emerges from our outline of the course of learning is the role of exercises in the attainment of understanding. Again there is no necessary conflict between the work of the classroom and the work of the practitioner. But again there may be some dissents.

It is not uncommon to hear accountants complain that recruits are unable to handle what to them are the simplest kinds of practical exercise. Flaws in the mode of academic teaching may be responsible for this, in part; we return to the question presently. But the expectation that a recent graduate should be able to carry out any simple exercise places much too great a burden on the teaching institutions. There are numerous ways of doing many tasks in practice; the way in which a given practitioner (or his client) does a given job is to a large extent idiosyncratic, contingent upon a variety of facts, beliefs, expectations and past and present circumstances. For *all* practitioners (a graduate may come into the service of *any* one) the variety is enormous; no classroom tuition could cover it. And it is unnecessary. Many of the things a recruit may be said to be unable to do, can be picked up in a short space of time, task-by-task, by the very doing. It certainly "costs" the practitioner something to give this instruction or direction in detail; but there are few jobs under the sun which can be undertaken by a man fresh from the classroom without costs of this kind, the costs of becoming familiar with the specific environment and character of specific acts.

But there may be flaws in the mode of teaching. There is at least some ground for believing that "techniques" are losing favour among some teachers. Some belabour the formula: we are more concerned with concepts and principles than with techniques of book-keeping. One should not put too strong an emphasis on the priority suggested in such statements. But it does indicate a difference in emphasis by comparison with the style of tuition which concentrates on book-keeping and statement preparation exercises. The flight from techniques however may go too far. One may suppose it has arisen from the belief that there are opportunities in the business world for two classes of people, those who think and those who do. This is a gross oversimplification. There may well be a class of people who do in a routine fashion, without much thought. The other class is the class of those who *do* with understanding, and who therefore should be able to construct the routines which others will follow. But notice, they are doers too.

It is highly improbable that anyone can understand a technical art without doing. A budding surgeon may learn about scalpels, saws and sutures; but he will not go far unless he learns how to manipulate them. When he can manipulate them without intense concentration he is able to give his attention to the real object of his work. We cannot learn to drive a car from a handbook. We must take the wheel, get accustomed to the kinaesthetic and external signals which doing one thing or another produces. When we can take in all these signals and respond to them without self-consciousness, we can give the greater attention to what is crucial, or to attaining the maximum efficiency and safety in driving. Similarly a budding accountant must learn to perform the common operations of his art, skilfully to the point of routine, but not as mere routine. Such elementary operations as double-entry book-keeping and aggregation arise from universal commercial realities; they must be done with an apprehension of what is real about them, not because they are traditional or habitual. I know of no textbook which shows clearly what may and what may not properly be aggregated in accounting: I do not therefore find it odd that so much false and misleading aggregation occurs in practice.

The flight from techniques may also have arisen from the belief that the university must produce men who will be researchers and teachers, knowing much about concepts and principles but little concerned with technique. This too is muddled. Advances in knowledge do not come from the bulk of the university's graduates. They come from very few. And often long after the few have mastered the established knowledge and technique of their undergraduate, and even their postgraduate, years. It seems inept to adopt a position geared to the few for the teaching of the many.

In any case it seems inept to adopt such a position for many or few. Ideally techniques are the expression of principles, and principles are the fruit of observation and experience. It seems folly to concentrate on principles and concepts as such when their function is to link specific kinds of acts with empirical circumstance. This kind of isolation, I feel sure, has given rise to the veneration of such unreal conceptions as "book value", "historical cost", "cost less depreciation" and so on, all terms which have no counterpart in any present market place, which the market place can get along very well without, and which accountants could get along better without. The only effective way of avoiding the land of Jabberwocky, of avoiding conceptions which have no real counterpart, of avoiding the error of supposing that in a given discipline a particular real phenomenon may be conceived in quite different ways, is by forcing attention on the relationship of principles to the techniques by which they are expressed in a manner consistent with real-world usage and circumstance.

Fact, Symbol and Feedback

The ends of practitioners and teachers may be alike; both practioners and students may best learn by doing; between these lies the heart of the matter. I presume that it is proper to distinguish what is right from what is wrong, and that it is possible to establish what is right and what is wrong. If you find the dichotomy "right—wrong" distasteful, you are at liberty to substitute "best—inferior". I shall take it for granted that professional men want to do what is best, and that teachers want to convey the best of present knowledge to their students. But in translating the wish into the deed I believe both have failed. As for practitioners, the evidence lies in the disquiet and dissatisfaction within and beyond the profession with what is presently done, and the diversity of practices employed. As for academics, the evidence lies in the extraordinary diversity of views one will find at the core of the teaching on any dozen campuses. Is it possible that the logic of both practitioners and teachers has failed them? I think it is.

If we wish to discover whether any act will procure an end we seek, and if we have no exact knowledge of the outcome, we may try it and see. We can test any simple act by reference to its tangible or observable consequences. This is the procedure of the laboratory: but it is also what we do in many cases within our ordinary experience. Let us undertake a simple "thought-experiment" of this kind.

Suppose that on 1 January you had just $500 of your own money. This constitutes your capacity to buy any goods on sale; it constitutes your relationship, as far as property goes, with the rest of the community. Suppose that you bought a parcel of shares with the whole sum, and that at 30 June those shares were being bought and sold at around $1000, and that nothing had happened to the purchasing power of money in the interval. You would be confident that at 30 June you were $500 better off than at 1 January, and that your relationship with the rest of the community at 30 June is represented by $1000, not $500. You could put your confident belief to a test, by going out and selling the shares. But there is no need to do that because the market's buying price is quoted. No ordinary mortal, and no accountant holding shares in his own right, would think otherwise than I have suggested. Nor would he think he was still as well off at 30 June as he was at 1 January if the quoted price of the shares at 30 June was $300. When we think about our own shares the proximity of the scrip and the market price prevent us from blunders about our relationship with the rest of the community and the gain or loss we have made. If you decide to hold the shares after 30 June, and the price subsequently goes up or down, this movement has nothing to do with what happened to your relationship with the rest of the community *up to* 30 June. What happens to your relationship after 30 June depends on your decision at 30 June to go on holding the shares. Now, if you were to ask an orthodox accountant—one who follows the customary procedures of accountants, and the customary doctrine of the textbooks—to draw up some accounts of your affairs he would draw them up in a way which would tell a different story. He would show that you were just as well off at 30 June as at 1 January, and that you had made no profit at all. If you are wise you will disbelieve and dismiss what he says; for it has nothing to do with what you know has happened and nothing to do with the actions you may then take. If you were wise you should also dispense with his services; for if he has not been able to tell you what has happened up to 30 June he will not be able to tell you what has happened between 30 June and 31 December.

If, when dealing with their own shares (and other assets), practitioners and teachers are guided by what they observe, why do they take such unusual and obviously wrong steps in making up the accounts of others? Why, when *dealing* with assets do they take notice of contemporary market prices to ascertain where they stand and what has happened, and yet in keeping the accounts of others, in writing books and articles, and in courses of instruction, they adopt an entirely different premise? It is not an act of charity on my part, but an attempt to understand, which obliges me to suppose that the adoption of this premise—the present relevance of out-of-date prices—is an unwitting mistake. Those who continue to make it seem to be under the influence of misleading verbal habits which should long since have been exposed among accountants, for they have repeatedly been exposed by others. We will analyse the sources of confusion.

First: accounting is not itself a practical art, though it is related to the practical art of commercial and financial dealing. It is related to buying and selling, borrowing and lending, investing and disinvesting, using and deferring the use of money and things, and choosing or rejecting courses of action entailing the use of money and things. But accounting itself is a symbolic art. Its object is so to represent the course of events that, in the absence of real things, others may know what has happened and what is the upshot. There should be no confusion over the "real things", referred to; anyone who has learned any accounting will know that the predominant class of acts in accounting consists of recording the prices of goods and services; and prices are real elements of commercial experience, whether we pay them or receive them or simply take notice of them. But the symbol is not the thing. We buy and sell things. We use symbols to *reflect* upon the possibilities or the consequences of buying and selling things. We cannot reflect upon these or any other things without the use of symbols, verbal, numerical or pictorial. As Peirce observed, "all thought is in signs". In practical affairs all thought about real things is in signs or symbols of those things. If the sign or symbol of the thing does not closely correspond with the thing, reflection cannot but be misdirected, and the action which flows from it cannot but be mistaken. In financial affairs the role of accounting is to provide a set of symbols of prices paid, received or noticed, symbols which are some of the premises of reflection on what has occurred or may be accomplished. The proper business of accounting is thus to secure that the signs correspond, as closely as possible, with prices paid, received and noticed or discovered. If we do not reflect upon what has been and what now is, we have no basis for envisaging what may be.

It is the intermediary role of accounting which is lost to sight. It is a serious loss. For it deludes people into believing that the test of whether a rule is right or wrong is to be found at the intermediate stage—what accountants do—whereas the proper test is at the reflection stage—what has the result of using the rule to do with the potential and actual actions of a buyer, seller, borrower, lender and so on.

As an intermediate function accounting suffers from three kinds of remoteness which impede the correction of its rules.

If there were a clear consequence of what is reported it could be discovered, sooner or later whether what was reported was correct and useful or not. But in the typical business there is no clear consequence. The flux of business, in which new actions and events and the consequences of old actions and events continuously overlap, prevents the observation of the consequence of deviations of the fact from the record at specific points of time. And, if every action is predicated on the contents of the formal record, the present external facts and the judgement of the actor, and as the upshot may be due to external events which the actor could not possibly know of at the time of action, it is impossible after the event to deduce the single cause or the complex of causes of the result. The mere complexity of the flux of events interferes with feedback and with perception of the quality of the rules used in accounting.

A second form of remoteness is the lapse of time between the preparation of accounting statements and the consequence of any action based on them, even if we could isolate such an action. A recipient and user of the statements will know, even if the statements were ideal, that the position and progress reported is already some distance past. He is unlikely (except in the most unusual circumstances) to suppose that the statements could have been incorrect in any sense. If he errs in action he is more likely to lay the blame on unforeseen circumstances than anything else; but, if he thinks of the financial statements at all, he is more likely to suppose that the lapse of time is inevitable and that it is only for that reason that the statements could have been a less than ideal basis for his expectations and actions. Again, the accountant will have no feedback.

A third form of remoteness is the distance between the accountant and the user, and the dispersion of users. To consider managers as users first, the accountant is not physically remote (though he may be quite remote in mental orientation). But as it is the practice of accountants to place on managers the onus of providing some important figures, there is unlikely to be any contention on the part of managers that the financial statements were faulty if they subsequently err in action. Managers are more likely to treat the preparation of periodical accounts as a necessary ritual, and to depend for managerial purposes, on other contemporary factual information accessible to them. Investors and financiers are, by contrast, quite remote. By reason of the complexity and temporal distance already mentioned they are seldom likely to attribute error in action on their part to defects in the financial information supplied them. But if they complain about the financial information (as some have done), accountants could point (as some have done) to the fact that important components of the statements were supplied by managers, or assert that the accounts are the accounts of the management, and brush the complaint aside as none of their business. Again no feedback; or in the last case mentioned, feedback ignored.

This excursion has been hypothetical. But it seems to fit very well the facts as we know them. The postulated reactions are in every case quite reasonable reactions. No blame is implied or intended. I have merely tried to show that, in the nature of things, accountants have no obvious and direct feedback which would induce them to modify their rules, as practitioners or teachers. No feedback means no learning by experience; that is the crux of the matter.

Linguistic and Logical Errors

There are also internal flaws of the linguistic and logical kind which I believe have caused confusion. In some sense they stem from and in another sense they reinforce the effects of the remoteness we have considered.

When an accountant opens an account, say for the shares in the example used previously, and reports a balance at the end of a period in the amount of the original purchase price, he presumes one of two things. Either he treats the holding of shares as the holding of so much money, for the holding of so much money would properly be treated in the accounts in the above way. But in this case he will have reacted in a manner appropriate to something the holder of the shares no longer possesses. He will have made an unwarranted mental substitution of one real thing for another real thing. Or he treats the accounting process as being concerned with the symbol, $500 in the illustration, not with the shares themselves and their prices. He will have mistaken the symbol for the thing. If he makes a mistake of either kind it is impossible that any action dependent on the information he supplies will be consistent with the relationship of the actor to the rest of the world.

It may seem that such elementary mistakes could not be made. A few examples are cited. It has been said that money is a common denominator in terms of which diverse objects—land, plant, inventories—may be represented in common terms. This is not so. Money is a common denominator in terms of which the *prices* of diverse objects at a given time may be represented in common terms. It has been said that an asset *is* a cost; hence accounting for assets is accounting for costs. This is nonsense. It has also been said that an asset *is* a service potential. This too is nonsense. Assets may *have* costs (e.g., purchase prices) and service potentials. But to say assets *are* costs or service potentials is equivalent to saying a car *is* $3000. This kind of substitution of the symbol for the thing, reification, is one of the common causes of error in thought and exposition; and through them, of error in action.

A second type of error in thought and discussion is of a closely related kind. It is the consideration of wholes and the oversight of components. Accountants seem to think of the products of accounting as whole summaries. In fact a financial statement is a collection of singular component statements—about the present amount of cash, receivables, payables and so on. Every singular component statement must bear the stamp of truth or usefulness in the context in which the whole statement is to be used. Otherwise aggregating them will lead nowhere. It is impossible to deduce anything from putting together the two statements: "I now hold $1000; I now hold some shares which I once bought for $500." Yet this is what many financial summaries assert.

There are more fallacies in the literature and practice of accounting than those I have mentioned here. My aim has been simply to show that the difficulties of learning by experience, by the feedback from what happens to actors when they use financial statements, are intensified by confusion of language and thought. But neither of these difficulties and dangers is inescapable and both may be avoided by forcing the attention back to reality.

We have shown that the sense of reality may be caught in a "thought experiment", which isolates a particular action and the mode of its representation. But a careful examination of what accountants do will provide evidence of misapprehension, on a grand scale, even of the facts of practice. It is quite commonly held that most firms in most countries do their accounting on what is described as the historical cost basis. If it were so we might be entitled to suppose that none of the hard facts of the market has been sufficient to dislodge it. But it is just not so. In some countries very large numbers of companies have abandoned the rule in respect of some assets; as when revaluations have occurred. In respect of inventories it has *never* been a fixed rule. In some countries the rule has been set aside by statutorily approved revaluations or revalorizations. In the United States, where the publicity rules are probably tighter than anywhere else, the requirement of the cost rule is circumvented by the use of L.I.F.O., and by other devices used as well in other countries; and the invention of the "pooling" doctrine on mergers is just another crutch to sustain the rule in spite of its weakness. Anyone who dares to suggest that the rule is generally endorsed and accepted is flying in the face of a mountain of facts. There would have been no such facts were it not that the circumstances and forces which influence commercial dealing have just had to be accommodated in accounting somehow.

All these divergences are open to observation by practitioners and teachers alike. In other fields the accumulation of anomalies is the signal for throwing out the extant doctrine or rules, and for finding an alternative which is more general in its coverage of experience (i.e., reducing the number of anomalies, and ideally removing them altogether). It seems inescapable that the beliefs both in the prevalence and in the propriety of the cost doctrine persist because of the use of verbal gymnastics which camouflage anomalies (as for example, the "flow" assumptions which support L.I.F.O. and F.I.F.O.) and because of the failure properly to categorize deviations from the cost basis of anomalies. My point, however, is that there is a form of feedback which is independent of the practices and experiences of particular firms, and which becomes apparent if we stand off and look at what is happening in accounting generally.

The upshot of my observations is that there is no conflict as to the ends sought by practitioners and teachers; that technical competence is a concomitant of understanding; but that when it comes to the means of developing the understanding—by observation and argument—there is much common ground between practitioners and teachers, most of it quicksand. That it should be so is not inevitable.

The Empirical and Logical Best

To demonstrate this I return to a question posed by a remark at an earlier point. I presumed that it is proper to distinguish what is right from what is wrong, and that it is possible to establish what is right and what is wrong (or what is best and what is inferior). I feel confident that both of these propositions will be hotly contested.

There is a widespread feeling that what is right (or best) in accounting is a matter of opinion. The words "opinion" and "judgement" are bandied about so freely among accountants that the ubiquity of the aforesaid feeling is not surprising. But any who hold this opinion, by the very holding of it, reject the force of experience and the power of reason, reject in fact what years of schooling were devoted to inculcating. If there is any sense in which experience of the world teaches us, it is in the direction of forming firm impressions of the empirical relations between things or between classes of things. We speak of those firm impressions as facts and of the relations as factual relations—meaning that they are not matters of opinion, but matters on which others can show us to be right or wrong. And if there is any sense in which logic extends our understanding, it is in the direction of enabling us to draw necessary conclusions from stipulated premises. If the premises are just those that have not been shown to be false, and if the process of drawing conclusions is free of flaws, we are entitled to regard the conclusions as established knowledge. We no longer regard them as mere matters of opinion.

Some will contend that at any time we do not have sufficient facts; that we do not know whether the subsequent discovery of additional facts will falsify a premise which has not yet been shown to be false; and therefore that we cannot safely draw conclusions. This is merely face-saving procrastination. No scientist yet has had, and no scientist will have, all the facts that are or will be available to his successors. But if men had not been painstaking in their observations, and bold in their conjectures and conclusions, they would never have formulated the principles and laws which enabled their successors to see more, and more clearly. We can only know what is best given the state of factual and derived knowledge at any time. Given that knowledge there is some set of principles which embraces it more perfectly than any alternative set. To teach those principles seems to be the proper aim of higher education at any time; to follow the rules which those principles imply seems to be the proper aim of the profession.

There are some who hold, however, that the proper function of the university is to expose students to many views, on the ground that they are able enough to choose for themselves what is the best. There can be no more confusing a policy than this; and there is reason to believe that this lack of rigour and definiteness lies at the root of the vacillation and inconsistency of much of present day practice. In no other field are the halting and mistaken steps taken in the early stages of knowledge paraded before students, much less on an equal footing with the best of present knowledge. But, "a science which hesitates to forget its founders is lost", said Whitehead.

From the available facts and the exercise of discrimination in argument it should be possible to distinguish what is best from what is inferior. But we still find it said that this or that is best for some purposes. Particularly is it said in defence of accounting on the historical cost basis. However, I know of no demonstration to the point that those purposes are not equally well served by another or other forms of accounting which are superior in other respects. The task of finding what is best is rather like finding where to put a specially shaped piece in a jigsaw puzzle. It must fit in with the rest of the picture not just by virtue of the coincidence of one angle or one side, but at all angles and all sides and on the face of the picture too. A set of accounting rules which satisfies one or two conditions is just not good enough. Scholars need, teachers need, students need and the world needs an accounting which satisfies the greatest number of conditions simultaneously. I would welcome any demonstration to the effect that continuously contemporary accounting, as I have expounded it, does not meet this test.

If this paper has seemed to meander all over the place it is because the commonly held ideas I have tried to examine are vagrant, undisciplined. I can best make amends for this by stating what seems to me to emerge from my reflections on the dissonance which I noticed at the outset and the misapprehensions I have mentioned by the way.

I cannot share the view that no common conclusion can be reached by observant and thoughtful professionals and teachers, on the best of present knowledge, or on the best accounting practice in the present state of knowledge. It requires no more than a thorough respect for the facts of commercial life and a thorough belief in the fruits of systematic thought, both of which have been elements of learning and experience for the greater part of the lives of all of us.

I do not believe that, for the purpose, we need any more facts than are now available to us. Some stare us in the face daily in what we do or what we see done; others can be unearthed with a modicum of care and effort. To see only the facts we wish to see is a piece of folly. Teachers who indulge in it will produce men ill-equipped to learn by experience; practitioners who indulge in it will leave clients ill-equipped to meet their own problems; neither can take professional pride in that kind of handiwork.

I do not believe that the logic of teaching and learning differs one whit from the logic of practice. Teachers and students may seem to be concerned with broad principles; but we only learn broad principles from seeing their particular instances or applications. Practitioners may seem to be concerned with particular cases; but whether or not they consciously recognize it, they all have recourse to broad principles of some kind in the solution of particular problems. What is crucial is that the most general principles shall be consistent with the circumstances in which they are to be used; for no one can reason from unreal premises to practically fruitful conclusions.

I believe that practitioners and teachers should regard their roles as mutually dependent and mutually supporting, as are warp and woof (without double entendre). So to regard teaching and practice is common in other professions which depend on advanced technical skill and knowledge. But there is no need to depend on analogy. "All knowledge of reality starts from experience and ends in it", said Einstein. The commercial world is the source of what it is proper to do in the counting house and in the classroom; it is also the only place in which conclusions reached by reflection and deduction can be tested. There is every reason therefore why practitioners and teachers and researchers alike should regard themselves as part of a common enterprise. But with different functions in some respects.

I believe that practitioners should concede or respect the right of teachers to reflect, to research, to re-examine, rather than attempt to duplicate, or outdo or supplant them. Embroiled as they are in commercial affairs, practitioners have neither the time nor the independence of their own immediate commitments to reflect upon what they and their colleagues do, to amass the facts which support significant generalizations, to test them and to formulate them as principles and systems of principles. Teachers and researchers should have both time and independence. I believe, however, that such conclusions as researchers reach should be put under the closest and most patient scrutiny by practitioners; for only under the closest scrutiny will conclusions be failed or affirmed; and only by patient scrutiny is there likely to develop that sympathy between researcher and practitioner which will secure the trial of a tentatively affirmed conclusion. To take part in this review is a proper function of professionals, and a proper involvement in the process of advancing knowledge, understanding and practice. There has, unfortunately, been too much stand-offishness on both sides hitherto.

I believe that teachers should strive for the respect of practitioners by common allegiance to the established canons of inquiry, and by deliberate choice of what is best and by deliberate rejection of the rest. If the house of learning is divided against itself it cannot stand. If it is cut off from the house of experience it will deserve to stand empty. A common logic and linked but different functions in the common pursuit of excellence in thought or practice will, I believe, quell the dissonance which now assails us.

INDEX OF NAMES

INDEX

* "Traditional" is used in the index to signify the type of modified historical cost system in common use.